THE ANTHROPOLOGY OF MEDICINE

THE ANTHROPOLOGY OF MEDICINE

From Culture to Method

LOLA ROMANUCCI–ROSS
DANIEL E. MOERMAN
LAURENCE R. TANCREDI, M.D.

AND CONTRIBUTORS

PRAEGER SPECIAL STUDIES • PRAEGER SCIENTIFIC
J.F. BERGIN PUBLISHERS

Library of Congress Cataloging in Publication Data

The Anthropology of medicine.

J.F. Bergin Publishers.
Includes index.
1. Medical anthropology—Addresses, essays, lectures. 2. Folk medicine—Addresses, essays,
lectures. 3. Materia medica, Vegetable—Addresses, essays, lectures. 4. Mental illness—Social
aspects—Addresses, essays, lectures. 5. Psychiatry, Transcultural—Addresses, essays, lectures. I.
Romanucci-Ross, Lola. II. Moerman, Daniel E. III. Tancredi, Laurence R. [DNLM: 1.
Anthropology, Cultural. 2. Medicine, Traditional. WB 50.1 R761a]
GN296.A57   1982   306'.46   82-15102

ISBN 0-03-062192-5

All rights reserved
J.F. Bergin Publishers, Inc.
670 Amherst Road
South Hadley, Massachusetts 01075

Published in 1983 by Praeger Publishers
CBS Educational and Professional Publishing
A Division of CBS, Inc.
521 Fifth Avenue, New York, New York 10175 U.S.A.

0123456789   056   987654321

Printed in the United States of America

Contents

Preface. The Cultural Context of Medicine and the Biohuman Paradigm

Medical systems emerge from human attempts to survive disease and surmount death, and from social responses to illness and the sick role. Descriptions and analyses of this process within the variety of world cultures define a field known as medical anthropology. Although this process is itself an ancient one—perhaps sixty thousand years old—with roots in the middle Paleolithic, the field of study is a relatively new one that began with systematic inquiries by anthropologists into health practices and explanations of disease in primitive and peasant cultures.

This volume represents the state of the art of medical anthropology, emphasizing what we have called the anthropology of medicine: a study of medical thought and problem solving, the acculturation process of the healer and physician in diverse cultural settings, and the social and cultural context of medicine. Our approach is through the perspective of cultural and medical anthropologists who have taught and worked with Western-educated physicians immersed in clinical and research medicine, as well as those who have worked with other healers and patients outside the bounds of modern biomedicine and surgery.

Anthropological field research is an experience in abstraction; it is an exercise in putting "particulars" into brackets as we search for universals in elements and the relations among them. In this sense we have chosen to fuse the particulars of Western medicine with those from other cultures for conceptual analysis in what we have called the anthropology of medicine. Beyond the surface differences, we try to expose similarities of deep structure, to demonstrate that there is a path beyond culture and that one may focus on method.

We believe that medicine, in a very real sense, stands astride both the cultural and biological dimensions of humankind; we believe that medicine is a kind of applied anthropology in the broadest sense of the term: action for human beings. As anthropologists who have learned a great deal from physicians and surgeons, we hope that the perspective we can bring to this complex cultural and biological exchange will be of value to those who, so much closer to the action, are in the very trenches we learn so much by observing.

This book, then, is designed for physicians and medical students, public health administrators and workers, and students in related health-science fields, as well as students and professionals in anthropology and social science who are interested in the practice or theory of health and healing. It is, in brief, a text for both the health sciences and anthropology.

For a century in the West, there have been two literatures regarding the health sciences. They have represented two different canons, or paradigms: the approaches of biomedical science and of behavioral science. To simplify somewhat, the biomedical paradigm tells us that, for example, tuberculosis is "caused" by *Myobacterium tuberculosis*, whereas the behavioral-science paradigm tells us that tuberculosis is "caused" by poverty and malnutrition. It is our contention that these two approaches can be integrated into one biohuman paradigm; further, we contend that the unifying factor is the concept of culture. By culture we mean the system of meaning— belief, knowledge, and action—by which people organize their lives. Such organization structures the diseases to which people are subject: as a simple case, schistosomiasis is a disease of irrigation agriculture; as a less simple case, the *windigo* psychosis of Algonquan Indians is a disease (characterized by homicidal behavior and cannibalistic fears) of a hunting people subject to great environmental fluctuations.

Diseases, however, are never experienced directly; "illnesses," cultural constructs of "dis-ease," are what people experience; illnesses are constructed of belief and knowledge, which vary with both space and time. A contemporary example might be "hyperactivity," an "illness" with associated treatment(s), which did not exist twenty years ago. People debate whether or not it is a new "disease," a response perhaps to new environmental toxins (i.e., food additives), or whether it was "always there," but not recognized. *Either case* provides an example (slightly different ones, to be sure) of the role of the cultural process in sickness and health. If it was always there, but not recognized, then we have a case where an illness was invented. If it is a new disease, we have a case where cultural concerns (for foods with this color or that) have created a novel physiological disorder.

The theoretical value of such an approach seems evident. Human beings are simultaneously cultural and biological creatures, and these two dimensions necessarily interact. The historical concern of (at least North American) anthropologists with these two factors—differentiating anthropology from sociology or history on the one hand and from psychology or biology on the other—means that the study of human health and healing, where people *attempt to influence directly the relationship between biology and culture*, is one rich with potential for learning fundamental things about what it means to be a human being.

Perhaps the greatest difference between these two paradigms and the greatest obstacle to their resolution lies in the notion of efficacy. What on earth is there to learn, the biomedical scientist wants to know, from the bizarre medical practices of the past? Grounded in the history of Western medicine, such a scientist is aware of the awesome array of tortures perpetrated on sick people in the past thousand years: bleeding and purging, whipping devils out of the insane, the presumably medicinal use of bat's blood and bear feces, of frog sperm and earthworms, gruesome tales of septic surgery on nonanesthetized patients, and so on. Physicians seem, sometimes, almost gleeful when they reminisce about some sixteenth-century surgeon dying of infection from a nick of his own knife.

We do not deny the terrifying state of medicine in Europe between the twelfth and eighteenth centuries. The difference lies in the fact that the anthropologist takes a broader view of the world, and sees pre-modern Europe as a very unusual and special case—one of the least healthy societies in human history—subject to dozens of new and terrifying diseases as a consequence essentially of two things: the great growth then of the population of both humans and domesticated animals. This "one–two punch" of domestication and urbanization created conditions for the evolution and communication of infectious disease organisms on a scale unprecedented in human history, well beyond the abilities of the most well-intentioned physician.

Consider, as an ideal comparison, the health status of Europeans and native Americans in the year 1480. Paleopathological evidence indicates that the native Americans were extremely healthy: they had a life expectancy longer than that of Europeans of the time; life was difficult, and people suffered from accidents, fractures, rheumatic conditions, and, perhaps, from trichinosis contracted from animals that they hunted. Scholarly debate rages regarding the origins of syphilis; some argue that it was introduced into Europe from America by members of Columbus's crew, others, that it was an indigenous Old World disease. It is, however, the *only* ambiguous case; all the other diseases transmitted from one continent to the other went westward: smallpox, measles, typhoid, tuberculosis, cholera, diphtheria, plague—the list seems endless. These diseases, which had ravaged Europe for generations, were well beyond the abilities of European physicians. They were also the single most important cause of the cataclysmic drop in native American population. The most recent available estimates suggest that, between 1490 and 1890, the native population of the area of the 48 continental United States dropped 90 percent, from 1.9 million to 200,000 (Thornton and Marsh–Thornton 1981). Similarly, it is estimated that Australian population dropped by four-fifths between 1788 and 1933 (White 1977). The poor health status of native peoples in colonial times was a consequence of colonialism, and not a measure of indigenous health.

That native Americans or native Australians had little medical wherewithal when confronted with cancer or influenza seems a misplaced criticism. What is most striking about non-Western medicine is how much people did with what they had. That many of the herbal remedies of the past have been supplanted by synthetic ones—many of which are, after all, modified natural products, such as, for example, aspirin—should hardly detract from the perspicacity of the original discoverers; and, as the chapters in this book, especially those by Etkin and by Elvin–Lewis, attest, there may be much more of value that we can learn from non-Western medicine to enhance the biochemical basis of modern medicine.

But, perhaps because of the relative lack of powerful specific drugs in the non-Western pharmacopoeia, it is clear that many of these peoples were far more sophisticated and far more inventive than we in manipulating the social and human dimensions of medicine. This aspect of non-Western medicine may ultimately have the most to teach us about healing. Once one recognizes that the *form* of medical treatment affects the *outcome* of treatment, one can hardly leave it to chance, any more than one can prescribe drugs (however effective) by chance. The chapters in this book demonstrate that this *is* the case, and they show some of the forms that medical treatment can take; they show as well how deeply medical systems are embedded in culture.

Human beings are simultaneously biological and cultural organisms. For physicians to achieve their goal—to optimize human health—they must be intently aware of this human duality. Our purpose is not to undercut the grounding of medicine in biology (tuberculosis *is* caused by a bacillus) but to assert that medicine has two feet, and that the other is grounded in culture (tuberculosis *is also* caused by poverty and malnutrition); moreover, and most important, these two dimensions are interconnected in many and complex ways.

As a very specific example, consider the character of medical diagnosis. Physicians, during the long years of training in which they gain their expertise, become increasingly members of the "medical subculture"—with a language, a system of values, and a conceptual framework for decision making—and, at least for a time, are separated from the arena in which they are later to be effective. Moreover, physicians must learn how to cope with the inevitable internal duality of medicine as both scientific and clinical. Whereas scientific medicine involves public research on aggregates, clinical medicine involves private treatment of individuals; the former is statistical, the latter idiosyncratic; the former is concerned with "the course of a disease," the latter with "the history of an illness." As clinicians confront patients, they have to mold them into categories, transforming unique constellations of experience, notions, beliefs, symptoms, and dis-ease into types, a "case of the measles," the proverbial "liver in Room 446." This is at best a disconcerting process. For patients, it is simultaneously clarifying and dehumanizing: whatever they "have" rules out another thousand possibilities, but the price they pay is that now they are no longer discrete sufferers, but members of a class. The loss of uniqueness is, at best, a double-edged sword.

And likewise for the physician: to diagnose is to classify and to predict a course and a treatment based on the vagaries of statistics and experience; it is to take what can always be a very serious risk. This risk has both structural and statistical dimensions. It is a structural risk in that validation is essentially derived from the response to treatment, which is temporally remote. It is a statistical risk in that "classic cases" are rare, in that medical theory must be manipulated to fit the unique characteristics of infinitely varying patients. To do this at all is to *ignore* much of what patients present and to select as *meaningful* a segment of their existence as being particularly diagnostic, that is, to ignore things that patients think are important, to dismiss some (perhaps much) of their lives as *unimportant*; this is by its nature a dehumanizing process. A mutual commitment of patient and physician to an intrinsically categorical process, an intrinsically dehumanizing process, is necessarily disconcerting; the process must inhibit people from acting in concert. And this must occur regardless of the cultural distance between physician and patient. Indeed, the experience of many physicians is that among the most difficult patients are other physicians; perhaps it is only that here the physician can more easily translate the patient's discontent—and, perhaps, less easily ignore it. This dehumanization can only be exacerbated by additional cultural differences in general education, class, ethnic origins, and so on.

Whatever else diagnosis may be, it is first a social process based on interpersonal communication between the scientifically knowledgeable physician and the concerned patient. The physician should understand why and when a person seeks medical attention, how he views his own sickness, how he reports his symptoms and interprets his feelings, and what changes in his life occur because of his illness or treatment. These factors are always influenced by the respective cultural backgrounds of patient and physician. Wide variation in patients' backgrounds and the cultural differences between doctor and patient may profoundly influence the diagnostic process and therapeutic course.

Yet if the patient cannot act in concert with the physician, how is the physician to control the course of the patient's disease? As the patient gives up his uniqueness for a diagnosis, he also gives up his independence. And his new dependence is on the physician. Dependence can take many forms. The skill with which the physician projects an appropriate, empathetic concern and strikes a responsive chord in the patient will affect the richness and utility of the interchange. If the process is to be dehumanizing, it may as well be as useful as possible. The therapeutic exchange can be so structured that the patient can develop a sense of trust and security while the physician can develop a sense of responsibility and confidence; this reciprocity can replace the prior independence and uniqueness of patient and physician. Trust and security in return for responsibility and confidence can only facilitate healing.

This relationship aside, the physician must remember that when a diagnosis is pronounced there should be no assumption that the patient understands it in the same way as the physician does. The patient may never have heard the word before; or, if he has, it is inconceivable that he understands the term as the physician does. And *it is the patient's understanding that will influence his response to treatment*, to one degree or another.

Furthermore, there is increasing evidence that a significant group of patients, even those among the highly educated lay public, are unable to comprehend the nature of the medical information provided to give an informed consent (Tancredi, 1982). Many of these patients may simply be inattentive during the session with the physician. This attitude may reflect either that patients desire to place the responsibility for critical decisions about their care on the physician, thereby effectively waiving the requirements of informed consent, or, more likely, that, during a health crisis, patients are so distraught that they are incapable of making objective decisions concerning their medical care. The physician has to be sensitive to the many medical and emotional factors affecting the patient and make the necessary adjustments in the flow of communication to enhance the patient's understanding of the medical information that is being given.

The technique of patient interviewing can be a highly honed skill—focused, but not rigidly structured; flexible, to adjust to the patient's perhaps abnormal attitudes and behavior (he is, after all, at least by his own definition, sick), but organized to elicit sufficient pertinent information in the available time to allow the physician room to take the diagnostic risk; and so organized that the patient has an *appropriate understanding* of the diagnosis.

It is ultimately only the pathologist who can know for sure what the patient "had." By then, of course, it is too late. This is not to deny biological mortality: it is rather to assert the need for more than simply biological medicine.

This book is comprised of some twenty chapters on recent research in medical anthropology, which we believe will provide a foundation for a biohuman medical paradigm by demonstrating how culture—human belief, knowledge, and action—structures the human experience of disease, affects the ways in which *both physicians and patients* perceive and define illness, and influences the matrices of decision-making in the inevitable subcultures attempting to communicate about problems of health care.

L. Romanucci–Ross
D. Moerman
L. R. Tancredi, M.D.

REFERENCES

Tancredi, L. R. "Competency for Informed Consent: Conceptual Limits of Empirical Data."
1982   *International Journal of Law and Psychiatry*, 5 (1982):51–63.
Thornton, R., and J. Marsh–Thornton. "Estimating Prehistoric American Indian Pop-
1981   ulation Size for United States Area: Implications of the Nineteenth Century Population Decline and Nadir." *American Journal of Physical Anthropology*, 55:47–54.
White, I.M. "Pitfalls To Avoid: The Australian Experience." I.M. White, *Heath and Disease*
1977   *in Tribal Society*. Amsterdam: Elsevier.

PART ONE

Interaction
of Medical Systems

THE INTERACTIONS OF DIFFERENT MEDICAL SYSTEMS PROVIDE A FASCINATING CONTEXT for understanding the relationships between the biology and culture of medicine. In any particular case, the relative proportions of diseases, medicines, and ideas about each which are exchanged is an empirical question, but the fact of exchange is undeniable.

The exchange of ideas about medical phenomena is no simple matter. The common conceit of the West—that the benefits of scientific medicine are obvious, as are the truths on which those benefits are based—is a conceit held by all peoples regarding their own medical systems. It was as true for the bleeding and purging physicians of the last century as it is for the neurosurgeons and cardiologists of our own. These ideas, associated as they are with fundamental principles of belief about the major cosmological issues of life and death, are themselves generally very deeply held. In the United States in recent years, major political and social conflicts have raged over what can be narrowly conceived as "medical issues." Abortion, the definition of death (or "medical death"), and the notion of "death with dignity" are all examples of such issues, where broad, deeply held beliefs influence medical matters.

A similar, and quite extraordinary, case involves the enormous social and ecological changes undergone by the Northeastern sub-Arctic Algonquian Indians in response to the introduction of European diseases (Martin 1978). Martin, in what is nominally a history of the fur trade, argues that the commercial involvement of Indians in the fur trade was more apparent than real. For a people whose essential notion of all illness was that it represented retaliation by the spirits of mistreated prey animals, the vast epidemics of European diseases (often occurring long before the Indians encountered actual Europeans) presented a serious enigma. They had not mistreated the animals; why, then, were the animals killing them? Martin's argument is, in effect, that the Indians decided that, for unknown reasons, the animals had declared war on them. Adopting, when available, the providential armaments of the newly appearing Europeans (guns and steel traps), they fought back. The result was the Indian involvement in the fur trade, and, not incidentally, the extermination of much of the animal life of North America.

The most extraordinary aspect of this case appears in recent ethnographic accounts of the descendants of these fur traders (Tanner 1979). They are today returning to a pattern very similar to the one they pursued four centuries ago, carefully harvesting animals, with appropriate reverence and ceremony. The great epidemics of the past are, of course, gone, and (vaccinated) hunters may be as healthy as were their ancestors. The war, it seems, is over; and, after four centuries of incomprehensible social change, at least some essential notions of health for these people *are unchanged*.

The chapters in this section all focus on the ways in which the conceptual portions of medical systems change (or do not change) as a result of culture contact.

Romanucci–Ross's discussion of medicine in Italy describes the contact of culture and subculture, and the "medicalization" of "folk" by "Western medicine"—the active attempt by official providers of health care to impose a standard structure on diagnostic and curing practices. Despite massive propaganda, and even apparent complicity—seen in repeated visits to state insurance doctors—traditional ideas of body image and dysfunction prevail. New factors embellish traditional folk notions, and metaphorical thinking yields "rational bases" for combining religious beliefs with the language and logic of science. A unified theory of health—based on an integration of a mind–body unit linked with community and ideology—persists, absorbing on its own terms the language of the official medicine.

In Kidwell's account of the relationship between Aztec and Spanish medicine, we find that these systems exchanged a broad range of items that facilitated the identification and cure of a variety of diseases. Indigenous plants were used by the conquerors for the diseases they found in the New World; more problematical for the host populations were the diseases brought to them. Analysis of the Spanish and Aztec sources from the period can isolate features of the cross-cultural transactions in cognition. Upon what bases could the exchange of information occur? In this case, herbal medicine became a primary focus of exchange. Even though the Spanish had the Galenic binary structure of "hot" and "cold," whereas the Aztecs classified plants by their uses, both groups found plants useful as food, medicine, and ornament. Aztec epidemiology and pharmacology fused with Greek and Galenic views; in time, the Mexican folk-medicine system emerged, perhaps the most fully syncretic medical system known.

As the Spanish incorporated Aztec medicines into their conceptualization of medicine, the Ningerum of New Guinea are shown by Welsch to be incorporating Western medicine into their system. Western medicine plays a complementary rather than a competitive role, and Welsch sees the emergent system as integrative. Looking at the distribution of therapeutic knowledge and expertise in the Ningerum community and the locus of diagnostic and therapeutic decision making, this process is placed in Watson's (1980) broader social theory of "consensual complementarity." Welsch demonstrates that the *process* of syncretization, as well as the resultant system, can be documented, if one can talk with individuals to assess motivation and thereby specify the operation of belief in individual instances.

The Ostiak of Siberia have had a rather different response to the external alteration of their medical culture, under the pressure of Soviet antireligious and public-health programs. Here we find the original *shaman*, a prototype used by many anthropologists to describe curers in other cultures. The Ostiak differentiate three different kinds of practitioners: the family *shaman*, a sort of general practitioner; the trance *shaman*; and the "big man," whose spiritual travels take him far and wide. The *shaman's* patient is a colleague in the medical event and helps by confessing wrongdoing; cure comes through abreaction and transference. Since the entire community participates in the process, this is a sort of community-mental-health approach to individually focused group therapy. In this case, a deliberate attempt by the Soviet authorities to extinguish this indigenous system has succeeded to the degree that the systems have developed an antagonistic, rather than complementary or syncretic, relationship. During collectivization in the 1930s, *shamans* were characterized as "deceivers"; the campaign was successful enough that they are now characterized by many as "drunks," capable of doing evil. This example matches the traditional notion of "acculturation": Ostiak notions of health today generally mirror those of the larger Soviet public-health movement. Even such distinctive aspects of the traditional system as the manipulation of altered states of consciousness are now widely disparaged.

These cases, then, represent a wide range of medical interaction. If the Mexican case represents a fully syncretic system, the Siberian case represents a more nearly acculturated one. If the Ningerum case represents an emerging syncretism, the Italian case represents a stable, unshakable one. Exactly what determines the ultimate outcome of the interaction of medical systems is not yet clear. However, it *is* clear that this interaction is a complex and difficult one, not susceptible to facile prediction.

REFERENCES

Martin, C. 1978. *Keepers of the Game: Indian–Animal Relationships and the Fur Trade*. Berkeley: Univ. of California Press.

Tanner, Adrian. 1979. *Bringing Home Animals: Religious Ideology and Mode of Production among Mistassini Cree Hunters*. New York: St. Martin Press.

Watson, James B. 1980. "Protein and Pigs in Highland New Guinea." Paper presented to the American Anthropological Association, 79th annual meeting.

1

Folk Medicine and Metaphor in the Context of Medicalization: Syncretics in Curing Practices

Lola Romanucci—Ross

Folk medicine differs from primitive medicine in a very important way; it is nested in a "pocket culture" within a larger national context, into which traditions of the politically dominant culture have seeped over historical time. The nation—state has also borrowed from its peasant enclaves in cultural-exchange situations. Folk culture is therefore a more open system of beliefs and behaviors than societies we call primitive, which are characterized by transmission of beliefs and behaviors in a closed system lacking the opportunities found in a situation of culture contact.

In analyzing interacting processes in a primitive culture, I noted a "hierarchy of resort of curative practices" (L.R. Schwartz 1969) and demonstrated that there exists a commonality in concepts of health and illness in societies having a certain level of technological and informational complexity. In the Admiralty Islands of Melanesia, one could observe and predict shifting game strategies in curing events when an individual was confronted by choices. Depending on the degree of acculturation, choice of healer and/or cure would begin with usage of either native or Western medical categories. Failure would determine the next attempt, which would use the healing science of the other culture. Thus, beliefs about diagnoses, illness, and healing were "arranged" in a syntactic sequence by patient and kin as they made decisions. They might begin with either Western or traditional curing practices and vacillate back and forth until the illness terminated. (Needless to say, minimal culture contact had begun in these primitive societies, but it was recent and scant

5

enough that the native culture was still "core," salient and visible to the investigator.)

In subsequent analyses (Romanucci–Ross 1978, 1979, 1981) it was discovered that the metaphorical thinking process of the group studied was superimposed on their "rational thought" system for everyday "logic." Using the specificity of the culture itself rather than external analyses, it was then possible to identify native perception and imagery and their effects on knowledge configurations in the Melanesian society whose curative practices were being analyzed.

There is a coding to be deciphered in the linkages between metaphorical thought and other knowledge configurations, and what was learned in Melanesia is applicable elsewhere. Shifting game strategies are to be found in peasant cultures and in complex Western societies as well. Here, too, we find cybernetic models in groups who have no name for it (Romanucci–Ross 1973). For the following discussion, we define *medicalization* as the structuring of information about health and illness in the culturally informed drama of the body–mind, and we will explore how such structuring begins to occur in several contexts. Providers usually impose "correct" structuring on consumers of health care and perpetuate it in their professions through codes of propriety in training, problem recognition, and problem solution in pathology and dysfunction; medicalization itself is genuinely a cultural process.

What are those illnesses that the peasant (or folk) recognize as such, and what do they consider symptom and syndrome? In folk as well as primitive societies, notions of health and illness are grounded in the total configuration of local knowledge. For our folk contemporaries, this configuration is contained in and influenced by "scientific medicine" (transformed by its uses for television, radio, newspapers, and magazines), as well as its own persistent traditional nucleus (itself transformed through verbal communication known as "oral tradition," which is subject to interpretation and therefore to change). However, the fragments of knowledge are not viewed as contradictory; what is learned from the modern media is conjoined with—or allowed to contain or to be contained by—the remnants of traditional knowledge of disorders of mind and body and their remedies. The above assertions about folk medicine apply generally, but to further develop this analysis we will focus in particular on a segment of Italian culture.

An Example from Central Italy

Peasant cultures retain historical links to the larger societies in which they exist, which have already progressed to cultural complexity in a process called *lateralization.* This means that certain strata in very different societies will resemble one another in structure and function more than they resemble other strata in their own political nation–state. How, then, does one attempt to evolve a method to look at the interlacing of imagery and perception and its selective and stylizing effects on knowledge configurations? Illness is always a negotiable event, and in this society in Central Italy it is particularly so. Persons who think that they may be ill seek confirmation or denial from others. The confirmation or denial of the sick role means the beginning of the journey—cure with all its attendant changes in responsibilities, prerogatives, and negotiable rites of passage.

The section of Italy investigated is situated in the province of Ascoli Piceno in the region called Le Marche. One folk healer discussed below, though in a rural area, is actually part of the referral network of urban physicians; she is an acceptable consultant in exchanges of medical information with them. Her patients take pride not only in this, but also in the fact that she has been studied by the center for parapsychology in Bologna. The latter fact alone validates her diagnoses as scientific.

The inhabitants of this region watch television, listen to the radio, and have access to the world of journalism; they also travel to other parts of the country, and about 11 percent of the people have been abroad. However, they still retain basic traditional folk beliefs about body image and preventive medicine, and they carry with them an internal calculator of "reality," including that wide spectrum of luck, from good to bad, that places illness as one category among other misfortunes.

Among the rural villages in which current research is being pursued,[1] the agricultural fields are found to contain Christian crosses made of cane and olive palm for the protection of crops from tempests. If you happen to be there on January 17, you will hear hymns sung to San Antonio d'Abbate for the protection of domestic animals from sickness and death. In a small village called Castel di Croce on a mountain called Castello, there is a huge ancient oak tree; it is said that if one breaks or cuts a small branch at the tip of the tree, a wind will be unleashed that will destroy the harvest of that entire zone. (The people in this region had not heard of *The Golden Bough*,[2] but it was not far from here that Frazer (1890) found in history the mythical events that led him through 12 volumes of the relationships among magic, religion, and scientific thought). The city of Ascoli Piceno had its own *mago* ("sorcerer"), known as Cecco d'Ascoli.[3] *Maghi* and *streghe* ("witches") are considered real and effective.[4] One will be told even today of a *mago* in the nearby province of Abbruzzi who went out with a coven and sacrificed a crow and a male goat, at which time the skies darkened and the rains came. The listener is sworn to secrecy, as there will be retribution from this *mago* if "the government" learns of the feat.[5] All secret societies, even such as the Masons, are unlawful in Italy.

Prevention and Initial Strategies in Health Care

Preventive medicine begins for the infant with the rite of baptism into the Catholic church. In addition, there are proper amulets for the evil eye (*il malocchio*); the infant must be protected from certain persons whose gaze, when brought to rest on another individual, will cause serious illness or even death through envy and jealousy.[6] In some of the smaller mountain villages, a branch of a certain type of pine tree is placed behind the door so that evil spirits cannot accost the child. A piece of material from the vestments of a priest will be placed in a pocket of the child's clothing. There are bad winds (particularly the *sirocco*), and bad airs (particularly night air), and the child must be kept bundled up, away from curious, admiring eyes. Umbilical cord, nail clippings, bits of hair, and other exuviae are disposed of with great care until the baby is "strong enough" to withstand envy and the technology of witchcraft that can be employed by use of these bodily bits to harm the child.

What is done in the event of illness? In the words of a physician in Ascoli, speaking to the author in 1979:

> First they go to a physician because it is gratis. When I was a young man they didn't go to a doctor because it cost money. They would go in those days after two or three days of a high fever. Now that the *Mutua* pays they go to one doctor after another, just to check on the diagnosis. The doctors know this, so they won't give the patient the same diagnosis but will give the same medications and counsel. Even though he came to the same conclusion as the preceding doctor(s), he knows the patient doesn't want this. If all these consults don't bring the desired results, after
> exhausting the supply of Mutua doctors, the patient will then go to the *mago*. But they will simultaneously take any and every medication, provided it is free of charge. Italy is replete with *malades imaginaires,* not in the sense of Moliere's play, but in the sense that they are constantly diagnosing each other and recommending cures. This is not surprising since—as you know, for you have described it elsewhere—here one lives almost exclusively in the opinion of others, along with sweat cures, mud cures, and inhalation cures. They even get 12,000 lire from the Mutua to spend on the way to these cures.[7]

The Mutua is the social security system that includes health care insurance. Other physicians voiced similar sentiments to me somewhat less cynically, but all agreed with this physician's "factual statements" about these journey–cures. This led me to question others to learn how the same events are perceived by nonphysicians.

Adults not in the medical profession stress the fact that many, if not most, patients are not ill at all, but are in unspoken collusion to get the signature that allows them to embark on these cures, from Mutua doctor to Mutua doctor and from health spa to health spa. Few find it dishonest: "The government always takes, it ought to give a little!"

As for medications, all receive them, accept them, even request them, according to the nonphysicians interviewed, but few "take" them; particularly not for ingestion are the psychoactive drugs. Here in this Italian province one does not medicalize that "anxiety that comes from not fitting in . . . the newcomer who cannot make friends . . . the woman who cannot get along with her daughter-in-law . . . the executive who cannot accept retirement . . . the inability to cope."[8] Rather, in this region, the life trajectory is staged in a variety of modelics specifically designed for the coping abilities needed. Thus, in the socialization process the child learns both from the family and from other institutions that the road ahead is strewn with difficulties and is also provided with many alternative mechanisms to confront these problems (Romanucci–Ross 1975).

Therapeutic psychoanalysis has had little or no success, despite attempts by a group situated in Rome to send Italian professors to certain provincial centers (Ascoli Piceno is one of them) in order to instruct school teachers and psychological counselors. There are difficulties selling the premises of psychoanalysis to a culture that considers repression to be good—in fact, the only possible basis for civility as well as civilization. Furthermore, it is believed that the unconscious is almost always evil and should be suppressed. Such are the uses of prayer, as the lives of saints (some from these parts) suggest.

The proverb used to illustrate survival strategies is couched in terms of health-care activities: *Campa cavallo che l'erba cresce* (an admonishment to a horse to concentrate simply on his personal efforts to keep alive—for as he does so, the grasses (sustenance) around him will one way or another, by natural or social necessity, keep growing). In the instancing of such a presupposition, Mr. F., a communist, signed up for one week of work absence during a religious festa, claiming that he had injured his chest lifting a heavy umbrella in the line of duty on his job in a public works department. The insurance doctor "recommended" it simply on the basis of Mr. F.'s claim that he could not work. This happens with frequency and, in fact, the notion of the local hospital is that it is to be used as a rest home. The "truly ill" are surrounded by those recovering from "nerves," and all are surrounded by relatives and friends bearing gifts of food and acolyte nuns selling food and flowers. The chapel is very prominent in this small hospital, and a representation of the Virgin reminiscent of Lourdes, presiding over a "gushing spring," iconically implies that miracles have occurred here.

My physician colleague during one field trip[9] was consulted frequently to "check out" medications, since it is a widely held opinion that Mutua doctors get paid according to the number of prescriptions and diagnosis cards filled out. It was asserted by those who came to us that Mutua medical personnel do not recall illnesses; rather, it is up to the patients to tell the doctors who they are and what the previous diagnoses were; it was considered that patients are merely given medications on hand, since the doctors expect that patients will not go out to purchase a truly proper drug. Whether this is so is not being affirmed or denied here: we merely state that this is an assertion so common that it borders on universal patient perception. Several scandals reported in the newspapers concerning doctors who stole from the Mutua, and who are now in prison, are adduced as evidence by patients that their perceptions are correct.

Some manage to convince the Mutua doctors that they need a rest in a mental hospital. The attainment of such certification for two months or so managed to save several widows of my acquaintance that amount of board and room, which they would otherwise have paid at a local convent. It also transformed them into interesting, sought-after, conversational guests when they came out into the real world again. Other "mental hospitals" visited were filled with the elderly, both male and female, alone in the world with no close relatives. Observable here was the recognition by both "patients" and caretakers alike that "madness" is a medical opinion that cannot be refereed by experts because there are no experts where there is no body of knowledge established and testable, and where one finds continuing variance of definition. Therefore, all played out with various degrees of merriment a Pirandello scene in which the caretakers seemed grateful to "the mad" for rendering them employable, and "the mad" replayed old roles of romantic reminiscences amidst flowers, colored ribbons, and sweets. Such conscious role playing was particularly enjoyed by all when there were visitors. I was with subtlety invited to join this trick on the "state" and the "science" of psychiatry at the Ricovero Ferucci in Ascoli Piceno. The "truly mad" are, of course, welcome here, since they validate the institution. It would be interesting to study the therapeutic effect (or intensifying effect) of such environs for the "truly mad."

It is asserted that medical-care delivery systems are used by personnel and patients alike to make illness and curing exploitable events, with the government paying the costs. Unfortunately, such beliefs do promote distrust of the state, of scientific advancement, and of future possibilities for good medical-care delivery. In 1976 it was proclaimed by many newspapers that the Mutua was "dying." It had not died several years later, but perhaps the reportage expressed desires shared by many.

An Interface of Folk and Western Medicine

It was at the suggestion of Dr. M. that I found Pasqualina, healer–diagnostician. Her house, a 45-minute drive from Ascoli Piceno, was somewhat modern and presentable. The large waiting room was crammed with 34 people, all engaged in diagnosing the patients next to themselves, who listened intently until it was their turn to diagnose the aches and disorders of their neighbor. Pasqualina seemed only moderately flattered that a *dottoressa* from the University of California wanted to observe how she worked; she had already been studied by several parapsychologists. When asked how she first discovered her gift of "seeing" and "knowing" she claimed to have "seen" her husband committing adultery, and later described the scene in great detail to him, even though she was far away at the time. (He is now her most devoted believer and apostle.)

Pasqualina diagnosed by auscultation, and by touching or almost touching body parts. She would actually palpate the soft tissue of the throat or testicles. Joints were examined by passive motion. Finally, her fingers back to the "almost touching" position, eyes closed, and lips trembling, she went into trance, a state preliminary to the end of the examination. She usually came out of the trance state with a shudder and wiped her face with a large handkerchief. On one occasion, she told me that a diagnosis was particularly exhausting, but that she had finally detected the problem.

Her patients, whatever their symptoms, come to her with self-diagnoses (often arrived at in the waiting room with the help of others) reflecting a body image that views two things as salient: one is the fixation on the function of one organ, particularly the liver or kidneys. The other is the concern with diet, couched in terms of receiving energy and losing energy from the body and mind as though these systems were a fixed lump sum. Any loss from total body weight or mass is considered a step toward extinction. One must build up the mass and density to avoid the always imminent diminution of forces ("the fat get thin—the thin die"). Exercise is not only not highly regarded but rarely discussed, and one does not find a notion of homeostasis with exercise as a physiologic weight stabilizer. Exercise, or any physical movement without an immediate utilitarian goal, is particularly discouraged for women. Any woman who even discusses the possibility of putting an interest in exercise into practice is regarded as a libertine, with tendencies toward lubricity. The young woman, once married, should evolve into a figure well upholstered, engirdled, and waistless, somewhat like a fortress which has kept its labyrinthine secrets even from a husband. Pasqualina, of course, endorses these views, and although she considers herself only a "psychic" with power of diagnosis, she is considered a healer by her patients, who attest that recovery begins from the moment she refers them to a physician in Ascoli.

Another healer, "Maria La Santa," was a living example of the syntactic structuring of folk symbols uniting religious passion, illness, and healing. Said by certain physicians to be an example of a true "hysteric," she worked as a part-time domestic despite the stigmata on her hands. She is now obese, but it is said that at one time she was considered comely. The pupil of one eye is noticeably larger than that of the other, so much so that the viewer in conversation with her suffers a slight hypnotic effect, becoming "light-headed." Her apparel suggests quasi-nun status, with matching black gloves to hide the stigmata, which are said to bleed on certain Fridays prior to religious holidays. Maria had her first vision of the Virgin at age 15. The apparition was surrounded by rays of scintillating light, as in the reported experiences of mystics. She knew then that despite her humble origins she would be a living reminder to others of the passion and the crucifixion, and it was only later that she learned she could heal the sick. Her house contains memorabilia of healing events, such as a cane left by a cured cripple, a death robe shed by a person whom she had liberated from the grip of death, dark glasses left by one whose sight she had restored.

Belief in her powers increases in intensity in direct proportion to the geographic distance from her. Her clients come mostly from the neighboring province of Abbruzzi, while the old man who lives next door laughed lasciviously as he described her powers over the physiology of male "clients" in the years of her attractive youth and suggested a slow spiritual evolution in the nature of her services.

Even her local neighbors who did not believe in her powers do believe in miracles at a distance; they noted, as I did, a *news* story in the local paper[10] reporting on the liquification of the blood of San Gennaro in Naples: "A little before 10:30 a.m. the ancient dried blood (from A.D. 305) began to liquify and drops of blood on the marble began to redden. This is a good augury." The locals have their own saint, San Emidio Rosso, a sixteenth-century German bishop, martyred in Ascoli, who protected the city from earthquakes and still does. San Emidio was beheaded and walked with his head in his hands to his present resting place, the baptistry that bears his name. A marble chopping block within contains dried blood that liquifies on his feast day and some other religious occasions. His powers are authenticated by distance, not in space but in time, and it is believed that in World War II he confused the bombers headed for Ascoli and had them bomb Ancona instead.

Cynosure Locals

We have alluded to two local examples of what are widely known in the culture as a mystic and/or a *sensitiva*. What are the characteristics of these persons? Some (but not all) of the following need to be present:

- Stigmata, or wounds that open and bleed. These are related to the passion of Christ and are to be found on the palms of the hands, the feet, and the ribs.
- A vision of a religious figure who has appeared to the person in the past, or the occurrence of a clairvoyant episode.
- Symptoms of a sense of weightlessness, "out-of-body experiences," "kidnapping of the soul," bouts of ecstasy, feelings of "being transported," and levitation. In these states, one "sees" and "knows."
- Exposure to flames without suffering burns when in an altered state of consciousness.
- Emanations of "odors of sanctity."
- Profound alteration in sense of time.
- Occurrences of revelations.
- Convulsions followed by paralysis.
- Hyperesthesia (oversensitivity to touch).
- Anesthesia and tremors.

Any or all of these validate for the sensitive or mystic, as well as for the patients, that the healing power derives from the deity. It is known that St. Catherine of Siena, St. Theresa, St. Francis, and St. John of the Cross had such experiences but did not necessarily use the power for healing; rather, they usually employed it for divine relevation and to convert nonbelievers to Christianity. Such powers ordinarily arrive "after a long and dolorous malady," and the ensuing mystical experiences "light the fire," spur the subject to action, and drive out doubt and desperation.

Who are these people? Usually they are of humble origin, often women, and sometimes those who had been elevated to high status but then suffered a decline in popularity. One such was a film star who became a healer, "laying on hands" several years before his death.

These healers function in a culture that has a great interest in emotional states—ecstatic, hysterical, dream states, hypnotic states, meditative states, and trance. Such states are not written off as irrelevant to the business of getting on with life in the world but are viewed as central to "meaning" in the teleological unravelling of one's destiny.

Borrowing from the Language and Logics of Science

Both in verbal communication and journalistic writings, individuals and groups in Ascoli adopt the language of contemporary science to describe healing techniques.

Emotional states create "bioenergetics," allowing the healer to absorb energy from the universe which can be transmitted to others. One 35-year-old male healer is said to absorb such bioenergetics from archaeological sites and is able to cure rheumatics, arthritics, and the like in a curative process known as "bioradiant therapy" or "biomagnetic therapy." In further emulation of scientific exchange, he claims that he went to the Philippines to study "spiritual surgery." He allows himself to be studied by physicians and psychologists so that "science" might learn about these laws that work themselves out in his person.

The persistent use of herbs and the vocabulary used to describe them is now enjoying a revival as the efficacious scientific use of nature's own pharmacopoeia. Decoctions of leaves of cypress, the people are now told (through local newspapers) are good for dysentery or intermittent fevers; the cyprus "fruit" is a vasoconstrictor, useful for menopausal symptoms and degeneration of the uterus and in prevention of hair loss.

Some will seek a pranotherapist. Further south in Bari there is a regional hospital where a 43-year-old parapsychologist practices this kind of healing. *Prana* in Sanskrit means "vital energy," and the pranotherapist usually claims that he "cures" but does not "heal." Hypnosis by him helps ulcerative colitis, and he has helped patients with arthrosis and with muscular dystrophy. He claims to have curative fluids in his hands, and some doctors in the hospital want him to put his hands over colonies of bacteria as an experiment in "hard science."

In a nearby province, there is a healing twosome, mother and daughter, who practice pranotherapy. The mother claims that she learned automatic writing from Mesmer. Her pen would flow and the signatures always became "Carlos Mirabelli." She had difficulty discovering who he was, but finally learned of someone by that name who had died before his time in an accident and presumably wanted her to continue his work. The daughter claims that, unlike her mother, she is "serenely detached" from her work, as a scientist should be, and that the heat radiating from her hands has cured even some skeptics but has on occasion failed to cure believers.

But here, too, there is a difference between the way therapists are perceived by those who deliver such therapeutic services and those who receive them. The healers gave this investigator intricate explanations of the principles involved, but the patients were interested only in the specifics and particulars of symptom and syndrome, cure or remission. They wished to be spared the explanatory principles.

We may summarize by emphasizing that the practitioners of folk healing borrow the terminology of medical science for symptoms and syndromes, and that of physics for the most recent "buzz words" and buzz concepts. They adopt as well the classificatory mode of viewing phenomena in the natural world and classify themselves as specialists. Their clients not only find this acceptable, but accept the "updating" as further validation of the powers of the folk healers. To them, the incorporation of traditional folk-medical practices into current therapies by these healers merely demonstrates that "scientific thinking" has found these old cures to have been effective, and that the healers were scientific all along but only recently joined the *communication* revolution.

The Mind–Body Unit: An Unexpressed Presupposition

Peasants as well as primitive people see the mind–body system as a unit. Body, person, family, and community systems are also connected. Thus, persons in subsystems interact with each other through complex causal loops in a hierarchy of systems: family, community, society. For any minor dislocation in a subsystem, this view maintains that one should investigate all possible dislocations throughout the hierarchy. With such an assumption, the kinds of questions which we avoid as meaningless can be confronted. Mind and body belong to the *same* system; they affect and are affected by each other. For this reason, the shaman or other healers serve both religious and medical needs of the individual and the community.

Here one finds an unquestioned connection between illness and sociomoral deviance (Romanucci–Ross 1969). European civilizations have occasionally been fettered by notions that certain illnesses "play out," metaphorically, ideas of good and evil. Sontag (1978) has described some of these notions, citing examples in literary works of several European countries.

In contrast to the unity of mind and body expressed in primitive and folk cultures, the mainstream of early Western thought and culture conceptually severed the person from society; this was followed quickly by our notion of mind–body dualism or two systems in one person. Considerable institutional investment through the millenia has kept the systems separated (churches and theological seminaries have generally been isolated from hospitals and medical colleges, certainly in the training of professionals). Products of a tradition such as ours are events in which minds inhabit bodies but persevere after bodies disintegrate, and mind–souls await incorporation into a new body. The latter assumption surfaces in our practical policy making, as, for example, in the abortion issue: when is a fetus a person? In our culture, bodies can operate in causality systems without inputs from mind, and attributes of a thing, body, or system can have a separate existence of their own; e.g., the patient "has" a mental illness such as schizophrenia.

This traditional dichotomy not only still persists in Italian culture today, but, indeed, certain parts of Italy can be said to have been the birthplace of such concepts. We need only allude to the medical school in Salerno (tenth and eleventh centuries), the first in Europe and the parent of the great medieval schools at Bologna, Padua, Montpellier, and Paris. Physicians in Italy today, in a "lateralization" with their colleagues in other Western cultures, join in workshops that tend to keep this dichotomy alive, even when the titles of these conferences announce a broader understanding of causality in illness and disease as their intended goals.

How Western Medical Thinking Contemplates Change

Numerous interdisciplinary workshops comprised of experts are now held both in the United States and in Europe on such phenomena as sociocultural risk factors for a given disease, or on what is now called behavioral medicine. (Such workshops have been attended by some of the physicians who interact in referrals from Pasqualina.) There is a familiar unfolding to these sessions; each participant makes a presentation from the vantage point of his expertise, as he sees it veering toward the sociocultural or behavioral–medical. "Data" are not lacking, for there are ample figures, charts, and measurements on the thing or event that the speaker has been trained to measure. Of course, interrelating what has been presented and heard is not a simple matter, for the training to present is the same as the training to receive. The resumé, usually by the conveners, will focus on the most biomedically oriented, reductionist model presented; it invariably bears little resemblance to any of the presentations on what might be called sociocultural behavioral vectors of the pathology in question. The most lauded presentation usually offers no linkages and the least hope for articulation between the various levels of explanation of the topic under discussion as it relates to human behavior. Yet in the resumé it is this presentation that is said to "provide the best hope of increasing our understanding." It is a turning inward and actually offers the least hope for the problem under discussion, as exemplified by a recent workshop in behavioral function in arteriosclerosis.[11] But it is not likely that "more" will be learned about the wide arc of causality that links behavior and arteriosclerosis, or any other malfunction, by focusing exclusively on internal small circuits of cause and effect. Exercise, stress, environmental pollutants, ingestion of food additives and drugs (casual or prescribed), and other culturally approved, tolerated, or recommended behavior modifiers were in this typical example once again totally ignored in the biochemical micro-model embraced with joy by the "scientists" expressing an interest in learning about human behavior and interaction. We will need much more internal analysis of the information we *have* before we can continue to talk productively about communication between health-care providers and consumers. Like symptoms joining in syndromal constellations, beliefs cluster, and scientific beliefs cluster just as adamantly as any other as they resist new modes of thought. It is a fact of our culture that we have too long ignored nonverbal communication and other aspects of linkage between segments of information. At the same time, there are social exhortations both within and outside of medicine to promote awareness of patient needs and patient education. Nevertheless, it would appear that clinical research studies are being designed that have *less* information than formerly on clinical endpoints affected by social functioning and occupational status. Fletcher and Fletcher (1979), in a study of frequency of research designs in the clinical literature, described 612 articles in three general medical journals from 1946 to 1976. They found a decline in longitudinal studies and an increase in cross-sectional studies. This decline results in a diminution of the information that provides sound data for clinical decision making, a trend that, in the Fletchers' view, "deserves critical attention." Obviously, both are needed, but the Fletchers are concerned with a growing neglect of longitudinal studies. To what can this be attributed? Nelson (1979) points out that there is an "epidemiology to publication" in medical science that would bring about such a trend. Rewarded are the "timely" conclusions (with no time for impeccable design and detailed description for the reader of what the researcher actually did). Hypotheses that have "failed" do not get published, so that one is tempted to work backward from the conclusions to the premises, using several variables—with several variables, the researcher will certainly always come up with something. There are professional as well as social pressures for success, and resistance engendered by introspection and criticalness of one's work do not promise "payoff." (I think of this as analogous to the hydraulic-resistance equation; the *flow* of published material is a function of *quality* times *drive* over the filter of introspection; flow equals pressure over resistance.)

There have been explorations for change. To look for sources for a cultural change in medical education, or facilitation in communication in health-care situations, is difficult, since the role models emerge contaminated from traditional training.

One forceful source for change lies with a group of persons who were never before as numerous, as articulate, and as accessible as they are today. They are promising agents for change in the enculturation of medical trainees. These agents are the chronically ill patients who achieve status in the eye of the medical student as bearers of an intractable illness. Through the years of chronicity these patients have learned the discourse, the stylistic techniques of interpreting pain; they have mastered the vocabulary of their illness in acculturation. They know about medications and their effects on them. As brokers and cultural mediators of this information, transformed by their own experience, they also teach colleagueship to medical students, residents, and postgraduate fellows. It was evident that this kind of communication was effective in promoting Pasqualina's medical-care delivery network; she learned from her patients and transmitted this information to their physicians, thereby greatly enhancing their effectiveness.

Occupational medicine provides another possible avenue in which the health-care provider might learn about the subject, i.e., the patient. In primitive societies we have noted that sickness is an event categorized with other disordered states; so, too, we learn through occupationally induced illness that people often consider job risks in the same category, and just as important, as unemployment. In a calculus that includes disasters of one sort or another, and with the time factor making one disaster more real and imminent than the other, we learn from the worker that the probability of incurable disease in the distant future is not an important immediate deterrent to keeping a relatively well-paid job. Thus, going beyond manifest differences in behavior, we find structural similarities among all "patients" in all cultures.

Some Conclusions

Culture is the structuring and processing of information, but it is also all the residues that accumulate over time and influence indirectly the structuring and processing. It would be well to develop a method to look at how imagery and perception interlace to exercise selectivity and stylizing effects on the generated knowledge configurations (Romanucci–Ross 1979). But for the present we can at least postulate transactions and exchanges within a social-relations context. Emerson (1976), speaking as a social exchange theorist, maintains that there is a reciprocity in the relation between experimenter and experimentee (p. 346). It is not, as commonly thought, a one-way flow of information that will result in a solution to the problem at hand. Even the recognition of the formality of the relationship between investigator and subject will affect outcome. However, we would like to add to Emerson's stimulating analysis the concept of a stream of consciousness in the exchanging parties. The consciousness continuums allow for points of real communication, but they also allow for many more points of mismatch of codes and messages. The physician has a body of information, constantly if minimally transformed as he goes from patient to patient. He interprets cross-sectionally what appears before him. The patient has a longitudinal experiential history of his own illness as he presents it, and his own calculus of mishaps, misfortunes, and optimization strategies for resolution of the problem.

In the psychology of operant behavior modelling, what has been looked at is the rewarding of compliance, but there is also a reward for noncompliance, certainly for humans if not for pigeons and rats. Firth (1967) stated a position, fashionable among some economists, that whatever a person does can be seen as motivated by maximization of that person's gain. Rewarding for compliance is a proposition that is not testable as currently stated.

Another approach might be the adoption of a model of power–dependence relations, as developed by Emerson (1964) from his experiments in social psychology. Emerson's theoretical model defines balance and imbalance in power relations and relational networks in the balancing process. He posits that the power to influence an actor (in our case the patient) is based on his dependency (urgency for treatment), which is related to motivational investment in the goals mediated by the power holder (physician in our case) and inversely proportional to the availability of these goals outside of the relationship (p. 298).

Within our problem orientation, medicalization can be viewed as the attempt by power holder to capture the motivational investment field, leaving the dependent patient with little other choice that he finds acceptable. This state of affairs has occasioned attempts, constituting islands of collusion between some patients and marginal healers, to begin counter acculturative movements in medical care. It is to be hoped that conventional Western allopathic medicine will, as it has in the past, assimilate what is scientifically valid from these movements into its own corpus of knowledge, and at the same time broaden its hypotheses about health and behavior in the cultural context. We share with cultural groups of less complexity and less internal diversity the shifting game strategies of confronting illness to regain health. Folk medicine and primitive medicine are on varying points of the medicalization continuum, but those engaged in all systems negotiate health care and identity while seeking to retain the option of alternativity in remedies to physical and mental disorders. The search for a formula of colleagueship between health-care providers and consumers appears to be universal.

NOTES

1. See Romanucci–Ross 1975. Anthropological field research in Italy was continued in four field trips of six to eight weeks' duration each in 1976, 1977, 1978, and 1979.

2. The theme of *The Golden Bough* is Frazer's theory of the development of modes of thinking; he visualized magic and religion evolving into science. For this region of Italy, he traced the origin of the myth of the divine king slain by a young man who had then to seize the mistletoe on the tip of a large oak. This unleashed social upheaval, with the young slayer becoming the new king and priest, thereby assuring fertility in crops, animals, and people.

3. Commonly called Cecco d'Ascoli, his name was Francesco degli Stabili (1267–1327). Professor of astrology in Bologna, he was condemned as a heretic and went to Florence in 1324, where he was burned at the stake in 1327. In Ascoli it is said that by his magic he threw up a bridge so that he might escape from that city; the bridge is still called *il ponte di Cecco.*

4. Singular and plural: *mago/maghi; strega/streghe.*

5. It is of interest that the Italian Penal Code, Article 661, punishes with three months of imprisonment and a 400,000-lire fine anyone "whoever publicly seeks with whatever imposture, even for no recompense, to abuse popular credulity if this should lead to the disturbance of public order." Laws are not usually needed for these areas of human interaction where there are no differences of opinion on common-sense judgment.

6. I have found remarkable similarities of belief and behavior surrounding "the evil eye" in Palgi's description of this phenomenon among Yemenite Jews. See Palgi, chapter 18 of this book.

7. The doctor was referring to a prior publication (Romanucci–Ross 1975).

8. The quotation is from Roche advertising to promote sales of Valium and Librium. Hearings before the Subcommittee on Monopoly of the Select Committee on Small Business, U.S. Senate, 21–23 July and 22 Sept. 1971 (concerning mood drugs, sedatives tranquilizers, and stimulants), p. 810.

9. John Ross, Jr., M.D., August–September 1979.

10. *Il Resto del Carlino,* 17 Aug. 1979.

11. "Workshop on Behavioral Science; Working Group on Arteriosclerosis," La Jolla, Cal. 15–16 Nov. 1979. The intent of the working group was implicit in the title. Psychologists, sociologists, and anthropologists were also invited to make presentations on behavior affecting arteriosclerosis, but the medical specialists who had convened the conference focused on one report on research on biochemical transmitters. It was felt by the conveners that "here" lay the promise for future discoveries on human behavior. The conference closed with the major convener promising to recommend "funding" for this sort of research on the biochemical and cellular lead to learn "more" about the effects of human behavior on arteriosclerosis.

REFERENCES

Emerson, Richard M. 1962. "Power–Dependence Relations." *American Sociological Review,* 27(1):31–41.

1964   "Power–Dependence Relations: Two Experiments." *Sociometry,* 27(3): 282–98.

1976   "Social Exchange Theory." *Annual Review of Sociology,* 2:335–62.

Firth, Raymond. 1967. *Themes in Economic Anthropology*. London: Tavistock.

Fletcher, Robert H., and Suzanne W. Fletcher. 1979. "Clinical Research in General Medical Journals: A 30-year Perspective." *New England Journal of Medicine*, 26 July, 180–83.

Frazer, Sir James. 1890. *The Golden Bough: A Study in Magic and Religion*, 12 vols., 3d. ed., revised and enlarged. London: Macmillan, 1911–15.

Nelson III, Rodney B. 1979. "Are Clinical Trials Pseudoscience?" *Forum on Medicine*, pp. 594–600.

Romanucci–Ross, Lola (a.k.a. L.R. Schwartz). 1969. "The Hierarchy of Resort in Curative Practices: The Admiralty Islands, Melanesia." *Journal of Health and Social Behavior*, 10:201–9.

1973   *Conflict, Violence and Morality in a Mexican Village*. Palo Alto: Mayfield.

1975   "The Italian Identity and Its Transformations." George de Vos and Lola Romanucci–Ross, eds., *Ethnic Identity: Cultural Continuities and Change*. Palo Alto: Mayfield, 198–226.

1979   "Melanesian Medicine: Beyond Culture to Method." Peter Morley and Roy Wallis, eds., *Culture and Curing: Anthropological Perspectives on Traditional Medical Beliefs and Practices*. Pittsburgh: Univ. of Pittsburgh Press, 115–138.

1981   "Metaphor and Medicalization: Hierarchy of Curing Practices Reconsidered." Paper presented at American Anthropological Association, 80th annual meeting.

In Press, "Medicalization and Metaphor: Strategies in Health Care and Their Meanings in Cultural Stability and Change." Martin de Vries, ed., New York: Reidel.

Schwartz, L.R. See materials listed under Lola Romanucci–Ross.

Sontag, Susan. 1978. *Illness as Metaphor*. New York: Farrar, Straus & Giroux.

2

Aztec and European Medicine in the New World, 1521–1600

Clara Sue Kidwell

Spanish settlers in the New World came bringing with them their customs, their foods, and their diseases. The New World represented a strange and even exotic place. It was primarily of interest to the Spaniards because of the material wealth of gold and silver that they dug from its bowels. However, although the gold and silver of the New World mines had a tremendous impact upon the role of Spain as a world power and upon the course of European history, the most lasting contributions of the North and South American continents to the European civilizations were not the minerals that represented wealth. Instead, it was the plants, primarily in the form of foodstuffs but also in the form of herbs for medical use, that were ultimately to provide a wealth far greater than the mineral wealth of the New World continents.[1]

In return for that wealth, the Spaniards gave to the native peoples of the New World many diseases—e.g., smallpox, typhus, cholera, and measles—and a life of slavery in the mines that largely decimated the Indian populations within approximately 50 years of the conquest.[2] Although there are many problems in calculating exact numbers of native populations at the time of conquest from which to calculate a rate of decline, the fact of the population decline due to disease is readily apparent.

The Spaniards, in their turn, suffered from what is often called "Montezuma's revenge," that is, gastrointestinal distress, as well as respiratory ailments induced by the living conditions in the New World. Agustin Farfan, a Spanish physician writing in Mexico in 1579, listed the principal afflictions of the Spanish residents of the New World as "flaqueza y indigestion del estomago" (weakness and indigestion of the stomach), "tauardete" [*sic*] (typhus), "dolor de costado" (tuberculosis), and "de la colica passion y del dolor de Ijada" (appendicitis).[3] Juan de Cardenas also devoted a chapter to the subject of Spanish ills in his *Primera Parte de los Problemas*

20

y Secretos Maravillosos de la Indias. Those ills included stomach problems, menstrual difficulties, rheumatism, liver trouble, and urinary difficulty.[4] Native populations were also subject to respiratory and gastrointestinal diseases, of course, but the Spanish seemed much more susceptible to the illnesses of the New World.[5] One disease with major social and economic importance for the Spanish was syphilis.[6] One of the important export items from New Spain to Europe was guaiacum, highly touted in Europe as a cure for syphilis.[7] The theory seemed to be that syphilis was indeed a New World disease, and thus its cure should be a New World plant.

Acculturation and Medical Practice

It was in the area of medical practices that early forces of cultural assimilation began to affect both cultures, European and native. The tradition of medical "simples" was well known to European settlers in the New World, and since herbal medicines formed an important part of the medical practices of the Aztecs, Incas, and other native peoples with whom the Europeans were coming into contact, it can reasonably be assumed that at least some of these herbal remedies were adopted by the Spanish colonists and thus constituted a case of reverse acculturation, the adoption of native practices by the conquering civilization.[8] But the differences in basic premises of culture underlying the methods of treatment in the European and the Aztec societies were so different in so many respects that one would expect much less exchange of therapeutic methods outside of herbal medicines.

A body of writings by European physicians and Aztec writers (or information supplied by Aztecs) concerning *materia medica* in sixteenth-century New Spain shows some of the processes of acculturation that were going on in medical practice. These writings are sources of medical information that demonstrate the differing viewpoints of two cultures toward medical practices (and, as well, the viewpoint of one culture toward another). From these writings one can determine the interaction that was going on between native and European physicians, the differences and similarities of their viewpoints, and the extent to which any true influences were being exchanged in the first 80 years of contact between the cultures.

The body of writings under discussion comprises the following: from the Europeans, the *Opera Medicinalia* of Francisco Bravo (1525?–1594?), published in 1570 in Mexico;[9] the great work on New World plants compiled by Francisco Hernandez (1517–1578) and published in part in 1628 under the title *Rerum Medicarum Novae Hispaniae Thesaurus . . . ;*[10] the *Tractado Breve de Anothomia y Chirugia . . .* , published in Mexico by Agustin Farfan (1531?–1604) in 1579 (with a second edition, *Tractado Breve de Medicina,* in 1592);[11] and *Summa y Recopilacion de Chirugia . . .* , by Alonso Lopez Hinojosos (1535–1597), published in Mexico in 1578 (with a second edition in 1595).[12] And from the Aztecs *Libellus de medicinalibus Indorum Herbis . . .* , written by Martin de la Cruz and translated from Aztec to Latin by Juan Badianus (both authors were Aztecs),[13] and the *Historia General de las Cosas de Nueve Espana,* compiled by Bernardino de Sahagun, a Franciscan priest, from

Aztec informants.[14] The intricate relationship among these various works provides a fascinating insight into the differences between New World native medical practices and European concepts of medicine, and the bases upon which exchanges of information could be made. The convergences and divergences of viewpoints constitute an important chapter in the development of medicine in sixteenth-century colonial America.

Communicable Concepts in Aztec and European Medicine

Aztec medicine was deeply embedded in the matrix of a culture that was highly religious in nature. Erwin Ackerknecht has commented on so-called primitive medicine that it is based essentially on supernaturalism with some rational elements, whereas modern medicine is based essentially on rationalism in spite of its magical elements.[15] An important aspect of medical practice among the Aztecs, for instance, was the ascription of causes of disease to the wrath of various deities. Xipe Totec caused skin diseases and was appeased in a yearly ceremony, in which sufferers of skin diseases walked in procession wearing the skins of sacrificial victims who had been flayed.[16] European medicine, on the other hand, was firmly rooted in the rational traditions of the Greeks, and the Galenic theory of the mechanism of the four humors and their balances in the body prevailed among European physicians. Attribution of qualities of hot and cold, wet and dry, was part of the Galenic tradition and linked European medicine with Aristotelian thought. Certainly all of the European physicians discussed here—Bravo, Farfan, Lopez de Hinojosos, and Hernandez—were firmly within the Galenic tradition of medicine. The Aztec writers, Badianus and de la Cruz, and the Aztecs upon whose information Sahagun based his work, represented a world view based upon the actions of the deities and their role in causing disease, as well as certain definite Aztec cultural values concerning fear, anxiety, and other emotional states that might be said to constitute illness.

Of the possible points of communication between the two systems of medical thought, two seem to be particularly important. The most obvious point of communication was a common belief in herbal medicines. The tradition of medical simples was well established in Europe, and the use of New World plants for therapeutic purposes would seem obvious. A second point of communication, which bears on the first, is the pragmatic nature of medical practice in the New World, where there were few physicians and where the Spaniards were confronted with new conditions relating to their health. Of the works under consideration, those of Bravo and Hernandez are most strongly based in the theoretical Galenic and Aristotelian tradition of European thought, whereas those of Farfan and Lopez de Hinojosos, although they subscribe to Galenic doctrines, represent more the orientation of the practicing physician confronted with new situations in a land where traditional European physicians were not readily available to large parts of the colonial population. In many ways the Badianus–de la Cruz manuscript, with its almost cook-book-like approach to medical prescriptions, is closer to the Farfan and Lopez de Hinojosos books than it is to the work by Sahagun, which sought to reflect the Aztec world view as a whole, which devotes limited attention to specific medical practices (book 10), and which treats the role of physicians (book 10), the nature of herbal medicines (book 11), and the role of deities as causes of illness (book 1) in different parts of the final version of the work.[17]

In terms of the historical connections among all of the works under discussion, there is evidence that the writers could have been in contact with one another in various ways, either directly or indirectly. Connections among the works by Bravo, Farfan, and Lopez de Hinojosos are established in the prefatory material of the three books. Bravo wrote endorsements for both Farfan's *Tractado Breve de Anothomia y Chirugia* and Lopez de Hinojosos's *Summa y Recopilacion de Chirugia.*[18] His endorsements may have been sought because of his reputation, which had been established with publication of his *Opera Medicinalia* (generally considered the first medical work published in the New World). Farfan also endorsed Lopez de Hinojosos's work.[19] Lopez de Hinojosos, in turn, was associated with Francisco Hernandez at the Royal Hospital for Indians in Mexico, where he practiced for 14 years.[20] The connection between Hernandez and Bernardino de Sahagun is very tenuous, but yet it appears that Hernandez might have used a section of Sahagun's work in his own book (although without proper attribution).[21] Sahagun, in his turn, was for a time associated with the College of Tlalolco, where Juan Badianus and Martin de la Cruz were students. Sahagun was at the college from 1536 to 1540 and again in 1545. There is no indication that he was directly associated with de la Cruz and Badianus, whose work, the *Libellus,* was completed in 1552.[22] However, Sahagun's interest in the collection of Aztec materials may well have indicated a more general interest in writings by Aztecs at the college.

Despite the historical conjunction of these writers, there is very little evidence that transmission of knowledge from Aztec to European sources, or from European to Aztec sources, was taking place during the first century of contact. Rather, the conjunction is more evidence that differing cultural traditions were coming into contact but that, except in the area of herbal medicine, little exchange was taking place between the two cultures in medical practices.

European Physicians and Their Interpretations

Of the writers under consideration, Francisco Bravo seems most clearly the European physician. His work is divided into four major parts: a discussion of typhus (which he calls "tauardeste" [*sic*]) and its treatments; a disputation in the form of a dialogue concerning the uses of venesection to treat the disease; a discussion of the doctrine of critical days in the treatment of disease; and a description of sarsaparilla, with a discussion of its qualities (Bravo maintained that the plant is hot and dry, rather than being cold as some maintained).[23] Bravo makes numerous references to Galen and also to Arabic writers—Avicenna and Rhazes—as well as to Fracastorio and Laguna, his closer contemporaries.[24] He makes no mention of native medical practices, and the herbal remedies that he does mention (except sarsaparilla) are of European origin. For example, a remedy for plague includes "rosis, violis, hordeo, lactucis, capitiabus papaveris, soliis salicis, et cannarum et cucurbitae" mixed in water.[25]

Francisco Hernandez, physician to Philip II of Spain, was sent by Philip to the New World to collect material on natural history. His work is more in the ency-clopedic traditon of natural histories and herbals that were appearing in Europe during the sixteenth and seventeenth centuries. Although he used the Aztec names of plants, reflecting a classification system based on use (*quilitl* as a suffix referred to plants used as foods; *yochitl* referred to ornamental plants; *patli* referred to me-dicinal plants; and economic plants useful for building and material objects were referred to by several suffixes),[26] Hernandez introduced his discussion with reference to the classification system of Theophrastus, who classified plants according to form: *arbor, herba, suffrutex,* and *frutex.*[27] Hernandez is much more concerned with de-scription of the form of plants, although he does include medicinal properties in some descriptions (*texaxapotla,* for example, when burned and its vapors breathed, cured sneezing and dried up phlegm in the eyes, nose, and mouth).[28] The drawings of plants in his work are much more naturalistic than those in the *Libellus* of Badianus and de la Cruz. His work is an important source of information on Aztec plants and, in some cases, their medicinal uses. However, it remained very much in the European tradition of descriptive natural history.

Farfan and Lopez de Hinojosos both follow European traditions in their references to humors, and to Galen and Guido as authorities.[29] However, both also made reference to herbal medicines used by Aztecs healers. In the 1579 edition of Farfan's work, he mentions, for instance, xoxocoyoles (for stomach disorders),[30] mechoacan (*iopmoea jalapa, Bryonia mechoacana,* as a purgative)[31] guayacan (*guaiacum officinale,* for "mal de Bubas")[32] and sarsaparilla (which, in agreement with Bravo, he describes as hot, its heat moving vapors in the body).[33] In the 1592 edition of the work, which is indeed more a major expansion of the section of medical practices than simply a new edition, he includes 59 native plants as remedies.[34]

Lopez mentions remedies newly described and discovered by experiments.[35] He mentions specifically guayacan, sarsaparilla, canafistola, and chichimecapatle as in-gredients in a cure for *alferezia* (epilepsy).[36] In regard to specific medical practices, both Farfan and Lopez mention bleeding as a curative technique, but Lopez says that he has not seen bloodletting as a practice among the natives.[37] However, specific mention of bleeding as a practice in the cure of headaches is made in Sahagun's work.[38]

As their treatises indicate, both Farfan and Lopez de Hinojosos are much more concerned with experience than theory. The endorsements for Farfan's book speak of his long years of experience as a physician (he evidently obtained his medical degree on 20 July 1567 from the *Real y Pontificia Universidad de Mexico.*)[39] Farfan and Lopez both describe their books as being intended for those who are far from cities and need to learn about remedies for illness and medical practices.[40]

In its general nature, the *Libellus de medicinalibus* of Badianus and de la Cruz is similar to the works of Farfan and Lopez de Hinojosos. It, too, is a description of medical practices, primarily based on herbal medicines. Its intended audience was Don Francisco de Mendoza, son of the viceroy of New Spain. The title of the book can be translated as "A Little Book of Indian Medicinal Herbs Composed by a Certain Indian, Physician of the College of Santa Cruz, Who Has No Theoretical Learning, But Is Well Taught by Experience Alone."[41] The emphasis is upon experience rather than upon theory, and the approach of the book is purely descriptive, including extensive recipes of herbal medicines. The book is organized in a straightforward head-to-foot manner, following the organization of the human body. The dedication of the work is very revealing in the attitudes of native physicians toward their Spanish overlords. Badianus and de la Cruz were, of course, educated at the College of Santa Cruz at Tlalolco, which was established by Franciscan missionaries to educate the sons of Aztec nobles. De la Cruz includes in the dedication the following statement:

> Indeed I suspect that you ask so earnestly for this little book of herbs and medicaments for no other reason than to commend us Indians, even though unworthy, to His Holy Caesarian Catholic Royal Majesty. Would that we Indians could make a book worthy in the King's sight, for this is certainly most unworthy to come before the sight of such great majesty. But you will recollect that we poor unhappy Indians are inferior to all mortals, and for that reason our poverty and insignificance implanted in us by nature merit your indulgence.[42]

The *Libellus* is enlivened with colored drawings of the herbs that are described, and the work contains such typical Aztec remedies as acozoyatl for treatment of one affected by a whirlwind.[43] It is interesting to note that conditions such as "fatigue, . . . lassitude suffered by officials holding public office," "fear . . . or faintheartedness," and "mental stupor,"[44] are included as conditions to be treated with herbal remedies. Although the work reflects Aztec traditions, it contains nothing of the rich religious traditions that underlay the practice of Aztec medicine. It reflects a European bias in its statements concerning the lowly status of the natives. Its concern for practical treatment rather than theory may represent a European orientation (Sahagun's book 10 follows the same head-to-foot orientation and statement of specific treatments) that ignored the religiously based aspects of Aztec medicine, but it may also reflect a kind of pragmatic orientation toward treatment of illness that is somewhat similar to the works of Farfan and Lopez de Hinojosos.

Conflict between Rationality and Religion

If Bravo and Hernandez represent the purely rational and theoretical tradition of European medicine, and Farfan and Lopez de Hinojosos represent both the rational and pragmatic aspects, Bernardino de Sahagun represents the conflict of rational thought and religious belief, belief in both Christian and Aztec culture. The initial charge to Sahagun, given by the provincial father Francisco de Toral, was that Sahagun should write in the Nahuatl language those things that he considered useful for the maintenance of Christianity and the work and ministering of Christian doctrines.[45] Sahagun gathered information from Aztec informants and cross-checked his information with Aztecs in various parts of the country. But his original intent was to use the information to convince the Aztecs of the errors of their past ways. He thus included after his description of major deities a tract condemning the worship of those deities:

> My children, perceive God's word, which is God's light. Thus will see those who live in darkness, who have lost the way; those who worship idols, who go with the sins of the devil, who is the father of lies. And thus will be known to them their gods and their lords which the word of God, which here, lying unfolded, revealeth how idolatry began. Likewise here are revealed many things concerning the error, misery, and blindness into which the worshippers of idols fell.[46]

Sahagun's work remains the standard source for descriptions of Aztec medical practices. It is interesting to note, however, that, like the work by de la Cruz and Badianus, Sahagun's work was not published in his lifetime. Indeed, it was not until 1830 that even a partial edition of the work was published.[47]

Medical Knowledge from the New World

In the contacts between medical practices in the New World and the Old, the major point at which exchange of information took place was in the area of herbal medicines. Indians were certainly treated by European practitioners in hospitals such as the Royal Hospital for Indians, where Hernandez and Lopez de Hinojosos worked together. But in terms of the overall structure of medical practices, European physicians did not adopt any of the religiously based ideas of the Aztecs concerning medical practices, and Aztecs did not immediately adopt any European practices that they did not already have.

An interesting example of the transmission of knowledge from Aztec to European sources is the plant *cacaloxochitl,* which is mentioned in Hernandez's *De Rerum Medicarum,* the *Libellus,* and Sahagun's *Historia General.* The physical description of the plant differs in the *De Rerum Medicarum* and the *Historia General.* The physical description in Hernandez reads as follows:

> It is a tree of medium size with leaves like citrus, but much larger and with abundant veins which run from the center vein to the edges. The fruits are one pod, very large and red; the flowers are large, beautiful and of pleasing, pleasant scent, and are the only part that is used; they are used to make nosegays, garlands and crowns, things much used among the Indians and held in such esteem that they never appear before a head person without offering beforehand some of these offerings. It makes milk. Cooled and congealed, and applied, it is a cure for the illness of the breast which comes from heat. Its marrow, taken in a dose in two drachms cleanses the stomach and the intestines.[48]

Sahagun describes the plant in the following terms:

> It is a bush that they call cacaloxochitl; it has leaves that are somewhat broad, and

somewhat long, and downy. It has branches straight and spongy, and the leaves and branches sometimes make milk, and this milk is sweet as honey. The flowers of this tree are beautiful. They are called also cacaloxochitl. They are bronze colored, of red, yellow and white. They have a delicate odor, and they comfort the spirit with their odor. Through the districts of Mexico one has these flowers, but those which come from warm lands are better; some are black. In former times these flowers were reserved for the lords.[49]

Badianus and de la Cruz do not give a written description of the plant, but their drawing shows a plant with red flowers and long, slender leaves. The veins mentioned in Hernandez's description do not appear in the drawing.[50] The flowers of the plants are part of a very elaborate herbal formula entitled, "Trees and Flowers for the Fatigue of Those Administering the Government and Holding Public Office."[51] That the plant is the same in all three sources, despite the discrepancies in written description, can be determined primarily by the fact that all three sources mention the same use for the plant, i.e., in relation to lords or high government officials. However, Badianus and de la Cruz mention a specific condition of those persons, fatigue related to holding high office, and the plant is thus treated as part of a remedy that would drive weariness away and would drive out fear and fortify the heart.[52] Hernandez and Sahagun do not attribute any medicinal properties to the plant in its use as an offering to high officials. They do mention other medicinal uses, however.

In the contacts between medical practices in the New World and the Old, the only major point at which exchange of information took place was in the area of herbal medicines. Those were adopted by Europeans seemingly as a matter of the practical necessities of dealing with the diseases and health conditions in the New World. Interest in Aztec culture was primarily ethnographic in nature (as in Sahagun's work), or was firmly embedded in the natural-history tradition of European academic inquiry (as in Hernandez's work). The very pragmatic nature of medical practice provided the only real point of contact between two very disparate systems of medical treatment. The importation of New World plants (such as guaiacum) to the Old World, and of Old World plants to the New World, and a mutual concern with the efficacy of herbal remedies, provided the only substantial evidence of cross-cultural medical practices.

NOTES

1. See Alfred W. Crosby, Jr., *The Columbia Exchange: Biological and Cultural Consequences of 1492* (Westport, Conn.: Greenwood Press, 1972), pp. 165–208, for a discussion of New World plants and Old World demography. See also Francisco Guerra, "Drugs from the Indies and the Political Economy of the Sixteenth Century," *Analecta medico–historica,* 1 (1966): 29–54.

2. William M. Denevan, ed., *The Native Population of the Americas in 1492* (Madison: Univ. of Wisconsin, 1976), 7.

3. Agustin Farfan, *Tractado Breve de Anothomia y chirugia, y de algunas Enfermedades, que mas comunmente suelen hauer en esta Nueua Espana. Compuesto por el muy Reuerendo padre Fray Augustin Farfan, Doctor en Medicina, y Religioso de la Orden de Sant Augustin. Dirgido al muy Reuerendo padre Maestro Fray Martin de Perea, Prouincial de la dicha orden de Sant Augustin.* (Mexico: Casa de Antonio Ricardo, 1579), 223–64.

4. Juan de Cardenas, *Primera Parte de los Problemas y Secretos Maravillosos de la Indias* (Mexico: Casa de Pedro Ocharte, 1591; reprint ed., Mexico: Imp. del Museo n. de arqueologia historia y etnologia, 1913), 185–86, 191, 193.

5. See Sherburne F. Cook, "The Incidence and Significance of Disease Among the Aztecs and Related Tribes," *Hispanic American Historical Review,* 26 (1946): 320–35.

6. Crosby, *Columbia Exchange,* pp. 122–64. Francisco Guerra, "The Problem of Syphilis." Fredi Chiappelli, ed., *First Images of America.* (Berkeley: Univ. of California, 1976), 22:845–51.

7. Charles H. Talbot, "America and the European Drug Trade," in *First Images of America,* ibid., 2:834–36.

8. Juan Comas, "Influencia Indigena en la medicina hipocratica en la Neuva Espana del siglo XVI," *America Indigena,* 14: (1954): 329.

9. Francisco Bravo, *Opera Medicinalia in quibus plurima extant scitu medico necessaria in 4 li. digesta, que pagina versa cotinentur, Authore Francisco Bravo Ofunesi doctore, ac Mexicano Medico (Mexico:* Apud Petrum Ocharte, 1570). A facsimile reprint edition of Bravo's work, *The Opera Medicinalia* (Folkestone & London: Dawsons of Pall Mall, 1970), with an introduction by Francisco Guerra, makes the work available for scholarly study. Guerra cites the *Opera* as the earliest medical work published in the New World (see his introductory statements, p. 2).

10. Francisco Hernandez, *De Rerum Medicarum Novae Hispaniae Thesaurus seu Plantarum Animalium Mineralium Mexicanorum Historia ex Francisci Hernandi Novi Orbis Medici Primarij relationibus in ipsa Mexicana Urbe conscriptis a Nardo Antonio Recchio Monte Coriunate Cath. Maiest. Medico et Neap. Regni Archiatro Generali Iussu Philippi II Hisp. Indar. Regis Collecta ac in ordinem digesta a Ioanne Terrentio Lynceo Constantiense Germ. Pho. ac Medico Notis illustrata Nunc primum in Naturaliũ rerũ Studiosor gratia et utilitatẽ studio et impensis Lynceorum. Publici iuris facta Philippo IV Magno Dicata* (Rome: Iacobi Mascardi, 1628). A new printing of the work, with a new title page, appeared in 1651. See Francisco Hernandez, *Nova Plantarum, animalium et mineralium mexicanorum historia A Francisco Hernandez primum compilata, dein a Nardo Antonio Reccho in volumen digesta, a Jo. Terentio, Io. Fabro, et Fabio Columna Lynceis notis, & additionibus longe doctissimis illustrata. Cui demum accessere aliquot ex principio Federici Caesi frontispiciis Theatri naturalis phytosophicae tabulae una com quamplurimus iconibus ad octigentus, quibus singula contemplanda graphica exhibentur* (Rome: V. Mascardi, 1651). The 1651 printing is much more readily available than the 1628. Hernandez, during his stay in Mexico, collected 17 volumes of material, which he transmitted to Spain, where Philip II deposited them in the Escurial. A fire in the Escurial destroyed the manuscript in 1671. A version of the manuscript was derived from a copy left in the mission at Huaxtepec and was published in 1615 by Francisco Ximenez under the title *Quatro Libros de la naturaleza, y virtudes de las plantas, y animales que estan recevidos en el uso de Medicina en la Neuva Espana, y la Methodo, y correccion y preparacion, que para ad mimmallas se requiere con lo' que el Doctor Francisco Hernandez escrivio en lengua Latina. Muy util Paratodo Generode gente q vive en estacias y Pueblos, de no ay Medicas, ni Botica. Traduzido y aumentados muchos simples, y Compuestos y muchos secretos curativos, por Father Francisco Ximenez, hijo del Conuento de S. Domingo de Mexico, Natural de la Villa de Luna del Reyno de Aragon.* A Nro R. P. Maestro Father Hernando Bazan, Prior Provincial de la Provincia de Sactiago de Mexico, de la Orden de los Prelicadores, y Cathedratico Iubilado de Theologia en la Universidad Real. (Mexico: Casa de la Viuda de Diego Lopez Davalos,

1615). Further published versions of Hernandez's work are based primarily on the 1628 (or 1651) edition of the summary by Reccho. The two modern editions of the work are *Historia de las Plantas de Nueva Espana,* 3 vols. (Mexico: Imprenta Universitaria, 1942–46), and Francisco Hernandez, *Obras Completas,* 5 vols. (Mexico City: Universidad Nacional de Mexico, 1960), which includes not only the Mexican work but Hernandez's translation of Pliny's *Natural History.* In 1790, an edition of Hernandez's work, based on the Reccho manuscript, appeared as *Opera, cum edita, tum inedita, ad autographi fidem et integritatem expressa, impensae el jussu regio.* (Matriti: Ibarrae heredum, 1970).

11. Farfan, *Tractado Breve.* The 1595 edition is *Summa y Recopilacion de Chirugia, Compuesto por mestro Alonso Lopez de Hinofoso, con un arte para Sangrar, y examen de Barberos, va anadido en esta segunda impresion el origen y nascimientes de las reumas y las enfermedades que dellas proceden, con otras cosas muy provechosas para acudir al remedio dellas, y del otras muchas enfermedades* (Mexico: Pedro Balli, 1595).

12. Alonso Lopez de Hinojosos, *Summa, y Recopilacion de Chirugia, con un arte para sagrar muy util y prouechosa. Compuesta Por Maestre Alonso Lopez, natural de los Inojosos. Chirugano y enfermero del Ospital de S. Iosephus de los Indios, destra muy insigne Ciudada de Mexico.* Dirigido al Lii. Y. R. S. Don P. Moya de Contreras, Arcobispe de Mexico y del cocejo de su Magest. (Mexico: Antonio Ricardo, 1578). The 1595 edition is *Summa y Recopilacion de Chirugia, Compuesto por mestro Alonso Lopez de Hinojoso, con un arte para Sangrar, y examen de Barberos, va anadido en esta segunda impresion el origen y nascimientes de las reumas y las enfermedades que dellas proceden, con otras cosas muy provechosas para acudir al remedio dellas, y del otras muchas enfermedades* (Mexico: Pedro Balli, 1595).

13. *Libellus de medicinalibus Indorum herbis, quem quidam Indus Collegii sancte Crucis medicus compusuit, nullis rationibus edoctus, sed solis experimentis edoctus, Anno domini sexuatovis 1552.* The manuscript was discovered in the Vatican library and finally published, first as *The de la Cruz–Badiano Aztec Herbal of 1552,* trans. William Gates (Baltimore, Md.: The Maya Society, 1939), and then as *The Badianus Manuscript (Codex Barberini, Latin 241), Vatican Library, an Aztec Herbal of 1552,* introduction, translation, and annotations by Emily Walcott Emmart (Baltimore, Md.: John Hopkins, 1940).

14. Bernardino de Sahagun, *Historia General de las Cosas de Nueva Espana,* 5 vols. (Mexico: Editorial Pedro Robredo, 1938). See also Fray Bernardino de Sahagun, *A History of Ancient Mexico (1547–1577),* trans. Fanny R. Bandelier from the Spanish version of Carlos Maria de Bustamenta, vol. 1 (Nashville, Tenn.: Fisk University, 1932). Subsequent editions of the work include *Historia General de las Cosas de Nueva Espana, escrita por Fr. Bernardino de Sahagun Franciscano y fundada en la documentacion en lingua mexicana recogida por los mismos naturales. La dispuso para la prensa en esta nueva edicion, con numeracion anotaciones y apendices Angel Maria Garibay K.,* 4 vols. (Mexico: Editorial Porua, 1956); *Historia General de las Cosas de Nueva Espana,* 5 vols. (Mexico: Editorial Pedro Robredo, 1938), and *General History of the Things of New Spain,* trans. Charles E. Dibble and Arthur J.Q. Anderson. Monographs of the School of American Research and the Museum of New Mexico, Nos. 13, 14 (Santa Fe, N.M.: 1950–65).

15. Erwin H. Ackerknecht, "Problems of Primitive Medicine," *Bulletin of the History of Medicine,* 2 (1942): 504.

16. Sahagun, *General History,* 2:16. See also Francisco Guerra, "Aztec Medicine," *Medical History,* 10 (1966): 320, for a general discussion of Aztec medical practices.

17. Sahagun, *General History,* 11:139–63, 53; vol. 12; 2:1–24.

18. Farfan, *Tractado Breve* (1579), p. 17, and Lopez de Hinojosos, *Summa y Recopilacion* (1578), 1–2.

19. Lopez de Hinojosos, *ibid.,* 3.

20. Joaquin Garcia Icazabalceta, *Bibliografia Mexicana del Siglo XVI Catalogo Razonado de Libros Impresos en Mexico de 1539 a 1600 con biografias de auteres y otras ilustraciones* (Mexico: Fondo de Cultura Economica, 1954), 235–36.

21. The connection between Hernandez and Sahagun is established in Ioannis Nieremberg's *Historia Naturae maxime peregrinae: Libris XVI distincta: In quibus rarissima Naturae arcana, etiam astronomica, & ignota Indarum animalia describuntur; Accedunt de miris et miraculosis naturis in Europa libri duo; item de iisdem in terra Hebraeis premissa liber unus* (Antverpiae: Ex Officina Plantiniana Balthasaris Moreti, 1635). Nieremberg attributed part of his book 2 directly to Hernandez. The manuscript source from which he drew these chapters seems to be no longer extant. However, the chapters in Nieremberg's book are virtually identical to the appendix to book 2 of Sahagun's *Historia General*. The material is a listing of religious ceremonies. See Nieremberg, pp. 142–44, and Sahagun, *General History*, 3:165–71. Leon–Portilla asserts that Nieremberg took the material from Hernandez without realizing that Hernandez had in turn copied it from Sahagun's manuscripts. It is surprising then that there are not more correspondences between the descriptions of plants in the Hernandez and Sahagun works. See Miguel Leon Portilla, *Ritos, sacerdotes y atavios de los dioses:* Introduction, paleografia, version & notas de Miguel Leon–Portilla (Mexico: Universidad Nacional Autonoma de Mexico Instituto de Historia: Seminario de Cultura Nahuatl, 1958), 21.

22. Sahagun, *History of Ancient Mexico*, pp. 3–9.

23. Bravo, *Opera Medicinalia*, pp. 2v–3, 167v, 273–74, 295v.

24. Ibid., pp. 4, 8, 273–74.

25. Ibid., p. 79.

26. De la Cruz, *The de la Cruz–Badiano Aztec Herbal*, p. xvii.

27. Hernandez, *De Rerum Medicarum*, pp. 8–9.

28. Ibid., pp. 29–30.

29. See, for example, Farfan, *Tractado Breve* (1579), p. 2, 4v, 107; Lopez de Hinojosos, *Summa y Recopilacion* (1578), pp. 1, 2.

30. Farfan, ibid., p. 7r.

31. Ibid., p. 55v.

32. Ibid., p. 217v.

33. Ibid., p. 87.

34. Comas, "Influencia Indigena," pp. 345–61.

35. Lopez de Hinojosos, *Summa y Recopilacion* (1578), p. 16.

36. Ibid., p. 70.

37. Farfan, *Tractado Breve* (1579), p. 77; Lopez de Hinojosos, ibid., p. 34v.

38. Scarification and bleeding were known to the Aztecs. The Badianus manuscript mentions a cure for veins swelling because of bloodletting, p. 281, in the heading of chapter 10, but the text does not include a specific cure as indicated by the heading of the chapter. Sahagun, *General History*, mentions bleeding the scalp as a cure for headache, 2:140.

39. Farfan, *Tractado Breve* (1579), pp. 1–2,; Comas, "Influencia Indigena," p. 344.

40. Lopez de Hinojosos, *Summa y Recopilacion* (1578), p. 16; Farfan, ibid., p. 17.

41. De la Cruz, *Libellus*, p. 205.

42. Ibid.

43. Ibid., p. 306.

44. Ibid., pp. 207–8.

45. Sahagun, *History of Mexico*, pp. 3–9.

46. Sahagun, *General History*, 2:34.

47. Sahagun, *History of Mexico*, pp. 13–14.

48. Hernandez, *Historia de las Plantas,* 3:806.
49. Sahagun, *Historia General* 3:276.
50. De la Cruz, *Badianus Manuscript,* pp. 276–77.
51. Ibid.
52. Ibid.

3

Traditional Medicine and Western Medical Options among the Ningerum of Papua New Guinea

Robert L. Welsch

The practices of these peoples in relation to disease are not a medley of disconnected and meaningless customs, but are inspired by definite ideas concerning the causation of disease. Their modes of treatment follow directly from their ideas concerning etiology and pathology. From our modern standpoint we are able to see that these ideas are wrong. But the important point is that, however wrong may be the beliefs of the Papuan and Melanesian concerning the causation of disease, their practices are a logical consequence of those beliefs.
—W.H.R. Rivers, 1924

This chapter considers the expectations, attitudes, and beliefs about Western medicine held by the Ningerum people of Papua New Guinea. My concern here is to show how the Ningerum perceive interrelationships between traditional and recently introduced Western curative practices. In particular I will argue that the Ningerum people's extensive use of Western medicine is closely related to their understanding of disease processes.

The Ningerum, a lowland rainforest people, became aware of the outside world barely 30 years ago. With the arrival of government, missions, and mineral exploration teams, the Ningerums' familiarity with Western ways has expanded rapidly. Despite a certain amount of ambivalence, they have endorsed the government's rule of law, their own local government council, national and local elections, wage labor, money, and economic development. Although economic development has been minimal (see Jackson, Emerson, and Welsch 1980) and money is scarce, they have access to government and mission stations, trading stores and imported goods, shotguns, primary schools, and Western-style medical care.

The Ningerum are a very traditionally oriented society. They have no cash crops, they send few of their children to school, few men are employed as wage laborers, and subsistence activities remain largely as they were before government control. Their pig feasts and other ceremonies are frequent social occasions, practiced very much in their traditional ways. In contrast to their response to other innovations, the Ningerum have rapidly and eagerly accepted Western medicine. Every Ningerum person uses Western medicine—although not necessarily for every illness. Moreover, if one considers villages with easy access to an aid post, one finds that the aid post orderly (APO) provides more medical treatments than all traditional practitioners combined.

Comparative Response to Western Medicine of Ningerum and BaKongo

Prior to the arrival of the Australian Administration, the Ningerum had an extensive repertoire of curative and diagnostic practices. Although they are now regular and heavy users of government- and mission-sponsored health-care services, they continue to use most of their traditional medical practices. Ningerum acceptance of Western medical care is fairly typical of what has occurred in other non-Western communities. Janzen's (1978:3) description of BaKongo responses to Western medicine is equally applicable to the Ningerum.

> The people of Zaire recognize the advantages of Western medicine and seek its drugs, surgery and hospital care, but contrary to what might have been expected, native doctors, prophets, and traditional consultations among kinsmen do not disappear with the adoption of Western medicine. Rather a modus vivendi has developed in which different forms of therapy play complementary rather than competitive roles in the thoughts and lives of the people.

Whereas the BaKongo response to Western medicine is the result of nearly a century of contact with introduced medical practices, the Ningerum response reflects barely a decade of regularly available Western medicines. In less than a generation the Ningerum have substantially changed their methods of treating a variety of illnesses. They have tried Western medicine, assessed its strengths and weaknesses, and incorporated Western medical services into a number of different treatment strategies. These strategies include both traditional and introduced treatments and regularly employ them together in a complementary fashion.

Non-Western Assimilation of Western Medicine: Overview

To the Ningerum, Western medicine initially appeared as an incomprehensible, alien, and perhaps undifferentiated means of dealing with sickness. But after 15 years of more or less regular access to aid posts and small rural hospitals, they no longer view Western medicine in these ways. In assessing the strengths and limitations of Western care, they have integrated aid-post and hospital treatment with their own traditional practices. In short, Ningerum people—as opposed to Western health workers—do not see Western and traditional medicine as in competition, in conflict, or contradictory. Instead of being an intrusive, discrete medical system that is poorly integrated into the local society and culture, Western medicine is part of a differentiated but nevertheless integrated system of health care, one that relies heavily upon both Western and traditional practices.

Analytically, many studies of illness behavior in rural non-Western settings implicitly (if not explicitly) consider Western medicine on the one hand and indigenous curing practices on the other as essentially discrete medical systems that in one way or another are in competition or conflict. The labels used to describe these medical practices, such as modern medicine, cosmopolitan medicine, folk medicine, and primitive medicine, imply fundamental differences between traditional and introduced practices, just as they suggest that each operates as a separate medical system. Such studies frequently view patients as deciding among alternative medical systems—rather than choosing from among alternative treatments—as if each were an undifferentiated system of treatment practices.

Medical professions in Western countries encourage this view of practitioners as working within different "medical systems." From the practitioners' perspective, their practices often do have a certain coherence that may justify labeling each as a separate medical system. They may, for example, have professional trade secrets, professional economic interests, and esoteric theories of pathology and etiology. Thus an anthropology of comparative medical systems is possible (e.g., Leslie 1976, Kleinman et al. 1976, and Moreley and Wallis 1978).

My concern here is with users rather than with practitioners. If we want to understand how users conceptualize different therapeutic options and select from among these options, we cannot assume that users distinguish between medical systems in the same ways as practitioners, or even that they necessarily distinguish between medical systems at all (which is not to say that they do not distinguish among different therapies and different therapeutic goals).

Treatment Choices in Western Medicine

The structure of Western medical consultation also encourages a view of medical systems as undifferentiated systems of treatment practices. Physicians generally make their own diagnoses and prescribe treatment in terms of these diagnoses; patients merely recognize and present complaints. Given such a situation, the patient's decision to consult a physician is logically the same whether the doctor prescribes antibiotics, a diuretic, or confinement. Where self-diagnosis is more typically the rule, as in Ningerum, these same treatments may constitute quite different courses of action for the patient. This is particularly true when patients select practitioners for specific kinds of treatment, based on their own self-diagnosis.

Attempts to account for observed treatment choices generally stem from a single kind of explanation, namely, that because Western medicine is an introduced medical system it is in some way less well integrated into the society and culture of the users than traditional practices. The usual task in explaining underutilization, noncompliance, and delays in seeking Western treatment has been to identify those areas where local beliefs and values, practices, role relationships, or economic requirements conflict with those of the Western system. There are many examples of this approach to treatment decisions: Adair and Deuschle (1970), Clark (1959), and Garrison (1977) consider a range of conflict areas; Cassel (1955), Carstairs (1955), Gonzalez (1966), Rubel (1960), L. Schwartz (1969), and Young (1976) examine conflicting beliefs, values, and expectations; Mitchell (1976) looks at differences between the general practice of medicine in the traditional and introduced medical systems; and Madsen (1964), Marriott (1955), Peck (1968), Press (1969), and Stanhope (1968) consider role relationships and socioeconomic factors. Each of these studies looks to one conflict area or another to demonstrate the poor integration of Western medicine within the local setting and thus explain underutilization as an artifact of the intrusive nature of Western medicine.

Although these studies offer valuable insights into how introduced medical practices do not always meet the needs of the users, their authors tend to have difficulty explaining how introduced medicine can and often does meet local users' needs. Explaining the tenacity of traditional beliefs and expectations in terms of the meaning system of the community does not help to clarify why non-Western peoples typically make heavy use of the Western medical system.

Paradoxically, studies accounting for the regular use of Western medicine for certain classes of illness often assume the same things about Western medicine's poor integration within the non-Western setting. They agree that Western and traditional medical systems differ in theory, in practice, and in practitioners' style, but argue that patients use Western medicine in spite of these differences—because they observe the empirical results of the superior Western medicine.

The strongest proponents of this view have been Erasmus (1952) and Foster (e.g., 1958), both of whom have argued that "in all societies people are remarkably pragmatic in testing and evaluating new alternatives, in deciding whether it is to their advantage to innovate" (Foster and Anderson 1978:245). While I do not for a moment doubt that people evaluate their available treatment options, I do question whether this evaluation is made without reference to indigenous illness beliefs. Foster and Anderson in essence argue that these practices are—for the users—a hodgepodge of poorly understood and meaningless practices. They say that the decision to use new practices is a pragmatic one, thus a decision made without reference to theory. Such decisions are "exercised on a situational basis" (1978:248), and subsequently, "all kinds of accommodations are made and all manner of rationalizations appear to justify continuing faith in the old system while simultaneously accepting the new" (1978:251). In short, because of their pragmatism when confronting new practices, non-Western people make decisions to use Western medicine in a haphazard and ad hoc way. Foster ends up in this untenable position because he insists that a community must view its own traditional practices and the newly introduced ones as discrete theoretical and practical systems. Underutilization is the result of slowly changing beliefs (and thus a conflict between the two systems) while the use of Western medicine is the result of empirical observations and human pragmatism that leave these introduced practices poorly integrated with the older, more traditional, practices.

My own observations of treatment choices in the Ningerum area suggest that introduced Western medicine is highly integrated into the local setting. Ningerum people have very definite ideas about how Western medicine works. These understandings are different from the theories of Western physicians, but are no more disconnected from Ningerum illness beliefs than are traditional medical practices. The observed pattern of aid-post and hospital attendance, including regular use of Western medicine as well as delays, noncompliance, and occasional nonuse, can best be explained in terms of the integration of the two medical traditions and in terms of the differing expectations that the Ningerum have of different kinds of treatment. Differences between Western and traditional Ningerum theories of illness exist, but Ningerum people are largely unaware of such differences. A single theory of illness accommodates Western as well as more traditional medical practices.

If we are to understand medical practices and thus the particular treatments that patients seek when they are sick, we must consider their beliefs about illness causation and pathology. But unlike Rivers, who was little concerned with the introduction of Western medicine in non-Western communities, I feel we should first seek explanations of *all* treatment choices in these same indigenous illness beliefs—whether the treatments chosen have their origins in indigenous or introduced medical traditions. The issue is not to show how indigenous and Western medical practices or principles are different: rather, our task should be to examine how non-Western peoples interpret and then make use of the new practices available to them.

To assume that Western medicine somehow stands apart from traditional curative practices and is poorly integrated within the local setting tends to lead analysis away from any understanding of how users actually conceptualized Western medicine and how these conceptualizations influence actual treatment choices. In short, I suggest a model of illness behavior that assumes a local interpretation of medical events and syncretism rather than conflict between a well-integrated traditional medical system and a poorly integrated new one.

Ningerum Contact With European Medicine

Approximately 4500 Ningerum people inhabit the hilly country immediately to the south of the Star Mountains on both sides of the border between Papua New Guinea and Indonesia. They are an interior lowlands people, practicing shifting cultivation and pig husbandry in a dense rainforest environment. Sago and bananas, the staple foods, are supplemented with tubers. Prior to European contact, the settlement pattern was one of individually dispersed homesteads, each containing a single extended family related by marriage and kinship ties to neighboring family groups. At the encouragement of both the government and the mission, the Ningerum formed villages, but continue to spend the larger portion of their time on their own family territories, away from the villages. These "bush houses" continue to be the families' primary residences, providing privacy and easy access to gardens and hunting territories.

Although some Ningerum were aware of Europeans in the early 1920s, government control and regular contact with Europeans did not begin until after 1950. During the early years following government control, many men had the opportunity to visit other parts of the country, working for wages as casual or contract laborers. Many were carriers for government and petroleum exploration patrols; others worked on plantations near Sorong, Port Moresby, and other centers; still others helped open government stations at Kiunga in 1951, Nomad River in 1962, and Ningerum in 1964. Today few have regular employment, per capita income is less than K10 ($15) per year, and the economy continues to be subsistence oriented. Knowledge of and interest in the outside world remains very limited.

Prior to the opening of Ningerum patrol post, access to Western medicine was minimal, consisting largely of infrequent patrols to control yaws or immunize the people against cholera and small pox. Government administrative patrols gave routine treatments during their annual visits and contract laborers generally had regular access to medical care. About 1960 the government opened an aid post in the neighboring Yongom area, which was accessible to some Ningerum people.

Creation of Aid Posts

Partly as a response to a localized but serious dysentery outbreak, the Australian Administration opened the first aid post in Ningerum Census Division in 1963. The aid post orderly (APO) was reposted within the first year and was not replaced until about 1965. Staffing continued to be irregular until 1968, but since then APO postings have been continuous. Permanent staffing does not mean, however, that an APO was always present in the village to treat the sick. APO visits to Ningerum station for supplies, recreation leave, in-service training, and other absences typically leave the aid post unstaffed for three to six months each year.

This original aid post was located at Bwakim village, half an hour's walk from Hukim village, where I lived for two years. Large numbers of deaths due to dysentery and influenza epidemics led Bwakim people to relocate both their village and aid post three times in the following ten years. In 1976 the villagers decided to move the aid post to Hukim, where most of the original Bwakim families now reside. Despite the periodic relocation of this aid post, it continues to serve the same families as it did in 1963.

In 1964 the government opened an aid post at Ningerum patrol post. About the same time the Unevangelised Fields Mission opened the third aid post serving Ningerum Census Division. At this time all of the APOs were Papuans from Western Province but none were Ningerum. Their training was fairly basic; they were expected to treat the most common medical problems, viz., malaria, acute respiratory infections, gastroenteritis and diarrheal diseases, cuts and sores. As the first level of rural health care, they were expected to refer more serious conditions to rural hospitals.

The aid post at Ningerum patrol post was eventually upgraded to a rural health center, which made referrals from the village aid posts more convenient than the three- or four-day walk to Kiunga Health Centre. Staffing at Ningerum Health Centre increased steadily during the 1970s, and in 1979 there was a staff of ten, all Papua New Guineans. Maternal–child health (MCH) clinics began in the area about 1970. These clinics are held in the villages; patrols visit the villages three to six times a year, providing prenatal examinations for pregnant women as well as immunizations and regular exams for children up to five years. Before 1978 these patrols were conducted by European nurses, but at present, nurses and APOs conduct alternate patrols. MCH patrols have been the only area of health care provided directly by Europeans rather than by Papua New Guineans.

Perhaps the most significant change in health care delivery has been the training of local people from the Ningerum area as health workers. Since 1972 four Ningerum men have completed APO training and one woman has recently finished nurse aide training. One of these APOs and the nurse aide are from Hukim village.

For the village people, training Ningerum men as APOs has led to a stronger identification with the aid post and has added to the feeling that the aid post is a Ningerum institution. Training as a health worker is highly valued and many young men are seeking sponsorship for APO training. Local people take a keen interest in the selection and sponsorship of APO trainees by their elected local government council.

The Organization of Traditional Medical Practices

Before considering the ways that Ningerum people interpret aid-post medical services, I want to examine, briefly, two aspects of how Ningerum curative practices are organized: (1) the distribution of therapeutic knowledge and expertise in the community; (2) the locus of diagnostic and therapeutic decision-making. The organization of medical care structures the social production of knowledge about illness and its treatment. It provides culturally meaningful guidelines for how medical decisions ought to be made and who should make these decisions.

Every society has a certain body of medical knowledge readily available to anyone who cares to know about it. This is the basis of nonspecialist treatment, practices that have often been called "home remedies," but are more usefully considered as "individual and family based care" (Kleinman 1976). The Ningerum have many "self-help" therapies that require no special skills or abilities, no special training, and no specialized knowledge. Anyone may perform them for themselves or their relatives.

These treatments include topical herbal preparations, warm baths, rest, healthful foods, and nettles, or the proper ways to stop external bleeding, dress cuts, and treat fainting. Family-based care often includes the use of simple divinations and rituals that will identify and banish attacking ghosts. It often uses ritual techniques having to do with men's cult secrets (these secrets are not available to women, but are part of the standard repertoire of male knowledge).

The Ningerum also have a variety of specialized therapeutic and diagnostic practices. These are used for illnesses that people fear might lead to permanent disability, chronic weakness, or death. A practitioner must be expressly instructed in the proper procedures, ingredients, and ritual formulae if the treatment is to be effective.

These medical treatments require a certain amount of skill that can only come with experience. As with other skills—including successful gardening, pig tending, hunting, feasting, and control over valuables—the Ningerum believe that therapeutic abilities require jealously guarded esoteric knowledge if they are to be done well. Individual aptitude is important, but uncommon, secret knowledge is essential.

Esoteric Knowledge

Esoteric knowledge is a source of power or control over external forces, and its possession makes one person's gardens more productive than another's, and some people's pigs fatter and less likely to run away. Access to uncommon knowledge produces fine hunters; it gives some men the means to put on fantastically successful feasts, allows some the ability to ensorcell their enemies or to change into various animals or to perform other extraordinary feats. Esoteric knowledge allows some men to acquire more wealth than others or to perform one of these specialized curative practices.

Instruction in the details of sucking out tiny ghost arrows or removing sorcery packets from a patient's body can only come from another specialist practitioner. Similarly, in order to perform an *anggun* ("burning bark") divination, or any of a dozen other therapeutic and diagnostic practices, one must be taught properly by someone who has the esoteric knowledge. Each skill is totally independent of all others, and, like all esoteric knowledge among the Ningerum, is customarily passed on from father to son. Men do not always teach their sons these closely guarded secrets, however, sometimes because they die first, but often for their own idiosyncratic reasons. As with other kinds of magic, therapeutic knowedge is property that can be given away or sold.

Ningerum society lacks "big men" in the classic New Guinea sense, just as traditionally there were no villages or other bounded political units larger than the extended family. Everyone engages in the same economic and social activities and there is little in the ordinary pattern of daily life to distinguish one man from another. In a social field consisting of men who are virtually identical to himself, a Ningerum man can only individuate himself through his own outstanding abilities and esoteric knowledge.

From the Ningerum point of view, individuals are born with nearly identical capabilities, but as children mature, subtle personal differences lead them to develop their own aptitudes and interests, eventually leading them into particular fields of individuation or specialization through the acquisition of esoteric knowledge and expertise. Uncommon knowledge is power; it is implicitly magical and extraordinary, even when it includes no ritual formulae and has purely instrumental goals. This knowledge rather than innate ability is what makes a fine hunter or a therapeutic specialist.

Individuals cultivate these extranormal abilities and learn the esoteric things they can from their fathers or whoever will teach them. They acquire reputations for having narrowly defined specialties, expertise that surpasses what others are able to do in activities in which everyone has some ability. They keep their uncommon knowledge secret, unless they decide to train someone else. On occasion others call upon them for assistance that requires their particular abilities; when someone is ill, the patient or close relatives will send for a friend or relative who knows the necessary curative practice.

What emerges is a pattern that Watson (1980) describes as "consensual complementarity." Through a general consent, individuals have their own specialties, and everyone knows who possesses what special types of knowledge. Ningerum people frequently would say about one practice or another, *"De kaa, ne kaa duwam"* ("He knows [how to do it]; I don't know").

While control over esoteric knowledge and consequent control over others has many implications for Ningerum social dynamics—which I will not go into here—the implications for Ningerum medical care are striking. While everyone in the community shares the ability and knowledge of nonspecialized treatment, only a select few can perform any particular treatment that might be used with very serious illnesses. Everyone understands the general principles and methods of specialist therapy.

Specialization of Traditional Practice

Ningerum practitioners are specialists with one or perhaps two therapies. They are not general practitioners in the way that practitioners appear to be in other parts of Papua New Guinea (cf. Johannes [1980], Glick [1967], Nelson [1971], Luzbetak [1958]). They do not have a broad inventory of curative practices available to them. Instead, Ningerum practitioners are selected because they can perform certain specialties; they are not consulted to make a diagnosis and then prescribe the appropriate therapy.

No Ningerum practitioner could treat every kind of illness, nor would a practitioner be asked to do so. Patients and their families must seek the treatments they feel are most appropriate to the condition: they must send for a practitioner—often a friend, relative or affine. By selecting the practitioner they are thus selecting the kind of treatment that will be performed. This places the diagnostic burden on the patient and the family; it makes self-diagnosis an inherent part of traditional practice. Without self-diagnosis or a family-based diagnosis a patient could not get appropriate treatment.

Ningerum individual and family-based care, then, penetrates into the more specialized sector of the overall system of health care. The patient and family manage the illness and take over much of the responsibilities we are accustomed to expect a practitioner to handle. The extended family, as the "therapy managing group" (Janzen 1978), makes nearly all of the diagnostic and therapeutic decisions—though it should be noted that the patients often make many decisions themselves unless the illness is particularly disabling. Unless the practitioner is a member of the extended family, the Ningerum practitioner merely performs the requested treatment and then leaves the patient. Subsequently, when it comes to evaluating the results of treatment, it is the patient and family that share this burden; a practitioner seldom makes further comment on the results of treatment. Everyone in the Ningerum community is free to speculate on the cause and nature of any symptomatic episode; there is no one to legitimate a diagnosis. For example, when Okmun (a woman in her 30s) came down with gastroenteritis after eating some pork that had been given by her affines, she was able to diagnose the condition herself. With the help of her family, she performed a nonspecialist ghost divination that indicated an affinal ghost was responsible for the illness. The family performed the appropriate nonspecialized ritual to send the angry ghost away and Okmun recovered the following day. Many other people in the village—who had not shared the pork and were somewhat jealous about it—had a different view. Several people confided to me that Okmun's illness was due to having eaten spoiled pork; in their view the illness had nothing to do with ghosts.

In other cases, where the symptoms are more threatening, a specialist may be called for immediately. When Akorem (a man of about 40) came down suddenly with bronchopneumonia, high fever, and chest pains he immediately diagnosed his condition as ensorcellment. He sent word to his classificatory brother to come and remove the sorcery packet lodged in his chest. When the brother did not arrive by the second day, a classificatory uncle arrived to perform the treatment. This uncle had not been asked to come; rather, he had heard that the illness was due to sorcery and came to assist when he heard that Akorem's brother was unavailable. The uncle said very little to Akorem or his family; after asking where the pain was, he smeared clay on Akorem's chest and removed the tiny sorcery packet, handing it to Akorem's wife. He waited until Akorem's wife began to wash the packet and study its contents, but then left without commenting on the contents or who might have been responsible. The packet contained tobacco and thus did not point to any one suspect, since many people could have stolen a discarded cigarette butt. Akorem had his suspicions as to the sorcerer's identity, but other people suspected a number of other people. Akorem went to the aid post twice during this episode, once before his uncle arrived, and then the day after the packet's removal. His subsequent recovery made the sorcerer's identity a moot point.

What is interesting in this example—although in no way unusual—is that Akorem's uncle, who was acting in the capacity of a specialist, did nothing to define or diagnose the illness condition. He merely performed the desired treatment and left, spending a total of ten minutes with his patient. The initial diagnosis and subsequent discussion of the sorcerer's identity were left entirely to Akorem and his family.

The Use of Traditional and Western Medicine

Ningerum people, old and young, educated and uneducated, continue to use traditional forms of treatment and feel that they are effective. This has not impeded their use of the aid post's medicines, which they also believe are quite effective. During the two years I lived in Hukim village, every person in the resident population used the aid post, and most attended quite regularly and frequently. Aid-post attendence did not lessen the importance of most kinds of traditional therapy, although several herbal treatments were used less frequently than in the past. In short, everyone used both traditional and aid-post treatments. Accepting one did not weaken their belief in the effectiveness of the other. While recognizing the separate origins of customary and aid-post treatments, the Ningerum never felt that one contraindicated the other. As in Akorem's case of bronchopneumonia, their treatment strategy was to employ treatments from both traditions together. I will consider this treatment strategy shortly.

Conditions treated at the aid post ranged from cuts, sores, coughs, headaches, and fever to more serious conditions, such as pneumonia, gastroenteritis, malaria, tuberculosis, and other disorders, some of which proved fatal. They used the aid post most frequently for minor complaints—but, of course, these are statistically the most common. The Ningerum used the aid post for chronic as well as acute illnesses, for internal as well as external conditions, for both mild and serious complaints, and for conditions that they explained as the result of both social and natural causes. There is no single criterion that correlates with the exclusive use of treatments from one or the other tradition, except availability.

Only conditions that persisted for several days—particularly if accompanied by much pain, disability, or worsening symptoms—generally received both traditional and aid-post treatment. With these more serious and persisting conditions, there was a noticeable tendency for patients to receive initial treatment from the APO rather than from a traditional specialist or family member, particularly if the patient developed symptoms while in the village.

A hierarchy-of-resorts model of treatment selection—such as that suggested by Romanucci–Ross (Schwartz 1969; Romanucci–Ross, in the present volume)—is relevant here, though the Ningerum hierarchy of resorts should be examined carefully before assuming it is identical to hierarchies found elsewhere. Superficially, the Ningerum data resemble the "acculturative sequence" of treatment choices that Romanucci–Ross observed in Manus as one of several treatment strategies (Schwartz 1969:204). The acculturative sequence in the Manus case begins with European treatment and proceeds to traditional therapies. Although it is tempting to interpret Ningerum interventions in this way, such an analysis would be overly simplistic and, more important, it would not elaborate upon local understandings of Western medicine. Thus, it would ignore the very aspects of treatment selection that Romanucci–Ross and others have attempted to elucidate by considering treatment sequences as hierarchies of resorts.

We cannot assume, as some researchers have done (e.g., Woods 1977), that the sequential order of treatment always reflects a ranking of treatment preferences. Similarly, we should not assume, as Kunstadter (1976) does, that different treatments are always therapeutic alternatives: they can easily be therapeutic supplements. There is no *a priori* reason why treatment strategies must follow an ordered sequence of trial and error, trying first one treatment and then another as different practices fail to cure the condition.

In cases such as Akorem's, the strategy was to use both a traditional specialist and the aid post simultaneously. Akorem would have preferred to have the customary treatment first, immediately followed by a course of treatment at the aid post. During the actual episode, he started treatment at the aid post while waiting for his classificatory brother to arrive. It was only by happenstance that he used the APO's medicine first; therefore one cannot assume that Western practice was the first resort; for the patient both *Western and traditional* practices are part of the same resort.

Treatment Strategies as a Function of Severity of Problem

Ningerum treatment strategies vary according to the degree of severity of the illness. Generally speaking, there are three levels of severity: trivial, serious, and life-threatening. Defining different levels of severity are different thresholds of pain, disability, and suddenness of onset. In addition, there are a number of culturally marked "significant symptoms"—such as vomiting, fainting, noticeable weight loss or swelling, and profuse bleeding—that indicate a serious or perhaps life-threatening condition regardless of the accompanying symptoms.

The Ningerum language does not have labels for these different levels of severity. Nevertheless, there are marked differences in people's responses to illnesses at each level of severity. Patients demonstrate the severity of their condition by the kind of sick role they assume. At the same time, relatives and friends respond to increasing severity by taking on more and more responsibility for therapy management and treatment decision making. For each level of severity there are different treatment options, and at each level these treatment options include both European and customary treatments. Treatment options for trivial conditions never include specialized traditional therapy. They may be either aid-post or customary treatments, although nowadays there is a heavy emphasis upon the APO's medicines.

Once a condition is defined as serious, the course of treatment nearly always includes some kind of traditional specialized therapy, although in most cases the treatment strategy includes other kinds of treatment that Ningerum people see as complementing the specialist's efforts. If the condition persists, a series of specialists may be called in, each with a separate treatment strategy that may include complementary nonspecialist care.

When a patient is in extremis, lying in his house recumbent and helpless, treatments of all kinds are administered in rapid succession by many different individuals. Each relative will offer whatever treatment he knows, whether specialist or nonspecialist, and the APO will usually make house calls to offer his own medications. Each individual may have their own diagnosis. Thus, by their nature, treatment sequences during life-threatening episodes lack a coherent treatment strategy, being more a collage of many individuals' last-resort efforts.

The Ningerum hierarchy of resorts does not emphasize the many differences between introduced and customary treatments: either or both may be used at each level of severity. The specific course of treatment has much to do with the nature of the symptoms experienced and the ways that the Ningerum people understand different etiologies and pathological processes.

Serious illnesses do not always develop dramatic symptoms suddenly, and life-threatening conditions almost never do. What initially appears as a simple headache may develop over several days into a high fever, rigors, and chest pain. In such cases the patient will initially seek treatment at the aid post for his headache. When debilitating symptoms develop, the patient and his family will redefine the condition as serious and will decide upon a new treatment strategy that includes specialist treatment (although often it will include a mix of aid-post and nonspecialist treatments as well). Patients do not say that the aid-post medication was ineffective; rather, they say that it was insufficient. In short, the Ningerum hierarchy of resorts consists of a progression of increasingly complex treatment strategies that correspond to increasingly threatening illness conditions.

The Relationship between Traditional and Western Medicine

Like other researchers in similar settings, I was struck initially by the many differences between Western medical practices and the more dramatic traditional forms of treatment, which included the magical removal of sorcery packets, divination, and exorcism of spirits. I recognized many differences between traditional and Western theories of illness causation and of how treatments were supposed to effect cures. After I had spent about six months in the village, it became increasingly apparent to me that many of these differences went unnoticed by the Ningerum. Such differences were not what they saw as most significant about the two medical traditions.

Villagers were largely unaware of Western biomedical theories of illness causation and the logic of Western treatments. They recognized differences between the two sets of practices in their materials and techniques, in the kinds of training required, and in their origins, but they seldom mentioned these differences. Instead, they repeatedly stressed the similarities and interchangeability of customary and aid-post medicine. Later it became clear to me that only certain traditional and aid-post treatments were fully comparable. In general, they felt that aid-post therapies were highly effective in assisting the body's ordinary regenerative process. In terms of what Ningerum see as the goals of treatment, Western medicines are virtually identical to many of their own nonspecialist treatments, treatments that are aimed at strengthening the body, restoring internal tissue damage, lessening pain, and so forth. The APO's medicines are not, according to the Ningerum, effective in exorcising spirits or in removing sorcery packets. The APO performs no treatments involving the men's cult, just as he never identifies ghosts.

APOs often come from other ethnic groups in the region, but they all share many of the Ningerum people's understandings about ghosts, sorcery, and the men's cult. APOs frequently attend men's cult feasts, divinations, and other rituals, just as I did. They are interested in learning Ningerum beliefs about these phenomena, and often participate in village conversations about them. Like the village people, APOs fear ambush from killers, assault sorcerers that are called *vada* in Motu and *sanguma* in Pidgin (see Williams 1932:124 and Glick 1973). Moreover, APOs observe many of the same precautions concerning ghosts, spirits, and sorcerers that village people do.

As I have discussed elsewhere (Welsch 1979), APOs seldom talk with patients about the theoretical basis of their treatments, nor do they tell their patients the specific effects they hope to achieve with any particular course of treatment. In most cases they merely administer the necessary medication, with instructions—or sometimes orders—to return if a second dose is required. Insofar as APOs discuss their medicines at all, it is to describe their treatments in terms of strengthening the body or the symptom-specific effects of various drugs. They never discuss aid-post medicines in terms of ghosts or sorcery, although patients are well aware that APOs know about these phenomena and that APOs do talk about ghosts and sorcery in other contexts. Thus, it is not surprising that villagers interpret aid-post medicines as aimed only at strength-giving and symptom-specific relief—that is to say, restoring ordinary body functions.

Some traditional treatments, such as nettles and certain ritual preparations, are intended to promote the patient's overall strength. Others, including several herbal preparations, venesection, and dressings for wounds, are topical, their objective is the relief of localized pain, or, alternatively, the restoration of impaired organs or tissues. Other treatments aim at etiologic agents responsible for the condition; for example, divination and exorcisms are intended to identify and send away attacking ghosts. Finally, some therapies, particularly men's-cult curing rituals, strive for all three of these effects at once; simultaneously they send off ghosts, relieve localized pain, and promote the patient's general strength.

The Ningerum insistence that Western and traditional treatments are essentially the same is a manifestation of their view that the two traditions are not discrete medical systems. Both Western and traditional practices are heterogeneous, and the selection of specific therapies is made in terms of the specific effects patients want to achieve. In the past, Ningerum people chose only traditional treatments—since that was all that was available. But they did not choose treatments randomly. They had specific goals in mind when selecting from the assortment of possible treatments. But the recognition persists that only traditional medicine can deal with ghosts, spirits, and sorcery.

If we consider the therapeutic objectives of Western and traditional practices (as the Ningerum understand them), there is only one medical theory and only one medical system. The concerns of Western therapies (as APOs present these concerns to the users) are easily subsumed into the traditional medical theory.

The Ningerum recognize differences in the ingredients and form of treatments in the two medical traditions, but they also see similar differences among customary treatments. Despite the many differences, all customary medical practices have one or more of the same three therapeutic goals. In the same way, Ningerum people interpret Western medical practices to have these same ends, and this is what people meant when they said that Western and traditional medicine are the same.

Selection of Appropriate Treatment

Traditionally, there are more or less standardized associations between certain symptoms (or combinations of symptoms) and various etiologies and pathological processes.

Fever, for example, unaccompanied by any other symptom, suggests exposure to intense sunlight, ghost attack, and several other possible explanations, but it is not a manifestation of sorcery. Accompanied by chest pain and coughing, a high fever might be explained as a secondary sign of sorcery. I regularly encountered patients with simple fever and would ask if anyone had treated the patient to remove a sorcery packet. Not surprisingly, I never encountered a case of simple fever treated in this way. Although I continued to inquire about this treatment option, just to be certain, my field assistants were puzzled by my questions. Finally, they asked me, "Why do you always ask about that? You have been here two years already; you know we never try to remove a sorcery packet for a fever."

This example is not unique. Most traditional treatments are used for a specified range of illness conditions. Ningerum people, like Americans, have very definite ideas about what kinds of treatments would be appropriate for any particular illness condition. Removing a sorcery packet from a febrile Ningerum patient is as inappropriate as prescribing laxatives for Americans suffering from migraine or decongestants for patients with swelling in their legs.

Since a range of medical treatments are available from the APO, one might assume that this unifying factor would lead the Ningerum to identify all Western treatments as part of a single alternative medical system. But their use of the aid post suggests that they differentiate aid-post treatments according to the conditions for which they are most appropriate, just as they differentiate traditional practices. Villagers make fewer distinctions among aid-post medications than do APOs, but they clearly recognize certain categories of treatment, each appropriate for particular kinds of illness conditions. These categories of APO medication include the following: cough mixture, stomach mixture, injections, tablets, ointments, bandages, linament, iodine, and *tinea* paint. Very few people could name any of the different kinds of tablets available at the aid post, although everyone was aware of differences in size, shape, color, taste, and dosage. They also know from the APO that some tablets are for pain, some are for fever, some for pregnant women, and so forth.

Patients regularly asked for a particular kind of medication by name, rather than describing their symptoms or case history. This was particularly true when they wanted cough mixture, stomach mixture, linament, bandaging, and occasionally even tablets and injections. When patients did describe their condition and mentioned particular symptoms, they often discussed the symptoms in a way that suggested they had a particular treatment in mind; they were not seeking a diagnosis and corresponding treatment from the APO. Patients occasionally told me before they went to the aid post the kind of medication they were going to get.

On numerous occasions a patient would mention only one or two symptoms when he was experiencing other symptoms as well. Unaware of other symptoms and assuming that the patient was suffering only from the symptoms mentioned, the APO usually gave the patient precisely the kind of treatment he sought. A full listing of symptoms might not be given, even when the APO took some interest in the case and asked many questions about the history. In some cases, patients had experienced chest pains and coughing or fever, and a relative had removed a sorcery packet the previous day. Although the patients still felt chest pain, they mentioned only the cough or fever; in such cases patients viewed the APO as a pharmacist or dispenser of medications, which patients had already decided they needed. Only in a few cases, where the illness exhibited unusual or puzzling symptoms, was the APO consulted in the role of diagnostician.

The APO is a single practitioner, but the Ningerum pattern of utilization would scarcely be altered if there were ten different APOs, each with a single specialty.

Causation and Treatment Strategies

In selecting and following a treatment strategy, Ningerum people also consider agents responsible for their discomfort and symptoms. These causal agents may be either natural or social—what Ackerknecht (1971) and others have seen as a contrast between natural and "supernatural" or natural and "sociomoral" causes. From the Ningerum point of view, both natural and social agents influence the body in much the same ways, and an analytical preoccupation with whether the cause of an illness is seen as natural or social merely confuses our understanding of Ningerum illness behavior. Analytically, what is more significant is how the Ningerum understand these agents to affect the body to produce illness.

In the Ningerum view, all causal agents originate outside the body and damage or obstruct normal functioning in some direct way. The agent may be ethereal or tangible, but the effects are always physiological. Food sorcery uses a magical technique to implant a foreign object within the body, and this sorcery packet damages tissues in much the same way that an axe or fire can damage skin and flesh. Eating rotten food or too much pig fat disrupts ordinary digestion, leading to diarrhea and nausea. Spirits and ghosts can cause pain, disable limbs, or disrupt digestion by striking, strangling, or binding their victim's limbs and internal organs. They can also implant foreign objects within the victim's body to cause pain and internal damage. The smells of sexual secretions and menstrual blood create within the body reactions that produce midline hernias and chronic hoarseness, respectively. Spirits can come at night, while people sleep, to consume their victims' vital fluids, producing fever and weight loss. Whatever the agency, all illness is the direct result of some physiological disruption.

The Ningerum recognize the regenerative ability of the human body and expect their bodies to gradually repair most damage inflicted by external agents. These regenerative powers can not, however, eliminate a causal agent that continues to obstruct normal functioning. Thus, they perceive a fundamental difference between illnesses due to agents acting continuously over a period of time and those due to an agent like a knife cutting the body, which has only a temporary effect. Once the knife is removed from a wound, the body can begin to repair the damage. Similarly, spirits sometimes capriciously cause pain, fever, or other discomfort, but, for reasons known only to the spirits themselves, they do not always continue their attacks. In such an instance, the body will return to normal over a relatively short period of time without intervention.

In contrast, a sorcery packet, once implanted, remains inside the body until it is removed. It will continue to disrupt normal functioning and will cause further internal damage. If left intact, the sorcery packet will cause irreparable internal damage, ultimately resulting in death.

Spirits may repeatedly consume a victim's vital fluids; if the spirit is not identified and sent away it will persist until the victim's condition degenerates to an irreversible and terminal state. Natural agents can also repeatedly impair the body; for example, chronic coughs were sometimes attributed to smoking, and several men had given up tobacco so that they would not exacerbate the condition.

"Negative" and "Positive" Treatments

The Ningerum understand all medical treatments to act in one of two ways: the treatment either checks the continued effect of the attacking agent or it helps promote the body's normal regenerative processes. The Ningerum distinction, thus, resembles what Glick (1967:44f) describes for the Gimi as the "negative" and "positive" mobilizations of power; the former aims at weakening the cause, while the latter enhances the patient's ability to resist these causal influences (see also Johannes 1980:51ff).

From the Ningerum perspective these two treatment actions are fully complementary. Removal of a sorcery packet merely eliminates the source of internal damage and stops the damage from becoming worse. This treatment does nothing to help the body return to normal. Rubbing the same patient with stinging nettles strengthens the body but does nothing to remove a sorcery packet.

During the cool rainy season many people in the village including myself developed symptoms of head cold. The Ningerum believed head cold to be caused by eating too many okari nuts, which have their season at this time. They feel that the soft husk around the nut irritates the membranes at the back of the throat, producing congestion and coughing. Repeatedly they told me that if I wanted to get rid of the condition, I would have to stop eating okari nuts for a few days. I suggested going to the aid post for cough mixture, a very popular medication despite its unpleasant taste. They laughed at me and said that if I did not leave the okari nuts alone for a while, nothing that I did would alleviate my condition. There was, thus, a clear distinction between treatments that dealt directly with the agents causing an illness and those that helped restore normal body functions.

Traditional treatments were sometimes aimed at the agents and sometimes at restoring the body, but aid-post treatments were nearly always discussed in terms of restoring normal functions. Ningerum people thus never viewed any aid-post treatment as the functional equivalent of removing a sorcery packet or an exorcism. Aid-post medications never competed with these kinds of treatments but were instead regularly used to complement such treatments.

While aid-post medicines do not compete with traditional treatments for ghosts or sorcery (although some APOs think they do), they do compete with a variety of treatments aimed at restoring body functions. Since aid-post medications are so convenient, they have in some cases lessened the importance of many herbal, nonspecialist preparations for trivial and moderately serious conditions. For this reason, young men today are frequently unfamiliar with many of the herbal preparations.

Patients often told me that after a sorcery packet had been removed, they went to the aid post to make their recovery faster; they would probably get better in any event, but the APO's medicines helped the process.

Multiple Treatments

When patients are gravely ill and show little sign of improvement, the treatment strategy changes again: many infrequently used treatments are performed, to remove a series of causal agents as well as to help restore the body with as many techniques as possible. Nearly all of the therapeutic repertoire of the Ningerum was used in such cases, both traditional and introduced practices—that is, those of the APO's medicines that the APO would administer. In these cases the Ningerum are not trying to find one treatment that will cure the patient; rather they are using a variety of different therapies together to help the patient's body in every possible way: increase strength, repair localized dysfunction, and deal with all possible causal agents that might be involved. Again, the emphasis is on complementary use of medical options.

APOs often complain that patients on a three- or five-day course of medication for malaria or pneumonia do not return for the full treatment; such patient noncompliance can be explained in terms of Ningerum ideas about the objectives and effects of treatment. As I have discussed elsewhere (Welsch 1979), Ningerum people generally expect any treatment to bring noticeable signs of improvement over a period of 24 to 36 hours (cf. Mitchell 1976 for a discussion of similar expectations among the Lujere). After receiving the first dose of antimalarial medicine or penicillin, patients often begin to feel better—particularly if a traditional specialist has also performed some treatment. In these cases patients often do not return for the full course of aid-post medication, explaining that they are feeling better and that their illness is finished. Once they are recovering from the illness, they believe that their bodies will return to normal as a matter of course. They experience signs of improvement and feel certain that the original causal agents no longer have a detrimental influence upon them. If persistence of symptoms is not very troublesome, further restorative treatment is considered unnecessary.

Cases of Conjunctivitis

The following three episodes of conjunctivitis illustrate how traditional and aid-post treatments can be either functional equivalents or complements.

Case 1. Tenong (a man in his early 30s) came down with conjunctivitis in both eyes. He attended the aid post regularly for several days, until the condition cleared up. When I interviewed him, Tenong was uncertain as to how he had come to develop the condition, nor was he particularly interested in speculating about its cause. He assured me that he had performed no other treatment and that the aid-post ointment had helped his eyes considerably.

Case 2. Several months later Tenong again came down with a similar infection in one eye. Again, the condition was neither debilitating nor very painful; it was probably less troubling than his earlier episode. During this episode Tenong developed the symptoms when he was away from the village, and he treated himself with the sap from a certain succulent shurb generally regarded by the Ningerum as an effective restorative for eye conditions. By the time he had returned to the village the illness was much better, and Tenong sought no further treatment. When I asked about this traditional treatment, Tenong insisted that it was the same kind of treatment as the APO's ointment. He told me that the two worked in the same way and that there was really no difference between the two. Tenong also explained that had the condition started when he was in the village, he would have gone to the aid post because it was more convenient; but since the eye infection had begun when he was away from the village, he used the customary treatment.

Case 3. Timop (a man in his late 20s) developed a more painful and debilitating case of conjunctivitis in both eyes, which he described in the same terms that Tenong had. Timop also sought treatment first at the aid post, when the pain was limited. He, like Tenong, received ointment. When the condition worsened, Timop continued to attend the aid post each day, but he decided that something more serious was wrong. Assisted by his wife, he performed a divination to determine whether ghosts were causing his illness. It indicated that three particular ghosts were responsible for his symptoms and that they were repeatedly poking him. The ghosts were angry and jealous about several minor incidents in the village. The ghosts were related to Timop's wife, and she performed the rituals necessary to expel each of the ghosts in turn. Timop's condition did not improve significantly over the next few days, during which time he had walked to Ningerum station for a meeting. At Ningerum he continued his treatment at the health center, and by this time his treatment included penicillin. Again he experienced no improvement and so performed another divination, which identified yet a fourth ghost. Timop sent this ghost away as he had the others. After several more injections his condition improved considerably and he resumed ordinary activities.

His explanation of the entire episode was that a relative's ghost had gotten angry and had begun the episode by poking him in the eyes. Other ghosts noticed Timop's weakened condition and began to do the same. The aid-post treatments would have helped his condition early on, he felt, except that every time he sent one ghost away another started aggravating his condition, giving him no rest. After sending all of the ghosts away, the medicines from the aid post and health center began to take effect and his condition returned to normal.

These three cases illustrate how some traditional treatments are functional equivalents to aid-post medicines, whereas others are not. Cases like these show that the major factor in deciding between functional alternatives is accessibility and convenience. In contrast, divinations and aid-post medications are functional complements that people use together for the best results. They are not therapeutic alternatives in the way that treatments aimed at symptom-specific effects often are. Moreover, these three cases illustrate how the degree of disability and pain is related to different treatment strategies, according to the Ningerum hierarchy of resorts and differential diagnoses of similar conditions. Timop's condition required some explanation in order to control the persistent causes of the symptoms, because the persistence of symptoms indicated continued influence from (in this case) ghosts.

There are, of course, conflicts between Western and customary Ningerum medical practices. APO complaints about noncompliance are only one of several possible examples. But if we emphasize the conflicts between Western and traditional practices we tend to lose sight of this syncretic integration of older and newer practices. Specifically, if we uncritically assume that Western and traditional medical theories are different, we may lose sight of how users conceptualize their medical options. We stand to learn a lot more about treatment decision making by examining the ways that people in non-Western communities conceptualize and integrate practices which, on the surface, would appear to be quite distinct. Once we have examined the ways that different communities interpret introduced medical practices and how they integrate these practices with basic ideas about illness, we can begin to understand the typical treatment choices. At that point in our analysis we will be in a position to understand the limited ways that conflicting medical theories and practices can modify more basic treatment strategies.

REFERENCES

Ackerknecht, Erwin H. 1971. *Medicine and Ethnology: Selected Essays*. Baltimore: Johns Hopkins Press.

Adair, John, and Kurt Deuschle. 1970. *The People's Health: Anthropology and Medicine in a Navaho Community*. New York: Appleton–Century–Crofts.

Carstairs, G. Morris. 1955. "Medicine and Faith in Rural Rajasthan." Benjamin D. Paul, ed., *Health Culture and Community*. New York: Russell Sage Foundation.

Cassel, John. 1955. "A Comprehensive Health Program among South African Zulus." Benjamin D. Paul, ed., ibid.

Clark, Margaret. 1959. *Health in the Mexican–American Culture: A Community Study*. Berkeley: Univ. of California Press.

Erasmus, John Charles. 1952 "Changing Folk Beliefs and the Relativity of Empirical Knowledge." *Southwestern Journal of Anthropology*, 8:411–28.

Foster, George M. 1958. *Problems in Intercultural Health Programs*, SSRC pamphlet no. 12. New York: Social Science Research Council.

Foster, George M., and Barbara Gallatin Anderson. 1978. *Medical Anthropology*. New York: John Wiley & Sons.

Garrison, Vivian. 1977. "Doctor, *Espiritista* or Psychiatrist?: Health-Seeking Behavior in a Puerto Rican Neighborhood of New York City." *Medical Anthropology*, 1:65–180.

Glick, Leonard B. 1967. "Medicine as an Ethnographic Category: The Gimi of the New Guinea Highlands." *Ethnology*, 6:31–56.

   1973   "Sorcery and Witchcraft." Ian Hogbin, ed., *Anthropology in Papua New Guinea: Readings from the Encyclopedia of Papua New Guinea*. Melbourne: Univ. of Melbourne Press.

Gonzalez, Nancy Solien. 1966. "Health Behavior in Cross-Cultural Perspective." *Human Organization*, 25(2):122–25.

Jackson, Richard, Craig Emerson, and Robert L. Welsch. 1980. *The Impact of the Ok Tedi Project*. Konedobu, Papua New Guinea: Papua New Guinea Department of Minerals and Energy.

Janzen, John M. 1978. "The Quest for Therapy in Lower Zaire." Berkeley: Univ. of California Press.

Johannes, Adell. 1980. "Many Medicines in One: Curing in the Eastern Highlands of Papua New Guinea." *Culture, Medicine and Psychiatry*, 4:43–70.

Kleinman, Arthur M. 1976. "Social, Cultural and Historical Themes in the Study of Medicine in Chinese Societies: Problems and Prospects for the Comparative Study of Medicine and Psychiatry." Arthur M. Kleinman et al., eds., *Medicine in Chinese Cultures*. Bethesda, Md.: National Institutes of Health.

Kleinman, Arthur M., et al., eds. 1976. *Medicine in Chinese Cultures*. Bethesda, Md: National Institutes of Health.

Kunstadter, Peter. 1976. "Do Cultural Differences Make Any Difference? Choice Points in Medical Systems Available in Northwestern Thailand." Arthur M. Kleinman, et al., eds., *Medicine in Chinese Cultures*. Bethesda, Md.: National Institutes of Health.

Leslie, Charles. 1976. *Asian Medical Systems: A Comparative Study*. Berkeley: Univ. of California Press.

Lewis, Gilbert. 1975. *Knowledge of Illness in a Sepik Society: A Study of the Gnau, New Guinea*. London: Athlone Press.

Luzbetak, L. J. 1958. "The Treatment of Disease in the New Guinea Highlands." *Anthropological Quarterly*, 31(2):42–55.

Madsen, William. 1964. "Value Conflicts and Folk Psychotherapy in South Texas." Ari Kiev, ed., *Magic, Faith and Healing*. Glencoe: Free Press.

Marriott, McKim. 1955. "Western Medicine in a Village of Northern India." Benjamin D. Paul, ed., *Health, Culture and Community*. New York: Russell Sage Foundation.

Mitchell, William E. 1976. "Culturally Contrasting Therapeutic Systems of the West Sepik: The Lujere." Thomas R. Williams, ed., *Psychological Anthropology*. Hague: Mouton.

Morley, Peter, and Roy Wallis, eds. 1978. *Culture and Curing: Anthropological Perspectives on Traditional Medical Beliefs and Practices*. Pittsburgh: Univ. of Pittsburgh Press.

Nelson, Harold E. 1971. "The Ecological, Epistemological and Ethnographic Context of Medicine in a New Guinea Highlands Culture." Ph.D. diss., University of Washington.

Peck, John. 1968. "Doctor Medicine and Bush Medicine in Kaukira, Honduras." Thomas Weaver, ed., *Essays on Medical Anthropology: Southern Anthropological Society Proceedings*, no. 1:78–87.

Press, Irwin. 1969. "Urban Illness: Physicians, Curers, and Dual Use in Bogota." *Journal of Health and Social Behavior*, 10:209–18.

Rivers, William H. R. 1924. *Medicine, Magic and Religion*. New York: Harcourt & Brace.

Rubel, Arthur J. 1960. "Concepts of Disease in Mexican–American Culture." *American Anthropologist*, 62:795–814.

Schwartz, Lola. 1969. "The Hierarchy of Resort in Curative Practices: The Admiralty Islands, Melanesia." *Journal of Health and Social Behavior*, 10:201–9.

Schwartz, Theodore. 1963. "Systems of Areal Integration: Some Considerations Based on the Admiralty Islands of Northern Melanesia." *Anthropological Forum*, 1(1):56–97.

Stanhope, John. 1968. "Competing Systems of Medicine among the Rao–Breri, Lower Ramu River, New Guinea." *Oceania*, 39:339–45.

Turner, Victor. 1968. *The Drums of Affliction: A Study of Religious Processes among the Ndembu of Zambia*. Oxford: Clarendon Press.

Wagner, Roy. 1972. *Habu: The Innovation of Meaning in Daribi Religion*. Chicago: Univ. of Chicago Press.

Watson, James B. 1980. "Protein and Pigs in Highland New Guinea." Paper presented to the American Anthropological Association, 79th annual meeting.

Welsch, Robert L. 1979. "Barriers to the Aid Post: Problems of the Very Isolated Community." Ralph Premdas and Stephen Pokwin, eds., *Decentralisation: 1978 Waigani Seminar*. Waigani, Papua New Guinea: Univ. of Papua New Guinea.

Williams, F.E. 1932. "Sex Affiliation and Its Implication." *Reprinted in* F.E. Williams, *The Vailala Madness and Other Essays*, ed. Erik Schwimmer. Honolulu: Univ. Press of Hawaii (1977).

Woods, Clyde. 1977. "Alternative Curing Strategies in a Changing Medical Situation." *Medical Anthropology*, 3(1):25–54.

Young, Alan. 1976. "Some Implications of Medical Beliefs and Practices for Social Anthropology." *American Anthropologist*, 78:5–24.

4

Doctors or Deceivers?
The Siberian Khanty Shaman
and Soviet Medicine

Marjorie Mandelstam Balzer

Introduction[1]

In a new spirit of respect for indigenous medicine, the United Nations World Health Organization has instituted a policy of training traditional medical practitioners in hygiene and midwifery, while at the same time encouraging certain ancient "folk" herbal and shamanic cures (Bannerman 1977: 16–17). Without denial of the real benefits of modern psychiatry and medical technology, health problems are increasingly studied in their historical, social, and symbolic contexts (Gillin 1948; Turner 1964; Romanucci–Ross 1977:481–87; Ohnuki–Tierney 1976, 1980; Kleinman 1979). It is especially appropriate to undertake such a study in Siberia, where "classical" shamanism has long and diverse roots.[2]

This chapter examines multiple ways in which illness is cognitively and behaviorally coped with by the Siberian Khanty, Ob Ugrians, often termed "Ostiak" in Western literature. Although Khanty ideas about sickness have been changing rapidly with the arrival of Soviet doctors, some traditional ideas about health and how to obtain it are still alive. These ideas center on the dramatic role of shamans, whose ecstatic trance journeys enable some Khanty to believe they can communicate with and control the supernatural.

Khanty concepts of health as essentially spiritual help to explain both traditional curing and modern attitudes toward medicine. Shamanic cures are directed at "spiritual" ailments of patients, usually believed to take the form of lost or stolen souls. In treating such afflictions, shamans have sometimes managed to get at the

54

heart of interlocked physical and psychological problems. The success of a shaman in doing this, however, depends upon his or her stature in a given community, and, given Soviet anti-religious propaganda, this stature is changing.

To put these changes in perspective, Khanty soul belief and correlations of moral behavior with health are discussed. Shamans and seances are then described, to illustrate the importance of shamanism in community relations and to illuminate how the symbolism of shamanic trance may contribute to curing. Ideas of Shirokogoroff (1935), Turner (1964, 1977) and Lévi–Strauss (1967) are adapted, and recent responses to Soviet medicine are analyzed. Modern Soviet attitudes have frequently undermined precisely the elements of shamanism which may have made it effective in traditional contexts, but key aspects of the Khanty shamanic symbol system survive.

The Relation of Souls and Morality to Health

Khanty souls have contrasting named functions and locations, which have led to categorizations of souls as "dual" (Karjalainen 1921:21; Raun 1955:50–71) or "multiple" (Chernetsov 1963:5; Sokolova 1976:57). The Soviet scholar Chernetsov (1963:5) argues that it is impossible to squeeze all Khanty concepts of the soul into a dualistic framework. I would add that we have yet to understand the scope of soul belief, given indications of "souls" or soul-aspects residing in many parts of the body (head, hair, skin, liver, heart), plus indications that souls guide human conscience, dreaming, sickness, and reincarnation (see Table 4.1).

Chernetsov (1963:3–45) has classified four main Ob-Ugrian souls as those representing material being, sickness, dreaming, and reincarnation. He suggests that

Table 4.1   Khanty Soul Beliefs

Soul or Soul Aspect	Gloss	Location	Image	Function
Is-chor *Is*	Material or shade	Shadow	Shadow	To stay with a person in life and stay with the grave in death; can cause nightmares; may be the conscience
Iləs Is-ilt	Sickness	Head or body surface	Mosquito; cuckoo; swallow; magpie	Health; stays with person while awake; leaves in sleep and can be stolen to cause sickness; shaman causes this soul to leave at will in trance
Uləm is	Dreaming	Head in sleep; forest in waking hours	Wood grouse; black cock	To enable dreaming, visions, and life; can cause nightmares
Lil	Reincarnation; breath	Head or hair	Bird: falcon?	Ancestral Khanty spirit enabling perpetuation of Khanty clans; can warn master in times of danger; is basis for divination of *liaksys* (ancestral namesake) name

SOURCES: Chernetsov (1963); Karjalainen (1921); Raun (1955); and Tegy and Kazym consultants.

a fifth soul, enabling physical strength, is exclusively the province of men (1963:5).[3] The sickness soul, *iləs*, is believed to live either in the head or "on the surface" of the body (Chernetsov 1963:13–14).

Khanty claim that when a person is awake and healthy, the sickness soul is invisible. However, when an individual is ill or asleep, this soul takes on the form of an insect or a bird. In sleep, the sickness soul naturally wanders. Usually this is considered safe, but sometimes the soul can be stolen, resulting in illness involving weakness, lethargy, and unconsciousness (Chernetsov 1963:15). Additional danger occurs if the sickness soul leaves while a host is not sleeping, as when someone has chills, sneezes, or takes fright. Shamans can see and recover sickness souls by letting their own *iləs* leave their bodies in trance.

According to Khanty consultants, most of the dangers that can befall a soul are considered unavoidable by the unfortunate victim. Soul theft is often attributed to a recently deceased relative longing for the company of the patient. Nonetheless, some examples of soul loss have traditionally been related to a patient's morality. Such concepts were common through the 1930s, and have limited currency today.

Khanty considered themselves safe from spiritual and therefore bodily harm only when ancestral idols had been treated well, when rules regarding ritual purity had been obeyed, and when ceremonies had been performed properly. Ancient concepts of well-being merged good health and fertility with fishing and hunting gains, since success in these goals reflected oneness with propitiated ancestors. Ancestral patrilineal clan spirits, called *menk* and *mis*, were believed capable of chastising Khanty for sins of disregard by soul theft. Evidence from early ethnographers Gondatti (1887:84) and Nosilov (1904:14) indicates that epidemics of smallpox were believed by Ob Ugrians to result from grave disrespect for spirits, possibly incurred by too much contact with Russians. Traditionally defined sins worthy of bringing on illness thus concerned both human–supernatural transgressions and interpersonal human relations. Serious crimes, such as incest or murder, were particularly considered to invite retaliation by ancestral spirits (cf. Bartenev 1896:85, 95).

Occasionally, health was thought to depend on maintenance of rapport with shamans. Revengeful shamans were believed capable of sending disease in the form of a physical object—like entrails, a worm, or hair—into their victim's body (cf. Shashkov 1864:99; Startsev 1928:93). But shamans, especially those known personally in a given community, were usually considered to be more doctor than witch. (A popular turn-of-the-century shaman assured Alexander Brem [1897:378] that, although his spirit helpers could be used to do evil, the shaman himself endeavored only to cure and to protect his community from "unclean powers.")

Shamans were traditionally able to attribute the sickness to the patients own behavior, to someone else, or to a dead relative. To accomplish this attribution, shamans solicited confessions from patients and family members. Such a confession was itself believed beneficial to health, and may indeed have had psychological benefits (cf. Frank 1961:51–52).

Shamans: Definitions and Classifications

Since shamans traditionally determined the nature of sickness and were major actors in seances to recover lost souls, Khanty considered them crucial for their personal well-being. But Khanty shamans, like most Siberian shamans, were more than medical practitioners. As mediators between the natural and supernatural, they made predictions, provided spiritual shields for the living in times of danger, acted as intelligence agents in times of interclan rivalry, and behaved as psychiatrists, entertainers, and judges.

Ugrian names for shamans reveal many nuances of meaning. The Northern Khanty call the shaman *semvojan*, or "seeing one," with suffixes *xo* or *ne* to denote man or woman. *Tsepanən-xoi* connotes a sorcerer as well as a medicine man in Vakh River dialects, while on the Vasyugan a shaman is referred to as a great or little magician, *jol* (Hadju 1968:170). Karjalainen (1927:245–305) mentions also *multə-xo* ("praying man") and *t'arttə-xo* ("prophet") for Tremyugan shamans. Still other widely used terms denote "men who fall into trances," with notions of heat and narcotic drunkenness as intrinsic to the trance state (Balazs 1968:53–75).

The traditional Khanty shaman was often a community leader, by virtue of personality, spiritual knowledge, and proven ability as a conductor of souls. But the degree to which shamans fulfilled leadership roles has varied according to the individual shaman. A classification of Khanty shamans should be based on their reputations and the range in which they operate, rather than on distinctions of "black" (evil) and "white" (good) identity.[4] Gradations of power can be seen to form a system over time whereby an apprentice shaman "graduates" to practice first in the family, then the locality (defined as extended patrilineal clan affiliations), and finally, in villages not affiliated by clan. While reality is undoubtedly not so systematic, descriptions of shamans by Khanty, Karjalainen (1927:245–95), Startsev (1928:90–91) and Minenko (1974:204) confirm this. Female shamans usually practice only at the family or local level (cf. Durrant 1979).

Training

Questions of shamanic power begin with who becomes an apprentice. Potential talent is believed inherent from birth, although it is often not discovered until the teens, when it is manifest in nervousness, dreaming, and sickness (Khanty consultants; cf. Dunin–Gorkavich 1911:48). While shamanic status is not necessarily hereditary, usually close older relatives who are themselves shamans discover and informally coach their sometimes reluctant candidates. Primarily, training involves learning how to send one's sickness soul into the world of spirits. To achieve a trance state, traditional shamans were taught how to use dried mushrooms, *Amanita muscaria;* alcohol and physical exertion seem to be more current (although less effective) means to alter consciousness.[5]

The apprentice learns how to control specific helper spirits, which come in trance—usually as animals and birds, but also as ancestral forest spirits. Soviet anthropologist Sokolova (1971:224) associates such helpers with clan "totems" of particular shamans (cf. Ridington and Ridington 1975:190–204). Through dreams or trance, the shaman also discovers how to obtain necessary magical accoutrements, such as reindeer-skin drums, felt hats, and iron or brass ornaments.

The most structured aspect of training involves memorizing songs and prayers, passed down by the shaman with whom an apprentice eventually works as an assistant. Service to a master shaman includes maintaining seance equipment and sometimes translating the shaman's trance exploits from mumblings into a dramatic story for the audience. This can give an assistant considerable power as well as practice.

There is no formal initiation or fixed training time for the Khanty shaman, although part of the trance process may involve the symbolic flesh cutting and bone reorganizing torture of an apprentice by spirits, to signify death and rebirth (Siikala 1978:22; cf. Eliade 1974:62–95; Nachtigall 1976:320). When a master considers an apprentice ready to perform, a small extended family seance is arranged for curing or prediction. Word of success spreads rapidly, making for a flexible system.

Family shamans are available on call for relatives and are rarely felt to be spiritually threatening to members of their community. Ugrian specialist Hajdu (1968:147) defines such shamans of lesser strength as "people with sensitive nervous systems who distinguish themselves by their skills in dream reading and in healing minor diseases." This kind of shaman might have some herbal knowledge, but little seance paraphernalia. Family shamans usually live from subsistence activities, rather than seance commissions. The Soviet ethnographer Startsev (1928:89) knew two such family shamans in the 1920s, one a young hunter of 26, the other an older head of a large household, "who hunted, made bows and arrows and boats, and in nothing differed from others." Most shamans alive today are probably on this level. One example is a Tegy woman, considered by several Russians as well as Khanty to be a shaman. She has little contact with Russians, refusing to learn their language, and is reputedly well versed in shamanic lore.

A more powerful type of shaman, operating at the local level, has a reputation for prediction and healing through trance with helping spirits. Such shamans would probably own a drum, bells, hats and some metal ornaments, depending on their location within Khanty territory and on possible Samoyed influences. They could control only a few helping spirits, making for modest seances devoid of "miracles" or prolonged trances. Shamans of this caliber usually have neither the desire nor the personality for broader practice. (A supplementary explanation might be that they do not use intense trance-producing narcotics, because of restricted access to them or to the knowledge involved in using them.) A current example of a shaman with a local reputation is a Tegy recluse in his 40s who lives in the forest and is feared by many but still summoned by a few Khanty believers.

The true shaman of wide reputation and power does not necessarily appear in every community or in every lifetime. This "big man" travels widely, in both this world and the spirit world. Hajdu (1968:147) defines a shaman of great repute to be one "who excels in communicating with spirits and superior beings and who practices magic and produces wonder-working powers." Such Khanty shamans are perceived capable of visiting both the upper and lower worlds of Khanty cosmology, of manipulating in one seance as many as seven spirit helpers including the bear, and of controlling the emotions of a large audience for two or three consecutive evenings.[6] They have many professional secrets, enabling them to perform logic-defying feats of physical endurance, ventriloquism, and dancing.

A big man shaman is a true man of iron, wearing a cloak filled with dangling metal ornaments calculated to attract helper spirits (cf. Businsky 1893:35; Pro-kof'yeva 1971:5–10). He beats an enormous drum, *koim,* which is believed to be transformed in trance into a horse or reindeer (cf. Roheim 1954:49; Dioszegi 1968:260–61). He "rides" his drum into mountainous upper and lower worlds, sometimes depicted in symbolic form on the drum itself (Czaplicka 1914:222). Often the back, handle, and beater of the drum are decorated with iron rings and figures representing spirit helpers. Iron, as a multifaceted symbol of strength, longevity, and spiritual power, is particularly appropriate for the shaman.[7]

Examples of big man shamans are rare today, because the climate of adulation required for a shaman to build a following is lacking. On the Vakh River, in the 1960s, a great shaman named Jorgen was buried by his clients, mostly old men who came from 150 kilometers around (Sokolova 1971:224). I heard of one shaman reputed to have been a phenomenal miracle worker operating out of Beriosovo. He was the father of the current local Tegy shaman. In addition, several Salekhard shamans have wide reputations for curing.

Traditional Khanty Shamanism

Complex beliefs enable performances of seances and help shape not only the personality and power of individual shamans, but also the culture of curing in a given community. Many researchers focus on the psychology and "miracles" of a shaman, rather than on the reasons these "miracles" are or were impressive to clients.[8] During a traditional seance, an enormous amount of communal energy was directed at solving a spiritual emergency, with an extended family often actively participating in chants and dancing (cf. Startsev 1928:94–96). The Khanty shaman, whether male or female, was and to some extent still is able to fulfill mediating roles and to manipulate important Khanty symbols of communication by being an artist and impressario, transforming a small hut into a scene of moving dramatic action (cf. Charles 1953:95–122; Revunenkova 1974:110).

There are often two stages to a Khanty shamanic cure. The first is a diagnosis stage, involving confessions and the summoning of spirit helpers to the cabin of a patient to discover the causes of the illness. The second stage consists of a shamanic trance journey into the upper or lower worlds. A trance journey may not be necessary, if helping spirits are able to accomplish a cure or suggest a sacrifice in the first stage.

A mid-nineteenth-century student of Siberian shamanism, Shashkov (1864:97–99) witnessed a Khanty seance that culminated in a sacrifice. The shaman's helping spirits directed him to order several reindeer from the patient's family as their price for a cure. The reindeer were dragged directly into the *yurt* of the patient:

> To the leg of one deer they fasten one end of a rope, the other end is held by the patient, and when the latter pulls the rope, they kill the deer. The head and horns are laid on the floor, the flesh is eaten and the sick man is anointed with fat [Shashkov 1864:98–99].

This sacrifice is significant because the patient took an active part in his cure. Anointing the patient is itself similar to the smearing of idols with fat and blood during shaman-led sacrifices to ancestors. Thus this patient was given the same kind of concerned attention that sacred ancestral idols were given. Today—because of Soviet restrictions against killing collective animals—animal sacrifices for curing, burial ritual, or ancestral grove worship are rare, but they are not entirely unknown (Balzer 1980:82).

Patient participation during traditional curing sessions was, and to some extent still is, also accomplished by confessions. A story told by Khanty to Obdorsk resident Bartenev (1896:85) illustrates the high value Khanty place on confession, although the story itself is probably apocryphal. During a difficult childbirth, female relatives of an expectant mother sent for a renowned shaman in panic and concern. The shaman entered the darkened, ritually-prepared birth hut and began to beat his drum, asking the unhappy patient in what way she had "sinned." She first said she had "masturbated," then that she had had "a relationship with a dog," and finally that she had "slept with her father" (Bartenev 1896:85). Only after this ultimate confession was the shaman satisfied, and the mother safely delivered of her child. This story probably served Khanty as a morality play, demonstrating graphically the necessity of full confession. A more current description of Ob-Ugrian birth rituals by Mansi ethnographer Rombandeeva (1968:80) stresses confessions of both mothers and fathers.

While confession of culturally defined "sins" by a patient or family members might help clear the air for a cure, further information regarding sources of sickness was acquired supernaturally. At the turn of the century, the Finnish ethnographer Karjalainen (1927:310–15) witnessed an impressive summoning of helping spirits on the Vasyugan River. At nightfall the shaman placed himself in the darkest corner of a low, crowded *yurt* and began to play a native lyre, *narsus*. First he contacted a fierce and somewhat impertinent flying messenger called "Stern Woman with the Handled Stick." When she arrived, he began to shake and ordered her to summon underground spirits. With each helper's arrival, the shaman sang to his audience about the journeys the spirits had made. He announced a bear spirit, claiming, "I hear the hairy humped beast of the Great Earth coming from under the first layer of the earth to the water of the second" (Karjalainen 1927:311).

After helping spirits of the underground were assembled, the shaman began to call forth celestial helpers, using his lyre and metaphorical speech. Each time a spirit entered the yurt, the shaman shook with its power and then renewed the music and rhythm of his dialogues. After seven spirits were called, one of them an important celestial horse that nearly knocked the shaman out with its cold breath, the shaman announced that a second evening would be required for him to travel on the grey horse to the spirit world (Karjalainen 1927:313).

Karjalainen (1927:318) stresses that the Vasyugan shaman was not possessed by spirits, but rather was inspired by their whispering in his ear. During seances, shamans were likely to sing praises of special spirits, to challenge them, and to advertise control over a range of spirit types. A song fragment collected by H. Paasonen on the Konda, at the turn of the century, brags, "I spirits (*tonxət*) a hundred, forest goblin (*menk*) a hundred have conjured" (Vertes 1968:119). Two kinds of classic song—myths were folk models for shamanic trance, one in which the shaman rescued a lost soul from greedy, fighting underworld spirits of the dead; and a second in which the shaman either flew by horse or turned himself into a white-winged bird to negotiate with sky deities (cf. Karjalainen 1927:245–331; Senkevich 1935:158).

In the 1920s, Khanty seances were still widely believed capable of solving spiritual problems. The skeptical Startsev (1928:94–96) saw a Vakh River seance, intended to recover the lost soul of a young child. The tightly packed session continued until 5 in the morning, with seven seances. During breaks, the shaman told his audience which spirits had come to him. With each seance, he became more energetic and "ferocious," while dancing, reeling, and tossing his drumsticks to the audience. He brought himself and his audience to a fever pitch with the ever-louder intensity of his drumbeats.[9] "Characteristic moments occurred when the shaman put the edge of his drum on the small of his back, on his left leg, and on his torso. He would touch family members [of the sick child] and yell" (Startsev 1928:95–96). When the sessions were over, the shaman had barely enough strength to promise that the child would be well.

Multiple Dimensions of Shamanism

Given the importance of patient and audience participation in seances, it is logical to view shamanism as potentially effective for community cohesion as well as individual health (see Table 4.2). Shirokogoroff's monumental work on Siberian Tungus psychology stresses the responsiveness of shamanism to community stress; he calls "the treatment of psychic troubles . . . the practical aim of shamanism" (1935:422). His analysis can be compared to that of Turner on the African Ndembu (1964:230–63), particularly because each sees curing complexes as aiding adaptive responses to tensions produced during culture change (cf. Shirokogoroff 1935:393).

For both Shirokogoroff and Turner, major benefits of Tungus and Ndembu seances are assumed to stem from improvements in community relations that result from confessions and symbolic enactments of emotional group solidarity. Turner (1964:237) concludes that Ndembu doctors "are well aware of the benefits of their

Table 4.2 Khanty Shamanism: A Feedback System of Symbolic Action

Players	SHAMAN →	PATIENT →	COMMUNITY →
Definitions	Mediator between natural and supernatural worlds	Sufferer from culturally defined and/or transcultural afflictions	Loose grouping of extended patrilineal families
Potential Benefits	Increased Reputation		
Level of Effectiveness	Personal — Technique	Cure — Physical, Psychological, Social	Problem Solving — Cohesion, Values, Cosmology
Descriptions	Unusual confidence in self, system; Leadership ability; Creativity; Nervousness; Renumeration. **Controlled trance:** *Amanita muscaria* hemp?; alcohol; dance. "Miracles". **Costume:** color; symbols; metal. **Drum:** cosmology model; transport metaphor; seance intensifier	**Physical:** Endorphin trigger?; Herbal medicine; Massage. **Psychological:** Abreaction; Transference; Suggestion; Hypnosis?; Dream analysis; Shock therapy? **Social:** Confession; Group attention: calling shaman; in seance	Social resentments aired. **Taboos enforced:** clan; sexual. **Respect:** ancestors; animals; spirits; elders; shamans. Soul belief. Hunting, fishing, reindeer losses explained. Individual restored to group. Sorcery discovered, punished. Culture change tensions eased, explained? **Beliefs enacted:** layered universe. **Spirit helpers:** bear; lizard; birds; *menk*; *mint*; *tonx*. Ancestral power. **Sacrifices:** horse; reindeer. **Offerings:** cloth; coins

62

procedures for group relationships, and they go to endless trouble to make sure that they have brought into the open the main sources of latent hostility in group life."

This applies to Khanty curing, although it is unwise to attribute to shamans control over all latent social problems. Social control varies with the personality, experience, and stature of a shaman. What the nonlocal shaman gains through a reputation as a "big man," he loses in lack of intimacy regarding local affairs. To compensate, a shaman's assistants and in-laws can act as informants, explaining marital problems, hunting shortages and extended-family tensions in a given community.

Theories about Shamanic Cures

Although traditional shamanism does indeed seem to be a form of group therapy, its successful treatment of individuals is more problematic. The intense communal and spiritual activity of seances can provide an incredible psychological boost by increasing self-confidence and jolting a patient out of depression (cf. Gillin 1948:387–400). Creatively handled symbols of common cultural experience, whether coded in shamanic paraphernalia or speech, can also help define and channel individual problems, beginning with diagnosis of afflictions, peaking in trance journeys, and ending with various prescribed postseance tasks. Whether this psychological effect is enough to unblock mental or physical anguish depends greatly on the patient and the complaint.

Lévi–Strauss (1967), stressing the value of repetitive, emotion-laden symbolism in shamanic chants, has provided an explicit discussion of how individual cognition may be shaped by culture in the curing process. The crux of curing is that a chaotic and painful experience is reorganized by the shaman for the patient, through processes of abreaction and transference, and fitted into a comprehensible familiar mythical system. This reorganization "induces the release of the physiological process" (p. 193). While Lévi–Strauss suggests that polynucleids in brain nerve cells could be affected, newer research indicates that brain chemicals such as endorphins (Beeson et al. 1979) may be triggered in the brain to willfully control pain. [10]

Curative Procedure

The details with which Khanty shamans regale their audiences may have a focusing effect on patients, similar to that which Lévi–Strauss suggests for Cuna Indians. As the shaman overcomes an obstacle-filled topography of the lower world, with a powerful bear spirit as a guide, the patient anticipates recovery of a lost sickness soul. When the shaman finally confronts a spirit of the dead with soul theft and offers the spirit food, money, and valuable cloth, it may be an enormous relief to the patient to know that the soul has been pinpointed. If a battle ensues, between shamanic helpers and spirits of the dead, this battle may be mirrored in the mind of a patient struggling with pain or drowsiness. Finally, when the shaman flies back to earth with the prized soul clenched firmly in his fist, the patient might sense a renewal of energy and confidence, made concrete when the shaman blows the soul back into the patient's ear (cf. Karjalainen 1927:305–15).

Generalizations about what goes on in a patient's mind are highly speculative, but in traditional contexts of faith and communal concern, some shamans were able to cure, at least temporarily, a respectable portion of their patients. It is possible that this was accomplished with the aid of tremendously powerful symbol manipulation. Shamans themselves may have had no inkling of specifically how their ecstatic journeys produced bodily cures. They were just as likely to go into trance for the lost soul of an infant, who could not mentally follow their exploits, as for an adult, who could. Thus, I am not attributing clairvoyance of scientific principles to shamans, but simply saying that the effect of their ecstacy was sometimes positive.

Although Lévi–Strauss's thesis is perhaps furthered by discovery of endorphins, aspects of his structural assumptions are still questionable. As his articulate critic Jerome Neu (1975:285–92) has pointed out, there is no direct homology, even for the Cuna, between the physical body and the supernatural world, so that there is little proof of universal structuralism by reference to either physical or "fantasy-physical" parallels with shamanic mythology. Similarly, "limited laws" of symbolism cannot be derived from physical correspondences (cf. Lévi–Strauss 1967:199).

Assuming that processes of abreaction and transference do occur during some shamanic cures, they undoubtedly are managed in different ways, with numerous powerful, culturally defined metaphors. For Khanty, abreaction could result from confession of cultural or even clan-specific taboos; from adroit removal of bloody hair out of a patient's body as evidence of sorcery; or from the blowing of a lost soul into a patient's ear. Transference could be accomplished not only during seances, but throughout a patient's potentially life-long relation with a family or local shaman (cf. Beck 1967:317, 321).[11]

World views reaffirmed in seances are also significant. The cosmology of a soul's journey or a shamanic initiatory trance may be similar for a number of Siberian peoples, but it differs considerably from that of the Cuna. Thus, a balance should be kept between awareness of similar widespread and effective forms of psychotherapy, and an understanding of the multiple symbol systems which are tapped in the process of therapy.

Indigenous views of health and of shamanic behavior may vary in their congruence with interlocked psychophysiological curing mechanisms. Thus success rates for cultures in which mythological chants are loudly dramatized and shamans are widely respected may be greater than for cultures where shamanic cures are secretly mumbled away from the patient (cf. Fortune 1932:144–47). Since cultures also emphasize different styles of curing, ranging from the more individually oriented to the more communal, there is further scope for variations in effectiveness. This in turn can change over time, as our own psychiatry reveals. Finally, various kinds of illnesses may lend themselves differently to symbolic manipulation. Difficult childbirth may be more susceptible to cure through psychologically triggered release of brain chemicals than tuberculosis.

In sum, shamanism can cure certain kinds of social and personal ills, working at once on the body politic, ancestral relations, and, perhaps, the culturally influenced mind of a patient.

Culture Change

An absolute prerequisite for an effective shamanic cure is faith, and this is difficult, but not impossible, to find today. Much belief in shamanism that currently exists in Northern Khanty villages seems to be a negative belief in the power of shamans to do evil. Whereas many Khanty shamans were traditionally thought to be restrained in misuse of their spirit powers, heightened community tensions—with increased Russian contact and antishaman propaganda—seem to have exacerbated Khanty ideas of the shaman as a sorcerer. This trend was particularly marked in the 1930s through the 1950s.[12] Any previous ability of shamans to restore community equilibrium in times of trouble, as suggested by Turner (1964) and Shirokogoroff (1935), was often overwhelmed by Sovietization, serious losses in World War II, displacement of Khanty communities, and efforts to settle nomadic Khanty reindeer breeders. This does not mean that Khanty culture has disintegrated, but rather that new emphases are being developed in other areas of cultural life, including rituals (Balzer 1980, 1981; Sokolova 1976).

A Contemporary Shamanic Treatment

Today many Soviet officials deny the existence of Khanty shamans, and, indeed, belief in shamans as either curers or sorcerers is waning. However, I was able to get the following account of a curing attempt in Tegy:

> There is a shaman, about 41 years old, who lives not far from here, separate, with his family. He has daughters who study. He is always drunk, and has been in jail. He came to this house one time and tried to cure an old woman who was living here. Everyone ran away when he came, except one woman who was very drunk, and a small child. The shaman cut the sick woman who had called for him. He cut her on the side of the neck, and blood ran down to her stomach. He stood at the door so no one could see just what he did. He raised his hands and motioned to the sky, to call his special evil spirits. You can tell he is a shaman by his evil eyes. Everyone knows he is a shaman. He takes an ax and shakes, when the spirits come to him, as he crouches on the ground.

There is much that is unconventional about this account. Shamans are not known for extreme blood-letting or for covert seances. The shaman's helping spirits are referred to here as "evil," whereas once only a few in uncontrolled contexts were considered frightening. A medium of divination (the ax) has become a weapon, while other crucial symbols of shamanic power (the drum, iron ornaments, special clothing) are missing from the account. The story of this disreputable shaman continues:

> This same man, earlier, lived in this very house. He tortured us. He was always drunk, and broke furniture. He speaks in shaman's tongues, and knows all the old shaman songs. He sometimes did not let us into our own home. He stood straight at the door, and stared, and said: "The spirits are helping me." The police chase him. He lived in Beriosovo, and his father was a big and very famous shaman. He is a swine shaman. He was kicked out of the Beriosovo collective and so he came here. His wife's brothers lived here . . . He lived there, but after a month and a half, they kicked him and his family out of their house. He cursed them, and I heard it: "From now on in this house, you will not live well, may there be blood on your floors." And after this, the brother of his wife shot himself and died . . . Then he moved in here . . . and finally the police chased him from here . . . He aided so many deaths . . . Probably one of his daughters too will become a shaman. How can people say there aren't shamans? Of course there are.

It is hard to measure how common such stories of shaman misbehavior and Khanty condemnation are, since there still seem to be a few shamans whom the Khanty revere and protect from prying ethnographers. This Tegy shaman seems to be disillusioned to the point of despair at the ridicule of his knowledge, but reputedly other shamans in the Arctic town of Salekhard have not lost their confidence. In general, the Soviet-spurred cycle of hiding and distrust has broken many of the mutually reinforcing bonds previously maintained by followers and shamans. Private seances are not necessarily effective, because an important aspect of curing involves the communal support given to patients and shamans. This kind of public–private distinction between effective hope-producing atmospheres in ritual curing is made by Frank (1961:62), who adds: "Even in private forms of healing, group and cultural factors are implicit" (cf. Kleinman 1979:364).

Shamans as Deceivers

The decline of shamanism among Northern Khanty began in the 1930s, with collectivization and agitation against shamans as "deceivers" (cf. Ankudinov and Dobriev 1939; Vdovin 1976:261–62). Soviet officials destroyed sacred idols (often of ancestral shamans) and took away drums and other equipment of shamans in raids. They used each illegal offense of shamans (for example, drunkenness, or *kulak* offenses of wealth and hoarding) as a reason to put them in jail. More positively, the government also initiated "red tents" with which doctors, nurses, and medical assistants traveled, giving modern medical aid. Earlier, distances required to reach hospitals were so prohibitive as to discourage their use by natives.

Judging by Startsev's accounts (1928:88–97), shamanism was alive and popular with both Khanty and Siberian Russian peasants in the 1920s. Senkevich, ten years later, had a much harder time trying to record shamanic songs: "The clever shamans not only don't want to sing them, but also in general hide their profession" (1935:158).

Looked at from the Soviet point of view, the campaign against shamans is understandable. Zealous revolutionaries from the south, bent on scientifically and collectively unlocking Siberian resources, had no use for the "wasteful" animal sacrifices encouraged by shamans. They considered shamans to be exploiters of peasants and natives, and accused them of demanding too much payment for services or forcing sacrifices solely for their share of meat. Such "kulak-shamans" were condemned at regional communist party meetings in the 1930s, which were geared toward training young Siberian natives to reject traditional political–religious elders.

It is logical in these conditions that some shamans went underground, others became alcoholics, and a few revolted. In the 1930s, under the leadership of the shaman Yarkin of Narikarsky, a huge sacrifice of horses was organized, in an effort to prevent collectivization (Kartsov 1937:120). Such activism was especially great on the Kazym and Sosva rivers, where there was even shaman-led destruction of Soviet encampments as well as more common refusals to attend schools. In addition, authorities claimed to have uncovered a plot to kill communist party workers, which led to arrests and court sentencing for many shamans and their followers (Kartsov 1937:120). Persecution turned the tradition which made shamans great into a dangerous badge of religious conservatism.

Today, local log-cabin hospitals are available in villages as small as Kazym.[13] Hospitals are accessible—even to nomadic breeders of reindeer—by helicopter and Ob River hydrofoil. Focus for curing is on hygiene, drugs, and surgery. Although modern medicine has been introduced, psychological roots of illness are rarely explored, and the shared world view on which shamanic mythology was based is being discredited. Communist ideology, although not totally rejecting psychiatry, precludes most psychological explanations of illness, whether Freudian or native. In the context of modern diseases, both Khanty and Siberian Russian villagers realize that Soviet medicine is often more effective than shamanic seances. Nonetheless, Soviet methods are not always chosen by the Khanty.

The Khanty Response

The first point to be made about current Khanty responses to Soviet medicine is that choices of cures are open to experimentation. If a local shaman is more accessible than a Soviet doctor, that shaman might be tried before the patient bothers to apply to a hospital. If a Soviet cure has failed, a Northern Khanty family might try to send for a nonlocal Salekhard shaman with a wide reputation. Recourse to shamans is kept a family secret, if possible, to avoid the displeasure of Soviet authorities. I learned of one blind woman who, having been treated unsuccessfully by both Soviet and Khanty practitioners, was putting her final faith in a new Soviet medicine which she had heard cured reindeer of eye problems. A progression of medical alternatives can theoretically lead to a systematic study of the "hierarchy of resort" (Romanucci–Ross 1977:481–87).[14]

A second factor, concerning contrasts in the curing milieu, partially explains Khanty difficulties in adjusting to Soviet medicine. The power of traditional focus on spirit-oriented cures, confession, drama, and communal participation in seances has been stressed. In Soviet hospitals, the family is confined to formal visits, and the patient is likely to feel isolated. There is an unaccustomed discomfort in the clean white rows of beds and the unfamiliar faces of other patients and staff. A modern cure entails the reverse of concerned group solidarity, which engulfs the patient in goodwill in an otherworldly, darkened, and impassioned atmosphere. It involves the crisp professional relationship of the patient with a usually Russian doctor and a few medical assistants.

I met a young woman in Kazym who was awkwardly waiting out an illness of her mother in the hospital, while her reindeer-breeding father stayed behind in their reindeer-skin tent. She told me she longed for the tundra and for her family, and that her mother also wished to go home. They, like most Khanty, had some confidence in the ability of Soviet doctors, but they resented the situation in which their family was placed. It was hard for them to understand why a cure for the body had to be divorced from cures for the souls of the mother and her family. It was likely that, when they returned to the tundra, a shaman would be asked to make sure that not only the symptoms but also the cause of the sickness had been treated.

Third, it has taken a long time for the level of confidence in Soviet medicine to be built to its current point. When Soviet doctors first came to the north, they were resented as part of the collectivization effort. They were confusing foreign figures, curing without communal ritual. They were also actively opposed by Khanty shamans who believed sincerely in their own abilities. In the early Soviet period, shamanic self-assurance was still nurtured by community approval, in a complex feedback system (cf. Boas 1930:20–41; Lévi–Strauss 1967:169–75; Table 4.2). Any defect of Russian medicine became a victory for shamanism. Startsev (1928:90) tells of a Russian medical assistant whose death was popularly attributed by Vakh River villagers to revenge taken by the local shaman for trifling with his drum. This very polarization prevented shamans, often especially intelligent and creative individuals, from becoming "culture brokers" in the new political and medical atmosphere (cf. Landy 1977:468–81).

Faith in Medical Systems

Even Western medicine requires some faith to be effective, particularly if cures entail the regular taking of drugs. The transfer of faith can involve an intense conversion with a successful cure, or more commonly a slow process of trial, suspicion, pain, and reward (cf. Frank 1961:76, 81, 98). Failures of "foreign" medicine when Russians were trying to win over the populace could not have helped the Soviet cause. Just as "red-tent" programs were beginning to be accepted, World War II, with its terrible losses of Siberian natives, occurred. "Why couldn't Russian medicine have saved more Khanty soldiers?" Khanty asked.

The issue of change in medical faith leads to a hypothesis concerning the ways Khanty think about medical problems. This suggestion is derived from Goodenough (1963:152) and Romanucci–Ross (1977:481–87). Goodenough notes that some Pacific natives coping with acculturation have cognitively divided sickness into white-man's and native categories. When they have a white-man's sickness, it can be treated with white-man's medicine. Otherwise, nature cures will suffice. I believe that the Khanty similarly differentiate choices about cures, but that not all sickness can be neatly pigeonholed into Soviet and Khanty categories. Thus, in practice Khanty may combine Western and native cures. Illnesses likely to be treated with native medicine are menstrual, birth, and sexual difficulties, as well as depression, lethargy, dizziness, blindness, soreness, and arthritis.

Syncretism, the merging of beliefs or symbolic actions from different cultures, is a natural part of cognitive adjustment, especially during intense periods of culture change. Its patterning often reveals a logic of its own, as when a prerevolutionary Khanty shaman painted images of St. Nicholas on his drum, claiming that the Russian Orthodox saint, renowned for his curing ability, had become the shaman's helping spirit (Shukhov 1916:31). Today, when Khanty combine respect for Soviet surgery with belief in lost souls, they may be demonstrating an underlying awareness that illness often involves the whole self—both body and mind. Shamanic theories and their accompanying symbolic actions are, as Lévi–Strauss (1967:173–74) has shown, relatively false, but they reach, nonetheless, important symbolic realms rarely glimpsed by modern medicine.

For many Khanty, these realms are based upon sacred correlations, such as birds and hair with souls; bears, horses, and reindeer with spirit messengers; and iron with strength and longevity. These Khanty symbols seem to be both multifaceted and dominant, rendering them flexible and long-lasting, with potential to take on new meanings (cf. Turner 1977:77). Other representations of the sacred, such as clan-related forest spirits (*menk* and *mis*) seem to have less meaning in the Soviet social environment. It is difficult to determine the degree to which ancient shamanic myths have meaning and power in new, limited curing contexts. There is still belief in shamanic ability to turn into a bird, and there is a continuing memory of marathon legends dealing with the travels of shamanic ancestors. I was told one myth about a shamanic cat ancestor who founded a forest grove still revered by some Kazym Khanty. Thus, a few key sacred symbols and myths have maintained a vitality enabling shamanism to survive "underground," but the richness of Khanty symbolism wanes with the death of each shamanic elder.

Conclusion

In conclusion, Khanty are increasingly turning to Soviet medicine. The communal atmosphere required for effective symbol-manipulating shamanic seances has been undermined both by Soviet persecution of shamans and by the advances of Soviet medicine. Faith in shamanic power has sometimes turned to fear, making failure of traditional medicine as self-fulfilling a prophecy as success once was. With changing world views has come syncretism and increased choice. A combination of factors governs Khanty choices about cures, including issues of convenience, family attention, shamanic reputation, and definitions of sickness as Soviet or native. Khanty consider shamans to be both doctors and deceivers.

ACKNOWLEDGMENTS

I am indebted to the International Research and Exchanges Board, which made 13 months in the Soviet Union (1975–76) possible, and also to IREX for providing preparatory fellowship funds in the summers of 1973 and 1974. Participation in a summer field trip to the Khanty–Mansisk area of Northern Siberia (1976) was made possible through Leningrad University. The American Association of University Women (Helen Wood–Pearl Hogrefe Fellowship), the Washington, D.C., Alumnae Association of Bryn Mawr, Sigma Xi, and the Harvard Russian Research Center have generously provided additional support. I wish to acknowledge helpful comments on portions of this material by Professors Frederica de Laguna and Jane C. Goodale of Bryn Mawr and by Professors Demitri B. Shimkin (University of Illinois), Jonathan Andelson (Grinnell), Michael Harner (New School for Social Research), Lydia Black (Providence), Evon Z. Vogt (Harvard) and Michael Fischer (Harvard). Doctors Ronald Dubner and Candace Pert of the National Institute of Health and Curator Ildiko Lehtinen (National Museum of Finland) deserve special thanks for their aid. I am also grateful to the Soviet scholars Rudolf Ferdinandovich Its (head and founder of Leningrad University's anthropology department), and Valery Andreevich Kozmin (expedition leader and professor at Leningrad University). They are not, however, responsible for my non-Marxist interpretations of data.

NOTES

1. This chapter combines ethnohistorical research with limited field data. For further information about sources, see Balzer (1979). Leningrad University's eight-member student-oriented 1976 ethnographic expedition to the Northern Ob River area (near the Arctic Circle) stayed in two Khanty villages: Tegy, a fishing collective, and Kazym, a reindeer-breeding center. Although Russian was the main means of communication, I learned key concepts in Khantesky and was able to seek my own consultants.

2. "Classical" forms of shamanism are recognized to be rooted in Siberia, especially among Tungus–Manchu peoples (Laufer 1917; Nowak & Durrant 1977:38; Harner 1973: xii; Siikala 1978:14–15), although the linguistic origins of the Tungus word *saman* are also sought in more southern, Turkic, traditions, in Sanscrit *sramana,* and Vedic *sram* (Shirokogoroff 1935:270; Demitri Shimkin, personal communication April 1979). The Ob-Ugrian (Khanty and Mansi) shamanism described here reveals both northern and southern influences (cf. Dioszegi 1978:135–62).

3. Given the complexity of Ob-Ugrian soul beliefs, the question becomes whether Khanty have one soul with many aspects or separate souls. Lydia Black believes that multiple manifestations of souls in Siberia represent "the relationship of parts to the whole" (personal

communication 16 Feb. 1978). Named distinctions are nonetheless made, and when asked about a gender-based discrepancy in souls an elderly Tegy woman explained: "Males are higher and females are lower. Males are stronger."

4. In some areas of Siberia, especially among the Mongolic Buriat and the Turkic Yakut, shamans are divided into "black," dealing with lesser and evil spirits of the lower or Eastern world; and "white," dealing with major, pure spirits of the upper or Western world (Krader 1954:334–37; Krader 1978:192; Zelenin 1936:294–98). Both can cure, but black shamans are also sorcerers.

5. I have no evidence of *Amanita muscaria* use today, but did see it growing near Kazym. Khanty consultants loathed all mushrooms and were appalled at the large numbers eaten by expedition members, but a few Khanty shamans may secretly maintain the mushroom tradition. Eye-witness evidence for Ugrian shamanic use of *Amanita muscaria* comes from Munkasci (1907), reprinted in Wasson (1968:306), Dunin–Gorkavich (1904:95), and Patkanov (1897:121). Czigany (1980:213) confirms the antiquity of mushroom use by Ob Ugrians. Khanty shamans may also have used hemp seeds thrown in fires to produce intoxication and a blue smoke (Balazs 1968:59–61; Zuev [1771–72] 1947:45). This is documented for Central Asia (Shimkin 1967:624).

6. The importance of the number seven and of a multi-layered cosmology in Khanty shamanism may reveal Tatar influences (Karjalainen 1927:245–331; Siikala 1978:224). Ob-Ugrian myths describe seven layers of the universe: three upper and three lower worlds, with the earth as central (Chernetsov 1935). Bears, key symbols of supernatural mediation, are still greatly revered throughout Siberia. In Tegy, I was told: "The bear understands everything. He is older than us all. He is the biggest, most important being in the world." (See also Balzer 1979; Hallowell 1926).

7. Iron and other metals may have once been impressive markers of trade wealth. The religious significance of metal in Khanty symbolism has been shown by Sokolova (1978) and Moszynska (1968), and is studied by Ugrian specialist Ildiko Lehtinen. Shaman accoutrements in National Museum of Finland collections are from Potanin, Alquist, and Karjalainen (e.g., numbers 4866:6; 1870:22; and 4934:216). Metal images of spirit helpers, associated either with shaman equipment or idols, include a bear, lizards, and birds.

8. There is a large literature on whether the shaman is "neurotic" or "schizophrenic." Proponents include Czaplicka (1914), Bogaras (1909), Zelenin (1936), Devereux (1961), and, with reservations for "shaman–saviors," LaBarre (1972). Opponents include Ackerknecht (1943), Honigman (1960), Nordland (1967), Opler (1959, 1961), and Murphy (1964). Beck (1967) and Torrey (1974) argue that the shaman is more psychiatrist than psychotic, whereas Eliade (1974) believes that shamans are cured psychotics. Silverman (1967) stresses that technically schizophrenic tendencies are put to good supportive–creative use in shamanist cultures (cf. Revunenkova 1974; Hultkranz 1978; and Peters and Price–Williams 1980).

9. Neher (1962) suggests that there are important trance-inducing effects of near-alpha brain wave frequencies in shamanic drumming, but the French ethnomusicologist Rouget (1980) forcefully refutes Neher's "reductionist" claims.

10. I am grateful to Doctors Ronald Dubner and Candace Pert at NIH for providing me with leads to possible biochemical responses of patients during shamanic seances. For discussion of endorphins, see Snyder (1977) and Foster and Anderson (1978:99–100). In fall 1980, the Mental Hygiene Institute, R.M. Bucke Memorial Society, and Department of Psychiatry of McGill University sponsored a conference in Montreal entitled "Shamans and Endorphins." Linkages of endorphins with pain control, memory, acupuncture, and shamanic trance were explored.

11. Theories of Freud (1949) and Sargant (1964) are not directly applicable, although abreaction, transference, and heightened suggestibility seem to occur during seances. Cathartic acting out of suppressed desires by a Khanty patient is rare. Other psychological techniques which may apply to Khanty shamanism include shock therapy (during sorcery object removal); hypnosis (from repetitive shamanic recitations of spirit arrivals); dream interpretation (during diagnosis and in shamanic training), and social reintegration (showing to a patient group concern). Similar native therapies are suggested by E. Fuller Torrey (1974:330–37) and Vincent Crapanzano (1973:212–29), with each cultural context altering the healing process (cf. Kleinman 1979:363–65).

12. A similar increase in "witch-fear" during a period of intense cultural change has been described among the Eskimo by Edmond Carpenter (1961:508–15).

13. In 1976, Kazym had about 270 families with a population of roughly 1300. Such figures are fluid because many Kazym Khanty use their houses as bases from which to go hunting, fishing, or reindeer breeding. There were 466 people in Tegy, living in about 180 houses. They had access to a small medical center in the village and a hospital in Beriosovo. For statistics on modern medical improvements, see Diachkov (1979:20–24).

14. Lola Romanucci–Ross (1977) explains that Manus frequently choose native medicine, basing decisions on a moral component of sickness, whereas choices of European medicine are often last resorts (cf. Landy 1977; Nichter 1978). Studies of "resort" must cope with haphazard elements of choice, and with sampling accurately enough to reflect cultural trends and change (Jon Andelson, personal communication, November 1979).

REFERENCES

Ackerknecht, Erwin H. 1943. "Psychopathology." *Bulletin of the History of Medicine,* 14:30–67.

1958   "Problems of Primitive Medicine [1942]. W.A. Lessa and Evon Z. Vogt, eds., *Reader in Comparative Religion.* Evanston: Row Peterson & Co., 342–53.

Ankudinov, N., and A. Dobriev. 1939. *Shamany Obmanshchiki* [Shamans as Deceivers]. Leningrad: Akademii Nauk.

Balazs, J. 1968. "The Hungarians Shaman's Technique of Trance Induction," trans. Stephen Dunn. V. Dioszegi, ed., *Popular Beliefs and Folklore Tradition in Siberia.* Uralic and Altaic Studies, vol. 57. Bloomington; Indiana Univ. Press, 53–57.

Balzer, Marjorie Mandelstam. 1979. "Strategies of Ethnic Survival: Interaction of Russians and Khanty in Twentieth-Century Siberia." Ph.D. diss., Bryn Mawr College. Ann Arbor: Univ. of Michigan Microfilm.

1980   "The Route to Eternity: Cultural Persistence and Change in Siberian Khanty Burial Ritual." *Arctic Anthropology,* 17:77–90.

1981   "Rituals of Gender Identity: Markers of Siberian Khanty Ethnicity, Status and Belief." *American Anthropologist,* 83(4):850–67.

Bannerman, R.H. 1977. "W.H.O.'s Programme." *World Health,* Nov.:16–17.

Bartenev, Victor. 1896. *Na Krainem Severe-Zapade Siberia* [In the Far North of Siberia]. Saint Petersburg: M.F. Paukina.

Beck, Robert J. 1967. "Some Proto-Psychotherapeutic Elements in the Practice of the Shaman." *History of Religions,* 6(4):303–27.

Beeson, Paul B., Walsh McDermott and James B. Wyngaarden. 1979. *Cecil Textbook of Medicine.* Philadelphia: W.B. Saunders Co.

Boas, Franz. 1930. "The Religion of the Kwakiutl." *Columbia University Contributions to Anthropology,* 10 (2).

Bogaras, Waldemar. 1909. *The Chukchee.* Memoirs of the American Museum of Natural History, no. 11. New York: Stechert.

Brem, Alexander. 1897. "Ostiaki-Idolpolkoniki" (Ostiak Idol-Worshippers). *Ezhemesiachnyia Literaturnyia Prelozheniia k Nive,* 2:347–83.

Businsky, P.O. 1893. *Kreschenie Ostiakov i Vogulov Pre Petre I* [Christianization of Ostiak and Vogul Under Peter I]. Kharkhov: Gub Pravleniia.

Carpenter, Edmund S. 1961. "Witch-Fear Among the Aivilik Eskimos." Yehudi A. Cohen, ed., *Social Structure and Personality.* New York: Holt, Rinehart & Winston, 508–15.

Charles, Lucile Hoerr. 1953. "Drama in Shaman Exorcism." *Journal of American Folklore,* 66:95–122.

Chernetsov, Valery Nikolaevich. 1935. *Vogul'skie Skazki* [Vogul Tales]. Leningrad: Soslitizdat.

    1963   "Ideas of the Soul among Ob-Ugrians," trans. Ethel Dunn and Stephen Dunn. Henry Michael, gen. ed., *Studies in Siberian Shamanism: Anthropology of the North,* vol. 4. Toronto: Univ. of Toronto Press. 3–45. (Original: "Predstavleniia o Dushe u Obskikh Ugrov." *Trudy Instituta Etnografiia,* 51(1959):114–59.)

Crapanzano, Vincent. 1973. *The Hamadsha: A Study in Moroccan Ethnopsychiatry.* Berkeley: Univ. of California Press.

Czaplicka, Marie A. 1914. *Aboriginal Siberia.* London: Oxford Univ. Press.

Czigany, L.G. 1980. "The Use of Hallucinogens and the Shamanistic Tradition of the Finno–Ugrian People." *Slavonic and East European Review,* 58:212–17.

Devereux, George. 1961. "Shamans as Neurotics." *American Anthropologist,* 63:1088–90.

Diachkov, V.I. 1979. "Sostoianie i Perspektivy Razvitiia Zdravookhraneniia v Iamalo-Nentskom i Khanty-Mansiiskom Avtonomykh Okrugakh Tumenskoi Oblasti" (Condition and Perspectives on the Growth of Health Care in the Iamal-Nenet and Khanty-Mansi Autonomous Districts of the Tumen Region). *Zdravookhranenie Rossiskoi Federatsii,* 4:20–24.

Dioszegi, Vilmos. 1968. *Tracing Shamans through Siberia,* trans. Antia Rajkay Babo. Oosterhout, The Netherlands: Anthropological Publications. (Original: *Samanok Nyomaban Sziberia foldjen,* Budapest, 1960)

    1978   "Pre-Islamic Shamanism of the Baraba Turks and Some Ethnogenetic Conclusions," trans. S. Simon. V. Dioszegi and M. Hoppal, eds., *Studies in Siberian Shamanism.* Budapest: Akademiai Kiado, 83–167.

Durrant, Stephan. 1979. "The Nisan Shaman Complex in Cultural Contradiction." *Signs,* 5(2):338–47.

Dunin–Gorkavich, A.A. 1904, 1910, 1911. *Tobol'skii Sever* [The Tobol'sk North], vols. 1–3. Tobolsk: Gub. Tip.

Eliade, Mircea. 1974. *Shamanism: Archaic Techniques of Ecstacy.* Princeton: Princeton Univ. Press.

Fortune, Reo. 1932. *Sorcerers of Dobu.* New York: Dutton & Co.

Foster, George M., and Barbara Gallatin Anderson. 1978. *Medical Anthropology.* New York: John Wiley & Sons.

Frank, Jerome. 1961. *Persuasion and Healing.* Baltimore: Johns Hopkins Press.

Freud, Sigmund. 1949. *An Outline of Psychoanalysis.* trans. James Strachey. New York: Norton. (Original: *Abriss der Psychoanalyse,* 1940.)

Gillin, John. 1948. "Magical Fright." *Psychiatry,* 11:387–400.

Gondatti, N.L. 1887. "Sledy Iazycheskikh Verovanii U Mansov" (Traces of Pagan Belief among Mansi). *Trudy Obshchestva Estestvenii Antropologii i Etnografii,* 8:49–73.

Goodenough, Ward. 1963. *Cooperation in Change.* New York: Russell Sage Foundation.

Hajdu, Peter 1968. "The Classification of Samoyed Shamans," trans. Stephen Dunn. V. Dioszegi, ed., *Popular Beliefs and Folklore Tradition in Siberia.* Uralic and Altaic Series, vol. 57. Bloomington: Indiana Univ. Press, 147–73.

Hallowell, A. Irving. 1926. "Bear Ceremonialism in the Northern Hemisphere." *American Anthropologist,* 28:1–175.

Harner, Michael. 1973. *Hallucinogens and Shamanism.* London: Oxford Univ. Press.

Honigman, John J. 1960. "Review of *Culture and Mental Health,* ed. Marvin Opler." *American Anthropologist,* 62:920–23.

Hultkrantz, A. 1978. "Ecological and Phenomenological Aspects of Shamanism," trans. S. Simon. V. Dioszegi and M. Hoppal, eds., *Shamanism in Siberia.* Budapest: Akademiai Kiado, 27–58.

Karjalainen, K. 1921, 1922, 1927. *Die Religion der Jugra-Volker,* 3 vols. Folklore Communications: 41, 44, 63. Porvoo: Finnish Academy of Sciences.

Kartsov, V.G. 1937. *Ocherk Istorii Narodov Severo-Zapadnoi Sibiri* [Essay on the History of the Peoples of Northwest Siberia]. Moscow–Leningrad: Gos. Sots.–Ekon. Izdat.

Kleinman, Arthur. 1979. *Patients and Healers in the Context of Culture.* Berkeley: Univ. of California Press.

Krader, Lawrence. 1954. "Buryat Religion and Society." *Southwestern Journal of Anthropology,* 10:322–51.

———— 1978 "Shamanism: Theory and History in Buryat Society," trans. S. Simon. V. Dioszegi and M. Hoppal, eds., *Shamanism in Siberia.* Budapest: Akademiai Kiado, 181–233.

LaBarre, Weston. 1972. "Hallucinogens and the Shamanic Origins of Religion." Peter Furst, ed., *Flesh and the Gods: The Ritual Use of Hallucinogens.* New York: Praeger, 261–78.

Laufer, Berthold. 1917. "Origin of the Word Shaman." *American Anthropologist,* 19:261–71.

Landy, David. 1977. "Role Adaptation: Traditional Curers under the Impact of Western Medicine." David Landy, ed., *Culture, Disease and Curing.* New York: Macmillan.

Lévi–Strauss, Claude. 1967. *Structural Anthropology,* trans. Claire Jacobsen and Brooke G. Schoepf. New York: Anchor Books.

Minenko, Nina Adamova. 1975. *Severo-Zapadnaia Sibir'* [Northwest Siberia]. Novosibirsk: Nauka.

Moszynska, V. 1968. "On Some Ancient Anthropomorphic Images from West Siberia," trans. Stephen Dunn. V. Dioszegi, ed., *Popular Beliefs and Folklore Tradition in Siberia.* Uralic and Altaic Series, vol. 57. Bloomington: Indiana Univ. Press 93–101.

Murphy, Jane. 1964. "Psychotherapeutic Aspects of Shamanism on St. Lawrence Island, Alaska." Ari Kiev, ed., *Magic Faith and Healing.* New York: Free Press, 53–83.

Nachtigall, Horst. 1976. "The Cultural–Historical Origin of Shamanism." A. Bharati, ed., *The Realm of the Extra-Human: Agents and Audiences.* Hague: Mouton, 315–22.

Neher, Andrew. 1962. "A Physiological Explanation of Unusual Behavior in Ceremonies Involving Drums." *Human Biology,* 34:151–60.

Neu, Jerome. 1975. "Lévi–Strauss on Shamanism." *Man,* 10(2):285–92.

Nichter, Mark. 1978. "Patterns of Resort in the Use of Therapy Systems and Their Significance for Health Planning in South Asia." *Medical Anthropology*, 2(2):29–56.

Nordland, Odd. 1967. "Shamanism as an Experiencing of 'the Unreal.' " C. Edsman, ed., *Studies in Shamanism*. Stockholm: Almqvist & Wiksell, 166–85.

Nosilov, K.D. 1904. *U Vogulov* [Among the Voguls]. Saint Petersburg: Suvorin.

Nowak, Margaret, and Stephen Durrant. 1977. *The Tale of the Nisan Shamaness: A Manchu Folk Epic*. Seattle: Univ. of Washington Press.

Ohnuki–Tierney, Emiko. 1976. "Shamanism and World View: The Case of the Ainu of the Northwest Coast of Southern Sakhalin." A. Bharati, ed., *The Realm of the Extra-Human: Ideas and Actions*. Hague: Mouton, 175–200.

    1980 "Ainu Illness and Healing: A Symbolic Interpretation." *American Ethnologist*, 7:132–51.

Opler, Marvin, K. 1959. *Culture and Mental Health: Cross Cultural Studies*. New York: Macmillan.

    1961 "On Devereux' Discussion of Ute Shamanism." *American Anthropologist*, 63:1091–92.

Patkanov, S.K. 1897. *Die Irtysch Ostyaken und ihre Volkspoesie*. Saint Petersburg: Suvorin.

Peters, Larry G., and Douglass Price–Williams. 1980. "Towards an Experiential Analysis of Shamanism." *American Ethnologist*, 7:397–418.

Prokof'yeva, E.E. 1971. "Shamanskie Kostiumy Narodov Sibiri" (Shaman Costumes of Peoples of Siberia). *Sbornik Museia Antropologii i Etnografii*, 27:5–10.

Raun, Alo. 1955. *The Ostyak and the Vogul*. New Haven: Human Relations Area File.

Revunenkova, E.V. 1974. "O Lichnosti Shamana" (On the Personality of the Shaman). *Sovetskaia Etnografiia*, 3:104–11.

Ridington, Robin, and Tonia Ridington. 1975. "The Inner Eye of Shamanism and Totemism" (1970). Denis Tedlock and Barbara Tedlock, eds., *Teachings from the American Earth*. New York: Liveright, 190–204.

Roheim, Geza. 1954. *Hungarian and Vogul Mythology*. Monographs of the American Ethnological Society, vol. 23. New York: Augustin.

Romanucci–Ross, Lola. 1977. "The Hierarchy of Resort in Curative Practices: The Admiralty Islands." David Landy, ed., *Culture, Disease and Healing*. New York: Macmillan, 481–87.

Rombandeeva, E.I. 1968. "Some Observances and Customs of the Mansi (Voguls) in Connection with Childbirth," trans. Stephen Dunn. V. Dioszegi, ed., *Popular Beliefs and Folklore Tradition in Siberia*. Uralic and Altaic Series, vol. 57. Bloomington: Indiana Univ. Press, 77–83.

Rouget, Gilbert. 1980. *La Musique et la trance*. Paris: Gallimard.

Sargant, William. 1964. *Battle for the Mind*. London: Pan Books.

Senkevich, V. 1935. "Skazka i Pesni Khantov" (Khanty Tales and Songs). *Sovetskii Sever*, 6(3–4):151–59.

Shashkov, S. 1864. *Shamanstvo V Sibiri* [Shamanism in Siberia]. Saint Petersburg: Morichegovskogo.

Shimkin, Demitri. 1967. "Pre-Islamic Central Asia." *Canadian Slavic Studies*, 1(4):618–39.

Shirokogoroff, Sergei. 1935. *Psychomental Complex of the Tungus*. London: Kegan Paul, Trench, Trubner.

Shukhov, I.N. 1916. "Reka Kazym i ee Obitateli" (The River Kazym and Its Inhabitants). *Ezhegodnik Tobol'skogo Gubernskogo Muzeia*, 26:1–57.

Siikala, Anna-Lenna. 1978. *The Rite Technique of the Siberian Shaman*. Folklore Communications, 220. Helsinki: Finnish Academy of Science.

Silverman, Julian. 1967. "Shamans and Acute Schizophrenia." *American Anthropologist,* 69:21–31.

Snyder, Solomon H. 1977. "Opiate Receptors and Internal Piates." *Scientific American,* 236(3):44–57.

Sokolova, Z.P. 1971. "Perezhitki Religioznykh Veronanii U Obskikh Ugrov" (Survivals of Religious Belief among the Ob Ugrians). *Sbornik Muzeia Antropologii i Etnografii,* 27:211–39.

1976 *Strana Ugrov* [The Country of the Ugrians]. Moscow: Mysl'.

1978 "The Representation of a Female Spirit from the Kazym River," trans. S. Simon. V. Dioszegi and M. Hoppal, eds., *Shamanism in Siberia.* Budapest: Akademiai Kiado, 491–501.

Startsev, Georgi. 1928. *Ostiaki: Sotsial'no-Etnograficheskii Ocherk* [The Ostiak: A Social–Ethnographical Study]. Leningrad: Priboi.

Torrey, E. Fuller, M.D. 1974. "Spiritualists and Shamans as Psychotherapists: An Account of Original Anthropological Sin. Irving I. Zaretsky and Mark P. Leone, eds., *Religious Movements in Contemporary America.* Princeton: Princeton Univ. Press, 330–37.

Turner, Victor W. 1964. "An Ndembu Doctor in Practice." A. Kiev, ed., *Magic, Faith and Healing.* New York: Free Press, 230–63.

1977 "Process, System and Symbol: A New Anthropological Synthesis." *Daedalus,* 106(3):61–80.

Vdovin, I.S. 1976. "The Study of Shamanism among the Peoples of Siberia and the North." A. Bharati, ed., *The Realm of the Extra-Human: Agents and Audiences.* Hague: Mouton, 261–73.

Vertes, E. 1968. "On the Trail of Ostyak (Khanty) Mythical Songs." V. Dioszegi, ed., *Popular Beliefs and Folklore Tradition in Siberia.* Budapest: Akademiai Kiado, 113–22.

Wasson, Robert Gordon. 1960. *Soma: The Divine Mushroom of Immortality.* New York: Harcourt, Brace & Janovich.

Zelenin, D.K. 1936. *Kul't Ongongov V Sibiri* [Cult of Idols in Siberia]. Moscow–Leningrad: Akademii Nauk.

Zuev. Vasilii F. 1947. "Opisanie Zhivushchikh Sibirskoi Gubernii V Beriosovskom Uezde, Inovercheskikh Narodov Ostiakov I Samoyedov" (Notes on the Inhabitants of Siberia in Beriosovo, the Natives Ostiak and Samoyed) (1771–1772). *Trudy Instituta Etnografii,* 5(1):1–95.

PART TWO

*Symbols
and Healing*

IN THE PREVIOUS SECTION, WE CONSIDERED THE RELATIONSHIPS BETWEEN SPECIFIC pairs of medical systems. In this section, we begin consideration of a more reflexive kind of exchange: what can we learn from the medical system of the non-Western world?

Lévi–Strauss (1967) describes in some detail how the shaman and the mythology shared by him and the patient alter physiological processes through the control of mental processes, dissolving the boundary between "self" and "other," and offering reintegration to the patient. The "shaman provides a language" (p. 198) and, like the psychoanalyst, allows the conscious and unconscious to merge. He does this through a shared symbolic system, and that is why a cured individual also improves the mental health of the group. Because of this, the patient performs a very important social function; he provides a definition for normalcy and he validates the system by calling into play the group's sentiments and symbolic representations to have them "become embodied in real experience" (p. 180–82). For these healers, the mind, the body, and the experiential field are "one."

The key to this whole social process is the relationship between the process and the consequences of healing; and this is one of the great loci from which we have much to learn from non-Western medicine.

The relationship between a healing act and the act of healing is a highly complicated one. Figure 1 sketches a few of the paths of consequence in the healing process. The patient experiences something amiss: his stomach hurts, he feels lonely or depressed, he develops a sore on his lip or a pain in his head. These symptoms may well, by themselves, have a series of consequences for the patient (path 1)—in the simplest case, they may frighten him and cause stress. In Figure 1, this "fear" is a "conceptual consequence," and the "stress" is a "physiological consequence" of the fear (path 7). Stress, producing an experience itself (path 8), can compound fear; the system contains a feedback loop. The universal human response to such a situation is a kind of analysis we call diagnosis. Either alone, or in consultation with family or therapist, the patient develops an explanation for his experience (path 2). Diagnosis itself has two types of consequences. The first is directly conceptual (path 3) and may vary greatly in degree. The diagnosis may be soothing ("Oh, it's just a fever sore") or terrifying ("Oh, it's skin cancer"). A soothing diagnosis may "damp down" the feedback loop, whereas a terrifying one may intensify it.

The second consequence of diagnosis (path 4) is "treatment," which has two types of consequences, conceptual and physiological. The variation in conceptual responses is, again, great, ranging from minor ("It's just a fever sore—use this ointment on it twice a day") to major ("It's skin cancer—let's try radiation and chemotherapy"). And, of course, different treatments can have different kinds and degrees of physiological consequences. There is here, however, a particularly interesting interaction between the two types of consequences. The ointment may contain an astringent that will help heal the sore; the evidence of healing can encourage the patient, reducing his anxiety via pathways 6–8–7. This process is often generalized so that people develop a kind of faith—"Ointments heal sores"—which can itself be generalized—"Medications heal illnesses"—which can simultaneously induce healing via pathways 5–7–8.

This entire process is deeply embedded in culture. Sickness, a fundamental assault on person and society, is a matter of the deepest human concern: affecting life and death, it can induce deep emotional arousal. Not surprisingly, the act of healing, often including intensely dramatic ritual, shares qualities of the "numinous" in re-

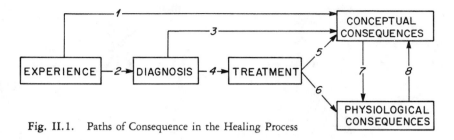

Fig. II.1. Paths of Consequence in the Healing Process

ligious experience—it can be ineffable, absolute, and undeniable (Rappaport 1979: 211–16). In simpler terms, the experience of healing can be highly marked.

But sickness raises other issues as well, less emotional, more cosmological. Undeniable experience combined with ultimate cosmology can simultaneously account, in cultural terms, for both. This fact is amply demonstrated in the chapters that follow. Finkler shows how spiritualist symbolic healing, "cleaning," is effective for treating a range of chronic diseases in Mexico. Rogers and Evernham describe the shaman tradition of the Digueño Indians and demonstrate the powerful role it plays for these people *even though it is no longer practiced*. Roberts develops a persuasive argument for the symbolic character of medicines, showing how a specific agent (the charred bones of immolated arsonists) represents a vast cosmological system in Tabwa therapeutics and witchcraft. Herrick shows in deep detail how the Iroquois choice of medicinal plants is bound up with their entire understanding of the origins and nature of their universe. Moerman considers the conceptual and subsequent physiological consequences of medical treatment by examining the placebo in Western biomedicine.

None of this is to say that the physiological consequences of medical treatment are not important; path 6 of Figure 1, the central domain of biomedicine, is a fundamental one (see Part IV of this book for detailed treatments of this path in non-Western medical traditions). It *is* to say that paths 1, 3, 5, and 7—that is, the conceptual consequences of sickness, diagnosis, and treatment—and their interactions are extremely important in understanding and controlling sickness. An integrated biohuman medical paradigm requires that all of these relationships be understood simultaneously. And biohuman medicine requires that they all be controlled to optimize the healing process.

REFERENCES

Lévi–Strauss, C. 1967. *Structural Anthropology*. New York: Doubleday.
Rappaport, R. 1979. *Ecology, Meaning, and Religion*. Richmond, Cal.: North Atlantic Books.

5

Studying Outcomes of Mexican Spiritualist Therapy

Kaja Finkler

Introduction

The aim of this chapter is to demonstrate how medical anthropological concerns reverberate with broader anthropological issues. The present focus is on nonmedical treatment outcomes and the ways in which they reveal a sociocultural group's cognitive model not readily apparent on first glance; how symbolic meaning casts back directly on the ecological environment and indirectly on historical conditions experienced by a population within a complex society.

Treatment outcomes were investigated in two spiritualist temples in a rural region of Mexico (Finkler 1980b, 1981a, 1981b).[1] The study, based on a series of follow-ups, deepens the scientific and clinical understanding of the healing process by unveiling the cultural requisites for restoring patients to a subjectively perceived premorbid state. Analysis discloses the culturally encoded model bearing on illness resolution.

Perusal of the literature reveals ample rationale for the investigation of nonmedical healing systems (Fabrega and Silver 1973; Kleinman 1980; Kunstadter 1978; Lieban 1973). As many scholars have observed, aside from being a basic research question, the cross-cultural study of ethnomedical phenomena emphasizes the "cultural construction of illness" (Kleinman 1980); the relationship of illness as a cultural category to other social and cultural phenomena (Colson and Selby 1974), and the light thrown by the anthropological study of health on the manner in which people perceive their world (Lieban 1973).

Widespread attention has thus been given to illness management, illness etiologies, and therapeutic choice. Concern has also focused on efficacy—the ways in which healers achieve therapeutic success (Young 1976); on how nonmedical practices and healing rituals aid in illness management in a culturally meaningful way (Garrison 1977; Gonzalez 1966; Harwood 1977; Kennedy 1967; Lieban 1977; Turner 1967); and on the role of cultural symbols in restoring patients to health (Lévi–Strauss 1967; Turner 1967).

Curiously, with few exceptions (Garrison 1977; Kleinman 1980; Jilek and Todd 1974), few attempts have been made to evaluate nonmedical treatment outcomes. Admittedly, establishing efficacy is rather a sticky problem (Young 1976). There are numerous difficulties in assessing therapeutic outcomes by nonmedical practitioners (Fabrega 1974; Mechanic 1968), primarily because disease is self-limiting; in large measure the body heals itself with or without therapeutic intervention. Yet, in spite of methodological difficulties and theoretical reservations, empirical investigation of treatment outcomes must be done because outcome studies lay open to view cognitive requisites of the healing process.

At this juncture it must be emphasized that the present discussion refers to patient-perceived outcomes of spiritualist treatments. Hence, the focus is on patient perception of symptom removal and patient attribution of recovery. No attempt has been made to evaluate medically changes in patients' biological or biochemical states resulting from spiritualist therapies. Thus, the emphasis is on cultural rather than biomedical criteria for illness resolution.[2] The systematic study of culturally perceived treatment outcomes provides an especially propitious area for examining the ways in which symbols work, and the degree to which such symbols elicit responses within a given cultural group.

Interestingly, while anthropological attention has been given to the power of symbols (Lévi–Strauss 1967), there has been less concern with inquiry into the proportionate power of symbols. That is, do all individuals in a given culture respond equally to the same set of symbols (e.g., Fernandez 1965; McCreery 1979)? Examination of treatment outcomes necessarily leads to this question. As will be noted, the empirical evidence tends to suggest that not all persons exposed to the same healing symbols respond to them similarly, and tends to pinpoint the types of individuals and syndromes that fail to respond to symbolic manipulation.

Additionally, empirical exploration of treatment resolution and recovery attribution brings into view not only those who fail to respond to healing symbols but also those who eschew symbolic manipulation of their illness, suggesting that not all members of a culture share the same symbolic requirements (cf. Fernandez 1965). The study, however, generates the hypothesis that, in prolonged illness, symbolic requisites for recovery become shared. It is postulated that symbolic requisites mitigating illness resolution accompany perduring illness episodes over time, suggesting that whereas illness amenable to speedy recovery is managed biomedically by physical manipulation, prolonged illness necessitates symbolic management of a type not furnished by biomedicine.

In keeping with proponents of the relationship between cognitive models and the ecological order (e.g. Rappaport 1979), it is suggested that in the region under study the environment fosters in many a perpetual state of illness unmanageable by modern medical practices, which requires culturally meaningful symbolic management. It is argued that current scientific medical modalities promote prolonged illness, resulting in advancement of nonmedical therapeutic regimes that rely upon symbolic removal of affliction.

Spiritualist temples are widespread throughout Mexico and in border towns of the United States.[3] In fact, it is a vigorous religious movement (Finkler 1981c) as well as a health-care delivery system. For these and other reasons (Finkler 1980b), investigation of spiritualist therapy is especially propitious for rendering insights into therapeutic outcomes and recovery attribution concomitant with their cognitive correlates.

To elaborate on these points, it is necessary to describe the investigation's setting, discuss briefly the healers and their treatment techniques, and explore the types of syndromes they attend and the success and failures of Spiritualist ministrations.[4]

The Setting

A brief description of the ecological and socioeconomic conditions of the region is necessary, because they form part of an interlocking matrix which renders meaning to recovery attribution cited by spiritualists' patients. As background to the Mexican spiritualists under study, a summary discussion of their beliefs is also presented.

Mexican Spiritualism

Spiritualist temples enjoy a large clientele (see also Lagarriga Attias 1978). In one of the temples where the study was done, an average of 83 persons were treated on any given curing day.

Mexican spiritualists believe in the trinity, the Father, Jehovah, the Son, Jesus Christ, and the Holy Ghost, Father Elias, who manifested himself to humanity in the person of a humble Mexican priest in 1861 (Finkler 1981c). They also speak of a millenium; this is not very well conceived, and not all spiritualists are aware of it. All, however, agree that humanity suffers a miserable fate on earth. Death is therefore regarded as a release of one's spirit, and the spirits of those who faithfully follow the teachings of spiritualism will not return to this earth. The reward is thus "nonreincarnation" of their spirits.

Ethical teachings are embodied in 22 precepts, which guide spiritualists in proper conduct between person and person, and between person and God. The first ten of these include, for the most part, the Biblical Ten Commandments, whereas the remaining twelve refer to areas of contemporary life such as enjoining members from drinking alcoholic beverages or from believing in witches and witchcraft. The latter is of special interest because it distinguishes spiritualist healers from the majority of their patients, who are nonadherents of spiritualism (Finkler 1980b). As will be seen, whereas many patients seeking spiritualist therapy attribute illness to witchcraft, spiritualists deny the existence of witchcraft. The group upon which this investigation is based regard illness either as stemming from natural causes or as induced by "dark spirits" who roam the heavens and have not been "given light" during a specially performed spiritualist ritual (Finkler 1981c). These dark spirits had once belonged to evil persons on this earth, such as drunkards, murderers, etc. According to some, such spirits are especially instrumental in causing chronic impairments of the type not cured by physicians.

Spiritualist denial of witchcraft is significant, then, for at least two reasons: first, because it has been emphasized that "the success of the doctor–patient relationship is in large part attributable to the extent the doctor and patient share common frames of reference" (Mechanic 1968:164). In this instance, patient and healer fail to share a basic premise of illness etiology. Second, spiritualist healers are important agents of ideological change—they shift the onus for illness from neighbors, friends, or relatives, to impersonal spirits. When Mexican spiritualists succeed in removing a patient's belief in witchcraft, they are not only healing the patient of the specific complaint but also promoting a more harmonious social environment in which the patient may function, thereby eliminating possible future tensions which may otherwise contribute to future illness episodes.

Ecological Conditions

But although spiritualists may be instrumental in altering the social environment of their patients, they have little, if any, effect upon the ecological or economic conditions of the region in which they are found. The temples where the study was done are situated in an agricultural region of the state of Hidalgo. The population there is comprised predominantly of peasants and wage laborers (Finkler 1974; 1978; 1979). Because the region is situated in a semiarid zone, agriculture is possible only because irrigation water is diverted from Mexico City (Finkler 1974).

The region enjoys a unique source of water, untreated sewage water[5] emanating from Mexico City. Because these waters have been used in the region for the past 60 years and because they flow into the ubiquitous irrigation canals where they also become stagnant, they are of special concern in the present discussion. Although the use of untreated sewage waters for irrigation contributes to high agricultural yields for the peasants of the area (Finkler 1974; 1978; 1980a), these waters afford a conduit for transmission of enteropathogens by several vectors. In fact, the waters carry an array of intestinal parasites (including vibrio, cholera, salmonella, shigella, endamoeba, and enterovirus, among others) (Heukelekian 1962). Moreover, these waters absorb chemical wastes on their way from Mexico City to the region; the effects of these wastes on crops and humans have not been ascertained. Whereas potable water flows through separate conduits, the degree to which the irrigation waters may contaminate the potable water supply is uncertain as well (Heukelekian 1962), but an ever-present danger of direct contamination exists.

Other environmental conditions contributing to poor public health in the region include the unsanitary living environment prevailing in the Mexican countryside. Since most village households and even those in the municipal towns lack indoor facilities, human wastes are left to be disposed of by domestic animals, including pigs and dogs. Other garbage is disposed of in town dumps, and flies prevail everywhere, particularly during rainy months.

Patterns of Health and Illness

As a result of these adverse living conditions, parasitosis is endemic to the region. Significantly, enteritis and diarrheas were the principal causes of morbidity in Hidalgo between 1973 and 1975. According to local doctors, there is a higher frequency of intestinal disease in the area than in Mexico as a whole.[6] But whereas the region differs epidemiologically from the rest of Mexico, the disease patterns found in the area under study do not differ from third world countries. In fact, as in other parts of the developing world, we are dealing with a "malnourished, anemic and parasite burdened individual" (Brown 1966:272). These conditions clearly weaken and attenuate the individual's resistance to other potential health hazards and produce a perpetual sense of discomfort, including fatigue, stomach distension, and head pain.[7] This is extremely important to keep in mind, because the subject population exhibits relatively high scores on a medical health questionnaire, the Cornell Medical Index (Finkler 1980b; 1981a). High scores measured by this instrument have been interpreted as reflecting an individual's psychological health (Abramson 1966; Brodman, et al. 1952); however, in the context of the adverse ecological and economic conditions of the population (Finkler 1974; 1980a), high scores on this questionnaire may have their origin in the generally poor physiological health of the population.

The socioeconomic situation of the population adds to the poor state of health. The peasants and daily wage workers predominating in the region are relatively indigent, owing, in large measure, to the local socioeconomic structure (Finkler 1974; 1978; 1980a; 1980c). While the land tenure system is outside the scope of the current discussion, it is important to emphasize that a large segment of the population holds *ejido* land, that is, land redistributed to the peasantry under Mexico's land reform program, as well as small parcels of privately owned land (Finkler 1974; 1978; 1980a). Inasmuch as access to *ejido* lands is conditional and the land is not owned outright, these lands are frequently a major source of both intracommunity and intercommunity tensions. The fact that *ejido* holdings add additional stress for *ejidatarios* (*ejido*-holders) is suggested by the fact that *ejidatarios* have statistically significantly higher scores on the medical health questionnaire than people who are not *ejidatarios* (Finkler 1981b).

The region is also experiencing intensive industrialization, which has brought with it new economic hardships, including expanding consumption needs, particularly the education of children. In fact, the recently created education requirements of a growing industrial nation have put great economic strains on rural households, adding to day-to-day tensions.

Additional sociocultural factors contributing to the underlying health problems in the female population include the high rate of alcohol consumption by males. Over and above the economic drain on household funds created by alcohol consumption, the women may also be subject to physical abuse, contributing to an overall ill state of health. In sum, it can be assumed that we are confronted with a population whose impoverished state of health is attributable to a combination of factors, including adverse ecological, economic, and cultural conditions.

Patients and Their Complaints

Three categories of patients seek treatment at the temple. I have designated them as *first comers, habitual temple users,* and *regulars* (Finkler 1980b; 1981a).

As a general rule, *first comers* include individuals who failed to respond to medical treatment and as a final recourse sought an alternative mode of health care. As is pointed out elsewhere (Finkler 1980b), *first comers* create an interesting symbiosis between medical practitioners and spiritualist healers by their reasoning regarding the etiology of their illness. In most cases, when an individual fails to be cured by medical doctors, the conclusion is reached that the illness was caused by witchcraft. A type of syllogism is produced which can be stated as follows: If doctors cannot cure the illness, it must be due to witchcraft. This type of reasoning creates a curious paradox because, as already noted, spiritualists repudiate the reality of witchcraft.

Successfully treated first comers become either *regulars* or *habitual temple users.* *Habitual temple users* comprise the majority of temple patients. This category refers to persons who, having been successfully cured once by spiritualist healers, return again on other occasions. In fact, out of 1,212 patients for whom I wrote prescriptions,[8] 89 percent were first comers or habitual temple users.[9] Habitual temple users seek treatment at the temple for culturally defined nonserious illnesses, usually disorders unaccompanied by fevers, including diarrhea and vomiting. Similar dysfunctions accompanied by fevers, as well as life-threatening afflictions requiring bed confinement, and sundry conditions accompanied by fevers, are considered grave impairments for which medical treatment is normally sought (Finkler 1980b; 1981a). Importantly, enteropathogens, which, as we have seen, are endemic to the area—but which are frequently asymptomatic, especially when not accompanied by fever—are not regarded as a serious illness.

On the whole, the majority of complaints presented by these two groups revolve around gastrointestinal impairments followed by musculoskeletal, respiratory, and gynecological disorders, as well as nerves, fevers, *susto* (sudden fright), mild children's disorders, teething, sweating, chills, colds, hiccups, and infants' crying (Finkler 1981b). Also, many first comers are initially exposed to temple healers immediately prior to impending surgery, when patients come to inquire whether surgery is indeed warranted (Finkler 1981a).

Approximately 15 percent of first comers and habitual temple users are patients who come to the temple seeking advice on how to deal with personal problems usually centered around male–female interpersonal relationships in general and husband–wife tensions in particular. But the majority of patients' complaints center around physical dysfunctions.

Regulars are converts to spiritualism who have adopted spiritualism as their religion and who participate frequently in temple rituals. Included are temple functionaries, curers, and persons who regularly attend spiritualist services on Sundays and on the five scheduled service days of each month. Regulars, unlike the other two groups, usually consult temple curers *first* in all cases of illness. Hence, when an illness befalls a regular's household, the ill individual immediately seeks treatment at the temple. However, if a cure is not effected within a brief span of time, then the patient resorts to medical services.

Regulars are recruited into temple participation by spiritualist healers because they display types of syndromes that differ in some respects from the other categories of patients. Unlike the latter, who tend to experience an assortment of psysiological and somatized conditions, regulars exhibit a variety of clinical symptoms more frequently associated with dysphoric states and chronic pain (Blumer et al. 1980; Sternbach 1974; Katon, Kleinman and Rosen n.d.(a), n.d.(b)), types of disorders diagnosed by spiritualist healers as illnesses of the spirit rather than of the body (Finkler 1981a).

Healers and Their Healing Techniques

Spiritualist curers heal through spirit protectors, who manifest themselves when the curer enters into trance. Each curer usually possesses the same spirit protector during the curer's career. Spirit protectors, it is believed, were at one time doctors or other gifted individuals who had not completed their mission on earth during their lifetime. These include individuals who may have died recently and others from the distant past. Commonly, among spirit protectors, there are Aztec and other Indian personages who had possessed great knowledge of healing during their lifetime.

Several curers, frequently but not exclusively women ranging in age from 20 to 60, sit side by side, each treating a different patient. In one of the temples under study, four to six curers usually work simultaneously; because of the large clientele there are two shifts, with each curer working on the average two hours a day. Some healers who have an especially large following, however, may work unceasingly for as long as four to six hours a day. Each curer sees an average of seventeen patients in two hours. Thus, each healer spends 7.1 minutes, on the average, with one patient. The actual time spent with each patient varies depending upon individual healers and the treatment given. Special types of treatments, which will not be dealt with here, may take as long as 45 minutes. However, during the normal course of the day a curer devotes between 4.7 minutes and 17.5 minutes to a patient. The patient is thus expedited rapidly and patient–healer interaction is relatively impersonal.

Stages in Healing

Healer–patient interaction can be divided into four phases (Finkler 1980b). The first phase, which lasts longest, is referred to by spiritualists as *desalojos* ("dislodgements"), whereas patients refer to it as *"limpia"* ("cleaning"). Some curers may spend as much as half the interaction time with the patient administering the "cleaning," during which they move their hands up and down the patient's body and recite a blessing. The symbolic meaning of the "cleaning" phase will be discussed later; at this juncture it is important to emphasize that this aspect of spiritualist treatment is regarded by patients as a major beneficial component of spiritualist treatment procedure.

During the subsequent phases, the interaction revolves around a patient's statement of symptoms and a healer's statement of remedies and recapitulation of required treatment. There is little demonstration of compassion or support for the sick person, other than by providing a prescription for the symptoms. These data counter the view, advanced by many, that personal relations with health practitioners are necessary for healing to take place (e.g., Fabrega and Manning 1973, Mechanic 1968). Interestingly, the most favored curers are not those who consign the longest time to the patient, but rather those who are "most spiritual," meaning that they concentrate on "cleaning" and massaging the patient.

Every patient presenting a physiological symptom is usually prescribed at least three categories of prescriptions: teas, baths, massages, and frequently also patent medicines. Teas and baths are prepared from 140 varieties of medicinal plants; of these 100 are native to the region, and others, commonly used throughout Mexico, can be purchased from herbalists at local pharmacies. The most commonly prescribed patent medicines are mild laxatives, tonics, and vitamins. Laxatives are important components of the treatment and are recognized by healers as an internal "cleansing" that complements the external one effected by "cleaning." In the words of one healer addressing a patient, "After a purge the stomach is like a child—everything is new."

Patients with interpersonal problems are usually instructed to place red flowers under their beds to eliminate or purify "their bad thoughts" or white flowers to protect them against evil thoughts or evil spirits.[10]

Whereas first comers and habitual temple users are usually treated summarily, regulars benefit from diverse types of temple therapeutic modalities. They, unlike other patients, enjoy more extensive and continuous interaction with the healers, including frequent "cleaning," and they may also be trained to become healers or temple functionaries. This training of regulars, which includes trancing and which leads to a change of roles, forms an intricate part of their therapy (Finkler 1981a).

Treatment Outcomes and Recovery Attribution

Detailed consideration is given to spiritualist treatment outcomes elsewhere (Finkler 1980b; 1981a). For the present discussion it is enough to say that out of 107 patients on whom follow-ups were done,[11] there were 35.5 percent failures; 25.3 percent successes; 19.6 percent inconclusives; and 19.6 percent miscellaneous. Treatment outcomes of first comers and habitual temple users were established by using the basic criterion of recovery: patient's relief from target complaint (Battle et al. 1966) or self-perceived symptoms and alleviation of behavioral incapacities. Hence *successes* refer to those patients who reported that they had followed the prescribed treatment and, at the time they were interviewed, had recovered from the symptoms for which they had sought treatment. In most cases, patients were able to pinpoint which aspect of temple therapy was instrumental in effecting their recovery. The majority of complaints in this group revolved around abdominal pains and general body aches. This group is comprised of equal numbers of first comers and habitual temple users.

Failures refer to patients who sought temple therapeutic intervention and followed the prescribed treatment, but who reported that they were not cured by it. In those instances, patients continued to suffer from the ailments for which they had come to be treated at the temple. One-third of this group is made up of patients with gastronintestinal disorders manifested clinically in blood in stools and diarrhea. The remaining two-thirds comprise a variety of maladies, including a medically diag-nosed case of terminal cancer, ear dysfunctions, kidney impairments, an abscess, senile deterioration, psychosis, and a case of female infertility. Of these, 60 percent were habitual temple users, treated successfully at the temple on a previous occasion, and 40 percent were first comers.

Inconclusives are patients who stated they had recovered but had also sought medical intervention for symptoms reported at the temple. The majority of individuals in this category experienced abdominal problems; there were also children suffering from fright and one woman afflicted with paralysis. Two-thirds of the group were habitual temple users; the remainder, first comers.

The *miscellaneous* category includes persons who, at the time of the follow-up visits, had failed to administer the prescribed treatment, and those from whom it was not possible to ascertain from their reports whether or not their condition had changed since the initial interview.

Significantly, the failure group scored higher on the medical-health questionnaire than the success group, suggesting that spiritualist healers have greater success with patients exhibiting fewer self-perceived symptoms as measured by the Cornell Med-ical Index (Finkler 1980b).

The research results reported here concerning first comers and habitual temple users reveal two important findings: First, recovery attribution is not related to the degree of experience with temple therapy, as one might have expected, inasmuch as both first comers and habitual temple users equally attested to treatment failure and inconclusiveness. Second, detailed examination of the sundry syndromes pre-sented at the temple (Finkler 1980b) suggests that four types of disorders tend to benefit from spiritualist therapy: (1) diarrheas probably not due to pathogens, (2) simple gynecological disorders, (3) somatized syndromes, and (4) mild psychiatric disorders analogous in type to those reported by others (Garrison 1977; Kleinman and Sung 1979).

Significantly, successfully treated patients tend to attribute recovery to "cleaning" received at the temple; even among the failures and inconclusives, many indicated that what they liked most about temple treatment was the "cleaning." We shall return to this point shortly.

By way of illustration, the following case of Irene demonstrates a somatized syndrome of brief duration with a favorable outcome by use of ordinary temple therapeutic measures.

Case 1: Irene, a Successfully Treated Case.   Irene, a 36-year-old woman, happily married, with two children, economically well situated, developed a severe pain in her right arm, back, and dorsal region of the head, the *cerebro*. She was afflicted with sleeplessness and a number of unspecified fears. Irene was treated by numerous doctors including an acupuncturist, and her condition was variously diagnosed as related to her lungs, her chest, and her coccyx. Finally, one physician declared that there was nothing wrong with her, yet she continued to experience the symptoms. After three months of treatment-seeking activity, a friend recommended the temple. After two treatments consisting of "cleaning" and massages, her ailment completely disappeared and she regained her usual cheerful mood. Following her recovery, Irene stopped going to the temple, but she referred several patients to the healers.

Irene's case suggests a mild somatized syndrome coinciding with her move to a relatively luxurious new house, totally isolated from friends and family. Significantly, she recalled that her father, whom she had attended, had suffered a similar pain in his right arm at his death 14 years ago. Irene's case seems relatively clear: a somatized depressive condition precipitated by the loss of a previous house in which she had been very happy. The loss of her old home became merged with the loss of her father, as evidenced by her symptoms, which reproduced those of her dead father. It is not uncommon for depressed individuals to reproduce complaints of deceased loved ones (Freedman and Kaplan 1972).

Irene's speedy response to routine temple treatments and cases with similar clinical syndromes contrast with individuals recruited into the ranks of regulars. Thus, whereas first comers and habitual temple users tend to react favorably to temple ministrations—i.e., teas, massages, baths, and "cleaning"—regulars fail to respond to these types of short-term therapeutic regimens. In effect, regulars are persons who tend to suffer from disorders not readily amenable to treatment by either medical or ordinary spiritualist therapy. Regulars maintain more extensive and continuous interaction with healers when they receive "cleaning." They are also trained to become healers or temple functionaries; thus they become involved in ongoing temple participation and exposed to trancing (Finkler 1981a). As is analyzed elsewhere at length (Finkler 1981a), a concatenation of these therapeutic modalities aids regulars to successfully function in and outside the confines of the temple, provided that they maintain continuous contact with the temple.[12] In contrast to Irene, Emiliano provides a compelling illustration of a regular whose symptoms are not eliminated but who is restored to functioning by means of several therapeutic modalities administered to regulars.

Case 2: Emiliano, a Temple Regular.   Emiliano, a 47-year-old Otomi–Spanish-speaking man, originates from the very poorest sector of Mexican peasant society.

He is married with five children. He resides in an inaccessible village; it and the nearby land that he tills are 30 miles from the temple.

Emiliano was brought to the temple by his wife a year after the onset of his illness. Previously he had sought treatment with physicians and in a spiritualist temple where he was given "cleanings," but he continued to suffer from his impairment. His symptoms included insomnia, severe headaches, lack of appetite, and pain and frequent numbness of the entire body. He urinated frequently, and he experienced pain in his kidneys and liver. He also developed a large ball-like lump behind the ear. Additionally, Emiliano reported that he dreamed many evil dreams, such as that he was being beaten up by his brothers and neighbors. He wanted to kill himself but was stopped by the thought of leaving his children fatherless. He described himself as having been very nervous, easily frightened, quarrelsome, and gross. He used crude language and easily lost his temper, especially when he got drunk. He customarily drank two to three liters of *pulque* (a local alcoholic beverage) and *cubas* (rum and Coke) daily. Life went badly for him. Two of his children had died and the other five suffered from many illnesses.

Emiliano, a docile man, was next to the youngest of 11 children, whose mother had died upon delivery of the eleventh child. His father remarried, but the stepmother treated her stepchildren abominably. He recalls how she used to strike them, how she let them run around dirty in unwashed clothes. At age 15, Emiliano left his village and moved to an industrial town about 25 miles north of Mexico City. There he worked as a mason for 30 years until returning to his village two years before the present study. Three of his adult children continue to live there.

He bought two hectares of land and some animals and built a little house on land he inherited from his father. He inherited one hectare of *ejido* land from his mother.

Soon after he returned to the village he fell ill. The onset of his illness corresponded to the time of a violent dispute with his neighbors and brothers over the boundaries of his land. He attributes his illness to the jealousies of his brother and neighbors. He knows they gossip about him and even accuse him of being a witch.

The doctors who had treated him took blood tests; the tests did not reveal anything wrong with him. In the temple that he attended previously he was given "cleanings," but he continued to suffer from his impairments unrelentingly. After a year of unsuccessful treatment with these health practitioners, he arrived in this temple. Initially, he came irregularly; he did not believe that he would be cured here, either, and his condition remained unchanged. After six months of sporadic attendance, the temple head suggested he remain in her house, situated as it is adjacent to the temple, so that he could receive treatments regularly and also save himself the exorbitant travel expenses from his village to the temple.

Upon taking up residence in the temple head's house, he was also ordered to enter "development," which entails trancing and preparation for becoming a temple functionary and healer (Finkler 1981a).

Emiliano described his trance experience poetically. Briefly translated here, he indicated that he *felt* a beautiful light appearing before him and that it felt good. He thinks it was the light of God—that it entered his body, gave it a spark, and removed his pain. Following each development session he felt happy, and he experienced the feeling as if a fresh breeze passed through his body.

Four months later, he was beginning to feel well most of the time. He no longer frightened easily or lost his temper; he had stopped being gross and quarrelsome, and he had stopped drinking regularly. He might take some pulque occasionally, but he no longer got drunk. He had also regained his appetite. The lump behind the ear diminished in size, and, although it was still visible, it was unobtrusive. He felt well when he was at the temple but when he returned to the village his body began to ache again. At the initial interview, Emiliano yielded a very high score (103 "yes" responses) on the health questionnaire, which measures both physical and emotional self-perceived symptoms. Four months after the initial interview, when the instrument was administered the second time as a follow-up, his responses on the physical section had not changed, but his score on the emotional section had decreased by 20 points. Emiliano attributed his recovery to the "cleanings" and to temple participation.

Discussion

It is noteworthy that patients attribute recovery to "cleaning."[13] Although not all individuals ascribed treatment efficacy explicitly to "cleaning," the symbolic significance of this phenomenon appears to be widespread both within and beyond the population studied. This assumption, of course, requires further empirical testing, but it also raises the question, why is "cleaning" beneficial for illness resolution within the Mexican context?

In keeping with this line of inquiry, three levels of explanation will be presented from three different perspectives. Yet, it must be emphasized that to distinguish these levels does not suggest separating them.

The psychotherapeutic explanation suggests itself because tactile communication of the type that takes place between healer and patient during "cleaning"—including constant massaging of the patient—is regarded as an important therapeutic component by some of the more recent schools of psychotherapy (cf. Krippner 1978).

Viewed sociologically, the act of "cleaning" a patient suggests a symbolic termination in public of the patient's sick role. The sociological theory of the sick role proposes that patients assume a sick role, usually for secondary gain (Parsons and Fox 1952); but eventually the role must be discontinued for daily life to continue. Sigerist (1977) astutely observes that "illness throws us off an accustomed track" (p. 389). Ultimately, the accustomed track must be regained; spiritualist healers symbolically efface the sick role in a culturally meaningful way, enabling the person to proceed with day-to-day affairs without further disruption. With symbolic termination of the sick role the patient is restored to a level of functioning, if only temporarily.

The preceding leads to yet another important consideration. It has been argued by some (Kleinman and Sung 1979) that whereas nonmedical practitioners may alleviate the course of culturally constituted expressions of symptoms, or the illness, they fail to alter the underlying physical and biomedical dysfunctions, or the disease (Kleinman 1980). Therefore, the same symptoms are likely to recur (Kleinman and Sung 1979). It is, however, likely that the same symptoms will re-emerge, not only because healers have failed to deal with the disease, but also because the living conditions will not have changed.Given the unceasing flow of untreated sewage waters in the irrigation canals and the relentless presence of vectors in the open garbage pits, gastrointestinal disorders will continue to flourish. The ecological enclave occupied by the population under study tends to promote, in many, a perpetually debilitated state, which biomedicine fails to permanently cure but which is temporarily relieved by symbolic manipulation.

"Cleaning" Restores Order

The foregoing remarks are linked with the third and perhaps most important level of analysis. From a cultural perspective, the proposition is advanced that "cleaning" nurtures symbolically a Mexican cultural imperative. The usual reference to "cleaning" in the literature is within the context of Mexican traditional healing practices (Ingham 1970; Madsen 1955). The symbolic significance of "cleaning" was unexpected. However, it suggests the cognitive correlate of recovery and the interrelationships among illness, healing, and sociostructural phenomena. The interface between sickness and social structure has been recognized by many scholars (Adams and Rubel 1967; Currier 1966; Ingham 1970; Lieban 1973; Turner 1967, 1968).

In the Mexican context, "cleaning" may be considered a form of external purification, which, as noted earlier, is sometimes recognized as complementary to the use of purges as a form of internal cleansing. Purification, as is proposed by Douglas, ". . . restores order on an inherently untidy experience" (1966:4). The "cleaning" act terminates the illness, the sick role, an untidy experience from the start. However, as argued elsewhere (Finkler 1980b), the order to be restored may bear not only on a personal level of experience, but also on the society in which the individual is found. Here we stand at the nexus of the individual health experience and the social structure, because the order that must be restored relates both to the illness episode and to the prevailing sociostructural framework of the society of which the person is part.

The Mexican experience of social disorder probably dates back to the cataclysmic effects of the conquest (Wolf 1959; Paz 1961) which ushered in a dictatorial presence and sociopolitical domination for a period of three centuries, culminating with the Mexican Revolution of 1910. But the revolution itself created upheavals, which perdured for over 25 years and which continue to abide in the memories of the older generation.

The more immediate forces currently impinging upon contemporary Mexico are being brought about by industrial acceleration in the whole of Mexico, as well as in the region where the study was carried out. As is the case in other industrially developing nations, industrialization in Mexico is being thrust upon what is basically an agrarian society adapted to agrarian rhythms and patterns of social organization (Adams 1967). Hence, whereas industrialization in Mexico has been going along at full speed, other societal institutions have not as yet been sufficiently developed to correspond with the requirements of an industrialized society, including infrastructural supports for the individual.[14]

Thus, the disorders an individual encounters in the course of life, whether produced by the ecological and sociostructural matrix of the individual or in a personal level of experience, or both, become relieved by symbolic manipulation through purification by "cleaning." Hence, the patient gains a respite, if only temporarily, before another illness episode strikes.

Patterns of Patients' Use of Spiritualist Healers

Two important questions of theoretical import still require examination. First, do all patients similarly respond to symbols furnished by spiritualist healers? Second, do all individuals in the region seek symbolic reordering for every illness episode? Turning to the first question, clearly not all temple patients' ailments are removed by a "cleaning." In fact, we have seen that only a minority of first comers and habitual temple users claim their symptoms have been alleviated. This obviously implies that not all illness episodes are amenable to spirtualists' therapeutic intervention. As noted earlier, the data suggest that individuals with fewer self-perceived symptoms are more likely to obtain relief from spiritualist treatment than persons with a greater number of expressed symptoms. Moreover, it was shown that persons such as Emiliano who are recruited to become regulars are individuals whose impairments are intractable to routine spiritualist therapy but who require ongoing ministration including temple participation and frequent exposure to "cleaning"[15] and ritual trancing (Finkler 1981a).

Concomitant with materials presented elsewhere (Finkler 1981a), Emiliano's case supports the contention that temple treatments tend only to minimize patients' perception of their symptoms and tend to restore the individual's behavioral capacities, provided, of course, that the patient continues to participate in healing rituals of which development forms an intrinsic part. Moreover, there are persons whose syndromes fail totally to respond to temple ministration, including "cleaning." Importantly, the present analysis of spiritualist treatment outcomes throws into bold relief the categories of syndromes that, as we have seen, fail to respond to temple therapeutic intervention, and patients who fail to be reached by the symbolic manipulations of spiritual healers. Observation of those who are selected to become regulars but who failed to respond to various temple ministrations and failed to be incorporated into the temple community lends support to the proposition that whereas temple treatment techniques assist individuals with dysphoria, mild psychiatric syndromes, and mild ongoing complaints, they clearly fail to help individuals incapacitated by psychotic syndromes. A corollary to this assertion is that whereas symbolic manipulation by healers is crucial for perceived treatment efficacy, a patient's *capacity to respond* to these symbols is equally crucial. Thus, although Turner (1967) rightly suggests that the healer must provide the proper symbols in order to effect therapy, it must also be acknowledged that not all patients or their syndromes have equal capacities to react to a set of symbols.

Analogously, symbolic manipulation can be equated to placebos within the healing context, as can hope, transference, and the doctor–patient relationship itself (Shapiro 1971; Beecher 1972), as well as much of medical therapeutics (Moerman 1979). We may assume that much in the same way that placebos have their limitations (Rhein Jr. 1980; Shapiro 1971), so does symbolic manipulation. Shapiro (1971) indicates that psychotic patients react negatively to the placebo effect, as they do to other types of nonpharmacological therapies (May 1976). Similarly, the data from the spiritualist temple suggest that patients inaccessible to symbolic manipulation totally fail to respond to spiritualist therapeutic intervention.

Interestingly, in two out of four such cases I encountered in the temple—senile deterioration and a young girl described by her mother as "crazy," with apparent intellectual and affective deficits—the temple head made strenuous efforts to involve the patients in training and trancing, and provided special elaborate rituals of "cleaning" and purification in addition to the routine massages, teas, and baths. These measures were unsuccessful (Finkler 1981a).

Conclusion

We may conclude, then, that the temple's complete failure to heal is associated as much with the limitation of its therapeutic regimen as it is with the patient and his/her failure to respond to cultural symbols.

Focusing on the second question raised earlier, and also posed by others (e.g., Fernandez 1965; McCreery 1979), bearing on the sharing of symbolic requisites, elsewhere (Finkler 1981b) I present a body of data demonstrating that not all inhabitants in the region resort to spiritualist therapy. In fact, within the same socioeconomic and sociocultural population segment there are those who are solely disposed to biomedical treatment. The findings suggest that differential commitment to the Catholic church delineates those who seek medical treatment from those who resort to both medical and spiritualist therapeutic intervention.[16] Evidently, those who seek medical therapy are subject chiefly to physical manipulation supplied by the medical model (cf. Kleinman 1980). These findings, then, imply that not all members of a sociocultural group are similarly impelled by cultural requisites, in this case symbolic cessation of the sick role by "cleaning." While this assertion is amply supported by the empirical evidence, using quantitative techniques I present elsewhere (Finkler 1981b), we should accept this conclusion only tentatively. The hypothesis must be advanced that those who seek only medical health care have not previously experienced the severely disruptive afflictions that necessitate the symbolic manipulation which touches us at our deepest level (Cassell 1976; Turner 1967). In fact, examination of 21 life histories drawn from a control group (n = 366) of ostensibly healthy individuals, who had no previous contact with spiritual healers, discloses that these individuals or their families have been confronted with few traumatic episodes such as loss of children, life-threatening disease, or even alcoholism. When life histories from the control group are compared with those of spiritualist adherents, they reveal that the controls managed to enjoy a less turbulent existence than spiritualist adherents prior to joining the temple.

In view of these findings, I postulate that a cultural imperative—such as, in the Mexican case, the restoration of order through purification—is shared by a large proportion of Mexicans. Such imperatives, however, become activated and come into play in the patient when life's equilibrium is fully upset by ongoing illness or other life trauma.[17]

Thus, those who resort to cosmopolitan medicine exclusively may never have experienced prolonged or recurring illness, the type that lingers on and throws us off our routine course—be it perpetual parasitosis, chronic pain related to depressive disorder (Blumer et al. 1980; Katon, Kleinman, and Rossen n.d.(a), n.d.(b); Sternbach 1974), or physical impairment. We may assume that even orthodox Catholics will resort to spiritualist healers in the event that they are faced with serious existential problems. In sum, whereas cultural imperatives associated with health restoration need not be shared within a given cultural group, they *become* shared with a prolonged illness experience, to which potentially all persons are exposed, which may be brought on by endogenous factors or be exogenous ecological or socioeconomic circumstances.

It has been argued that in the region under discussion, ecological and socioeconomic stressors contribute to an ongoing state of poor health, which calls for closure by symbolic manipulation of a type not furnished by biomedicine. Paradoxically, contemporary medical technology also adds to illness chronicity by prolonging the illness state and thereby producing situations calling for symbolic manipulation. It is said that we no longer die of the disease that affects us, but suffer from it. In the words of Pellegrino (1979), "the human and personal consequences of living with illness in which drastic treatments prolong life without curing is already a dominant concern" (p. 262). Therefore, in light of contemporary medical technology, it can be assumed that therapeutic regimes of the spiritualist variety providing symbolic ministration will continue to flourish in adverse ecological environments or owing to advanced medical technology itself.

To conclude, although the focus has been on a symbolic paradigm elicited by the study of treatment outcomes in one segment of a population in Mexico, it is likely that similar cognitive orientations prevail in other areas of the country as well. Moreover, there is some suggestion in the literature that health restoration associated with the theme of purification is found in other cultures (e.g., Janzen 1978; Hudson 1975). Further, it is possible that the imposition of order is not only a cultural imperative found in two or three cultures but a universal human imperative (Berger 1969; Leach 1976; Young 1977). These are empirical questions, which medical anthropological investigations can adequately illuminate given the existential dilemma of illness; thus, study of therapeutic outcomes is especially suitable for shedding light on theory and praxis.

To summarize, in essence my argument has been, first, that empirical studies of treatment outcomes shed light on requisites for recovery and health care, and, second, that cognitive models encoded in recovery attribution are meaningful within the context of the historical and ecological backgrounds becoming shared with common experience of affliction. Furthermore, it is anticipated that the extant symbiosis between biomedicine and alternate healing systems of the spiritualist kind will continue to gain strength as medical technology continues to increase its capacity for treating illness without curing it.

ACKNOWLEDGMENT

I very gratefully acknowledge the generous support of the National Science Foundation (grant no. BNS77/13989 and grant no. BNS80/13077) for this research and for making this analysis possible.

NOTES

1. The investigation upon which this study is based forms part of a much broader study of therapeutic outcomes and treatment-seeking behavior using traditional anthropological techniques as well as socioeconomic interview schedules and medical questionnaires administered to a sample of 1045 persons at two spiritualist temples, a doctor's office, four government health centers, and in a control group. For an extensive discussion of the methodology and data-collecting procedures, see Finkler (1980, 1981a, 1981b).

2. It can be argued that the biomedical model of disease is a culturally produced model as well (Comaroff 1978; Kleinman 1980), which has only recently been developed in the West (cf. Rosenberg 1979). From an applied perspective, it is important to establish patient-perceived criteria of treatment outcomes, because normally patients relinquish the sick role on the basis of their self-perceived state of health rather than on criteria used by physicians.

3. There are at least eight temples in the region. The movement is known to be widespread (Lagarriga Attias 1975; Madsen 1967), but it is not known precisely how many spiritualist temples there are in the entire country or in the United States. Temples are said to exist in Houston, Los Angeles, and San Francisco, as well as in border towns. Based upon figures of a random and partial count provided to me by the Mexican government, there were 115 temples in central Mexico alone; based upon my count this figure is but one-fifth of the number dispersed throughout Mexico. I expect that spiritualism as a religious movement will continue to spread, because it is linked with increased social stratification.

4. Only a summary of the empirical results is being presented here. For a complete and detailed report of the findings pertaining to treatment outcomes, see Finkler (1980b; 1981a).

5. Sewage waters are defined as "waters of domestic and industrial liquid wastes, and include rain waters, run-off sewage waters, and subsurface drainage waters" (Heukelekian 1962:6; translation mine).

6. Other diseases include respiratory and cardiovascular dysfunctions. For mortality and morbidity statistics in the entire country, see Laurell (1979).

7. The symptoms may be vague or even asymptomatic, but more often intermittent diarrhea, constipation, flatulence, and abdominal cramps occur (*Merck Manual* 1977). Anyone experiencing the condition, as I have, will attest to these discomforts, along with a sense of perpetual fatigue.

8. During the field stay I was being prepared to become a healer, and as part of my preparation I assisted the healers by writing prescriptions prescribed by them to patients during consultation (Finkler 1980b). My initial contact with spiritualist curers took place in 1974 while I was working on other research problems (Finkler 1978, 1979, 1980a). This was followed by a brief investigation in 1975 (Finkler 1975, 1976, 1977). The data in this study are based upon 22 months of fieldwork 1977–1979 supported by the National Science Foundation.

9. Of the sample interviewed, approximately 26 percent were first comers, the remaining 74 percent included habitual temple users of whom 27.1 percent have been coming from one to twelve months; 25.5 percent, one to seven years; and 21.4 percent have been seeking treatment intermittently for from eight to twenty years. Both temples were established in the 1960s, but the temple heads have worked as curers for many years previous to the founding of the temples.

10. Flowers are also important in spiritualist religious rituals. A spiritualist temple altar is adorned exclusively with flowers. Interestingly, flowers were also ritually important in the preconquest period (Duran 1971: Doris Heyden, personal communication 1979). Like spiritualist mobilization of Aztec and other Indian spirits as spirit protectors, spiritualist emphasis on ritual use of flowers suggests a recognition of ties with the preconquest past.

11. Follow-ups were done 7–15 days and 30–45 days after temple treatment; for more details see Finkler (1980b).

12. For a detailed discussion of the physiological, psychological, sociological, and cultural effects of spiritualist therapy, see Finkler (1981a) and Kiefer and Cowan (1979). The recent discoveries of endorphins and enkephalins adds yet another dimension to these findings.

13. In addition to those on whom follow-ups were done who attributed recovery to "cleaning," approximately 18 percent of 1212 patients personally observed in front of healers during my apprenticeship cited "cleaning" as their chief reason for coming to the temple.

14. For a more extensive analysis demonstrating the ways in which the lack of infrastructural support relates to illness, see Finkler (1980b).

15. When I was recruited into becoming a temple regular I was continuously urged to have a "cleaning" because "it restores one."

16. Another important variable is knowledge of the existence of spiritualists and, for two other variables distinguishing the two groups, see Finkler (1981b).

17. Life traumas are often instrumental in producing sickness; see Jacobs and Ostfeld (1977) and Lloyd (1980:11).

REFERENCES

Abramson, J.H. 1966. "The Cornell Medical Index as an Epidemiological Tool." *American Journal of Public Health,* 56:287–98.

Adams, Richard N. 1967. *The Second Sowing.* San Francisco: Chandler.

————, and Arthur J. Rubel. 1967. Sickness and Social Relations. Robert Wauchope, ed., *Handbook of Middle American Indians,* 6. Austin: Univ. of Texas Press.

Battle, C., et al. 1966. "Target Complaints as Criteria for Improvement." *American Journal of Psychotherapy,* 20:184–92.

Beecher, Henry K. 1962. "Pain, Placebos and Physicians." *Practitioner,* 189:141–55.

Berger, Peter L. 1969. *The Sacred Canopy.* Garden City, N.Y.: Anchor Books.

Blumer, Dietrich, et al. 1980. "Systematic Treatment of Chronic Pain with Antidepressants." *Henry Ford Hospital Medical Journal* (Detroit), 28:15–21.

Brodman, Keeve, et al. 1952. "The Cornell Medical Index-Health Questionnaire. III. The Evaluation of Emotional Disturbances." *Journal of Clinical Psychiatry,* 8:119–24.

Brown, R.E. 1966. "Medical Problems of the Developing Countries." *Science,* 153:271–75.

Cassell, Eric J. 1976. *The Healer's Art.* Philadelphia: J.B. Lippincott.

Colson, Anthony, and Karen E. Selby. 1974. "Medical Anthropology." Bernard J. Siegel, ed., *Annual Review of Anthropology,* vol. 3, 245–62.

Comaroff, Jean. 1978. "Medicine and Culture." *Social Science and Medicine* 12(4B): 247–54.

Currier, Richard L. 1966. "The Hot–Cold Syndrome and Symbolic Balance in Mexico." *Ethnology,* 5:251–63.

Douglas, Mary. 1966. *Purity and Danger.* London: Routledge & Kegan Paul.

Duran, Fray Diego. 1971. *Book of the Gods and Rites and the Ancient Calendar.* Norman: Univ. of Oklahoma Press. [Original: circa 1590.]

Fabrega, H. 1974. *Disease and Social Behavior.* Cambridge: MIT Press.

Fabrega, H., and P.K. Manning. 1973. "An Integrated Theory of Disease: Ladino–Mestizo Views of Disease in the Chiapas Highlands." *Psychosomatic Medicine,* 35:223–39.

Fabrega, Horacio, Jr., and Daniel B. Silver. 1973. *Illness and Shamanistic Curing in Zinacantan.* Stanford: Stanford Univ. Press.

Fernandez, James W. 1965. "Symbolic Consensus in a Fang Reformative Cult." *American Anthropologist,* 67:902–28.

Finkler, Kaja. 1974. *Estudio Comparativo de la Economia de dos Comunidades de Mexico.* Mexico: Sep INI Series, Institute Nacional Indigenista.

1975 "Mediums and Curers: An Alternate Road to Health." Paper read at the Detroit Psychoanalytic Society, 19 Nov.

1976 "Spiritualism in Rural Mexico." *Actes du XLII Congrès International des Américanistes,* vol. 6. Paris: International Congress of Americanists, 99–105.

1977 "El Cuidado de la Salud: Un Problema de Relaciones de Poder." *America Indigena,* 37:435–56.

1978 "From Sharecroppers to Entrepreneurs: Peasant Household Production Strategies under the *Ejido* System of Mexico." *Economic Development and Cultural Change,* 27:103–20.

1979 "Applying Econometric Techniques to Economic Anthropology." *American Ethnologist,* 6:675–81.

1980a "Land Scarcity and Economic Development: When Is a Landlord a Client and a Sharecropper His Patron?" Peggy F. Barlett, ed., *Agricultural Decision Making.* New York: Academic Press.

1980b "Non-Medical Treatments and Their Outcomes." *Culture, Medicine and Psychiatry,* 4:301–40.

1980c "The Effects of Differential Policies on Social Integration in One Region of Mexico: A Historical Perspective." *Central Issues in Anthropology,* 2:51–68.

1981a "Non-Medical Treatments and Their Outcomes; Part Two: Focus on Adherents of Spritualism." *Culture, Medicine and Psychiatry,* 5:1–38.

1981b   "A Comparative Study of Health Seekers: Or, Why Do Some People Go to Doctors Rather than to Spiritualist Healers?" *Medical Anthropology*, 4.

1981c   "Dissident Religious Movements in the Service of Women's Power." *Sex Roles Journal of Research*, 7:481–95.

Freedman, Alfred M., and Harold I. Kaplan. 1972. *Diagnosing Mental Illness*. New York: Atheneum.

Garrison, Vivian. 1977. "Doctor, *Espiritista* or Psychiatrist: Health-Seeking Behavior in a Puerto Rican Neighborhood of New York City." *Medical Anthropology*, 1:65–180.

Gonzalez, Nancy. 1966. "Health Behavior in Cross-Cultural Perspective." *Human Organization*, 25:122–25.

Harwood, Alan. 1977. *Rx: Spiritists as Needed*. New York: John Wiley & Sons.

Heukelekian, H. 1962. *Informe Sobre el Uso de las Aguas Negras y las Superficiales en el Valle de Mexico y la Region de el Mezquital*. Hgo. Secretaria de Recursas Hidraulicos, Comision Hidrologica de la Cuenca del Valle de Mexico.

Hudson, Charles. 1975. "Vomiting for Purity: Ritual Emesis in the Aboriginal Southeastern United States." Carole E. Hill, ed., *Symbols and Society*. Athens: Southern Anthropological Society.

Ingham, J.M. 1970. "On Mexican Folk Medicine." *American Anthropologist*, 72:76–87.

Jacobs, Selby, and Adrian Ostfeld. 1977. "An Epidemiological Review of the Mortality of Bereavement." *Psychosomatic Medicine*, 39(5):344–57.

Janzen, John M. 1978. *The Quest for Therapy in Lower Zaire*. Berkeley: Univ. of California Press.

Jilek, Wolfgang G., and Norman Todd. 1974. "Witchdoctors Succeed Where Doctors Fail: Psychotherapy among Coast Salish Indian." *Canadian Psychiatric Association Journal*, 19:351–56 (reprinted in Ino Rossi, John Buettner–Janusch, and Dorian Coppenhaver, eds., *Anthropology Full Circle*. New York: Praeger, 1977, 400–3).

Katon, Wayne, Arthur Kleinman, and Gary Rosen. n.d.(a). "Depression and Somatization, A Review. Part I."

n.d.(b).   "Depression and Somatization, A Review. Part II."

Kennedy, John G. 1967. "Nubian Zar Ceremonies as Psychotherapy." *Human Organization*, 26:185–94.

Kiefer, Christie W. and Jonathan Cowan. 1979. "State/Context Dependence and Theories of Ritual." *Journal of Psychological Anthropology*, Winter: 53–83.

Kleinman, Arthur. 1980. *Patients and Healers in the Context of Culture*. Berkeley: University of California Press.

———, and L.H. Sung. 1979. "Why Do Indigenous Practitioners Successfully Heal?" *Social Science and Medicine*, 13B:7–26.

Krippner, Stanley. 1978. "Psychic Healing: A Multidimensional View." James L. Fossage and Paul Olsen, eds., *Healing*. New York: Human Sciences Press.

Kunstadter, Peter. 1978. "The Comparative Anthropological Study of Medical Systems and Society." Arthur Kleinman, Peter Kunstadter, E. Russell Alexander, and James L. Gale, eds., *Culture and Healing in Asian Societies*. Cambridge: Schenkman, 393–406.

Lagarriga Attias, Isabel. 1975. *Medicina Tradicional y Espiritismo*. Mexico: Sepsetanta.

1978   "Tecnicas Catarticas en los Templos Espiritualistas Trinitarios Marianos." *Estudios Sobre Etnobotanica y Antropologia Medica*, (3):115–26.

Laurell, Asa Cristina. 1979. "Work and Health in Mexico." *International Journal of Health Services*, 9:543–68.

Leach, Edmund. 1976. *Culture and Communication.* Cambridge: Cambridge Univ. Press.

Lévi–Strauss, Claude. 1967. "The Effectiveness of Symbols." Claude Lévi–Strauss, *Structural Anthropology.* Garden City: Anchor Books, 181–201.

Lieban, Richard W. 1973. "Medical Anthropology." J.J. Honigmann, ed., *Handbook of Social and Cultural Anthropology.* Chicago: Rand McNally, 1031–72.

1977 "Symbols, Signs and Success: Healers and Power in a Philippine City." R.D. Fogelson and R. Adams, eds., *The Anthropology of Power.* New York: Academic Press.

Lloyd, Camille. 1980. "Life Events and Depressive Disorder Reviewed. II. Events as Precipitating Factors." *Archives of General Psychiatry,* 37:541–47.

Lock, Margaret M. 1980. *East Asian Medicine in Urban Japan.* Berkeley: Univ. of California Press.

Madsen, William. 1955. "Shamanism in Mexico." *Southwestern Journal of Anthropology,* 2:48–57.

1967 "Religious Syncretism." Manning Nash, ed. *Handbook of Middle American Indians,* vol. 6. Austin: Univ. of Texas Press, 361–91.

May, Phillip R.A. 1976. "Rational Treatment for an Irrational Disorder: What Does the Schizophrenic Patient Need?" *American Journal of Psychiatry,* 133:1008–12.

McCreery, John L. 1979. "Potential and Effective Meaning in Therapeutic Ritual." *Culture, Medicine and Psychiatry,* 3:53–72.

Mechanic, David. 1968. *Medical Sociology.* New York: Free Press.

Merck Manual. 1977. 13th ed. Rahway: Merck, Sharp & Dohme Research Laboratories.

Moerman, Daniel E. 1979. "Anthropology of Symbolic Healing." *Current Anthropology,* 20:59–80.

Parsons, Talcott, and Renee Fox. 1952. "Illness, Therapy and the Modern American Family." *Journal of Social Issues,* 8:31–44.

Paz, Octavio. 1961. *The Labyrinth of Solitude.* New York: Grove Press.

Pellegrino, Edmund D. 1979. "The Socio-Cultural Impact of Twentieth-Century Therapeutics." Morris Vogel and Charles E. Rosenberg, eds., *The Therapeutic Revolution.* Philadelphia: Univ. of Pennsylvania Press, 245–66.

Rappaport, Roy A. 1979. *Ecology, Meaning and Religion.* Richmond: North Atlantic Books.

Rhein, Reginald W., Jr. 1980. "Placebo: Deception or Potent Therapy?" *Medical World News,* 21:39–47.

Rosenberg, Charles E. 1979. "The Therapeutic Revolution: Medicine, Meaning and Social Change in Nineteenth-Century America." Morris J. Vogel and Charles E. Rosenberg, eds., *The Therapeutic Revolution.* Philadelphia: Univ. of Pennsylvania Press, 3–25.

Shapiro, Arthur K. 1971. "Placebo Effects in Medicine, Psychotherapy and Psychoanalysis." Allen E. Bergin and Sol L. Garfield, eds., *Handbook of Psychotherapy and Behavior Change.* New York: John Wiley & Sons, 439–73.

Sigerist, Henry E. 1977. "The Special Position of the Sick." David Landy, ed., *Culture, Disease, and Healing.* New York: Macmillan, 388–94.

Sternbach, Richard A. 1974. *Pain Patients.* New York: Academic Press.

Turner, Victor. 1967. *The Forest of Symbols.* Ithaca: Cornell Univ. Press.

1968 *The Drums of Affliction: A Study of Religious Process among the Ndembu of Zambia.* Oxford: Clarendon Press.

Wolf, Eric. 1959. *Sons of the Shaking Earth.* Chicago: Univ. of Chicago Press.

Young, Allan. 1976. "Some Implications of Medical Beliefs and Practices for Social Anthropology." *American Anthropologist,* 78:5–24.

1977 "Order, Analogy and Efficacy in Ethiopian Medical Divination." *Culture, Medicine and Psychiatry,* 1:183–99.

6

Shamanistic Healing among the Diegueño Indians of Southern California

Spencer L. Rogers and Lorraine Evernham

This chapter will center on the Diegueño shamanistic healing complex in both traditional and contemporary practice. Diegueño resoluteness in attempts to maintain traditional healing complexes is as profound today as in 1925 (Kroeber 1925), albeit more difficult.

The people with whom we are concerned under the caption Diegueño do not comprise a culturally unified population. Rather, there are a series of groups, all of whom spoke variations of the same Yuman language and among whom many but not all cultural details were practiced in common. The term "Diegueño" was first applied by the Spaniards to designate the Indians who dwelt around the mission of San Diego de Alcalá. Various native names are associated with these people, e.g., Comeya, Kamya, Tipay, Ipai, and Kumeyaay (Hedges 1975:71–77; Luomala 1978:592, 605–8). The label "Diegueño" is retained here for the reason that it is deeply established in the literature (Hodge 1907; Kroeber 1925; Encyclopaedia Britannica 1977), and to consult most documents under any other designation or its many varied spellings would be problematic.

The Place of the Shaman in Diegueño Cosmology

Shamanism can perhaps best be defined as a technique for dealing with the supernatural. The shaman is a repository of knowledge and a master of methods pertaining to the control of mysterious powers and forces that affect the affairs of humankind. Before discussing the Diegueño shaman's training and techniques and the results of his ministrations, it is important to consider briefly the structure of his universe, his view of cosmic forces, and his role in confronting the mysterious powers. The shaman's viewpoint was essentially practical. While he seems usually to have been conversant with the mythic narratives of creation and spirit beings appropriate to his culture, he was primarily involved with the utilitarian issues of curing sickness and averting disaster. In order to accomplish these ends he drew upon sources of power from the cosmic realm.

The aboriginal California psychic world was permeated with mystic supernatural powers. Mysterious power gave origin to the universe and occurs in the universe in three levels. The upper world is a region of primordial spirit beings, the creator gods, the sun and moon and spirit beings of higher order than lesser spirits. The second level, the here world, is the center of the universe. This floats in space and is surrounded by emptiness. In this realm humans live, as do certain spirit beings that manifest themselves to humanity at times. The third world, the underworld, is the realm of strange creatures of grotesque form, usually reptilian or amphibian, or distorted human-like creatures which usually work evil toward human beings. They live in caves, caverns and springs (Bean 1975:25–26).

Mysterious power may reside in living and nonliving beings, but it exists more in some entities than in others. Elements of the environment may normally be neutral in the power sense, but at times may surge up and be a recognizable entity and force. Power endows its possessors with human-like qualities of feeling, emotion, and capriciousness. A tree or an animal may become charged with power and take on a degree of anthropomorphism. Humans are continually afraid of the operation of power in their environment, maliciously unleased through black magic and witchcraft. Again, power may be released for human betterment, as in the healing of illness, the circumventing of a hazardous situation, or the avoidance of a threatened disaster. The universe is in a continual balance between the entities that incorporate and manipulate power. Humans can adjust this interaction by using power that can be derived from the cosmic realm. Humans can obtain power in various ways: by meticulously observing the rules of avoidance and obligation, or through a vision induced by hallucinogenic plants or by fasting, drumming, and chanting. A person who acquires power has the supernatural qualities of a shaman. The medicine man knows how to deal with power and has a personal power potential that gives him the ability to deal with the rites of passage and the transient crises of sickness, bewitchment, and violations of taboo.

The Diegueño Indians' world was complex. Their daily lives were continual encounters with the many loci of power in their living realm. Ordinary individuals, in their efforts to find a comfortable path between the heavily charged possible centers of power surrounding them, had but one authentic and dependable resource: the knowledge and personal capacity of a shaman. The shaman was the tribal specialist in handling the dangerous potentials of supernatural power and was expert in interpreting the revelations that came from his access to this power. The Diegueños believed in somewhat personalized supernatural powers, such as their culture hero Chaup, but they did not pray to these (Waterman 1910:276–77). They sought aid for their ills not through appealing to divinities but through power manipulation, and this was in the province of the shaman.

Other Curing Crafts

While the shaman was the specialist in things supernatural and the elite healer of illness, organic and psychic, a secondary curing craft developed among the Diegueño, as in most cultures. Persons accomplished in this field were knowledgeable with regard to the uses of herbs and some inorganic items in healing injuries and various minor ailments, and were able to reduce fractures and treat through massage. A number of natural medicaments were known in Southern California. Barrows identifies 11 medicinal herbs for the Cahuilla (Barrows 1900:77–79); Kroeber cites 20 for the Luiseño (Kroeber 1925:650); and Sparkman cites 26 out of 95 herbs used by the Luiseño as being medicinal (Sparkman 1908:228–34). Owen lists 73 vegetal substances employed as curatives by the people of Santa Catarina, Baja California, a recent group that has retained many traditional Diegueño culture elements (Owen 1962: 110–16). If we eliminate those of more recent introduction from Owen's list we still have 26 that are probably of ancient traditional usage. Some of these were probably used by shamans, whereas others may have been household remedies.

The Training of the Shaman

Diegueño shamans were not educated for their profession in any formal manner. The older medicine men selected boys from nine to fourteen years of age as likely candidates for the shamanistic role, although there is occasional mention of women in the profession (Willoughby 1963:57, 60). Candidates were chosen purely for their interest, concern about magic and healing, and precocity in dreaming (Toffelmier and Luomala 1936:199). Of outstanding importance was their ability to have prophetic dreams. Physical condition was not a prime factor; a blind person might become a shaman (Spier 1923:312). Although dreaming and trances were highly important in Diegueño shamanism, there seems to have been no tendency to regard persons suffering from neurotic disorders to be suited for the profession, as was the case in Siberia (cf. Czaplicka 1914:172–73).

The initiation of a shaman was a major supernatural experience. Prior to his initiation, a neophyte shaman was given training under the direction of an older shaman, who imparted to this protegé the lore and techniques of the profession. Before his initiation, the student shaman was required to go through a period of fasting, and during this time he was told by his instructor the significance and character of the dreams that he would experience during his final initiation rite. On sundown of the appointed day the neophyte was given a decoction of datura to drink; this induced a series of hallucinatory dream experiences that included seeing mythologic beings and mythic animals. The ancient Aztecs called the plant *Datura meteloides,* "toloatzin," hence the Spanish word "toloache." The Spanish also referred to this plant as "*yerba del diablo,*" or "devil's weed." In Europe it is still known by this name, whereas in the United States it usually goes by the name "jimson weed." The species generally available in Southern California is *Datura meteloides;* older and somewhat confused species designations are *Datura wrightii* and *Datura inoxia* (Munz 1974:830–31).

Datura meteloides, a plant of the nightshade family, contains tropane alkaloids, which affect the central nervous system, causing deep sleep and loss of consciousness (Schultes and Hofmann 1979:42, 111). Scopolamine is a depressant that causes drowsiness, sleep, and amnesia. Atropine paralyzes the muscles that contract the iris diaphragm of the eye. Overdose can cause delirium and coma. As a ritual narcotic, datura is effective, since it causes sleep with vivid dreams of fanciful and grotesque beings and events.

Initiation

The initiate was put into a drowsy state—at first semiconscious—during which time the instructor suggested the content of the dreams the student was about to experience and interrogated him as to the doctrine that had previously been imparted to him. The neophyte's dreams that followed were in part the result of immediate suggestion, but also combined with this was probably the latent symbolic dream content in his unconscious mind. His dreams seem to have included his receiving an animal guardian spirit, songs, cures, the identification of power items, and the ability to interpret dreams. After he awakened, the shaman initiate had the sense of beginning a new life, enhanced with the power that he had just received, as evidenced by the dreams of entities and states that were beyond normal experience and sensation. He must have asked himself the logical question of the origin of the strange otherworldly creatures, personages, and visual states that he had just experienced. The answer, implanted through the suggestion of his mentor, was that these came from the cosmic realm. He accordingly felt that he, as a shaman, was now a conduit through which mysterious cosmic power could enter the human realm, and be used to remedy the affairs of human beings in their continuous and defensive interplay with the forces that caused sickness, famine, and strife of all kinds. He felt this power within him, but did not as yet have the privilege of using it. He was required to go through an internship, during which time he worked with older shamans and was required to undergo stringent food and behavioral taboos. He was probably instructed in some of the detailed methods, skills, and dogma that would be required in his forthcoming years of practice. He learned the details of conducting ritual, the technique of dealing with a patient in such a way that tensions of his unconscious mentality could be brought to the conscious level, and the thaumaturgic techniques of disease object removal, along with other aspects of suggestive therapy.

After this internship, the novitiate emerged as a qualified shaman with an effective battery of suggestive therapeutic methods at his disposal. He also held a body of folklore that tied him to the symbolism and values of his culture and united him to the ancient traditions of his society. Moreover, although this was in his mind a minor aspect of his proficiency, he had been taught the healing value of some herbs and other natural medicaments available in his area. The beginning shaman was now advanced to a position of high social prestige that would continuously grow with his successful cures and other demonstrations of ability. He was now not an ordinary mortal, but an instrument of the supernatural.

Sanctions on Shamanic Practice

Yet the Diegueños were a practical people, and the proof of supernatural power was in the effective exercise of that power. If a shaman could not heal, he must not have power. If an older shaman failed to heal, this was evidence that his power was waning. Failure to cure a patient might mean that the shaman claimed to have power that he did not have, and so was doubly culpable: for failure to heal and for deception. Shamans who were unsuccessful, particularly in dealing with endemic diseases in the region, were said to have been killed with arrows shot by relatives of the deceased victims of the disease. The doctor's only hope of retaining his prestige—or perhaps of surviving—after a failure to heal, was to come forth with a ready explanation of his failure in terms of superior magic executed by someone foreign to the area. Since magic was regional, a shaman of one area would not claim to understand the magic of another territory. This type of alibi might have been accepted.

One of the hazards in the shaman's career was that he might be considered guilty of witchcraft and using black magic. If his power enabled him to do good things, why could he not, if he chose, use his power to injure and perhaps kill his enemies? With the Cupeño, neighbors of the Diegueño, and presumably with the Diegueño as well, the shaman could not only understand and manipulate natural phenomena, but could throw his power into an enemy, causing death (Strong 1972:253). With the Diegueño, disease-causing objects could be thrust into the body of a victim by black magic. Also, items formerly in contact with the person of a prospective victim, such as hair, could be used as an instrument of black magic in causing harm to a victim. This caused great fear of leaving around any items that could be obtained by a possible enemy (Waterman 1910:280).

Shamanic Specialization

In times past, particularly in Northern California, there was a considerable degree of specialization in shamanism. Bear shamans, rattlesnake shamans, weather shamans, and dream shamans are reported, as well as diagnosticians and healing shamans. Bear doctors, as among the Pomo, were commonly not healers but evil witches who practiced malignant magic (Kroeber 1925:259). Rattlesnake shamans had a special relationship to rattlesnakes and knew the ways of curing people who had been bitten by rattlesnakes. Weather shamans could bring rain, and dream shamans interpreted dreams and, in particular, reported the cures for illnesses revealed in dreams. Diagnosticians did not cure, but determined the cause of an illness, after which the patient was turned over to a healing doctor. In Southern California, however, there was considerable simplification of the shamanistic profession. There were apparently neither bear doctors nor weather shamans among the southern Diegueños. Both rattlesnake and curing shamans were prevalent among all Diegueño groups (Spier 1923:313–15). Specialized diagnosticians were not reported for the Diegueños; the healing shaman made his own diagnosis before he began his curing ministrations.

Diegueño Epidemiology

Disease, as in most cultures, may have had a variety of causes, some of which were natural and did not need complex explanation, such as minor mishaps and lesser body ailments. Other and more grave illnesses, however, required diagnosis by an expert in the supernatural. The Paipai of Northern Baja California, who have preserved many ancient Diegueño beliefs, state as the main causes of illness witchcraft, accidents, upsetting the balance of nature and modern medical concepts such as cancer and measles, the latter being of least importance in their scheme of analysis (Owen 1962:62–64). This classification will be reflected in the discussion of hierarchy of resort in curative practices later in this chapter.

Some other neighboring peoples may throw light on the concept of disease among the Diegueño, for whom the recorded evidence is meager. Father Boscana, describing the culture of the Juaneños of San Juan Capistrano, stated that among these people diseases were attributed to the effects of particles or objects introduced into the body, such as hairs of various animals, bones, stones, briars, and sticks, which produced pain and infirmity (Boscana 1933:71). Such disease-causing items were apparently cited by the Diegueño shaman as the immediate or proximate causes of disease, whereas other, more remote forces—such as black magic and witchcraft— were also used to explain illness (Rogers 1944:559–64). It is quite probable that both types of cause were recognized; a remote cause bringing about the proximate cause, such as witchcraft being used to inject a disease-producing object into the sufferer's body (Waterman 1910:280). Among the Cahuilla there was a firm belief in witches. They thought that witches would turn people into horses and ride them into the mountains. They also thought that evil spirits caused sleeplessness (Bowers 1888:6). Some neighboring groups have reported, in addition to witchcraft, dream poisoning by the spirits; and, among the Yuma, soul loss has been cited (Forde 1931:185). It is well established that the Diegueño believed in disease-object intrusion as a cause of illness, since sucking and the display of a removed object was a common therapeutic method (Kroeber 1908:5; Engelhardt 1920:181). One cause of disease reported for the contemporary Diegueño is in "travelling rocks." These are interesting and attractive rocks that a person picks up. The rock travels from the hand up the arm and through the body. If it reaches the heart, the individual dies. This form of sickness is peculiar to Indians and must be diagnosed by an Indian doctor. Rocks are thought of as hazardous, and a witch's power is believed to reside in his collection of rocks (Almstedt 1977:19). Stones were endowed with the capacity for evil: "Sometimes a witch would put a special stone in a spring and you would hear voices and see things if you drank from it. If you stayed around, you would not be able to think any more. All Indians are scared of bad springs" (Cuero 1968:49).

The shaman's diagnostic and healing ability was often involved with dreams, both his own and those of his patients. Doctors obtained their power from dreams. The power might be good or bad. If the power was good, the recipient would heal anyone who was in need of his services. If the power was bad, the possessor of this power would make people sick and threaten them with illness if they did not give him food (Cuero 1968:51). Healing songs came to shamans in dreams. Dreams on the part of a doctor might come from a dead relative, giving the doctor the knowledge that he needed (Toffelmier and Luomala 1936:202).

"The Interpretation of Dreams"

The shaman's diagnostic technique often involved the interpretation of his patient's dreams, categorized by type. One type was considered meaningless and without significance, such as those caused by overeating or undernourishment. The second type included "common dreams," dreams of any content, that did not disturb the dreamer on awakening. Some of these had a standard converse interpretation as being prophetic: for example, a dream of a particular relative dying, which meant the death of another relative, or a dream of a dog or coyote bite, which forecast a rattlesnake bite. Some dreams were portents of good luck. If a husband and wife both dreamed of snakes, they would have many children. A dream of straight, clean arrows meant imminent good fortune. The third type of dreams caused alarm in the dreamer and led him to consult a shaman for interpretation. Such dreams involved a dead relative, which the shaman interpreted as meaning that the dead relative's spirit wanted something, such as the burning of an object that should have been ritually burned during a funeral rite, but was not. Certain dreams were guides to the shaman in recognizing particular types of mental disorder: e.g., sex dreams accompanied by apathy, loss of appetite, and other atypical behavior indicated specific problems. Dreams of incestuous relationships between brother and sister and between cousins were regarded as equally reprehensible. Homosexual dreams were not considered particularly meaningful. Although Dieguéno shamans treated lesbian women, dreams were not the basis of the diagnosis. Love dreams about persons of one's own sex were not given serious consideration. Homosexual men were not regarded as subjects for treatment; they were dealt with as weak and amusing.

Lincoln classifies dreams as "individual," or unsought spontaneous dreams occurring in sleep, and "culture-pattern" dreams, which are induced (Lincoln 1935:22). The three categories of dreams enumerated for the Dieguéno are apparently of the "individual" type. "Induced" dreams would be those of the shaman, furthered by hallucinogenic drugs and, during the shaman's initiation, suggestion on the part of other shamans. The shaman's diagnostic dreams and the patient's dreams—prompted by the shaman's interrogations and suggestion—could also be classified as "induced" dreams.

Practicing the Art of Medicine

The Diegueño shaman's techniques involved both preparatory and therapeutic procedures. The beginning of each healing session was a period of singing and dancing, which brought about rapport between the shaman and the supernatural power, and also established a setting for suggestive therapeutic ministrations. The shaman's personal activities consisted of preparatory singing, dancing, and dreaming to put him in contact with the supernatural powers upon which he would draw in order to acquire the healing force. His method in treating the patient was not only a diagnostic method for the doctor's own guidance, but also a therapeutic method, since it enabled him to bring the patient's stresses from the unconscious to the conscious level and to prepare the patient for the suggestions used in further treatment. The shaman's manipulatory procedures were dextrous and impressive. He would massage, fan, and blow upon the patient's body. His preeminent technique was ostensibly sucking or blowing from the patient's body an object, such as a pebble or thorn, which he claimed to be the cause of the disease. Sucking was done either directly with the mouth or with the aid of a tube of hard black stone through which the doctor sucked or sometimes blew, on the theory that the disease was either sucked out or blown away. The tube was sometimes filled with wild tobacco (probably *Nicotiana attenuata* Torr.) (Lewis and Lewis 1977) and lighted, the smoke being blown over the patient. As a purported result of the sucking or blowing, the disease-causing object was produced—with dramatic ceremony—and displayed to the patient and onlookers. The two prime therapeutic methods of the Diegueño shaman, interrogration and object removal, are worthy of further discussion.

Interrogation was conducted with the shaman's supernatural authority. Respect for the shaman's status and fear of his powers made the patient unlikely to try to conceal the details of his life, which were being probed by the shaman. Issues explored included violations of taboos, failure to comply with obligations, and failure to show suitable deference to persons and symbols of authority. The doctor was able to bring the causes of the patient's inner stimulus tensions into conscious consideration. In an aboriginal society, where life was a continual contest for adjustment in complying with intricate rules of avoidance and obligation, along with the placation of supernatural entities and forces, every person probably had internal stresses resulting from known or suspected derelictions. The shaman's questioning involved a catharsis with resulting abreaction that formed a useful therapeutic device. The shaman's interrogation and the patient's admission of derelictions relieved the suffering person of the mental stress that resulted from his knowledge or suspicion that he had violated a rule of behavior and was paying the penalty through his illness. Freud (1961:82) comments on the struggle for reduction of anxiety, the constant effort to keep the inner stimulus tensions in a moderated and controlled state. In an aboriginal society, such as that of the Diegueño, where taboos and obligations were powerful instruments of social control, to bring such tensions into a conscious state and perform a subsequent curing rite would have been sound therapy.

Object removal was a forthright method of benevolent deception. The shaman was skilled in the technique of hiding, in his hand or mouth, the items that he would ultimately produce with theatric ostentation as the causes of the disease. The dynamic effect of producing the disease-causing object as an observable entity was twofold. The patient was given a vivid suggestion that his illness was at an end: the cause had been removed. Moreover, the attending relatives and concerned onlookers were convinced that a highly accomplished doctor had performed his supernatural duty.

A Diegueño shaman's account of his own technique is as follows:

> Sometimes I blow and sometimes I rub, but I do not use herbs much. I have been given the power to cure with my hands. I spit and blow on my palms and cure with these. I feel with my hands: if the patient's body is cold, I rub it until it is warmed. Then when I feel that he is warm I let him go [Spier 1923:312].

Occasionally it appears that curing was accomplished by strictly magical and symbolic methods. A case is reported where a sick man of the Diegueños was stretched out on the ground for the treatment. Several persons gathered around him and motioned three times upward, each time expelling breath. They danced around him three times, singing, and at the end of the song sat in a circle around him. Next, the oldest woman present urinated in a pottery cup, and the urine was sprinkled over the patient with an eagle feather. This procedure has been interpreted as a magical device by which the advanced age of the woman was mystically transferred to the patient as an aid to his recovery (Waterman 1910:280).

Nonshamanic Healing Skills

In addition to the more elite shamanistic techniques, there was a body of healing skills utilized at times by the shamans, but also available to those of lesser status, including older women, "herb women," who were accomplished in simple medication. Their areas of practice involved bruises, sore throats, inflamed eyes, earaches, and burns in particular. These were dealt with mainly by the use of herbal remedies. Accidents, disorders of the nose and eyes, and perhaps even fevers and broken bones were commonly dealt with by "herb women." It is quite clear, however, that the more obscure and grievous maladies were referred to the shaman with his supernatural insight and mystical authority (Rogers 1976:23).

A question that must eventually be considered is: How successful was the Diegueño shaman in his efforts to heal? Although statistical data are impossible to compile, some recorded comments help to give us an impression as to the shaman's success in curing the sick. Such statements as, "My father was a good shaman and as far as I know he never lost a case," are recorded (Spier 1923:312). There are also numerous instances where it was said that the patient "got well" or that the disease "never bothered" the patient again (Almstedt 1977:13).

Another line of evidence lies in the fact that the shamanistic career was not altogether an easy way of life. The shaman was obligated to live a somewhat restrictive existence and was required to subject his own convenience to community needs. The prospective shaman undoubtedly realized this and also knew that his success as a healer would be vital to his prestige, material rewards, and perhaps, in earlier times, to his personal survival (Forde 1931:199). Yet there were many shamans; by one estimate, one out of every ten men entered some phase of the profession (Toffelmier and Luomala 1936:199). That such a high proportion of the male population became shamans indicates that success was to be expected.

Medical Care and Culture Change

In the first section of this chapter, we dealt primarily with the knowledge of the Diegueño Indians as recorded by explorers, priests, and travelers from the discovery of California by Europeans until the first contacts of the Indians with trained ethnologists early in the current century. In this section, we discuss interviews and observations that have revealed attitudes toward disease and healing on the part of the living descendants of the "mission" Diegueños. Ongoing fieldwork within the Diegueño community, both urban and in the reservation setting, over the past two years, has revealed that the traditional Diegueño shaman is no longer practicing. Open-ended interviews and participant observation were the research methodologies employed to ascertain the status of Diegueño shamanistic healing today.

Traditionally, the Diegueño shaman fulfilled the role of healer, or medicine man. Although the shaman was not representative of the sum total of health-care delivery, he certainly was the central figure. Today there is no one to replace him. However, the following descriptions, taken from field notes, will reveal the extent to which shamanistic belief systems maintain a powerful influence in Diegueño society today. The survival of these beliefs further demonstrates the importance and effectiveness of the shaman in traditional Diegueño society.

Contemporary Cases

Funeral rites are still held today in very much the same way they were performed traditionally. The influence of the Roman Catholic church has modified the ritual to include a mass and the presence of a priest, a role traditionally filled by the shaman. Burial rather than cremation has become the rule. The Catholic wake closely resembles the traditional Diegueño mourning ceremonies. A recent funeral was held in the "traditional," post-contact form, including a rosary, mass the following morning, and burial in the graveyard. The person's most important belongings were buried with him rather than burned, as had been the tradition before contact. After the burial the grave was strewn with swaths of new cloth, cigarettes, playing cards, and new clothes for all those present who were not related to the family to take home for "souvenirs." Following the burial there was a huge meal for all those in attendance. Essentially, all the traditional customs were observed. However, there was no wake, because "many of the older people were not up to it."

About two months after the funeral, one of the immediate family members reported that she had not been feeling well since the funeral. She had not been able to swallow her food easily, had no appetite, felt nauseous, and coughed up a yellowish liquid at night. She had lab tests performed and nothing could be found. Although she was experiencing physical manifestations of illness, the doctors could find nothing wrong with her. She said she felt it was more a spiritual illness than a physical one. But the Roman Catholic church, of which she is a member, was of no help. She said she thought perhaps her illness was the result of not performing all the proper rituals for the funeral. There had been no wake and not all of her relative's possessions had been disposed of. Her interpretation can be traced to the traditional Diegueño belief of disease causation: that negligence concerning certain tribal obligations could lead to illness. In just such a situation as this, the shaman would have been called upon to ascertain the cause of the illness.

Contemporary Use of Dreams

Dreams are still regarded as a significant means of understanding illness today. Dreams of dead relatives were prevalent and were considered extremely important. Traditionally, if a person had recurrent dreams of a dead relative, the services of the shaman were employed to determine why the spirit was lingering. These dreams were believed to occur because the spirit wanted something that had not been included in the burning of the property at the funeral. The shaman's role was to determine what the spirit wanted, so that the patient would no longer have disturbing dreams. Another relative of the deceased, in the events cited earlier, had recurrent dreams of playing "peon" (a Diegueño gambling game) with the dead man. It was felt by the other family members that these dreams occurred because the spirit wanted something that had not been buried with him. However, they were at a loss as to what it could be and lamented the fact that there were no "dream doctors" who could resolve the situation.

One consultant directly related her state of ill health to a very clear dream she experienced. She dreamed she was sleeping on her couch and woke up to find a golden snake lying beside her in a friendly way. She found this dream to be significant because snakes are very important in Diegueño cosmology. They are generally feared and are considered powerful beings. She had never killed snakes; in fact, she went out of her way to avoid harming them. In one version of the Diegueño myth, the snake, referred to as Sky-Rattlesnake, is the main character. Sky-Rattlesnake lived in the ocean and was a very powerful being. It was said that he was the first shaman. Snakes were also important in the ground paintings that described the world as the Diegueño knew it. The *awik* cult or snake cult was represented in the painting. In addition to *awik* creatures, which are shown by a line bent at a right angle, other species of snakes are also shown. These paintings were part of the *toloache* ceremony (Waterman 1910:303).

The consultant considered this dream extremely important and actively pursued an interpretation of it, exemplifying the persistence of the shamanistic healing complex. She stated that "there are no medicine men left who can interpret dreams." Neither the priest nor the Western medical doctor could fulfill the role of the shaman.

The "Hierarchy of Resort" of Digueños

This case is reminiscent of the "hierarchy of resort of curative practices" (Roman-ucci–Ross 1969). In the case presented, a hierarchy of action appears to exist for the Diegueño as well. The consultant first saw her priest, and later, when the physical symptoms became overt, she turned to consultation with a Western medical doctor. When neither of these resources produced positive results, she consulted a *curandera* from Mexico. The consultant related that formerly she had seen a *curandera* in Baja California on a somewhat regular basis, but indicated that now she was so busy that she preferred to see a healer on this side of the border. By the completion of five visits, the curing process had caused her physical symptoms to disappear, and the consultant indicated that she felt, in her words, "in balance again." Though unable to interpret the dream the *curandera's* treatment consisted of "spiritual surgery" to remove a "blockage," a *limpieza* to cleanse the soul and remove bad thoughts that other people may have sent her way, and some herbal pills and teas.

Even though shamanistic healing in the traditional sense has declined, beliefs related to disease causation remain particularly strong, and herbal remedies are still widely used. Although the use of plants was traditionally in the realm of "herb women" rather than the shaman, his was the ultimate authority. Some sources state that the use of herbs proliferated in the community as the shamans became fewer in number. According to one Diegueño woman, when there were more medicine men they held all the knowledge of plants and their uses, but as they decreased in numbers the people began to acquire the knowledge of plants so that they could take care of themselves (Almstedt 1977:9). Many of these plant remedies are in common usage today in Diegueño households. Some of the more commonly found plants are creosote bush (*Larrea tridentata* Sessé and Moc., Cov.) (Altschul 1973:127) for colds and flu; elderberry (*Sambucus caerulea* Raf.) for fevers and menstrual cramps; white sage (*Salvia* apiana Jeps.) (Altschul 1973:252; Owen 1962:113) for colds and coughs; yerba santa (*Eriodictydon californicum*) (Lewis and Lewis 1977:301) for colds and coughs; and cottonwood (*Populus fremontii* S. Wats.) for swollen ankles and feet (see also Munz 1974). An exhaustive discussion of Diegueño ethnobotany is not within the scope of this work, but it is important to emphasize that plant remedies are still used widely as an alternative modality of treatment.

Conclusion

The rapid acculturation that the Diegueño have experienced has not allowed them to create replacements for the traditional institutions that have disappeared. This is felt most acutely in the health–illness network. To date, the shamanistic healing complex has not been equalled by institutions such as the government health clinics, for modern health-care delivery does not provide the integration of mind, body, and spirit. Beliefs regarding disease causation and relationships between animate and inanimate parts of the universe and between the living and the dead are still very much alive. The shaman held the knowledge of the power that directed all the relationships of the universe.

Current Health Problems

The major health challenges facing Diegueño Indians today are diabetes, obesity, hypertension, alcoholism and other substance abuse, mental illness, dental disease, and chronic upper-respiratory disease. Meeting these challenges goes beyond a discussion of health-care models. Sustained contact with Europeans began with the establishment of the Mission of San Diego de Alcalá in 1769. Major changes in the lives of the Indian population occurred as a result: the local population was rapidly depleted by smallpox, tuberculosis, and other diseases, and was relocated by the Spanish missionization process. Disruption of entrenched socioeconomic patterns began with first contact and has continued ever since, with significant deleterious effects. The division of the Diegueño into reservation and urban factions, fostered largely by economic necessity, has had a disruptive influence on social organization, especially in regard to traditional communal (mutual aid) patterns. There are tremendous conflicts between families, clans, generations, and the sexes—conflicts that for the most part did not exist before the midpoint of this century. Interests and perspectives that were once communally shared have been replaced by factors of isolation, distrust, and uncertainty. The economic base for the Diegueño people as a culture, as well as for individuals, is tenuous at best.

The shamanistic healing complex used to provide a way of dealing with the complexities, perplexities, and negative aspects of human existence. The specialties of the shaman—which, regrettably, have been lost—included the treatment of both mental and physical illness. As a culture, the Diegueño are out of balance with their world, the natural harmony necessary for their survival has become discordant, and there is virtually no way to reestablish either balance or harmony.

The World Health Organization has defined health as "a state of complete physical, mental, and social well-being and not merely the absence of disease or infirmity." Traditionally, the Diegueño shaman pursued the same goal for his patients: the balance of the three worlds—the synchronization of body, mind, and spirit. This definition of health holds true today among Diegueño people. Among those Diegueño people consulted during the course of this research, it was emphasized.

Modern health-care delivery systems do have the potential to assist in reestablishing harmony for the Diegueño community. Although they cannot hope to replace fully the shamanistic healing complex, they can incorporate some aspects of this complex into the scope of their services. Herbal medicines and traditional treatments, culturally relevant preventive health education, and the encouragement of the health center as a cultural and social center for Diegueño are feasible. A report on a recent mental-health project sponsored by the Sycuan Tribal Council and the Indian Health Service stated: "We do know that the Western model of treatment based on the medical model has not been effective for Indian people, and we must develop alternative methods of treatment. This most surely can be developed through the use of more traditional methods" (1979).

As one 82-year-old Diegueño woman aptly stated, "These scientists are disturbing the balance of the stars and the earth, and that is why there is so much sickness." As reinforcement of these findings, interviews with Diegueño people during the course of this research indicate that the Diegueño want to see increased use of traditional ways of healing.

REFERENCES

Almstedt, Ruth Farrell. 1977. *Diegueño Curing Practices.* San Diego Museum Papers, no. 10. San Diego: Museum of Man.

Altschul, S. von Reis. 1973. *Drugs and Foods from Little-Known Plants; Notes in Harvard University Herbaria.* Cambridge, Mass.: Harvard Univ. Press.

Barrows, David Prescott. 1900. *The Ethnobotany of the Cahuilla Indians of Southern California.* Chicago: Univ. of Chicago Press.

Bean, Lowell John. 1975. "Power and Its Application in Native California." *Journal of California Anthropology,* 2(1):25–33.

Boscana, Geronimo. 1933. *Chinigchinich, a revised and annotated version of Alfred Robinson's translation of Father Geronimo Boscana's historical account of the belief, usages, customs and extravagensies of the Indians of this Mission of San Juan Capistrano called the Acagchemem tribe.* Santa Ana, Cal.: Fine Arts Press.

Bowers, Stephen. 1888. "A Remarkable Valley and an Interesting Tribe of Indians." Unpublished manuscript. Files of Spencer L. Rogers.

Cuero, Delfina. 1968. *The Autobiography of Delfina Cuero, a Diegueño Indian, as Told to Florence C. Shipek.* Los Angeles: Dawson's Book Shop.

Czaplicka, M.A. 1914. *Aboriginal Siberia: A Study in Social Anthropology.* Oxford: Clarendon Press.

DuBois, Constance Goddard. 1908. "The Religion of the Luiseño Indians of Southern California." *University of California Publications in American Archaeology and Ethnology,* 8:69–186.

Encyclopaedia Britannica. 1977. Micropaedia, s.v. "Diegueño."

Englehardt, Zephyrin. 1920. *The San Diego Mission.* San Francisco: James H. Barry Co.

Forde, C. Daryll. 1931. "Ethnography of the Yuma Indians." *University of California Publications in American Archaeology and Ethnology,* 28(4):83–278.

Freud, Sigmund. 1961. *Civilization and Its Discontents,* trans. and ed. James Strachey. New York: W.W. Norton & Co.

Gifford, E.W. 1931. *The Kamia of Imperial Valley.* Smithsonian Institution Bureau of American Ethnology Bulletin, no. 97. Washington, D.C.: U.S. Government Printing Office.

Hedges, Ken. 1975. "Notes of the Kumeyaay: A Problem of Identification." *Journal of California Anthropology,* 2(1):71–83.

Hodge, Frederick Webb. 1907. *Handbook of the Indians North of Mexico,* s.v. "Diegueños." Smithsonian Institution Bureau of American Ethnology Bulletin, no. 30, part 1. Washington, D.C.: U.S. Government Printing Office.

Kroeber, A.L. 1908. "A Mission Record of the California Indians: From a Manuscript in the Bancroft Library." *University of California Publications in American Archaeology and Ethnology,* 8(1):1–27.

———— 1925 *Handbook of the Indians of California.* Smithsonian Institution Bureau of American Ethnology Bulletin, no. 78. Washington D.C.: U.S. Government Printing Office.

Langdon, Margaret. 1975. "Kamia and Kumeyaay: A Linguistic Perspective." *Journal of California Anthropology,* 2(1):64–70.

Lewis, Walter H., and Memory P.F. Lewis. 1977. *Medical Botany.* New York: John Wiley & Sons.

Lincoln, Jackson Steward. 1935. *The Dream in Primitive Cultures.* London: Cresset Press.

Luomala, Katherine. 1978. "Tipai–Ipai." Robert Heizer, ed., *Handbook of North American Indians,* vol. 8. Washington D.C.: Smithsonian Institution, 592–609.

Moriarty, James Robert. 1965. "Cosmogony, Rituals, and Medical Practices among the Diegueño Indians of Southern California." *Anthropological Journal of Canada,* 3(3):2–16.

Munz, Phillip. 1974. *A Flora of Southern California.* Berkeley, Los Angeles, & London: Univ. of California Press.

Myerhoff, Barbara G. 1966. "The Doctor as Culture Hero: The Shaman of Rincon." *Anthropological Quarterly,* 39(2):60–72.

Owen, Roger Cory. 1962. "The Indians of Santa Catarina, Baja California Norte, Mexico: Concepts of Disease and Curing." Ph.D. diss., Univ. of California at Los Angeles.

Rogers, Spencer. 1944. "Disease Concepts in North America." *American Anthropologist,* 46(4):559–64.

———— 1976 "Healing Practices of the Diegueño Indians." James Moriarty, ed., *The People Cabrillo Met.* San Diego, Cal.: Cabrillo Historical Association, 21–30.

Romanucci–Ross, Lola (a.k.a. L.R. Schwartz). 1969. "The Hierarchy of Resort in Curative Practices: The Admiralty Islands, Melanesia." *Journal of Health and Social Behavior,* 10:201–9.

Romero, John Bruno. 1954. *The Botanical Lore of the California Indians; with Sidelights on Historical Incidents in California.* New York: Vantage Press.

Schultes, Richard Evans, and Albert Hofmann. 1979. *Plants of the Gods: Origins of Hallucinogenic Use.* New York, St. Louis, and San Francisco: McGraw-Hill Book Co.

Schwartz, L.R. See article listed under Lola Romanucci–Ross.

Sparkman, Philip Stedman. 1908. "The Culture of the Luiseño Indians." *University of California Publications in American Archaeology and Ethnology,* 8(4):187–234.

Spier, Leslie. 1923. "Southern Diegueño Customs." *University of California Publications in American Archaeology and Ethnology,* 20(16):295–358.

———— 1933 *Yuman Tribes of the Gila River.* Chicago: Univ. of Chicago Press.

Strong, William Duncan. 1972. *Aboriginal Society in Southern California.* Banning, Cal.: Malki Museum Press. (First published in 1929. University of California Publications in American Archaology and Ethnology. Berkeley: Univ. of California Press.)

Sycuan Tribal Council. 1979. *Sycuan Mental Health Project.* San Diego, Cal.: Sycuan Tribal Council and the Indian Health Service.

Toffelmier, Gertrude, and Katherine Luomala. 1936. "Dreams and Dream Interpretation of the Diegueño Indians of Southern California." *Psychoanalytic Quarterly,* 5:195–225.

Waterman, T.T. 1910. "The Religious Practices of the Diegueño Indians." *University of California Publications in American Archaeology and Ethnology,* 8(6):271–358.

Willoughby, Nona Christensen. 1963. "Division of Labor among the Indians of California." *Reprints of the University of California Archaeological Survey,* 60:7–79.

7

Anarchy, Abjection, and Absurdity: A Case of Metaphoric Medicine among the Tabwa of Zaire*

Allen F. Roberts

The Event

On 10 October 1960, two young men named Kiyumba and Mulobola[1] rode their bicycles from Kirungu to Chief Kaputo's village, ostensibly to purchase reed mats to resell at Kirungu market. In fact, their intention was to steal tax moneys held by the chief's clerk; Kiyumba would set fire to the chief's residence, and while everyone's attention was fixed on the blaze, Mulobola would break into the clerk's and steal the funds. Kiyumba did his part, without realizing that the chief himself was napping inside. Women saw him do this, and sounded the alert. Mulobola, frightened by the ensuing commotion, took flight, while Kiyumba was captured by the chief's men. Kiyumba was thrashed till he admitted his plan and told where his partner would probably be waiting for him, on the road back to Kirungu. Mulobola, too, was apprehended, and both were beaten senseless. Chief Kaputo sent his car to fetch his judge, then visiting a nearby village; the judge later told me that by the time he arrived at the chief's, the thieves were in a pitiful state. He could do nothing, at that point, to alter the course of the event.

Accounts vary as to what occurred next. The official inquest[2] found that "in a paroxysm of anger," Chief Kaputo Lambo ordered that the two men be burned alive. As though summing up the event, the report concludes that "a very important detail should not be overlooked . . . : Kiyumba was found bearing an MNC Lumumba card." My informants skipped over this detail. The judge said that he saw Kanengo, the chief's counselor and a noted practitioner of traditional medicine (*mfumu*, pl. *wafumu*,) take a long, sharp knife and lead young men from the village

---

* In memory of Minnie G. Curtis.

in carrying the two thieves to the bridge across a nearby stream. The judge later learned that the two had been burned alive. As Nzwiba, another practitioner and close informant, said, "this [the culprits' ashes] is what is called *kapondo*. *Wafumu* practitioners from all over went and got *vizimba* medicines then. Many, many went there, and those who have *kapondo* will show it to you if you ask, and will say it came from that time at Chief Kaputo's. If you say you want to buy some, ah, you buy it."[3]

The Historical Context

With Independence on 30 June 1960, the Congo began a series of convulsions, relatively mild at first, that would lead to unparalleled tragedy. A week after Independence, the Force Publique mutinied; several days later, before a rumored intervention by the Soviet Union could occur, United Nations troops arrived in the Congo; and almost concurrently, Katanga seceded. Through July and August, Katangans lived in fear of an expected invasion by the Congolese National Army (ANC); in August, Kasai also seceded and sought federation with Katanga. In September, the ANC occupied several key centers in Kasai, and many civilians were killed. President Kasavubu divested Prime Minister Lumumba of his powers, and vice versa; Colonel Mobutu declared both parties "neutralized" till the end of the year. On 10 October Lumumba was confined to his official residence, with UN troops assuring his security by occupying the gardens around the house, while ANC forces menaced all within the periphery of the property they surrounded.

Tabwa living along the southwestern shores of Lake Tanganyika were within the old province and new state of Katanga, and were among the earliest and most ardent supporters of Tshombe's breakaway government, providing several of its first ministers and other high officials. The tumultuous nature of these first months of double independence was the backdrop for the questioning of much more local authority; unrest would grow among Tabwa around Kirungu, as factions long denied power within the colonial hierarchy of chiefs attempted to wrest control from their adversaries. With international, national, regional, and local tensions so high, an attempted robbery was not especially remarkable; the judiciary could not focus attention upon such an event in such times. Instead, the Belgian Magistrat Instructeur noted that one of the perpetrators had allegedly possessed the party identity card of those against whom Katangans were fighting for independence, and the matter was dropped without Chief Kaputo, his counselor Kanengo, or anyone (but the two thieves) receiving the least punishment.

The Actors

It is difficult to say much about the two thieves. Present-day residents of Chief Kaputo's village remember the event, but nothing of the young men; I did not contact their families. Although others in the area who engaged in overtly political, insurrectionist actions during these same years are well known and still celebrated locally, these two are not. It seems most likely that the general state of alarm prevailing throughout Katanga, and the attraction of a strongbox containing 8,000 francs in tax receipts proved too great a temptation for the two, who sought only private gain. They were not (or were not allowed to become) "social bandits"— men acting with public (or at least factional) approbation in social protest against forces commonly perceived as "the oppressor" (see Hobsbawm 1965, 1981). The magistrate, trying to justify (or at least to pass over) both their assassinations and the lack of pursuit by an overtaxed Katangan judiciary, seems to imply that they *were* social bandits, acting in the name of a political party subversive to the Katangan state. Rather, they were deemed criminals by Chief Kaputo's people, men without regard for order as personified by the chief whose life they had wantonly threatened in the course of their attempted robbery.

Chief Kaputo Lambo (dead in the mid-1960s) was known as an irascible fellow whose ambitions for power within his local political arena knew few bounds. He tried to replace an inferior chief in the colonial hierarchy, whose insistence of superiority by tradition and precolonial history had long chafed him; when this effort was foiled, with great loss of face, Kaputo saw to it that he was physically abused by soldiers. It is still believed that Kaputo had great medicines at his disposal, including an ability to send "lion" to maim or kill his enemies. Such powers are associated with Kanengo, his closest henchman.

Until his death in the late 1970s, Kanengo was widely renowned for two capacities: his knowledge of Chief Kaputo's history, for which he was consulted in all affairs in which the legitimacy of the chief's rule was questioned; and his knowledge of medicines. When my wife and I knew him he was living in exile from Kaputo's chiefdom, after protracted quarrels with the man who succeeded to the chair at the death of Kaputo Lambo. As a gauge of his marginality, Kanengo's house—far from any village and located deep in a swamp—was the only round (hence, "traditional") one we saw in four years among the Tabwa. He was known as the greatest practitioner of mfumu in the area, and the most difficult cases were taken to him. A kinsman of his who had violent psychotic episodes was kept in stocks in the same yard in which others—there for treatment, or living with Kanengo—were seated or seeing to everyday chores. Kanengo told us that he had tried all his means to heal the young man, but was resisted at every turn; we were left with the distinct impression that the old man would "solve" the problematic case whether or not the disturbed nephew survived his cure. He suggested that my wife (an anthropologist studying traditional medicine, who as a paramedic ran a small clinic of Western medicine) give injections of his traditional medicines to his kinsman and other difficult cases. This and his attempt to involve us in his conflict with the seated Chief Kaputo (by telling others *we* wanted to divest him of power, and as expatriots would see that it happened) left us very uneasy in our dealings with Kanengo.

Kanengo was also one of only two Tabwa we ever knew who was reputed to have been (or still be?) in the Kazanzi society (BaKazanzi). This society was introduced to the central Luba around the turn of the nineteenth century by Luba traders visiting the Songye (Reefe 1981:118) and spread to the lands along the Luvua and Lukuga rivers (Lebaigne 1933).[4] It was popular among northern Tabwa (or "Holoholo") at the turn of the present century (Schmitz 1912:278) and was encountered among ("Luba-ized") western Tabwa (or "Hemba") slightly thereafter (Colle 1913:528). An elderly informant once came upon a seance of the society at Chief Rutuku's near the Lubilaye (and counts himself lucky to have escaped unscathed!), but said that the society never spread farther south than that. The BaKazanzi may have survived the first decades of the 1900s, but in an attenuated form, being replaced by new religious organizations more apt in the context of established colonialism (e.g., BuGabo, Ukanga). It did not disappear altogether. As one old man remarked with acerbity, "It lasted long after the Belgians came; even when they finally left [in 1960], they didn't know how to 'see' sorcerers, so how could they 'see' Kanzanzi adepts?"

Among Luba, the Kazanzi eliminated avenging ghosts by disinterring corpses, burning fagots in the opened graves to prevent the spirits' return, and incinerating the remains for later use as medicines (Lebaigne 1933; Joset 1934). All Tabwa I questioned contended that Kazanzi adepts among them killed and ate sorcerers identified by diviners and/or the poison oracle (and denied that war enemies, the elderly, slaves, or others of "lowly condition" would also be consumed, as stated in Colle 1913:540). With macabre detail, Tabwa recount how adepts would be summoned by a chief to eliminate one designated a sorcerer. Using the strength of their medicine called *niembo* or *buyembe* (as in Colle 1913:541; Burton 1961:171), they would secrete medicines in the headpad the victim used to carry loads, and this would cause the soul (*roho* in Swahili, *mutima* in KiTabwa) to leave the body. The sorcerer would be powerless against this, and his/her body would then go to the Kazanzi camp. The adepts, their faces crimson with *nkula* powder ground from Pterocarpus bark (this a "symbol of blood" [*mfano ya damu*], as I was told), would dance about and begin to dissect the victim, beginning with the legs, as the victim looked on vacuously. When the sorcerer finally fell, his/her flesh would be eaten, openly, it was said, in contrast to the secret manner in which sorcerers consume the flesh of their victims. Colle reports that as they did this, they would imitate the hyena's cry (1913:539). The bones would be burned and used as medicines. BaKazanzi also danced publically, performing incredible feats such as piercing their cheeks. In the past, they held regular ceremonies during the dark of the moon (Schmitz 1912:281).

The Action

The execution of the two thieves at Chief Kaputo's is most easily explained as the result of "a paroxysm of anger"; that the chief's house was set afire, and that he himself was asleep inside at the time, would seem due cause for retribution. The severity and form of the method, the choice of executioner, and the ultimate meaning of the act as reflected in what became of the relics, are not so simply explained.

A common Tabwa adage is that "theft and sorcery are of one path." The perpetrators of either manifest a disregard for others' sanctity, act in contradistinction to community, and therefore taunt and threaten social life. Sorcery for Tabwa is a "solar" activity; God and the sun are both said to be sorcerers in their lack of limit (hence, figuratively, of pity [*uruma*]) and through their association with death. God is said to feast upon humans "like goats," and the sun kills crops and hence humans when it shines unabated. Yet the sun is recognized as necessary to life, the order of which is synonymous with a god called *Leza Malango* ("Almighty Intelligence").

Opposed to these phenomena is the marked discontinuity of the life cycle. Kinship is considered a phenomenon expanding outward from a central point where there emerged, either from a deep body of water or a subterranean passage, the first human beings. As generations passed, humankind spread out to populate the lands surrounding this point. Such a concept is given representation (or found) in spirals such as that of *mpande* conus shell disks, once an important symbol of chiefship and still revered as an ancestral shrine item.[5] The *mpande* is of a paradigm with the moon, as is most clearly indicated in a Tabwa myth in which they can be interchanged (A.F. Roberts 1980:426–27). Each turn of its spiral is analogous to the "belt" of a chief; succession is called "to wear the belt" (*kuvaa mukaba*), and the succession of generations can be imagined as concentric circles, each succeeding generation encompassing previous ones. A paradox of existence is that while life is eternal, in that the "belt" is always inherited (except in the case of executed sorcerers), it is finite in that each individual is born and dies (ibid.:98–101). Sorcery is an action opposing such expansion, as those who superficially appear supportive kinsmen or neighbors nefariously rob their victims of vitality and finally "eat their flesh." Sorcerers, when caught and executed, are not succeeded, and every attempt is made to obliterate them physically and from memory (*kufuta*). Thieves with so little regard for life and property would be meted out condign punishment, and Tabwa are hard pressed or loath to draw a distinction between sorcerers and thieves in cases of the sort.

Kanengo was the executioner of the two young men, a role for which his cultic background had prepared him technically and for which his personality was attuned. Several of the traits characteristic of Kazanzi adepts are especially apt in this case, and may be elaborated.

Colle reported that as the BaKazanzi partook of their ghastly repast, they uttered the cry of the hyena. A reference to this animal, in turn, allows a clearer understanding of the place of Kazanzi adepts in their contemporary society. Specifically, *baendo* joking partners, who see to the burial of members of their opposite clans, are called "hyena"; and the classificatory grandchildren who orchestrate the burial of a chief are assigned the term even more explicitly. Those who act as *baendo* and bury someone one day, will receive the same service from their opposites another. The cutting insults they offer must be tolerated, as they, too, will be returned on a later occasion. This sort of exchange is called *vizambano,* and the image Tabwa evoke in explaining the term is of boys wrestling, first one on top of and pinning the other, then the one on the bottom reversing his partner. Such alternation finds its obvious analogy in that of the seasons, and the fierce but jocular behavior of the "hyena" is that of dry-season heroes seeing to the bloody business of change.

The burial of a chief is performed in a lunar idiom, the period of his reign analogous to the light of the moon, his death to the tenebrous two or three days prior to the new moon. It is no coincidence that the Kazanzi adepts, too, chose this time for their celebrations. For Tabwa, moonlight is thought auspicious, as it allows one to discern predators lurking on the periphery of the community or along one's path; on the other hand, the dark of the moon, called *kamwonang'anga,* is a liminal time, fraught with danger. The name means "the one seen by the *ng'anga* or practitioner": the moon is "still there," but can only be seen by those with supernatural vision. The moon is a *mulozi* or sorcerer then, as it effects its apparent journey from the east, where its final sliver was seen, to the west, where it will newly appear; during *kamwonang'anga,* Lake Tanganyika, whipped by high winds, unleashes its most treacherous furies, and the most pernicious beasts are in evidence. In contrast, game and fish may be seen in especially large numbers, but they will elude their pursuers; they have been "closed" by the moon, as people say (A.F. Roberts 1980:111–18). The moon, then, usually lights a person's way, or "leads" the person, just as a chief is ordinarily the "father of his people" and looks to their succor. Yet, on a regular basis, the hidden side of the moon—like that of a chief—will predominate. As Father Theuws has written of beliefs held by people closely related to the Tabwa, "the moon is ambiguous as is life itself: . . . to be and become, to live and to die are but two faces of the same reality" (1968:11). Tabwa chiefs are leaders of their people but they are also deemed the greatest sorcerers of the land. Theirs is the marginality of privilege. They do not kill and eat victims like other sorcerers, but they do condone the practice in their community. It is said that sorcerers will bring a portion of the meat of their victim to the chief, who will sell it to other sorcerers, thus drawing a direct profit. For Tabwa, lunar and solar tropes are used to order and understand life; but neither is univocal; each has two sides, and when the positive of one predominates, often it does so in contradistinction to the other, and vice versa.

The Hyena and Its Metaphoric Significance

The spotted hyena, *Crocuta crocuta,* is a *solar* animal, and so opposed to the moon and those of its idiom. A Tabwa myth tells of a hyena fetching the sun and bringing it to the universe. The sun is said to be unchanging, hence unmarked (whereas the moon has phases and period); it is sexless, and not personified, as is the moon. The trait of the spotted hyena making it most sun-like through metaphor is its apparent lack of sexual dimorphism. Observers as early as Aristotle commented upon this, and as noted in the twelfth-century *Bestiary*, the spotted hyena's "nature is that at one moment it is masculine and at another moment feminine, and hence it is a dirty brute" (White 1960:3).[6] Beidelman has reviewed the spotted hyena's other odd characteristics noticed by many African observers and given moral sense via metaphor: they have an odd posture and gait, with front legs longer than back; their "grotesque and somewhat humanoid calls [have been] described by some writers as demonic"; they "paste" an odoriferous substance from anal glands to mark territory; and they chew up and digest bones left as refuse by other predators, so that their droppings may be white—and "hot," as Tabwa say—as a consequence (Beidelman 1975:190; see also Sapir 1981). Important for Tabwa in conjunction with this last is the hyena's *malosi*, the singular vision that they believe allows the beast to see carrion at great distances; metaphorically, this would assist "hyena" in perceiving sorcerers. Like hyenas, Kazanzi adepts are reputed to have exhumed corpses, especially of those "proven" sorcerers by the poison oracle, and to have obliterated them (just as hyenas consume bones, the final vestige of vital form). Finally, hyena anal hairs *may* have been a transform for the kizimba of the rainbow-producing serpent, Nfwimina. If for Kaguru such "liminal qualities make hyena the witches of the animal world" (Beidelman 1975:190), for Tabwa these same allow "hyena" to turn *against* the sorcerers with whom they are somewhat consonant. Sorcerers in the social realm, like hyenas in the natural, are betwixt or altogether outside of the categories by which life is ordered (cf. Turner 1967:97 and passim). Being quintessentially "between," they bespeak transition, both negative (sorcerers robbing crops' or kin's vitality) and positive ("hyena" restoring order by destroying sorcerers).

After a Tabwa chief is buried,[7] classificatory grandchildren—whose "souls are red" like the camwood powder and Lady Ross's turaco plumes they sport—are said to lust for blood, and a moment called *kisama* is begun. All goods on their way back from the water course beside or under which they have buried the chief are broken or confiscated; chickens, goats, and even small children are slaughtered; and adult kinsmen of the chief are captured, mistreated, and held for ransom. The chief's surviving kinsmen hasten to placate them, and, their rampage stopped, the same "grandchildren" choose a successor. It is they who sing "he returns, he awakens, he awakens" as they circle the hut where the successor is hidden, bidding him to "reappear" like the new moon.

In this act they echo the role of the cosmic serpent Nfwimina, which stops the rains with the rainbow, yet assures their return with the smoke of the dry season's last and most important bushfires. Tabwa place a medicine bundle at a point in the woods which they intend to make the center of a fire lit from several sides; it is hoped that all four cardinal winds will join to bring the fire to a flaming circle, trapping game at the center where the medicines have been hidden. An element of this *nsipa* bundle[8] is the belt of an executed sorcerer (*mukaba wa mulozi*), and the pyric circle of the bushfire repeats its message of destruction and contraction, so opposed to the expansion of the generations. Another *kizimba* used in the bundle is that of Nfwimina, the solar serpent; and when the circle closes, annihilating all brought within its constricting perimeter, the column of smoke that rises above the point is said to be Nfwimina itself, standing on the tip of its tail, its head toward the heavens. This moment is one of several vital transformations: wild animals become meat (even "cooked" meat!), and the column of smoke causes clouds to "build" (*kujenga*), carrying the first rains, which will in turn extinguish the bushfires.

The "hyena" have staged the death of the chief (which is hidden from the populace till the decomposition of the corpse is such that the skull falls from the body), the *kisama* interregnum, and the reapparition, just as the dry-season heroes bring back the wet. "Hyena" had other roles in Tabwa society, in which their dread propensities had an ultimately moral denouement. One didactic tale recorded by Schmitz among northern Tabwa recounts how Kimbwi, the hyena, changed into a person and accepted a baby from a negligent mother intent on going off dancing, only to smash the baby's head on a rock (1912:268). Although there were theriomorphic lions (and Tabwa terrorists who assumed this disguise), aside from random stories in which an odd circumstance might be explained (unconvincingly for many listeners) by sorcerers assuming some other animal's form, Tabwa do not speak of hyena-men. That is, when they speak of "hyena," this is a figurative term, one with social connotations for Tabwa, but not evidence of a belief in metempsychotic transformation to this beast.

As "hyena," then, the Kazanzi adepts—like classificatory grandchildren burying a chief—oversaw a transformation important to the continuity of social life. As a "stabilizing institution," they were " 'saviors to the whole community' " (Reefe 1981:205, 118 citing W.F.P. Burton). Unlike the "grandchildren," they were summoned by will rather than circumstance, by a desire to eliminate a sorcerer rather than by the death of a chief. They reduced the sorcerer to nothing. It is not clear whether they engaged in the anthropophagous orgies early missionaries did and Tabwa still do attribute to them; this may have been feigned as a part of their showmanship, of which the piercing of their cheeks while they danced was another example. A few colonial authorities denied the existence of the practice (Lebaigne 1933), but most repeated or rephrased the ghoulish details of Father Colle and other missionaries as though absolute truth (e.g., Administrateur Territorial 1919). Such a clearcut "failure to comprehend that they were dealing with inverted moral orders, rather than descriptions of concrete happenings" (Arens 1979:153), had political motivations and consequences best elaborated elsewhere.[9] More significant was the adepts' obliteration of the sorcerer, their dismembering of the cadaver (or, perhaps, of the yet-living), incineration of its bones, and their transmutation of the circumstance and substance into an elemental meaning for use in medicines. The disruptive were then brought back into order and put to the service of the community, I would suggest, in the same way that the smoke from the last and most intense bushfires, catalyzed by the nsipa bundle with its vizimba of a sorcerer's belt and Nfwimina, brings the clouds of the season's first rains.

The Meaning

The elements of Tabwa traditional medicine are of two clearcut categories, *miti* ("trees" in KiTabwa) plant substances, and *vizimba* (s. *kizimba*), or what Richards has called "activating agents" (1969). These latter are mostly parts of animals, references to place (e.g., a pebble from the mountaintop wherein resides an Earth spirit) or to circumstance (e.g., a piece of root traversing a path upon which one has tripped). A few may be termed relics, in that they are parts of human beings whose essence or history may be typified. To possess knowledge of these is suspicious; to *use* them, much more so, and always subject to situational interpretation, either condemned as sorcery, or deemed pardonable when resorted to in "self-defense."

As C.D. Roberts has written, "the transformative capacity of any kizimba is referred to by people not as its 'strength' (*nguvu*), but as its 'meaning' (*maana* in Swahili)" (in press). When the two thieves were burned alive, their bones were taken and used as the *kapondo* kizimba. Different informants explain kapondo in various ways according to their level of esoteric knowledge and their descriptive flair; an overarching or underlying meaning can be discerned in them all. Kiuma, a chief's son in his 60s who is *not* a practitioner, said that kapondo is when someone dies alone in the bush of hunger or lack of care; this, he stated, is what Nfwimina is, and furthermore both are the same as a woman who has never menstruated or had children, a "woman–man." Others, among them practitioners, articulate this knowledge, distinguishing among these parts; all *are* related, and a relic of a *musala* or amenorrheal woman *is* a transform of the kizimba of Nfwimina, the rainbow-breathing solar serpent (whose story Kiuma did not know; see A.F. Roberts 1980:244–49). These are related to but not the same as kapondo. Another non-practitioner said that this was someone who lives alone in the woods without fields or a house, and who steals from others; such a person's "head is not right" (*kichwa si sawa, hata*). He went on to describe a case of this when he was a boy, of a woman who lived in the hills like an animal, with hair and fingernails exaggerated to the point of bestiality. As an aside, it may be added that Kanengo (the executioner of the two thieves) once said that crazy people are like Mbote "pygmies": they run about in the woods and will sleep anywhere.

Other Examples of Alienation

Practitioners offered more elaborated explanations. Kabemba (the only person with *muyembe* medicines like Kanengo's whom we ever met) said kapondo is a person walking alone fallen upon and killed for no reason. Kalwele (a renowned practitioner living at Chief Kaputo's) said this is someone who has been "taken" by a possessing spirit (*pepo*), a usage repeated by others (see C.D. Roberts 1981); when I said that the same term had been used in reference to the two thieves, he noted that to burn a chief's house one must have been possessed by a bad spirit or *shetani* (from "Satan"). All of these explanations bespeak mental and/or social alienation, hence absurdity, discordance. Yet by being contrary to reason, by being antistructural, they are part of a greater whole demanding dialectic to define reason.

The word *kapondo* is from a verb meaning to pound, grind, or crush, as one does with manioc or corn in a mortar.[10] Derivatives bridging metaphorically from this root range in sense: "to dispirit," "to be shunned," "a night thief," "a woman who eats well without the knowledge of her husband" (who presumably does not!), "din or tumult." All touch upon reduction and disindividualization.

Most informants' exegeses, like these dictionary definitions, deal with solitude, isolation, or seclusion. Dying alone is absurd, since a "proper" death is in the arms of kinswomen whose warmth and ministrations reflect the afflicted person's life-long participation in kinship and other close relations. Dying of hunger while alone underscores the abjection, for Tabwa are diligent farmers and responsible providers who would not be so careless with self or others—even complete strangers—except in the most dire of circumstances. Such a person is *lost,* from human contact and the succor it implies. Being killed while a solitary traveler, for no reason due to past history, is equally absonant with a social universe in which all acts are willed and have a history that is determinable through divination, if not already common knowledge. Kiuma's assertion that *kapondo,* Nfwimina the solar serpent, and the amenorrheal woman are all the same plays upon the unmarked nature of them all.

The alienation in the examples given is more evident when individuals are deranged (their "heads are not right") or possessed by spirits to the exclusion of an ordinary self. Eating alone is a rejection of the commensal norm important to Tabwa for everyday survival and proclaimed as an attribute of Tabwa chiefs (Kaoze 1950) as opposed to Luba or Luba-ized ones, who eat in seclusion. Tabwa see this as the height of greed, which, as a threat to life, is a definitive characteristic of sorcery; to choose to eat alone, then, is evil, while to be forced to eat alone is pitiable. Din and tumult are opposed to harmony in the aural realm, just as solitude is a "pounding down" (also from *kuponda*) of the obligations and prerogatives that make an individual *distinctive* within a community interrelated by kinship, marriage, and neighborliness.[11]

The two thieves at Chief Kaputo's displayed a singular disregard for person and property. The firing of *anyone's* house is a heinous act, and when the residence is the chief's, brings an added sense of anarchy. Solitude, eating alone, and din are all of a paradigm with anarchy, each having its own context against which it is the disorderly foil. The thieves' anarchy was checked, however, by the old "hyena," Kanengo the aged Kazanzi adept, and his young followers. Kapondo, too, represents this completion, this ultimate restoration of order after absurdity.

The substances which are made vizimba are employed as I understand tropes in rhetoric to be used.[12] Roots by the thousand cross one's path, yet a particular one on a particular occasion "causes" one to stumble; a piece of this root is taken for use in medicines, as the reduction of that set of circumstances which includes the trip and the tripping, but also such other elements as a sense of destiny, the interference of vengeful ghosts or sorcerers, pain (in the toe) and the knowledge that such a seemingly inconsequential injury can lead (through secondary infection)

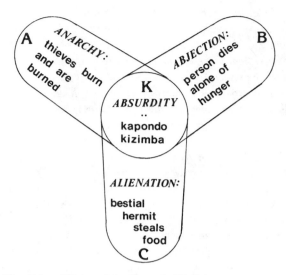

Fig. 7.1. Origins of the Kapondo Kizimba

to eventual loss of limb or life. Through a synecdochal process, the particular root is chosen that represents the whole of these circumstances, and it will "foreground those aspects of the whole that are not only distinctive but are also taken as essential or directly relevant to the topic" (Sapir 1977:16). It is still a piece of root (without regard to botanical identity) and as such metaphorically joins the separate domains "root" and "fate" or whatever ultimate meaning the *kizimba* possesses.

The charred bones of the two thieves are still just that as well: charred bones like all other; but their transmutation has led to a sense beyond that of ordinary skeletal remains. This is a sense which may be derived from other circumstances than the anarchic threat as in the event described here. Each of these others will be synecdochically reduced, then each stands metaphorically in relation to the others, through the common mediator of the kizimba (see Figure 7.1: A:K, B:K, C:K = synecdoche; AK:BK:CK = metaphor; K + L + M + other vizimba: amulet X = metonomy). The kizimba has a single meaning (in this case, kapondo's is absurdity, I would assert), although each kizimba is a paradigm for its various sources; kapondo can then be mixed metonymically with other vizimba/paradigms in the preparation of complex medicines (where "metonym" implies the juxtaposition within a single domain—the medicine bundle or amulet—of distinct items).

The Eventual Use

Substances used as vizimba are often difficult to obtain, and may be purchased from distant practitioners at significant expenditure of money, time, and energy. Only a tiny quantity is required (perhaps a cubic centimeter of charred bone, for instance) and this will serve many, many times, since each medicine bundle or amulet contains the merest shaving of the bone, a dusting from something else, a smudge of yet another. In other words, these elements or their combination are not iconic, and one cannot know their identity and meaning unless told; instead the assemblage of vizimba are "A poetry which, contrary to Auden, makes everything happen, a domain in which the expressive and the instrumental are in some profound sense united as are the material and immaterial aspects of reality" for Tabwa (C.D. Roberts [in press]).

The kapondo kizimba is an ingredient in important concoctions, the constitutions of which were revealed to us only after several years of working with the same practitioners. It is an element of the *kiito* medicine horn of Tabwa snare hunters, and used to be employed in the *kinkungwa* horn of members of the now-defunct Mowela big-game hunting guild. It is added to medicines prepared "to throw someone in the bush" (*kumutupa mutu mu pori*), that is, to rid the patient of an avenging ghost. It can be employed in the *mwanzambale* protective amulet, as *muyembe* practitioner Kabemba explained, and this kizimba in conjunction with the many others of the device will make a solitary person seem as though many. "If you are alone and someone comes to test (*kupima*) the strength of his medicines against the strength of yours [as sorcerers do in trying to conquer even the hardiest of practitioners], they will see that in your medicines many things are mixed, each and every quality or meaning." In other words, the solitude of the kapondo's source is put to use, to make hunted animals bereft of direction or wiles, or to thwart aggressive sorcerers by having "solitude" under control and "closed" within one's amulet.

There are other less salubrious uses. As Nzwiba explained,

> Now these *vizimba* that they go and take from your fellow man, ah, we see this tends to be sorcery. For they take the kizimba from that one who has died, and they invoke it: "Now, you kizimba, I want so-and-so to be killed." So it is certain that afterwards he will die, the kizimba will agree that the person will die. . . . For instance, if he had taken a kapondo kizimba, a bone or something of someone who has died, he puts this with other medicines and begins to invoke there, saying, "This man has not done right by me, I want him to die the same way you died," then won't he die? Because he has prayed to the person who has already died to do this, he [the victim] will die or have another kind of accident. . . because the one who died agrees to the business for which it has been called.[13]

Any of these uses may be deemed sorcery, depending upon the situation. Hunters are said to ensorcel (*kuloga*) their game, and amulets like *mwanzambale* are considered to be protective by their possessors, but offensive by critics. The absurdity of kapondo—its meaning (*maana*) as a constituent of medicines—is brought to bear on animal or human targets, plucking them from their apparent destinies and assuring them another fate they desire less, yet one which allows the greater community to continue in restored harmony. Individuals who possess and deploy kapondo are intervening in the course of events, and such hubris must always have its detractors as well as its supporters among those denied and gaining advantage, respectively. The hubristic, in turn, are *of* society but not altogether *in* society. Like the hyena, they are masters of transformation and transition, necessary yet dread.

ACKNOWLEDGMENTS

Four years' anthropological fieldwork was undertaken from late 1973 to late 1977 with financial support from the National Institute of Mental Health (no. 1–F01–55251–01–CUAN), the Committee on African Studies and the Edson–Keith Fund of the University of Chicago, and the Society of the Sigma Xi. A first draft of this paper, entitled "*Kapondo*: The Use of Political Synecdoche in Tabwa Traditional Medicine," was prepared for the "Sovereignty, Sickness and Health in Africa" panel of the 1981 African Studies Association meetings, chaired by Randall Packard. As this work has evolved, helpful comments have been received from J. Knight, O. Kokole, D. Merten, D. Moerman, R. Packard, T. Reefe, and C. Roberts, some of which have been incorporated here. Despite such generosity, all responsibility for this paper's content remains my own.

NOTES

1. All names have been changed except that of Kirungu, the central town of Tabwa lands along the southwestern shores of Lake Tanganyika in the Zaire Republic. Common Tabwa names have been chosen, and are employed in the writing of C.D. Roberts (1980, 1981, in press) and of the present author to refer to the same individuals.

2. A single document concerning this incident was discovered quite by chance in the archives of the Bureau des Affaires Culturelles, Division Régionale des Affaires Politiques in Lumbumbashi: W. DeBruyn, Magistrat Instructeur, "Avi d'ouverture d'instruction," Parquet du Tanganika, Etat du Katanga, 7 Nov. 1960.

3. Nzwiba, interview of 14 May 1976 at Nanga; other relevant interviews with the chief's judge, Kanengo, and other interested parties were conducted on a visit to Chief Kaputo's in March 1977.

4. I disagree with Reefe's assertion that "the presence of the bambudye and bakasandji secret societies and subsequent transformation of oral traditions in frontier areas to the Luba, like those of northern Tabwa suggest that the loyalty of distant client-lineages and villages was changing into a more substantial sense of belonging to a common polity" (1981:153). Although there *is* a linguistic and cultural *aire* of which Luba, Tabwa, and other groups are members, among whom ideas and practices have long been traded easily, evidence that these chiefdoms (e.g., Tumbwe's) were "client-lineages and villages" of a centralized Luba empire is scant and unconvincing. Rather than belonging to "a common polity," that there were Tabwa Kazanzi adepts may reflect the borrowing of beliefs and behavior patterns deemed powerful because of their alien origin. The most effective medical practitioners, practices, and substances known to Tabwa my wife and I consulted still come from Luba beyond the hills and rivers to the west (or, less frequently, from across Lake Tanganyika).

5. Other spirals important to Tabwa cosmology are discussed in C.D. Roberts (in press), in A.F. Roberts (1980:353–74), and in idem (in preparation).

6. Female spotted hyenas have an elongated clitoris visually identical to the male's, and a sham scrotum; the clitoris becomes erect during greeting, as does a male's penis, and field biologist Kruuk admits that he can distinguish between male and female adolescents only through close anatomical inspection (1974:210–11). The vagina is at the end of the clitoris, and coitus occurs when, in estrus, the entrance swells and the clitoris does not become erect; these points are reviewed in A.F. Roberts 1980:265–74.

7. Although many Tabwa ceremonies and rituals are no longer practiced as they were precolonially, most informants believe that chiefs are still buried in the manner mentioned here, and a *kisama* interregnum follows; no direct observation was possible.

8. "Nsipa" is a term used for the bundle of medicines buried in a central place in a new village, to attract residents and to keep them content in staying. Cunnison has described these among southern Tabwa along the Luapula (1956).

9. In a future paper, tentatively entitled "'Sinister Caricatures': 'Cannibalism' among Belgians and Africans in the Congo," the Kazanzi society among colonized and the Mitumbula among colonizers will be contrasted, as to political history and essence.

10. Van Acker 1907:54; Van Avermaet and Mbuya 1954:533–34; White Fathers 1954:619; Kajiga 1975:611; Johnson 1971:384. In KiTabwa -*ponda* can also mean "to insult, to dance fast"; *muponda* is the wild dog, *Lycaon pictus,* and *kiponda* a "night thief," according to Van Acker. In both KiLuba and CiBemba (which in turn are closely related to KiTabwa), derivatives refer to rebellion, insurrection, and the "underground" (*maquis*).

11. Not coincidentally, Tabwa and others in the area used to create a din when the moon was "eaten" during eclipse. See Heusch 1972:72–82, for an elegant discussion of how this is an action to "separate the sky and the earth," to maintain the discrete nature of cosmic principles.

12. I rely here upon J. David Sapir's "Anatomy of Metaphor" (1977), in which he holds that "metaphor states an equivalence between terms taken from separate domains"; "metonymy replaces or juxtaposes contiguous terms that occupy a distinct and separate place within what is considered a single semantic or perceptual domain"; and "synecdoche, like metonymy, draws its terms from a single domain; however, one term always includes or is included by the other" (p.4). Figure 6.1 is also derived from his (p. 20).

13. The place and meaning of invocation in the Tabwa medical process, as well as the usefulness of the rhetorical analogy in the explication of the process, will be expounded upon in the writings of C.D. Roberts.

REFERENCES

Administrateur Territorial. 1919. Untitled administrative report from Albertville, 22 Jan. 1919. Archives of the Sous-Région du Tanganika, Kalemi (Zaire).

Arens, W. 1979. *The Man-Eating Myth.* New York: Oxford Univ. Press.

Beidelman, T. 1975. "Ambiguous Animals: Two Theriomorphic Metaphors in Kaguru Folklore." *Africa,* 45(2):183–96.

Burton, W.F.P. 1961. *Luba Religion and Magic in Custom and Belief.* Annales du Musée Royal de L'Afrique Centrale, Sciences Humaines, no. 35.

Colle, P. 1913. *Les Baluba.* 2 vols. Anvers: Albert Dewit.

Cunnison, I. 1956. "Headmanship and the Ritual of Luapula Villages." *Africa*, 26(1):2–19.

DeBruyn, W. 1960. "Avis d'ouverture d'instruction." Judicial report, Parquet du Tanganika, Etat du Katanga, 7 Nov. 1960. Archives of the Bureau des Affaires Culturelles, Division Régionale des Affaires Politiques, Lubumbashi.

Heusch, L. de. 1972. *Le roi ivre, ou l'origine de l'Etat.* Paris: Gallimard.

Hobsbawm, E. 1965. *Primitive Rebels.* New York: Norton.

1981 *Bandits.* New York: Pantheon.

Johnson, F. 1971. *A Standard Swahili-English Dictionary* (1st ed. 1939). London: Oxford Univ. Press.

Joset, G.A. 1934. "Etude sur les sectes secretes de la circonscription de Kinda, district du Lomami—territorie des Baluba." *Bulletin de la Société Royale Belge de Géographie*, 58(1):28–44.

Kajiga, B. 1975. *Dictionnaire de la langue swahili.* Goma: Librarie des Volcans.

Kaoze, S. 1950. "Histoire des Bena–Kilunga." G. Nagant, ed., *Une société de l'Est du Zaire, les Tusanga depeints par Eux–Mêmes.* Paris: Mémoire de Licence, Ecole Pratique des Hautes Etudes.

Kruuk, H. 1974. *The Spotted Hyena: A Study of Predation and Social Behavior.* Chicago: Univ. of Chicago Press.

Lebaigne, L. 1933. "Sectes Secretes." Administrative report from Albertville, 13 July 1933. Archives of the Sous-Région du Tanganika, Kalemie.

Reefe, T. 1981. *The Rainbow and the Kings: A History of the Luba Empire to 1891.* Berkeley: Univ. of California Press.

Richards, A. 1969. *Land, Labour and Diet in Northern Rhodesia.* London: Oxford Univ. Press.

Roberts, A.F. 1980. "Heroic Beasts, Beastly Heroes: Principles of Cosmology and Chiefship among the Lakeside BaTabwa of Zaire." Ph.D. diss., University of Chicago.

In Preparation "'Comets Importing Change of Times and States': Ephemera and Process among the Tabwa of Zaire." Submitted for publication.

Roberts, C.D. 1980. "*Mungu na Mitishamba:* Illness and Medicine among the BaTabwa of Zaire." Ph.D. diss., University of Chicago.

1981 "*Kutambuwa Ugonjuwa:* Concepts of Illness and Transformation among the Tabwa of Zaire." *Social Science and Medicine*, 15B:309–16.

In Press "Emblems and Imagery: Analysis of a Tabwa Diviner's Headdress." D. Ben–Amos, ed., *Verbal and Visual Arts in Africa.* Bloomington: Indiana University Press.

Sapir, J.D. 1977. "The Anatomy of Metaphor." J. David Sapir and J. Christopher Crocker, eds., *The Social Use of Metaphor: Essays on the Anthropology of Rhetoric.* Philadelphia: Univ. of Pennsylvania Press, 3–32.

1981 "Leper, Hyena, and Blacksmith in Kujamaat Diola Thought." *American Ethnologist*, 8(3):526–41.

Schmitz, R. 1912. *Les Baholoholo.* Anvers: Albert Dewit.

Theuws, T. 1968. "Le Styx Ambigu." *Bulletin du Centre d'Etudes des Problèmes Sociaux Indigènes*, 81:5–33.

Turner, V. 1967. *The Forest of Symbols.* Ithaca: Cornell Univ. Press.

Van Acker, A. 1907. *Dictionnaire kitabwa–francais, francais–kitabwa.* Musée Royal du Congo Belge, annals, series 5, Ethnographie–Linguistique.

Van Avermaet, E., and B. Mbuya. 1954. *Dictionnaire Kiluba–Francais.* Musée Royal du Congo Belge, annales, Sciences de l'Homme, Linguistique.

White, T. 1960. *The Bestiary.* New York: Putnam.

White Fathers. 1954. *Bemba-English Dictionary.* Capetown: Longmans, Green.

8

The Symbolic Roots
of Three Potent Iroquois
Medicinal Plants

James W. Herrick

Introduction

The goal of this chapter is to understand the potency of three medicinal herbs from the perspective of a member of traditional Iroquois culture. Understanding the potency of these three plants will require more than a knowledge of pharmacodynamics. Their potency does not derive from their biochemical properties alone, but rather, is due to their position within the Iroquois cosmology. In short, the basis for their power is largely symbolic and conceptual.

Three Potent Herbs

Lobelia cardinalis (Cardinal Lobelia) is a plant that, to the traditional Iroquois people, is as powerful as its spiked, scarlet flowers are compellingly beautiful. It is found growing in or near the water—in wet places and swamps and along streambanks. The native name for this plant (ʔawɛətaːkəh or "wild flower") is nondescript, giving no clue as to its uses or powers.[1] It is, however, said to be "one of the highest plants." As in the case of anything with much power, it is seen to be capable of effecting both beneficial and harmful results. Keeping it indoors with other herbal medicines may result in their becoming "spoiled." It is best kept outdoors. At the same time, it is believed to strengthen other medicines when mixed with them. Gathering abscesses in the breast, stricture caused by "having connections" with a woman during her menses, canker and fever sores, cramps, cracking and caking

134

breasts, swollen glands on the neck and under the arms, bad stomachs caused by consumption, and epilepsy in both men and women are among the ailments it is said to cure. It may also be used as an emetic "for when someone gives you something bad to eat." Along these same lines, it is thought effective in treating "any pain or trouble caused by witchcraft." Sickness caused by grieving is cured by a medicine having this plant as an ingredient. And it is believed to have the power to compel individuals to carry out acts against their will. Steeped in water, then sprinkled on one's person or on an item one wishes to sell, it will compel another or others to be attracted to you or your wares. Because of this plant's reputed powers, it is not surprising to find it among the ingredients in the powerful "substitute" Little Water Medicine (that is, the LWM made from plants that have been substituted for very rare or no longer existing animal substances).

As the Iroquois name of *Ipomoea pandurata* suggests, the roots of ʔɔkwe ʔokteæʔ (meaning "human roots") resemble the human figure. Common English names include Man Root and Morning Glory. This climbing, tenaciously clinging plant (also called "can twist bushes") is believed to have much magical potency. Native herbalists warn against its being touched by children. If one rubs one's fingers with it and strikes someone, that person will be killed. It is said to have been used by hunters in the past, allowing them to carry two deer with ease. As a medicine, it "gives you strength" and, by virtue of its being a blood purifier, "is good for all kinds of diseases." More specifically, it may be used in the treatment of coughs, liver ailments, headaches, and upset stomachs. And it is said to be good for tuberculosis or coughs with blood. The highly sacred and secret "substitute" Little Water Medicine has this plant listed among its ingredients. Fenton (1936) reports that a decoction of this plant and sunflower seeds is taken by those assembled in the Longhouse during the spring and fall curing rites of the False Faces. Like any other very powerful thing of this world, it may be manipulated by an evil-minded person (a "witch" or ʔotkɔʔ) for the purpose of harming others. Its human-shaped roots make it especially good for such purposes. Finally, it is believed that this plant is so powerful that one may become harmed simply by coming into contact with it. It, in itself, is "witch" (ʔotkɔʔ).

"Big Root" or ʔokteækowanɛs is sometimes called "Bullfrog's Sitting Place." The Latin and common English names for this plant are *Nuphar luteum variegatum* and Yellow Pond Lily, respectively. The roots of this aquatic plant are large and pock-marked. Undoubtedly, this latter characteristic is responsible for its being considered effective against the dreaded smallpox. Other serious illnesses for which this plant is believed to be of curative value include heart trouble, "pains in the chest that make you hold your breath," tuberculosis, epilepsy, swollen abdomens and lungs, fainting in girls said to have "bad blood," and "witchcraft diseases" in general. It is also believed to cause tuberculosis. If its roots are sliced and allowed to stand in cold water, the water may be sprinkled about one's home to drive away troublesome ghosts. Hanging its roots indoors will ward off witches, making blind those that intrude. One may divine the sources of witchcraft by giving a decoction of it and four other plants to someone suspected of such evil practices. If the suspect spits

Table 8.1   Themes Deriving from Events in the Creation Myth

Event	Theme
Sky World	
1. Sky Woman falls to earth	Sky World is prototype of earth life
	Dreams compel fulfillment
	Basic cultural ways brought from Sky World
Earth	
2. Sky Woman gives birth to a female child	
3. Daughter then gives birth to twins	The earth is to be influenced by good and evil
4. Wicked grandmother repudiates Good Twin (Creator)	
5. Father Turtle teaches Good Twin domestic activities	
6. Grandmother and Good Twin bet for control of food supply	Good triumphs over evil, but requires good luck
7. Struggle between Flint and Creator; Flint loses contest of power	Good triumphs over evil; evil can be made to do good through imitation and appeasement; smoke is vehicle to Sky World
8. Creator assigns duties to Moon, Sun, Thunderers, etc.	Spirits in Sky to assist humans
9. Creator and Flint return to Sky World via different paths	Good-minded humans to follow the Creator; evil-minded to follow Flint
Earthly Human Events and Visits by the Creator	
10. Humans multiply, but wander aimlessly; there are no ceremonies	Ceremonial life needed for meaningful existence

out the medicine, raves, and uses foul language, the person is a witch. Like *ʔɔkwe ʔokteæʔ*, this plant is *ʔotkɔʔ* whether or not it is used by an evil-minded person.

The Story of Creation

There exist several versions of the Iroquois creation myth (cf. Hewitt 1903, 1928; Speck 1949; Wallace 1972). Certain cultural themes, however, are found in each (See Table 8.1).

In an earth-like world beyond the sky, Sky Chief, owner of the Tree of Light, dreams that he uproots the Tree and casts down into the hole in the sky dome all living things. His dream is guessed by community members and supernaturals, but to avoid destruction of life, he pushes his pregnant wife (Sky Woman) into the hole and repositions the Tree.

Sky Woman, with basic cultural items in hand, drifts downward through the sky and lands on the back of a huge turtle floating in the earth's primal sea. As she walks about, the earth expands. Now called Earth Woman, she gives birth to a

Table 8.1   continued

Event	Theme
11. Creator gives Four Sacred Rites	Four Sacred Rites please supernaturals; imitation of activities in the Sky World pleases supernatural beings
12. Gift of Stirring Ashes Rite	People must be roused to unite their minds in repeated thanks; they must rejoice at life
13. Gift of the White Dog Sacrifice	Purity needed to communicate with Creator; Tobacco and smoke are vehicles for messages to the Sky World
14. Gift of Thanksgiving Address	All spirit forces require repeated thanks
15. Gift of love/peace	Peace and love needed for uniting minds in repeated thanks
16. People become negligent; disease, social decay	Without ceremonies, life is endangered
17. Rainbow appears; Creator gives Berry and Maple ceremonies; value of love and peace restated	Creator will continue to protect humans; signs given
18. Continued social decay; ceremonies neglected	Flint's influence increases; two divergent paths well established
19. Disease and death travel earth unrestricted	Disease and death are faceless entities created by Flint to destroy humans
20. Creator losing control; provides medicinal herbs as stopgaps; gifts of corn, beans, squash	Herbs used on individual bases to counter Flint's disease and death; easily acquired wild food sources dwindle; humans must work harder to cultivate their sustenance
21. Deaths increase; people become distraught and neglectful	Unclear minds of bereaved interfere with uniting minds in ceremonies; ceremony given to clear minds of bereaved
22. Quiet youth proposes division of humans into groups	Imitation, mutual aid, clans, moieties, love, peace, and clear minds allow humans to perform ceremonies

daughter who, in turn, dies giving birth to twin boys—one (the Creator) is good, the other (Flint) is evil.

While the Creator learns domestic activities from his father and proceeds to create things on the earth and in the sky to assist humans, Flint goes about thwarting his brother's efforts and creating the dangerous and obnoxious things of the world. A contest of power ensues between the brothers. The Creator wins, and Flint concedes to help humans combat his evil creations if they wear masks in his imitation and burn Sacred Tobacco. The brothers return to the Sky World by way of divergent paths in the sky.

The creation story then turns to humans on earth as they encounter and, with the Creator's assistance, overcome the problems that threaten their existence. Much of the Creator's assistance is in the form of rites and ceremonies (Four Sacred Rituals, Stirring Ashes, White Dog Sacrifice; Midwinter, Berry, and Maple ceremonies) which must be performed to thank and please Him and other supernaturals in the

Sky World. The gifts of love and peace are given so that minds may be united in the performance of these ceremonies.

After each of the Creator's visits to earth, the people fall back into a state of ceremonial neglect, making them increasingly vulnerable to the evil creations of Flint. At one juncture, the Creator creates a rainbow to symbolize His continued support for humans. But through repeated ceremonial neglect, Flint gains more control of the earth to the point that the Creator must provide humans with earthly measures for countering disease, starvation, and the sorrow of death. Medicinal herbs are provided, and corn, beans, and squash (with their appropriate ceremonies) are given to supplement dwindling wild food sources. Grief-stricken minds may be cleared through ceremonial means. Finally, to enhance their chances of earthly survival, the Creator (disguised as a quiet boy) suggests that humans imitate the diversity found among animals by dividing themselves up into groups (clans) that may then engage in mutual aid. With this, the story ends. Themes deriving from its events are presented in Table 8.1.

Ceremonies and Rites: The Thanking, Begging, Appeasing, and Renewal Complex

As a result of the actions of the Creator and Flint, the Iroquois people found themselves in the position of having to (1) maintain and renew, through supplication and repeated thanks, the beneficial things and events given to them by the Creator, and (2) honor, beseech, placate, and nurture Flint. These acts could be carried out through any of the interrelated ceremonies and rites that were also given to the people by the Creator. Were these actions not carried out, all that was good on the earth would cease to exist, and the evil works of Flint would come to dominate, resulting in the demise of the Iroquois people (see Table 8.1).

Among the yearly cycle of ceremonies we find: Midwinter (January or February), Our Sustenance and Bush (late winter, early spring), Maple (March), False and Husk Faces (spring), Seed Planting (early May, June), Moon and Sun, After Planting, and Strawberry (June), Raspberry, Green Bean and Thunder (summer), Little and Green Corn (late August, September), Our Sustenance (late summer, early fall), False and Husk Faces (fall), and Harvest (October). These ceremonies are made up of various speeches or invocations, dances, songs, or chants (with drum, rattle, or flute accompaniment), games, drinking, feasting, and specialized acts (e.g., stirring ashes, confession, guessing dreams, sprinkling water on people, feeding). Some of these rites go into forming what have come to be called "medicine societies." The functions of these societies will be discussed later.

For several reasons, analysis will emphasize the rites performed at the Midwinter Ceremony. This ceremony could be considered the most important and inclusive of the regularly scheduled ceremonies. It contains all of the Four Sacred Rituals (Great Feather Dance, Skin Dance, Men's Personal Chants and Bowl Game), as well as nearly every other ritual available for renewing the powers of the entire spectrum of spirit forces in the cosmos. It is also the ceremony at which we find members of the various medicine societies meeting to renew the powers of their respective rites. Finally, it well illustrates the interrelatedness of ceremonial, ritual, and, ultimately, "medical" matters in traditional Iroquois culture. It is in understanding these interrelationships that we will begin to understand the use of medicinal herbs.

To aid in understanding the traditional Iroquoian conception of ceremonial, ritual, and medical matters, activities in Table 8.2 have been divided up into various categories. For example, some ritual activities are "regularly scheduled." Such rites constitute the activities of the ceremonies carried out throughout the year. These activities are of three types: (1) groups of people performing rites for nonhuman spirit forces (GRP/SF); (2) groups performing rites for certain classes or groups of human beings (GRP/GRP); and (3) groups performing rites for individual persons (GRP/IND). Certain other rites are performed as needed, or "on demand." Included here are four types: groups for spirit forces (GRP/SF); (2) groups for human groups (GRP/GRP); (3) groups for individuals (GRP/IND); and (4) individuals for individuals (IND/IND). The column on the far right of Table 8.2 contains various medicinal tools that may be used by individual health-actors as they treat their patients (or victims). It should be noted that herbs are but one of several such tools.

Regularly Scheduled Rites

Many of the scheduled rites comprising the Midwinter ceremony (see *a–m*, Table 8.2) are concerned with renewal through communal thanks and supplication, as well as a general rejoicing at the powers of the entire range of nonhuman spirit forces, with special emphasis on the Creator. But some of these rites (e.g., those carried out by the medicine societies, see *n–w*, Table 8.2) center around remembering, beseeching, placating, and nurturing the powers of certain spirits which, although inherently powerful and potentially harmful, may be transformed into being the benefactors of humans.[2] Included among these spirits are: (1) the medicine animals, such as the Bear, Buffalo, Otter, and Eagle—with the Society of Mystic Animals (*yi:ʔto:s*) centering on remembering, celebrating, appeasing, and feeding the spirits of these powerful animals, including the medicine bundles made from them that constitute the Little Water Medicine; (2) the magic animals, such as the White Beaver, Blue Panther, Great Horned Serpent, the Pygmies, Exploding Wren, Great Naked Bear, and others, and the charms made from them—all of which are "sung for" by members of the Pygmy Society; (3) the linked False and Husk Face societies, with the former representing a wide range of potentially harmful spirits (e.g., Flint, Forest Spirits, Stone Giants, Whirlwind Spirit; see theme 7, Table 8.1) and the latter representing powerful supernatural agriculturalists and spirits of fertility that act as heralds for the wooden False Faces; and (4) the spirits of the dead, which are placated and fed during the Feast of the Dead (Parker 1909).

All of the rites discussed above (*a–w*, Table 8.2) also contain elements that are concerned with a communal celebration or renewal of the existence and powers of

Table 8.2.   The Ceremonial–Ritual–Medical Continuum in Iroquois Culture

	Regularly Scheduled			Performed on Demand				Medicinal Tools
	GRP/SF	GRP/GRP	GRP/IND	GRP/SF	GRP/GRP	GRP/IND	IND/IND	
Longhouse Events: Rites of renewal, thanks, supplication and beseechment								
a. Confession		a^1	a^2	a^3	a^4	a^5	Self-treatment	Herbs
b. Opening Address								Tobacco
c. Stirring Ashes							Lay treatment	Sweat lodges
d. Dream Guessing								
e. Feather Dance								
f. Skin Dance								Fasts
g. Personal Chants							Herbalist	
h. Bowl Game								Feasts
i. Tobacco Invoc.								
j. Eagle Dance								
k. Our Sustenance								
l. Social Dances							Clairvoyant	Speeches
m. Ritual Games		m^1	m^2	m^3	m^4	m^5		

Medicine Societies: Rites of propitiation and renewal

n. Soc. Mystic Animals
o. Little Water Medicine Society
p. Otter Society
q. Bear Society
r. Buffalo Society
s. Eagle Society
t. False & Husk Face Societies
u. Women's Society
v. Pygmy Society
w. Feast of the Dead

Dances

Songs

Ritual objects

Charm holders

Games — LWM Bundle Holders

Animal-derived charms

Plant-derived charms

Magical objects (e.g., stones)

Incantations — Witch

n^1 ——————— n^2 ———— n^3 ———— n^4 ———— n^5

w^1 ——————— w^2 ———— w^3 ———— w^4 ———— w^5

human beings, or certain classes of humans (see a^1–w^1, Table 8.2). These classes of humans and the rites associated with celebrating and renewing the powers of them include the following: the entire nation (as in the case of a communal guessing of an individual's dream involving a very powerful, offended spirit force, cf. Wallace 1972:72, 73); the entire community or society (Thanksgiving Address, Stirring Ashes Rite); chiefs and Faithkeepers (Personal Chant); one's family (Personal Chant, Stirring Ashes); friends (Personal Chant, Eagle Dance, Bowl Game); men (Otter Society); women (Women's Society); the cured (any rite used to cure individuals); those in need of curing at some future time (any of the medicine society rites); and the dead (Feast of the Dead).

Also included under "group for group" activities would be any of the rites of the medicine animal societies (Bear, Buffalo, Eagle, Otter), as well as those performed by the Society of Mystic Animals (SMA). The SMA has as its function the general celebration and renewal of all the cures effected by the medicine animal society rites, or the charms fashioned from them (including Little Water Medicine bundles). Certain of the rites of the SMA also allow those cured by the released power of the Little Water Medicine to renew, through celebration, their cures. So, in addition to remembering, placating, and nurturing the spirits of certain potentially harmful creatures (the medicine animals), the welfare of those who have benefited or will benefit from the powers of these creatures (i.e., the "cured" and "future cured") is also preserved through performing the rites of the various animal medicine societies at Midwinter. The same would hold true for those having been cured by the spirits of the False and Husk Faces (cf. Wallace 1972:81) and the spirits of those magic animals sung for by members of the Pygmy Society.

Just as the entirety of spirit forces in the cosmos (GRP/SF) and certain groups of humans (GRP/GRP) may benefit from various of the regularly scheduled, collectively performed rites of the Midwinter ceremony, so too may individual persons (GRP/IND). Either through a dream or on recommendation by a clairvoyant, an individual may receive curative benefits by attending or participating in the rituals of any one of the medicine societies (see n^2–w^2, Table 8.2), or *any other prescribed rite* (see a^2–m^2, Table 8.2) of the Midwinter ceremony. Foster (1974:154), for example, reports that "the songs of the Skin Dance may be sung without the chanted middle section, as an individual curing rite during the first part of Midwinter." Also, when performed at Midwinter, "[the War Dance] is a cure for a variety of ailments, including vague disposition" (Kurath 1968:50). Even social dances may have curative functions (cf. Wallace 1972:72).

Rites Performed on Demand

The regularly scheduled ceremonies—especially the ones held at Midwinter—recharge, renew, and preserve the divinely given powers of the cosmos, which might then be tapped for assistance throughout the year. However, certain problems could not wait for one of the ceremonial occasions—and so cultural mechanisms developed that could be utilized "on demand" (see Table 8.2)

Few ethnographic examples involving a group of people collectively performing rites for spirit forces "on demand" have been found (see $a^4–w^4$, Table 8.2). One explanation for this is that the spirit forces that would be influenced under such circumstances would already have been sufficiently acknowledged, thanked, and beseeched during parts of the yearly cycle of ceremonies. Furthermore, in the performance of particular rites (e.g., the Opening Address, the Great Feather Dance, the Skin Dance) at the periodic ceremonies, special emphasis is given to the spirit force or forces deemed most important at a particular time of year (cf. Foster 1974:117).

Because the behaviors of the Moon and Sun are fairly stable and predictable, and because the cycle of ceremonies is conducted at various critical times of the year, there are few occasions when these spirit forces are called upon out of a sense of urgency. This is not to say, however, that this is not done for other spirit forces that reside in the sky. In writing about cultivation ceremonies, Waugh (1916:23) reports that ". . . invocations or prayers to the Thunder Men [rain makers] may be offered at any or all of the meetings, i.e., the cultivation ceremonies, as may seem desirable. If the weather is too hot or dry, *special gatherings may be called* for such invocations and are considered highly effective and beneficial" (emphasis added).

Dealing with Spirit Forces "on Demand"

Examples of collective efforts to deal with spirit forces on demand are more clearly in evidence when considering the spirit forces around which the Pygmy Society and Little Water Medicine Society center. Both societies make use of hunting charms or medicine bundles. The charms of the Pygmy Society are useful in effecting cures and good fortune; but, as is true of any powerful event or thing in traditional Iroquois culture, they may also be used in evil ways (i.e., they are "witch"). They may be utilized by evil-minded, jealous, or envious persons (i.e., by witches, the people who have had their minds successfully seduced by Flint) to harm others, or they may act malevolently on their own power. The latter is likely to occur when someone who is in possession of one (or has knowingly or unknowingly inherited an obligation to a charm) has neglected it (i.e., did not "feed" it or did not perform other specific rituals designed to placate it). It might then bring about misfortunes involving a series of serious illnesses or deaths in one's family (Shimony 1970:252, 253). To counter these charm-induced misfortunes, it is necessary to perform a Pygmy Society dance and hold a feast of the Society of Mystic Animals in order to appease and quiet the slighted ("hungry") spirit of the charm.

Another case of a group acting to influence spirit forces on an improvised basis is found in the application of the Little Water Medicine powder. After the powder is applied to an injury or wound by a LWM bundle holder, there is a period of confinement for the patient, followed by a meeting of LWM Society members. They then sing for and "release" the medicine—i.e., they perform a rite that allows the medicine to be effective in curing the patient. The LWM also has to be sung for communally three times a year to renew its powers (see o^1, Table 8.2). As in the case of the Pygmy Society, individual LWM bundle holders are required to please (by singing for and feeding) their bundles several times a year, lest the bundles feel neglected and turn on ("eat") the bundle holders' loved ones. These rites are in addition to the meetings held by LWM Society members to renew the medicine's strength. Ritual obligations to LWM bundles may also be knowingly or unknowingly inherited (Fenton 1979).

Just as scheduled collective efforts intended to influence spirit forces through thanks, beseechment, and placation are indirectly being performed for all humans or classes of humans, so too are the unscheduled efforts. When certain of the scheduled rites are extracted and performed on demand to meet the exigencies of a particular time during the yearly cycle of subsistence activities, it is one's lineage, clan, moiety, village, or nation that will ultimately benefit if these efforts are successful. When medicine society members call a meeting to appease the spirit of some powerful charm that has been neglected or manipulated to harm someone, not only do individuals benefit, but groups or classes of humans as well, such as families.

Group Work on Behalf of an Individual

At the "group for individual" on-demand level (GRP/IND), we find full expression of the flexibility and inventiveness that is built into traditional Iroquois culture. Here, any segment of any Longhouse event (e.g., any of the rites in Table 8.2 in the category *a–m*), a Death Feast, or any of the rituals comprising any of the medicine societies might be used as needed for the benefit of an individual. Upon dreaming about any of the above rituals, or upon the recommendation of a clairvoyant, an individual will organize the performance of these extracted rituals as a medicine for him- or herself (Shimony 1961).

Although a *group* of persons is being used to help an *individual*, the groups themselves benefit from these activities as well. Those who "make friends" (as in the social dances) or unite their minds (as in a ritual event) by participating in this type of "medical" activity gain, just as the family of the individual who helped to sponsor it does.

Individual Work on Behalf of an Individual

We turn now to cases involving an individual being concerned, as necessity demands, with the welfare of an individual (IND/IND). Included here would be (1) self-diagnosis and treatment; (2) a nonexpert (friend or relative) or lay health-actor (cf. Polgar 1963) engaged in the diagnosis and treatment of another person; (3) an "herbalist"; (4) a clairvoyant or fortuneteller, who can communicate with the spirit world; (5) individuals in possession of medicine bundles or charms, who may use them either to enhance the good fortune of themselves or another, or to harm another; and (6) a witch (or "witch doctor," cf. Parker 1928), who becomes engaged in using counter-witchcraft techniques to benefit an individual who has been witched (see Rioux 1951 and Snyderman 1949).

It should be noted that these individual healers do not constitute mutually exclusive categories. A person engaged in self-treatment might also be an herbalist or a clairvoyant; and a charm holder or clairvoyant could, if so inclined, become involved in countering the effects of witchcraft. In order to understand how these individual healers function it is necessary to relate them to various symptoms of misfortune and beliefs regarding their theorized causes. When this is done, we may take a closer look at the the use of both animal- and plant-derived medicines in the hope of understanding the relative potency of each and, more importantly for this chapter, the sources of their potency. Before doing this, however, an attempt should be made to understand the concept of medicine from the traditional Iroquoian point of view.

Traditional Iroquois Conceptions of "Medicine"

In a footnote to his account of the creation story, Hewitt (1928:610, 611) reports the following: "In archaic use the name for medicine is also the name of the mind or soul. It is derived from the verb stem meaning to beg, to crave; as a noun it is the agent of the begging, craving. The agent of the begging, etc., is the soul, and the cause of the craving, etc., is the thing desired by the guardian spirit for the welfare of the body and mind."

Shimony (1961:276) states that "everything about [a] ceremony, each part and the whole is 'medicine' and . . . . if one part is not functioning, the medicine is weakened to that degree." Speck (1949) reports that certain objects may be "medicine" (e.g., feathers in the Eagle Dance), but implies that these objects become medicine only after they have become charged with curative powers through the performance of various ritual acts.

To Parker (1928:9), "medicine was simply the magic necessary to secure certain results; first to bring back to the patient the departed spirits of health; second, to propitiate it for neglect; third, to drive out and placate the evil spirit that had come to cause the trouble." He adds that it was the combination or "formula" of various medical things and events that was responsible for success, not the actual things or events per se.

One definition useful in understanding both Iroquois and many other non-Western conceptions of "medicine" is as follows: medicine involves the exertion or manipulation of the inherent power or life-force (soul) possessed by any person or persons, place, thing, or event for the purposes of maintaining, restoring, or upsetting the inherent, balanced power or life-force of any other person, persons, thing, or event. Using such a definition I have argued (Herrick 1976, 1978) that any communally performed ritual or group of rituals for any purpose could be considered "medical" in nature. Therefore, it could be argued that the term "medicine" in medicine society is misleading. Any Longhouse rite (i.e., *a–m*, Table 8.2) may be performed for the purpose of attempting to restore or maintain balance to the life-force of any person, persons, place, thing, or event. Also, it will be remembered that if the people are unable to unite their minds and perform rites and ceremonies (especially the Four Sacred Rituals) for the Creator, they will lose his protection and risk allowing Flint to increase his control over the earth. Disease is one of Flint's creations. All calendrical rites and ceremonies could, therefore, be considered preventive medicines. Conversely, medicine societies are as religious in nature as Longhouse events are medical.

If a rationale were sought for separating what have come to be called medicine societies (See *n–w*, Table 8.2) from other ritual acts, it would be that the agents of misfortune associated with these societies were, in ancient times, inherently evil or harmful. Gifts from the Creator and the ceremonies and rites designed to ensure the continuance of these gifts and his protection are, on the other hand, inherently good (see Table 8.1).

In discussing traditional Iroquois conceptions of medicine, a word should be said about the special place of water in the Iroquois cosmos. There are numerous references to the lifegiving and life-sustaining powers of water in the myths and legends of the Iroquois, and it cannot be overlooked that water plays a central role in both the preparation (steeping, boiling, scrying) and application (drinking, feeding mushes, applying poultices, spraying, sprinkling) of animal- and plant-derived medicines. Significant, too, is the observation that many of the more powerful medicinal plants are found growing in or near the water.

The impression is received that water, very much like smoke, is regarded as some sort of medium through which spiritual forces may become united with earthly substances.

Even in ceremonial or religious matters, the role of water as a spiritual medium may be observed. Linguistically, for example, the verb root -*at(C)éh-/-at(C)ɛ-* (meaning "to benefit someone through a medicine ceremony") can be transformed into a noun meaning "a medicine ceremony" (*ʔotɛ:shæʔ*) by addition of a nominalizer. However, when this same verb root is combined with a nominalizer and with the verb root meaning "to be in the water" (-*o*-), the noun formed means "he's preparing the ceremony" (*hotésyɔ:ni:h*) (Chafe 1967:42).

Traditional Etiologic Beliefs

Wallace (1972:62) follows Hewitt (1928) in contending that the Iroquois traditionally believed disease could arise from three sources: natural injuries, witchcraft, and unfulfilled desires of the soul. From my own ethnomedical and ethnobotanical fieldwork and the accounts of other ethnographers (most notably Waugh;[3] Parker 1909, 1928; Fenton;[4] Speck 1949; and Shimony 1961, 1970) I have concluded that that the first of these three etiologic categories ("natural injuries") is better understood in terms of the categories "witchcraft" and "taboo violation."

The world of the traditional Iroquois was one dominated by animistic and ani-

Table 8.3.   Symptomatic Severity and Theorized Etiology as Related to Health Actor Used

Theorized Etiology	Severity of Symptom		
	Mild	Serious	Severe
Taboo violation	S / L / H	L / H / C	H / C
Unfulfilled desires	S / L / H	H / C / C	Ch
Contact with *otk*	S / L / H	H / C	C / W / W / Ch
Witchcraft		H / C	C / W / B / Ch	W / W

NOTE: S = Self-treatment; L = Lay treatment; H = Herbalist; C = Clairvoyant (recommends W, B, Ch, or medicine society or Longhouse rites); B = Little Water Medicine Bundle Holder; Ch = Charm Holder; W = Witch (for counterwitchcraft)

matistic beliefs, and involved an interplay of spirit forces that pervaded every living and nonliving thing and event of the cosmos. Unfortunately, the term "natural" in "natural injuries" somehow implies that spirit forces were not involved. This was, and still is, not the case. Accidents and battle wounds could clearly be interpreted as the results of someone's malicious attempt to bring misfortune into another's life. One would be especially vulnerable to witchcraft if the Creator's protection were lost through ceremonial neglect (see Table 8-1). Wounds might also be the result of being out of favor with a spirit force associated with war (the Sun or Thunderers), through neglect of a charm, or by neglecting one's guardian spirit.

A truer indication of native disease etiologic categories is, I believe, represented in Table 8.3. "Taboo violation" is used in the broadest sense of the concept. Any societal or cultural prohibition established by tradition could be included here—be it the killing of a bear or otter without first properly thanking the spirits of these animals; not "feeding" one's hunting charm; not avoiding a "witch" plant; profane singing of sacred songs; ridiculing the False Faces; neglecting to purge one's body in the spring or fall; eating food prepared by a menstruating woman; failing to thank or beseech properly a spirit force; neglecting the ghost of a relative; or failing to properly rejoice at any of the gifts given to humans by the Creator (cf. Stone 1935).

To appreciate the interrelatedness, artificiality, and imposed nature of such etiologic categories, one need only consider that both "not fulfilling one's desires" and "coming into contact with things or events considered evil" constitute violations of taboo. Either goes against a traditionally established cultural prohibition. Having "connections" with a menstruating woman would involve both taboo violation and contact with evil. Dreaming of a False Face or a medicine charm—both of which are evil—would also involve an overlapping of categories. Similarly, unknowingly coming into contact with something that is evil (e.g., a charm buried near one's house) would involve both witchcraft and contact with evil.

More significant than these oftentimes overlapping native etiologic categories are the relationships that obtain between them and the various symptoms of misfortune or illness experienced by individuals. Symptoms, per se, do not automatically suggest a theorized cause, although certain classes of symptoms are more frequently associated with particular etiologic categories than others. To have meaning in terms of diagnosis and treatment, they have to be considered in conjunction with the behavioral history of the unfortunate person. Included here would be such things as previous curative attempts, the contents of dreams, the behaviors of one's close kin, interpersonal relations with fellow societal members, adherence to the ways established by the Creator, participation in various ritual and ceremonial activities, and so forth. Communal and individual behavioral acts are as involved in *acquiring* illness or misfortune as they are in the process of treatment.

Symptomatic Correlates of Native Disease Etiologies

Because "taboo violation" is the most inclusive of the etiologic categories presented in Table 8.3, it is seen to have the widest range of possible symptomatic correlates. Although symptoms associated with violations of the established ways could be severe (if the violation was serious, such as offending a powerful spirit force that then communicated its desire for appeasement to an individual soul), most in this category would be relatively mild in nature. They would involve mild discomfort of short duration, would be localized, and would tend to manifest themselves externally. A child getting diarrhea because its mother had committed adultery, or an adult suffering from chills and fatigue because of bad blood resulting from the failure to purge oneself in the spring and fall, exemplifies these types of symptoms.

Treatments for these milder types of illnesses appear to be more naturalistic and empirical, in that various herbal remedies are more likely to be used in their treatment. It is important to remember, however, that spiritual matters are involved at all levels of treatment for all types of misfortune. The spirits of plants, for example, must always be "reminded of their duties" to humans, and tobacco must always be burned as the spirits are begged for assistance.

The symptoms associated with unfulfilled desires of the soul could conceivably be as varied and as mild as any of those credited to taboo violation (see Table 8.3). Any sort of misfortune or symptoms of any degree of severity could be linked with the symbolic content of any dream, the only limitations being those imposed by the bounds of one's or another's imagination. However, the more serious the symptoms (either in the sense of being more intense or of a longer duration), the more likely the unfulfilled desire would be thought to involve some potentially dangerous spirit force: perhaps one of the medicine/magic animals or a charm fashioned from them, a False Face, or the angry ghost of a family member would be responsible. Any of these would require the performance of appropriate Medicine Society rites (see *n–w*, Table 8.2). In such cases it would be likely to find longstanding wasting diseases, chronic illnesses, depression, chronic anxiety, loneliness, and illnesses of the psychosomatic and psychogenic varieties. These symptoms might also be linked with witchcraft, just as certain symptoms more frequently associated with witchcraft (e.g., sore eyes) might be credited to the desires of a powerful medicine animal (such as sore eyes and the spirit of the Otter; cf. Shimony 1961:272).

In cases involving contact with things or events deemed evil, we are dealing with any of the many troublesome or obnoxious creations of Flint (bats, spiders, insects, dead bodies, poisonous plants, etc.). Also included here are charms made from parts of powerful animals, magical objects (e.g., white stones possessed by the Pygmies), or powerful plants (such as those used in making the "substitute" Little Water Medicine).

Shimony (1970:252), in her discussion of charms associated with the Pygmy Society, reports that "there is a beetle or 'fatal insect' . . . which lodges in the face, neck and spine, and 'eats' through these organs." Statements such as this well illustrate the more serious nature of illnesses thought to be brought about by contacting things or events that are inherently evil. This is not to say, however, that mild symptomatic discomfort could not be attributed to this theorized cause (see Table 8.3). Acne, for example, is thought to be caused by "worms in the face," while "worms in the teeth" account for tooth decay. Generally speaking, however, symptoms attributed to coming into contact with evil things tend to be both of a localized, irritating, annoying nature and of a more serious nature. Boils, cysts, cramps, warts, symptoms of venereal disease, stomach aches, mouth sores, piles, and bad (contaminated) blood would be found here. As discussed above, some of these symptoms would necessarily involve two or more etiologic categories. "Going with" or being kissed by a woman during her menses, for example, involves both a taboo violation and coming into contact with evil. Stricture, or difficulty in urinating, and mouth sores are also linked with these acts.

More serious or severe illnesses might also be credited to contact with an evil thing. In such instances, we would be likely to find False Faces or charms and the powerful spirit forces that they represent being implicated, either by their own actions or by malicious manipulation by a person. Dreams of Pygmies and their charms, the False Faces, or any of the medicine animals might have similar results. In all cases, extremely serious or severe symptoms, including death, would be observed. The tendency, however, would be for symptoms to be more vague and debilitating, and to affect the sick person's entire family. Also included here would be certain behavioral symptoms, such as despondency, laziness, irresponsibility, infidelity, and bad luck in general.

Severe symptoms associated with taboo violation and contact with evil things (directly or through dreams) also characterize illnesses believed to be the result of witchcraft. This is understandable in light of the fact that the concept *ʔotkẹ̃ʔ* refers not only to "evil," but to "witch" as well (Chafe 1967). Vague debilitating illnesses specifically linked with acts of witchcraft include sore eyes, swellings, blindness, paralysis, dizziness, convulsions, insanity, alcoholism, accidents (especially those involving broken bones or deep wounds), loneliness, love sickness, infidelity, and infertility.

Health-Actor Use in Relation to Theorized Etiology and Symptomatic Severity

Unless one has reason to suspect a more powerful or dangerous spirit force to be responsible for one's unfortunate predicament, self-treatment or lay health-actor treatment would be undertaken in cases of mild illness or misfortune (see Table 8.3). Even today, most families will have a member or friend with at least a rudimentary knowledge of the use of certain herbs—herbs that reduce fever; induce sweating, vomiting, urination, or defecation; stop diarrhea; soothe sore throats; expel phlegm; tranquilize; stimulate; cleanse the blood; stop toothache, and so on. If such a person is unavailable, or if the patient's condition is such that a person with expert knowledge of plant medicines is needed, then an herbalist would be called on. Such experts would be sought especially if symptoms were of a more serious nature, with the patient still having no reason to believe that a powerful, neglected or offended spirit force was in any way responsible for the patient's misfortune. If one or more of the plant medicines does not effect a cure, it will be because a powerful spirit force (i.e., one of the spirit forces around which the medicine societies center; see $n-w$, Table 8.2) is hindering its curative action. A curing rite addressed to the suspected spirit force would then have to be carried out by members of the appropriate medicine society (Speck 1949:58).

Self-diagnosis would be possible if, for example, an unfortunate individual's behavioral history included a dream of a powerful or angry spirit force, or if he or she knowingly possessed a charm that is suspected of feeling neglected. Self-diagnosis, however, is not self-treatment. In both cases, the treatment needed would require the rites of a medicine society. The angry, inherently harmful spirit force would have to be appeased.

Should mild symptoms persist after self-treatment, lay health-actor treatment, or treatment by a socially recognized herbalist, then the unfortunate or sick person would most likely consult a clairvoyant. This course of action would be carried out especially if the person had no idea as to the cause of the problem. But it might also be done in order to confirm any of the patient's suspicions based on a self-review of past behaviors. Magical means of diagnosis (e.g., scrying with LWM powder, divining with special plants or tea leaves) would then serve only to reinforce causes discovered as the clairvoyant interrogated the patient for waking and dreaming clues to the malady.

Depending on the behavioral history of the patient, the nature of the symptoms, and the degree of symptomatic severity, the clairvoyant might recommend that an extracted Longhouse or medicine society rite be performed as soon as possible (a^5-w^5,

Table 8.2). The clairvoyant might also recommend that the patient participate in or sponsor a particular rite ($a^2–w^2$, Table 8.2) at the next regularly scheduled ceremonial.

In some cases, the clairvoyant might reveal that the patient is the victim of witchcraft. A person ("witch doctor") might then be recommended for purposes of performing counterwitchcraft, or the clairvoyant might simply divine the identity of the witch so that it could then be sought out and killed by the victim.

Some unfortunate events connected with witchcraft require more immediate, less retaliative, measures. Deep wounds or broken bones resulting from accidents or, in earlier days, warfare, might be treated with Little Water Medicine powder. Under these circumstances, the services of a bundle holder would be called for. Put in water, then sprayed by mouth or sprinkled directly on the wound or fractured bone, the mysterious powder would work its miraculous curative powers.

Use of Plant- and Animal-Derived Medicines within the Ceremonial-Ritual Complex

In general, all plants may be considered earthbound spiritual tools used to assist or supplement the spirits of more powerful spiritual forces that reside in the sky and, ultimately, beyond it. The powers of plants and all other spirit forces are, as discussed earlier, "recharged" during the regularly scheduled ceremonials and rites. Not surprisingly, we find that the Creator has, in his persistent efforts to assist humans, provided each earthbound medicinal tool with structural features signifying its use or uses (see Table 8.1).

Included among the least powerful herbal medicines are the various plants used as spring and fall purgatives. These same plants are sometimes used by those who are to participate in the rites of various ceremonies. Both purified minds (accomplished through rites of confession) and purified bodies are needed in order to successfully communicate with the spirit world—especially with the Creator.

Certain plants are given the name "game medicines." The misfortune being treated or prevented by the use of such medicines would be "poor performance while participating in a game" or "losses" of various games. These medicines (1) give physical strength or endurance to a game participant—with some of these game medicines acting as purifiers of the body; (2) give an advantage to one player over another through magical means; or (3) magically give objects (e.g., peach stones used in the Bowl Game, snowsnakes) special characteristics that will benefit their users. Those that produce an unfair advantage by magical means qualify as "witching" medicines and are among the more powerful game medicines.

Planting medicines are used to help corn and other plants grow, the misfortune in this case being poor crop production. Most of these types of medicines are used on corn. Seeds are soaked in a decoction made from certain herbs. This is believed to increase the corn's vitality, assist in its growth, and protect it from worms, birds, and other creatures (Waugh 1916).

Closely related in function to corn medicines are the weather and fertility medicines. Both are concerned with life-giving and sustaining functions, and may be viewed as being earthbound supplements to the duties of the Moon (growth of plants and children and childbearing), and the Thunderers (rain makers that assist in the growth of plants). The Hanging Fruit (there existing a mystic community of function between childbearing women and fruit-bearing plants; cf. Hewitt 1928:610) and Husk Faces (cf. Fenton 1936:12) are also symbolically linked with fertility among humans.

Herbs used as fertility medicines are primarily concerned with affecting the woman's blood so that conception may occur. This association between blood and fertility conforms to the more general belief that the moon dictates menses and is also involved with childbearing.

Weather medicines are employed as tools to make thunder and, hence, rain. Some are said to make a thundering sound before it rains, while others must be mixed with the bark from trees that have been struck by lightning.

Love medicines are those that may be used to attract someone of the opposite sex. They make one appear to be attractive in general or attractive to a particular person. Plants having ensnaring or catching characteristics, or those that are in themselves extremely beautiful, are used for such purposes. In a sense, the use of love medicines (like some game medicines) constitutes a type of witchcraft in that a person is being compelled, through magical means, to do something against his or her will. Also, there is the possibility of making someone love a person who will never return these feelings. The loneliness and despondency resulting from this malicious act are easily recognized as being the symptoms of witchcraft. As in all cases of witching medicines, there are antilove or antiwitching herbal medicines that may be employed to counter the effects of love medicines.

As discussed earlier, it is the Feast of the Dead that is concerned with the ritual "feeding" and appeasing of ghosts of the dead. There are, however, specific herbal medicines that may be used to ward off bothersome ghosts. Some of these medicines are burned; some are burned, then rubbed under the eyes (especially if the ghosts are keeping a person from sleeping); some are boiled and drunk; some are boiled in water and then sprinkled about the rooms once inhabited by the dead person; some are used in making a wash for the hands and face; and still others work when the roots of the plant are hung in the house. Grief medicines are boiled and drunk to induce vomiting.

Forces of Divination

Clairvoyants may be considered pivotal health-actors in the sense that they can readily bridge the gap between the waking and dreaming (spirit) worlds. A similar role exists for those plants that are used for divination. Plants used in such a way, however, may be used by anyone—just as anyone might attempt to self-interpret dreams. Clairvoyants, because of their special abilities, are simply recognized as being more adept at using plant divination medicines.

A few divination plants simply "make you dream" after your hands and face are washed with a decoction made from their stems or roots. Sometimes one need only place a certain root under one's pillow. More specialized plants can be used to detect bewitchment or something that might be the result of bewitchment, such as unfaithfulness. To detect unfaithfulness, the root of a certain plant is cut lengthwise and the two sections are placed next to each other. Each section is given a name: the wife's or husband's and the suspect's. If, through time, the roots dry and intertwine, suspicions are verified. The same procedure can be used to divine whether or not two people are romantically right for each other. Still other divination plants may be used by the skilled clairvoyant (e.g., by floating certain roots on water in a vessel) for the purposes of detection, diagnosis, or prediction. In all cases, divination plants facilitate contact with the spirit world.

In matters of war and hunting, medicines that ensure "good luck" are used. In ancient times, charms were used for such purposes. As discussed earlier, they were fashioned from parts of magic or medicine animals. The use of such charms and bundles well illustrates the association made in traditional Iroquois culture between factors of good luck, a potential for danger or harm, hunting–warring activities, and the need for especially powerful medicines to supplement the protection given by individual guardian spirits and the Creator.

There are also plants considerably less powerful than charms that are used as hunting medicines. With some of these, a decoction made from roots or leaves is either drunk (to make the hunter vomit) or used as a wash for fishing line, traps, bows, or rifles. Some are said to take away the human scent, some attract animals in a magical way, and others remove the contamination of contact with a menstruating or pregnant woman. To decontaminate hunting tools, the roots of certain plants are put on hot coals and the rifle or bow is held in the resulting smoke. Certain hunting medicines might qualify as antiwitchcraft medicines in that their use may neutralize witchcraft designed to spoil hunting.

Finally, there are those plants that are in themselves considered evil. In keeping with Flint's flair for creating the unpleasant things of this world, such plants are seen to possess the following characteristics: they are thorned or barbed, they have obnoxious odors or tastes, they are poisonous or are thought to be poisonous, or they are seen to grow on graves. These plants, like other things that are inherently evil, may work on their own or may be manipulated by an evil-minded person. Similarly, it is possible to use these plants for good purposes; i.e., to cure symptoms associated with witchcraft.

It is worth noting that many of the more potent Iroquois medicinal herbs are thought to be effective in treating certain of the more serious introduced diseases (e.g., smallpox and tuberculosis) and diseases that have come to be associated with Europeans (e.g., cancer, heart disease, and syphilis). These and other diseases were no doubt seen as but one more indication that Flint was increasing his control over the earth, and that the end of time was drawing nearer. The timely appearance of Handsome Lake at the end of the eighteenth century—the early reservation period and a time of widespread social decay and cultural collapse for the Iroquois people (cf. Wallace 1972)—was clearly the result of the Creator's persistent and patient efforts to once again save the "genuine people" (cf. Wallace 1972) and could be seen as further evidence of the Creator's patience and his persistent efforts to protect the "genuine people" from being completely destroyed by his equally persistent, evil-minded brother (see Table 8.1). Thanks to Handsome Lake, their minds could once again be united in ceremony. And, once again, they would survive.

Conclusion

If the reader has understood how the traditional Iroquois conceived of the cosmos and the workings of various things and events in it, it will immediately become obvious why the three plants described at the beginning of this chapter may be considered among the most powerful. It should be kept in mind, however, that herbal medicines are but one small part of a whole series of individually and collectively performed acts designed either to maintain, *restore,* or, in some cases, upset the good fortune or good health of a person, persons, place, thing, or event. It is the sum total of all such acts that constitutes the medical system of the traditional Iroquois people.

NOTES

1. All native words used are of the Seneca language, following Chafe (1967).
2. Each medicine society will also have a legend regarding its origin. Some of these are included in Hewitt and Curtain (1918).
3. Unpublished field notes, 1933–1942.
4. Unpublished field notes, 1912–1918.

REFERENCES

Chafe, Wallace L. 1967 *Seneca Morphology and Dictionary*. Washington, D.C.: Smithsonian Press.
Fenton, William N. 1936 "An Outline of Seneca Ceremonies at Coldspring Longhouse." *Yale University Publications in Anthropology*, 9:3–23.
1940 *Masked Medicine Societies of the Iroquois*. Washington, D.C.: Smithsonian Institution Annual Reports, no. 3624.
1953 *The Iroquois Eagle Dance: An Offshoot of the Calumet Dance*. Bureau of American Ethnology Bulletin, no. 156.
1962 "This Island, the World on the Turtle's Back." *Journal of American Folklore*, 75:283–300.
1963 "The Seneca Green Corn Ceremony." *Conservationist*, 18:20–22.
1979 "The 'Great Good Medicine'." *New York State Journal of Medicine*, 79:1603–1609.

Foster, Michael K. 1974 *From the Earth to Beyond the Sky: An Ethnographic Approach to Four Longhouse Speech Events.* Mercury Series, Ethnology Division, paper no. 20. Ottawa: National Museum of Man, National Museums of Canada.

Herrick, James W. 1976 "Placebos, Psychosomatic and Psychogenic Illnesses and Psychotherapy: Their Theorized Cross-Cultural Development." *Psychological Record,* 26:327–42.

    1977 "Iroquois Medical Botany." Ph.D. diss. SUNY Albany.

    1978 "Powerful Medicinal Plants in Traditional Iroquois Culture." *New York State Journal of Medicine,* 78:979–87.

Hewitt, J.N.B. 1903 *Iroquoian Cosmology,* First Part. Bureau of American Ethnology Annual Report, 1899–1900.

    1928 *Iroquoian Cosmology,* Second Part. Bureau of American Ethnology Annual Report, 1925–1926.

Hewitt, J.N.B., and J. Curtain. 1918 *Seneca Fictions, Legends, and Myths.* Bureau of American Ethnology Bulletin, no. 32.

Kurath, G.P. 1968 *Dance and Song Rituals of Six Nations Reserve, Ontario.* National Museum of Canada Bulletin 220, Folklore Series 4. Ottawa: Department of the Secretary of State.

Parker, Arthur C. 1909 "Secret Medicine Societies of the Seneca." *American Anthropologist,* 11:161–85.

    1913 *The Code of Handsome Lake, the Seneca Prophet.* New York State Museum Bulletin 163.

    1928 *Indian Medicine and Medicine Men.* Toronto: Archeological Report of the Minister of Education, Annual Reports.

Polgar, Steven. 1963 "Health Action in Cross-Cultural Perspective." H.E. Freeman, S. Levine, and L.G. Reader, eds., *Handbook of Medical Sociology.* Englewood Cliffs, N.J.: Prentice-Hall, 397–419.

Rioux, M. 1951 "Some Medical Beliefs and Practices of the Contemporary Iroquois Longhouses at Six Nations Reserve." *Journal of the Washington Academy of Sciences,* 41:152–58.

Shimony, A.A. 1961 *Conservatism among the Iroquois at the Six Nations Reserve.* New Haven: Yale Univ.

    1970 "Iroquois Witchcraft." D. Walker, ed., *Systems of North American Witchcraft and Sorcery,* 239–265. Moscow: Univ. of Idaho Press.

Snyderman, G.S. 1949 "The Case of Daniel P.: An Example of Seneca Healing." *Journal of the Washington Academy of Sciences,* 39:217–20.

Speck, Frank, 1949 *Midwinter Rites of the Cayuga Longhouse.* Philadelphia: Univ. of Pennsylvania Press.

Stone, E. 1935 "Medicine among the Iroquois." *Annals of Medical History,* 6:529–39.

Tooker, Elisabeth. 1970 *The Iroquois Ceremonial of Midwinter.* Syracuse: Syracuse Univ. Press.

Wallace, Anthony F.C. 1958 "Dreams and Wishes of the Soul: A Type of Psychoanalytic Theory among the Seventeenth Century Iroquois." *American Anthropologist,* 60:234–48.

    1972 *The Death and Rebirth of the Seneca.* New York: Vintage.

Waugh, F.W. 1916 *Iroquis* [sic] *Foods and Food Preparation.* Canada Department of Mines, Geological Survey, Memoir 86. Ottawa: Government Printing Bureau.

9

Physiology and Symbols: The Anthropological Implications of the Placebo Effect

Daniel E. Moerman

How can we account for the effectiveness of non-Western medical treatment? What can we learn about the effectiveness of Western healing through comparative study?

One of the foremost dilemmas in ethnomedicine is understanding how it is that the manipulations of the shaman or healer actually influence the physiological state of the patient. Many studies, including several of my own, have devoted much energy to the study of the effectiveness of native pharmacology. The standard exercise is to show that pharmaceuticals in use have "appropriate" physiological impact. And many tribal peoples cooperate with this exercise by having at their disposal enormous pharmacopoeias; Wyman and Harris (1941) reported 515 species of medicinal plants for the Navaho alone as long ago as 1941. My dictionary of native American medicinal plants includes 1288 different plant species from 531 different genera from 118 different families used in 48 different cultures in 4869 different ways (Moerman 1977). In a less standard exercise, comparing those medicinally *used* plants with *available* plants, I have been able to demonstrate substantial selectivity among families by native Americans. The three most heavily utilized families (Asteraceae, Rosaceae, Ranunculaceae) account for 29 percent of medicinal items in my dictionary, but only 15.9 percent of the genera in the Flora North America list of some 17,000 species (Shetler and Skog 1978). The three *least* heavily used families, in terms of their availability (Poceae, Orchidaceae, Acanthaceae), account for 1 percent of items in my dictionary, but 12 percent of genera in FNA (Moerman 1979). But we can also be certain that neither native therapists nor their patients saw pharmaceuticals as any more important in therapy than the song, dance, and din that accompanied treatment. While several investigators (most notably Victor

156

Turner) have provided brilliant symbolic analyses of these more dramatic aspects of treatment, few have attempted to understand the healing quality of such symbolic dimensions to treatment.

This bimodal quality of native treatment often baffles Western observers. One notes approvingly the intelligent study, the deliberate consideration, and the long empirical tradition employed as the Navaho healer gathers 30 or 40 herbal medicines—many of them "rational," "effective" drugs. But despair follows, when the subsequent infusion is fed to and washed over the patient—*and* a half dozen singers and friends who are participating in the ritual. What kind of effectiveness is this? The Navaho healing ritual, focused on a sweat–emetic rite, coupled with chants and beautiful sandpaintings, is said by Reichard to be like "a spiritual osmosis in which the evil in man and the good of deity penetrate the ceremonial membrane in both directions, the former being neutralized by the latter" (Reichard 1970:112). Such a rich metaphorical structure, part of the whole Navaho cosmological system, is simultaneously healing and barely intelligible to Western "biomedical" understanding.

Bimodal Quality of Western Biomedicine

Yet there is an impressive array of evidence of similar processes, with similar effects, in our medical practice. This bimodality in treatment is probably universal. My argument is that the *form* of medical treatment as well as its content can be effective medical treatment, that medical treatment must be understood bimodally, in terms of both its specific and general dimensions, and that we have only a rudimentary capacity for simultaneously understanding both modes.

In Western medical and surgical contexts, what I refer to as general medical therapy is usually referred to as the "placebo effect." Various investigators (Beecher 1961; Frank 1975:195) attribute between 35 percent and 60 percent of the effectiveness of contemporary biomedicine to this placebo effect. In the shaman's context, some investigators attribute *all* effectiveness to general medical therapy, although this clearly devalues empirical pharmacological traditions dating back to Middle Paleolithic times (Solecki 1975).

Even though the general effectiveness of treatment is recognized occasionally as a substantial component of the healing process, biomedicine founders in its attempts to account for the phenomenon. This follows, I believe, from the naive dualism of contemporary medical science, which characteristically assumes a fundamental mind–body dichotomy in its conceptualization of the human organism. And since disease is an affliction of the "body," whereas perception (of treatment) is an aspect of the "mind," and since the only available mediators of this dichotomy are as ineffable and "unscientific" as the "soul," biomedicine tends simply to ignore, or even deny, the significance of general medical therapy (see Engel 1977).

Even in neuroendocrinology, where recent ingenious work (important enough to warrant a clutch of Nobel prizes) has shown that the hypothalamus, a central portion of the brain, is simultaneously a central portion of the endocrine system (the "body"), authors insist on maintaining this naive dualism; the hypothalmic neurons that produce hormones (which regulate pituitary function) are routinely called "transducer cells" (Wurtman 1971).

There is a wide range of phenomena that compels us to reject this dualism. In addition to the findings of neuroendocrinology, we might mention phenomena as diverse as "psychosomatic" illness, biofeedback (Stoyva et al. 1972), host–pathogen interaction (Solomon 1969), Eastern meditative techniques (Datey et al. 1969), and, just for fun, fire handling (Brown 1976; Kane 1976). General medical treatment as I have defined it falls within this class, wherein conceptual, meaningful, cultural, categorical events influence physiological process.

Anthropologist James Fernandez has eloquently demonstrated the power of the metaphor, a "strategic predication" that can move us, that is, change our behavior (Fernandez 1971:43). I argue that metaphor can heal, that meaning mends. I will consider in some detail one case where we can see some consequences of meaningful human performance in Western biomedicine.

Placebo Surgery

One of the most common causes of death in the United States is myocardial infarction, or heart attack. The traditional biomedical understanding of this disease is that it is caused by ischemia, or local anemia, which is caused by atherosclerosis, a buildup of lipids or fatty tissues in the coronary arteries. The heart attack is typically understood to be caused by thrombosis, that is, blockage of the narrowed artery by a blood clot. Heart muscle, deprived of oxygenated blood, dies; the heart goes into fibrillation, and the patient dies.

In milder forms, coronary arteriosclerosis may cause angina pectoris, a crushing pain beneath the sternum, radiating out over the left side of the body. Small doses of nitroglycerine dissolved under the tongue provide dramatic and rapid relief from the severe pain of angina; this has been the medical treatment of choice for over 100 years. Curiously, no one seems to know how nitroglycerine works. The drug has a potent relaxing effect on smooth muscle tissue, notably of the blood vessels; it rapidly reduces blood pressure. However, there is no clear agreement as to how this relates to the analgesic quality of the drug (Nickerson 1970).

Angina pectoris, a grave and dangerous disease, is highly responsive to inert treatment. This is all the more surprising since the theory of sclerotic arteries and random blood clots, what one can think of as the "rusty plumbing" theory of heart disease, would seem to leave little place for such unlikely findings. Benson and McCallie have recently reviewed the literature on placebo effectiveness in angina (1979). Examining the histories of a series of treatments subsequently demonstrated to be inactive and then abandoned, they note a consistent pattern: "The initial 70 to 90 per cent effectiveness in the enthusiasts reports decreases to 30 to 40 per cent 'base-line' placebo effectiveness in the skeptics' reports" (Benson and McCallie 1979:1424). Thus, for this grave disease, skeptics can heal 30 to 40 percent of their patients with inert medication; enthusiasts, 70 to 90 percent. Either case, given the existing theory of rusty plumbing, seems remarkable!

The logic of this theory has yielded several other interesting approaches to angina. The surgical metaphor, by analogy with the manipulation characterized by splinting limbs, removing broken teeth, or cleaning wounds, is a powerful one for a people confident of the physical basis of illness. The placebo consequences of surgery were noted 20 years ago by Beecher (1955, 1961) and have recently been elaborated by Frank (1975). And, in recent years, a number of more heroic surgical procedures have been developed to deal with angina. Since the problem (pain, and ultimately infarction) is presumed to be due to a constricted blood supply, why not reroute some blood supplies, "bypassing" the constricted areas and "revascularizing" the muscles at risk? Several indirect revascularization techniques involving rerouting various arteries were developed, in the 1930s by Beck, and in the 1940s by Vineburg (Meade 1961:480–515). Although Beck's procedure attained modest popularity, the first widely used surgical approach to angina was the bilateral internal mammary artery ligation (BIMAL). The internal mammary arteries arise from the aorta and descend just inside the front wall of the chest, ultimately supplying blood to the viscera. Following anatomical research by Fieschi, an Italian surgeon, which indicated connections between various ramifications of these arteries and the coronary circulation, several other Italian surgeons developed a procedure in which the arteries were ligated below the point where branches diverge to the myocardium in order to enhance this flow and supplement the blood supply. The operation was first performed in the United States by Robert Glover and J. Roderick Kitchell in the late 1950s (Glover 1957; Kitchell et al. 1958). It was quite simple, and since the arteries are not deep in the body, could be performed under local anesthesia. The physicians reported symptomatic improvement (ranging from slight to total) for 68 percent of their first sample of 50 patients, in a 2-to-6-month follow-up. The operation quickly gained some popularity.

But, in part due to its simplicity, it was not to last. Two research teams independently carried out double-blind studies comparing the BIMAL with a sham procedure, in which the entire operation was carried out except that the arteries were not ligated (Cobb et al. 1959; Dimond et al. 1960). In both studies, patient follow-up evaluation was carried out by cardiologists unaware of which patients had been ligated and which had not. In both studies the nonligated patients reported the same substantial subjective relief from angina as ligated patients (see Table 9.1). Most patients, ligated or not, reported substantially reduced need for nitroglycerine. Both studies concluded that the results of the operation could be accounted for by placebo effects, and therefore should be discontinued.

In sum, the surgery did not work for the reasons that it was done, and it quickly disappeared from the surgeons' repertoire. The question for *us* is, how *did* it work? How did it relieve this severe systemic pain?

A major breakthrough in the surgical approach to angina came in the 1960s with the development of "direct" revascularization, in which veins from elsewhere in the body (now routinely the saphenous vein from the leg) are grafted directly into the aorta and then into the appropriate coronary arteries beyond their obstruction.

Table 9.1.   Improvement of Patients Undergoing Actual and Sham Surgery

| Improvement | Study Number | | | | | | | | |
| | Ligated | | | | | Sham | | | |
	1	2	3	Row No.	Total Percent		2	3	Row No.	Total Percent
Substantial	29	5	9	43	66		5	5	10	83
Slight	15	3	4	22	34		2	0	2	17
Total	44	8	13	65	100		7	5	12	100

SOURCES: Study 1: Kitchell et al. 1958 (44 patients under 70 years of age: substantial improvement = "asymptomatic" or "moderate improvement"); Study 2: Cobb et al. 1959 (substantial improvement = subjective improvement > 40%); Study 3: Dimond et al. (substantial improvement = subjective improvement > 50%).

NOTE: Statistics for row totals (underscored): chi square = 1.3935; significance = .2378.

Contemporary Use of Coronary Bypass Surgery

While it is hard to know exactly how many of these operations are done, various estimates suggest that between 80,000 and 100,000 are now performed annually, at a cost of between $10,000 and $15,000 each; coronary bypass is at least a billion-dollar-a-year business. Although the operation has become very popular, it remains highly controversial. Many surgeons are, clearly, deeply committed to the tremendous value of the procedure. Its logic is obvious, its effects dramatic.

Numerous studies indicate that the operation is highly successful, reducing symptoms (i.e., pain) in 80–90 percent of patients with severe stable angina pectoris. However, there are other measures of the effectiveness of such a procedure. A recent review by Ross considered symptom reduction, improved ventricular function (based on exercise electrocardiogram), and increased survival time; "Symptomatic improvement is present in 85% of patients, but ventricular function is improved in only 20% at most" (Ross 1975:500). Neither Ross nor anyone else (including the large-scale Veteran's Administration study [Murphy et al. 1977]), has been able to demonstrate that the procedure extends life except perhaps for those patients with chronic stable angina and occlusion of the left main coronary artery (Murphy et al. 1977: 621). One large study has shown that, although the operation clearly alleviates symptoms, it has little rehabilitative effect on patients. Among 350 patients studied, "There was no improvement in return to work or hours worked after surgery" (Barnes et al. 1977).

But the most interesting aspect of coronary artery bypass surgery is that several authors have noted that "some patients undergoing coronary artery bypass have improvement of angina despite the fact that all grafts are occluded" (Gott et al. 1973:30). A recent study examined 446 bypass patients who underwent coronary arteriography subsequent to their surgery. Of these, 54 had no functioning, patent grafts. Both groups displayed similarly impressive functional improvement. The authors conclude that coronary bypass surgery patients "experience impressive symptomatic improvement regardless of completeness of revascularization . . . [and] the late survival of unsuccessful revascularization patients is more favorable than pre-dicted from previous natural history data. [This] suggests that factors other than coronary bypass surgery may play a role in the long-term survival of coronary artery disease patients undergoing surgery" (Vlades et al. 1979).

Ross, in the review cited earlier, concludes, gently enough, that "the situation is complex and . . . increased blood flow to the ischemic [occluded] area is not the only possible explanation for symptomatic improvement" (Ross 1975:503). Other explanations have been proposed, including the notions that surgery actually causes minor myocardial infarction in the angina-producing region (that is, causes a "heart attack"), or that surgery denervates the angina-producing region.

Why Does Coronary Bypass Surgery Work?

This means that although the surgery works, *it does not necessarily work for the reasons that it is done.* The rationality of the procedure is apparently unconnected with its effectiveness. In the 1880s, when James Mooney analyzed the use of a series of Cherokee drugs, he concluded, "'We must admit that much of their practice is correct, however false the reasoning by which they have arrived at this result" (1891:328). The same would appear to be the case for coronary bypass surgery.

How can cutting two little incisions over the second intercostal space alleviate the pain of the angina pectoris? How can coronary bypass patients with occluded grafts experience this profound relief? The logic of these procedures is persuasive, if erroneous. And it is this logic that is propounded to the patient by the surgeon. And, thereby, an obvious remaining explanation for the effectiveness of bypass surgery, or BIMAL, is general or placebo effectiveness. Bypass surgery, especially, is, from a patient's point of view, a cosmic drama, following a most potent met-aphorical path. The patient is rendered unconscious. His heart, source of life, fount of love, wracked with pain, is *stopped!* He is, by many reasonable definitions, dead. The surgeon restructures his heart, and the patient is reborn, reincarnated. His sacrifice (roughly $10,000) may hurt as much as his incisions. Remembering that angina can be a remarkably stable, nonfatal condition (see Gott et al. 1973:7–15 on "patient selection") and considering the substantial subjective components in pain iself, it seems reasonable to conclude that the general metaphorical effects of this surgery are at least as decisive in its anomalous effectiveness as are graft-patency rates (Frank 1975).

Recent research on the etiology of coronary artery disease has shown that angina and infarction may be caused by coronary artery spasms (Maseri et al. 1978), which may in turn be caused by neurological impulses or emotional stress. Angina and heart attacks, then, are not random mechanical events, but are rather the results of neurological or mental processes—the system is a complex one open to cortical influence, increasing our confidence that it is subject to symbolic influences.

In modern Western biomedicine as well as in tribal healing, whether by design or default, the *form* of medical treatment, internal or surgical, can be effective medical treatment. Recall the characteristic American medical treatments of the period immediately preceding the biomedical revolution of the 1880s: most conditions were treated with calomel (mercurous chloride), a powerful purgative, or with venesection, minimally a symbolic operation, the laying on of steel (Shryock 1966:245). These two treatments probably had some specific physiological impact. Such stress might trigger a general immunological response. But in all likelihood it was the dramatic, general, metaphorical elements in these treatments that were decisive in any effectiveness the physician had. Such effectiveness adheres to modern treatment.

Healing and Philosophy

We have no generally accepted theoretical paradigm within which we can evaluate and interpret such human experience. Even the growing literature on holistic medicine seems essentially empirical, cataloging experience on biofeedback, host–pathogen interaction, stress and illness, and so on (Pelletier 1977). And consonant with that empiricism is a kind of religiosity: those who venture beyond the empirical seem almost inevitably to begin speaking mythopoetically of archetypes, gods, or souls (Hillman 1964). Even the more scholarly of them, we feel, are straining against the temptation to break into song.

Dualism

This follows, I think, from a naive dualism, the ethnometaphysic of our time. With a thinking and unextended mind, and an unthinking and extended body, in Descartes' formulation, there is no ground for interaction of these human quanta, or onta, save some ephemeral mystical spiritual soul (Stent 1975).

Philosophical attempts to resolve this dilemma come in many forms, one as likely as the next, each one reasonable in its own terms, each one fundamentally flawed in terms of the others. Idealism and behaviorism are two most powerful monisms, denying one or the other of our quanta. Although idealism resolves the mind–body dilemma by denying body, it also denies the reality of the external world; solipsism seems too high a price to pay for this solution. Behaviorism resolves the dilemma by denying mind, by denying mental life. Among the strongest of such positions is that taken by the philosopher J.J.C. Smart: "When I 'report' a pain, I am not really reporting anything. . . , but am doing a sophisticated sort of wince" (Smart 1959:11). Such a position denies the existence of an autonomous inner life, not to mention the possibility of culture.

Among several more sophisticated varieties of dualism are parallelism and interactionism, and several combinations. They are similarly flawed; for a classic philosophical dogfight on the matter, see *Consciousness and the Brain* (Globus et al. 1976).

Person Theory

The most interesting recent philosophical consideration of this problem is, I think, Brody's (1977) defense of Strawson's (1958), Kenny's (1973), and Grene's (1976) "person theory." This persuasive theory simultaneously meets many of the challenges of the standard philosophical positions, and can be extended to meet many of the concerns of the anthropologist. It is one philosophical position in this debate that has a central role for culture. At the risk of oversimplifying, I will briefly summarize Brody's argument, and indicate how it meets the anthropological requirements of a cultural epistemology, and how it provides a framework for understanding what I have called general medical therapy.

Denying the primitive qualities of the quanta "mind" and "body," this theory asserts that there are two kinds of entities, "material bodies" and "persons," to which two kinds of predicates, "mental" and "physical," can be attached. "Material bodies can correctly have ascribed to them only physical predicates, while persons can have applied to them both physical and mental predicates" (Brody 1977:93). Thus, the two "I's" in the sentence "I am happy that I am six feet tall" refer to the same "person." The critical logical feature of this position is that "the concept of person is more basic than the physical and mental predicates ascribed to it" (ibid.); this is a unitary conceptualization of the human organism, which does not have to account for either of those quanta in terms of the other, yet lets us talk about humans in an intuitively familiar manner. In this formulation, "persons" are understood as animals possessing the capacity to use symbols in special ways, specifically in structuring experience, and generally in participating in culture, an anthropological commonplace. In this context, there is no longer in principle an anomaly in understanding how performance can influence physiological state:

> If being a dweller within culture is a special way of being an animal, it should not be anomalous if this characteristic were found to influence other animal capacities— including the capacities to undergo changes in bodily status and function. Experiencing symptom change due to the placebo effect is therefore the bodily expression of the person's participation in the healing context as a culturally determined, symbolic phenomenon [Brody 1977:102–3].

Let me restate this position in general terms. To be a person is to have a mind. To have a mind means that one is able to use symbols. Symbols are most evident in language. Private symbols are impossible in the same sense that private language is impossible—were it private, it would not be language. Therefore, being a person is essentially a *social* phenomenon and requires the prior existence of other persons. (I note parenthetically that the quantum "person" need not even be confined to one individual body [Crocker 1976]). "The ability to use [mental] predicates self-referentially follows from the ability to use them at all" (Brody 1977:111), that is, to use them regarding others. Hence, self-consciousness is a differentiating process, a process of noting meaningful contrasts, of noting differences that make a difference, not merely an indexing or naming process. Considering the process where a person makes determinations about health, we can perhaps, following Kleinman (1973), equate "disease" with "difference," and "illness" with "a difference that makes a difference," that is, a meaningful difference. It is at this point in the process that diagnosis, either by the patient (based on widely shared symbolic norms) or by the healer (based on more private, or more technical or more sophisticated sacred norms), becomes critical. For it is at this point that the inchoate disease becomes a meaningful quantum illness, hence understandable, and, within the limits of animal mortality, finally controllable. And likewise for the treatment of illness through performance, remembering Fernandez (1971), medical metaphors are those strategic mental predications that can "move" us, that is, apply physical predications, in a process we call "healing."

Objections

Consider a curious and poetical objection in a recent essay by Erde, a philosopher of medicine. He contrasts some contemporary dualisms with a variation of this person theory in a sort of double *reductio ad absurdum* proof. He argues that dualism commits us to much that is incredible, a position with which I would agree. But he further argues that the unitary position does likewise: it

> implies that the body is animate . . . [I]f the body is also a character within the drama, if we personify the body and it becomes an agent unto itself, we might understand that it could produce physical illness from within . . . . the implication is that what we call "bodily illness" may be meaningful in the sense made current by Freud regarding neuroses, dreams, and slips of the tongue . . . . [I]f a man is a unity, somatic illness is as meaningful as any illness . . . and should be understood by the sick individual and the physician perhaps even before it is determined whether it should be treated by . . . secondary material means . . . [Erde 1977:187, 189].

This, Erde concludes, is "incredible."

It seems to me to be eminently credible, and even, from an anthropological and semiotic point of view, properly intuitive.

Medical Therapy, Specific and General

From this perspective, I propose these somewhat more formal definitions of specific and general medical therapy. Specific therapy is that healing activity influencing the physical predicates of persons; general therapy is that influencing (wittingly or otherwise) the mental predicates of persons. Such a view places these alternative experiences on an equal ontological footing, compatible and comparable in effect. It also affords a guide to clear talk *about* such experiences. Thus the sentence "I feel better: I have less heart pain" breaks down into "I feel better because I have more blood in my myocardium and because I have a restructured heart." The relative impact of these two predicates on the subject is, in any individual case, open to analysis, and, before the fact, each is open to manipulation, control, and skill.

Of course, this does not solve the problem of general effectiveness in detail, any more than it does for specific effectiveness; how a given drug precisely influences a given organ is a complex research question and the same may be expected in understanding the particular influence of any general therapy. But it *does* mean that there is no obstacle *in principle* to understanding such effectiveness through properly designed studies. Recent studies by Levine and others implicating endorphins in placebo analgesia are a brilliant beginning in this research (Levine et al. 1978).

Such studies could have great anthropological significance, since they could provide the context for confronting a much more fundamental problem. When one human (a healer) draws on the codified empirical experience and the moral and meaningful imperatives of his culture in order to manipulate the physical and mental predicates influencing the personal well-being of another (a patient), we face directly an intimate locus of the most general anthropological concern for understanding human beings as simultaneously organic and symbolic beings. And if health is somehow reflected in fitness, in relative reproductive efficiency, we are on the verge of a theory of the evolution not of medicine, but of the human capacity itself.

Meaning mends. Study meaning, and we learn about mending. But study mending, and we might learn about meaning. These are some of the implications of the study of physiology and symbols.

REFERENCES

Barnes, Glenda K., et al. 1977. "Changes in Working Status of Patients Following Coronary Bypass Surgery. *Journal of the American Medical Association,* 238:1249–52.

Beecher, H.K. 1955. "The Powerful Placebo." *Journal of the American Medical Association,* 159:1602–6.

1961   "Surgery as Placebo." *Journal of the American Medical Association,* 176:1102–7.

Benson Herbert, and David P. McCallie. 1979. "Angina Pectoris and the Placebo Effect." *New England Journal of Medicine,* 300(25): 1424–29.

Brody, Howard Allen. 1977. "Persons and Placebos: Philosophical Dimensions of the Placebo Effect." Ph.D. diss. Michigan State University, East Lansing. Ann Arbor: Univ. of Michigan Microfilm.

Brown, Carolyn Henning. 1976. "Ritual Power and Danger: Hindu Firewalking in Fiji." Paper presented at the Annual meeting of the American Anthropological Association, Washington, D.C.

Cobb, L.A., G.I. Thomas, D.H. Dillard, K.A. Marendino, and R.A. Bruce. 1959. "An Evaluation of Internal Mammary Artery Ligation by a Double Blind Technic." *New England Journal of Medicine,* 260:1115–18.

Crocker, J. Christopher. 1976. "The Mirrored Self: Identity and Ritual Inversion among the Eastern Bororo." *Ethnology,* 15:129–45.

Datey, K.K., S.N. Deshmukh, and C.P. Dalvi. 1969. " 'Shavasan': A Yogic Exercise in Management of Hypertension." *Angiology,* 20:325.

Dimond, E.G., C.F. Kittle, and J.E. Crockett. 1960. "Comparison of Internal Mammary Artery Ligation and Sham Operation for Angina Pectoris." *American Journal of Cardiology,* 5:483–86.

Engel, George. 1977. "The Need for a New Medical Model: A Challenge for Biomedicine." *Science,* 196:129–36.

Erde, Edmund L. 1977. "Mind–body and Malady." *Journal of Medicine and Philosophy,* 2:177–90.

166   PART TWO • SYMBOLS AND HEALING

Fernandez, James. 1971. "Persuasion and Performances: Of the Beast in Every Body . . . and the Metaphors of Everyman." *Daedalus,* 110:39–60.

Frank, Jerome. 1975. "Psychotherapy of Bodily Illness: An Overview." *Psychotherapy and Psychosomatics,* 26:192–202.

Globus, Gordon G., Grover Maxwell, and Irwin Savodnik. 1976. *Consciousness and the Brain: A Scientific and Philosophical Inquiry.* New York: Plenum.

Glover, Robert P. 1957. "A New Surgical Approach to the Problem of Myocardial Revascularization in Coronary Artery Disease." *Journal of the Arkansas Medical Society,* 54:223–34.

Gott, Vincent L., J.S. Donahoo, R.R. Brawley, and L.S. Griffith. 1973. "Current Surgical Approaches to Ischemic Heart Disease." *Current Problems in Surgery,* no. 10.

Grene, Marjorie. 1976. " 'To Have a Mind. . .' " *Journal of Medicine and Philosophy,* 1:177–99.

Hillman, James. 1964. *Suicide and the Soul.* New York: Harper & Row.

Kane, Stephen. 1976. "Holiness Fire Handling: A Psychophysiological Analysis." Paper presented at the annual meeting of the American Anthropological-Association, Washington, D.C.

Kenny, A.J.P., H.C. Longuet–Higgins, J.R. Lucas, and C.H. Waddington. 1973. *The Development of Mind.* Edinburgh: University Press.

Kitchell, J.F., R.P. Glover, and R.H. Kyle. 1958. "Bilateral Internal Mammary Ligation for Angina Pectoris." *American Journal of Cardiology,* 1:46–50.

Kleinman, Arthur. 1973. "Medicine's Symbolic Reality." *Inquiry,* 16:206–13.

Kleinman, Arthur, and L.H. Sung. 1976. "Why Do Indigenous Practitioners Successfully Heal? A Follow Up Study of Indigenous Practice in Taiwan." Paper presented at the Workshop on the Healing Process, Michigan State Univ., East Lansing, April.

Levine, J.D., N.C. Gordon, and H.L. Fields. 1978. "The Mechanisms of Placebo Analgesia." *Lancet,* (2):654–57.

Maseri, Attilio, et al. 1978. "Coronary Vasospasm as a Possible Cause of Myocardial Infarction." *New England Journal of Medicine,* 229:1271–77.

Meade, Richard H. 1961. *A History of Thoracic Surgery.* Springfield, Ill. Charles C. Thomas.

Moerman, Daniel E. 1977. *American Medical Ethnobotany: A Reference Dictionary.* New York: Garland.

1979   "Symbols and Selectivity: A Statistical Analysis of Native American Medical Ethnobotany." *Journal of Ethnopharmacology,* 1:111–19.

Mooney, James. 1891. "The Sacred Formulas of the Cherokee." Seventh Annual Report of the Bureau of American Ethnology, 301–97.

Murphy, M.L., et al. 1977. "Treatment of Chronic Stable Angina." *New England Journal of Medicine,* 297:621–27.

Nickerson, Mark. 1970. "Vasodilator Drugs." Lewis S. Goodman and Alfred Gilman, eds., *The Pharmacological Basis of Therapeutics,* 4th ed. New York: Macmillan, 745–63.

Pelletier, Kenneth R. 1977. *Mind as Healer, Mind as Slayer: A Holistic Approach to Preventing Stress Disorders.* New York: Delta.

Reichard, Gladys. 1970. *Navajo Religion.* New York: Bollingen Foundation.

Ross, Richard S. 1975. "Ischemic Heart Disease: An Overview." *American Journal of Cardiology,* 36:496–505.

Shetler, S., and L. Skog. 1978. *A Provisional Checklist of Species for Flora North America,* Monographs in Systematic Botany, vol. 1. St. Louis: Missouri Botanical Garden.

Shryock, Richard H. 1966. *Medicine in America: Historical Essays.* Baltimore: Johns Hopkins Univ. Press.

Smart, J.J.C. 1959. "Sensations and Brain Processes." *Philosophical Review*, 68:141–56.

Solecki, Ralph S. 1975. "Shanidar IV, a Neanderthal Flower Burial in Northern Iraq." *Science*, 190:880–81.

Solomon, George F. 1969. "Emotions, Stress, and the Central Nervous System." *Annals of the New York Academy of Science*, 164 (2):335–42.

Stent, Gunther S. 1975. "Limits to the Scientific Understanding of Man." *Science*, 187:1052–57.

Stoyva, Johann, T.X. Barber, L.V. DiCara, et al. 1972. *Biofeedback and Self Control, 1971.* Chicago: Aldine.

Strawson, P.F. 1958. *Persons.* Minnesota Studies in the Philosophy of Science, vol. 2. Minneapolis: Univ. of Minnesota Press.

Vlades, M., et al. 1979. " 'Sham Operation' Revisited: A Comparison of Complete vs. Unsuccessful Coronary Artery Bypass." *American Journal of Cardiology*, 43:382.

Wurtman, R.J. 1971. "Brain Monoamines and Endocrine Function." *Neuroendocrine Research Program Bulletin*, 9:172.

Wyman, Leland C., and Stuart K. Harris. 1941. *Navaho Indian Medical Ethno-Botany.* Univ. of New Mexico Bulletin no. 336. Albuquerque: Univ. of New Mexico Press.

PART THREE

Empirical Analyses
of Non-Western
Medical Practices and
Medical Ecology

NON-WESTERN FOLK OR TRIBAL MEDICAL SYSTEMS USE A BROAD RANGE OF BOTANICAL and other elements in the treatment of the sick. That these herbal systems reside within complex and medically significant ideologies (as for the Iroquois, described in the previous section) in no way mitigates the fact that the herbs themselves are significant as medicines.

Humans have been experimenting with medicinal plants for a long time. Indeed, although one cannot be certain that they were used medicinally then, the fact that most of the pollens found by Soleki with the Middle-Paleolithic burial of Shanidar IV were from plants still in use medicinally by the local Iraqi population suggests that they were so used. One of the plants identified was *Ephedra,* source of ephedrine, a substance widely used in modern medicine as an antihistamine. Several of the other plants also have substantial demonstrable active principles (Solecki 1975).

That cases like these are not simple luck, that people carefully select medicinal plants and do not merely choose them at random, has now been demonstrated twice, by independent researchers, in analyses of different continents. But, Hu, and Kong (1980), analyzing the use of 4941 species of Chinese medicinal plants, and Moerman (1979), analyzing the use of 1288 species of native North American medicinal plants, have both concluded (by somewhat different techniques) that medicinal plants *used* are nonrandom selections of plants *available*. Work designed to compare these continental selections is under way.

The long tradition of identification and analysis of medicinal plants in popular practice is represented here in its most sophisticated form in the paper by Elvin–Lewis. She has identified a broad range of analgesic, antibacterial, hemostatic, and astringent substances in 186 species of plants used around the world for cleaning teeth.

There is more involved in health, however, than the plants used to improve it. Pelto and Pelto, in their comprehensive review of the relationship between nutrition and culture, demonstrate clearly the obvious notions that health is a consequence of nutrition, and that nutrition is a consequence of culture, and the much less obvious notion that the development of agricultural and industrial food systems since the end of the upper Paleolithic has led to a general decline in the state of human health.

In a closer analysis of one West African society, Etkin and Ross argue that diet is, as well, tied not only to the maintenance of health, but to the amelioration of disease, as they argue that a number of elements in the Hausa diet can actually affect the course of malaria. The difference between "drugs" and "food" is ultimately one of concept, not content. In a similar vein, Keith and Armelagos demonstrate the widespread incidence of therapeutic quantities of naturally occurring antibiotics in various non-Western diets.

There is a wealth of knowledge and belief, explicit and implicit, in the non-Western world regarding healing. Not all, or perhaps even much, of it may ever be of significance for Western medicine—but some of it may be. All of it is useful in our attempt to understand how humans live. The combination of such possibility with such certainty is sufficient reason to continue the serious pursuit of understanding of these other systems of health care.

REFERENCES

But, P.P., S.–Y. Hu, and Y.C. Kong. 1980. "Vascular Plants Used in Chinese Medicine." *Fitoterapia,* 51:245–64.

Moerman, D. 1979. "Symbols and Selectivity: A Statistical Analysis of Native American Medical Ethnobotany." *Journal of Ethnopharmacology,* 1:111–19.

Solecki, R. 1975. "Shanidar IV, a Neanderthal Flower Burial in Northern Iraq." *Science,* 90:880–81.

10

Culture, Nutrition, and Health

Pertti J. Pelto and Gretel H. Pelto

Introduction

As a subject of anthropological investigation, food cross-cuts a variety of research concerns, from symbolic to biological studies. Not only is a dependable and adequate supply of food essential for the maintenance of human health, but food is universally subject to symbolic and ritual interpretation and political and economic manipulation. The significance of food as a vehicle for studying human social and biological conditions was well understood by Audrey Richards, whose classic study *Hunger and Work in a Savage Tribe* (1964) provided a holistic analysis of food and nutrition among the Southern Bantu. The idea of food as an organizing principle for anthropological analysis was also stressed by Malinowski in his introduction to Richards' book: "The principle which underlies a great deal of what is said in this book is that only a synthesis of facts concerning nutrition can give a correct idea of the economic organization of people, of their domestic life, of their religious ideas and ethical values." (Malinowski, in Richards 1964:xiii). This chapter is devoted to the exploration of some main points concerning the interface between culture and nutrition.

Foods as Nutrients

While humans consume food, our bodies require and utilize nutrients. From a biological standpoint, foods can be regarded as mere carriers of nutrients and non-nutritive elements whose organoleptic and symbolic qualities are irrelevant, except as they promote or inhibit consumption. The nutrients required for the maintenance of health and growth are classified into six broad categories: proteins, carbohydrates, lipids, vitamins, minerals, and water. Within these classes, further distinctions are made, for example, between fat-soluble and water-soluble vitamins, and between simple, compound, and derived lipids. Including water and oxygen, there are approximately 42 to 44 different nutrients that have been identified as essential to adequate nutrition, and it is likely that others will be added to the list with time (Briggs and Calloway, 1979:10).

One of the most significant facts about food as carriers for nutrients is that nutrients are very unevenly distributed in food. Most fruits, for example, contain virtually no protein or fat, and their vitamin and mineral composition varies from one type to another: oranges are an excellent source of ascorbic acid (vitamin C) and a moderately good source of potassium; bananas contain significant amounts of potassium, but are a poor source of ascorbic acid. Foods also vary widely in the quality or utilizability of their nutrients. Several naturally occurring substances bind certain minerals into insoluble compounds that cannot be absorbed by the body. Thus, the phytates in unrefined grain products affect the availability of calcium and zinc, as does oxalic acid in spinach and rhubarb. The amino acid pattern determines the quality of protein in a food, in which the amino acid in lowest supply is the limiting factor. Protein-containing foods vary greatly in their protein quality; the quality is further influenced by digestibility, which varies from one type of food to another and is also influenced by food preparation techniques.

In our contemporary world, nutritionists' solution to the complexities of the relationship between foods and nutrients is to advocate a diverse and "balanced" diet. If different nutrients are distributed in greatly different proportions in different kinds of foods, then the best strategy to ensure adequate nutrition is to eat a variety of foods. To help people select wisely, nutritionists have devised food classification schemes, which place foods in broad categories on the basis of more or less similar nutrient composition. In United States schools today students are taught the "four food groups," whereas earlier students were taught about the "seven food groups." In other countries different schemes prevail. In Finland, for example, nutrition education emphasizes selecting foods from primary, secondary, and tertiary sources, categories that cross-cut, to some extent, the American classification scheme.

Another key element in the matter of nutrition–culture interaction is that nutritional requirements vary from one individual to another and from one environment to another. Among individuals, sex, age, and physiological status (including pregnancy, lactation, growth, and illness) affect requirements. The extent to which genetic differences in growth potential and growth pattern affect nutrient requirements is presently a hotly debated issue, with significant political implications. Less controversial is the concept that environment influences nutrient requirements, in part because of temperature- and humidity-related factors and in part because of different morbidity risks. Activity levels also have a significant effect on requirements. Thus, the assessment of dietary adequacy on a societal level requires a great deal of information, and generalizations about nutrition–culture interactions with respect to dietary adequacy should be made with caution.

Human Food Systems

Without benefit of nutritional sciences, human societies have evolved a variety of strategies for providing their members with food. The wide variation in contemporary and historical cultures is a function of the complex cultural and ecological determinants of human food systems, in conjunction with the physiological and genetic characteristics of our species. Compared to other animals, human food systems are distinctive in a number of ways.

1. Many species have solved the nutrient-food dilemma by evolving food intake patterns based on a narrow range of high nutrient-density foods and/or anatomical-physiological adaptations that promote efficient metabolism and absorption. In contrast, humans are extremely omnivorous, utilizing many more kinds of plants and animal foods than do most other species. The list of plants used by hunter–gatherers often runs to more than a hundred, some being utilized as primary food resources, others for flavoring, preservative, or ritual purposes (cf. Bicchieri 1972; Lee and DeVore 1968).
2. Humans invest a great deal of time and energy in food transport and storage, compared to most other animals. The dependence on stored food and importance of large-scale harvesting for future consumption varies in different food systems, but even most hunting–gathering groups have some stored provisions and both transportation and storage-related technology.
3. Humans expend a great deal of effort preparing foods—cooking, mixing, flavoring, and embellishing meals. The use of fire and the origin of cooked food, which sets humans apart from other animal species, has its roots in our proto-human past, for there is evidence of the use of fire in the caves of Choukoutien, China, where hominid fossils as well as the remains of many other kinds of animal and plant foods have been found (Howell 1970).
4. Humans regularly share and exchange food, and societies have often developed elaborate schemes for food exchange. For most other species, food sharing is limited to parental feeding of infants and/or mate-feeding during infant care, although Teleki (1973) has reported occasional food sharing and even "begging" among chimpanzees. In human societies, food sharing and exchange have economic and ecological significance, and the circulation of food is also central to many symbolic and ritual practices.
5. To the best of our knowledge, only humans have food taboos, which regulate the consumption of edible foods through prohibition. Although other animals certainly recognize or distinguish "food" from "nonfood" and exhibit idiosyncratic and species-specific preferences, the human cognitive overlay affects food selection to an extraordinary degree (cf. Simoons, 1967).

Until recent centuries, most human groups obtained their basic foods from their local environments. The particular plants and animals available in given regions, plus histories of technological development in conjunction with cultural and social processes, have created a fascinating array of food patterns in different parts of the world. The extent to which these food systems provide people with adequate nourishment is a function of a number of factors, including the diversity of foodstuffs, their nutritional qualities, characteristics of the environment, and sociopolitical structures that regulate or control access to food.

Nutrition in Hunting–Gathering Societies

Because *Homo sapiens* evolved as a nomadic or seminomadic hunting–gathering species, the nutritional status and food intake patterns of contemporary hunting–gathering people hold a special fascination, and the study of nutrition in hunter–gatherers past and present helps us to understand nutrition-related health problems in the contemporary world. Like other types of food systems, hunting–gathering systems demonstrate a wide range of food selection, from the heavily animal-protein-dependent diet of Inuit (Eskimo) people of the high Arctic to the largely vegetarian groups of the California Coast and the American West. The !Kung San of the Kalahari desert in Southwest Africa, whose food intake is probably the most carefully documented of any hunting–gathering group, represent an intermediate level of omnivorous adaptation, with approximately 40 percent of calories from meat (Lee 1979:205). Lee attributes the security of !Kung life to "the fact that vegetable food and not meat is the primary component of their diet." He suggests further that "This fundamental aspect of their subsistence the !Kung share with the vast majority of the world's tropical and subtropical hunter–gatherers for whom plant foods are primary and meat secondary" (p. 158).

In the past decade there has been a substantial growth of new techniques for dietary reconstruction (Wing and Brown 1979) and for assessing the nutrition and health status of prehistoric populations (Cassidy 1980). Demographic and health studies in living populations of hunter–gatherers have added further data to the emerging picture of nutrition (Lee 1968; Scudder 1971). The combined force of these multiple data sources suggests that

> these peoples have more than adequate food supplies of large variety and suffer mal-
> nutrition very much less than do agriculturalists. . . . Further, there is growing
> evidence that specific nutritional disorders—beriberi, sprue, even kwaskiorkor—did
> not appear until humans began living on diets consisting largely of grains. Several
> authors have speculated that some of the problems of malnutrition seen in modern
> agriculturalists result from an incomplete selective adjustment of the human organism
> to grain diets since the beginning of the Neolithic [Cassidy 1980:118–20].

Two studies of prehistoric New World populations have helped to clarify the picture of health and nutrition in hunter–gatherers compared to agriculturalists. Cassidy (1980) has contrasted an early hunting–gathering population in Western Kentucky with a late agriculture population in Eastern Kentucky, and Cook and Buikstra (1980) studied the transition from hunting–gathering to agriculture in the Illinois River region. Multiple sources of evidence from both studies point to the superior nutritional adaptation of the hunter–gatherers. Life expectancy is greater for hunter–gatherers (Cassidy 1980:138); the association of severe dental lesions with very high childhood mortality among the horticulturalists in the Illinois River region suggests that malnutrition and infectious disease were more severe in the period after the shift to agriculture; lesions in the cranium that *may* indicate iron deficiency anemia were found only in the agriculturists and not in the hunter–gatherer population in Kentucky.

Reviewing the evidence for hunter–gatherer nutritional status, the general anthropological consensus appears to be that diets were diverse, based on a wide range of plant and animal foods, with great seasonal fluctuations in food selection; and that, barring major disasters caused by severe drought or other unusual climatic conditions, the nutritional status of hunting–gathering peoples was good to excellent. As Cassidy has suggested, "It is a curious and bitter paradox that humans, in the transitional periods of food production, exchanged many components of good physical health for opportunities to increase cultural complexity. The development must have been so slow as to blind experiencers to its occurrence. Indeed, we are only now, as we come out on the other side of what might be called 'agricultural–superiority ethnocentrism,' in a position to realize the fatal bargain we, as agriculturalists, seem to have made." (Cassidy 1980:142)

The First Food Transition: Plant and Animal Domestication

The first broad and sweeping transformation of human food patterns started with small hunting–gathering bands in the Middle East who developed greater dependence on the wild grains that grew in profusion in some favored areas. Flint and obsidian "sickles," stone grinding slabs and other grain-processing materials have been found in a number of archaeological sites in Israel, Syria, Iraq, and other upland areas of the "Fertile Crescent." Some of the remains of emmer wheat and barley from these sites appear to be genetically changed from the purely wild strains (Cohen 1977:134-136). Another archeological feature that increased in the period from fifteen thousand to twelve thousand years ago is the presence of underground storage pits. Storage facilities do not prove that wheat, barley, and other grains were grown deliberately, but they do demonstrate increased utilization and dependence on grain harvests. They also imply greater sedentarism, with all the health risks and social complexities associated with more permanent settlement.

Sedentariness appears to have reduced the opportunities for hunting big game, although it is probable that the larger wild herds in the Middle East had already been depleted as human population expanded. In any case, the archaeological record indicates a shift toward eating waterfowl, fish, small reptiles, crustaceans, molluscs and other small game. At the same time, the increasingly rich fields of grain attracted certain types of animals that were early candidates for domestication. Pigs, goats, sheep, and cattle became the regular domesticates of the Middle East farmers and their use as domestic food-on-the-hoof spread gradually into Europe, Africa, and eastward.

The Neolithic transition occurred at different times in various parts of the Old World. The complex of wheat, barley, and domestic animals gradually spread northward in Europe, but only reached England and Scandinavia many thousands of years after full domestication of food was achieved in the Middle East. Similarly, the earliest evidence of agriculture in China occurred only about six thousand to seven thousand years ago. The first cultigens were probably varieties of millet, but rice was soon added to the basic farming pattern in many areas (Chang 1970). On the other hand, plant domestication in Southeast Asia seems to have occurred at approximately the same time as in the Middle East. As in the Middle East, the transition from the first evidence of human control of food crops to full-scale domestication covered a period of several thousand years.

In the New World, the domestication of plants and animals developed entirely separately from the Old World Neolithic and the primary domesticated plants were also quite different. Throughout large areas of North America and Middle America there is good evidence of a shift from primary dependence on animals to greater reliance on vegetable foods. In some areas of the Southwestern United States, heavy dependence on wild vegetable materials is indicated by grinding stones dated from as early as eight thousand to nine thousand years ago (Cohen 1977:178–80).

The earliest domestication of plant foods north of the Isthmus of Panama appears to have been about eight thousand years ago in several areas of Mexico. Gradually, domesticated maize (*Zea mays*) became the chief food plant of most of the area stretching from Central America into the river valleys of the Midwest and far north into New York State. Squash, the "second leg of the Mexican cooking pot," was domesticated at about the same time as maize, while the domestication of beans, the "third leg," occurred somewhat later (Cohen 1977:215). In South America the transition from hunting–gathering to dependence on domesticated food sources undoubtedly took different pathways in different ecological zones, but the archeological traces concerning the domestication of potatoes, manioc, sweet potatoes, peanuts, and other crops are very sketchy. The Middle American trinity—maize, beans, and squash—made its appearance in South American communities at least 4,000 years ago, but the patterns of diffusion southward from Mexico are largely unknown.

The pattern of agriculture in the Americas took a very different form from developments in the Old World, in part because of the differences in potentially domesticable plants and in part because of the lack of domesticable animals. However, all over the world the transitions to sedentary cultivation and animal keeping seem to have developed in reciprocal interaction between increased population pressures and the genetic–environmental possibilities offered by the significant cultivable food resources.

The Second Food Transition:
World-Wide Circulation of Cultigens

Until the Age of Discovery, beginning in the fifteenth century, complexes of domesticates spread slowly within their respective continental regions; the Old and

New Worlds were totally isolated from each other. Columbus's voyages to the West Indies changed that dramatically. The first arrival of Old World crops in the Americas was in 1494, when Columbus's second voyage brought "1,200 men, seeds and cuttings for planting wheat, chickpeas, melons, onions, radishes, salad greens, grape vines, sugar cane and fruit stones for the planting of orchards. The early results were marvellously encouraging" (Crosby 1972:67).

The most dramatic food change introduced by the Europeans was the importing of cattle, horses, sheep, goats, and pigs. In the Americas these animals had few natural enemies or competitors; on many of the islands of the West Indies the pigs and cattle that escaped their owners rapidly developed into wild herds. In the centuries since the first Europeans invaded the Americas, the food systems of the New World have been transformed into an eclectic mixture of the word's cultigens and animal domesticates. Navaho Indians have now been sheepherders for so many generations that their economy has the appearance of an ancient indigenous pattern. Similarly, the Indians of the Great Plains changed their economic system drastically when they took up extensive use of horses, profiting from the animals that strayed from Spanish explorers.

The impact of native American foods on the Old World also has been dramatic and far-reaching, though the process was much slower. In Europe, American foodstuffs were at first regarded with suspicion and disdain. For example, "in 1774 the hungry citizens of Kolberg refused to touch [potatoes] when Frederick the Great of Prussia dispatched a wagonload to relieve famine" (Tannahill 1973:259).

Maize, manioc, and potatoes are the American crops that have perhaps had the most significance as staples throughout the world. Some authors have argued that the infusion of new crops from the Americas into the Old World made large increases in population possible because of their impact on food supplies (cf. Crosby 1972). Ho (1955) has analyzed the history of food production in China, noting that by 1937 China's dependence on rice had dropped from about 70 percent to 36 percent. By that time American cultigens made up at least 20 percent of Chinese food production. Ho states: "During the last two centuries, when rice culture was gradually approaching its limit, and encountering the law of diminishing returns, the various dry land food crops introduced from America have contributed most to the increase in national food production and have made possible a continual growth of population" (Ho 1955:191–92). In addition to effects on population, the second food transition had many other effects, including changes in cooking styles and food culture.

The Third Food Transition: Commercialization of Food

Like the other major transitions in human food use, the present day "commercialization of food" has its origins in earlier times and has proceeded in different patterns in different parts of the world. Its major features are:

1. The development of extensive and elaborate food processing technology for commercial purposes.

2. The rapid expansion of commercial sale of prepared meals—in restaurants, fast-food establishments and vending machines.
3. The conversion of food production into "agri-business" and extensive mono-crop agriculture in much of the world.
4. The extensive *de-localization* of food resources, so that previously subsistence-oriented farmers in many parts of the world now purchase a major portion of their food in commercial stores and markets, even though they may still be engaged in farming.

The third major food transition is now going on. Major sectors of the rural hinterlands in Africa, Asia and South America have not yet experienced its full impact, and the effects of industrialized, urban environments have not yet run their course. As the transition proceeds, the amount of self-provisioning by households declines and the proportion of even partially self-provisioning households in a region is reduced. Thus, one index of the commercialization of food in an area is the ratio of purchased food to total food consumed per capita.

The outlines of the contemporary revolution in human food patterns is complicated by the variety of cross-currents generated by people who seek some reprieve from rampant delocalization. In some sectors of industrial populations this takes the form of greatly increased reliance on home gardens and other local resources. Concern with "organic" and "natural" foods is also part of the complex of responses to the major trends in contemporary food use patterns.

In many areas of the Third World the current changes appear to be having negative consequences on nutritional status, even when delocalization brings new food resources into an area. In some cases the societal transformations referred to under the general rubric of "modernization"[1] (cf. Poggie and Lynch, 1974) mean that high nutrient-density, low-cost food products are exported from an area, while low-density, high-cost substitutes are brought in. Two cases involving local animal protein illustrate this process.

The Skolt Saami of Finnish Lapland

The Skolt Saami (formerly called Lapps) of northeastern Finland have depended on trading posts for supplies of flour, sugar, salt, and a few other commodities for decades, even centuries. However, until the middle 1960s their dietary mainstays were reindeer meat from their own herds and large quantities of fish from local lakes and streams. Fruit and vegetable consumption was minimal, although most families gathered considerable amounts of blueberries and lingonberries in the fall, with some households maintaining stores of berries through most of the winter.

In the past two decades the dietary picture changed rapidly for the Skolts. With the introduction of the snowmobile, reindeer herding was mechanized and meat prices rose rapidly, to levels of seven or eight dollars per pound, even in local reindeer-herding areas. At the same time, many families lost their reindeer herds because of the major economic and ecological changes that accompanied the shift to mechanized herding. Thus, most families could no longer rely on reindeer meat as a dietary mainstay. Fishing was intensified somewhat, but local lakes were already overtaxed, so the consumption of locally caught fish also suffered a decline.

Meanwhile, improved transportation facilities made it easier for local stores to stock dairy products, fruits, vegetables, and many other commercial items that had hitherto been unknown in the Skolt community. By 1978 almost all families were heavily dependent on the local store for weekly, if not daily, food supplies. Most women had given up baking bread and coffee bread, as these items were easily obtained from the store. A variety of moderately priced sausages, popular throughout Finland, became typical fare among the Skolts, and their use of potatoes and other vegetables increased, taking the place of reindeer meat and fish. The local food system is now almost completely delocalized. In fact, most of the reindeer meat produced in the area is shipped out to commercial establishments in the south (Pelto 1973; Pelto and Moshnikoff 1978).

The changes in the Skolt diet over the past 20 years are large scale, and have both positive and negative elements. There is clearly a great increase in the use of sugar and other refined carbohydrates. The commercial sausages are high in fat, sodium, preservatives, and other additives. On the other hand, the Skolts, for the first time, have plenty of milk for their children. They have probably increased their consistency of ascorbic-acid intake (e.g., in citrus fruits), and their diets have become more diverse.

The Miskito of Nicaragua

Like many other communities off the mainstream of the modern industrialized world, the Miskito peoples of eastern coastal Nicaragua had ample sources of food, especially protein foods, from their immediate local environment. Traditionally their main sources were green sea turtle, other marine life, deer, and other forest game. They grew root crops and a few vegetables in their gardens. Local stores supplied additional staples, but a very large portion of their foods came from natural and local sources (cf. Weiss 1980; Nietschmann 1973).

The Miskito were introduced to wage labor early in this century with the advent of logging and rubber tapping. Through the decades they experienced a series of economic booms, followed by periods when wage labor was not available. During such times the Miskito turned back to their local environment for food. Today the situation has changed drastically. In late 1968 a commercial company set up a factory to process green turtles for soup (Weiss 1980:163). The Miskito turtle hunters now sell most of their catch to the companies, from whence it finds its way to elite restaurants in North America and on the Continent.

As with the reindeer meat of the Skolt Saami, the value of the dietary mainstay of the Miskito has become so costly that many people can no longer afford to eat turtle. The local stores in the Miskito area are not as well stocked as appears to be the case among the Skolts, and the main foods that people are buying are flour, sugar, and rice, which together account for more than 60 percent of average caloric intake. A number of other changes are occurring at the same time. Formerly the Miskito shared their catch and their harvests with kin. Now sharing is much reduced, and the households that do not have able-bodied turtle hunters and foragers find themselves in increasingly serious circumstances.

Nutrition and the Diseases of Civilization

The major transitions in food systems during the course of human history have been associated with massive changes in social, economic, and political conditions. Large-scale changes in dietary patterns have also accompanied these processes. Given the speed of these changes and the significance of nutrition for health, it is reasonable to hypothesize that some contemporary diseases may be the result of disjunctions between the human biological system, evolved in our hunting–gathering past, and the food patterns now found in much of the world. In many ways our hunter–gatherer constitutions may be out of step with contemporary eating patterns, despite our enormous flexibility and capacity to adapt.

One of the most pervasive effects of modern sedentary lifestyles, especially in more affluent countries, is the increased prevalence of obesity. In industrialized nations the level of energy output required in daily living has been significantly reduced for most people, but caloric intake has remained the same or even increased. Composition of diets has also changed, as people consume more fat and refined carbohydrates and less fiber and complex carbohydrates.

At the same time, during the twentieth century there has been a continuing trend toward slimness as an ideal for both male and female beauty. In Europe and North America, and in much of the rest of the world as well, fashion models and celebrities are expected to be very thin. Interestingly, cultural definitions of ideal height/weight ratios in terms of attractiveness are quite congruent with medical opinion and actuarial data on healthiness and life expectancies. Although some debate remains about the advantages of carrying a few extra pounds of stored energy, most statistics appear to support the generalization that "slimmer is healthier."

Obesity, and the dietary patterns that tend to accompany it, have been implicated in several of the most pervasive and serious contemporary diseases: diabetes, hypertension, and cardiovascular disease. To date, relationships between cancer—the other major scourge of modern times—and diet have been less investigated. It would be an oversimplification to suggest that "in the old days our ancestors ate the right things; now our eating is all wrong." Although it is true that contemporary populations eat much more refined carbohydrates, including sugar, than did our ancestors, high intake of animal fat was probably characteristic of many hunting–gathering groups living in harsh climates. The apparent paradox, that what was adaptive in ancient times is not necessarily good for us today, requires that we understand the problems in modern diets in terms of a complex system, involving activity levels, combinations of foods consumed, seasonal and other fluctuations, and other features of ecological systems.

Diabetes, Diet, and Modernization

Diabetes mellitus is a disease that is becoming more prevalent as people adopt modern life-styles. While prevalence rates seem to be holding steady in industrialized, European populations, there have been dramatic increases, to extraordinarily high prevalence levels in many acculturating groups (cf. Eaton 1977). At the extreme, for example, are the Pima and Cocpah Indians of Arizona, where surveys have shown diabetes rates as high as 84 percent of the population over 35 years old (Genuth et al. 1967; Henry 1969). In Africa, diabetes was formerly regarded as a rare disease, but newly urban groups (e.g., Bantu peoples in Capetown) have rates in some areas that are 40 times as high as the rates in rural areas.

How is the increase in diabetes related to changing biocultural conditions? The anthropologist Neel (1962) has hypothesized that diabetes has a genetic foundation reflecting an effective adaptation to hunting–gathering. This "thrifty genotype" involves a genetic predisposition that includes rapid insulin metabolism, efficient utilization of blood glucose, increased ability to convert excess calories to fat, rapid physical development, and early menarche. These biological characteristics were adaptive for hunter–gatherers, but under modern conditions the same genotype, geared to high production of insulin, constantly stimulated by high intake of carbohydrate, leads to exhaustion of the insulin–glucose regulative system and hence to diabetes.

Part of the problem appears to be related to heavy consumption of refined sugar, which passes more readily into the blood stream and thus puts excessive demands on the insulin secretion system. The dietary picture is not simply a matter of "sugar," however. Crapo et al. (1977) have found that the human physiological system has quite different responses to different forms of complex carbohydrates. They found that glucose and insulin responses to cooked potatoes, for example, were much greater than responses to rice and corn. Other dietary components that have been implicated in the complex puzzle of diabetes include chromium (which some researchers have identified as the active component of a so-called glucose tolerance factor), zinc, and dietary fiber (Hambridge 1974; Maurer 1979; Boyle et al. 1977).

Higher stress levels, as well as dietary factors, may be involved in the increased prevalence of diabetes. Increased secretions of epinephrine and other hormones during stressful situations are known to raise blood glucose levels. Equally important, people often respond to psychosocial stress by eating. Eating and drinking are among the most common tension-reduction responses among both children and adults.

A recent experimental study has produced striking evidence of the effects of "civilization" on hunter–gatherer biocultural adaptations (O'Dea et al. 1980). A multidisciplinary team located a small group of Australian aborigines living in urban conditions who still retained the knowledge and skills necessary for survival in their previous hunting–gathering way of life. In the urban area of Derby their diet was mainly composed of stews, made from unenriched white flour, vegetables, and fatty meat. The meal was washed down with sweet tea; consumption of beer and port was also quite high. Researchers estimated the composition of the urban diet to be "carbohydrate 50% (half of which was derived from sugar); fat 40% and protein 10%" (O'Dea et al. 1980:4). Most of the group were overweight, and their insulin response levels were notably higher than those of the white population, indicating serious potential to develop diabetes.

The Mowanjum ex-hunter–gatherers agreed to spend three months back in their former habitat in the Kimberley region of northwestern Australia (May–July 1977). There they recapitulated their earlier way of life as closely as possible, although they used guns, steel axes, and simple fishing tackle instead of the aboriginal equipment. Their diet in the hunting–gathering "experiment" was composed of "meat (kangaroos, reptiles, birds) and fish with varying supplements of carbohydrate (yams, palm hearts, bush honey) . . . [Diet composition was] estimated to be: carbohydrate 20% at most; fat, 30% at least; protein 50%. Caloric intake was high" (O'Dea et al, 1980:4). It is interesting to note that the Mowanjum people consumed most of the food at one major evening meal, following their earlier traditional eating pattern.

The effects of the experiment were striking. The return to a hunting–gathering life-style clearly changed their physiological patterns in the directions predicted by epidemiological and clinical studies on the "diseases of civilization." After three months of foraging life, levels of obesity were reduced (although not back to "ideal" height/weight ratios), insulin response levels dropped significantly, and triglycerides were markedly lower.

Nutrition, Hypertension, and Cardiovascular Disease

Hypertension and cardiovascular pathologies—such as stroke, myocardial infarction, and other catastrophes—are conditions that are often regarded as the epitomy of the "diseases of civilization." Like maturity-onset diabetes, cardiovascular diseases have a complex etiology, involving obesity, dietary factors, lack of exercise, stress, and other variables. Unlike diabetes, many of the manifestations, including hypertension, can be asymptomatic for years.

Obesity has been strongly implicated in the etiology of elevated blood pressure, and most of the factors that contribute to obesity are also involved in hypertension. Thus, stress can be seen as a direct contributor to hypertension, as it is to obesity and diabetes, and a number of studies have demonstrated clear links between stress factors (including stressful life events) and elevated blood pressure (Harburg et al. 1973; Dressler 1979).

Among dietary factors, the role of sodium in affecting blood pressure has received considerable attention. Sodium intake has increased greatly in modern times, and contemporary people consume hidden sodium in food preservatives and flavoring agents. The large increases in sodium intake represent a radical departure from hunting–gathering conditions, for it is generally postulated that "humans evolved in a low-sodium, high potassium environment" (Meneely and Batterbee 1976).

Despite the body of circumstantial evidence, there are a number of problems in linking sodium intake to the etiology of hypertension. It is extremely difficult to measure sodium intake accurately, and it is also difficult to identify "low-salt" users for controlled comparisons.

Certainly, the most widely publicized nutritional factor in relation to cardiovascular disease and hypertension is cholesterol. Current biomedical opinion generally recognizes the role of saturated fats in the etiology of these conditions, but the mechanisms that link fat intake to disease, the role of other dietary components, genetics, exercise, and stress are all hotly debated and poorly understood. What is not debated is that cardiovascular diseases have increased markedly with the advent of modern life-styles and that changing dietary patterns play a role in the changing epidemiological picture.

A classic study that demonstrated the effects of urban migration was carried out by Scotch (1963), who compared blood-pressure levels in Zulu urban migrants to levels in people who were living in traditional rural communities. In his careful analysis, Scotch identified a series of psychosocial stresses that help to explain the elevated blood pressures of the urban dwellers. A recent study of migrants from Tokelau to New Zealand also illustrates the effect of migration. The migrants— particularly males—were found to be uniformly higher in diastolic and systolic pressures for nearly every age group. Since the researchers had effective controls for genetic relationships among the migrants and nonmigrants, they were able to assess the relative effects of genetic and sociocultural factors (Ward and Prior 1980).

The data from the Tokelau study and from other studies that combine careful genetic assessment with analysis of the environmental factors (including diet) show that in any population the risks of hypertension, cardiovascular disease and other "diseases of civilization" are not equal for all members of migrating or modernizing groups. Hereditary differences in "original risk" play an important role in the interaction with nutritional and other lifestyle variables (Lewitter 1980).

Other Diseases of Modern Life

The triumvirate—obesity, diabetes, and cardiovascular disease—are but a portion of the inventory of the diseases of civilization. Many neoplasms can be related to progressive industrialization and urbanization of lifestyles, and some may be associated with dietary factors. Many respiratory ailments can be linked to modernization; some may also have links to dietary factors, through food allergies that precipitate asthmatic attacks.

Gallstones are thought by many medical authorities to be another symptom of civilization, quite possibly related to dietary factors. Gallstones are composed of cholesterol, bile pigment, calcium, salts, and protein. The main evidence linking them to human cultural evolution is in the observation that they "are seldom found in primitive people living in their native reserves and undertaking active physical work" (Davidson and Passmore, 1971:552).

Dairy Products and Modern Life

In much of the industrialized world, consumption of dairy products is a major part of food intake; milk, cheese, butter, and eggs are regarded as important and desirable staples. (Even most vegetarians, who may eschew both animal meat and fish, find dairy products acceptable because they do not require the killing of animals.) Adult consumption of milk products, however, is a relatively recent addition to the human diet, for, like domesticated food crops, they became available only after humans had acquired domesticated animals as regular food sources. Even after domestic animals had become a routine dietary item, milking was probably not practiced on a regular basis for several millenia.

Many peoples in the world do not consume milk products, notably in tropical Africa and eastern Asia. Various cultural and ecological explanations have been offered to explain "antimilk" attitudes and practices. For some Africans and Asians, milk is regarded as a disgusting animal fluid like urine. Other attitudes include objections to "stealing the food of the young animals," as well as revulsion at the idea of manipulating an animal's udder.

In some areas there are sound ecological reasons for the lack of dairy animals, particularly where their presence would require intensive land use for fodder that would be uneconomical in comparison with crops for direct human consumption. In recent years it has become evident that there is also a physiological basis for some people's resistence to milk use. In many populations a large percentage of adults lack sufficient amounts of the enzyme lactase, which is essential for digesting lactose, the sugar in milk. Some lactase-deficient persons are able to consume milk without serious problems, but many others experience cramps, diarrhea, and nausea.

Lactase, must, of course, be present in infants if they are to utilize their mother's milk; however, in nonhuman mammals, and in many human groups, lactase activity diminishes markedly or disappears after weaning (Simoons 1980). The phenomenon of adult lactase in humans is therefore somewhat aberrant in comparison with the "usual" mammalian pattern.

Simoons (1980), McCracken (1971), and others have hypothesized that genetically "aberrant" individuals—those with adult lactase capability—would have had a selective advantage in societies where animal milk was a potentially important food resource. Thus, as the use of dairy products increased in these animal-keeping societies, there was a gradual increase in the numbers of adults who could ingest milk without experiencing ill effects. The gradual spread of genetically lactose-tolerant persons throughout Europe, parts of Africa, and southern Asia followed the expansion of dairying.

Many nutrition programs after World War II provided milk to people with little or no previous traditions of milk use by post-weaning children and adults and to populations with high rates of lactase deficiency. Whereas many people could consume some milk without problems, others developed unpleasant symptoms and rejected the "new" food. However, it is also important to note that the problem can be confounded by other factors. Serious diarrhea can also destroy the body's capacity to synthesize lactase, causing a temporary lactose intolerance. Since gastrointestinal infections are endemic in many areas of the Third World, problems that appear to involve genetically based lactose intolerance may arise from other factors. Therefore, it is important to be cautious in condemning milk as the source of the problem.

Undernutrition and Culture Change in the Modern World

Although many people in the modern world confront the health hazards of obesity, diabetes, and cardiovascular disease, the largest nutrition problem today is undernutrition. Our contemporary food systems leave many millions of the world's people without adequate food to nourish their bodies. At the extremes of undernutrition are the diseases of marasmus and kwashiorkor. Marasmus, or starvation, caused by a lack of calories and protein, is characterized by severe wasting and leads ultimately to death. The other fatal disease of undernutrition, kwashiorkor, is caused by a shortage of protein without severe caloric deficit. In contrast to marasmus, in which the individual looks emaciated, kwashiorkor is characterized by edema (swelling), especially in the face and lower extremities, which masks the absence of body fat. There are also serious metabolic changes that occur in kwashiorkor, and it is more rapidly fatal, if untreated, than is marasmus.

Many medical researchers before the 1930s believed that kwashiorkor was due to parasitic infections. It was also variously diagnosed as "infantile pellagra," "fatty-liver disease," or congenital syphilis until 1933, when Cecily Williams, a physician working in Ghana, adopted the term "kwashiorkor" as she came to recognize the complex of nutritional and sociocultural factors involved in the disease. Kwashiorkor means "the disease of the deposed baby when the next one is born" (Williams 1935).

Among the events that can precipitate kwashiorkor are the termination of breast-feeding, which, in many traditional cultures, is brought about by a new pregnancy or childbirth. However, infections can also precipitate the disease, particularly among children experiencing serious, chronic undernutrition. The additional protein needs engendered by the infection can push the child into a downward spiral, with progressively greater malnutrition due to diarrhea and loss of appetite.

Psychosocial stress may also arise in connection with stressful weaning, especially if weaning is accomplished through withdrawal of the mother. Thus, there is a possibility that the vulnerable child, already undernourished, may experience loss of appetite and thus be pushed progressively toward greater nutritional deficits (Geber and Dean 1956).

Although the nutritional factors and physiological processes are different in marasmus, cessation of breast-feeding may also be a factor in marasmus. Marasmus is likely to occur when the young infant is weaned prematurely from the breast onto a nutritionally inadequate substitute. Risks of marasmus are particularly high in newly urbanizing populations in developing countries. According to Davidson and Passmore (1971):

> The urban influences which predispose to marasmus are a rapid succession of preg-
> nancies and early and abrupt weaning, followed by dirty and unsound artificial feeding
> of infants with very dilute milk or milk products, given in inadequate amounts to
> avoid expense. Thus the diet is low in both calories and proteins . . . repeated in-
> fections may develop, especially of the gastrointestinal tract . . . [p. 388].

Less extreme than marasmus and kwashiorkor but affecting very large numbers of people are conditions of undernutrition manifest as stunted growth, inadequate weight, and a host of associated consequences. Undernutrition is not a new condition in human life; however, the current situation, which may be called "the commer-cialization of food," is associated with very different cultural dynamics than were operative during the Neolithic period. The increasingly high cost of food production, the concentration of control over productive land into fewer and fewer hands, the conversion of most food into the status of a commodity, increasing population pressure and the worldwide shift of population concentrations to urban areas, the political nature of food policy at national and international levels, the norms and styles of consumption in the affluent nations—all of these factors, and others, contribute to the present situation.

During the past decade there has been a growth of anthropological concern with problems of undernutrition, and there is an increasing number of case studies that help to elucidate the cultural processes involved in the great human tragedy of undernutrition. For example, Gross and Underwood (1971) demonstrated how the introduction of sisal in northeast Brazil brought about increased nutritional stress for the peasant population. A number of anthropologists have studied the social context of infant nutrition (cf. Marchione 1980). Others have examined the effects of economic development projects on nutritional status (Dewey 1980; DeWalt 1979; Hernandez et al. 1974).

Breast-Feeding and Bottle-Feeding: The Not-So-Tender Dilemma

No nutritional issue has occasioned as much heated debate and discussion as the matter of breast-feeding *versus* bottle-feeding. Bottle-feeding typifies the "third food transition," for it involves the development of a high technology food product, disseminated primarily through commercial channels that are highly delocalized. When we seek to disentangle all the factors influencing people's choices and be-haviors with regard to infant feeding, we find that breast milk substitution embodies many of the complexities of modern life.

The positive advantages of breast milk and breast-feeding in contrast to bottle-feeding include the following:

1. As a product of evolution, it can be assumed that human milk is finely adjusted to the full array of infant nutritional needs.
2. Human milk contains antibodies that convey significant protection against a wide range of infections.
3. Breast-feeding minimizes exposure to bacterial and other contaminants that may occur in bottles, mixing receptacles, and nipples.
4. If carried out with sufficient intensity, lactation prolongs the period of post-partum amenorrhea and increases the time interval between births.
5. Breast-feeding is relatively convenient.
6. The cost of feeding a mother the additional calories she needs for lactation is significantly less than the costs of any available substitutes.
7. Additional advantages involve maternal–infant interaction, particularly related to the development of mother–infant "bonding."

In earlier centuries mothers who could not or did not want to breast-feed had only one option: they could find a substitute "wet nurse." The use of wet nurses was common among upper-class women in some cultures, perhaps because they saw themselves as having more important tasks (Wallace 1972) or because the ability to hire a wet nurse somehow conveyed social prestige.

Near the end of the eighteenth century the conical glass infant feeding bottle was invented, with "a tubular mouthpiece enclosed in an overlapping finger of linen, parchment or wash-leather." The new technology was not rapidly adopted; both lay and medical opinions were against the use of artificial feeding. The London obstetrician Underwood commented, "I am convinced that the attempt to bring up children by hand proves fatal in London to at least seven out of eight . . ." (Duncum 1947:1141).

The bottle was not the only significant technical development affecting infant feeding. Sweetened condensed milk, manufactured by Gail Borden, was first available commercially in the United States in the 1850s, followed by canned, evaporated milk 30 years later.

In the first half of the twentieth century bottle-feeding spread rapidly in the United States and Europe. By the end of World War II only one mother in four was breast-feeding in the northeastern United States (H. Meyer 1968). After the 1950s the trend continued until bottle-feeding leveled off at slightly over 80 percent of the population. Recently there has been a return to breast-feeding (or at least to the initiation of breast-feeding), especially among middle-class women (Hendershot 1980:3).

In the Third World the shift from breast-feeding to bottle-feeding has been a post-World-War-II phenomenon. It has been found that the pattern of adoption of artificial feeding follows the same pattern as in the industrialized world: urban higher-income women are the first to make the shift, followed by low-income women (WHO/UNICEF 1981). In rural areas, breast-feeding continues to be the norm in many countries. In the Philippines, 33 percent of urban upper-income mothers had *not* breast-fed their youngest infant; the comparable figure for urban poor women was 15 percent. In Guatemala, the figures were 23 percent and 9 percent, respectively (ibid.). The percentages of women who shift to bottle-feeding soon after an initial period of breast-feeding are much higher (Winikoff & Baer 1980).

Why are so many women in the world adopting bottle-feeding? The reasons, which are many and varied, include the following:

1. Bottle-feeding can be done by other caretakers.
2. Some women believe that their milk is inadequate or somehow inferior.
3. Breast-feeding is regarded (in the community) as undignified or even "disgusting."
4. Breast-feeding is thought by some people to disfigure the breasts or interfere with sexual activity.
5. In some instances health-care professionals and health practices discourage breast-feeding.
6. Bottle-feeding is perceived as "modern."
7. "Lactation failure" or perceived failure, brought about by a complex of behavioral, physiological, and psychological factors, is involved in some early weaning from the breast.
8. Experiences of discomfort from cracked nipples, engorgement, or breast infection lead to early weaning.

According to a number of surveys, the need to return to work is seldom given by women as the primary reason for bottle-feeding (Winikoff and Baer 1980), but women's economic activities undoubtedly play an important role in decisions about infant feeding (G. Pelto 1981).

Supplemental Feeding and Weaning

Different cultures show considerable variation in the timing and types of supplemental foods given their youngest members. Variations are also considerable from one family to another within seemingly homogeneous communities. Some people introduce foods other than breast milk to their babies soon after birth (Johnston 1977). Others give supplemental foods only after many months of full reliance on mother's milk. Nerlove (1974) has demonstrated that in traditional cultures, the timing of supplemental feeding varies systematically (across cultures) with the relative economic importance of women's roles. Where women's work is crucial in food production or in other economic pursuits, there are clear tendencies toward earlier supplementation.

Many developing countries now have programs aimed at improving supplemental feeding practices in order to offset the often serious decline in nutritional status of infants around the age of four to six months. The well-known product *Incaparina,* developed by the Institute of Nutrition of Central America and Panama (INCAP), was one of the first efforts to provide new types of supplemental foods.

Food Taboos and Restrictions

Humans are unique among mammals in the extent to which we construct taboos prohibiting the use of foods. The prohibitions against pork among millions of Jews and Muslims and the prohibitions against eating animal meat observed by large numbers of Hindus are particularly intriguing examples, because these foods are regarded as especially desirable by many other cultural groups. Our concern here, however, is limited to the nutritional implications of food restrictions.

Nearly all human groups have some culturally-imposed restrictions on eating foods that are considered completely edible by other groups. Such taboos may be applied to the whole society (all Jews must avoid pork) or parts of the society (taboo animals of particular clans or kin groups), or for particular periods of time (Lenten fasting among Catholics).

Pregnancy and Childbirth Taboos

In many societies pregnancy and childbirth is a time of food restriction. Food taboos of this sort appear to restrict intake when it is particularly important for women to maximize their intake of calories, protein, and other critical nutrients. However, any researcher or policy planner who is confronted with evidence of food taboos should be wary of drawing hasty conclusions. The degree of restrictiveness varies considerably within populations. For example, Eichinger Ferro–Luzzi (1980) interviewed 1200 women in Tamilnad, South India, concerning food avoidances. Of the total of 1059 nonvegetarian women, 61 reported avoiding meat during pregnancy; 65 of the 998 fish-eaters did not eat fish during pregnancy, and some others abstained from crabs, shark, catfish, and some other species. The reasons given were that those foods were "hot" and might induce abortion (Ferro–Luzzi 1980:102). Over 80 percent of the women avoided papaya for the same reason. A series of beliefs concerning papaya linked this fruit with abortion, early onset of menarche, and possible regulation of the menstrual cycle.

Postpartum avoidances in Tamilnad included meat, fish, milk products, and eggs, as well as a variety of fruits. For most of the women, the normal period of food avoidance was 40 days. A number of vegetables were avoided because they were thought to be "cold." Interestingly, the lists of avoided foods varied, and most individuals did not avoid the full list. The results from this survey in Tamilnad suggest something of the variations in interpretation that may occur concerning the applicability of usually held proscriptive principles.

For Malaysia, Wilson (1980) has reported on a series of restrictions derived from the humoral belief system, which classifies foods in terms of their hot and cold properties. Based on dietary intake data, Wilson concluded that the restrictions of fruit and vegetables for postpartum women are "inimical to the woman's health, since her nonpregnant status with regard to vitamins and minerals is often equivocal" (p. 73). She suggested the possibility "that a lowering of nutritional status following birth of the child may contribute to the fetal and neonatal deaths . . ." (ibid.).

A contrasting view is presented by Laderman (1979), based on research in a Malay village on the east coast of the Malay Peninsula. She found that "diet during pregnancy did not suffer because of beliefs and taboos. In fact, a woman's diet during pregnancy was essentially the same as that of the rest of the adult population" (abstract). Laderman reports that the Malay women did indeed espouse a humoral system of beliefs concerning "hot" and "cold" foods, but that the classification of specific foods varied from individual to individual. Further, many informants believed that mixing "hot" and "cold" foods produced a neutral quality, and many foods were classified as "neutral."

"Male" and "Female" Differences in Food

Although temporary food restrictions, infrequently honored, are unlikely to have major effects on nutritional status, permanent patterns of differential consumption, whether formalized into taboos or practiced from habitual expectation, can certainly have significant consequences. As an expression of power relationships, differential access to food characterizes many societies—from differences in class and caste to differences between men and women or between adults and children.

Many societies reserve meat mainly for men. Among the Chagga in Tanzania, the men explained to anthropologist M.-L. Swantz and her associates that "Man butchers the cow, woman could not do it, so it is his right to eat it, too" (1975:32). The Chagga men further asserted that "women can eat such foods as bananas and green vegetables (*kitalolo,*) gruel (of *mbege*), sugar cane and mangoes, which men cannot eat, so why should men not eat meat which they can eat" (ibid.:32–33).

Rosenberg (1980) reviewed the ethnographic literature on sex differentials in food use and found such practices to be widespread in both simpler and more complex societies. "In most traditional societies . . . women's diets are inferior to the men's. These diet patterns are often sanctioned by religious beliefs and built into the prestige structure of the society" (pp. 198–99). Food differentials, with specific restrictions against female access to certain foods, do not disappear readily under conditions of economic change and modernization.

Sex differentials are often reflected in the ratios of malnourished male to female children. In the Chagga case, Swantz and associates examined data on 47 cases of kwashiorkor at a nutrition clinic; 30 of the cases were female, whereas only 17 were male children (1975: appendix). Similarly, the large imbalance in the sex ratio in India (260 million males and 213 million females in the 1961 census) suggests differential child care, including differential feeding practices.

Food as Cause and Cure of Illness

In many cultures food is used not only to maintain spiritual health (through sacred fasting and the observance of taboos), but also to maintain and restore physical health. The concept of food-as-medicine has been a feature of Western medical traditions since the time of Hippocrates. The Chinese conceptual system of *yin* and *yang* may be the origin of the Hippocratic humoral theory, although similar concepts, phrased as the complementary relationships of "hot" and "cold," are found in Ayurvedic and pre-Ayurvedic medical traditions in India (Logan 1977; Foster 1976). The central idea is of a harmonious balance of body fluids, vital organs, food intake, and physical activities.

Humoral theories of hot–cold harmony are widespread in Latin America, Southeast Asia, and India.

The examples given above of "hot" and "cold" foods in relation to pregnancy and childbirth in India and Malaysia illustrate the specific ways in which food choices can be organized in relation to bodily states. McKay (1971) has described a situation in which adherence to humoral theory appeared to have clearly negative consequences. In the area of Ulu Trengganu in West Malaysia, he found that about 10 percent of the 1- to 3-year-old children had symptoms of xerophthalmia, a serious eye disease caused by vitamin A deficiency, which, if uncorrected, can lead quite abruptly to blindness. The mothers interpreted the eye symptoms as an indication of "worms" in the eye, a locally recognized disease. It was widely believed that "cooling" foods (green and yellow vegetables and fruits) could make the condition worse. As McKay suggests, "The curious and unfortunate effect of this belief is to decrease the marginal intake of Vitamin A at the very time the child is in most dire need of it" (p. 70). McKay noted a contrast between lay opinion and the views of local folk practitioners, who recommended "a whole chicken liver broiled in the sap of the papaya or an egg baked in a certain kind of tuber," and commented, "Alas, this striking folk wisdom in therapeutics seemed far less widely accepted than the folk folly that produced carotene restriction . . ." (p. 71).

On the other hand, some researchers have examined the implications of the humoral system in Mexico and felt that it is biologically adaptive, "especially in prevention of heatstroke and heat cramps, because it includes physiologically realistic rules for behavior during work in a hot climate" (McCullough 1973:32). McCullough found, for example, that peasant farmers in the Yucatan added pinches of salt to their drinking water, in compliance with the humoral theory that plain water is dangerously cold, after one has been heated through hard work and sunshine. Addition of the salt theoretically "neutralized" the coldness of the water.

Food That Cures

The most dramatic example of a "food that cures" is the role of citrus fruits in curing scurvy. Scurvy, rickets, pellagra, and beriberi can be considered "diseases of civilization," which are particularly associated with the "Age of Discovery" and the "second food transition." Until Europeans became involved in extensive sea-going expeditions, scurvy was apparently a rare disease. It was not recognized by Greek, Roman, or medieval medical writers (Davidson and Passmore 1971:424).

In 1497 scurvy killed 100 men of Vasco de Gama's crew of 160, as they sailed around the Cape of Good Hope to India. Most sailing expeditions from the sixteenth through the eighteenth centuries were beset by scurvy, even though some apparent cures for scurvy were discovered as early as 1535!

The history of scurvy is a striking lesson concerning the gaps between scientific knowledge and effective utilization, for a number of cures for scurvy were identified and remained for the most part unused. Swedes used a decoction of spruce or pine needles effectively in the sixteenth century. More important, a Scottish naval surgeon, J. Lind, published a complete *Treatise on Scurvy* in 1753, describing his controlled experiments using fresh oranges and lemons with scurvy patients. Yet it was "not until 1795, 42 years after the publication of Lind's treatise, that his pupil Sir Gilbert Blane persuaded the Lords of the Admiralty to put his precepts into practice and thus immediately abolished scurvy from the Royal Navy" (Davidson and Passmore 1971:425).

As in the matter of scurvy, the concept of "foods that cure" is most clearly identifiable when the illness in question is caused by a nutritional deficiency. The "miracle" foods are simply those that supply the missing nutrient (or nutrients) in sufficient quantity to overcome the deficiency. Pellagra and beriberi, like scurvy, are diseases brought about by changing food patterns, in which the treatment ultimately arrived at was to supply the missing nutrients.

By the middle of the twentieth century it had become evident that many aspects of modern food processing — milling, grinding, refining, and preserving—produce illness because they remove significant nutrients from our foods. In contrast to the diseases of civilization discussed earlier, the terrible deficiency diseases—beriberi, pellagra, rickets, and scurvy—are caused by the deficiency of a single nutrient. Thus the cure is at hand, in the form of specific components of food—thiamine, niacin, vitamin D, and ascorbic acid.

The Health-Food Movement

For many people the health-food movement is an alternative and answer to doubts about both our current food culture and perceived deficiencies in the medical system (Kandel and Pelto 1980). Although there is great diversity of ideology and dietary practices among people who identify themselves as health-food users, some common features are evident, including the following: (1) avoidance of refined carbohydrates, especially white sugar; (2) avoidance of foods with sodium-based additives; (3) avoidance of saturated fat, especially meat (and, in many cases, avoidance of meat altogether); (4) avoidance of "junk foods," whose inventory ranges across a variety of factory-produced cookies, cakes, and other snacks, to hot dogs and even pizzas; and (5) utilization of whole grains, fruits, and vegetables.

The vegetarian sectors of the health-food movement include a wide range from the intensely vegetarian macrobiotics to lacto–ovo-vegetarians, who use eggs and dairy products, as well as many people who will also include fish in their diet, but not animal meats. Strict vegetarians in the industrialized nations often refer to the spiritual writings of Hindu scholars and Oriental philosophers, though they may also refer to modern medical data in support of their abstention from foods derived from the animal world. (Certain Christian groups, notably Seventh Day Adventists, also have religious doctrines concerning vegetarianism.)

The clearest medical gain from vegetarianism is the reduction in animal fat, reflected in low serum cholesterol among vegetarians (Hardinge 1962). American vegetarians also tend to be slimmer than their nonvegetarian peers (Taber and Cook 1980) and have lower blood pressure (Sachs et al. 1974). On the other hand, strict vegetarian diets (without eggs or dairy products) increase the risks of deficiencies in vitamin B_{12}, iron, and calcium. For small children, such diets may also incur risks of insufficient protein intake.

Malnutrition in the Modern World

As discussed earlier, a major characteristic of many contemporary national food systems is that people cannot obtain adequate calories, protein, and other nutrients. As the magnitude of the problem has become more apparent to people in government and international agencies, a great deal of effort has been devoted to analyzing the causes of hunger. Because the problem is one of inadequate food, the dominant themes in the analysis have tended to focus on one or another of three major causes of the problem of hunger: (1) poverty, so income must be increased; (2) food shortage, so more food must be produced; and (3) maladaptive dietary patterns, so more nutrition education must be made available.

Perhaps because so much human suffering is involved, the debates about which cause is *the* main cause have tended to be bitter and acrimonious. The fundamental "correctness" of the economic explanation seems so clearly apparent in the association between poverty and undernutrition as to appear nonproblematical. Yet, as a total explanation, it fails to explain some significant conditions of undernutrition. For example, Gokulanathan and Verghese (1969) studied 390 children in an industrial belt in Kerala, India; they found significant numbers of children of the middle and upper socioeconomic classes with evidence of malnutrition. The authors felt that the growth retardation of children in these middle and upper-income families "is due to factors other than poverty and the lack of availability of food materials."

There is increasing interest among nutrition programs in capitalizing on the knowledge of community people who are able to cope effectively with nutritional maintenance in the face of poverty. For example, as part of the "Family Nutrition Improvement Program" in Indonesia, a training manual for field workers includes an exercise in which "village mothers with healthy children and limited resources share how they feed their children with a group of village women. Their practices are discussed and compared with other women's feeding practices and with recommendations from the manual" (Anon. 1981:1).

Does the present situation mean that something has gone wrong with humankind, that one of the most fundamental of all adaptive responses—eating—is no longer well tuned to biological needs and realities? Behind some of the current writing about food, especially the literature of the health-food movement, is the assumption that in earlier times people "ate naturally" and selected diets wisely. Many people still refer, with wistful faith, to the classic study in the 1920s in which Clara Davis claimed to demonstrate that newly weaned infants, if given full choice, would *naturally* choose a balanced diet (Davis 1928, 1939). Aside from the fact that the infants in the experiment did not obtain adequate nutrition (cf. Munro 1966), the most interesting aspect of this famous experiment is that the infants had no "junk food" to choose from. They were offered no candy, no sugar-coated cereal, no Twinkies, soda, or fruit drink, no potato chips or hotdogs. As Munro has suggested, the cafeteria offered to Dr. Davis's infants was a loaded deck—it practically insured a balanced diet. If the infants had, indeed, selected from the cafeteria at *random*, they undoubtedly would have had excellent nutrient intake.

Claude Fischler (1980) has addressed the issue of inappropriate (unhealthy) forms of eating in modern societies. In part he attributes the problem to what he refers to as "gastro-anomy." Modern individuals are left without clear sociocultural cues as to what their choice should be—as to when, how, and how much they should eat. Food selection and intake are now increasingly matters for individual, not social, decisions, and they are no longer under ecological or seasonal constraints. But individuals lack reliable criteria to make these decisions, and therefore they experience a growing sense of anxiety (Fischler 1980:948).

The delocalization of food in the current food transformation is one factor producing this "gastro-anomy." However, the bewildering changes in available foods, including the varieties of processed and "quick" foods, are only part of the equation. The other factor is the transformation of the social systems themselves, including changes in commensal activities, as Fischler suggest. As a larger proportion of the individual's food intake occurs in the form of snacks, informal meals, and commercially purchased food, family and kin group cultures have less effective control of individual diets. Or, to put it the other way around: individuals get less help from their social networks of kin and non-kin in their dietary choices.

An anthropological theory of nutrition is just beginning to develop from the combined efforts of cultural and biological anthropologists. At present we have only minimal understanding of the ways in which food systems have evolved and how they function. It is clear, however, that the current situation, world-wide, presents a significant challenge to our cultural mechanisms of adaptation.

REFERENCES

Anonymous. 1981. "Usaha Perbaikan Gizi Keluarga." *Mothers and Infants*, 1(2):1.

Bicchieri, M.G., ed. 1972. *Hunters and Gatherers Today*. New York: Holt, Rinehart & Winston.

Boyle, E. 1977. "Chromium Depletion in the Pathogenesis of Diabetes and Atherosclerosis." *Southern Medical Journal*, 70: 1449–53.

Briggs, George M., and Doris Howes Calloway. 1979. *Bogert's Nutrition and Physical Fitness*. Philadelphia: Saunders.

Cassidy, Claire M. 1980. "Nutrition and Health in Agriculturalists and Hunter–Gatherers: A Case Study of Two Prehistoric Populations." N.W. Jerome, R.F. Kandel, and G.H. Pelto, eds., *Nutritional Anthropology*. Pleasantville, N.Y.: Redgrave, 117–47.

Chang, K.C. 1970. "The Beginnings of Agriculture in the Far East." *Antiquity*, 64: 175–85.

Cohen, A.M. 1961. "Prevalence of Diabetes among Ethnic Groups in Israel." *Metabolism*, 10: 50–54.

Cohen, Mark N. 1977. *The Food Crisis in Prehistory: Overpopulation and the Origins of Agriculture*. New Haven: Yale Univ. Press.

Cook, Della, and Jane Buikstra, 1980. "Health and Differential Survival in Prehistoric Populations: Prenatal Dental Defects." *American Journal of Physical Anthropology*, 51:649–64.

Crapo, P.A., G. Reaven, and J. Olefsky. 1977. "Postprandial Plasma-Glucose and -Insulin Responses to Different Complex Carbohydrates." *Diabetes*, 26: 1178–83.

Crosby, Alfred W., Jr. 1972. *The Columbian Exchange: Biological and Cultural Consequences of 1492*. Westport, Ct.: Greenwood Press.

Dahl, L.K. 1977. "Salt Intake and Hypertension." J. Genest, E. Koiw, and O. Kuchel, eds., *Hypertension*. New York: McGraw–Hill, pp. 548–59.

Davidson, S., and R. Passmore. 1971. *Human Nutrition and Dietetics*, 4th ed. Edinburgh and London: E. & S. Livingstone.

Dewey, Kathryn G. 1980. "The Impact of Agricultural Development on Child Nutrition in Tabasco, Mexico." *Medical Anthropology*, 4(1):21–54.

DeWalt, Kathleen, M. 1979. *Nutritional Strategies and Agriculture Change in a Mexican Community*. Ph.D. diss. University of Connecticut, Storrs.

Dressler, William. 1979. "'Disorganization,' Adaptation and Arterial Blood Pressure." *Medical Anthropology*, 33:225–48.

Duncum, B.M. 1947. "Some Notes on the History of Lactation." *British Medical Bulletin*, 5:1141.

Eaton, Cynthia. 1977. "Diabetes, Culture Change, and Acculturation: A Biocultural Analysis." *Medical Anthropology*, 1(2):41–63.

Ferro–Luzzi, G. Eichinger. 1980. "Food Avoidance of Pregnant Women in Tamilnad." J.R.K. Robson, ed., *Food, Ecology and Culture*. New York and London: Gordon & Breach, 101–8.

Fischler, Claude. 1980. "Food Habits, Social Change and the Nature Culture Dilemma." *Social Science Information*, 19(6): 937–54.

Foster, George M. 1976. "Disease Etiologies in Non-Western Medical Systems." *American Anthropologist*, 78:773–82.

Gokulanathan, K., and K. Verghese. 1969. "Sociocultural Malnutrition (Growth Failure in Children due to Sociocultural Factors)." *Journal of Tropical Pediatrics:* 118–24.

Gross, Daniel R., and Barbara A. Underwood. 1971. "Technological Change and Caloric Costs: Sisal Agriculture in Northeastern Brazil." *American Anthropologist* 73:725–40.

Hambridge, K.M. 1974. "Chromium Nutrition in Man." *American Journal of Clinical Nutrition*, 27:505–14.

Harburg, E., et al. 1973. "Socioecologic Stressor Areas and Black–White Blood Pressure." *Detroit Journal of Chronic Diseases*, 26:595–611.

Hardinge, M., et al. 1962. "Nutritional Studies of Vegetarians: Dietary Fatty Acids and Serum Cholesterol Levels." *American Journal of Clinical Nutrition*, 10:516–24.

Hendershot, G. E. 1980. "Trends in Breastfeeding." *Advanced Data*, Vital and Health Statistics of the National Center for Health Statistics. PHS no. 59. Washington, D.C.: U.S. Public Health Service.

Hernandez, M., C. P. Hidalgo, J.R. Hernandez, H. Madrigal, and A. Chávez. 1974. "Effect of Economic Growth on Nutrition in a Tropical Community." *Ecology of Food and Nutrition*, 3:283–91.

Ho, Ping-ti. 1955. "The Introduction of American Food Plants into China." *American Anthropologist*, 57(2):190–95.

Howell, F.C. 1970. *Early Man*. New York: Time–Life Publishers.

Hypertension Task Force. 1979. *Report of the Hypertension Task Force*, vol. 2: *Scientific Summary*. NIH Publication 79–1624. Washington, D.C.: U.S. Department of Health, Education, & Welfare.

Johnston, J. 1977: "The Household Context of Infant Feeding Practices in South Trinidad." Paper presented at the annual meeting of the American Anthropological Association.

Kandel, Randy F., and Gretel H. Pelto. 1980. "The Health Food Movement: Social Revitalization or Alternative Health Maintenance System?" N.W. Jerome, R.F. Kandel, and G.H. Pelto, eds., *Nutritional Anthropology*. Pleasantville, N.Y.:Redgrave, 327–64.

Laderman, Carol C. 1979. *Conceptions and Preconceptions: Childbirth and Nutrition in Rural Malaysia*. Ph.D. diss., Columbia University, New York.

Lee, Richard B. 1968. "What Hunters Do for a Living, or How To Make Out on Scarce Resources." R.B. Lee and I. DeVore, eds., *Man the Hunter*. Chicago: Aldine, 30–48.

   1979   *The !Kung San: Men, Women and Work in a Foraging Society*. Cambridge: Cambridge Univ. Press.

———, and Irven DeVore, eds. 1968. *Man the Hunter*. Chicago: Aldine.

Lewitter, F., P.V. Tishler, and F.E. Speizer. 1980. "The Families of Adult Twins as a Genetic Epidemiological Tool." *Medical Anthropology*, 4:385–96.

Logan, Michael H. 1977. "Anthropological Research on the Hot–Cold Theory of Disease: Some Methodological Suggestions." *Medical Anthropology*, 1(4):87–112.

Mamarbachi, D., and P.L. Pellett. 1980. "Observations on Nutritional Marasmus in a Newly Rich Nation." *Ecology of Food and Nutrition*, 9:43–54.

Marchione, Thomas J. 1980. "Factors Associated with Malnutrition in the Children of Western Jamaica." N.W. Jerome, R.F. Kandel, and G.H. Pelto, eds., *Nutritional Anthropology*. Pleasantville, N.Y.: Redgrave, 223–73.

Mata, Leonardo J. 1978. *The Children of Santa Maria Cauque*. Cambridge, Mass.: MIT Press.

   1978   "Breastfeeding: A Main Promoter of Infant Health." *American Journal of Clinical Nutrition*, 31:2058–65.

Maurer, A.C. 1979. "The Therapy of Diabetes." *American Scientist*, 67: 422–31.

McCracken, F.D. 1971. "Lactase Deficiency: An Example of Dietary Evolution." *Current Anthropology*, 12: 479–518.

McCullough, J.M. 1973. "Human Ecology, Heat Adaptation and Belief Systems: The Hot–Cold Syndrome in Yucatan." *Southwestern Journal of Anthropology*, 29: 32–36.

McKay, David A. 1971. "Food, Illness and Folk Medicine: Insights from Ulu Trengganu, West Malaysia." *Ecology of Food and Nutrition*, 1:67–72.

Meneely, G.R., and H.D. Batterbee. 1976. "High Sodium-Low Potassium Environment and Hypertension." *American Journal of Cardiology*, 38:768–86.

Meyer, H. 1968. "Breastfeeding in the United States." *Clinical Pediatrics*, 7:708–15.

Meyer, P. 1980. *Hypertension: Mechanisms and Clinical and Therapeutic Aspects.* Oxford: Oxford Univ. Press.

Muñoz de Chávez, M., P. Arroyo, S.E. Perex Gil, S. Hernandez, S.E. Quiroz, M. Rodriquez, M.P. de Hermelo, and A. Chávez. 1974. "The Epidemiology of Good Nutrition." *Ecology of Food and Nutrition*, 3: 223–30.

Neel, J.B. 1962. "Diabetes Mellitus: A 'Thrifty' Genotype Rendered Detrimental by 'Progress'?" *American Journal of Human Genetics*, 14:353–62.

Nerlove, S.B. 1974. "Women's Workload and Infant Feeding Practices: A Relationship with Demographic Implications." *Ethnology*, 13:125–214.

Nietschmann, Bernard. 1973. *Between Land and Water: The Subsistence Ecology of the Miskito Indians, Eastern Nicaragua.* New York: Seminar Press.

O'Dea, K., R.M. Spargo, and K. Akerman. 1980. "Some Studies on the Relationship between Urban Living and Diabetes in a Group of Australian Aborigines." *Medical Anthropology*, 4(1):1–20.

Paul, O. 1977. "Epidemiology of Hypertension." J. Genest, E. Koiw, O.Kuchel, eds., *Hypertension.* New York: McGraw-Hill.

Pellett, Peter L. 1981. "Malnutrition, Wealth and Development." *Food and Nutrition Bulletin*, 3(1):17–24.

Pelto, Gretel H. 1981. "Perspectives on Infant Feeding: Decision-Making and Ecology." *Food and Nutrition Bulletin*, 3(3):16–29.

Pelto, Pertti J. 1973. *The Snowmobile Revolution: Technology and Social Change in the Arctic.* Menlo Park, Cal.: Cummings.

———, and Satu Mosnikoff. 1978. "Skolt Sami Ethnicity and Cultural Revival." *Ethnos*, 43(3–4):193–212.

Poggie, John J., Jr., and Robert N. Lynch. 1974. *Rethinking Modernization: Anthropological Perspectives.* Westport, Ct.: Greenwood Press.

Rawson, I., and V. Valverde. 1977. "The Etiology of Malnutrition among Preschool Children in Rural Costa Rica." *Journal of Tropical Pediatrics and Environmental Child Health*, 22:12–17.

Richards, Audrey I. 1964. *Hunger and Work in a Savage Tribe.* Cleveland: Meridian Books, World.

Rosenberg, Ellen M. 1980. "Demographic Effects of Sex-Differential Nutrition." N.W. Jerome, R.F. Kandel, and G.H. Pelto, eds. *Nutritional Anthropology.* Pleasantville, N.Y.: Redgrave, 181–204.

Sachs, F., et al. 1974. "Blood Pressure in Vegetarians." *American Journal of Epidemiology.* 100:390–98.

Scudder, T. 1971. "Gathering among African Woodland Savannah Cultivators, a Case Study: The Gwembe Tonga." *Zambian Papers*, no. 5.

Scotch, Norman A. 1963. "Sociocultural Factors in the Epidemiology of Zulu Hypertension."
    American Journal of Public Health, 53: 1205–13.

Simoons, F.J. 1967. *Eat Not This Flesh*. Madison: Univ. of Wisconsin Press.

    1980   "The Determinants of Dairying and Milk Use in the Old World: Ecological,
    Physiological and Cultural." J.R.K. Robson, ed., *Food, Ecology and Culture*. New
    York and London: Gordon & Breach, 83–92.

Stemmerman, G. 1970. "Patterns of Disease among Japanese Living in Hawaii." *Archives
    of Environmental Health*, 20:266–72.

Swantz, Marja-Liisa. 1975. "Socioeconomic Causes of Malnutrition in Moshi District." Re-
    search Paper no. 38. Bureau of Resource Assessment and Land Use Planning.
    University of Dar es Salaam.

Taber, Louis A.L., and Richard A. Cook. 1980. "Dietary and Anthropometric Assessment
    of Adult Omnivores, Fish-Eaters and Lacto–Ovo-Vegetarians." *Journal of the Amer-
    ican Dietetic Association*, 76:21–29.

Tannahill, Reay. 1973. *Food in History*. New York: Stein & Day.

Teleki, Geza. 1973. *The Predatory Behavior of Wild Chimpanzees*. Lewisburg, Pa.: Bucknell
    Univ. Press.

Wallace, Anthony F.C. 1972. *Rockdale: The Growth of an American Village in the Early Industrial
    Revolution*. New York: Alfred A. Knopf.

Ward, Ryk, and Ian Prior. 1980. "Genetic and Sociocultural Factors in the Response of
    Blood Pressure to Migration of the Tokelau Population." *Medical Anthropology*,
    4(3):339–66.

Weiss, Bryan. 1980. "Nutrition Adaptation and Cultural Maladaptation: An Evolutionary
    View." N.W. Jerome, R.F. Kandel, and G.H. Pelto, eds. *Nutritional Anthropology*.
    Pleasantville, N.Y.: Redgrave, 147–79.

Williams, Cecily D. 1935. "Kwashiorkor." *Lancet*, 2:1151–55.

Wilson, C.S. 1980. "Food Taboos of Childbirth: The Malay Example." J.D.K. Robson, ed.
    Food, Ecology and Culture. New York and London: Gordon & Breach, 67–74.

Wing, E.S., and A.B. Brown. 1979. *Paleo-Nutrition: Method and Theory in Prehistoric Food
    ways*. New York: Academic Press.

Winikoff, B., & E. Baer. 1980. "The Obstetricians Opportunity: Translating "Breast Is
    Best" from Theory to Practice." *American Journal of Obstetrics and Gynecology*, 138
    (1):105–17.

World Health Organization. 1981. *Contemporary Patterns of Breast-Feeding*. Report on the
    WHO collaborative Study on Breast-feeding. Geneva.

11

The Antibiotic
and Healing Potential
of Plants Used
for Teeth Cleaning

Memory Elvin–Lewis

Plant species in the form of sticks (roots and twigs), sponges, fruits, and gums are still used for teeth cleaning, particularly in rural areas of Africa, the Middle East through to the Asian subcontinent, and, to a lesser degree, Oceania and the Americas. Certain species are carefully selected for this purpose, not just because of their appealing flavor and texture, but also with the belief that their use maintains good dental health. Moreover, some have added therapeutic value, in that they are preferred when dental pathology exists, and thus are used for the purpose of healing and strengthening affected gums, in remedies for toothache, or to treat oral mucosal infections. Many of these species are also selected for medicinal purposes that are frequently associated with their healing, analgesic, hemostatic, and astringent characteristics, all properties that could be associated with their popularity for dental hygiene. Although selection of specific species may be influenced by availability, economics, social pressure, or even religion, this method remains a viable alternative to Western techniques in a large portion of the Third World (Elvin–Lewis 1979, Elvin–Lewis et al. 1980a; Adu-tutu et al. 1979; Elvin–Lewis, 1980a).

Since dental disease is the result of microbial interactions with the host, it is important first to review how various plant components could affect these odontopathic processes. Plants selected for teeth cleaning may possess an antibiotic capacity that either kills or limits the growth of these organisms, inhibitors that affect their enzymatic processes, lectins that prevent their attachment to structures in the oral cavity, and substances that promote healing and reduce inflamation, pain, and bleeding.

For example, the predominant organisms that cause tooth decay are either Gram-positive cocci (*Streptococcus* spp) or rods (*Lactobacillus* spp) or acid-fast organisms belonging to the Actinomycetales. These organisms possess a number of mechanisms that aid them in causing tooth decay. Their organelles, called pili, allow them to specifically adhere to the teeth or other organisms in plaque, and their enzymes—like glucosyl, transferase, and levan sucrase—act in the presence of sucrose to produce insoluble polymers of glucose (glucans, mutans) and fructose (levans), respectively. These polymers stick to tooth surfaces, serve as the plaque matrix in which organisms proliferate, and also provide secondary bacterial colonizers of plaque with food. These bacteria possess dextranases or levanases that first break down these polymers to their respective glucose or fructose moieties, which are then further processed in the glycolytic cycle to produce energy for the microorganisms and lactic acid as an end product. Other organisms may ferment sucrose directly with the same result. This acid accumulates in plaque and finally dissolves the calcium apatite of enamel, and, with other proteolytic enzymes, breaks down the supporting protein matrix of the tooth structure to form a carious lesion. Even without more sugar, these organisms can continue the cariogenic process by utilizing polysaccharides they have stored in intracellular vaculoes precisely for this contingency.

Thus, the anticariogenic potential of these plants is based upon the presence of antibiotics that affect the growth of cariogenic bacteria or prevent pili attachment (Gibbons 1982), tannins that inhibit the action of glucosyl transferases (Paolino et al. 1980; Elvin–Lewis et al. 1980b), and fluorides that affect glycolytic enzymes associated with either acid or intracellular polysaccharide production (Brown and Konig 1977; Hamilton 1977).

Periodontal disease is a progressively destructive disorder of the gums and supporting alveolar bone that results from the interaction of gingival plaque organisms and their products with the host and its defense mechanisms. Clinically, it first appears as bleeding, sore gums (gingivitis) and develops in severity until teeth are lost from lack of supporting tissue. Organisms that cause this disease are those associated with the carious process as well as others that reside in the gingival sulcus, often in the preferential absence of oxygen, such as a number of Gram-negative rods within the Bacterioidaceae, spirochetes, and spirilla. These organisms contain endotoxins in their cell walls that elicit inflammation and also produce enzymes that lead to tissue and bone loss. Plants that affect this process may do so through their antibiotics, lectins, or enzymatic inhibitors as described for caries, and may also contain astringent compounds like tannins that arrest bleeding, steroidal saponins that reduce swelling, and other substances, including some alkaloids, that reduce pain or promote healing.

Pulpal infections often develop after invasion of pulpal tissue by organisms from an associated carious or periodontally affected tissue, or less frequently, through the blood stream. Infection with these organisms causes inflammation and pain, and, in association with necrotic bacterial enzymes or loss of the tooth through periapical abscess formation, may result in nerve death. Plants and their oils used in root-canal therapy possess compounds that reduce pain, inflammation, and bacterial infection.

The successful herbal treatment of oral infections is associated with selection of plants that contain compounds that reduce pain and inflammation and are astringent and antibiotic for the bacteria, yeast, or virus involved. Thus, plants successfully used to treat the yeast infections of *Candida albicans,* like thrush, have astringent and antifungal capabilities. Little is known regarding the antiviral properties of plants used to treat herpetic infections, but often those with healing and analgesic properties are selected. The etiology of canker sores, aphthous stomatitis or aphthae, remains an enigma; however, these lesions respond to steroidal therapy, and plants used for their treatment may contain similar components like steroidal saponins.

Observations associating the dental health of populations with the use of plants for teeth cleaning were first made in West Africa. There, where this technique is popular, caries rates are extremely low; and clinical evaluation of Ghanaians using plants for teeth cleaning suggests that the potential to confer good dental health (estimated by the degree of tooth retention) can be correlated with the selection of one species over another (Elvin–Lewis et al. 1980a). Moreover, the antibiotic nature of these plants is an important feature in their empirical selection, since this clinical data on their use can be correlated with results obtained from their antibiotic potential (El–Said et al. 1971; Elvin–Lewis et al. 1974; Fadulu 1975).

Therefore, it is important to understand the antibiotic nature of plants used for teeth cleaning for several reasons. One is to establish a rationale for their preference, and perhaps efficacy, and another is to identify species that contain compounds that could be utilized to improve Western dental health. Attempts in emerging nations to achieve optimal dental-health care by imposing Western techniques has always been difficult for financial and other reasons. These data may provide the information necessary to establish needed cooperation between practitioners of traditional and modern dental hygiene. This is important not only in Africa and Asia, where both methods are being practiced without careful evaluation, but also in countries of the Caribbean and Central America, where knowledge of traditional forms of teeth cleaning is rapidly disappearing and is not being replaced by modern Western practices for financial reasons.

These data will be presented according to the phylogenetic groups to which the species belong. The rationale for this is as follows: Certain orders of angiosperms are more closely related than others by the nature of their position on the evolutionary scale, and they frequently share common dental and medicinal uses and related compounds (Lewis and Elvin–Lewis 1977). Thus, it is convenient to consider together those species belonging to one phylogenetic group. The groups are sequentially numbered to denote the degree of evolution from primitive to advanced characteristics in the dicotyledons (Groups 1–11) and monocotyledons (Groups 12–15). One hundred and seventy species are known for teeth cleaning, and their families can be found in some orders of each group with the exception of Group 12.

Phylogenetic Group 1

The American chewing stick, *Sassafras albidum* (Lauraceae), has had many uses in the folk culture of America. Today, in western Kentucky, Tennessee, and the mountains of North Carolina it is still used for teeth cleaning. Prior to the discovery that the **safrole** (Fig. 11.1*a*) in its oil causes liver cancer in rats (Segelman et al. 1976), the oil was used as a disinfectant in root-canal therapy, to treat toothache, and as a flavoring in root beer. Studies with its leaves (Madsen and Pates 1952), oil, and twigs have shown that the plant possesses broad-spectrum antimicrobial activity closely approximating that found for one of its components, **eugenol.** The inhibitory spectrum affects many bacteria, including some associated with caries and pulpitis. **Eugenol** is still used today in modern dentistry for disinfecting root canals, but is usually isolated from oil of cloves. Also, the use of the oil for toothache could have been related to a number of alkaloids or other compounds that might have analgesic or antibiotic properties (Leung 1980). Also, the **tannin** content in oil of cloves may exert either an anticariogenic or hemostatic effect.

None of the Menispermaceae used in West Africa as chew sticks have been examined for their antibiotic potential, although their medicinal uses include the treatment of swollen and infected wounds, as carminatives, and for cough (Dalziel 1937; Irvine 1961). However, studies among other related genera suggest that such a search would be worthwhile. In this family, a number of antibiotics have already been identified, including the alkaloid **berberine** (Fig. 11.1*b*), which is present in the Southeast Asian species *Arcanelisa flava,* American goldenseal, *Hydrastis canadensis* (Ranunculaceae), and European barberry, *Berberis vulgaris* (Berberidaceae); berberine has broad-spectrum antimicrobial activity and also affects protozoa. Also derived from another Ranunculaceae are **Substances A and B** from *Aristolochia* and *Asarum* species, with broad-spectrum properties (Korzybski et al. 1967).

Phylogenetic Group 2

The American chewing stick, *Liquidambar styraciflua* (Hamamelidaceae) or sweet gum, is still used today by farmers in the Southern United States for teeth cleaning (Elvin–Lewis 1979) and may be soaked in water or brandy before use (Krochmal and Krochmal 1973). Also, its gum is chewed by rural American Blacks with the belief that it whitens the teeth (Elvin–Lewis 1979), and was once used by white pioneers for a number of medicinal purposes, including the alleviation of pain and inflammation of herpetic lesions. This gum is the source of commercial storax, which is a stimulating expectorant (Friar's Balsam) and has been used topically in the treatment of canker sores, trench mouth, and herpes simplex (Osal and Farrar 1955; Leung 1980). Studies with extracts of its twig and twig bark have shown that it possesses a broad-spectrum antibiotic activity, including effects against bacteria and yeast with the potential to cause caries, thrush, and skin infections. Of the number of components isolated from storax, **cinnamic acid** (Fig. 11.1*c*) has been shown experimentally to be incorporated into the glycoside phenolic **arbutin** (Fig. 11.1*d*), 6-coumarin glucose, and subsequently coumarin, glucovanillin, and **salicin** (Fig. 11.1*e*) (Tyler et al. 1976). Since phenolics usually have antimicrobial and antiherpetic properties, and salicin has anti-inflammatory and analgesic qualities, these compounds may contribute to the healing capacity found in the plant.

In the Southeastern United States, the Cherokee and others once preferred twigs of the black or cherry birch (*Betula lenta,* Betulaceae) for teeth cleaning, and other native Americans utilized related species in remedies for cough, as well as for their astringent, analgesic, and healing properties (Elvin–Lewis 1979). *Betula lenta* has not been studied specifically for its antimicrobial activity. However, it is the source of sweet birch oil, composed primarily of the aromatic ester **methyl salicylate** (Fig. 11.1*f*), a compound known to reduce fever, pain, and inflammation, but with a toxicity greater than other salicylates (Leung 1980). Pharmaceutically, it has been used as a counterirritant in the treatment of arthritis and neuralgia, as a fragrance for perfumes and cosmetics, and as a wintergreen flavoring (Osal and Farrar 1955; Leung 1980). It is possible that other species were also used for teeth cleaning; among these *B. davurica* (Frisbey et al. 1954), *B. paprifera* (MacDonald and Bishop 1953), and *B. populifolia* (Frisbey et al. 1953) inhibit Gram-positive and acid-fast bacteria, a feature that may account for the use of *B. populifolia* by the Maritime Algonquin for the treatment of wound infections (Chandler et al. 1979).

Broad-spectrum activity has also been found for *Alnus glutinosa* (Betulaceae) (Frisbey et al. 1953), the inner bark of which was favored by ancient Britons for teeth cleaning. The anticancer agents **betulin** and **lupeol** have been isolated from the related species *A. oregonus* (Lewis and Elvin–Lewis 1977), although antibiotic agents per se have not been isolated from the genus.

Phylogenetic Group 3

In North Africa, twigs of *Achyranthes aspera* (Amaranthaceae) are used for teeth cleaning (Lewis and Elvin–Lewis 1977), as are infusions of its roots in China (Perry 1980). It is used medicinally for its astringent, hemostatic, analgesic, and healing properties, and has been found to contain achranthin, oleanolic acid, a **sapogenin**, potash (Perry 1980), and alkaloids. Similarly, the root of *Aerva tomentosa* (Amaranthaceae) is used in the Red Sea area for teeth cleaning; and elsewhere, roots of other species are used to treat skin infections and swelling (Dalziel 1937; Perry 1980). Antimicrobial tests have yet to be carried out on those used for teeth cleaning, but surveys among other Amaranthaceae have shown that at least one species, *Amaranthus retroflexus* (but not others—*A. blitum, A. caudatus, A. chlorostachys, A. hypochonriacus, A. tricolor,* and *A. viridis*), possesses antimicrobial activity against a Gram-positive (*Staphylococcus aureus*) and a Gram-negative (*Escherichia coli*) bacteria (Gottshall et al. 1949). Also, within this phylogenetic group, *Rheum officinale*, and *Cassia reticulata* of p ylogenetic group 7, have yielded an antibiotic oxyanthroquinone dye called **rhein** or cassic acid (Fig. 11.1*g*), which strongly inhibits the growth of Gram-positive (*Staphylococcus aureus, Bacillus* spp) and acid-fast (*Mycobacterium* spp) organisms but not Gram-negative bacteria (Kavanaugh 1947). The medicinal uses of those plants selected for teeth cleaning imply that they may also contain an antibiotic similar to that of rhein, since Gram-positive bacterial inhibition is an important characteristic necessary for the successful treatment of many skin infections.

Phylogenetic Group 4

Members of the Clusiaceae, used in West Africa for teeth cleaning, are also employed to heal, to treat pain, cough, and tumors, and for astringent, diuretic, and aphrodisiac purposes. In Ghana, *Garcinia* species are preferred because they clean efficiently, refresh the mouth, are mild to the gums, and serve to enhance the stimulatory effect of the cola nut. In this respect, *G. afzelii* and the closely related *G. epunctata*, known in Akan as "Nsodkodua," were favored by 60.2 percent of the population and *G. kola* or "Tweapea" by another 19.6 percent. This preference was closely correlated with the high incidence of tooth retention for individuals favoring these species, i.e., Nsodkodua (86 percent) and Tweapea (82 percent) (Elvin–Lewis et al. 1980a), and the broad-spectrum antibiotic activity (including activity against organisms with cariogenic potential) they possess (El–Said et al. 1971; Elvin–Lewis et al. 1974; Fadulu 1975). The antimicrobial spectrum of these species closely resembles that of the antibiotic morellin, isolated from an Indian species, *G. morella*. Morellin (Fig. 11.1*h*) is an antibiotic pigment with broad-spectrum but highly toxic properties (Murthy and Roa 1961), but is a more likely candidate than the other antibiotics, the alpha and beta gutiferrins (Fig. 11.1*i*), which only inhibit Gram-positive bacteria (Rao and Rao 1961). However, in the case of the West African species, the toxicity of the antibiotic compounds they contain may not be as great as those of *G. morella*.

Within the African Ebenaceae a number of *Diospyros* species are used for teeth cleaning, and these and others are employed for their astringency, to heal, and to treat cough or worm infestations (Irvine 1961; Lewis and Elvin–Lewis 1977; Perry 1980). Only one chewing-stick species, *D. tricolor*, has been evaluated for its effect on odontopathic organisms (Elvin–Lewis et al. 1974). Although *D. tricolor* was found to inhibit only *Actinomyces viscosus*, this finding appears significant since other species of *Diospyros* are known to inhibit the related *Mycobacterium tuberculosis*, also of the Actinomycetales, including those that yield the antibiotic plumbagin (Fig. 11.1*d*) (Lucas et al. 1955, Irvine 1961). Moreover, *D. tricolor* has a high fluoride content, and thus its extracts can also impair acid production of cariogenic streptococci without inhibiting their growth (Elvin–Lewis et al. 1974).

The American Ericaceae, *Gaultheria procumbens*, once used for teeth cleaning, is a component of an herbal mountain tea and the source of the wintergreen oil used in flavoring (Lewis and Elvin–Lewis 1977). The oil is almost 98 percent methyl salicylate, which differs isomerically from sweet birch oil or the synthetic component

(Leung 1980). The broad-spectrum antibiotic components of this plant have not been identified (Sanders et al. 1945; Gottshall et al. 1949), but methyl salicylate (Fig. 11.1*f*) may have anti-inflammatory and analgesic properties.

Phylogenetic Group 5

In spite of the fact that none of the species in the West African Cistales and Capparidales used for teeth cleaning have been examined for antimicrobial activity, data obtained from genera of the same families suggest that such a potential exists. A similar association may be made with the analgesic nature of some of these plants. For example, broad-spectrum activity is characteristic of a number of genera in the Flacortiaceae (*Flacourtia, Gynocardia, Taraktogenos, Azara, Hydnocarpus*) (Osborn 1943; Lucas et al. 1955), and seeds of *Hyndocarpus* are the source of the lipid chaulmoogra (Fig. 11.1*j*) and hydnocarpus oil (Fig. 11.1*k*), once used in the treatment of leprosy (Perry 1980). Similarly, antimicrobial activity against the Gram-positive organisms *Mycobacterium* and *Candida* is known for a number of *Viola* species of the Violaceae (Osborn 1943; Hayes 1947; Pates and Madsen 1955; Frisbey et al. 1953, 1954). **Gaultherin,** a methyl salicylate (Fig. 11.1*f*), and **salicylic acid,** both with analgesic and anti-inflammatory properties, have also been identified in members of the family. Among genera of the Passifloraceae, *Passiflora* species are known to inhibit a broader spectrum of organisms (Osborn 1943; Lucas et al. 1955) than *Opiscaulon cissameiloides,* which inhibits only Gram-positive organisms (Osborn 1943). A variation in inhibitory spectra is also evident for genera of the Capparidaceae; e.g., *Isomeris* and *Steriphoma* inhibit Gram-positive (Osborn 1943; Hughes 1952), and *Cynadropsis,* Gram-negative, organisms (Taniguchi et al. 1978).

In the Salicaceae, a number of *Populus* species (including *P. deltoides,* the cottonwood) were used by the Cheyenne and others in the southeastern United States for teeth cleaning (Elvin-Lewis 1979) and in their medicine for the treatment of cough and alleviation of pain (Leung 1980). Today, *Populus* is the source of commercial toothpicks and balm of Gilead buds, which are used as an ingredient in cough medicine (Leung 1980). A number of active components have been isolated from this genus, including the analgesic and anti-inflammatory **salicin** and **populin** (a benzoyl salicin) and antibiotics like **trichocarpin** (Fig. 11.1*l*), which inhibits fungi, **cinnamic acid,** which inhibits *Mycobacterium tuberculosis,* and **bisabolol,** which affects both *M. tuberculosis* and Gram-positive and Gram-negative organisms (Korzybski et al. 1967).

Phylogenetic Group 6

This phylogenetic group is well represented as a source of teeth-cleaning plants throughout the world (Lewis and Elvin–Lewis 1977; Elvin–Lewis 1979; Lewis 1980). Those in the Malvales are primarily used in West Africa, although *Hibiscus* is also preferred in Fiji. These species are also used in folk remedies of these regions to heal, to treat pain, fever, and constipation, and as abortificants (Dalziel 1937; Irvine 1961; Perry 1980). A number of active principles have already been isolated in *Hibiscus* and *Gossypium* (cotton) species of the Malvaceae, including salicyclic acid, with known analgesic and anti-inflammatory properties, and **polyphenols** (Sadykov 1972), which could be the source of the antibiotic activity determined in the chewing-stick species *Hibiscus rosa-sinensis* (Leven et al. 1979). Also within the Sterculiaceae, medicinal uses of *Waltheria indica* suggest that its **tannins** are important, as may be the stimulating alkaloids theobromine and caffeine in species of *Cola*. However, no antibiotic activity has been found for genera in this family (Osborn 1943) or for those used as chewing-sticks in the Tiliaceae (Lucas et al. 1955; Taniguchi et al. 1978). In the Urticales, however, genera in the Moraceae have yielded a number of antifungal **phenolics** that include **chlorophorin** from *Chlorophora excelsa,* which is similar to mycophenolic acid, and **tetrahydrostilbene** (Fig. 11.1*m*) from the osage orange (*Maclura pomifera*) (Lewis and Elvin–Lewis 1977; Korzybski et al. 1967). A number of antibiotic bitter acids have been isolated from hops (*Humulus lupulus,* Cannabaceae), which also belong to this order. Of these, the cyclic ketones, lupulon (Fig. 11.1*n*) and humulon (Fig. 11.1*o*) have the greatest antimicrobial activity for Gram-positive and acid-fast organisms. More specifically, species of fig (*Ficus*), which are sometimes used for teeth cleaning, or whose latex is chewed as gum in Africa and Central America to treat wounds or to eradicate intestinal worms, have been found to contain the enzyme ficin, which can digest the intestinal parasite *Ascaris* (Korzybski et al. 1967).

Genera in the Euphorbiales used for teeth cleaning in Africa are used there and in Southeast Asia to treat pain, fever, cough, and bleeding and for its astringency. Also, *Alchornia* are used to treat buccal ulcerations; *Drypetes,* toothache; and *Jatropha,* bleeding gums (Perry 1980). Broad-spectrum activity has been found for *Alchornia cordifolia* (Buadu and Boakye–Yiadom 1973) and other species belonging to genera used for teeth cleaning, like *Phyllanthus* (Frisbey et al. 1954; Taniguchi et al. 1978) and *Mallotis* (Jensen and Hess 1951). Overall, antibiotic activity is widespread in the Euphorbiaceae, and, as might be expected in such a large family, the spectrum of inhibition is variable (Madsen and Pates 1952; Lucas et al. 1955; Pates and Madsen 1955; Leven et al. 1979). Antibiotics active against Gram-positive and acid-fast bacteria have been identified; they are **selobicin** from *Croton sellowii* (De Lima and Caldas 1954) and **urensin** from *Cnidoscolus urens* (Silva et al. 1958).

In the Rhamnaceae, *Gouania lupuloides* and *G. polygama* are still used in the Caribbean Basin by persons of African descent for teeth cleaning; they are referred to as chaw sticks, *Lianne Savon,* or *bon dent.* The use of *G. lupiloides* was recorded in colonial literature by Barton (1817) as follows:

> In powder, it forms an excellent dentifrice; its aromatic bitter producing a health state of the gums, and the mucilage it contains working up by the brush into a kind of soap like froth. A tincture also is prepared from it, and much recommended, diluted with water, as a wash or gargle, in cases of salivation or disease of the gums. The principal use to which the chaw stick is applied, however, is a substitute for the tooth

brush itself. For this purpose, the extremity of a piece of a branch, which is usually about the thickness of the finger, is softened by chewing, and then rubbed against the teeth. In this manner a tooth brush and with it, a powder is obtained, equal, if not superior, to any in use in Europe.

Nowadays, an alcoholic extract called "Chewdent" is commercially available, as a mouthwash and, in thickened form, as a dentifrice.

Examination of both an alcoholic extract of *G. lupiloides* and the commercial product, Chewdent, for antimicrobial activity indicates that its use for teeth cleaning is justified. It affects a wide range of microorganisms, including those that have been associated with dental disease (Elvin–Lewis 1980b). Its antibiotic spectrum is not unlike that of *Ceonothus* spp. that have the capacity to inhibit acid-fast, Gram-positive and, to a lesser degree, Gram-negative organisms (Frisbey et al. 1953; Carlson et al. 1948). This species, and also *G. longipetala* in West Africa, contains saponins, which probably contribute to the healing capacity of the genus (Irvine 1961).

Phylogenetic Group 7

All plants used for teeth cleaning in this group belong to the order Rosales. In the Rosaceae, the two species cited as chewing sticks have yet to be examined (Lewis and Elvin–Lewis 1977), but antibiotic activity, especially for Gram-positive organisms, is probable, since it is widespread in the family (Frisbey et al. 1953; Nickell 1959; Leven et al. 1979). Antibiotics have already been identified in the Rosaceae, especially from species with commercial value. These include **phloretin** (Fig. 11.1*p*), present in the bark and root of apple (*Malus*), pear (*Pyrus*), and plum (*Prunus*) trees in the form of the glucoside **phorizin**, which has broad-spectrum activity (MacDonald and Bishop 1953). Also, the lactone, parascorbic acid, isolated from the ripe fruit of European mountain ash, has antibacterial activity (Kuhn et al. 1943; Lewis and Elvin–Lewis 1977).

Within the Connaraceae, the fruit of *Cnestis ferruginea*—used by children of Ghana and Sierra Leone for teeth cleaning—has broad-spectrum activity, as do others in the family with medicinal value; but not the one (*Agelaea obliqua*) known as a chewing stick (Boakye–Yiadom and Konning 1975). No antibiotics have yet been identified in this family.

Among the Fabaceae, subfamily Faboideae, *Meletia zachiana* used in Ghana for teeth cleaning has broad-spectrum antibiotic activity. This is not unexpected, since several antibiotic substances have already been isolated from members of this subfamily and include **dalbergion I and II** (*Dalbergia nigra*) (Figs. 11.1*q* and 11.1*r*) and **dicumarol** (*Melilotus*) with broad-spectrum activity; **phaseollin** (*Phaseolus vulgaris*) (Fig 11.1*s*) and an undefined substance (*Vicia faba*) with antifungal activity. Ethyl gallate, also isolated from *Arbutus unedo* (Group 4) and from *Haematoxylum campecianum* (Caesalpiniodeae), *Acacia adonsonii,* and *A. seyal* (Mimosoideae), specifically inhibits certain *Mycobacterium*. Other antibiotic substances likely exist in *Acacia,* since broad-spectrum antimicrobial activity, particularly for Gram-positive organisms that can cause dental disease, were found for the chewing sponge, *A. pennata,* and for two commercial Gum Arabic specimens obtained from either *A. senegal* or *A. seyal.* It is not understood why the dental health of those who prefer *A. pennata* is not as good as that of those chewing-stick users who choose species with similar antimicrobial spectra (Elvin–Lewis et al. 1980a). It has been suggested that the choice of these soft, astringent, and foamy sponges for teeth cleaning may be due to preexisting periodontal disease, in much the same way as other *Acacia* species are selected in India, and are thus not the cause but the treatment for the problem. *Acacia* also contains astringent cachotannic or catechol tannins and organic fluorides (Hall 1972; Peters and Shorthouse 1972), and these too may exert anticariogenic effects like those described for tea (Elvin–Lewis et al. 1980b).

Phylogenetic Group 8

Studies on the antimicrobial potential of the African Combretaceae used for teeth cleaning have shown that *Terminalia ivorensis* and *T. glaucescens* (El-Said et al. 1971; Fadulu 1975) possess broad-spectrum activity that includes an inhibitory capacity for oral organisms implicated in caries, pulpitis, and periodontal disease (Lewis and Elvin–Lewis 1977). This antibiotic spectrum is consistent with the clinical observations made on individuals using either *T. glaucescens* (Manley et al. 1975) or *T. ivorensis* (Elvin–Lewis et al. 1980a). In both reports, dental health was good, and in spite of a high incidence (72 percent) of yellow teeth acquired from the plant dye, no caries activity was detected. However, tooth retention among this group is lower (74.9 percent) than in groups preferring other chewing sticks with a similar antimicrobial spectrum, e.g., *Garcinia* species (each 84 percent). One reason may be that *Terminalia* is used as fibrous chewing sponges rather than chewing sticks, and thus this technique of teeth cleaning is not as effective as the use of certain chewing sticks. Although comparative clinical data are lacking to support this assumption, it is noteworthy that Ghanians who prefer *Acacia* chewing sponges also have a lower incidence of tooth retention (75.6 percent) (Elvin–Lewis et al. 1980a).

In the Myrtaceae the most important species to dentistry is *Syzygium aromaticum,* the source of clove oil that contains the analgesic and antiseptic eugenol (Fig. 11.1*t*), and eugenol acetate that acts like an antihistamine, as well as other components (Leung 1980). Clove oil is a common folk remedy for toothache, and eugenol is used in dentistry today to treat dry socket (postextraction alveolitis) and, with zinc oxide, in root-canal therapy. The spectrum of antimicrobial activity for eugenol is broader than for extracts of *Syzygium, Eugenia,* and *Psidium* species (Frisbey et al. 1954; Lucas et al. 1955).

Phylogenetic Group 9

In the Polygalaceae, the West African *Carpolobia* spp. used for teeth cleaning have not been examined for their antimicrobial spectrum; however, the related American species, *Polygala lutea,* is inhibitory to Gram-negative organisms and *Candida albicans* (Pates and Madsen 1955). Consistent with their medicinal uses, a number of *Polygala* throughout the world have been found to contain the analgesic compound **methyl salicylate** (Fig. 11.1*f*) and saponins with antimicrobial potential (Lewis and El-vin–Lewis 1977; Perry 1980).

Within the Rutaceae, *Citrus* spp. are used for teeth cleaning, to treat toothache and oral infections, and for other healing and analgesic purposes. Broad-spectrum antimicrobial activity has been identified in oil of lemon (*C. lemoni*) (Pételot 1952) and in the oil and other plant parts of the grapefruit (*C. paradisi*) (Pates and Madsen 1955). Similar dental uses have been reported in Africa for *Clausena anisata,* and its ability to heal, reduce pain, and expel intestinal nematodes has been attributed to its essential oil, primarily the phenolic ether **anethole** (Fig. 11.1*u*) and **methyl chavicol.** Specific active components have also been identified in a number of *Fagara* species utilized for their analgesic and counterirritant properties in the treatment of toothache, canker sores, rheumatism, snakebite, and cough. *F. zanthoxyloides,* a popular Nigerian chewing stick, has been found to contain antibiotics like **chel-erythrine, 1,6 canthine,** and **berberine** (Fig. 11.1*b*). Moreover, some of these compounds are also found in the related genus *Zanthoxylum.* For example, the North American toothache tree, *Z. clava-herculis,* contains **berberine** (Fig. 11.1*b*), and an African species, *Z. elephantiasis,* contains **1,6 canthine** (Odebiyi and Sofowara 1979; Lewis and Elvin–Lewis 1977). By inference, another member of the Rutaceae, *Teclea verdoorniana,* preferred in Ghana by the Akwapin (Elvin–Lewis et al. 1980a), may also contain similar antibiotics, since its antimicrobial spectrum is identical to *F. xanthoxyloides.*

The popularity of *Azadirachta indica* (Meliaceae), which is used for teeth clean-ing—its oil is used for antihelminthic, insecticidal, healing, and anti-inflammatory purposes—is consistent with the broad-spectrum antibiotic activity found in its twigs and oil (Patel and Trivedi 1962). Studies on the efficacy of *A. indica* used as a chewing stick are lacking; however, the reduced gingival inflammation associated with use of the dentrifice Neem (Rathje 1971), which contains components of Neem oil, may be related to its ability to raise the oxidation potential of the gingival sulcus, as *A. indica* does with erythrocytes infected with malaria plasmodia (Etkin 1979). Should this phenomenon occur, the number of anaerobes causing gingival irritation would be reduced, with a corresponding improved health of the gums. Moreover, a number of **triterpenoids,** characterized also as steroidal saponins, have been isolated that may account for an additional anti-inflammatory capacity (Cole et al. 1981).

Broad-spectrum antibiotic activity has been found for the mango, *Mangifera indica,* which is used in India and Panama for teeth cleaning (Lewis and Elvin–Lewis 1977). In Southeast Asia, the resin is used to treat canker sores; and in West Africa, the bark and leaves, with their astringent **tannin,** are used to relieve toothache, sore gums, and sore throat. Other genera share similar medicinal uses, including the American sumac, *Rhus glabra,* which probably contains tannins like other *Rhus* and has been found to have broad-spectrum antimicrobial activity associated with anacardic acid (Fig. 11.1*v*), isolated from *Anacardium occidentale.*

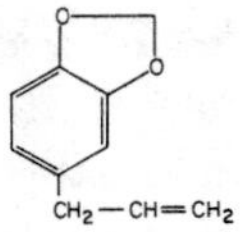

(a)

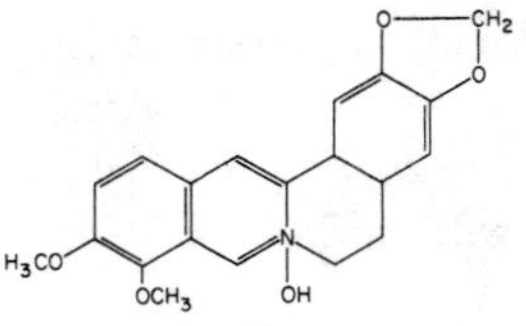

(b)

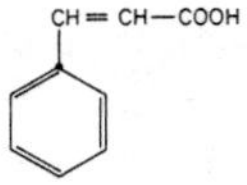

(c)

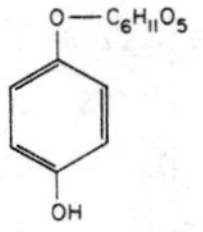

(d)

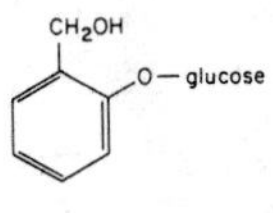

(e)

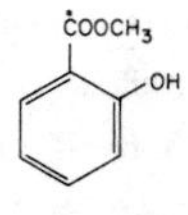

(f)

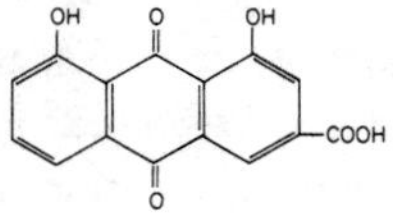

(g)

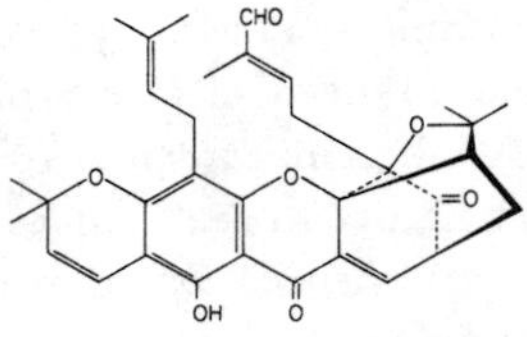

(h)

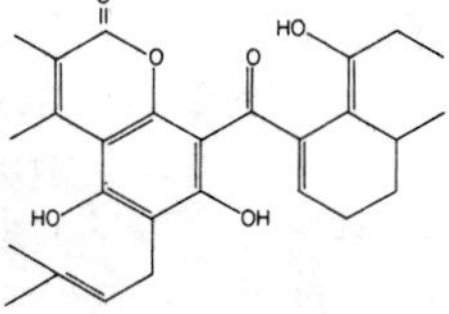

(i)

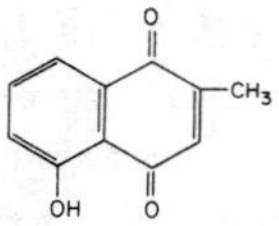

(j)

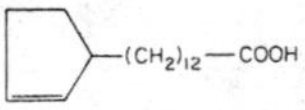

(k)

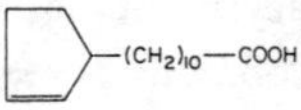

(l)

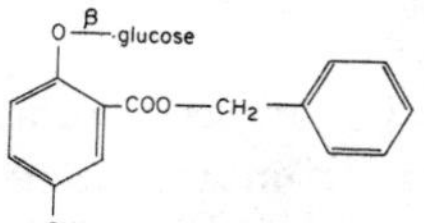

(m)

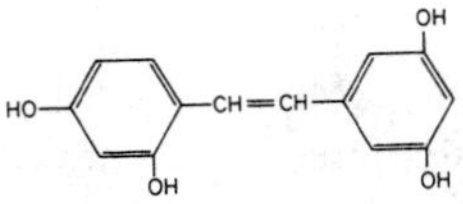

(n)

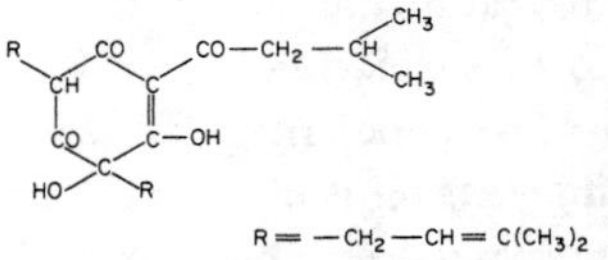

(o)

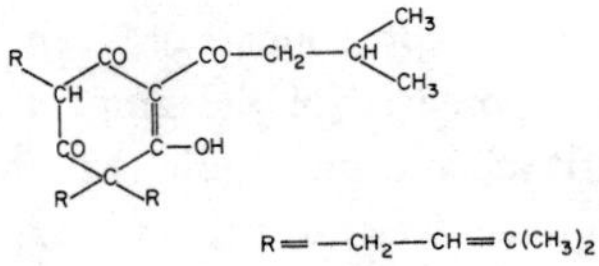

(p)

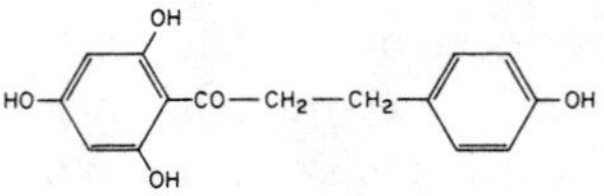

(q)

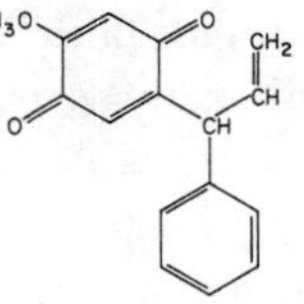

(r)

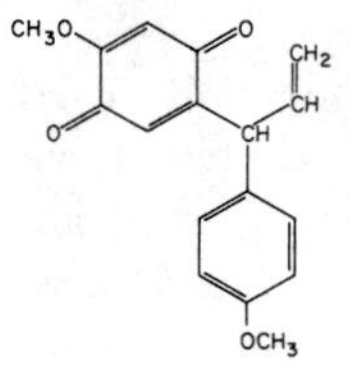

(s)

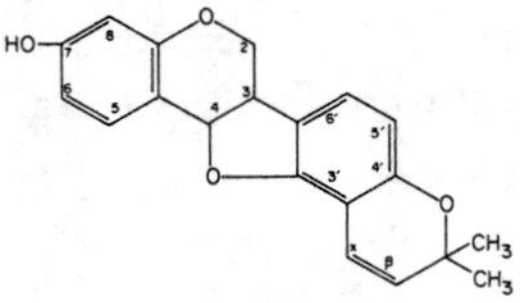

(t)

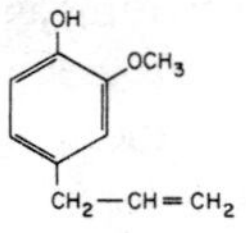

(u)

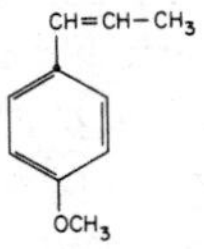

Fig. 11.1. Structures of Chemical Formulas.

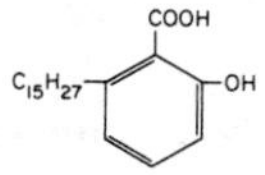

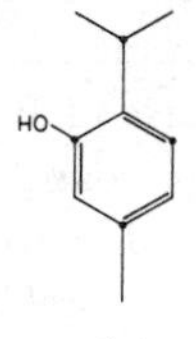

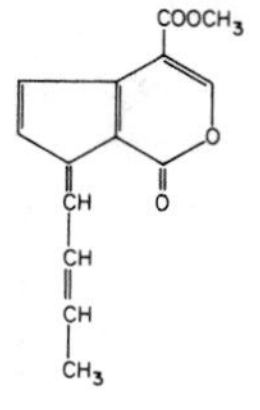

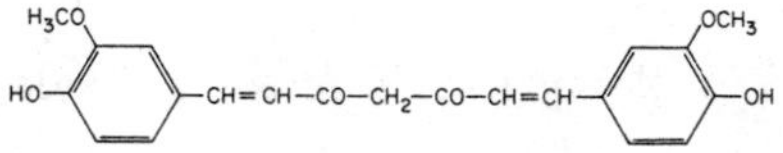

Juglans regia is used for teeth cleaning in Pakistan and for a number of medicinal purposes related to its healing and astringent potential. *Juglans nigra* yields juglone (Fig. 11.1w) (Gries 1943), which is active against a number of Gram-positive bacteria and fungi (La Grange 1956) and which has therapeutic value in the topical treatment of fungal skin infections (Korzybski et al. 1967). In the same family, the value of *Caryaa* spp, once used by those in Appalachia and the Choctaw, may not be as limited as its antibiotic spectrum suggests, since its high tannin content may exert an anticariogenic effect like the tannins of tea (Elvin–Lewis et al. 1980b).

Phylogenetic Group 10

The astringent and healing properties of the African Olacaceae, used as chewing sticks or to treat toothache in West Africa, may be related to the tannins, sapogenins, and cyanogenetic principles (with possible antibiotic activity) isolated from them (Irvine 1961). Broad-spectrum antimicrobial activity has been found for a number of *Ligustrum* spp (Oleaceae) (Winter and Willeke 1952; Lucas et al. 1951; Osborn 1943), although data on *Ligustrum medium*, once used by the Ainu of Japan, is lacking (Lewis and Elvin–Lewis 1977).

Within the same order, the popularity of *Salvadora persica* (Salvadoraceae) throughout Africa and Asia is not consistent with the limited antimicrobial spectrum detected in aqueous extracts for oral organisms (Elvin–Lewis 1982). It is possible, however, that the enzymatic action of saliva on the isothicyanates of this species can release unstable products that exert antimicrobial activity. Other factors in its selection may be its high chloride content, which could remove tartar and other stains from the teeth, silica, which would act as an abrasive, a resin, which could form a coat over the enamel to prevent tooth decay, and Vitamin C, which would promote healthy gingiva. Clinical observations on its efficacy for teeth cleaning are limited (Attar 1979), and those with the dentifrice Sarakan, incomplete.

On the basis of its antimicrobial activity, the choice by American Blacks in colonial times of the common flowering dogwood, *Cornus florida,* has merit and is consistent with the reports of Barton (1802) of its efficacy for cleaning the teeth and "preserving the gums sound and hard." The **cornin-verbanilin** content of *C. florida* is related to its ability to reduce fevers, although its antibiotic substances have yet to be determined (Osal and Farrar 1955).

Phylogenetic Group 11

Antibiotic activity among families used for teeth cleaning in this group are widespread, and the antimicrobial, antifungal, and antiprotozoal properties associated with their species have been reviewed in detail elsewhere. Specific studies on species known for teeth cleaning, or even their genera, are, however, extremely limited, and thus one can only assume that most would yield antimicrobial substances. For example, in the Rubiaceae, the African species *Massularia acuminata* and *Oxyanthus speciosus* were found to possess broad-spectrum activity, which included a number of oral organisms with cariogenic potential (El–Said et al. 1971; Elvin–Lewis et al. 1974; Fadulu 1975). On the other hand, a lack of activity has been determined for *Nauclea latifolia* and other species of *Mussaenda* and *Psychotria* (Osborn 1943). In the sunflower family, the Asteraceae, *Vernonia amydalina* was found in two studies to be capable of inhibiting the growth of organisms from saliva (El–Said et al. 1971; Fadulu 1975), but in another analysis did not affect some oral streptococci or other test organisms. The only specific antibiotic substances identified in genera used for teeth cleaning are **eugenol** (Fig. 11.1*t*) and **thymol** (Fig. 11.1*w*), present in species of *Osimum* of the Lamiaceae. However, antibiotics as well as a number of medically active substances have been identified in the Apocyanaceae and Loganiaceae. Antibiotics in the Apocynaceae include **alamandin,** isolated from *Allamanda violaceae*—with broad-spectrum antimicrobial, antifungal, and antiprotozoal properties (De Lima and Caldas 1954); and **plumercine** (Fig. 11.1*x*), isolated from *Plumeria multiflora*—with broad-spectrum antimicrobial and antifungal properties (Little and Johnstone 1950, 1951).

Phylogenetic Group 13

The use of the peduncle of the coconut palm *(Cocus nucifera)* and the date palm *(Phoenix dactylifera)* of the Arecaceae (Palmae) can occur wherever these plants are cultivated in the tropics. They are probably selected for convenience and the bristle that is formed. The roots and milk of the coconut have been used to eradicate intestinal worms (Lewis and Elvin–Lewis 1977) and its oil is used to treat caries (Pételot 1952), but extracts of the plant are negative in antibiotic tests (Cardoso and Santos 1948). The medicinal uses of the date palm are unknown; however, in North Africa, the plant is employed in tanning (Irvine 1961).

Similarly, the pedicel of *Pandanus* (Pandanaceae) is commonly used for teeth cleaning in Tahiti, Tonga, and Samoa (Elven–Lewis 1979). Medically, the genus is used to heal and treat cough and for its astringent, intoxicant and abortifacient properties, but no substances have been identified that could be correlated with an antibiotic potential.

Phylogenetic Group 14

Among the Poaceae, the use of sugar cane (*Saccharum officinarum*) for teeth cleaning in Africa, the West Indies, Hawaii, Samoa, and Fiji has not always been associated with high caries rates (Campbell 1975; Elvin–Lewis 1979; Elvin–Lewis et al. 1980a), as other studies suggest (e.g., Kunzel et al. 1973). The correlation of sugar-cane use with dental caries is related to a number of other factors. Thus, if cane is used for teeth cleaning without also being used as a major supplement to nutrition with refined carbohydrates, the **phytates** it contains could act to neutralize the acid produced by fermentation of its sucrose by cariogenic organisms (Edgar and Jenkins 1974), in spite of the fact that antibiotic activity is absent (Osborn 1943). Moreover, its fibrous nature allows it to act like both floss and a brush in removing plaque and food debris. In Ghana, for example, a number of our subjects ate cane with impunity, but did not suffer from the high caries rates one would expect; thus, the fastidiousness of their teeth-cleaning methods, and the chewing sticks they selected, were positive factors in preventing the disease from becoming rampant (Elvin–Lewis et al. 1980a). The reverse condition appears to be true in rural areas of Haiti and other parts of Central America, where because dental hygiene is poor, high caries rates are common among those ingesting large amounts of cane.

The use of stalks of wild rice, *Zizania aquatica* (Poaceae), for teeth cleaning among Indian tribes like the Ojibwa and Chippewa still occurs during the season of its harvest. At other periods, its popularity for dental hygiene is unknown, as are any efficacious principles it may contain (Elvin–Lewis 1979).

In the Zingiberales, the pounded peduncle and inflorescence of the plantain, *Musa sapientum* (Musaceae), with charcoal is preferred in Ghana by Ashanti women and their children for teeth cleaning (Adu-tutu et al. 1980). In this group, dental health is excellent, and 93.8 percent of those interviewed had intact teeth (Elvin–Lewis et al. 1980a). The plant contains a broad-spectrum antibiotic potential. However, the data are unclear whether the parts used for teeth cleaning share in this activity (Spencer et al. 1947). Moreover, **lectins** isolated from the fruit and skin of the banana have been found to prevent the adherence of cariogenic streptococci to the apatite component of teeth (Gibbons 1982). Thus, both antibiotics and lectins may be responsible for the anticariogenic effect observed among populations selecting this method of teeth cleaning. *Curcuma* species (Zingiberaceae) have also yielded an antibiotic curcumin (Fig. 11.1y) that has broad-spectrum antimicrobial and antifungal properties (Korzybski et al. 1967).

Phylogenetic Group 15

In the Liliales, the small stems of *Vellozia equisteloides* (Velloziaceae) are used in Tanzania for teeth cleaning. In a related family, the Liliaceae, allicin (Fig. 11.1z) and allistatin have been isolated from garlic (*Allium sativum*); they have broad-spectrum antimicrobial and antifungal properties. Baraloin, isolated from aloe (*Aloe barbedensis*), is active against *Mycobacterium tuberculosis* (Lewis and Elvin–Lewis 1977).

Conclusion

Many plants selected for teeth cleaning have been identified as having antibiotic and healing compounds (Table 11.1). In instances where these studies have not been detailed, data acquired from investigations with other members of the genus, family, or phylogenetic group provide clues that could help in delineating the antibiotic substances further. However, to select those species worthy of further analysis, field studies are essential, since they provide the necessary clinical correlation of efficacy. In this way, the worth of folk dentistry in providing new and useful compounds for modern dental hygiene will be realized.

Table 11.1.   Medicinal Properties of Plants Used for Teeth Cleaning

Antibiotic Activity Against:	Types of Active Substances:
Bacteria (Gram-Positive, Gram-Negative, Acid-Fast)	Alkaloids
	Resins
Fungi	Lectins
Yeasts	Tannins
Helminths	Saponins
Protozoa	Phenolics
Neoplasms	Chloride
	Fluoride
Healing Properties:	
Vitamin C	
Salicylates	*Abrasive Properties:*
Essential Oils	Silica

REFERENCES

Adu-tutu, M., Afful, Y., Asante–Appiah, K., Lieberman, H., Hall, J., and M. Elvin–Lewis. 1979. "Chewing Stick Usage in Southern Ghana." *Economic Botany*, 33:320–28.
Attar, Z.A. 1979. "Ancient Arab Toothbrush-Missawak." *Dental Survey*, 55:13–15.
Barton, B.S. 1802. "Journal of Benjamin Smith Barton on a Visit to Virginia." *Castanea*, 3(1938): 85–120.

Barton, W.P.C. 1817. "Vegetable Materia Medica of the United States." *Medical Botany*, 1:555–56.

Boakye–Yiadom, K., and G.H. Konning. 1975. "Incidence of Antibacterial Activity in the Connaraceae." *Planta Medica*, 28:397–400.

Brown, W.E., and K.G. Konig. 1977. *Cariostatic Mechanisms of Fluoride*. New York: J. Karger.

Buadu, C., and K. Boakye–Yiadom. 1973. The Antibacterial Activity of Some Ghanian Chewing Sticks. *Ghana Pharmaceutical Journal*, 1:150–51.

Campbell, G.D. 1975. "Virtual Absence of Dental Caries in One Context of High Sucrose Intake." International Sugar Research Symposium, *Dental Caries: A Review of Current Research on the Prevention of Cavities*, 29–36.

Cardoso, H., and M. Santos. 1948. "Studies on the Presence of Antibiotics in Plants." *Brasil-Med*, 62:67–70.

Carlson, H.J., Douglas, H.G., and J. Roberstson. 1948. "Antibiotic Agents Separated from Plants." *Journal of Bacteriology*, 55:241–48.

Chandler, R.F., Freeman, L., and S. Hoopers. 1979. "Herbal Remedies of the Maritime Indians." *Journal of Ethnopharmacology*, 1:49–68.

Cole, T.H., Muller, E., and H. Becker. 1981. "Chewing Sticks—Zahnholzer." *Pharmazie in unserer Zeit*, 10(5):150–56.

Dalziel, J.M. 1937. "The Useful Plants of West Tropical Africa." Appendix to J. Hutchinson and J.M. Dalziel, *Flora of West Tropical Africa*. London: Crown Agents for the Colonies.

De Lima, G.O., and J.M. Caldas. 1954. "Alamadina, Novo Antibiotico Ativo contra Protozoarios, Isolado de Allamanda Violaceae (Apocynaceae)." *Anais da Sociedade de Biologia Pernambuco*, 1:19.

Edgar, W.M., and G.N. Jenkins. 1974. "Solubility-Reducing Agents in Honey and Partly-Refined Crystalline Sugar." *British Dental Journal*, 136:7–14.

El–Said, F., Fadulu, S.O., Kuye, J.O., and E.A. Sofowara. 1971. "Native Cures in Nigeria. II. The Antimicrobial Properties of the Buffered Extracts of Chewing Sticks." *Lloydia*, 34:172–74.

Elvin–Lewis, M. 1979. "Empirical Rationale for Teeth Cleaning Plant Selection." *Medical Anthropology*, 3:431–54.

    1980a "Plants Used for Teeth Cleaning throughout the World." *Journal of Preventive Dentistry*, 6:61–70.

    1980b "Chewing Sponges for Teeth Cleaning." *Journal of Preventive Dentistry*, 6:273–84.

    1982 "The Therapeutic Potential of Plants Used in Dental Folk Medicine." *Revue d'Odonto-Stomatologie Tropicale—Tropical Dental Journal*, in press.

———, Hall, J.B., Adu-tutu, M., Afful, Y., Asante–Appiah, K., and D. Lieberman. 1980a. "The Dental Health of Chewing Stick Users of Southern Ghana: Preliminary Findings." *Journal of Preventive Dentistry*, 6:151–59.

———, Keudell, K., Lewis, W.H., and M. Harwood. 1974. "Anticariogenic Potential of Chewing Sticks." *Journal of Dental Research*, 53:277.

———, Vitale, M., and T. Kopjas. 1980b. "Anticariogenic Potential of Commercial Teas." *Journal of Preventive Dentistry*, 6:273–84.

Etkin, N.L. 1979. "An Indigenous Medical System among the Hausa of Northern Nigeria: Laboratory Evaluation of Potential Therapeutic Efficacy of Antimalarial Plant Medicinals." *Medical Anthropology*, 3:401–30.

1980   "Indigenous Medicine in Northern Nigeria. 1. Oral Hygiene and Medical Treatment." *Journal of Preventive Dentistry*, 6:143–49.

Fadulu, S.O. 1975. "The Antibacterial Properties of the Buffer Extracts of Chewing Sticks Used in Nigeria." *Planta Medica*, 27:122–26.

Frisbey, J.M., Roberts, J.C., Jennings, R., Gottshall, Y., and E.H. Lucas. 1953. "The Occurrence of Antibacterial Substances in Seed Plants with Special Reference to *Mycobacterium Tuberculosis* (Third Report)." *Michigan Quarterly Bulletin*, 35:392–404.

1954   "The Occurrence of Antibacterial Substances in Seed Plants with Special Reference to *Mycobacterium Tuberculosis* (Fourth Report)." *Michigan Quarterly Bulletin*, 36:477–88.

Gibbons, R.J. 1982. "Bacterial Adherence to Oral Tissues: An Overview." *Journal of Dental Research*, 61:168.

Gries, G.A. 1943. "Juglone: The Active Agent in Walnut Toxicity." *Northern National Growers Annual Report*, 34:52.

Gottshall, R.Y., Lucas, E.H., Lickfeldt, A., and J.M. Roberts. 1949. "The Occurrence of Antibacterial Substances Active against *Mycobacterium Tuberculosis* in Seed Plants." *Journal of Clinical Investigation*, 28:920–23.

Hall, R.J. 1972. "The Distribution of Organic Fluorine in Some Toxic Tropical Plants." *New Phytology*, 71:855–71.

Hamilton, I.R. 1977. "Effects of Fluoride on Enzymatic Regulation of Bacterial Carbohydrate Metabolism." *Caries Research*, 2 (supp. 1):262–91.

Hayes, L.E. 1947. "Survey of Higher Plants for the Presence of Antibacterial Substances." *Botanical Gazette*, 108:408–14.

Hughes, J.E. 1952. "Survey of Antibiotics in the Wild Green Plants of Southern California." *Antibiotics and Chemotherapy*, 2:487–91.

Irvine, F.R. 1961. *Woody Plants of Ghana*. London: Oxford Univ. Press.

Jensen, L.B., and W.R. Hess. 1951. "Preservation of Food Products." U.S. Patent No. 2,550,253 (24 April)

Kavanaugh, F. 1947. Activities of Twenty-Two Antibacterial Substances against Nine Species of Bacteria. *Journal of Bacteriology*, 54:761.

Korzybski, T., Kowszyk–Gindifer, Z., and W. Kurylowicz. 1967. *Antibiotics: Origin, Nature and Properties*, vol. 2. New York: Pergamon Press, 1146–1651.

Krochmal, A., and C. Krochmal. 1973. *A Guide to the Medicinal Plants of the United States*. New York: *New York Times* Book Co.

Kuhn, R., Jerchel, D., Moewes, F., Moller, E.F., and H. Lettre. 1943. "Uber die Chemische Natur der Blastokoline und Ihre Einwirkung auf Keinmende Samen, Pollenkorner, Hefen, Bakterien Epithelgewebe und Fibroblasten." *Naturwissenschaften*, 31:468.

Kunzel, W., Borrotos, R.C., Lanier, S., and F. Soto. 1973. "Auswirkungen Habituellen Zuckerrohrkauens auf Kaires Befall und Paradontazustand Kabanischer Zucker-rohrarbeiter." *Deutsche Stomatologies*, 23:554.

LaGrange, G.A. 1956. "L'Action Antibiotique de *Juglans regia*." *Compte Rendu Societé de Biologie*, 150:613.

Leung, A.Y. 1980. *Encyclopedia of Common Natural Ingredients, Used in Food, Drugs and Cosmetics*. New York: John Wiley & Sons.

Leven, M., Berghe, D.A.V., Mertens, F., Blietinck, A., and E. Lammens. 1979. "Screening of Higher Plants for Biological Activities. 1. Antimicrobial Activity." *Planta Medica*, 36:311–21.

Lewis, W.H. 1980. "Plants Used as Chewing Sticks." *Journal of Preventive Dentistry*, 6:71–73.

Lewis, W.H., and M. Elvin–Lewis. 1977. *Medical Botany*. New York: John Wiley & Sons.

Little, J.E., and D.B. Johnstone. 1950. "Plumericin." *Chemical Engineering News*, 3:300.

1951 "Plumericine: An Antimicrobial Agent from *Plumeria multiflora*." *Archives Biochemistry*, 30:445–52.

Lucas, A., Frisbey, J.M., Gottshall, Y., and J.C. Jennings. 1955. "The Occurrence of Antibacterial Substances in Seed Plants with Special Reference to *Mycobacterium Tuberculosis* (Fifth Report)." *Michigan Quarterly Bulletin*, 37:425–36.

Lucas, A., Lickfeldt, R., Gottshall, Y., and J.C. Jennings. 1951. "The Occurrence of Antibacterial Substances in Seed Plants with Special Reference to *Mycobacterium Tuberculosis*." *Bulletin of the Torrey Botanical Club*, 78:310–21.

Madsen, G.G., and A.I. Pates. 1952. "Occurrence of Antimicrobial Substances in Chlorphyllose Plants Growing in Florida." *Botanical Gazette*, 113:293–300.

Manley, J.L., Limongelli, W.A., and A.C. Williams. 1975. "The Chewing Stick: Its Uses and Relationship to Oral Health." *Journal of Preventive Dentistry*, 2:7–9.

Murthy, D., and N.P.L. Roa. 1961. "Structure of Morellin." *Experimentia*, 17:445.

Nickell, L.G. 1959. "Antimicrobial Activity of Vascular Plants." *Economic Botany*, 13:281–318.

Odebiyi, O.O., and E.A. Sofowara. 1979. "Antimicrobial Alkaloids from a Nigerian Chewing Stick (*Fagara Zanthoyloides*)." *Planta medica*, 36:204–7.

Osal, A., and G.L. Farrar. 1955. *The Dispensatory of the United States of America*, 25th ed. Philadelphia: J.B. Lippincott.

Osborn, E.M., 1943. "On the Occurrence of Antibacterial Substances in Green Plants." *British Journal of Experimental Pathology*, 24:227–31.

Paolino, V.J., Kashket, S., and C.A. Sparagna. 1980. "Inhibition of Dextran Synthesis of Tannic Acid." *Journal of Dental Research*, 59:389.

Patel, R.P., and B.M. Trivedi. 1962. "The in Vitro Antibacterial Activity of Some Medicinal Oils." *Indian Journal of Medical Research*, 50:218–22.

Pates, A.L., and G.C. Madsen. 1955. "Occurrence of Antimicrobial Substances in Chlorphyllose Plants Growing in Florida. II." *Botanical Gazette*, 116:240–61.

Perry, L. 1980. "Medicinal Plants of East and Southeast Asia: Attributed Properties and Uses." Cambridge, Mass.: MIT Press.

Pételot, A. 1952. "Les Plantes Medicinales du Cambodge, du Laos et du Viet-Nam. I. Archives Recherches Agronamie Pastoral." *Vietnam*, 14:1–408.

1953 "II. [Ibid.]." *Vietnam*, 18:1–284.

1954a "III. [Ibid.]." *Vietnam*, 22:1–347.

1954b "IV. [Ibid.]." *Vietnam*, 23:1–307 (Indices).

Peters, R.A., and M. Shorthouse. 1972. "Fluorocitrate in Plants and Food." Phytochemistry 11:1337–1338.

Rao, K.V.N., and N.P.C. Rao. 1961. "Alpha and Beta Guttiferins." *Expermimentia*, 17:213.

Rathje, R. 1971. "Influence of Neem Tree Extracts on Inflammatory Changes of the Gingiva." *Quintessenz*, 22:5.

Sadykov, A.S. 1972. "Polyphenolic Compounds of *Gossypium* and *Hibiscus* Species." Rangaswami, S., and S. Rao, eds., *Some Recent Developments in the Chemistry of Natural Products*. New Delhi: Prentice–Hall, 256–64.

Sanders, D.W., Weatherwax, P., and L.S. McClung. 1945. "Antibacterial Substances from Plants Collected in Indiana." *Journal of Bacteriology*, 49:611–15.

Segelman, A.B., Segelman F.P., Karliger, J., and R.D. Sofia. 1976. "Sassafras and Herb Tea: Potential Health Hazards." *Journal of the American Medical Association*, 236:477.

Silva, E., De Lima, G., and M.M. De Alburquerque. 1958. "Primeriras Observacoes sobre um Antibiotico com Propriendades de Indicator Acido-Basico Isolado de *Cnidoscolus urens*—Eupoorbiaceae." *Revista do Instituto de Antibioticos Universidade do Recife,* 1:125.

Spencer, C.F., Koniusz, F.R., Kaeka, E.A., Kuehl, F.A. Jr., Phillips, R.F., Walti, A., Folkers, K., Malanga, C., and A.O. Seeler. 1947. "Survey of Plants for Antimalaria Activity." *Lloydia,* 10:145–74.

Taniguchi, M., Chapya, A., Kubo, I., and K. Nakanishi. 1978. "Screening of East African Plants for Antimicrobial Activity." *Chemical and Pharmaceutical Bulletin,* 26:2910–13.

Tyler, V.E., Brady, L.R., and F.R. Robbers. 1976. *Pharmacognosy,* 7th ed. Philadelphia: Lea & Febiger.

Winter, A.G., and I. Willeke. 1952. "Untersuchunger uber Antibiotika aus Hoheren Pflanzen. IV. Hemmstoffe im Herbstilichen Laub." *Naturwiss,* 39:45–46.

12

Naturally Occurring Dietary Antibiotics and Human Health

Margaret Keith and George J. Armelagos

The widespread prescription of antibiotic drugs in the 1950s was expected to revolutionize Western medicine. The physician would no longer be servant to nature, but would become its master (Marti–Ibanez 1958:20). The term "magic bullet" was employed to describe the *specific* nature of microorganisms causing antibiosis; i.e., diseased cells were targeted for destruction by an antagonistic, but closely related, substance, whereas—ideally—healthy cells were left untouched. It was anticipated that these wonder drugs would cure all diseases: bacterial, fungal, and viral. Use of antibiotics in animal feeds would eradicate animal disease and close the gap between poor and wealthy nations.

That the expectations of the "antibiotic era" in Western medicine will never be realized is now apparent. Although many disease patterns were disrupted, the evolution of resistant strains of microorganisms was unforeseen. Researchers are now suggesting that overprescription of antibiotics itself has facilitated the development of resistance to antibiotics.

Failure to obtain the anticipated results was due to a misunderstanding of the nature of human–biotic relationships and to underestimation of exposure to antibiotics in supposedly virgin populations. Evidence for antibiotic resistance in virgin populations in Borneo (Davis and Anandan 1970), the Solomon Islands (Gardner et al. 1969), and other human and animal communities (Maré 1968) suggests the existence of naturally occurring antibiotics. Large-scale screening of plant material to determine antibiotic activity was undertaken as early in the "antibiotic era" as 1943 (Osborn), at which time 2300 species of plants were tested against pathogenic organisms, and 63 genera showed inhibitory action. It was subsequently pointed out that inhibitory activity was often accompanied by toxicity to humans and that plant material was therefore not as therapeutically valuable as substances of "microbial origin" (Nickell 1959:281–82); nevertheless, the rush was on to find naturally occurring substances that could be patented as human medicine. After systematic survey of the Pteridophytes (ferns and fern allies), it was reported that 64 percent of the sample examined had antibiotic activity (Banerjee and Sen 1980). Of these, 41 percent were inhibitory to Gram-positive bacteria alone, in agreement with the folk-medicine usage of ferns for staphylococcal and streptococcal infections (ibid.:292). In a study of Aztec medicinal plants, deMontellano (1975) found that 16 of the 25 plants analyzed were empirically effective (i.e., when evaluated within the Aztec medical paradigm). Another 4 plants "may possibly have been active" (p. 220)—an 80-percent concordance with the goals of the therapeutic measures.

Ivan Polunin (1976) cautions against the "moldy-bread-on-wounds-means-they-had-antibiotics" school, and claims that any medical practice must be judged within its own system. That is, its validity depends upon its ability to produce the results claimed within the context of the system itself. Frederick Dunn, on the other hand, points out that the system of primitive herbalists has evolved through centuries of trial and error, not differing qualitatively from the experimental procedures of modern chemotherapeutics (1976). Further, Laughlin states that the remarkable success of our species was due at least in part to local solutions of medical problems (Laughlin 1963:116–140). We do not here attempt to defend the empirical efficacy of any system. We are concerned with the effects of exposure to naturally occurring antibiotics, whether intentional or not. This approach gives rise to a different set of questions for anthropological populations.

What antibiotics exist in the natural environment of a given population? What cultural factors either buffer or enhance exposure? And what effect would exposure have on health and disease patterns, either short or long term?

Before concerning ourselves with cultural practices affecting exposure, a brief discussion of the ecological requirements of antibiotic-producing microorganisms themselves is in order.

Antibiotics

Antibiotics in the broadest sense of the term are substances that inhibit life processes. Their action ranges from disruptive (bacteriostatic) to fatal (bacteriocidal); effective dosage varies according to the source of the antibiotic and to the competing microorganism. They are, in fact, toxins—the antibiotic substance is produced to exclude competing species from a food source. The *toxicity* of a given substance, however, is a function of its capacity to produce a reaction when tested by itself. The anthropologist must be concerned with the *hazard* of the given toxic substance, i.e., its ability to produce a reaction under the conditions of exposure.

Antibiotics are generally classified according to the type of organism producing them, since the chemical structure is often unknown (Korzybski et al. 1967:8). More than one-half of all known antibiotics are derived from the Actinomycetes (soil microorganisms). This group includes streptomycin, the tetracyclines, erythromycin, and chlormycetin, the most active and, generally, the most effective of all antibiotics. They are a natural defense system against the thousands of soil microbes each of which produces a specific toxin directed against its most likely natural competitor (ibid.:6). Approximately 100 million microbes exist in a single cubic centimeter of soil. They cause the decay of organic materials into inorganic forms, thereby performing the valuable function of removing dead bodies, garbage, and other wastes from the environment—and incidentally forming plant nutrients in the process. Antibiotics exhibiting antitumoral activity are derived from this group (ibid.:2).

Other sources of antibiotics include bacteria, Fungi imperfecti, Basidio mycetes, algae, lichens, and higher plants and animals (ibid.:1). Penicillin is produced by the Fungi imperfecti group and is the least toxic to humans of the commercially utilized drugs. It does of course produce an allergic response in susceptible individuals.

Animal sources include maggots, insects, molluscs, blood, pigs' hooves, slime of snails, etc. (Korzybski et al. 1967:1535–46). Whether or not the active substance is then available to humans is dependent upon dietary restrictions, mode of preparation, etc.

The locus of action of antibiotics is the basis for its specificity of action and is essential to therapeutic use for humans (Woodruff 1980:1227). Antibiotics act by inhibition of cell-wall synthesis or protein synthesis, by disruption of bacterial membranes of nucleic acid polymers, or by enzymatic action (ibid.). Action on bacterial cells rather than mammalian cells is critical to its therapeutic value for human use.

Toxicity may also be due to interference with normal symbiotic relationships with human microflora, e.g., disruption of intestinal microorganisms, which are necessary for synthesis of vitamins. Extended exposure may result in deficiencies; broad-spectrum antibiotics such as tetracycline are particularly likely to cause such disruptions.

Ecological and Methodological Considerations

The study of Banerjee and Sen (1980) raises a number of areas of concern for investigators of archeological populations. They note that there is "considerable variation in the distribution of antibiotic substances within the plant" (p. 293); one must test the specified plant part to make definitive statements as to its efficacy. Seasonal variations in antibiotic activity were noted (p. 294), and ecological conditions were shown to modify activity; e.g., the *epiphytic* habit of the *Drynaria quercifolia* is responsible for its antibiotic activity. *D. quercifolia* growing on *Cocos nucifera* exhibit no activity, whereas *D. quercifolia* growing on *Strychnos nux-vomica* is active against tuberculosis, as claimed in the folk medicine of the region. State of maturity, genetic changes, and strains of test microorganisms contribute to test results. Discrepancy between laboratory results and the claims of folk medicine may even be due to the incorrect identification of plants by the herbalist (p. 296). Misidentification may have been a problem when a population migrated to a similar, but not identical, econiche.

In testing for antibiotic activity, the extracting solvent and dilution itself will affect results. For example, Bhakuni et al. (1969, 1971) and Dhawan et al. (1977) did not find any activity in the 42 species of ferns examined by them, in contrast to the 64 percent exhibiting antimicrobial properties when examined by Banerjee and Sen (1980). They claim that the discrepancy is because previous studies used only one solvent and at high dilution. The question remains: do the proper conditions for the antibiotic substance exist in a natural state? If extractable in an aqueous solution, for example, one might expect the method of preparation of foodstuffs or medicinal herbs to be boiling.

Cultural Factors Influencing Exposure to and Effects of Antibiotics

The ubiquitous nature of antibiotics might lead one to suspect that humans are constantly subjected to pharmacologically active substances; such is not the case. Many cultural factors influence both the growth of antibiotics and subsequent exposure to them.

The shift from a hunting–gathering mode of subsistence to agricultural, with the concomitant emphasis on food storage, greatly increased the possibilities for growth of antibiotic substances in dietary items. Both length and method of food storage affect the microclimates that affect the selective advantage of any given microorganism over another. Tetracyclines require a warm, dry, alkaline environment (Bassett et al. 1980). The introduction of metal bins for storage of coffee facilitates storage, but the resultant buildup of moisture increases the possibility of contamination by Cladosporium or Aspergillium (Hiscocks 1965:17). Relative humidity may also cause insect infestation, and the material of the storage bin itself may interact with microorganisms present (Majumder et al. 1965:30–32).

Food processing may either free a substance for absorption in the human gut or destroy it. Dietary antibiotics may also be antagonistic to one another. Indeed, food items themselves may curtail action of an antibiotic, e.g., the well-known tetracycline-binding properties of dairy products effectively prevent absorption of tetracycline from the intestinal tract.

Pratt and Dufrenoy (1953) warn that "with the exception of the alkaloids, quinine and emetime, many natural compounds are not selective and are therefore too toxic for systemic use, since effective dosage would be expressed in milligrams rather than micrograms per ml." (p. 358). They suggest that the potential value of such substances would be in antifungal activity, particularly in the control of topical microflora (ibid.).

In the case of plant material it is necessary to know what parts are utilized. The alkaloid *Tomatin* is extractable from the leaves of certain varieties of tomato plants (ibid.). *Tomatin* is an active bacteriocide, but leaves are not generally consumed. One might then investigate their use as a topical antibiotic.

An analytical approach could then be applied to anecdotal evidence for antibiotic use in anthropological populations. Perhaps the radish–onions–garlic diet of workers in Cheops's pyramid was a key factor in preventing infectious disease. Perhaps heparin, an antimicrobial agent in liver tissue (Rosett et al. 1980:30), did affect the health of recipients of human gladiator liver (Majno 1975:401–2). Table 12.1 lists a variety of items commonly proposed as having antibiotic properties, along with the substances responsible for antibiotic activity.

That antibiotics were available to an archeological population and did influence health and disease patterns there is evidenced by tetracycline labeling in the skeletons of Sudanese Nubians, an agricultural population that cultivated the flood plains of the Nile A.D. 350–550 (Bassett et al. 1980). It had been stated in a previous study that the infectious disease rate of this group was notably low (Armelagos 1969).

The Nubian Example

When tetracycline enters the human digestive tract, it is bound by bivalent and trivalent metals (e.g., calcium, phosphorus) and absorbed as a salt onto those surfaces of bone that are actively mineralizing at the time of exposure. The compound so deposited then fluoresces indefinitely in the bone in discrete areas, including osteons, osteocyte lacunae, Volkmann's canals, and circumferential lamellae on the subperiosteal and endosteal surfaces. These represent areas of both primary and secondary mineralization; mature osteons remain unaffected. The fluorophors are then visible at 500 mm under a fluorescence microscope.

That the tetracycline in the Nubian sample was incorporated in vivo, and not as a postmortem mold infestation, is shown by several factors. First, the fluorescence occurs on discrete surfaces, corresponding exactly to those of clinically labeled bone, and not as the diffuse fluorescence resulting from mold infestation. Second, osteons were identified that were the result of interrupted dosage or interrupted growth, i.e., an unlabeled area is visible between labeled lamellae. Third, "feathered"— incompletely mineralized—osteons were identified. This phenomenon is the result of either an in-vivo diffusion barrier (Frost 1961) or osteocytic osteolysis (Hoshino and Nomura 1969), also an in-vivo process.

The Source of Tetracycline

Wheat, barley, and millet were staples of the Nubian diet, and beer and bread comprised 70 percent of their caloric intake, as it does today. It is interesting to note that Egyptian medical papyrii have different names for those grains stored for making bread and those grains stored for making beer. Since the source of the grains

Table 12.1.   Naturally Occurring Antibiotics Cited in Ethnopharmacopoeias and Tested for Biological Activity

Antibiotic	Biological Source	Entities Principally Active against
Allicin*	Garlic, onion	Bacteria
Anacardic acid	Cashew	Bacteria; fungi; yeast
Anemonin (dimer of protoanemonin)	Pasque flower	Bacteria; fungi; yeast
Asiatic acid	Asiatic pennywort	Mycobacterium leprae
Asiatioside	Asiatic pennywort	Mycobacterium leprae
Benzoic acid	Urogenital gland of beaver	Bacteria
Benzoyl†	Nasturtium	Staphylococci
Berberine	Barberry	Bacteria; fungi
Blood	Whole blood of dog (probably leukocytes that are active)	Brucella suis and some other bacteria
	Processed blood of human, cattle, or sheep	Bacteria
	Hydrolyzed blood of human, cattle, or sheep	Bacteria
Cassic acid (see Rhein)		
Castoreum	Urogenital gland of beaver	Bacteria
Centellic acid	Asiatic pennywort	Mycobacterium leprae
Centelloside	Asiatic pennywort	Mycobacterium leprae
Centoic acid	Asiatic pennywort	Mycobacterium leprae
Cepnaranthine	Stephania cepharantha	Mycobacterium tuberculosis var. hominis and other bacteria
Cheiroline	Wall flower	Bacteria; fungi
Chlorophorin	Iroko fustictree	Bacteria
Coumarin (see Dicoumarin)		
Crepin	Hawksbeard	Bacteria
Curcumin	Tumeric	Bacteria; trichophyton gypseum
Datiscetin	Datisca cannabina	Bacteria; plasmodium sp.
Defensoate*	Garlic	Bacteria
Destruin		
Dicoumarin	Tonka bean, yellow sweet clover, common red clover	Bacteria
Dicoumarol (see Dicoumarin)		
Eriodin	Yerba santa	Bacteria
Erythrin	Red blood cells	Bacteria
Galangine‡	Honey	Bacteria
Gastric factor	Gastric contents of human, dog, rat, or mouse	Bacteria
Helicidin	Helix spp. (land snails)	Hemophilus pertussis
Heparin§	Liver	Bacteria; fungi

Table 12.1 continued

Antibiotic	Biological Source	Entities Principally Active against
Humulon	Hop	Bacteria
Juglone	Species of walnut	Bacteria
Kojic acid**	Rice mold	Bacteria
Lactenin	Milk	Lactobacilli and other bacteria
Lupulon	Hop	Bacteria
Lycopersicin	Currant tomato	Bacteria; fungi
Lysozyme	Egg albumen	Bacteria
Mammalian tissue factors	Extracts of various organs such as: cecum of rabbit and dog; thymus of dog, pig, cattle; pancreas of cattle and pig	Anthrax organism and other bacteria
Patasorbic acid	European mountain ash	Micrococcus phyogenes var. aureus; Trypanosoma equiperdum
Phenols	Urogenital gland of beaver	Bacteria
Phloretin	Apple	Bacteria
Pinosylvine	Scotch pine	Bacteria; fungi
Podophyllin	Common May apple	Fungi
Protoanemonin	Pasque flower	Bacteria; fungi; yeasts
Pterygospermin	Horseradish tree	Bacteria
Puchiin	Chinese water chestnut	Bacteria
Purothionin	Wheat flour	Bacteria; yeasts
Quercitin	Various higher plants	Bacteria
Quinine	Cinchona	Plasmodium vivax; P. falciparum
Raphanin*†	Radish	Bacteria
Rhein	Senna, rhubarb	Bacteria
Rutin (rhamnoglycoside of quercitrin)	Buckwheat	Bacteria
Simaroubidin	Orinoco simaruba	Endamoeba histolytica
Solanine		Fungi; yeasts
Spleen factor	Human beings and cattle	Streptococci
Tomatin (pure form of tomatime)	Currant tomato	Bacteria; fungi
Tomatine (formerly called Lycopersicin)	Currant tomato	Bacteria; fungi
Trilobin	Japanese snailseed	Mycobacterium tuberculosis var. hominis
Umbellatine	Himalayan barberry; Sikkim barberry	Paramecium sp.; Leishmania tropica
Urine, normal, fresh	Human beings	Bacteria

SOURCE: Platt and Dufrenoy (1953), except as otherwise indicated by footnotes.
*Korzybski et al. (1967).
†Böttcher (1964).
‡Majno (1975).
§Rosett and Hodges (1980).
**Kinosita and Shikata (1965).

was the same, the difference was either in the method of storage, length of storage, or both. We know that grains were stored in mud bins and clay pots (Adams 1977).

The source of contamination of the grains was the Nubian soil itself; streptomycetes (produced by Actinomyces) comprise 60–70 percent of Nubian soil microorganisms (Waksman 1967). These are the mold-like bacteria from which nonsynthetic tetracyclines are derived. Streptomycetes have a selective advantage over other soil bacteria in a hot, very dry, alkaline environment—just the conditions that obtain inside the storage bins and pots. By culturing modern grains on Nubian soils under various experimental conditions, streptomycetes were isolated at 55°C., dry heat (Bassett et al. 1980); streptomycetes are sources of naturally occurring tetracyclines. Some cultures exhibited obvious antibiotic behavior.

Antibiotic activity would have been advantageous to the brewing process, since tetracycline kills off competing bacteria but allows fermentation by yeast. Modern German breweries take advantage of this fact by introducing tetracycline-impregnated filters into the brewing process. It is likely that over time the Nubians realized the adaptive nature of contaminated grain to the beer-making process, if not also to its effect on their health and disease parameters.

Removal of grain from storage on a frequent basis would also have contributed to the maintenance of the streptomycetes in an immature state; i.e., sporation would have been disrupted, and the antibiotic-producing phase would have been maintained by "shear" action.

The Effect of Antibiotic Exposure on the Nubian Population

The X group—that is, the population during the period of Sudanese Nubian development that occurred after the breakup of the Meroitic Kingdom and before the Christian unification, A.D. 350–550—is characterized by a high frequency of parasitic infestation, specifically head lice, the vector for typhus and relapsing fever (Armelagos 1969). Dietary iron deficiency is also well documented (Armelagos 1968; Carlson et al. 1974). One might expect then to find "normal" to high incidence of infection lesions, which are generally a correlate of parasitic and nutritional stressors. However, only about 8.5 percent of the X group exhibits infectious lesions (Armelagos 1968). Periodic ingestion of therapeutic levels of tetracycline could have affected infectious disease processes, as tetracycline is a broad-spectrum antibiotic effective against Gram-negative and Gram-positive Rickettsiae, spirochetes, bacteria, and some viruses.

Although periodic ingestion of small amounts of tetracycline would have had the most beneficial effect on infectious disease vectors, extended exposure of any given population to antibiotics may ultimately have deleterious effects. Modern studies have shown that side effects of tetracycline therapy include temporary inhibition of bone growth in infants, vitamin B depletion (Kucers and Bennett 1975), interference with phagocytic activity (ibid.), inhibition of spermatogenesis (Timmermans 1974), and interference with protein synthesis (Kucers and Bennett 1975, Jackson 1963).

Recent studies have also shown that extended exposure to an antibiotic results in the evolution of resistance factors (R factors), which negate the effects of the antibiotic. The occurrence of R factors in antibiotically virgin populations has been demonstrated (Davis and Anandan 1970, Gardner et al. 1969). Exposures to naturally occurring antibiotics are most likely responsible.

Periodic exposure to this broad-spectrum antibiotic may explain the observed low infectious disease rate in this population, which was subjected to a number of stressors usually resulting in a high rate of infectious disease. Continued exposure may have resulted in the evolution of R factors.

The Nubian study is but one possible approach to the problem of exposure to natural antibiotics. The investigator looking at disease patterns in anthropological populations must be aware of the environmental and cultural factors affecting exposure, as well as effects on demographic variables.

ACKNOWLEDGMENTS

The analysis of tetracycline in the skeletal series was partially funded by the University of Massachusetts Biomedical Research Support Grant RR07048. We would like to acknowledge the help of Mary Jane Saunders, Guy Marrocco, Peter Hepler, and Otto Stein.

REFERENCES

Adams, William Y. 1977 *Nubia*. Princeton: Princeton Univ. Press.

Armelagos, George J. 1968. "Paleopathology of Three Archeological Populations from Sudanese Nubia. Ph.D. diss., University of Colorado.

1969 "Disease in Ancient Nubia." *Science,* 163:255–59.

Banerjee, R.D., and S.P. Sen. 1980. "Antibiotic Activity of Pteridophytes." *Economic Botany,* 34(3):284–98.

Bassett, E.J., M.S. Keith, G.J. Armelagos, D.L. Martin, and A.R. Villanueva. 1980. "Tetracycline-Labeled Human Bone from Ancient Sudanese Nubia (A.D. 350)." *Science,* 209:1532–34.

Bhakuni, D.S., M.I. Dhar, M.M. Dhar, F.N. Dhawan, and B.N. Mehrotra. 1969. "Screening of Indian Plants for Biological Activity. Part II." *Indian Journal of Experimental Biology,* 7:250.

———, M.I. Dhar, M.M. Dhar, F.N. Dhawan, B.N. Methrotra, B. Gupta and R.C. Srimal. 1971. "Screening of Indian Plants for Biological Activity. Part III." *Indian Journal of Experimental Biology,* 9:91.

Böttcher, Helmut. 1964. *Wonder Drugs: A History of Antibiotics.* Philadelphia: J.B. Lippincott.

Carlson, D.S., G.J. Armelagos, and D.P. Van Gerven. 1974. "Factors Influencing the Etiology of Cribra Orbitalia in Prehistoric Nubia." *Journal of Human Evolution,* 3:405–10.

Davis, C.E., and J. Anandan. 1970. "The Evolution of R Factor." *New England Journal of Medicine,* 282:117.

deMontellano, Bernard O. 1975. "Empirical Aztec Medicine." *Science,* 188:215.

Dhawan, B.N., G.K. Patnaik, R.P. Rastogi, K.K. Singh, and J.S. Tandon. 1977. "Screening of Indian Plants for Biological Activity. Part IV." *Indian Journal of Experimental Biology,* 15:208.

Dunn, Frederick. 1976. "Traditional Asian Medicine and Cosmopolitan Medicine as Adaptive Systems." C. Leslie, ed., *Asian Medical Systems: A Comparative Study.* Berkeley: Univ. of California Press.

Frost, H.M. 1961. "Feathering." *Henry Ford Hospital Medical Bulletin,* 9:103–14.

Gardner, P., D. Smith, H. Beer, and R.C. Moellering. 1969. "Recovery of Resistance (R) Factors from a Drug-Free Community." *Lancet,* 2:774.

Hiscocks, E.S. 1965. "The Importance of Molds in the Deterioration of Tropical Foods and Feedstuff." G.N. Wogan, ed., *Mycotoxins in Foodstuffs.* Cambridge: MIT Press.

Hoshino, T., and T. Nomura. 1969. "Feathering and Osteocytic Osteolysis." *Clinical Orthopedics,* 65:110.

Jackson, F.L. 1963. "Mode of Action of Tetracyclines." R.J. Schnitzer and I. Hawking, eds., *Experimental Chemotherapy,* vol. 3. New York: Academic Press, 103–17.

Kinosita, R., and T. Shikata. 1965. "On Toxic Moldy Rice." G.N. Wogan, ed., *Mycotoxins in Foodstuffs.* Cambridge: MIT Press.

Korzybski, T., Z. Kowszuk–Gindifer, and W. Kurylowicz. 1967. *Antibiotics: Origin, Nature and Properties,* vols. 1 and 2. Oxford: Pergamon Press.

Kucers, A., and N.M. Bennett. 1975. *The Use of Antibiotics: A Comprehensive Review with Clinical Emphasis.* London: William Heinemann Medical Books.

Laughlin, W. 1963. "Primitive Theory of Medicine: Empirical Knowledge." I. Gladston, ed., *Man's Image in Medicine and Anthropology.* New York: International Universities Press.

Majno, Guido. 1975. *The Healing Hand: Man and Wound in the Ancient World.* Cambridge, Mass.: Harvard Univ. Press.

Majumder, S.K., K.S. Narasimhau, and H.A.B. Parpia. 1965. "Microecological Factors of Microbial Spoilage and the Occurrence of Mycotoxins on Stored Grains." *Mycotoxins in Foodstuffs.* Cambridge: MIT Press, 27–47.

Maré, I.J. 1968. "Incidence of R Factors among Gram Negative Bacteria in Drug-Free Human and Animal Communities." *Nature,* 220:1046.

Marti–Ibanez, Felix. 1958. *Men, Molds and History.* New York: M.D. Pubs.

Nickell, Louis G. 1959. "Antimicrobial Activity of Vascular Plants." *Economic Botany,* 13:281.

Osborn, E.M. 1943. "On the Occurrence of Antibacterial Substance in Green Plants." *British Journal of Experimental Pathology,* 24(6):227.

Polunin, Ivan. 1976. "Disease, Morbidity and Mortality in China, India and the Arab World." Charles Leslie, ed., *Asian Medical Systems.* Berkeley: Univ. of California Press.

Pratt, Robertson, and Jean Dufrenoy. 1953. *Antibiotics,* 2d ed. Philadelphia: J.B. Lippincott.

Rosett, W., and G.R. Hodges. 1980. "Antimicrobial Activity of Leparin in Liver and Lung Tissue." *Journal of Clinical Microbiology,* 11(1):30.

Timmermans, L. 1974. "Influence of Antibiotics on Spermatogenesis." *Journal of Urology,* 112:348–49.

Waksman, S.A. 1967. *The Actinomycetes: A Summary of Current Knowledge.* New York: Ronald.

Woodruff, H. Boyd. 1980. "Natural Products from Microorganisms." *Science,* 208:1225.

13

Malaria, Medicine, and Meals: Plant Use among the Hausa and Its Impact on Disease

Nina L. Etkin and Paul J. Ross

Introduction

The literature is replete with examples in which Western and indigenous medical systems are competitively juxtaposed and only exiguously effective in promoting the maintenance and/or restoration of optimal health (for examples, see Foster 1976; Landy 1977; Logan 1973; Scott 1975). But there exist as well other instances, prominent among them China and India (Leslie 1976, 1977), in which two such medical systems operate together to offer the advantages of both to health-care consumers. We concur with many others in suggesting that the therapeutic merits of indigenous and Western-scientific treatment modalities are not in all (and perhaps in no) cases mutually exclusive. Nonetheless, although the therapeutic value of Western medical treatment is generally considered to have been amply demonstrated, the efficacy of indigenous therapies remains virtually unexplored. Although many extol the psychosocially integrative—and occasionally symptom-mitigating—support offered by indigenous practitioners (e.g., Crapanzano 1973; Edgerton 1971; Horton 1967; Nelson 1971; Young 1974–75), the same confidence has not been afforded their pharmacopoeias.

In recognition of the fact that traditional healers and their pharmacopoeias constitute the basic core of primary health care for more than two-thirds of the world's population (WHO 1978), and that to date the specificity, mode of action, and clinical efficacy of indigenous plant medicines have not been demonstrated in a manner congruent with the standards established by the pharmacognostic and pharmacological sciences, the importance of empirical research on indigenous medicines is being increasingly emphasized in many sectors (Lewis and Elvin–Lewis 1977,

231

Penso 1977, Rowson 1969, Swain 1972). A growing number of research institutions, national governments, and international agencies such as the World Health Organization are actively promoting laboratory examination of the pharmacological and other properties of indigenous medicines, in an effort to effect a coordinated and comprehensive evaluation of the applications and efficacies of medicinal plants used throughout the world (Penso 1977, Schultes 1972, WHO 1975, 1978).

The research reported here is consistent with such recommendations in addressing interrelationships among indigenous medicines, disease, and diet in northern Nigeria. Presented first are the results of laboratory evaluations of the potential efficacy of elements of a Hausa herbal pharmacopoeia used in the treatment of malaria infection. Our data suggest that some of these plants have therapeutic value against malaria, insofar as they may increase levels of intraerythrocytic oxidation, a phenomenon previously demonstrated to suppress fulminant plasmodial infection. These observations are then placed within a broader ecological framework through consideration of the nutritional role played by some of these same plants. By so doing, we illustrate the same positive functions afforded by these botanicals when they are used in emically nonmedical contexts such as alimentation. This examination of the multiple roles of botanicals as constituents of both an indigenous diet and an herbal pharmacopoeia contributes to our understanding of the range of behaviors that must be considered for comprehensive investigations of biocultural adaptations to disease.

Indigenous Pharmacopoeias and Malaria Infection

The more traditional research strategies applied in the study of indigenous medicines assign positive or negative therapeutic values on the basis of efficacy in the treatment of simple, discrete symptoms. For example, in other communications (Etkin 1980, 1981), we have reported potential therapeutic efficacy for a number of Hausa plant medicines used in the treatment of various diseases affecting the teeth and oral tissues. Empirical investigation based on constituent analyses recorded in the pharmacological literature revealed a variety of phytochemical constituents with known antibacterial, inflammation-suppressive, and anticariogenic properties. The efficacy proposed for this portion of the Hausa herbal pharmacopoeia is consistent with the observations of Elvin-Lewis (1979, 1980, and this volume) and coworkers (1974). Their data suggest that among some Asian and African populations, the relatively high standard of oral health (determined by clinical dental examinations) can be at least partially attributed to the use of some of the same Hausa plant medicines that we examined. Similarly, our investigations of plants used in the Hausa treatment of gastrointestinal and related disorders discerned the presence of phytochemical constituents with potentially therapeutic properties such as antibiotics, emollients, anthelminthics, and others (Etkin and Ross n.d.).

By contrast, the research reported here on the empirical evaluation of Hausa antimalarial plant medicines affords an opportunity to assess the potential efficacy of therapies applied in the treatment of diseases characterized by interrelated and externally indiscernible symptom complexes. As we have discussed elsewhere (Etkin 1979), examination of the indigenous treatment of symptom-complex disorders such as malaria infection is particularly important in view of the high rates of morbidity that generally attend such diseases when compared with relatively simple, symptom-discrete disorders, and also because it is precisely in the prevention and treatment of these complex diseases that one often finds most competition between Western and indigenous treatment modalities (Beals 1976; Dunlop 1974–75; Foster 1973, 1976; Janzen 1978; Lambo 1971), a fact that has far-reaching policy implications for medical development programs.

Pharmacologic analyses of indigenous antimalarial medicines as reported in the literature have, for the most part, considered only those plants described specifically for treatment of the malaria symptom complex in its entirety. Attention has apparently not been directed toward those plants used for only single or related symptoms, for other diseases, or for emically nonmedical purposes such as alimentation, hygiene, and cosmetic application. These pharmacologic investigations have primarily been constituent analyses designed to detect the presence of quinine-like alkaloids or compounds that mimic the structure, and ostensibly the activity, of other synthetic antimalarial drugs (Bowman et al. 1968, Goodman and Gilman 1970, Goth 1970, Popp et al. 1968). Since no such substances have been reported for plants used in the Hausa treatment of malaria (Ekong 1968, El-Said et al. 1968, Malcolm and Sofowora 1969, Spencer et al. 1947, Watt and Breyer–Brandwijk 1962), we directed our analysis toward laboratory examination of other pertinent biochemical parameters.

The plants whose analysis is described in this chapter constitute a subsample of some of the more common Hausa medicines (listed in Table 13.1) used in the treatment of one or more components of the malaria symptom complex. These components include the periodic fevers that characterize malaria infection, as well as more obscure indicators such as spleno-hepatomegaly, icterus, hemoglobinuria, and anemia. By accounting for medicines used to treat the full range of symptoms (either singly or in some combination), one can approach a more comprehensive evaluation than one could achieve if one were to restrict analysis to only those plants used when all symptoms appear together to indicate what Western medicine designates as malaria (a symptom cluster which indigenous practitioners do not necessarily recognize as a single entity).

Study Site and Data Collection

An extensive investigation of the uses and efficacies of indigenous medicines, as well as a nutrition survey, was initiated during 18 months' residence in a Hausa–Fulani agricultural hamlet of 400 residents located approximately 50 km. southeast of Kano City in northern Nigeria. Data collected during this study provide the basis for an ongoing series of evaluatory investigations and laboratory analyses currently

Table 13.1 Hausa Antimalarial Plant Medicines

Species (Family)	Common Name "Hausa Name"	Medicinal Application	Dietary Utilization	A	B	C
Abrus precatorius L. (Papilionaceae)	Indian liquorice "Idon zakara"	Whole plant used to treat periodic fevers and jaundice	Whole plant is edible; leaves are sweet, used as flavoring	+	+	+
Acacia albida Del. (Mimosaceae)	Winter thorn "Gawo"	Bark used in treatment of fever and jaundice				+
Acacia arabica Willd. (Mimosaceae)	Egyptian mimosa "Gabaruwa"	Fruit pulp and pods used as fever cure; root and leaf mixture to treat fever	Leaves, fruit, and seed are edible; the gum is occasionally chewed	+	+	+
Adansonia digitata L. (Bombacaceae)	Baobab tree "Kuka"	Leaves, seeds, fruit, and bark used to treat fever; bark is a treatment for jaundice	Fruit, seeds, leaves, young root, and bark are edible	+	+	
Anogeissus leiocarpus Guill. & Perr. and *A. schimperi* Hochst. (Combretaceae)	"Marke"	Leaves used in cure for jaundice; bark used for fever remedies	Infusion of bark and stem buds is made into beverage; gum is edible	+	+	
Azadirachta indica A. Juss. (Melaiceae)	Neem tree "Darbejiya"	Leaves and bark used in fever medicines and for periodic fevers	Flowers are edible as stomachic and dietetic	+		
Balanites aegyptica Del. (Zygophyllaceae)	Desert date tree "Aduwa"	Root used in cures for periodic fevers; fruit used in fever medicines; leaves are treatment for jaundice	Fruit, seeds, leaves, flowers, and occasionally resin are used in foods	+	+	+
Bauhinia reticulata D.C. (Caesalpiniaceae)	Camel's foot tree "Kargo"	Leaves, root, and bark are fever medicines; root used to treat spleen disorders	Leaves and pods are edible; root bark chewed to impart red color to teeth and lips	+	+	+

234

Species	Local name	Medicinal use	Food use			
Cassia goratensis Fres. (Caesalpiniaceae)	"Runhu"	Leaves and fruit pods used to treat fevers	Leaves and fruit are edible; leaf infusion taken as refresher	+	+	+
Cassia occidentalis L. (Caesalpiniaceae)	Coffee senna "Majamfari"	Leaves used to treat periodic fevers, jaundice, and fevers; roots are fever medicines and are used in cures for hepatic disorders	Young leaves and unripe fruit pods are edible; root decoction taken to enhance appetite; seeds are used in beverages	+	+	+
Cassia tora L. (Caesalpiniaceae)	Foetid cassia "Tafasa"	Leaves used in treatment of fevers	Leaves widely used as vegetable and in soups; seeds for drinks, and eaten in times of scarcity	+	+	+
Celosia laxa Sch. & Thonn. and *C. trigyna* L. (Amaranthaceae)	"Nannaho"	Whole plant used for treatment of periodic and other fevers	Leaves cooked in soups and as vegetable.	+	+	+
Chrozophora senegalensis A. Juss. (Euphorbiaceae)	"Damagi"	Leaves are medicine for fevers				
Cochlospermum planchonii Hook (Cochlospermaceae)	"Balagande"	Root used in fever medicines and to treat jaundice	Seeds are edible; root is added to foods to impart yellow color	+	+	
Cochlospermum tinctorium Rich. (Cochlospermaceae)	"Rawaya"	Bark and root used in treatment of jaundice	Root is mixed in cooking oils or food to impart a yellow color	+	+	
Commiphora kerstingii Engl. (Burseraceae)	"Dali"	Leaves taken as medicine for jaundice				
Eragrostis cilianensis Lut. (Graminae)	Stink grass "Bunsurum fage"	Whole plant is medicine for fevers	Seeds are edible	+	+	+
Ficus syringifolia and *F. polita* Vahl. (Moraceae)	"Durumi"	Leaves are used to treat fevers	Young leaves are cooked in soups	+	+	+

Table 13.1. Con't

Species (Family)	Common Name "Hausa Name"	Medicinal Application	Dietary Utilization	A	B	C
Ficus thonningii Blume (Moraceae)	Loincloth fig tree "Cediya"	Leaves are fever and jaundice remedies; bark used to treat spleno- or hepatomegaly	Young leaves are cooked in soups; fruit is edible	+	+	+
Guiera senegalensis Lam. (Combretaceae)	"Sabara"	Leaves are medicine for fevers and are common vehicle for other remedies	Leaves are included in soups and are added to gruels as an appetizer	+	+	+
Hibiscus sabdariffa L. (Malvaceae)	Red sorrel "Yakuwa"	Seeds, fruit, and leaves taken as fever medicine	Leaves and calyces are commonly used as vegetables; fruit, seeds, and seed oil are edible	+	+	+
Ipomoea spp. (Convolvulaceae)	Stream calabash "Duman rafi"	Whole plant taken in treatment of fevers				
Moringa pterygosperma Gaertn. (Moringaceae)	Horseradish tree "Zogali"	Leaves are used in medicines for fevers and jaundice	Leaves widely used in soups and as vegetables; fruit pods, roots, and seed oil are edible	+	+	+
Parkia filicoidea Welw. (Mimosaceae)	African locust bean tree "Dorawa"	Leaves and fruit pulp used in treatment of fevers; bark is a medicine for jaundice	Leaves, fruit pulp, seeds, and flowers are edible; bark infusions are drunk as a tonic	+	+	+
Prosopis africana Taub. (Mimosaceae)	Ironwood "Kirya"	Leaves and bark are remedies for fevers	Seeds are edible	+		

Species	Common name	Uses	A	B	C
Sarcocephalus esculentus Afz. (Rubiaceae)	African peach "Tafashiya"	Leaves and root are medicines for fevers, jaundice, and hemoglobinuria; bark is taken to treat periodic fevers and jaundice / Fruit is edible; the wood in infusion is drunk as a tonic	+		
Sclerocarya birrea Hochst. (Anacardiaceae)	"Danya"	Fruit taken in treatment of hemoglobinuria / Fruit and seeds are edible	+	+	+
Securidaca longipedunculata Fres. (Polygalaceae)	Violet tree "Sanya"	Roots used to treat periodic fevers; seeds and roots are a medicine for fevers / Infusion of the root bark is drunk as a tonic	+	+	
Striga senegalensis Benth. (Scrophulariaceae)	"Soki"	Whole plant is a remedy for anemia and jaundice / Whole plant used in cooking vegetables and legumes, to soften them	+	+	+
Strychnos spinosa Lam. (Loganiaceae)	Monkey orange "Kokiya"	Fruit and roots are used as medicines for fevers / Fruit and leaves are edible	+	+	+
Tamarindus indica L. (Caesalpiniaceae)	Tamarind tree "Tsamiya"	Leaves, fruit, bark, and root are taken for treatment of fevers; leaves and bark are medicines for jaundice; flowers are a remedy for jaundice and hepatomegaly / Leaves commonly cooked as vegetable and used in soups; fruit, seeds, and flowers are edible; bark and pod infusions drunk as tonics	+	+	+
Ximenia americana L. (Olacaceae)	Wild olive "Tsada"	Leaves, young twigs, and roots are remedies for fevers / Leaves, fruit, and seed oil are edible	+	+	+

NOTE: In column A, + means that one or more parts of this plant are used as food; in column B, + means that the same part(s) of the plant serve(s) both as medicine for one or more symptoms of malaria and as food; in column C, + means that the plant part(s) in column B is/are maximally utilized during the period of high malaria risk at the end of the rainy season.

being conducted to examine the potential therapeutic efficacy of certain components collected from the Hausa herbal pharmacopoeia.

As we have documented elsewhere (Etkin 1979, 1980, 1981), the indigenous herbal pharmacopoeia provides the only substantive source of medical care for members of this population. It is compatible with—and is used concurrently and in many respects indistinguishably with—therapeutic practices that derive both from Islam and from historically antecedent religion the foundation of which lies in a cult of spirit possession (*Bori*). This continued reliance on indigenous treatment, in an area where Western medicine is typically in short supply and in any case not actively sought, constitutes an important rationale for the evaluation of therapeutic and other properties of medicines used routinely by the indigenous population.

Information regarding attitudes and beliefs relevant to disease etiology, classification, and treatment modalities was collected in order to develop a normative description of the most commonly perceived disease symptoms or symptom complexes and their appropriate treatments. Extensive interviews were conducted with individuals who are considered by other members of the population, and who perceive themselves, to be most conversant in matters relevant to health and disease. Fourteen adults, five women and nine men, constitute the group of principal respondents. Included among them is a woman whose knowledge of plant medicines is sufficiently comprehensive that her expertise as a chief herbalist is recognized throughout the entire district. Other respondents represent rather more narrow foci of medically relevant knowledge: a barber–surgeon, several midwives, and locally designated "specialists" in particular treatments such as venereal disease therapies, weaning medicines, cures for bewitchment, and others. These respondents, and in fact many of the adult villagers, also demonstrated knowledge of at least several treatments for a variety of complaints that include colds, febrile states, epidermal inflammations and infections, digestive disorders, and other common afflictions.

Interviews were loosely structured around: (1) a catalogue of 637 plants, which individuals described with reference to physical descriptions for each plant, its availability, and any medicinal or other applications associated with it; and (2) a list of 808 disease names, symptom descriptions, and related terms, for which respondents described commonly used indigenous treatments, including preparation procedures, additional constituents of composite preparations, approximate dosage, repetition of applications, and alternatives used in the event the medicine does not effect symptom remission and/or cure. These plants are listed alphabetically by genus and species designation in Table 13.1, which also includes a summary of specific portions of the plants used in medicinal and dietary contexts. The medicinal applications of indigenous flora as reported for this population are to a high degree congruent with other surveys of Hausa medicinal plants conducted by Adam (1972), Ainslie (1937), Ayensu (1978), Dalziel (1937), Githens (1949), Hambali (1973), Oliver (1960), and Prietze (1913–14).

Samples of commonly used medicinals were collected with the assistance of the chief herbalist and her assistants. Plants were air dried in the field and sent to the United States for future laboratory evaluation. To establish precise taxonomic identification, pressed (voucher) samples accompanied each plant species collected. (Presently, these are housed in the African collection of the herbarium at Shaw Botanical Gardens in St. Louis, Mo.) The samples collected from the Hausa herbal pharmacopoeia constitute the basis for the laboratory analyses to be discussed next.

Biomedical Evaluation of Hausa Antimalarial Plant Medicines

The discussion that follows first outlines the rationale for the methodology developed to assess the chemotherapeutic value of the antimalarial plant medicines. Discussed next are the specific laboratory procedures that were carried out and the experimental results.

A series of analyses were designed to assess the capacity of these plant medicines to alter the oxidation-reduction, or "redox," status of red blood cells. The significance of this particular feature of red cell metabolism in the course of malaria infection was elucidated in our earlier research on parasite and host cell biochemistry during plasmodial infection (Etkin 1975; Etkin and Eaton 1975), and is briefly summarized below.

Examples of specific redox phenomena important in erythrocyte metabolism are the reversible conversions among (1) the (reduced) enzyme cofactors nicotinamide adenine dinucleotide (NADH) and nicotinamide adenine dinucleotide phosphate (NADPH) and their oxidized counterparts, NAD and NADP; (2) the compound glutathione (GSH) and its oxidized counterpart GSSG; and (3) hemoglobin and an oxidized form of the protein, methemoglobin.

The principal function of the red blood cell is to carry large quantities of molecular oxygen without itself becoming oxidized by it, with red cell integrity dependent upon the suppression of chemical equilibrium with molecular oxygen. Key erythrocytic components such as sulfhydryl-containing enzymes and the ferrous iron of hemoglobin exist in an oxygenated environment, which would, if equilibrium were reached, become oxidized. Excess oxidation is harmful to the red cell, and, when not compensated, produces a variety of damaging effects that may cause lysis of the red cell.

In normal erythrocytes, several interrelated reductive processes counteract intracellular redox equilibrium, and thus ensure red cell survival. These mechanisms include the maintenance of hemoglobin, glutathione, and NADH and NADPH in high titres of their reduced forms relative to concentrations of their oxidized counterparts. The activities of the pentose phosphate shunt, one of two alternative glucose catabolizing pathways, are largely responsible for preventing and repairing oxidant damage to the red cell. This process is summarized in Figure 13.1, which illustrates that the first step of the shunt is responsible for generating reducing (anti-oxidant) potential in the form of the enzyme cofactor NADPH. This, through conversion to its oxidized complement (NADP), maintains glutathione in its reduced form, which, in turn, neutralizes hydrogen peroxide (H_2O_2), a powerful intracellular oxidant, by converting it to water (H_2O). Subsequent steps in the pentose shunt generate additional reducing potential, and NADPH and NADH both are important in preventing formation of high levels of methemoglobin, as indicated toward the bottom right of Figure 13.1. (In Fig. 13.1, reactions of the pentose phosphate shunt are circumscribed by the broken line, and the following abbreviations are used: G-6-PD = glucose-6-phosphate dehydrogenase; NADPH and NADP = reduced and oxidized forms, respectively, of nicotinamide adenine dinucleotide phosphate; NADH and NAD = reduced and oxidized forms, respectively, of nicotinamide adenine dinucleotide; GSH and GSSG = reduced and oxidized forms, respectively, of glutathione; H_2O_2 = hydrogen peroxide; Hb = hemoglobin; Met Hb = methemoglobin.)

The red cell enzyme catalase additionally protects against excessive oxidation by mediating the detoxification of hydrogen peroxide:

$$P - Fe^{+++} - OH + H_2O_2 \qquad P - Fe^{+++} - OOH + H_2O$$
(Catalase)   (Complex I)

$$P - Fe^{+++} - OH + H_2O_2 \qquad P - Fe^{+++} - OH + H_2O + \tfrac{1}{2}O_2$$
(Complex I)   (Inactive Complex II)

Catalase will react with one molecule of H_2O_2 to form Catalase Complex I and water. Complex I can react with and neutralize a second molecule of H_2O_2 in an irreversible reaction that produces inactive Catalase Complex II, water, and molecular oxygen. As indicated in Figure 13.2, if the compound aminotriazole (AT) (which does not occur normally in red cells) is added to the system, it will react with Complex I to form an inactive and easily detected catalase: AT compound. Thus, in the presence of AT, diminution of catalase activity demonstrates the presence of the oxidant H_2O_2. As Figure 13.2 demonstrates, catalase neutralizes H_2O_2, forming Catalase Complex I, which, in the presence of aminotriazole (AT), will be inactivated. Thus, diminution of catalase activity when AT is present demonstrates the occurrence of H_2O_2.

In order to clarify these considerations of redox reactions in red blood cells, we reiterate several points. Those deviations from a normal redox balance that result in excessive intracellular oxidation jeopardize the integrity and continued functioning of the red cell. Elevated and potentially damaging oxidation is indicated when: titres of NADP and NAD are high relative to their reduced counterparts, NADPH and NADH; methemoglobin levels rise; GSH concentrations decrease; and catalase activity is diminished in the presence of aminotriazole.

In the course of monitoring red cell parameters such as these, we observed an increase in red cell oxidation attendant upon plasmodial infection (Etkin and Eaton 1975). In-vivo methemoglobin concentrations were significantly higher in malaria-infected experimental animals relative to controls, and infected erythrocytes were markedly more sensitive to additional oxidant stress. Moreover, catalase activity in infected red cells was markedly inhibited by aminotriazole, indicating the presence of H_2O_2. In all cases, the degree of oxidation was related directly to the severity of infection. Additionally, isolated parasite suspensions were capable of oxidizing the cofactors NADH and NADPH. These data suggested that malaria-infected

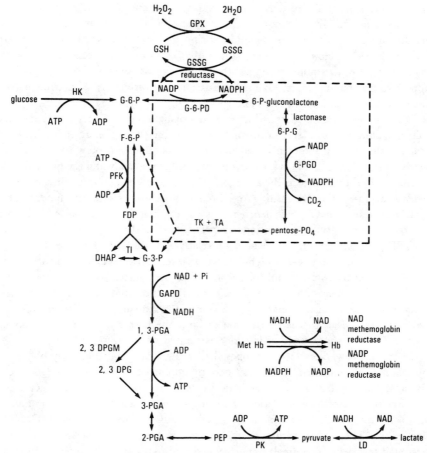

Fig. 13.1 Catabolism of Glucose in Human Erythrocytes. SOURCE: Harris and Kellermeyer (1970:471).

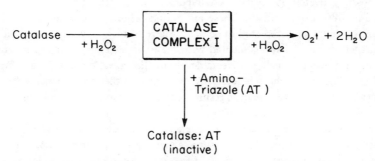

Fig. 13.2. Reaction of Catalase with Hydrogen Peroxide and Aminotriazole. SOURCE: Etkin and Eaton (1975:222).

erythrocytes are exposed to considerable oxidant stress and that at least some of the oxidants generated are of parasitic origin. This is consistent with other reports in the literature that note GSH depletion during plasmodial infection (Fletcher and Maegraith 1970, Homewood and Neame 1980). As discussed below, these data combine with other studies to suggest that, whereas plasmodial parasites themselves appear to generate oxidants, excessive oxidation may ultimately be detrimental to the continuation of malaria infection.

We proposed that the increased intracellular oxidation that occurs during malaria infection might explain the biochemical basis for the protection against fulminant malaria afforded by some inherited deficiencies of glucose-6-phosphate dehydrogenase (G-6-PD). G-6-PD is the enzyme responsible for catalyzing the first reaction of the pentose phosphate pathway (Fig. 13.1), the red cell's most critical line of defense against oxidative insult. And from this it follows that the fundamental metabolic lesion in G-6-PD deficiency is an insufficient production of reducing compounds necessary for prevention or repair of oxidant damage. As a consequence, G-6-PD-deficient erythrocytes would be relatively intolerant of the oxidation associated with malaria infection. Thus, in normal red cells, oxidants are neutralized, allowing efficient parasite multiplication, subsequent infection of new host cells, and the development of fulminant disease. On the other hand, in G-6-PD-deficient and other oxidant-sensitive erythrocytes, cumulative oxidant damage to the infected red cell would lead to the destruction of both the host cell and the developing parasite, so that the severity of infection is limited.

Eaton and coworkers (1976) proposed that the same conditions may obtain in normal red cells rendered oxidant-sensitive by imposition of a vitamin E deficiency. (Because vitamin E functions metabolically as an antioxidant, its deficiency leads to excessive intracellular oxidation, resulting in an intraerythrocytic environment that is, with respect to redox status, metabolically analogous to that in G-6-PD deficiency.) Their work with malaria infection in vitamin-E-deficient mice demonstrated that deficient animals were more resistant to plasmodial infection. Further, illustrating that the suppression of malaria infection was in this case specific for vitamin E deficiency, they observed that when E-deficient animals were later resupplemented with the vitamin, susceptibility to fulminant malaria infection was restored.

A possibly related observation was reported for undernourished nomadic populations in sub-Saharan Africa. These are groups whose diets normally are low in vitamin E, and who were noted to be relatively resistant to severe malaria infection. When their diets were supplemented with grain, an excellent source of vitamin E, recrudescence of previously undetectable plasmodial infections occurred (Murray et al. 1976). This can perhaps be partially explained by the same phenomenon—that is, elevated intracellular oxidation resulting from vitamin E deficiency may suppress malaria infection (Eaton et al. 1976).

The same reasoning probably also explains the mode of action of a number of synthetic antimalarial preparations, such as primaquine, paludrine, and other drugs that act on the endoerythrocytic form of the parasite and that also generate oxidants

(Beutler 1969, Bowman et al. 1968, Cohen and Hochstein 1965). That is, their efficacy in malaria prophylaxis and therapy may be ascribed to their ability to generate oxidants.

The foregoing observations combine to elucidate the clinical significance of redox perturbations during malaria infection, by demonstrating that the imposition of substantial oxidant stress by a variety of endogenous or exogenous factors can be of therapeutic value in plasmodial infection.

In view of this cumulative evidence, we have undertaken investigations to assess the oxidizing potential of a number of medicines used in the Hausa treatment of malaria. We suggest that plants which can raise levels of intraerythrocytic oxidation may be effective in limiting plasmodial infection. This could occur by promoting oxidant damage that would lead subsequently to lysis of infected red cells, to release immature parasite forms incapable of continuing the infection. To our knowledge, no other examination of indigenous pharmacopoeias has investigated this parameter. This offers what we consider to be a unique and important approach, which can be integrated with other methods to achieve a more comprehensive evaluation of plants used by indigenous populations.

Laboratory Methods and Results

The first set of experiments was designed to estimate the capacity of Hausa anti-malarials to generate methemoglobin, a sensitive measure of erythrocyte oxidant damage. Extracts were prepared from macerated plant materials in solutions of isotonic saline and neutralized to physiologic pH. Normal red cell hemolysates in dilute hemoglobin suspensions were incubated at 37° C. in equivolume ratios with the extracts, and methemoglobin concentrations were determined after two hours' incubation. Data are summarized in Table 13.2, with two-hour methemoglobin concentrations expressed as percentages of the sample of *G. senegalensis* No. 11, the only sample in which all hemoglobin had been oxidized to methemoglobin at the end of the incubation period. Control samples accumulated no significant amount of methemoglobin, with final concentrations at an expected 0.5 percent of total hemoglobin. These data suggest the presence of oxidizing properties in these medicinal plants and indicate the relative capacity of each to generate methemoglobin.

As a second measure of oxidizing potential, we examined these plants to determine their capacity for oxidizing glutathione (GSH). Oxidation of GSH to GSSG is indicated by diminution of GSH concentrations over time. Extracts and hemolysates were prepared as for the methemoglobin studies. Reduced glutathione (GSH) was added to the hemolysates and combined with plant extracts, so that the starting GSH concentration for all samples was 2.0 millimoles (mM). Samples were incubated for two hours at 37° C., and residual GSH was measured at 30, 60, and 120 minutes. Results are summarized in Table 13.3, with sample numbers corresponding to plants in Table 13.2, and with residual GSH espressed in millimolar concentrations. Control samples showed virtually no change in GSH levels (as expected), with final two-hour determinations ranging between 1.9 and 2.0 mM.

Table 13.2.　Methemoglobin Generation by Plant Extracts

	Sample	Percent
1.	*Acacia arabica*—root	56
2.	*Azadirachta indica*—leaf	42
3.	*A. indica*—bark	9
4.	*A. indica*—root	7
5.	*Cassia occidentalis*—root	78
6.	*C. occidentalis*—leaf	68
7.	*Cassia tora*—leaf	35
8.	*C. tora*—root	29
9.	*Cochlospermum tinctorium*—root	51
10.	*Guiera senegalensis*—root	47
11.	*G. senegalensis*—leaf	100
12.	*Securidaca longipedunculata*—root	29
C.	Controls	0.5

Table 13.3.　Influence of Plant Extracts on Glutathione (GSH) Stability

Sample	Time Elapsed			
	0 min.	30 min.	60 min.	120 min.
1.	2.0 mM	1.3 mM	0.9 mM	0.2 mM
2.	2.0	1.2	0.7	0.1
3.	2.0	1.7	1.6	1.4
4.	2.0	1.8	1.7	1.8
5.	2.0	1.9	1.7	1.5
6.	2.0	1.9	1.6	1.0
7.	2.0	0.4	0.4	0.1
8.	2.0	1.5	1.3	0.9
9.	2.0	1.8	1.7	1.2
10.	2.0	1.8	1.5	1.5
11.	2.0	0.5	0.1	0.1
12.	2.0	1.8	1.5	1.7
C.	2.0	1.9	1.9	1.9

Table 13.4.　In-vivo Effects of Medicinal Plants on Malaria Infection

	Sample	Parasitemia, Day 7
1.	*Acacia arabica*—root	0%
2.	*Azadirachta indica*—leaf	0%
7.	*Cassia tora*—leaf	83%
11.	*Guiera senegalensis*—leaf	1%
C.	Controls	87%

On the basis of both the methemoglobin generation and GSH depletion studies, it appears that some of the Hausa antimalarial plant medicines have significant oxidant-generating activity in vitro. The mere presence of oxidants in these plants cannot, of course, demonstrate their efficacy in malaria therapy. But these preliminary data do suggest that some of the plants might have therapeutic merit, a possibility we considered worthy of further examination. Therapeutic efficacy could take the form of increasing intracellular oxidation, thereby making it likely that malaria-infected red cells would succumb to oxidant damage and be destroyed before parasites have had a chance to reach maturity.

In light of these results, we extended investigation of several plants that demonstrated particularly high in-vitro oxidizing activity on hemoglobin and GSH, in order to examine their effects in vivo. Studies were designed to assess the therapeutic efficacy of these medicinal plants in an analog of human malaria, murine *Plasmodium berghei* infection (studies of which represent much of the basic experimental work in human malaria therapy [Peters 1980, Aviado 1969]).

Malaria infection in the laboratory is routinely passed by injecting healthy subjects intraperitoneally with *Plasmodium*-infected red cells obtained from heavily parasitized animals. Our next series of investigations interrupted this process with an incubation phase, in order to expose parasites to the medicinal plant extracts. Infected erythrocytes were incubated with neutralized extracts from plants numbered 1, 2, 7, and 11 (cf. Table 13.2), then injected into healthy experimental subjects in order to monitor any effects such preincubation may have on the normal course of infection. Specifically, we measured the time that elapsed before the infection reached patency and the duration of infection prior to death, these being standard evaluations used in testing antimalarial drugs (Peters 1980).

As depicted in Table 13.4, after seven days, mice injected with parasites exposed to samples 1 and 2 were not infected; those injected with parasites exposed to sample No. 11 sustained only very mild infections, whereas those injected with parasites incubated with sample 7 mimicked controls (i.e., showed no antiplasmodial activity in vivo), with rates of parasitemia in excess of 80 percent of total number of red cells infected.

These observations did not permit us to rule out the possibility that some undetected toxic factors were responsible for killing the parasites during the preinjection incubation. In order to elucidate this, our most recent studies were designed to simultaneously evaluate toxicity and assess therapeutic activity in vivo. Twenty-four hours following the standard intraperitoneal injection of infected red cells, experimental subjects received by the same route of administration a daily dose of neutralized plant extract in approximate equivalence to the proportional quantity ingested by humans in the course of therapy. Preliminary results indicate strongly against toxicity for all extracts tested, but do not unequivocally demonstrate definitive therapeutic activity. Methodology for this phase of investigation is currently being refined, and the in-vivo analyses of therapeutic efficacy continue at the present time.

These preliminary studies on a sample of the Hausa antimalarials lend support to, albeit cannot yet confirm, our hypothesis that some of the plants may have value in the prevention and/or therapy of plasmodial infections. Such efficacy can be neither firmly established nor refuted until these medicinals are subjected to more extensive and sensitive analyses and, eventually (in cases that so warrant), to clinical trial in human malaria infection. The most conclusive tests, and those that provide focus and direction for future investigations of the Hausa antimalarials, would include more refined analyses that, first, can fractionate the specific constituents responsible for the in-vitro oxidant activity reported here and second, can determine whether the ingestion of these oxidizing plants effectively raises intraerythrocytic oxidation to levels that can interfere with malaria parasite development. Our investigations continue in this direction, and we submit the foregoing with principal emphasis on the proposed merits of its methodologic conceptualization and approach.

Also important, in addition to the biomedical analysis of these plants, is a consideration of other dimensions of the indigenous utilization of ambient flora. To this end, we extend examination of these plants to their evaluation as elements of diet, in order to achieve a more comprehensive understanding of the physiologic impact of the indigenous use of plants in a broad ecological context.

Interrelations among Indigenous Medicines and Diet

As indicated in Table 13.1, among the 35 indigenous plant species commonly used by the Hausa in the treatment of one or more symptoms of malaria infection, a sizable proportion (89 percent = 31 of the 35) are also used in a dietary context. Among these there exists 80 percent concordance (28 of the 35) for the same plant part serving as both medicine and food. Further, among these plants for which the same parts serve as antimalarials and foods, 82 percent (23 of the 28) are maximally available during the period of peak risk of malaria infection.

We begin this section with a brief overview of the general interactions between disease and nutritional status. This is followed by a methodologic description of a nutritional survey conducted among the study population. Some of the results of this survey are then discussed in conjunction with observations on the epidemiology of malaria infection in northern Nigeria.

Nutrition and Disease

Clinical, biochemical, and epidemiological studies have demonstrated that, in general, nutrition and disease impact significantly upon each other. A common observation in this regard is that various states of malnutrition are synergistic with infectious disease. That is, pathogenic processes tend to be more severe in poorly nourished hosts, and infections frequently aggravate symptoms of extant malnutrition. Most of the data that support such generalizations have been generated by studies conducted with experimental animals in controlled laboratory settings. Although it is clear that interactions between nutrition and infection are equally important in human health and disease, little is known of the general, let alone specific, relationships that actually obtain in nonexperimental contexts. An observation frequently reported among human populations is that whereas nutritional patterns may have no discernible effect on the frequency with which an infection occurs, dietary insufficiencies may exacerbate their severity. And, conversely, infectious diseases—indirectly and attendant upon various physiologic and cultural parameters—often precipitate or intensify symptom expression in existing cases of marginal nutritional depletion. (The foregoing is a summation of several comprehensive reviews: Chandra 1976, Katz and Stiehm 1977, Martorell 1980, Schneider 1971, Scrimshaw et al. 1968, Suskind 1977.)

Because the general relationship between human nutrition and disease has been typically viewed as a synergistic one, few studies have examined potentially antagonistic relationships between dietary patterns and the incidence or expression of infection, whether considered generally or for specific pathogens. Thus, aside from the diffuse and often vague notion that an adequate diet diminishes the risks of morbidity and mortality due to disease, there is to date no clear evidence that other features of diet—whether they be additions or exclusions of certain foods or nutrients—have a negative influence on the course of disease. Discussion now is addressed specifically to this issue of antagonism.

Two general types of antagonistic relationship between nutritional practices and specific pathogens can be considered. These are situations in which prevention or suppression of an infection can be attributed to (1) the routine inclusion, or (2) the absence of, specific foods or nutrients in the diet. We are aware of very few studies that demonstrate either of these relationships.

As for the former, several relevant examples can be cited. Kliks (1975) has suggested that the dietary ingestion of chenopod seeds (*Chenopodium ambrosoides*), which contain anthelminthic substances, may account for the absence of intestinal worm infection which was adduced from studies of parasite-free coprolites of a prehistoric population in Lovelock Cave, Nevada. Katz and Schall (1979) have proposed that the dietary utilization of fava beans (*Vicia faba*) may, by virtue of increasing erythrocyte oxidant sensitivity, limit the severity of malaria infection among some Mediterranean populations (cf. discussion earlier in this chapter). Similarly, with reference to chronic rather than to infectious disease, it has been suggested that the routine inclusion of plants known to have antiplatelet effects— such as garlic (*Allium sativum*), onion (*A. cepa*), and Cantonese black tree fungus (*Auricularia polytricha*)—may account for relatively low rates of atherogenesis and coronary heart disease among some populations (Hammerschmidt 1980; Makheja et al. 1979). Another commonly cited example that addresses a genetic disorder is Houston's (1973) proposal that the symptoms of sickle-cell anemia are mitigated by consumption of cassava and other cyanate-containing foods (although Lambotte [1974] has more recently raised important objections to this argument). In all four cases, the possibility is examined that the incorporation of certain foods into the diet may be beneficial over and above what such foods contribute in the standard nutrients important for resisting disease—i.e., protein, vitamins, minerals, and calories.

The second general type of antagonistic relationship between nutrition and disease is one in which the deficiency of some nutrient proves advantageous in preventing or suppressing a particular infection. Prominent examples in this regard include the reports of Kretschmar (1967; with Voller 1973) of suppressed plasmodial infection among individuals fed only with milk. Antagonism in this case is attributed to the absence in milk diets of para-aminobenzoic acid (PABA), a critical component of the B vitamin complex requisite for parasite synthesis of nucleic acids and for other metabolic activities. Additionally, as previously discussed in this chapter, both a vitamin E deficiency and the generally poor state of nutritional health noted among subjects of a famine relief program (Murray 1976) have a suppressive influence on malaria infection. At least the former, and perhaps both, instances of plasmodiostasis can be attributed to the sequelae of increased red cell oxidation (Eaton et al. 1976). This second set of examples of antagonistic relationships between nutrition and infection serves to illustrate cases in which the lack of one or more nutrients proves beneficial in limiting infection.

We offer evidence from our study suggesting the occurrence of both types of antagonistic relationship in suppressing fulminant malaria infection. We demonstrate in the ensuing discussion that for a period of the year during which the population experiences maximum risk for malaria infection, short-term fluctuations—characterized by the increased use of certain foods and the diminished use of others—may serve to minimize the severity of plasmodial infection.

Nutritional Survey

A nutritional survey of eight households, incorporating a mean total of 46 residents, was conducted in order to document dietary inputs for each household. The survey, comprising both questionnaires and weight measures of unprocessed foods, was implemented for 24-hour periods, randomly selected twice per week per household, for 48 consecutive weeks. This coincided with the end of one harvest and the beginning of the next, these being the most meaningful delineators of the annual agricultural cycle.

The eight households surveyed were selected both to maximize cooperation and to represent the range of variation in socioeconomic status for the study population. For each of the three daily meals, all foods were weighed prior to cooking and other modes of preparation. Independent and repeated analyses of all types of food consumed by the study population included weight and volume measures for all ingredients, tabulated sequentially through all stages of preparation to final cooked (or otherwise modified), consumable form. This allowed for extrapolation from the household unprocessed weight measures to quantified approximations of nutrient values (of calories, protein, etc.). Foods (meals and "snacks") consumed by adult household members and obtained from market or other intra- and extravillage sources were also r corded and were evaluated in the same manner, using collateral data such as cost per unit prepared food, fluctuating market and other prices, and the like.[1]

A more detailed presentation of methods and results of this nutritional survey will appear in future works. Our interest at this juncture is simply to describe the overall yearly fluctuations in relative quantities of different food types and their constituents, particularly with reference to grain-based foods versus those prepared from leafy and other vegetative plant parts. These data, integrated with other factors pertinent to the environmental context of malaria infection, provide the basis for the following discussion.

Epidemiology of Malaria in Northern Nigeria

Malaria is endemic in northern Nigeria. For the population studied, the risk of plasmodial infection is greatest in August–October, a pattern typical of much of the sub-Saharan savanna dominated by a unimodal pattern of rainfall (Wernsdorfer 1980).

In this region the annual cycle includes a 3–4 month rainy season and an 8–9 month dry season. In most years, the onset of rains in June is followed by a progressively increasing soil saturation, which results subsequently in the establishment of standing pools of water and other suitable breeding sites for the anopheline vectors of malaria. By August, there are enough mosquitos for continued development of plasmodial parasites and their transmission to susceptible human hosts. Nonetheless, the incidence of fulminant and debilitating plasmodial infection reported for this region is relatively low.[2] This is not to imply that malaria infection per se does not exist, but instead to note that infections tend to be relatively moderate. This apparent suppression of infection may be ascribed to a number of factors, one of which—the efficacy of indigenous antimalarials—has been discussed in preceding sectons of this chapter. Another potential contributor to relatively low rates of malaria parasitemia, certain features of diet, will be considered next.

Malaria Epidemiology and Dietary Patterns

In view of the precipitation patterns that characterize this region, agricultural populations routinely experience marked fluctuations in the seasonal availability of food crops. For example, the sorghum (*Sorghum* spp) and millet (*Pennisetum* spp) grains that constitute the principal staple crops in this area are sown in late May through early June and harvested from approximately the middle of September through November, subsequent to which they are stored in granaries within each family compound. Chief legumes cultivated in the region are groundnuts (*Arachis hypogoaea*) and cowpeas (*Vigna unguiculata*). Their sowing occurs at the end of June and beginning of July, with final harvests corresponding closely to the schedule of the later-maturing grains (sorghum). Maximum availability and lowest market costs for all these products coincide, not surprisingly, with their harvest. Their supplies are then gradually diminished throughout the remainder of the dry season and beginning of the rainy months, with market prices for replacements generally rising in accordance. The only exception to this pattern of fluctuating availability for principal food crops is cassava (*Manihot utilissima*), which is available year round, reflecting its xerophytic adaptations and the fact that if not all roots of a plant are harvested, it will continue as a transannual ("perennial"), providing edible rootstock for as long as three years.

The patterning in types and quantities of foods consumed corresponds closely with fluctuations in availability and costs. Variation is greatly restricted subsequent to harvest, when grains are readily available for consumption in the form of the flour-based foods that are preferred by the population. An elaboration of the diet—that is, an increase in the variety of foods eaten and in the sources for, and preparation forms of, these comestibles—becomes more pronounced through the progression of the dry season and commencement of rains. Figure 13.3 is a crude index depicting the frequency with which nongrain foods contribute to total caloric intake and illustrating the increasing dietary reliance on nongrain foods as the year progresses. (In Figure 13.3, the frequency with which nongrain foods contribute to household diets is expressed as a percentage of total caloric intake. The mean caloric value of nongrain foods is 21 percent, with a range between 15 and 28 percent. Means are given over four-week periods.) The reasons for the dietary elaboration outlined in Figure 13.3 and its implications are severalfold.

The occurrence of dietary elaboration during the rainy season is supported by consideration of various ecological and cultural parameters. The depletion of stored staples from the previous harvest contributes to a greater reliance on market purchases of raw grains and on consumption of foods prepared outside the home—either by village women, who sell cooked foods and "snacks" from their compounds, or by market vendors. These sources amplify the range of variability in the household's diet, a range that would otherwise be restricted to only those products reaped during the last harvest. Moreover, the frequency and duration of market attendance increase during the progression of the dry season and beginning of the rainy months. The population is thereby exposed to a greater array of foodstuffs from other areas, and this also affects food acquisition behaviors other than those directed at "necessary" purchases for household meals. Other factors that account for increases in dietary variability toward the end of the dry season include an increased number of ceremonies, which, in the public celebration of life-cycle events, involve intra- and intervillage food exchanges and redistributions. Although grains predominate in the diet throughout the year, the steady increase in market costs—which reach their maximum during the latter part of the rainy season—dissuades many individuals from replacing their diminished grain stores. Instead, they rely more heavily on other, less preferred, but more easily obtained, foods.

Another feature of dietary elaboration that characterizes the rainy season is the increased availability of wild and semi-cultivated "vegetables,"[3] chiefly various annual and perennial species of leafy plants. These are to a large extent "free goods," as those growing on public grazing lands, paths, or other nonprivately owned land, can be collected without obligation.

Although these plants can be dried and stored, and are consumed throughout the year in varying quantities, their most frequent use coincides with the last two

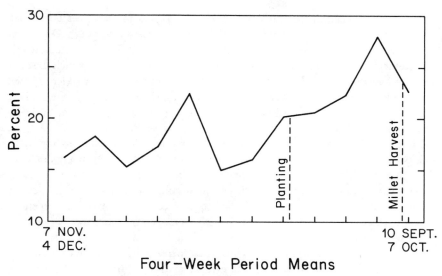

Fig. 13.3. Calory Sources Other Than Grains

months of the rainy season. This can be attributed to at least three factors. First, their availability is increased: compared to the cereals, they mature earlier and are then available for collection or in markets, where the cost of the fresh materials, and especially of any dried products from the previous year, is low relative to that for grain. Second, they help to diffuse remaining grains during a period of shortest supply by being increasingly added to cereal-based mixtures; hence, they are compatible with grain-based dishes. Third, concomitant with the decreasing supply of grain, these vegetable foods provide a welcome substitute for the readily available cassava, which figures increasingly in the diet immediately prior to the grain harvest as a necessary but undesirable substitute for cereals. Grain-based dishes are augmented by the addition of leaves and other vegetable plant parts and by the substitution of cassava for at least one meal, usually at midday, in order to reserve grain for the most important meal, in the evening. Vegetable dishes may also be prepared in preference to cassava, which is itself a substitute. Thus, the amount of vegetables consumed increases at the end of the rainy months.

The leaves and other tender parts of several species are especially favored; from among the plants listed in Table 13.1, these include: *Cassia tora, Celosia laxa, C. trigyna, Hibiscus sabdariffa,* and *Moringa pterygosperma.* (The only one of these especially favored vegetables that does not appear in Table 13.1—i.e., that is not used in the Hausa treatment of malaria—is *Hibiscus cannabinus.* Its dietary use is interchangeable with that of *H. sabdariffa,* which is included in that list.) The leaves of other species that figure more significantly as seasonings and for soups also appear in Table 13.1. Most important among these are *Adansonia digitata, Parkia filicoidea, Tamarindus indica;* a secondary group includes *Cassia occidentalis, Ficus polita, F. syringifolia, F. thonningii,* and *Guiera senegalensis.*

Some of the plants listed in Table 13.1 are also used in medicines other than antimalarials, the most notable among them being *Guiera senegalensis*. One of its Hausa names, *uwar magunguna* ("mother of medicines"), reflects its common role as a vehicle for various medicinal preparations, prominent among which are preventives and therapies for rainy-season diseases the Hausa etiology of which is based in exposure to *damina* ("dampness"), *raba* ("dew"), and so on. Also of note in these examples of maximal wet season utilization is the dietary application of *Striga senegalensis*, which is used as a softener in cooking vegetable foods.

Figure 13.4 demonstrates the increased use of vegetables in the diet, expressed as a percentage of days in a four-week period on which they appear in a household's diet. (Grain in one quantity or another appears in each household's diet for every day examined, and, therefore, at 100 percent would appear above the top of the graph as a horizontal straight line. The mean percentage of days that vegetable foods appeared in the household diet is 28, with a range between 1 and 71 percent.)

As noted earlier, the period of highest risk from malaria infection coincides with the end of the rainy season, during which time increases in vegetable consumption and decreases in grain consumption are most marked. This is demonstrated in Figure 13.5, where grams of grains and vegetables consumed per capita per day are depicted as deviations from respective means (given over four-week periods). We draw attention to the period indicated as high malaria risk, at right, where the quantity of grains consumed reaches its lowest level, and the quantity of vegetables one of its highest levels. We suggest that these interrelated aspects of dietary patterning both may have antagonistic effects on malaria infection. Such antagonism would help to explain why, despite the high risk, plasmodial infections that occur tend to be relatively mild.

We suggest that the results of studies on the Hausa herbal pharmacopoeia, presented earlier in this chapter, have important implications for nutritional studies, insofar as some of the same plants that serve as medicines in another context are also used as foods, as they become readily available at the end of the rainy season. If we accept the efficacy of certain plants when they are used as medicines, we can also accept that they serve a therapeutic and perhaps preventive function when used as foods. Although to date only a portion of these plants have been evaluated for oxidant-generating activity, we submit that the preliminary results demonstrate the significance and utility of this investigative approach. Utilization of certain oxidant-promoting plants in both medicinal and dietary contexts, during a period of the year when the risk of malaria infection is highest, may have a compound effect in limiting this infection.

The decrease in grain consumption that also occurs during this critical period may play a related role in helping to suppress malaria infection. We cite the study of Murray et al. (1976), which reported populations with atypically low rates of malaria infection who experienced increased rates of parasitemia subsequent to dietary supplementation with grains—rich in vitamin E—during a famine relief program. Eaton et al. (1976) proposed that the initially low rate of malaria infection could be ascribed to a vitamin E deficiency, which they demonstrated to be antag-

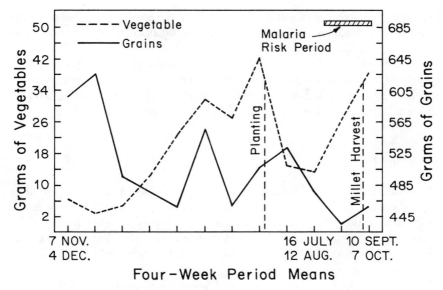

Fig. 13.4. Frequency of Vegetable Use in Diet

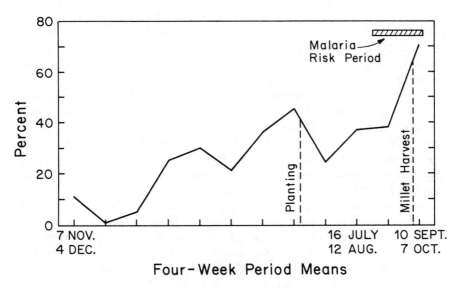

Fig. 13.5. Grams of Grains and Vegetables Consumed per Capita per Day

onistic to plasmodial development. Regardless of the specific explanation for this observation, it has been demonstrated that suppression of malaria infection coincides with periods of decreased grain consumption.

We propose, then, that the decreased consumption of vitamin-E-rich grains, concurrent with increased consumption of vegetable foods, at least some of which appear to generate oxidants, may have the combined effect of increasing intraerythrocytic oxidation to levels that can effectively suppress malaria infection.

Conclusion

The ecological constraints of a savanna-based agricultural regime characterized by marked seasonal variations necessitate an elaboration of diet through the progression of the rainy season. Increased utilization of certain vegetables is one feature of this diversification in the variety and sources of foods consumed, and it is most pronounced during the end of the rainy season, a period coinciding with the few months during which risk of malaria infection is greatest.

Considering these observations within a broader ecological framework, we can integrate these features of nutrition and disease with the results of investigations on specific indigenous treatment modalities for plasmodial infection. Significantly, we note that a number of Hausa medicinal plants used to treat malaria infection also constitute important dietary elements at the end of the rainy season. Our laboratory evaluations of Hausa antimalarials demonstrated that some of these plants may have therapeutic value in malaria infection, insofar as they may increase levels of intracellular oxidation. They could serve the same positive function when used in emically nonmedical contexts, such as nutrition. Moreover, and still with reference to oxidative processes, we have presented additional data suggesting that any plasmodiostatic activity that can be ascribed to these plants may be intensified by the decreased grain consumption that occurs along with increased use of oxidant-generating plants.

As we suggested earlier, the relatively low incidence of fulminant malaria infection in this region may be ascribed to a number of protective circumstances that function individually or in some combination to limit the extent of parasitemia. We can clearly rule out Western medical intervention for the particular population studied. On the basis of our investigation of the Hausa herbal pharmacopoeia, it appears that indigenous treatment modalities may have some suppressive effect on malaria infection. Further, we have made the proposal—and offered evidence in its support— that a nutritional model can also be invoked to account for some therapeutic and preventive effects. The extent to which adults in this population are protected by a nonresidual (acquired) immunity and by inherited red blood cell disorders such as G-6-PD deficiency and hemoglobin S is not known; but if these occur with significant frequencies, they also can be expected to confer some benefit in limiting the extent of infection in affected individuals. More extensive investigations, in conjunction with examination of clinical parameters, would help to clarify the extent to which any or all of these are important in affecting the incidence and expression of malaria in this population.

While our examinations to date have been confined to analyses of the possible effects that the medicinal and dietary utilization of certain plant species may have on malaria infection, the same rationale and some of the same methods can also be applied for considerations of plants used in other contexts and for examination of other diseases.

By focusing on these plants for an investigation of biocultural adaptations to disease, we perceive them within a rather broad conceptual sphere as ingestible plant products, rather than exclusively as "medicines" or "foods." With this approach, we propose to extend considerations of ingestible plants beyond the disciplinary boundaries that have traditionally circumscribed nutritional studies on the one hand and examinations of indigenous medicine and infectious disease on the other.

ACKNOWLEDGMENTS

A portion of the research on which this paper is based was funded by a grant-in-aid of research from Sigma Xi, the Scientific Research Society of North America, by the National Science Foundation #SOC 74-24412, and by the Graduate School of Washington University, St. Louis. The authors gratefully acknowledge the assistance of Ibrahim Muazzamu, Sarkin Kausani, and Jawa Karyar Kausani.

NOTES

1. We recognize the obvious merits inherent in a research design that would have (1) utilized a larger, randomized survey sample, and (2) measured the quantities of foods actually consumed by each individual. However, our experiences and observations (and an abortive pilot study), during six months' residence in the village prior to initiating the nutritional survey, demonstrated conclusively that such methods were infeasible. This reflects the large amount of time entailed in conducting such surveys, the intrusive nature of such measures, and the marked degree of privacy that the Hausa ascribe to eating behaviors. In light of this, informed compromises in research design were necessary, and any resultant shortcomings are to some extent balanced by the depth of the data base and its high degree of reliability.

2. The scope and locus of the study described here were such that it was impossible to conduct even the simplest laboratory procedures or other types of clinical examination. Thus, conclusions regarding the prevalence and severity of plasmodial infection are drawn from reports of the WHO Malaria Research Centre in Kano State, district government dispensary personnel, and published studies of malaria epidemiology in northern Nigeria (e.g., Dietz et al. 1974, Wernsdorfer 1980, Hamon and Coz 1966, Schram 1971). These are congruent with the observations made by the authors and reported by the local population with reference to duration and relative degree of incapacity of disease episodes experienced.

3. "Vegetables" here means plant structures other than lignified stem and radix; for the most part, this includes leaves, young stems, and buds, and, where so indicated, the reproductive structures, including flower petals and calyces, fruits, and seeds.

REFERENCES

Adam, J.G., N. Echard, and M. Lescot. 1972. "Plantes Médicinales Hausa de l'Ader (République du Niger)." *Journal d'Agriculture Tropicale et de Botanique Appliquée,* 19:259–399.

Ainslie, J.R. 1937. *A List of Plants Used in Native Medicine in Nigeria.* Imperial Forestry Institute Paper no. 7. Oxford: Oxford Univ. Press.

Aviado, D.M. 1969. "Chemotherapy of *Plasmodium berghei.*" *Experimental Parasitology,* 25:399–482.

Ayensu, Edward S. 1978. *Medicinal Plants of West Africa.* Algonac, Mich.: Reference Publications.

Beals, Alan R. 1976. "Strategies of Resort to Curers in South India." Charles Leslie, ed., *Asian Medical Systems.* Berkeley: Univ. of California Press, 184–200.

Beutler, Ernest. 1969. "Drug-Induced Hemolytic Anemia." *Pharmacological Review,* 21:73–103.

Bowman, W.C., M.J. Rand, and G.B. West. 1968. *Textbook of Pharmacology.* Oxford: Blackwell Scientific Pubs.

Chandra, R.K. 1976. "Nutrition as a Critical Determinant in Susceptibility to Infection." *World Review of Nutrition and Dietetics,* 25:166–68.

Cohen, G., and P. Hochstein. 1965. "*In vivo* generation of H_2O_2 in Mouse Erythrocytes by Hemolytic Agents." *Journal of Pharmacology and Experimental Therapeutics,* 147:139–43.

Crapanzano, Vincent. 1973. *The Hamadsha: A Study in Moroccan Ethnopsychiatry.* Berkeley: Univ. of California Press.

Dalziel, J.M. 1937. *The Useful Plants of West Tropical Africa.* London: Crown Agents for Overseas Governments and Administrations.

Dietz, K., L. Molineaux, and A. Thomas. 1974. "A Malaria Model Tested in the African Savannah." *Bulletin of the World Health Organization,* 50:347–57.

Dunlop, David W. 1974–75. "Alternatives to 'Modern' Health-Delivery Systems in Africa: Issues for Public Policy Consideration on the Role of Traditional Healers." *Rural Africana,* 26:131–39.

Eaton, John W., James R. Eckman, Elaine Berger, and Harry S. Jacob. 1976. "Suppression of Malaria Infection by Oxidant-Sensitive Erythrocytes." *Nature,* 264:758–60.

Edgerton, Robert B. 1971. "A Traditional African Psychiatrist." *Southwestern Journal of Anthropology,* 27:259–78.

Ekong, D.E.U. 1968. "The Chemist's Approach to the Study of African Medicinal Plants." Paper presented at the Symposium on African Medicinal Plants, Lagos, Nigeria, 19 Feb.

El-Said, F., E.A. Sofowora, and M. Olaniyi. 1968. "A Study of Some Nigerian Plants Used as Fever Cures." Paper presented at the Symposium on African Medicinal Plants, Lagos, Nigeria, 19 Feb.

Elvin–Lewis, Memory. 1979. "Empirical Rationale for Teeth Cleaning Plant Selection." *Medical Anthropology,* 3:431–55.

1980 "Plants Used for Teeth Cleaning throughout the World." *Journal of Preventive Dentistry,* 6:61–70.

———, K. Keudell, W.H. Lewis, and M. Harwood. 1974. "The Anti-Cariogenic Potential of African Chewing-Sticks." *Journal of Dental Research,* 53:125.

Etkin, Nina L. 1975. "The Human Red Cell, Glucose-6-Phosphate Dehydrogenase Deficiency, and Malaria." Ph.D. diss., Washington University, St. Louis, Mo.

1979 "Indigenous Medicine among the Hausa of Northern Nigeria: Laboratory Evaluation for Potential Therapeutic Efficacy of Antimalarial Plant Medicines." *Medical Anthropology,* 3:401–29.

1980 "Indigenous Medicine in Northern Nigeria. I. Oral Hygiene and Medical Treatment." *Journal of Preventive Dentistry,* 6:143–49.

1981 "A Hausa Herbal Pharmacopoeia: Biomedical Evaluation of Commonly Used Plant Medicines." *Journal of Ethnopharmacology,* 4:75–98.

———, and John W. Eaton. 1975. "Malaria-Induced Erythrocyte Oxidant Sensitivity." G.J. Brewer, ed., *Erythrocyte Structure and Function.* New York: Alan R. Liss, 219–32.

———, and Paul J. Ross. (n.d.). "Food as Medicine and Medicine as Food: An Adaptive Framework for the Interpretation of Plant Utilization among the Hausa of Northern Nigeria." *Social Science & Medicine,* in press.

Fletcher, K.A., and B.G. Maegraith. 1970. "Erythrocyte Reduced Glutathione in Malaria (*Plasmodium berghei* and *P. knowlesi*)." *Annals of Tropical Medicine and Parasitology,* 64:481–86.

Foster, George M. 1973. *Traditional Societies and Technological Change,* 2d ed. New York: Harper & Row.

1976 "Medical Anthropology and International Health Planning." *Medical Anthropology Newsletter,* 7:12–18.

Githens, Thomas S. 1949. *Drug Plants of Africa.* African Handbooks, no. 8. Lancaster: Univ. of Pennsylvania Press.

Goodman, Louis S., and Alfred Gilman, eds. 1970. *The Pharmacological Basis of Therapeutics,* 4th ed. New York: Macmillan.

Goth, Andres. 1970. *Medical Pharmacology,* 5th ed. St. Louis, Mo.: C.V. Mosby.

Hambali, Muhammadu. 1973. "Extractives from Hausa Medicinal Plants." Paper presented at the International Symposium on Traditional Medical Therapy, Lagos, Nigeria, 10–16 Dec.

Hammerschmidt, Dale E. 1980. "Szechwan Purpura." *New England Journal of Medicine,* 302:1191–93.

Hamon, J., and J. Coz. 1966. "Epidémiologie Générale du Paludisme Humain en Afrique Occidentale: Répartition et Fréquence des Parasites et des Vecteurs et Observations Récentes sur Quelques-uns des Facteurs Gouvernant la Transmission de cette Maladie." *Bulletin de la Société de Pathologie Exotique,* 59:466–83.

Harris, J.W., and R.W. Kellermeyer. 1970. *The Red Cell,* rev. ed. Cambridge, Mass.: Harvard Univ. Press.

Homewood, C.A., and K.D. Neame. 1980. "Biochemistry of Malarial Parasites." Julius P. Kreier, ed., *Malaria,* vol 1: *Epidemiology, Chemotherapy, Morphology, and Metabolism.* New York: Academic Press, 345–405.

Horton, Robin. 1967. "African Traditional Thought and Western Science." *Africa,* 37:50–71.

Houston, Robert G. 1973. "Sickle Cell Anemia and Dietary Precursors of Cyanate." *American Journal of Clinical Nutrition,* 26:1261–64.

Hunsicker, Lawrence G. 1969. "The Pharmacology of the Antimalarials." *Archives of Internal Medicine*, 123:645–49.

Janzen, John M. 1978. *The Quest for Therapy in Lower Zaire.* Berkeley: Univ. of California Press.

Katz, M., and E.R. Stiehm. 1977. "Host Defense in Malnutrition." *Pediatrics*, 59:490–95.

Katz, S.H., and J. Schall. 1979. "Fava Bean Consumption and Biocultural Evolution." *Medical Anthropology*, 3:459–76.

Kliks, M. 1975. *Paleoepidemiological Studies on Great Basin Coprolites: Estimation of Dietary Intake and Evaluation of the Ingestion of Anthelminthic Plant Substances.* Berkeley: Univ. of California, Archaeological Research Facility, Department of Anthropology.

Kretschmar, W. 1967. "The Significance of p-Aminobenzoic Acid for the Course of Infection and Immunity in Malaria of Animals *(Plasmodium berghei)* and Man (*P. falciparum*). III. On Those Fed on Milk." *Tropical Disease Bulletin*, 64:592.

Kretchmar, W., and A. Voller. 1973. "Suppression of *Plasmodium falciparum* Malaria in Aotus Monkeys by Milk Diet." *Zeitschrift für Tropenmedizin und Parasitologie*, 24:51–53.

Lambo, T. Adeoye. 1971. "Problems of Adjustment between Traditional and Modern Methods of Medical Practice." Special Seminar on the Traditional Background to Medical Practice in Nigeria, 20–23 April 1966, Institute of African Studies, University of Ibadan, Occasional Publication no. 25, 79–82.

Lambotte, C. 1974. "Sickle-Cell Anemia and Dietary Precursors of Cyanate." *American Journal of Clinical Nutrition*, 27:765–66.

Landy, David. 1977. "Role Adaptation: Traditional Curers under the Impact of Western Medicine." D. Landy, ed., *Culture, Disease, and Healing.* New York: Macmillan, 468–81.

Leslie, Charles. 1976. "The Ambiguities of Medical Revivalism in Modern India." C. Leslie, ed., *Asian Medical Systems.* Berkeley: Univ. of California Press, 356–67.

 1977   "Pluralism and Integration in the Indian and Chinese Medical Systems." D. Landy, ed., *Culture, Disease, and Healing.* New York: Macmillan, 511–17.

Lewis, Walter H., and Memory P.F. Elvin–Lewis. 1977. *Medical Botany.* New York: John Wiley & Sons.

Logan, Michael H. 1973. "Humoral Medicine in Guatemala and Peasant Acceptance of Modern Medicine." *Human Organization*, 32:385–96.

Makheja, A.N., J.Y. Vanderhoek, and J.M. Bailey. 1979. "Inhibition of Platelet Aggregation and Thromboxane Synthesis by Onion and Garlic." *Lancet*, 1:781.

Malcolm, S.A., and E.A. Sofowora. 1969. "Antimicrobial Activity of Selected Nigerian Folk Remedies and Their Constituent Plants." *Lloydia*, 32:512–17.

Martorell, Reynaldo. 1980. "Interrelationships between Diet, Infectious Disease, and Nutritional Status." Lawrence S. Greene and Francis S. Johnston, eds., *Social and Biological Predictors of Nutritional Status, Physical Growth, and Neurological Development.* New York: Academic Press, 81–106.

Murray, M.J., A.B. Murray, M.B. Murray, and C.J. Murray. 1976. "Somali Food Shelters in the Ogaden Famine and Their Impact on Health." *Lancet*, 1:1283–85.

Nelson, Cynthia. 1971. "Self, Spirit Possession and World View: An Illustration from Egypt." *International Journal of Social Psychiatry*, 17:194–209.

Oliver, Bep. 1960. *Medicinal Plants in Nigeria.* Ibadan, Nigeria: Nigerian College of Arts, Science and Technology.

Penso, G. 1977. "Problemi Relative all'Uso delle Piante Medicinali nel Mondo." *Bolletino Chimicofarmaceutico,* 116:506–19.

Peters, Wallace. 1980. "Chemotherapy of Malaria." Julius P. Kreier, ed., *Malaria,* vol. 1: *Epidemiology, Chemotherapy, Morphology, and Metabolism.* New York: Academic Press, 145–283.

Popp, F.D., J.M. Wefer, D.P. Chakaroborty, G. Rosen, and A.C. Casey. 1968. "Investigations of African Plants for Alkaloids, Antimalarial Agents, and Antineoplastic Agents." *Planta Medica,* 16:343–47.

Prietze, Rudolf. 1913–14. "Arzneipflanzen der Haussa." *Zeitschrift für Kolonialsprachen,* 4:81–90.

Rowson, J.–M. 1969. "Drogues et Plantes Médicinales de l'Ouest Africain." *Annales Pharmaceutiques Françaises,* 27:439–48.

Schneider, Howard A. 1971. "Nutrition and Resistance to Infection." S. Margen and N.L. Wilson, eds., *Progress in Human Nutrition,* vol. 1. Westport, Conn.: AVI, 75–79.

Schram, Ralph. 1971. *A History of the Nigerian Health Services.* Ibadan, Nigeria: Ibadan Univ. Press.

Schultes, Richard Evans. 1972. "The Future of Plants as Sources of New Biodynamic Compounds." T. Swain, ed., *Plants in the Development of Modern Medicine.* Cambridge, Mass.: Harvard Univ. Press, 103–24.

Scott, Clarissa S. 1975. "Competing Health Care Systems in an Inner City Area." *Human Organization,* 34:108–10.

Scrimshaw, N.S., C.E. Taylor, and J.E. Gordon. 1968. *Interactions of Nutrition and Infection.* World Health Organization Monograph Series no. 57.

Spencer, C.F., F.R. Koniuszy, E.F. Rogers, J.S. Shavel, Jr., N.R. Easton, E.A. Kaczka, F.A. Kuehl, Jr., R.F. Phillips, A. Walti, K. Folkers, C. Malanga, and A.O. Seeler. 1947. "Survey of Plants for Antimicrobial Activity." *Lloydia,* 10:145–74.

Suskind, R.M., ed. 1977. *Malnutrition and the Immune Response.* New York: Raven Press.

Swain, Tony. 1972. "The Significance of Comparative Phytochemistry in Medical Botany." T. Swain, ed., *Plants in the Development of Modern Medicine.* Cambridge, Mass.: Harvard Univ. Press, 125–59.

Watt, John Mitchell, and Maria Gerdina Breyer–Brandwijk. 1962. *The Medicinal and Poisonous Plants of Southern and Eastern Africa,* 2nd ed. London: E. & S. Livingstone.

Wernsdorfer, Walther H. 1980. The Importance of Malaria in the World." Julius P. Kreier, ed., *Malaria,* vol. 1: *Epidemiology, Chemotherapy, Morphology, and Metabolism.* New York: Academic Press, 1–93.

World Health Organization. 1975. *Health Manpower, Development, Training and Utilization of Traditional Healers and Their Collaboration with Health Care Delivery Systems.* Executive Board Publication no. 57/21.

———— 1978 *The Promotion and Development of Traditional Medicine.* WHO Technical Report Series 622.

Young, Allan. 1974–75. "The Practical Logic of Amhara Traditional Medicine." *Rural Africana,* 26:79–89.

PART FOUR

*Psychiatry
in Modern Medicine:
Problematics for Its
Transcultural Applications*

THE INTERSECTION OF CULTURAL VALUES WITH MEDICINE IS MOST PRONOUNCED WITH psychiatry. Other fields of medicine, such as internal medicine, rely on a relatively objective, statistically defined body of information for determining the difference between illness and health. Because it is concerned with disorders of mood, thought, and behavior, psychiatry must eke out of the panorama of everyday life, including social interactions, patterns of behavior that reflect psychological disturbances. These disturbances are often not obvious, because they involve an infusion of the symbols, imageries, and metaphors of the culture into the content of the specific patterns. This makes psychiatry problematic; the nature of the disorders that are the focus of its attention must inevitably involve manifestations of certain cultural characteristics. The dilemma is that of differentiating patterns involving cultural symbolism that are evidence of disorder from those that are merely idiosyncratic to the culture itself. From one perspective, it is as though one were looking at a colony of a thousand viruses in a petri dish and attempting on the basis of physical characteristics alone to determine which of these viruses are aberrant. The psychiatrist must examine certain personality features and behavioral patterns against the backdrop of a culture that enriches the patterns, and, at the same time, separate basic diversions from the norm.

Problems of Interpretation in Psychiatry

Unlike internal medicine or other fields of medicine, psychiatry cannot rely on laboratory tests to substantiate clinical symptomatology and evidences of deviation. It must rely almost totally on perceptions of the dissonances existing with the mood, thought, and behavior of the patient, as these are set against the canvas of culture. Slippage in perception and interpretation can occur at several points. Two seem most germane. First, there is the margin of distortion of those who are in the position to determine what constitutes a statistical deviation. The perceiver involved in this determination, often the psychiatrist or psychiatric epidemiologist, stands back and observes the culture—devising, perhaps in part intuitively, some notion of normative standards of behavior—and then conceptualizes behaviors that are distinctly deviant. Second, there is the basic tension in the dynamics between culture and personality. This relationship of culture and personality poses many questions similar to those involving mind–body dualism. The most important of these is whether the personality deviation, though manifesting itself through cultural symbolism, represents something separate from culture; i.e., does the presence of a mental disease or defect stand outside of the influences of culture? Or, perhaps, phrased another way: does the notion of mental health inevitably involve culturally biased value judgments? And in keeping with this argument, is it possible to conceptualize valid generalizations about defects in physiology or in the process of socialization that might produce similar psychological distress, might be called mental illness, and might be irrespective of the culture of the individual?

"Culture–Personality Dualism"

As with the dualism of mind and body, the dualism of culture and personality is relegated to reinterpretation at every stage in history. As mind–body dualism is breaking down in contemporary times with new knowledge of the biochemistry and biophysiology of mental processes, so, perhaps—through the benefits of major anthropological developments—the presumed dualism of culture and personality may be breaking down. We are learning more about the nature of the interaction of culture with pattern disorders. Many anthropological studies have addressed questions like whether the symptoms that psychiatry conceptualizes as evidence of mental illness are invariant in their nature, or are culturally linked—if not culturally specific (De Vos 1961). Some studies have examined the extent to which a society may pattern the actual mental disorder or may produce the personality types through child-rearing and subsequent development of the individual. Others, as demonstrated by Devereux (1956), have pointed out that the culture may actually perpetuate mental dysfunction in certain roles by rewarding it. Similarly, according to other investigations, a culture may produce psychiatric disorders differentially in segments of the population, perhaps by placing such segments in certain stressful roles. In *Civilization and Its Discontents*, Freud (1930) emphasized the complexity of culture and its relationship to the development of the personality. He recognized this complexity and in many respects set the stage for the development of a psychosocial notion of mental illness.

It seems clear from the work of both psychiatrists and anthropologists that there is a strong dynamic relationship between culture and the way in which mental illnesses are classified, as well as between culture and personality formation. In "On Madness, Deviance, and Culture," Romanucci–Ross discusses how concepts like normality and abnormality evolve and the extent to which cultures establish their own definitions of the normal mental state. Through her focus on Melanesian and other societies, she examines the issue of social tolerance of deviant acts, and suggests that certain behaviors tend to be institutionalized as within the scope of acceptable conduct, whereas others may be institutionalized as within the scope of unacceptable—sick, deviant—conduct. She addresses the crucial issues of relativism and cultural bias in the definition of mental illness.

Phyllis Palgi deals with similar concerns in her enlightening discussion of Yemenite traditions. She discloses the extent to which a society or culture must rely on causative factors outside itself for understanding the inexplicability of mental disease. Spirits (*shedim*) serve important roles, in that they allow the culture to understand how major deflections from acceptable conduct can occur, and provide a handle—exorcism—for society to cure itself of these influences. Since deflection from the norm is theorized to result from external causes, tolerance of deviation may be even more rigid and restrictive than under other theories. As a result, the nosology or classification of deviant behavior or mental disease is broader in scope in such a society. Both Romanucci–Ross and Palgi reveal the importance of culture in the characterization of mental diseases, the manner in which they are handled by a society, and the distinctions that exist between normality and abnormality.

Jen-Yi Wang's chapter, "Psychosomatic Illness in the Chinese Cultural Context," demonstrates even more strikingly the degree to which the culture shapes individual responses to psychological problems. Wang examines the thesis that the Chinese have a strong inclination to deny psychological difficulties, expressing them instead as physiological disorders. Once reified into a physiological symptom, these emotional problems can be subjected to physical (medical) treatment. Underlying the need to somatize psychological problems is the fact that the Chinese culture attaches a severe stigma to psychological or emotional problems. By treating mental disease with the same methods that would be used to treat physiological illness, the disease is seen as something outside of purely the emotional problems of the patient. Much of the reason for this stigma is the importance that the Chinese place on self-discipline and control. To accept psychological and mental problems as something separate from their physiological manifestations, is to accept the notion that individuals can lack self-discipline, despite their desire to the contrary or the social sanctions strongly pushing in the opposite direction. This introduces another important issue—the extent to which culture may impact on psychiatric disorders through the sanctions and strictures that it imposes on acceptable behavior. By regulating acceptable behavior strictly, as in the case of the Chinese culture, behavior would be viewed as inappropriate and evidenced as disordered even if it involves only a minimal deflection for self-control and be considered appropriate behavior in other cultures with less rigid sanctions.

Cultural Values and the Goals of Psychiatric Treatment

In addition to the epistemological questions of the definition of mental illness, there is also a close relationship between cultural values and the goals of psychiatric treatment. In his chapter, "Psychotherapy: Brave New World or Requiem?" Grant states that outcome studies of psychotherapy are beginning to clarify the "curative factors in treatment." The need for such studies has emerged from the great discrediting of psychotherapy in recent years, which Grant feels reflects the movement toward a medical model in psychiatry and criticism regarding mind–body dualism. Other issues of a political, philosophical, and economic nature, particularly the cost of such treatment, are also seriously threatening the survival of psychotherapy. Compared with therapies in other areas of medicine, the assessment of psychotherapy is more subjective. When a patient suffers from diabetes and is tested by a laboratory to have a blood sugar of over 120, the goal of medical treatment is clear cut, that is to reduce the blood sugar, compensate for other metabolic changes and educate patients in appropriate diet and self-treatment. In psychiatry, there are no laboratory tests that can act as barometers for establishing the degree of illness and the rate of improvement. Therefore, the criteria that have often been applied to the effectiveness of psychotherapy are highly value-laden, which makes it nearly impossible to assess its impact on patients.

The Four Major Goals of Psychiatric Treatment

The four major goals of psychiatric treatment are to relieve symptoms, provide support for the patient, assist in the definition of identity and self-actualization, and bring about an adaptation of the patient to the requirements of society. The first of these, relieving symptoms, would appear to be the least value-laden of the goals of psychiatric treatment. But on further analysis, it is apparent that values enter into the criteria for determining whether symptoms have been relieved. For example, the obsessive–compulsive patient who sees a psychiatrist because he is suffering from severe anxiety and "nervousness" might be quickly relieved of his symptoms by having a tranquilizer prescribed. From the long-term perspective, the psychiatrist might examine ways of altering the behavior of the patient so as to minimize the development of symptoms. Once this step of analysis occurs, biases will enter into how the psychiatrist shapes the therapeutic objectives. Obsessive–compulsive disorder, as with manic–depressive disease, may be seen among the most highly productive members of society. The psychiatrist may be so strongly directed toward minimizing these characteristics that they are dealt with at the expense of the patient's creative productivity. In treating, therefore, the underlying disorder aggressively, the psychiatrist may actually result in regressing the patient to the cultural norm, even though his purpose is simply that of relieving symptoms.

The second goal of therapy is to provide psychological support. For example, in treating the housewife–mother who is suffering from anxiety and doubts about her role, therapists who see their role as that of supporting the patient may be serving simply as a palliative, that is to say, assuring that this woman will remain in her current position. The value presupposition underlying this therapeutic decision would be that it is good to be married, to be a mother, to assume all of these household tasks full time, and to be almost totally responsible for the care of one's children.

A third possible goal of treatment—and the one perhaps most problematic from the anthropological perspective—is that of assisting patients to find their "identity," or "self-actualization." How we conceptualize what it is to be actualized is very much shaped by cultural notions of success against the backdrop of failure. The psychiatrist or therapist, often imbued with middle-class values, may be inclined to conceptualize self-actualization as achievement within a relatively narrow range of human possibilities.

The last goal of treatment—that of adaptation to society—has been the object of considerable criticism by a wide range of thinkers. One difficulty, of course, has been that we have never really resolved the distinction between those behaviors that we view as flowing from mental illness and those—such as taking drugs, engaging in criminal or delinquent acts, and suicide, to name a few—that we view as relatively unrelated to mental illness. Many would argue that these latter behaviors are evidence of structural personality defects. Others taking a more conservative position on free will might argue to the contrary, that is that people who engage in such criminal activities have control over their conduct and do not operate under the influence of some mental disease. There is considerable overlap between behaviors labeled criminal and those labeled sick.

On a less conspicuous level, decisions to force treatment on patients, designed to return them to a level where they can function within the social system, also address the issue of conformity and social control. In his chapter, "Psychiatry and Social Control," Tancredi addresses some of the legal and philosophical issues that are now confronting the psychiatric profession, most particularly, those dealing with the right of involuntarily committed patients to refuse medication. This question addresses directly the rights of the individual versus the rights of society and involves sociocultural values and ethics.

Evaluation of Efficacy of Treatment

Another value-laden aspect of psychiatric therapy is the role of cultural notions in defining and assessing the efficacy and effectiveness of such therapy. Whether or not a treatment works on a mental patient depends on the extent to which that mental patient is socializable. As has already been pointed out, we don't have any physiological or biochemical basis for differentiating mental diseases, let alone for determining whether the treatment course is efficacious. Hence the assessment of psychiatric treatments, both verbal and non-verbal, involves cultural values that determine the "conformity" of the individual. Is the patient in a position to be able to go out into society and to function, even, if need be, in a minimal way? This decision must involve examining the patient's mood, thought, and behavior from the perspective of how it will mesh with that of the society at large. Once again, societal values come directly into play in determining the destiny of those individuals who are considered outside the norm. In effect, culture is involved in the development of a psychiatric nosology, and understanding of the etiology of psychiatric diseases—perhaps through the nature of child-rearing behaviors in that society—and the devising of goals used to assess the effectiveness of various treatments employed by the psychiatric profession.

The chapters in this part address many of the issues that have been laid out in this brief introduction. By no means are the issues resolved. The nuances are made clear in many of the chapters, but, at best, more questions are raised, any one of which could lead to a profound examination of anthropological, psychiatric, and philosophical issues. The main thrust of these chapters is examination of the variety of ways that culture can impact on behaviors designated as mental illness. Another important aspect is the delineation of the complexity between culture and personality development. A final important issue underlying much of the discussion is whether the concept of mental health inescapably involves culturally biased value judgments or whether it can be the result of valid generalizations of certain conduct and distresses, separable from cultural bias. This question remains essentially unresolved. Increasingly, through psychiatric research, it appears that certain serious conditions may have a bio-genetic basis, which would give greater weight to the separability of mental illness and culture. Research on the biological and genetic basis of schizophrenia and manic-depressive illness seem to suggest strongly that certainly these very serious psychiatric disorders may have their etiology in some biochemical aberration. This discovery does not necessarily negate the importance of culture as an etiological agent or certainly a factor that augments the patient's condition. With regard to the less serious mental diseases or emotional difficulties such as character disorders, neurosis and even problems with living, the relationship between culture and personality can be quite pronounced and may argue against the generalizability of these disorders separate from cultural influences (Spiro 1951).

REFERENCES

Devereux, George. 1956. "Normal and Abnormal: The Key Problem in Psychiatric Anthropology." *Some Uses of Anthropology: Theoretical and Applied.* Washington, D.C.: Anthropological Society of Washington.

De Vos, George. 1961. "Symbolic Analysis in the Cross-Cultural Studies of Personality." B. Kaplan, ed., *Studying Personality Cross-Culturally.* Evanston, Ill.: Rowe, Peterson.

Freud, Sigmund. 1930. *Civilization and Its Discontents.* New York: Jonathan Cape & Harrison Smith.

Spiro, Melford E. 1951. "Personality and Culture: The Natural History of a False Dichotomy." *Psychiatry,* 14:19–46.

14

On Madness, Deviance, and Culture

Lola Romanucci–Ross

There is a documentary film about a state hospital for the criminally insane, including the activities of inmates, psychiatrists, and attendants.[1] The camera focuses on psychiatrists conferring among themselves and interviewing inmates—and on their regimens and curing techniques—and on inmates relating to one another. What are the parameters of a system called "a state hospital for the criminally insane"? The questions that follow, generated by a viewing of the film, are germane to the whole range of considerations of mental illness from the sociocultural point of view: Why "mental" hospital? Should interventions in a life include *any* measures to prolong a patient's life, regardless of the patient's wish to die? Do the hospital personnel and their behavior, both routine and interventive, appear "sane" to an outside observer? What is a criminal act, and when is a "criminal" insane? Is the psychiatrist who perseverates to a male patient that he should desire "a mature healthy female" describing a normal state? Who is labeling whom, and why?

Cultural psychiatry, or the formulation of psychiatric phenomena in cultural terms, was an outgrowth of psychoanalysis, which used the results of anthropological fieldwork with primitives in understanding the neurotic patient.[2] Such studies of "culture and personality" not only enriched the analysis of anthropological fieldwork but also informed psychoanalysis and psychiatry of the diverse cultural applications of these concepts. Syndromes of disordered behavior in other cultures led anthropologists to rethink their own and fostered an attempt at a new epidemiology of disordered mental states in Western society, a new epidemiology concerned with the role of communication and disorders of communication in a complex culture. What generally applicable conclusions can be drawn from any study of the distribution of disordered states in a population at a given place and time? How are definitions of these disordered states constructed; that is, what populations are not included, and what types of pathologies are missed by such exclusions? How are ethnic differences managed or ignored in symptom reporting? What is "observer agreement"? What of studies that seriously raise the question: does culture change *induce* mental illness? Conversely, then, does cultural stability promote mental health?

Our European Heritage

The thirteenth to the fifteenth centuries in Europe were distinguished, in hygienic terms, by the disappearance of leprosy. In France alone, there had been over 20,000 leprosariums. As leprosy faded, the attitudes that had been reserved for lepers were now heaped on the "mentally ill." Previously, such individuals had been taken out of the towns and villages, where they were found to be troublesome, and placed on working river boats called "ships of fools." There, as they worked, some got better, some got sick and died. When hospital prisons came into being, the former leprosariums became filled with those condemned by the law—primarily young men who had disappointed their families, and men and women without work—as well as with "the insane." Here they were shackled in an even more stringent policy of containment; here the mad were more fully exploited as a source of cheap labor, and here also the notion of public display of the insane raised revenue for the state and provided an affirmation of the sanity (and social correctness) of the onlooker.

While society was classifying certain behaviors as undesirable and trying to solve the problem of the proper context for mad persons, physicians were attempting to develop an intellectual framework for understanding them. In a recent review of insanity in the Age of Reason (end of sixteenth to end of eighteenth century), one scholar (Foucault 1965) has tried to put mental illness into proper perspective in the European heritage. Retrieving original documents, especially those that had escaped notice in previous historical writings, he emphasizes that the language of psychiatry as it evolved in the European tradition became a monologue of men of reason about madness. It was determined that nonreason had to relate to reason, and so the logic of the insane was considered a perversion of sane logic, but nonetheless *based* upon it, a fitting summary from the Age of Reason.

Modern psychotherapy in Western culture continues in this tradition, although anthropologists have drawn attention to other cultural views of madness and its cure. Since a real understanding of "insane logic" may not be possible until diverse modes of thinking take us beyond the duality—sane and insane—of Western culture and its insistence on "rational explanations," it may be useful to contrast some group processes in other cultures, as they define madness and deviant behavior that is usually "medicalized" in the West.

Group Process in Definition of Insanity

Any cultural group must establish the place of madness in its socially approved behavioral repertoire. The village of Mokereng in the Admiralty Islands of New

Guinea provided an opportunity to observe a definition of insanity *in process* over a period of time. The events surrounding one case brought forth from this cultural group all of their notions about mental illness and deviant behavior. How did they communicate about mental illness among themselves, to the "patient," to the anthropologist residing among them? The following is quoted from a fieldwork notebook:

> At the morning medical line-up, Hitawari tells me that her husband Lapak has cast her out and is keeping her three children. She is agitated, weeping, she vomits, tells me that she is sorry to be trouble but wants to assure me (as she was about to ruin my life and fieldwork for several weeks, I thought) that the nuns and priests had assured her that she had done no wrong. She often sleeps in the church (*lotu*), and she wants to die.
>
> Village people view this scene, and they begin today to tell me that Hitawari is crazy (*long-long* in Pidgin English). Her brother agrees with her husband. Potihin, the village Chief, tells me she has had craziness attacks before; for example, she once attacked his daughter with a fishing spear and then ran about the village naked, having cast off her wrap-around skirt (*lap-lap*). Her brother and his wife had not spoken to her for some time because she had used the "curse of the father's sister." Because a woman marries out of the clan in these Admiralty Island cultures and is disinherited, she is given spiritual ascendancy and she can curse her brother's children. Yet it is very unlikely that she will use this, for brother and sister are the sacred dyad in Manus. Her curse: "Just as I did not finish school, you will not finish school. Just as I became crazy, you will become crazy." Hitawari had then wanted to retract the curse, but all villagers said to her, "You are crazy and therefore don't have the power to withdraw it."[3]

This incident at medical line-up began a continuing dialogue with the Mokereng villagers on their social definition of insanity. Such severe deviance had not been encountered in recent memory in the village, and the process of a definition of deviance apparently had not previously been fully recorded in an isolated primitive group. The villagers and I had our "symposia" under the huge callophylum ironwood tree, as the men carved and worked on canoes and the women took care of babies. The tapes and notebooks recorded these valuable data daily.

"Crazies"

The village chief had given the subject much thought, since his daughter was an epileptic. He had carefully scrutinized the brains of dogs and a kind of opposum they ate. He had seen a photograph of New York City, and he had seen the American Navy Conglomerate at Mokereng Bay during World War II; he had, even then, decided that living with too many other people had to drive you crazy, for how could you have enough rules to tell you how to behave properly toward all of them? He knew that if he lived in New York, he would lose his mind. All those folks would surely drive him to pull off *his* lap-lap, forcing him to run naked in the streets.

What sorts of things did Hitawari (our "patient") do that the village considered insane? She walked into the house holding a sick child while the anthropologist was eating and complained of the child's ear injury. With seemingly inexhaustible energy and strength, she threw huge rocks and branches into the ocean, "house-cleaning" the beach. She kept villagers awake all night as she ran around and prayed while entering houses. She made much use of flowers, planting them, sleeping near them, putting them on tables, and gesticulating with them as she taunted her husband. She replied to barking dogs, and she directed obscenities towards persons whom the rules of her culture obliged her to avoid. She alluded to intimacies with a cross-cousin.

What to do about her? Potihin was sure he could cure her by passing the victory leaf under her nose, but he was concerned that if something went wrong he would be blamed. Therefore he would do nothing. In the old days, they would have killed her, he asserted, and that was really the correct thing to do.

Villagers attributed her madness to a "time of the full moon"; all dreaded its approach since Hitawari fulfilled this prophecy monthly. That was the immediate cause. Add the inordinate fretting over her husband's infidelity (with a young woman of the village, Suzy) and too much thinking about religion and God. A cure could be effected by bloodshed: "the blood should flow on both sides" and hopefully Hitawari would be killed. This could be done by trickery or by poison.

Hitawari had said, "They say I am crazy, but I know perfectly well that I am not. If I were crazy I would be now running naked about the village without my lap-lap." No one in the village doubted that she was insane, although the degree of insanity was measured on a scale calibrated by the degree of kinship to Hitawari. Thus, her close kin called her disturbances mild, but the kin of her husband, or of Suzy, scored her as raving mad. Those who would benefit by her demise told her that she was full of bush devils and would surely die soon, and they taunted her by pulling her religious medal from her neck.

She was sent to the Territory psychiatrist, an Australian physician, who referred her to a hospital at Rabaul, New Britain, far from her village, where her behavior was diagnosed as *schizophrenia*. It is not known whether she eventually returned, or was helped or not, but she did achieve a state of pregnancy there, an imminent hazard for a New Guinea woman, hospitalized far from her family, with no males to guard her.

The events that led to this outcome and to the inability of the villagers to relate to Hitawari's constructs of her problem are significant. Hitawari had been away at school in New Britain, in a Catholic junior high school. She had learned that Catholics take marriage very seriously and had adopted many English customs. But as the villagers discussed the intolerable, if sometimes amusing, deviance of Hitawari's behavior, it had little effect on their judgment to be informed that, for example, Europeans put flowers on tables with no intention of eating them; Europeans talk to dogs; Europeans sometimes pray out loud; and European women sometimes insult their husbands. As they cast Hitawari in the crazy role, they refused to hear her shouts, "All I want is my children." Unthinkable, as there is much invested in which side, husband's or wife's, gets the children. But she challenged them all, and forced an audience, especially at night, by keeping the entire village from a night's rest. This of course made them more adamant in labelling her "mad." She responded with counter-escalation in a true progressive differentiation of opposing stances, which rushed to its inevitable conclusion of changing the interaction[4] system completely by forcing Hitawari out of it. Memories of these events will provide "data" in the village memory bank of what constitutes crazy behavior and its proper outcome in the future.

In the past in this culture, the solution to the problem had been expulsion by death or banishment of the person considered insane. It was therefore easy in a culture contact situation to adapt to the style of the dominant culture and to *ritually* expel the mad Hitawari to an insane asylum on another island.

We now turn from a "primitive" to a peasant culture for contrast.

Mexican psychoanalysts have pointed out that denial is one of the most important defense mechanisms for the Mexican.[5] Although aspects of deviant behavior in the village will be discussed later, it should be noted that over a three-year period of observation and previous periods described to the researcher (Romanucci–Ross 1973), no one in the village had been considered insane by others. Much behavior occurred that was considered a response to depressing circumstances, leading to counter-depressive strategies that could be viewed as preventing "mental illness." For most of the inhabitants of this Mexican rural village, life was viewed as a long hard task, insufficient and infrequent rewards being coupled with meager environmental resources. Although interpersonal relations frequently led to frustration, deprivation, anguish, and disappointment, individuals were expected to return from these frequent and prolonged "bad experiences" and to ward off or compensate for depression.

The term "depression," of course, has several meanings, both for the professional and the lay person. However, whether or not depression is experienced subjectively depends upon levels of expectation, both positive and negative. In the village, expectations for good outcomes were set so low (improbable), and for bad outcomes so high (probable), that real-life experiences, however harsh, would never exceed these upper and lower limits. Such pessimistic attitudes were culturally established. This resulted in a constriction of patterns of the permissible, with all behavior predicted on low expectations. All of the fantasy, both social and personal—including proverbs, stories, ballads, humor, and films—helped persons growing up in this culture to set their reference levels of expectation. Tragedies emphasized separation from the mother, from children, from the group, indeed from life itself, but these were treated lightly, as though one could profitably exchange the whole lot "for a drink of tequila." So, in the process of becoming a member of the culture, the individual in this way also internalized the mechanism for calibrating and dampening the resonance of events.

Therefore, in this folk culture, the repertoire considered normal by the group included a wide variety of both depressive and manic behavior. In contrast to the primitive setting where rigid rules define the acceptable in everyday life, we see here a permissiveness in which acts that might be considered insane or criminal are *not* so defined.

"Mental Illness"

No observer is separate from the flow of events, since the moment one reflects on anything, the reflection is mediated by the experience of self and of others. Both doctor and patient bring to their encounter a set of expectations for this event. In the medical act, the patient comes as supplicant, accepts the definition of the situation, and is ready to accept the professional's view of the problem and its solution. He pays for this privilege, as the doctor allows the patient to be out of control and does not shun his illness. The physician will tell society that it is not the patient who is the vector of his disease; rather, it is a virus, a bacillus, an enzyme defect. By extension to psychic disturbances, it is not the patient who is acting badly, it is his mental illness, or his alcoholism, that is to blame.

Psychiatry considers itself and is considered part of medicine; it places disorders of behavior into a medical model of dysfunction. The medical model has typically excluded the complexities of communication and its cultural determinants in its readiness to classify and to postulate cause and effect. However, *how communication occurs* is the data base for mental illness. For this reason, it may be contended that the understanding of mental illness can never exclude the role of communication and that, even if mental illness were proven beyond doubt to be of biochemical origin, concepts of the self, the other, and communication distortion would still be central to diagnosis and treatment (Szasz 1961).

Whatever the shortcomings of Szasz's book, *The Myth of Mental Illness* did call attention to the view that a medical model for the dysfunction of mental illness is not an accurate one. Szasz maintained that by attempting to define the condition of insanity in terms of illness, as understood by doctors, psychiatry has impeded its own progress. Szasz emphasized that the manifestations of mental illness always constitute problems in living and problems in communication, which are never independent of cultural norms or of the effects of observation. Therefore, he contended, psychiatrists have a need to learn about language, symbolic communication, and the cultural determinants of behavior.

Other Deviant Behavior

A medicoreligious cult in Southern Italy (*Tarantismo*) provides an example of how culture can arrange appropriate settings for its deviant behavior (De Martino 1961). In this type of "illness," the "patient" asks for and receives help in the form of group therapy, which consists of dancing, feasting, and color display, all of which lead to possession, trance, and healing. The culture, out of accumulated generations of knowledge of its carriers, has provided forms through which certain ordinarily disapproved behavior can be exhibited. Such behavior, in its communication to others, provides for release of stress. Emotional burdens of the individual, which the culture will not acknowledge publicly, are thereby shared with others in a ritual performance.

Because the use of historical materials and archeological evidence for interpretation of the present has its dangers, anthropology looks at such current activities in primitive or isolated groups to learn how and why such forms have become institutionalized. The past was filled with events that were not recorded, and those who recorded events had their own interpretations as they reconstructed them. By studying small societies, anthropologists are able to isolate an event, observe its emergent complexities, and define the dynamics of interactions that are occurring within a reasonably circumscribed setting. They can directly observe new behavioral forms as these forms acquire labels and shape attitudes. As attitudes crystallize almost immediately around an event, some forms of "deviance" are born. A dramatic example follows.

Drunkenness

The initial public use of alcohol and the behavior associated with the "drunken" state in a primitive culture provides an opportunity to learn how proper behavior for an altered state is learned. Such an opportunity occurred at the first drinking party in a primitive village in New Guinea during which the development, communication, and "crystallization" of behavioral cues evolved for the drunk and the sober, the performer, and the audience (Schwartz and Romanucci–Ross 1974). All of these were affected by the context, both political and cultural. Antidiscrimination laws had been passed, so alcohol could be sold to natives in the Australian territory, and the few men in the village who had worked at one time for Europeans had observed the effects on the latter of "taking in the spirit." This in itself took on a heavy significance in the light of their religion, which made much of spirits entering the body and possessing the thoughts and acts of the human receptacle, now no longer in control of his words, thoughts, and deeds. That the missionaries of all Christian sects had forbidden—or, at the very least, frowned upon—drinking introduced an ingenious mode of anti-European rebellion in the very act of taking a drink.

As the party progressed and the script unfolded, no one knew the next line or movement, but all searched diligently in the eyes of others for glances of approval or shock. Those few men now intoxicated "spoke in tongues," as in their religious ceremonies, producing English phrases (much to everyone's total surprise) and shouting mock orders to each other in the European manner (obscenities included). Avoidance-behavior rules were violated; for example, some men asked women to dance. Those who vomited elicited caring and nurturant behavior; they had become Dionysian heroes, acting out for others what was most repressed. But the drinkers did not venture beyond limits, the limits of tolerable behavior being carefully set by all of the participants and observers. Several other drinking parties followed this one. However, the parameters had been set by the first party, and in subsequent parties only minor variations were introduced or were absent.

The interpretation of drunkenness by the villagers in the instance recorded was affected by established notions governing other extreme or unusual forms of behavior, such as mental illness, physical illness, possession, and trance. Although alcohol had direct sensorimotor effects and effects on the personality, the behaviors attributed to being "drunk" were not *limited* to these effects. Thus, there was collusion between the intoxicated individual and his audience in defining, shaping, and validating his altered states of behavior and consciousness.[6]

When do states become defined as deviant or problematic? It will be useful to the health professional to examine very briefly two important forms of deviance from the anthropological perspective: alcoholism and suicide.

Alcoholism

In Western cultures, alcoholism is generally considered an illness, and the alcoholic, or "patient," is an individual whose consumption of alcohol interferes with normal function, especially productivity. No state had yet been defined as "alcoholism" in the primitive culture described above. However, with the intake of "spirit" the drinker gained "soul," and after many drinks he lost "soul" as he passed into stupor. Therefore, it can be predicted that in that culture dunkenness will eventually come to be considered a cause of illness, because it is a state of instability tending toward soul gain or loss; that is, it represents a state of system imbalance.

Alcoholism has also been defined in larger political and cultural contexts. Through the eyes of the dominant culture, alcoholism in a subdued minority is a label that provides proof of not-quite-human status. In the late 1950s and early 1960s, American Indians in Chicago had a very high rate of alcoholism, which many Chicagoans looked at within the total cultural context of "job-loss" and other socially undesirable behavior. To urban whites, these states were all part of one syndrome: maladaptation. They saw it as nonintegrative and abrasive. Administrators saw alcoholism among the Indians as representing poor orientation to time and space in the urban setting. Drunken acts often brought the Indians into court where, although sullen and silent, they were usually labelled "wild men" who should be returned to the reservation. Here, there was no "illness," nor had a definition of alcoholism as illness been permitted for Indians in the courts. In the city-sponsored "House for Alcoholics" they seemed to enjoy acting as they thought whites wanted them to act—uninhibited and wild. However, in the Alcoholics Anonymous (AA) meetings, Indians were not sullen but tranquil; they spoke openly and freely and did not shy away from eye contact. Here were American Indians not encountered in the books of history or anthropology.

The AA system of treatment has certain premises about alcoholism that resemble the orientation of some religious systems regarding the place of the person in the world. This theme has been elaborated upon by Gregory Bateson (1972) who considers it a fallacy to look for the problem and cure of an alcoholic in his normal life, that is, when he is sober. Diagnosed in that dimension, the alcoholic will be seen as "immature," "oral," "passive," and/or "aggressive." Thus, advice to the alcoholic usually takes the form of an appeal to his sobriety state: "Get control"; "solve your problem." Ideally, according to Bateson, a theory about alcoholism should provide a converse matching between sobriety and intoxication, so that sobriety and drunkenness can be looked at as phases of the *same* system. Therefore, the usual attempt to reform the alcoholic by pitting the individual against himself, as the immature victim of his addiction, has to fail. The first step, as knowingly or unknowingly recognized by AA, is for the alcoholic to accept his existential status as a person who is powerless against alcohol.

Once more, then, we arrive at the theme of the psychosomatic unit, this time in dealing with alcoholism. Self, others, and environment as a configuration (still maintained for us by our primitive contemporaries) provide the framework within which deviance can be more fully understood.

Suicide

Suicide is explicitly either approved or disapproved by most cultures; so too, its complement—violent acts directed toward others. Approval or disapproval constitutes a form of social control. Suicide or violence provides a personal resolution to stress, or a personal rejoinder to excesses and restraints in social interaction. We examine such acts within the context of selected characteristics of several types of societies.

Anthropologists often study societies that lack written records, and the anthropologist usually works closely with informants. However, in statistical studies in which it is assumed that a large number of cases will yield data for meaningful generalizations, personal motivations tend to "drop out" in explanations of behavior. In the study of suicide, the methodological problem is that the informant cannot be interviewed. The intended suicide and the "suicidal personality" are not the same as the completed suicide. In understanding suicide, both the psychodynamics of the individual and the sociocultural milieu must be analyzed. In primitive societies, it is occasionally possible to tape-record a suicide "report," such as the following, translated verbatim from the Melanesian:

> I am Pondis of Male and I want to tell you a story of Katim. There were 30 men of Pwekeh, all in their village. They used to cook their taro and their sago, and they never had met. They heard a frog from a lake and didn't know a woman had hung herself from a tree there. The woman died first, then she stayed on the crown of the tree. They were fishing at night and saw her. She was an attractive woman and all decorated. They had put dogs' teeth and shell money on her body. They looked upon her and all desired her. All right, they loosened the woman and brought her down, and they all copulated with her. Then they went back and caught about 100 frogs. The ghost of the woman walked ahead and they followed to their homes. One old man saw the ghost of this woman from his house and he thought, "Now just what were these 30 men up to that this woman's ghost has appeared."

They offered the old man frog meat, but he refused, saying, "Eh, I am not about to eat those frogs. I saw that woman walking ahead of you." They ate the frogs, their wives did not, and the old man did not. Suddenly, their bodies couldn't keep still; they ran about the house of the betel nut, the house of the coconut right over there. Then they went to the bush and cut bamboo and made music with bamboo flutes. They played music and the sun went down. I think it was about four o'clock. They played their flutes on 30 different branches of the Callophylum tree. They played and felt great sorrow and they watched the sun go down. Now two of them loosened the vine with which they used to bind up their long hair—we call that vine Sahapay—tied one end to a branch and the other end around their necks and hung themselves. Two hung themselves and died, and the 28 who remained did the same thing. Now the meaning of these 30 hanging themselves is that they had intercourse with this woman who hung herself from a tree, and the ghost of this woman made them do this. It was to pay them back for what they did. That's all, the story is finished.[7]

This story has certain elements that are typical for Melanesian societies, and this material is useful in beginning to understand suicide there. The element of shame for sexual acts is central, because it was learned later that the woman had also hung herself for a sexual trespass. Sexual acts are members of a *class of acts* that emphasize the rule in that culture that one must not take what is not paid for; for in Melanesia symmetry exists in exchanges of property and actions. This myth provided a prepared script for proper future actions under certain circumstances. The myth was validated as truth because the teller could specify exactly the places in which the acts occurred. Suicide, then, provides an acceptable means of escaping unbearable sorrow or suffering and in this part of the world people may hang themselves to show mourning or to carry out a prescribed "right course of action" (Berndt 1962). Thus, suicide may terminate marital dissension, illness, sorcery, spinsterhood, criticism by other villagers, or fear of attending a court. One young man from Manus District hung himself when falsely accused of stealing £5 from the Australian naval commander's desk. When a man makes a suicide gesture, he cries out, so that often other men will run to save him, but females complete suicide more frequently because there is more social pressure for it and no interference with the attempt. Should a wife refuse sexual intercourse sought by her husband, he may publicly shame her to suicide. Victims of sorcery usually hang themselves, for sorcery is a severe social sanction, a message threatening total exclusion from the group; in such a case, the native curer is consulted, and he tells the victim how to bring about his death.

Homicide

What of homicide among these people? Here again we have no statistics, but there was much of it over territorial rights, over a slight insult—real or imagined—or simply for spite. There is no cultural disapproval either of suicide or homicide. In fact, much local humor was concerned with people killing themselves or others. When a man was mourning his wife's death, he would sometimes make himself feel better simply by going out and killing someone else, randomly selected, one death being balanced by another.

Context of Suicide and Homicide

In the Melanesian culture, persons relate to each other as members of classes or groups, marked by their place in the kinship or tribal structure. In such a context, interactions are actually between classes or sets of people, not between individuals (who can be readily replaced by other members of their group), and the situation is thus perceived by individuals in that culture. Within a more complex society, institutions are characterized by a distinct pattern of *interpersonal* relationships. To examine suicide and violence in this context, we may look at a city in Italy (Romanucci–Ross 1975). Here relationships depend on giving and receiving favors, an interactive pattern that shows remnants of feudal structure, and here there are very formal rules of responsibility and dependency for everyday living and for life crises. The consciousness that suicide is a possibility is considered an index of civility, urbanity, and "evolvedness"; as proof of this, it is pointed out that Southern Italians do not even consider this existential choice (in the usual invidious comparison between North and South). Who is most likely to commit suicide in this society? The aged, the woman who has more responsibility than she can bear in raising a family, or perhaps a woman with these responsibilities who is ill and has no one to help her. In generalization, then, the suicide is the person who can no longer do anyone a favor, and who cannot ask for help because the favor cannot be returned. Many situations are encountered in which shame could have been a powerful motive for suicide but is not. For example, when incest is discovered a chorus of protestations proclaim that it is better to kill oneself than commit such an act, but in fact incest *does* occur and those involved do *not* kill themselves, even when exposed. There are also other situations in which cultural messages (verbal or iconic) would advise suicide, but it is a prescription that is not followed. What mental mechanisms intercept these messages, and why does the guilty individual not take such a public moral prescription seriously, as primitives do? Pirandello, the Sicilian playwright, noted that Italian culture poses life's challenge to the person in this fashion: you live in a milieu layered alternately with fiction and reality—can you find your way in and out of those layers and survive? And, indeed, here is a culture with elaborate, seemingly contradictory codes about what is really important: what are acceptable and rewardable roles, and what are unrewarded gratuitous acts. The outsider notes that individuals in this culture present a happy exterior, even though they reiterate that "life is miserable and nothing will go right in the end." The individual feels that since the "real" rules are hidden from him he can hide the "real" person.

As in Mexico, we see here in Italy a counter-depressive strategy, in which the person and the group have expectations keyed so low that reality is always an upgrading and pleasant surprise. Cases of violence and killings noted in the Mexican setting were among the highest for any country over a 30-year period (Romanucci–Ross 1973), but there were no suicides. There are deterrents to suicide in both (Catholic) cultures; suicide is a "mortal sin." One can be poor, but if one has "respect" one can make it through life. In the Central Italian city that was studied (Romanucci–Ross 1975), suicides were rare, occurring only when the person felt no longer needed or respected and the social rules no longer justified existence.

Those close to the suicide never analyze the cause beyond saying, "The cause was mental disequilibrium." This is a culture where justifications for existence are searched for in the eyes of others.

Japanese culture is distinguished for its ritualized suicide.[8] Specific to traditional Japan was the self-disemboweling required of a warrior under certain circumstances (*seppuku*), which epitomized self-discipline and total commitment to role. The suicidal act (*junshi*) was performed by the faithful retainer who followed his lord in death. Advice suicide (*kangen seppuku*) was a way to coerce others to obey a command. This was used, for example, by a general to compel his own troops to surrender to the Americans at the end of World War II. Then there were the *shinju*, or "true heart" double suicides, in real life as well as in themes of tragic dramas. Suicides after scoldings, after industrial accidents, mistaken prescriptions by service personnel, or in order to relieve a spouse of a burden, have been common even in recent times.

Contrasts in Suicide Behavior

Suicide in Melanesia is characterized by injured status. It is always related to a sense of pride and is used for status validation. In primitive societies there is an absence of conflicting codes of behavior, because the definition of the self is related to the group validation of role, and individual responses are always mediated by group identity and group expectations. In certain contexts of more complex cultures, suicide is found to be filled with personal meaning through affirmation of role, as in the examples from Japan, where strong motivations to obliterate shame still exist. As in primitive societies, where it is group-mediated motivation that drives a person to suicide, so even within modern Japanese society the high suicide rate can be viewed as related to this causality, since many of the rigid codes of feudal society persist; here, also, suicide may be viewed as a function of intense integration into the group and high meaning of group values (de Vos 1973).

In contrast, parts of Italy and Mexico where suicide rates are low contain some remnants of feudal structure, but nevertheless are characterized by flexibility of personal choice of expression and by the inclusion in the society of some institutions that are prescriptively counter-suicidal. These include the supports provided by the church, the family, and the kinship and godparent network. Thus, in Italy suicide is the last resort of the elderly and a few others who perceive their options in "this earthly life" as truly gone.

In the classic statistical study of suicide in French society (Durkheim 1897), a negative correlation between suicide and the individual's integration into a group is postulated. In our contemporary American and other European societies, many continue to accept the view that a person will be motivated to end his life when he feels unintegrated into a group process—familial, religious, or social. Thus, there is concern in our own culture that suicide and accidents are the leading causes of death in our adolescent and young adult populations, and in an uncritical extrapolation of Durkheim's theories, many express the view that our industrial urbanized society *necessarily* "alienates" the person. In this vein, many social scientists have concluded that as a society becomes too loosely structured, suicide rates rise because the individual feels alone and unsupported. One study of a country exhibiting very high suicide rates postulated that mother–child interaction patterns failed to provide a sense of nurturance; that is, not having received nurturance, one is not able to give it (Hendin 1964). This type of study, based on analysis of individual interactions, is diametrically opposed to the sociological analyses, which maintain that only the "rate" of suicide in a large population will elicit the true causative variables. In the multi-ethnic, layered American society, however, rates of suicide do not provide complete information, since motivations will not be readily apparent. What people are killing themselves, and why, in our culture?

It has been noted that in our loosely structured American society the young person can quickly reach a state of hopelessness. Certainly the highly *visible,* strong group affiliations that motivate suicide in the societies discussed earlier are lacking. Clearly young people in America are opting for suicide as an "out" in numbers that surpass those in other cultures. Who is providing the images for the "success" they feel unable to achieve? Do we lack proper group supports (family structure, church, clubs, schools) that can provide options for life? Though not always explicitly stated, there is a strong motivating set of group values imposed on the young; it informs them that the way to success is in the acquisition of material goods, power over others, and early fame. Of course, group supports for the development of personhood still exist, but such supports pale in the barrage of multi-media advertising and commercialism that compel the young person to seek a more powerful and rewarding reality—to seek membership in the invisible group that is now setting standards of success (Henry 1965). Since only a few can achieve this, a sense of worthlessness is instilled in many. To state that in Western culture suicide occurs in the alienated person is a descriptive statement that needs qualification; it is not an explanation. We must begin to use for explanation the insights from anthropological, sociological, and psychological studies.

What Is Deviant, What Is Normal?

It has been found in surveys that when different psychiatrists see the same behavior, they agree on the diagnosis about 95 percent of the time. This felicitous occurrence is called "scorer agreement." Such an outcome might be predicted, however, since the individuals doing the scoring have gone through a similar educational process, in which they learned to recognize and label similar behaviors in a uniform way. Thus, "men of reason" talking about madness must eventually arrive at a consensus about what constitutes abnormal behavior and how to talk about it. It is this discourse, then, that becomes frozen into textbook "science."

Professionals and lay persons alike have a vast storehouse of cultural imagery to use in setting frames within which to communicate about insanity; madness and other forms of deviance have been attributed by most cultures to a great number of causes. These often are categorized in terms of "too much" of certain inputs into sociocultural systems and hence into personality: too much authority, too much religion, too much fantasy, too much freedom. Alternatively, the causes may be phrased by negation, as "not enough": not enough personal choice in alternative actions, not enough freedom of worship, not enough reality-orientation, not enough established norms for proper behavior. Once more we find that every culture has established ideas of system balance for what it deems the normal mental state. In the 1920s and 1930s, anthropologists began to investigate deviance in studies since enriched by research and theoretical views from psychoanalysis and medicine, as well as by more anthropology. Erich Fromm (1955) stressed that entire cultures or societies could be considered "crazy" or deviant, compared to a standard of behavior construed to be optimal for the resolution of problems of the human condition. He singled out our cultures of the urban–industrial complex as particularly alien to human mental health and self-fulfillment. In the experience of seeking but not finding the self in such a cultural milieu, the individual turns to alcohol, drugs, suicide, or a state of madness.

In declaring mad persons to be "ill," psychiatry allows them to achieve patienthood and thereby to receive therapy, caring, and nurturance. But the label of mental "illness" carries with it a significant reduction in individual rights and responsibilities (Tancredi, Chapter 15), and what began as a well-intentioned scientific and value-free advance also turned out to have important negative consequences. Even when all is circumspect in the diagnosis of insanity, the subsequent hospitalization and therapy—the entire process—is a *political* experience (Tancredi, ibid.). The example given earlier to illustrate the process of a social definition of insanity is also a description of a process called "political," that is, how—given conflicting goals and limited resources within a group—the more powerful "manage" the others in order to prevail.

Suicide, drinking behavior, and alcoholism are illustrations of how meanings of behavior change in cross-cultural contexts. We have examined simpler societies because in them are found, more visible, all the threads of the social fabric of more complex societies; we can then begin to formulate rules for transferring or transforming concepts or percepts, developed in the simpler models, to look for the underlying structure of events and behavior within the complexity of the society in which *we* are contained.

The "rate" of mental illness and deviance in any society is a statement about decisions made about cases; it does not define "actual" cases. In effect, much of the psychiatric process has to do with the physician's acculturation of the patient to psychiatry's grammar, vocabulary, logic, and definitions of cause and effect. In cultures such as Mexico or Italy, the limits of sanity are quite narrowly defined, but the limits of social tolerance are quite broad, and there are a great number of control mechanisms. As an example, in Mexican rural culture a public declaration of a serious conflict actually protects the adversaries, alerting the public as to who is to be blamed (incarcerated) if any misfortune should befall the other. Almost all cases of violence there were associated with inebriation, a state of consciousness that easily leads to misperception or miscalculation of the motives of others (Roman-ucci–Ross 1973).

The problem of personal normalcy is many-sided and complicated. "Normal" has been defined in a range of values about a mean of a distribution curve. This is easily done for height and weight in a tested group, but it is difficult for "personality." We look for learning theories for help, but there is no universal agreement as to what constitutes universal principles of learning, as we still try to design "culture-free" psychological tests.

For a culture-free definition of sanity, we could single out those individuals in any culture who are pursuing a course of action with the ability to assess both the behavior expected of them and the rewards or punishments for personal choices and a willingness to pay the price for those choices. Problematic is the position that a total society can be insane, as it pits "culture against person" into performing activities contrary to what is best for the human condition; for it is only within the society and by means of the culture that has rendered us "human" that the concept of "the human condition" can be understood or even discussed at all.

NOTES

1. *Titticutt Follies,* 1967. Zipporah Films, 54 Lewis Wharf, Boston, Mass. 02110.

2. The field of cultural psychiatry is well defined in the pioneering works of Sapir, Freud, Benedict, Mead, Linton, G.H. Mead, Devereux, and Henry. Its uses and applicability to specific societies in historical and social contexts is exemplified in the works of Fromm, Devereux, Bidney, Hallowell, DuBois, Opler, Spiro, and Henry. For studies of the epidemiology of disordered states in cross-cultural contexts, see Wittkower, Leighton, Stoller, Murphy, Weil, and Odegard. Mead, Edgerton, Levy, Schwartz, Romanucci–Ross, and Gonzalez–Pineda have done studies on culture change and mental illness. Gregory Bateson has made important contributions to the understanding of that which is "mental" in mind–body system and symbolic interaction within a cultural–social structure.

3. Anthropological Field Notes for American Museum of Natural History Expedition to the Admiralty Islands and New Guinea, 1963–1967, L. Romanucci–Ross. Expedition financed by NIMH. Investigators: Margaret Mead, Ted Schwartz, and Lola Romanucci–Ross.

4. Bateson 1936. See epilogue on *schismogenesis.*

5. For substantive contributions of Mexican psychoanalysis, see Gonzalez–Pineda, Ramirez, and Fromm. For details of field research cited here, see Fromm and Maccoby (1970) and Romanucci–Ross (1973).

6. Anthropological Field Notes, op. cit. note 3.

7. Ibid.

8. See De Vos, Wagatsuma, Mishima, and Bellah.

REFERENCES

Bateson, Gregory. 1936. *Naven.* Stanford: Stanford Univ. Press.
1972 *Steps toward an Ecology of Mind.* San Francisco: Chandler.

Bellah, Robert. 1965. "Ienaga Saburo and the Search for Meaning in Modern Japan." Marius Jansen, ed., *Changing Japanese Attitudes toward Modernization.* Princeton: Princeton Univ. Press, 360–423.

Benedict, Ruth. 1934. *Patterns of Culture.* New York: New American Library.

1946   *The Chrysanthemum and the Sword.* Boston: Houghton Mifflin.

Berndt, Ronald M. 1962. *Excess and Restraint: Social Control among a New Guinea Mountain People.* Chicago: Univ. of Chicago Press.

Bidney, David. 1953. *Theoretical Anthropology.* New York: Columbia Univ. Press.

De Martino, Ernesto. 1961. *La Terra del Rimorso: Contributo a una storia Religiosa del Sud.* Milan: Saggiatore.

De Vos, George. 1973. "Role Narcissism and the Etiology of Japanese Suicide." George De Vos, ed., *Socialization for Achievement: The Cultural Psychology of the Japanese.* Berkeley: Univ. of California Press.

Devereux, George. 1951. *The Reality and Dream: Psychotherapy of a Plains Indian.* New York: International Univ. Press.

Dubois, Cora. 1944. *The People of Alor.* Minneapolis: Univ. of Minnesota Press.

Durkheim, Emile. 1897. *Suicide.* Glencoe: The Free Press (1951).

Foucault, Michel. 1965. *Madness and Civilization: A History of Insanity in the Age of Reason.* New York: Random House (originally published in French as *Histoire de la Folie,* 1961).

Freud, Sigmund. 1950. *Totem and Taboo.* London: Routledge & Kegan Paul.

1930   *Civilization and Its Discontents.* London: Hogarth Press.

Fromm, Erich. 1941. *Escape from Freedom.* New York: Farrar & Rinehart.

1955   *The Sane Society.* New York: Holt, Rinehart & Winston.

————, and Michael Maccoby. 1970. *Social Character in a Mexican Village.* Englewood Cliffs, N.J.: Prentice–Hall.

Hallowell, A.I. 1955. *Culture and Experience.* Philadelphia: Univ. of Pennsylvania Press.

Hendin, Herbert. 1964. *Suicide and Scandinavia: A Psychoanalytic Study of Culture and Character.* New York: Grune & Stratton.

Henry, Jules. 1965. *Culture against Man.* New York: Vintage Books.

Kardiner, Abram. 1945. *The Psychological Frontiers of Society.* New York: Columbia Univ. Press.

Kiev, Ari, ed. 1969. *Social Psychiatry.* New York: Science House.

Linton, Ralph. 1936. *The Study of Man.* New York: Appleton Century.

Mead, G.H. 1938. *Mind, Self and Society.* Chicago: Univ. of Chicago Press.

Mead, Margaret. 1928. *Coming of Age in Samoa.* New York: William Morrow.

1935   *Sex and Temperament.* New York: William Morrow.

Mishima, Yukio. 1958. *Confessions of a Mask.* New York: New Directions.

Opler, Marvin K., ed. 1959. *Culture and Mental Health: Cross-Cultural Studies.* New York: Macmillan.

Ramirez, Santiago. 1958. *El Mexicano: La Psicologia de sus Motivaciones.* Asociacion Psicoanalitica Mexicana, Monografias Psicoanaliticas, Mexico, Pax.

Romanucci–Ross, Lola. 1973. *Conflict, Violence and Morality in a Mexican Village.* Palo Alto: Mayfield.

1975   "Italian Identity and Its Transformations." G. De Vos and L. Romanucci–Ross, *Ethnic Identity in Cultural Continuity and Change.* Palo Alto: Mayfield.

Sapir, Edward. 1948. *Selected Writings in Language, Culture and Personality,* ed. David Madelbaum. Berkeley: Univ. of California Press.

Schwartz, Theodore, and Lola Romanucci–Ross. 1974. "Drinking and Inebriate Behavior in the Admiralty Islands, Melanesia." *Ethos,* Fall: 213–32.

Spiro, Melford E. 1951. "Personality and Culture: The Natural History of a False Dichotomy." *Psychiatry,* 14:19–46.

Szasz, Thomas. 1961. *The Myth of Mental Illness.* New York: Harper & Row.

Wagatsuma, Hiroshi, and George deVos. 1973. "Alienation and the Authors: A Tryptych in Conformity and Deviancy in the Japanese Intellectuals." G. De Vos, ed., *Socialization for Achievement.* Berkeley: Univ. of California Press.

Wittkower, E.D., H.B.M. Murphy, and N.A. Chance. 1961. *Cross-Cultural Inquiry into the Symptomology of Depression: A Preliminary Report.* Montreal: Proceedings of the Third World Congress of Psychiatry.

15

Psychiatry and Social Control

Laurence R. Tancredi, M.D.

The past 20 years have brought about changes in the treatment of the mentally ill comparable in societal impact to the liberating of mental patients from the hospitals of Bicêtre and Salpêtriére by Philip Pinel, the founder of modern psychiatry.[1] Prior to the time of Pinel, in the latter part of the eighteenth century, mental patients and the retarded were housed with the criminally insane and actually placed in chains. By freeing the mentally ill, Pinel brought about a drastic change in society's perception of mental illness; this launched a trend in the treatment of the mentally ill that continued to evolve in the nineteenth and twentieth centuries with the establishment of specialized treatment centers or hospitals for the mentally ill, and the separation of these patients from the senile, destitute, and criminal.

Since the 1960s, mentally ill patients have reaped the benefits of another major shift in society's perception of the way in which such patients should be treated and the extent to which they should be afforded rights in accord with others in society. The main thrust of the civil rights movement for the mentally ill over the past 20 years has been to increase the rights of such patients to refuse treatment. The first phase of this trend was focused on involuntary confinement in mental institutions. In the mid-50s, two significant therapeutic developments made possible the wide-scale deinstitutionalization of mentally ill patients.[2] The first of these was the increasing and widespread use of psychotropic medications, particularly neuroleptics (such as thorazine, etc.) and antidepressants, which were found to be highly effective in the treatment of the seriously and acutely ill. These drugs were able to calm and tranquilize highly agitated and potentially violent patients, reduce the potentiality of suicide among the seriously depressed, and actually bring about changes in the thinking processes of seriously disturbed schizophrenic patients. Until the introduction of psychotropic medications, the armamentarium of psychiatry was limited to some physical procedures, such as electroshock and, in the mid-twentieth century, lobotomies; verbal treatments, such as psychotherapy and psychoanalysis, which had limited utility in the treatment of the psychotically ill; and milieu therapy within the institutional structure. With psychotropic medications, large numbers of patients could be rendered manageable and ultimately more receptive to the broad spectrum of psychological and social therapies. Psychotropic medicines also made possible the second major development in the 1950s that allowed deinstitutionalization of the mentally ill: the emergence of social psychiatry or the so-called therapeutic community. The community-based model for providing care made possible a shift away from the institutional context. With proper medication, patients could be treated frequently in the community through outpatient and day-care programs, living either with their families or in half-way houses.

Legal Ramifications

Indeterminant Commitment

These two major trends in psychiatry allowed for—and made necessary—a reconsideration of the now-antiquated laws relevant to the commitment of the mentally ill, which remained as a significant impediment to deinstitutionalization. Two major changes occurred in the 60s and 70s relevant to these laws. First, there was a shift away from indeterminant commitment—that is, legal procedures by which patients could be placed in institutions for almost unlimited periods of time, with minimal, if any, periodic review of their status.[3] Under such procedures, many patients were placed in mental institutions and remained there for as long as 18 to 20 years, receiving limited if any treatment during that period and undergoing limited periodic review. The changes in the statutes and cases relevant to involuntary commitment have essentially eliminated the arbitrary and indiscriminate use of indeterminant commitment.

Incompetency and Involuntary Commitment

The second major change that occurred with reexamination of the commitment statutes was a breakdown of the traditional merger of involuntary commitment with incompetency. Before the changes in the laws, mentally ill patients who were involuntarily committed to mental institutions were deemed to be incompetent to perform the full range of legal actions that the remainder of us enjoy in society. For example, they could not vote, enter into marriage, get divorced, sign wills, or engage in business transactions. Legislative reforms eliminated the automatic association of involuntary commitment with incompetency, and it became necessary to assess the potential competency of the involuntarily committed patient for each act in question. Generally, patients were allowed to freely communicate with others outside of institutions, and to receive phone calls; if they had the competency, they could sign wills and enter into business negotiations. Each of these acts required its own specific individual and contextual analysis; a joint judgment of committability and incompetency was no longer legally or ethically acceptable.

Criminal Due-Process Rights

In addition to these significant alterations brought about by the mental-health-law movement, there was also the application to patients of many of the due-process rights accorded the accused in the criminal system. Many states changed their statutes, and in others, cases were brought, dealing with the rights of patients to notice, a hearing, counsel, freedom from self-incrimination, and a significant narrowing of the statutory criteria justifying involuntary commitment. Until these reforms in the 60s and 70s, the mentally ill could be committed in many states on the basis of "in need of care and treatment" or "for their own welfare," or, as in one state, for "nonconformity." The legal changes of the 60s shifted the legal focus to objective criteria for justifying involuntary commitment of the mentally ill, criteria based predominantly on dangerousness to self or others or grave disability. This narrowing of the criteria for commitment of the mentally ill significantly reduced the number of persons who could be committed to mental institutions, and resulted in an expansion of the full range of behaviors that were legally acceptable outside of the institutional structure. Those patients who were considered seriously mentally ill, but who were not dangerous to themselves or others or gravely disabled, were allowed to live freely in society and even choose freely whether they would accept psychiatric treatment.

Deinstitutionalization

The deinstitutionalization movement has had a major impact in the number of residents in institutions across the United States. In 1955, there were over 560,000 residents in institutions in this country. This number declined at least 56 percent between that year and 1973, when the number of patients in institutions was slightly more than 248,000.[4] Much of this represents a decrease in the average length of stay of patients in institutions, although there was a slight increase in the number of first admissions to state institutions and a greater increase in readmission rates. The elderly, on the other hand, generally experienced a decrease in admissions to institutions. Again, as would be expected, the rate of out-patient episodes or visits significantly increased during the same period.

Goals

The traditional expansive social goals justifying the commitment of the mentally ill came under increasing attack during the 60s and 70s. Commitment had been perceived as fulfilling the following four goals: (1) protection of society from the potentially violent acts of the mentally ill; (2) protection of individuals who are disturbed from their own irresponsible actions—suicide or other self-harm; (3) provision of treatment for those who are in need of it; and (4) relief of the family as well as society of the difficulties of taking care of such individuals.[5] Of these goals, only the first—protection against the potential dangerousness of the individual to others—would be considered acceptable according to the standards of John Stuart Mill, who in his essay "On Liberty" stated unequivocally that "the only purpose for which power can be rightfully exercised over any member of a civilized community, against his will, is to prevent harm to others." In that same essay, he was explicit and adamant on the fact that there is not sufficient warrant in exercising power over an individual for "his own good either physical or moral."[6]

Notions of the Person

Recent cases extend even further the rights of the mentally ill to control their own lives and to limit what is done to them. These cases involve the right of the mentally ill to refuse psychotropic medication, even when these patients are involuntarily committed to mental institutions. The importance of these cases rests not only on the fact that they have expanded considerably the rights of the mentally ill, but that they have introduced concepts such as self-determination and the right to a protectable interest in one's own thinking processes even to persons who are disordered. These notions, which are generalizable, focus essentially on three critical issues. The first of these, long recognized by cultural anthropology, is the relativism of concepts such as normal and abnormal among cultures, and the extent to which these concepts are not only not absolute but are tied closely to societal intent,[7] which at certain stages in the historical development of a culture may be more rigid and limited and at others more expansive. Second, the concepts that have been evoked in the right-to-refuse-treatment cases and that are implicit in the commitment cases address directly the close nexus between psychiatry as a medical discipline and social or cultural values. Third, these notions presuppose a theory of personhood. That is to say, they imply that notions such as self-determination and self-actualization are predicated on an ethical priority and refer directly to the existence of some core eidetic concept of "individual," from which the content of the actualized self is derived.

The Case of Rennie v. Klein

The two most recent cases addressing these rights of the mentally ill are *Rennie v. Klein*[8] and *Okin v. Rogers*.[9] In the first, the district court—deciding on the basis of the right to privacy—articulated an elaborate procedural approach for dealing with patients not in an emergency situation who have been involuntarily committed and who refuse medication. In such situations, the patient has the right to notice of a hearing, a patient–advocate who may be a lawyer, and an informal hospital hearing before a third party, an ostensibly disinterested, independent psychiatrist. In part the requirement for a second psychiatric opinion may be viewed as an attempt on the part of the court to improve the quality of care in the New Jersey state hospital system. The psychiatrist, who serves the role of a consultant, reviews the case and makes the final determination regarding medication based on four factors: the physical threat of the patient to the staff or to other patients in the institution; the patient's ability to decide a particular treatment on his or her own; the nature and extent of the risk of permanent side effects from the treatments being proposed (this is particularly important with regard to the phenothiazines such as thorazine, which are known to cause tardive dyskinesia—involuntary movements of the mouth and jaw—that may be permanent disabilities; and, lastly, the availability and existence of less restrictive alternatives. The patient's right in this case was predicated on the right to privacy, which essentially means the right of individuals to have control over their own bodily integrity, a right that has been applied in recent years to a wide variety of situations such as marital relationships, contraception, abortions, and obscenity, to name a few. A critical concept underlying the articulation of the right to privacy is that of self-determination: that individuals have the capacity and the will to control what is done to them both physically and psychologically.

The U.S. Court of Appeals (Third Circuit), on reviewing this case, upheld the constitutional right to refuse treatment, but rejected both the requirement for an adversarial hearing before an independent psychiatrist and the need to apply the four patient-rights oriented criteria. Instead, the court determined that the decision should be made by the medical director, primarily on therapeutic considerations. [See *Rennie v. Klein*, 653 F.R.2d 386 (1981).] The controversies introduced by this case between patients' rights and therapeutic discretion should be resolved in the U.S. Supreme Court decision in *Mills v. Rogers* (originally *Okin v. Rogers*).

The Case of Okin v. Rogers

In the second case, the *Okin* case, the court took a much stronger position and stated, in effect, that involuntarily committed patients have an absolute right to refuse medication, except where there is a substantial likelihood that the patient may be dangerous to self or others. This argument has also been used in other cases, most particularly those involving the use of experimental psychosurgery to control violent behavior.[10] In addition to arguing on the basis of the involuntary patient's right to privacy, the *Okin* case added another dimension, the First Amendment right to freedom of speech. Freedom of speech, it is argued, requires unfettered production of thought or generation of ideas. The court concluded that the capacity to think and to decide is within the scope of the First Amendment and is a fundamental freedom in our society. Consequently, the fact that a seriously ill patient may produce disordered or bizarre thoughts does not in itself warrant the imposition of medication against that patient's will. Again, this concept has as an underlying presupposition an acceptance of self-determination, along with an expansion of the matrix of societal tolerance, altered only to the extent of the patient's substantial dangerousness to self or others.

The *Okin* case was appealed to the U.S. Court of Appeals for the First Circuit, which in November 1980 issued its decision regarding the right to refuse treatment; this agreed in part, but not completely, with the lower court's decision. The Court of Appeals upheld the notion that there was a constitutional right to refuse antipsychotic drugs based on the right of privacy, which includes the right to control what is done with one's body. However, the Court of Appeals did not consider the First Amendment right to freedom of speech and the generation of ideas, which was clearly stated in the lower court's decision. The Court of Appeals also excluded from consideration as antipsychotic medication the antidepressants and lithium carbonate (used in treatment of manic–depressive disorder)—focusing, therefore, almost completely on the neuroleptics, which are capable of producing tardive dyskinesia. Finally, the Court of Appeals expanded the definition of "emergency," when even competent, involuntarily committed patients can be given antipsychotic (neuroleptic) medications against their will. In the lower court, an emergency was defined as "substantial likelihood of physical harm to patient, other patients or staff." The Court of Appeals stated that the definition of "emergency" should be more flexible, with the psychiatrist taking the primary role in defining it. On Jan. 13, 1982, this case was argued before the United States Supreme Court.[11]

Legislative Responses

In Utah, alternatives to dealing with the issue of patients' rights to refuse medi-cation, even though involuntarily committed, were proposed by the legislature, which decided that persons can be involuntarily confined only if they are also viewed as lacking the ability to engage in a "rational decision-making process regarding the acceptance of mental treatment." In a subsequent case on this statutory provision, a federal court concluded that if, at the time of the original commitment, a finding is made that the patient is incompetent to decide about treatment matters, the patient cannot thereafter assert a constitutional right to refuse treatment, even if it involves psychotropic medication.[12]

Relativism of Normality–Abnormality

As we have already suggested, recent developments in the rights of the mentally ill reflect three suppositions regarding mental illness. The first of these is the relativism of the normal–abnormal polarity. Theorists concerned with psychiatric labeling have contended for some time that the perception of various behaviors as evidence of mental illness is largely context-specific. This is to say that the perception that certain clusters of behavior are representative of schizophrenia is relative to the social context of the evaluation. As pointed out by D. L. Rosenhan,[13] psychiatric nosology used for diagnostic purposes discloses more about the environment within which the diagnosis is made than about the patient. In his study, using graduate students in psychology, Rosenhan demonstrated that perfectly normal patients pre-senting at a mental institution with one symptom—that of auditory hallucinations—are often perceived as psychiatrically abnormal and channeled into the mental institution. Rosenhan states, like other critics of labeling, that once the diagnosis of schizophrenia or other mental illness is applied to the patient, others in the environment—including family, friends, and people closely or intimately related to the patient—respond to the patient as though the diagnosis were correct. Eventually, influenced by others, the patient buys into the external perceptions.

This thesis, of the relativism of mental illness as acted out in the labeling process, demonstrates a fluidity and almost arbitrariness that has now been substantiated in some subsequent studies. (See, for example, Romanucci–Ross's chapter in this section, "On Madness, Deviance, and Culture," for a strong statement of the validity of the concept of relativism.) Jane Murphy, an anthropoligist at the Harvard School of Public Health, contrasted two distinctly non-Western groups, the Eskimos of Alaska and the Yorubas of rural Nigeria,[14] demonstrating that labels for insanity exist in both these cultures and that insanity is a condition that is considered to influence the inner state of mind of the afflicted individual, essentially beyond the individual's control. Furthermore, the labeling of individuals as "insane" in these disparate cultures is not based on one characteristic but on a cluster of "interlinked phenomena." Hallucinations, delusions, behavioral aberrations, and disorientation in combination appear to signify that the individual is "losing his mind," even though the content of these manifestations, such as the nature of the delusions or hallucinations, is inevitably colored by cultural beliefs and reflects cultural symbols.

This would also be consistent with the epidemiological findings that schizophrenia rates in various countries in Europe, Asia, and North America are comparable, despite differences in the populations under study and subtle distinctions in the definitions of the disease condition.[15] With regard to this first underlying presupposition—that is, the relativism of normality and abnormality—there appears to be increasing evidence that the relativism of these states has been considerably exaggerated by sociologists and psychologists involved in labeling theory, and that there is a demarcation between sanity and insanity, predicated on symptom manifestations, that is comparable in various cultures of the world.

Psychiatrists as Social Control Agents

The second underlying presupposition is that psychiatry reflects the cultural norms of the environment. This presupposition is inextricably connected with the first. Also implied in this second notion is the idea that psychiatry serves the societal purposes of a system of control of "deviant" behavior, similar to other social-control systems such as law and religion.[16] There is probably greater validity in this argument with regard to the goals of psychiatric intervention than with regard to the development of a psychiatric nosology. As already pointed out in the previous argument, various cultures are comparable in the symptom complexes and manifestations that they perceive and use to distinguish between sanity and insanity.

Terms like "schizophrenia" may to some extent be panchrestons—concepts that explain everything—as described by Thomas Szasz;[17] on the other hand, the remarkable comparability of prevalence rates of this condition in various cultures, augmented by the increasing evidence of biochemical alterations that may be related to the development of such symptom complexes, suggests that there may be more homogeneity in "schizophrenia" than previously believed. Developments such as the discovery of elevated levels of cerebrospinal fluid norepinephrine in schizophrenic patients, particularly those with conspicuous paranoid features,[18] the suggestion of other neurohumeral changes in both schizophrenia and manic–depressive illness,[19] and, most recently, the discovery of the interchangeability between stress and amphetamines in sensitizing individuals to development of a psychotic syndrome,[20] give a firmer basis to the classification of schizophrenia as a disease. These discoveries, interlacing biochemical and biophysiological changes with the development of the conspicuous complexes that present as schizophrenia—the psychosis induced by amphetamines or other stimulants resembles paranoid schizophrenia—at best undercut some of the criticism often made that psychiatry is purely reflective of sociocultural norms and, consequently, of cultural relativism between normality and abnormality. Of course, the direct relationship of these neurochemical and biological changes to the pathogenesis of schizophrenia has yet to be fully explained.

There appears to be greater strength in the criticism that the goals of psychiatric intervention reflect cultural norms. R. D. Laing has argued that treatment of mental illness may be understood as essentially the seduction of patients into abandoning their own experiential and subjective perspective of themselves and the environment for the ostensibly objective perspective of the therapist.[21] This is achieved, in large part, by the therapist's interpreting away the perceptions and experiences of the patient, by applying a meaning to those interpretations that may very well be other than that actually intended by the patient. This viewpoint can be additionally elucidated by examining the underlying ethical notions of the therapist regarding the value of human existence. Freud considered the goals of life to be "lieben und arbeiten"—to love and to work[22]—a pronounced utilitarian ethic. A therapist may be oriented toward these same value-laden objectives. Others, such as Franz Alexander, take the position that the principal objective is that of adaptability, assisting the patient to adapt to the environment.[23] This is perhaps a more direct asseveration than Freud's of the importance of sociocultural norms and values in the definition of the goals of psychiatric intervention. The argument seems compelling, overall, that psychiatric intervention has as one of its primary objectives, even if not explicitly, some element of assisting the patient in a posture of conformance to the social context.[24]

On the other hand, the fact that psychiatry may be tied to sociocultural norms does not necessarily make it less scientific. To the extent that the development of the individual is by no means predicated wholly on what the individual brings ontologically into this world, but requires an ever-engaging dynamic relationship with the environment and interpersonal experiences, then a science that attends to the understanding of personal development must be sensitive to the intersubjective experience characteristic of that sociocultural milieu. From a philosophical perspective, this would be consistent with phenomenological notions that human beings are both constituted and constitutive of their intersubjective experience. As with any scientific endeavor, paradigms or models for observing and understanding data are essential, and these models are influenced by the framework of perceptions of the culture at particular points in history.[25]

Right to Autonomy

The third and most complicated issue raised by recent cases asserting the rights of the mentally ill, and by critics of the regressive and conforming function of psychiatric intervention, is the overriding right of patients to autonomy, self-determination, and self-actualization. These concepts are particularly difficult to understand as they apply to the mentally ill, but are no less problematic when examined on their own merits. The notion of self-determination or self-realization has its roots in the eudaimonistic tradition, which places an ethical priority on self-actualization, presupposing that within every individual there exists an entity, a daimon, that is essentially responsible for the uniqueness of that individual and that merely needs to unfold. The conditions of the world or sociocultural milieu in which we live are not always compatible with the emergence of that inner self, so that one can never achieve full actualization in this existence, but in time—through learning to know one's inner destiny and adhering to the rules thereof—individual uniqueness can be progressively understood.[26] This notion, emerging from eudaimonism, has been popularized in recent years by the humanistic psychology of thinkers such as Abraham Maslow.[27]

The extreme individuality suggested in this tradition nearly precludes a meaningful comprehension of what is meant by self-actualization. For example, when does this process occur, and how do individuals know that they are in touch with inner uniqueness, inner destiny? What criteria, or guideposts, can be used as a framework for individual development and personal growth? If we accept the idea that an individual has an inner teleology or directiveness, what limits should be placed by society on the nature of its expression or manifestation? On a less dramatic but equally significant level, what nosological basis can be made for egocentricism or narcissism? These conditions become almost desirable in a value system that emphasizes self-actualization. What validity, to go one step further, can then be given to any taxonomy of mental illness? Could these conditions not simply be a manifestation of self-actualization? Do we accept the notion that homicidal maniacs, although requiring control by society because of the impact that they may have on others, may not be judged on ethical or moral standards because they may be fulfilling an inner destiny or actualization?

The Role of Others

Perhaps even more perplexing is that this definition of personhood and the suggestion of an identity subterranean within the individual minimizes the roles of others in the social system. Some might argue that a theory of personhood requires some attention to the capacity of the individual to experience intimacy and care for others in society. This would be a very different thesis, as it would involve some concept of sociocultural identity as it interacts with the individual. Even more interesting are the descriptions of identity and personhood suggested by some of our great literary figures, such as Virginia Woolf. She viewed the self as an "elusive will o' the wisp, always just ahead on the horizon, flickering and insubstantial, yet induring."[28] Woolf saw personal identity as always in a state of flux, changing its contours as it responds to the forces and influences surrounding it. Further, she explained that even the past or history of the individual, upon which any momentary identity is predicated, does not remain static either. It is dynamically altered, changed, and redefined by the consciousness that recalls it at any point in the historical development of the person.

If the ethical priority of self-actualization is accepted, as defined in the eudai-monistic tradition, emphasis would be placed squarely on individuality, specifically on the necessity of inner directiveness for understanding the core of one's identity and one's personal destiny. Taking the perspective that personhood somehow relates to capacities for expressive intimacy and caring, as well as the not-incompatible view expressed by Woolf that identity is forever altering itself on the basis of external forces, then influences from the culture act to shape the determination of self. Recognizing the conceptual difficulties of a purely eudaimonistic notion of self-actualization—which provides little in the way of criteria for understanding when one is in touch with inner destiny as opposed to distortions of it—as well as the growing awareness (through linguistic analysis and interpretive sciences like hermeneutics) of the extent and pervasiveness of the interchangeable features of person and culture, a theory of personhood can be formulated, predicated on the importance of relationships with others and the potentiality for care and intimacy. Such a formulation seems both scientifically and philosophically sound. This interpretation would be consistent with the earlier observation that psychiatric nosology is no less valid because it is affected by the values of the culture.

If we accept that psychiatric nosology has some validity in the definition of mental illness, then the unresolved issues regarding personal identity are those of the significance of privacy and autonomy and the distinction between prediathetic and diathetic in assessing the basis for rights of self-determination. The cases dealing with the right of even involuntarily committed psychiatric patients to refuse psychotropic medication are based primarily on the rights to privacy, freedom of expression, and autonomy, as well as self-determination. Prior to the onset of disease, the individual rests on a foundation of self-determination that may be quite different from that experienced in the diathetic or diseased state. Which of these potentials for personal development should be protected by society and, in particular, by the law?[29] The belief that—in the name of free individual expression—it is essential to expand the matrix for societal tolerance of deviant behavior, even to the point of limiting treatment for the seriously disturbed, must take into account critical differences in that expression based on the presence or absence of illness. The Mill proposition that it is only in the case of dangerousness to others in society that the state has a right to intervene does not address the issue of differences in levels of intellectual and emotional potentiality that arise from the onset of a mental illness and that go to the very essence of the individual's capacity to understand their environment and their relationship to it, and to comprehend the full import of self-determination.

I am not arguing for the mandatory imposition of medication to patients involuntarily committed to institutions. Instead, I am suggesting that somewhere between the way in which psychiatric institutions operated in the past—which was to freely impose such medication even contrary to the patient's wishes—and the baseline argued for in recent cases—that only in the event of an emergency characterized by dangerousness to self or others should medication be applied—there is a threshold level that perhaps more appropriately represents the justification for involuntary medication. The goal should include some consideration of the importance of returning a seriously ill patient to a position, if not exactly prediathetic, at least in the direction that would allow for an enhanced understanding of the patient's own potentiality for self-determination in the way in which it is most meaningful, the capacity to opt for engaging in the world, experiencing intimacy both in interpersonal relationships and in work, and for caring for others in society.

The Current Dispute

In effect, we are left with an awareness of the various incentives operating to determine how the mentally ill should be handled in our society. On one side are those who argue that mental illness is a myth, that it is the imposition of the sociocultural norms of the majority on a minority, and that it is a device used by psychiatry to control deviant behavior and to regress individuals to a state of conformance in society. On the other side are those who argue that mental illness, although perhaps exaggerated in scope to some extent in the past, does exist, that it affects the very essence of an individual's thinking and ability to understand the individual's own capacities for self-development and relationships in the world, and that an ethical obligation exists not to control these individuals, except in cases of dangerousness to self and others, but to assist them to arrive at a true awareness of their own potentiality. To achieve this, it may be necessary to resort to the use of medication. By no means has the debate been resolved by this discussion. The intention in this chapter has been to elucidate some of the conceptual underpinnings of the present movement toward emphasis on the rights of the mentally ill and of the countervailing arguments for the application of a therapeutic model to these patients. Neither of these positions is value-free; both arise from social and ethical notions of what are just and acceptable goals for the individual in society.

The pendulum has clearly swung noticeably in the direction of asserting the rights of the mentally ill, and, to some extent, of the rights of these individuals to be mentally ill. Now, as in *Rennie v. Klein* on appeal, it is swinging back to the values of imposing the therapeutic model on such individuals. This will be achieved primarily because of exigencies of a social and economic nature, which will rely on the utilitarian ethic for resolution. These exigencies are the degree and immediacy of the impact of nontreatment on social order. Chief among these are statistics suggesting that the mentally ill engage in a higher incidence of criminal behavior—including violent offences[30]—than others in the population. The studies are somewhat conflictual on this issue;[31] however, the association of mental illness with criminal behavior may be particularly significant if it is firmly established in studies directed at assessing the social impact of the deinstitutionalization of the mentally ill, a phenomenon of very recent development. And lastly, a recent study attempting to evaluate the cost of schizophrenia to society estimates it to be somewhere between $11.6 and $19.5 billion annually, most of which represents the lack of productivity of schizophrenic patients.[32] The expense of maintaining these patients in the community may result in a considerable increase in the overall social cost. The extent to which patients have the right to refuse treatment will influence their degree of nonproductivity in society and—if increased—will inevitably result in an increase in the cost of maintaining them. Although this right reflects the impact of the expanding matrix of societal tolerance for deviance and for mental illness, a process justified on legal and philosophical grounds, this matrix may nonetheless be constricted for social, economic, and policy reasons.

The underlying analytical issues discussed in this chapter deal with the delicate interface of psychiatry, law, and culture, and they will remain important despite the changing matrix of tolerance of the mentally ill patient in the community and society. I have raised only a few of the underlying psychosocial and philosophical questions regarding mental illness. Clearly, there is a need for more attention to these questions, and for the development of a modern theory of mental illness that takes into account not only psychosocial but also biochemical and biophysiological processes, so that a more scientific basis will exist for informing policy makers regarding the nature of mental illness, the various levels of competency of patients, and the ways in which they may most appropriately be treated—or not treated—so as to maximize their individual development and yet meet the critical needs of society.

NOTES

1. M. Foucault, *Madness and Civilization* (New York: Vintage Books, 1965), 38–64.

2. M. Greenblatt and E. Glazier, "The Phasing Out of Mental Hospitals in the United States, *American Journal of Psychiatry* 132 (1975): 1135.

3. L.R. Tancredi, J. Leib, and A. Slaby, *Legal Issues in Psychiatric Care* (New York: Harper & Row, 1975).

4. Greenblatt and Glazier, "Phasing Out," pp. 1135 ff.

5. A.A. Stone, *Mental Health and Law: A System in Transition* (Washington, D.C.: National Institute of Mental Health, 1975), 43 ff.

6. J.S. Mill, *On Liberty*, ed. C.V. Shields (Indianapolis: Bobbs–Merrill, 1956), 13 ff.

7. Jürgen Habermas, *Knowledge and Human Interests* (Boston: Beacon Press, 1968). See

also M.H. Hollender and T.S. Szasz, "Normality, neurosis and psychosis," *Journal of Nervous and Mental Diseases* 125 (1957): 599.

8. *Rennie v. Klein,* 476 F. Supp. 1294 (D.N.J. 1979).

9. *Rogers v. Okin,* 478 F. Supp. 1342 (E.D. Mass. 1979). See also *In re Boyd,* 403 A.2d 744 (D.C. 1979).

10. Kaimowitz v. Department of Mental Health, 1 *Mental Disability Law Reporter* 147 (Cir. Ct., Wayne Cty, Mich., 1973). *See also In re* Mental Health of K.K.B., 609 P.2d 747 (Okla. 1980).

11. Rogers v. Okin, 478 F. Supp. 1342 (E.D. Mass. 1979); *cert. granted* and case argued *sub nom.* Mills v. Rogers, No. 80-1417 (U.S.S.Ct. Jan. 13, 1982).

12. *See* Utah Code Ann. Sec. 64-7-36 (10).

13. D. Rosenhan, "On Being Sane in Insane Places," *Science* 179 (1973): 250; E. Schur, *Labeling Deviant Behavior: Its Sociological Implications* (New York: Harper & Row, 1971); T.S. Szasz, *The Myth of Mental Illness: Foundations of a Theory of Personal Conduct* (New York: Hoeber–Harper, 1961).

14. J.N. Murphy, "Psychiatric Labeling in Cross-Cultural Perspective," *Science* 191 (1976): 1019.

15. W. Dunham, *Community and Schizophrenia: An Epidemiological Analysis* (Detroit: Wayne State Univ. Press, 1965), 18, 19.

16. A.E. Slaby and L.R. Tancredi, *Collusion for Conformity* (New York: Jason Aronson, 1975).

17. T.S. Szasz, "The Problem of Psychiatric Nosology—A Contribution to a Situational Analysis of Psychiatric Operations," *American Journal of Psychiatry* 114: (1957): 405.

18. C.R. Lake, D.E. Sternberg, D.P. Van Kammen et al., "Schizophrenia: Elevated Cerebrospinal Fluid Norepinephrine," *Science* 217 (1980): 331.

19. A.E. Slaby, L.R. Tancredi, and J. Lieb, *Clinical Psychiatric Medicine* (New York: Harper & Row, 1981).

20. S.N. Antelman, A.J. Eichler, C.A. Black et al., "Interchangeability of Stress and Amphetamine in Sensitization," *Science* 207 (1980): 329.

21. M. Siegler, H. Osmond, and H. Mann, "Laing's Models of Madness," *British Journal of Psychiatry* 115 (1969): 947. See also M. Siegler and H. Osmond, *Models of Madness, Models of Medicine* (New York: Harper & Row, 1976).

22. J. Rickman, ed., *A General Selection of the Works of Sigmund Freud* (Garden City, N.Y.: Doubleday, 1957).

23. A.M. Freedman, H.I. Kaplan, and B.J. Sadock, *Comprehensive Textbook of Psychiatry* (2d ed.), vol. 1 (Baltimore: Williams, Wilkins, 1975), 64–65.

24. A.E. Slaby and L.R. Tancredi, *Collusion for Conformity* (New York: Jason Aronson, 1975), 33 ff.

25. M. Foucault, *The Order of Things* (New York: Pantheon, 1970). See also M. Foucault, *The Archeology of Knowledge* (New York: Pantheon, 1969).

26. D.L. Norton, *Personal Destiny: A Philosophy of Ethical Individualism* (Princeton, N.J.: Princeton Univ. Press, 1976), 16 ff., 158 ff.

27. A.H. Maslow, *Toward a Psychology of Being* (New York: Van Nostrand, 1962).

28. Virginia Woolf, *Moments of Being,* ed. J. Schulkind (New York: Harcourt, Brace & Jovanovich, 1976), 12 ff., 73 ff.

29. See L.R. Tancredi, "The Right To Refuse Psychiatric Treatment: Some Legal and Ethical Considerations," *Journal of Health Politics, Policy and Law* 5 (1980): 514.

30. A. Zitrin, A.S. Hardesty, E.I. Burdock et al., "Crime and Violence among Mental Patients," *American Journal of Psychiatry* 133 (1976): 142.

31. See J.R. Durbin, R.A. Pasewark, and D. Albers, "Criminality and Mental Illness: A Study of Arrest Rates in a Rural State," *American Journal of Psychiatry* 134 (1977): 1.

32. J.G. Gunderson and L.R. Mosher, "The Cost of Schizophrenia," *American Journal of Psychiatry* 132 (1975): 901.

16

Psychosomatic Illness in the Chinese Cultural Context

Jen-Yi Wang

Recent visitors to China have reported that the incidence of mental illness in the country is extremely small (Sidel and Sidel 1973). Indeed, for many years, the Western stereotype of the Chinese has been that of a calm, self-restrained, and even phlegmatic people (Veith 1955). This characterization neatly fits the so-called Apollonian type, but it is an assumption not to remain unquestioned. What makes the Chinese relatively less prone to mental illness than others? Does Chinese culture provide people with more adaptive strategies? Or have mental problems been disguised for outsiders, and expressions of mental illness been interpreted as purely physical problems?

Some of the recent studies by both Chinese and Western psychiatrists have focused on psychosomatic symptoms among the Chinese (Tseng 1975, Kleinman 1977, 1980). It was found that many Chinese are inclined to somatize their psychological problems and to express them through physiological disorders. Not purporting to exclude other possibilities, the following discussion will center around the psychosomatic phenomenon of the Chinese people and will show how the culture interacts with the social structure to influence ideas and behavior relative to mental disorders.

The Chinese have long believed in the relation between one's mood and physiological state. A study of Chinese classic novels explicitly demonstrates the belief that strong emotion always leads people to sicken or to die. The following sentences from one of the most famous classic novels, *All Men Are Brothers*, written in the sixteenth century, are typical:

> He was so angry that several times he fainted from his anger. . . . His anger has risen so that he is ill of it and lies upon his bed, and his life cannot be long assured. . . . "Today I am killed by anger"—and when he had finished speaking he let his soul go free [Klineberg 1938].

298

Not only anger, grief, sorrow, and regret may lead people to sicken or die. In classic love stories lovers are always sick because they miss each other; once they are heart-broken, they die very soon. These themes of sickness and death appear repeatedly. In the Ching Dynasty, the great novelist Tsao Sheh-ching (曹雪芹), created a female figure who, in his work *The Dream of the Red Chamber,* has influenced generations of Chinese. The girl in the story has a very sensitive nature; she is smart, but also narrow-minded. Ever angry at others for unimportant matters, and innately weak, she is always sick. As in other love stories, as soon as she knows that her lover has to obey his parents' order to marry another girl, she dies. Many Chinese view her with great admiration; for over two centuries, the girl's name is a symbol of all smart, beautiful, and weak women. Sickness here is not a shortcoming; on the contrary, it is a virtue possessed by characters of traditional Chinese beauty. Though the Chinese, influenced by Western ideas, have started to appreciate healthy girls today, it is still common to show fainting caused by grief or even death caused by anger in contemporary television programs or movies in Taiwan.

A study of traditional Chinese medical literature reveals an early awareness of the mind–body relationship and a profound understanding of psychosomatic medicine (Veith 1955). One example can be drawn from the diagnosis made by a doctor for another woman in *The Dream of the Red Chamber,* which shows that the patient's sickness is caused by worry. Her anxiety is damaging her spleen[1] and results in the imbalance of *Yin* and *Yang* and five elements (gold, wood, water, fire, earth) in her body. The doctor believes that the patient can be cured by medicine. Interestingly, although Chinese traditional doctors are aware of the relationship between affective problems and illness, they treat the mental illness by the same methods used to combat physiological sickness. Therefore, in one Chinese acupuncture book the writer claims that even mental illness and neurasthenia, which are caused by affective disorders, can be treated by acupuncture (Chuang 1972). Even now, mental hospitals in China use traditional Chinese medicine and acupuncture in addition to all Western psychiatric methods.

One might argue that perhaps physiological causes are implicated in mental disorders. Freud refrained from generalizing too widely from his observations because of his uncertainty about the extent of the constitutional or somatic component in melancholia (Mendelson 1960). Cannon (1974) conjectured that underlying such conscious feelings there may be actual physiological disturbance, as exemplified in voodoo death, or that the physiological patterns of people with and without psychiatric symptoms may be different. However, the "twin studies" that focus on heredity in affective disorders do not exclude the significance of environmental factors (Price 1968). Among these factors, cultural influence plays a significant role.

Chinese Responses to Illness

In Chinese cases, many people have a strong fantasy about their illness. Although they are totally well, they deeply believe that they are sick, and ask doctors to do all sorts of check-ups for them (see Appendix, case 7 [Tseng 1975] and case 4

[Kleinman 1980]. On the other hand, we find that the family members of patients with major mental illness have a strong tendency to deny the fact. They either keep patients at home for prolonged periods[2] or take them to visit physicians (Lin et al. 1978). Many studies suggest that the severe stigma attached to mental illness by the Chinese may be responsible for this duality (Lin et al. 1978, Kleinman 1980). This kind of denial occurs not only with major mental illness, but also with minor emotional problems. In one study 70 percent of the patients who were later documented as suffering from mental illness initially presented to the psychiatry clinic at the National Taiwan University Hospital with somatic complaints (Tseng 1975). Another study carried out in the same clinic found that among 25 patients with the depressive syndrome,[3] 88 percent initially complained only of somatic complaints. Contrasted with this, among a parallel group of 25 patients assembled at the Massachusetts General Hospital, only 4 percent of 25 depressive patients presented somatic complaints in the absence of dysphoric affect, whereas 16 percent reported somatic complaints along with dysphoric affect as their chief complaint (Kleinman 1977). Li's survey of the shrines of Taiwanese shamans also shows that, of the 126 clients who visited for physiological illness, 65 percent had psychophysical problems (Li 1972). All these studies demonstrate clearly that Chinese people are inclined to express their mental problems in a physiological way. Kleinman has noticed that it is extremely difficult to elicit personal ideas and feelings from the Chinese, because they reduce the intensity of anxiety, depression, fears, and the like, by keeping them undifferentiated in language. However, he thinks that the vagueness in expression is a socially legitimized and usually "un-self-conscious" cognitive mechanism for coping with disordered or difficult emotions, which "function[s] to reduce or entirely block introspection as well as direct expression" (Kleinman 1980). I do not agree that indirect expression arises primarily from "un-self-conscious" mechanisms, but rather from social relationships or culturally shared attitudes that "consciously" hinder people from direct expression of their affective problems.

We now focus on the various reasons for the Chinese practice of manifesting their mental problems as physical problems. First let us define our range of discussion. Since depression, neurosis, hysteria, schizophrenia, etc., are all psychopathological terms used by Western psychiatrists, and since the Chinese do not classify mental problems in such detail, I will use here the more general term "affective disorder" to include all sorts of mental problems of the Chinese people, ranging from non-psychopathological, emotional disorders to major mental illness. All of these share a common feature: they are masked by physiological complaints and are hardly accepted as purely psychological problems by the people. Although some people are conscious of the possible relations between their affective and somatic problems, most of them are not.

Child-Rearing Practices

Findings from studies of Chinese child rearing are helpful to our discussion. The Chinese pattern of socialization is characterized by oral indulgence, interdependence and lack of privacy in bowel training, emotional control, and respect for authority; the early years are also marked by indulgence as compared to the strict disciplining that begins at school age. Generally speaking, the birth of a child, especially a male, is cause for much satisfaction and celebration in a Chinese household. Parental cares and anxieties about the survival of their offspring are expressed in oral indulgence, "for liberal feeding is about the only recourse beyond prayer that exists for a people with pre-modern notions about medicine and hygiene" (Solomon 1971). As soon as the child cries, Chinese parents give him food. Solomon (1971) suggests that the considerable indulgence in infancy and early childhood, and the affection expressed through the giving of food, "seem to be the basis of an 'oral calculus' in the way that Chinese approach interpersonal relations throughout life" (p. 42). This "oral calculus" might be related to the Chinese liking for medicinal tonics and their tendency to somatize psychological problems and treat them with medicine (Tseng 1972).

Chinese culture does not emphasize traits of cleanliness, order, and punctuality, which are seen by Freudian psychologists as proceeding from strict bowel training. On the contrary, Chinese parents are rather permissive about toilet training. They take care of a child's eliminative activity for him/her before a child can walk by anticipating his/her needs and encouraging movement through whistling. Later on, little children are often seen wearing bottomless trousers. Solomon thinks that because elimination is such a "public" function (the child has a bowel movement with the help of an adult or older sibling), failure to perform properly creates anxieties about the child's relation to the adult or sibling who was helping. One develops a sense of the interdependent quality of even the most personal activities, and, with it, a basic concern for how one performs before others, a sensitivity to shame (Solomon 1971). The interdependent relationship exists not only between parents and children, but also between close friends. Moreover, sensitivity to shame partly accounts for the powerful force of conformity in Chinese culture. The studies of both Solomon and Wolf, conducted primarily in different social classes[4] among the Chinese people, suggest that there is considerable reserve in the expression of affection between parents and children (Solomon 1971; Wolf 1970). Parental models from which children learn tell them that inner feelings are not to be expressed, except in highly guarded ways, and that, in public, emotions should be masked behind the forms of propriety. Teasing and bullying also teach the child the virtue of defense through emotional impassivity. Therefore, to a Chinese, an important aspect of social identity is self-discipline. A person must exercise self-control, especially of the emotions. This restraint of feelings is even more important than improper behavior, especially where one has been taught to depend on external authority for guidance as to what is correct or incorrect behavior (Solomon 1971). Thus, direct expression of strong feelings is seen as rude and disgraceful. This explains the serene quality found in classic Chinese painting and music. Furthermore, due to the cultural stress on emotional control, Chinese children gradually learn to be sensitive to the feelings of others and to be sophisticated in expressing their own. If the child fails to learn this, troubles arise from neglecting others' "real" feelings behind their mask.

When a child, particularly a male child, reaches school age, he encounters an abrupt change in treatment. The years of indulgence are all over; now parents start to see him as reasonable, and harshly demand good school performance from him (Solomon 1971, Wolf 1970). Solomon believes that the tension between the indulgence of infancy and the subsequent harsh discipline of youth creates the contradiction between individual and group life. The attitudes of strong self-esteem and self-worth developed in early oral gratification run counter to the parental goals of developing in their children a strong commitment to the purposes of the family group.

In the foregoing paragraphs, we have briefly discussed the relation between Chinese child training and the Chinese personality. The "oral calculus" and the stress on emotional control might be associated at an unconscious level with the psychosomatic phenomena in our discussion. However, besides the more individual experiences we have also seen the emphasis on nonprivacy, interdependence, and group conformity. The following discussion of the Chinese social structure will provide us with another dimension in understanding the forces that play upon the Chinese early in their experience, and that lead most Chinese to conform, consciously or subconsciously, to their social norms.

Social Structure

The Chinese anthropologist Hsu has suggested the concepts of psychological homeostasis and the Chinese idea of *jen* as complementary tools for understanding "personality." Because the idea of personality is a Western concept rooted in individualism and stressing what goes on in the individual's psyche, the word has obscured the understanding of the human being's relationships with others. However, the word *jen,* or personage, puts emphasis on interpersonal transactions. It sees the nature of the individual's external behavior in terms of how it fits or fails to fit the interpersonal standards of the society and culture (Hsu 1971). In nonindividualistic societies, the proportion of one's characteristics that comes out of social pressure might be no smaller than that of early child experience. Therefore, individual behavior is greatly influenced by status and role.

Familism

One of the significant features of Chinese social structure is familism, i.e., the individuals' places in life are closely associated with parents, siblings, and relatives. Therefore, most of the social ethic centers around how to be a child, a sibling, or a parent. The pattern of father–son interaction is the basic model for others, and it also extends to the relationship between superiors and inferiors in the political sphere. However, outside the primary family, the boundaries of one's kin group and other social groups are vague. All behavioral norms for the interactions in this vague area are based on personal relationship, namely, what degree of closeness is

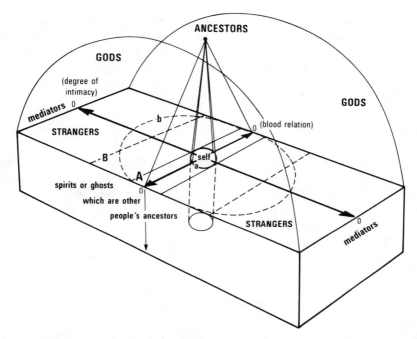

Fig. 16.1. "Heaven Is Round; Earth Is Square"

established between two individuals. Therefore, interpersonal transactions are guided not by absolute rights and privileges, but by reference to the relative intimacy of the parties. It has been suggested that the social network in Chinese society is like concentric circles[5] with oneself in the center. Beyond the primary kin group, social relationships are very flexible. Thus, for the Chinese the only concrete and controllable moral entity is the self (Fei 1948). From this point of view, the significance of self-control and self-cultivation in Chinese society can be better understood. Figure 16.1 is a diagram of the basic social network of a Chinese individual as a guide for interpersonal transactions. In Figure 16.1, Circle A represents the primary family; Circle B represents the kin group; Rectangle A represents close friends (sometimes treated as fictive kin); Rectangle B represents friends. Except for Circle A, which has a firm boundary, all the boundaries of the groups are flexible.

Kleinman has noticed correctly that ideas and feelings of the Chinese are frequently divided into those held to be superficial and public and those held to be deep and private (Kleinman 1980). As to the former, society demands that individuals act properly according to their social status; as to the latter, they are carefully controlled and revealed only to the most intimate friends. Social status not only defines one's public conduct, but one's emotions as well. Hence in the classic *Book of Filial Piety,* one reads, ". . . . when they [parents] are ill, he [the filial son] feels the greatest anxiety; in mourning for them, he exhibits every demonstration of grief; in sacrificing to them, he displays the utmost solemnity" (Veith 1955). In contemporary Taiwan, we can still find those who hire crying professionals for their parent's funeral and amplify the cries through speakers to exhibit their deep grief.

Self-Control in Chinese Morality

The foregoing discussion on socialization practices and Chinese social structure have led us to the focus of emotional self-control, which has been one of the basic moral criteria for thousands of years. Although we are not clear about the origin of the emphasis, the central ideas of the great Chinese tradition, Confucianism, can be seen as being fostered in the same cultural background, interacting with the folk tradition[6] and enhancing what the folk culture stresses. Therefore, a discussion of the Confucian concept of human nature will elucidate further the reason why self-training and emotional control are emphasized.

Confucius had an idea that men are by nature alike; but they grow wide apart in their actions. He did not explicitly talk much about human nature, but he admitted that both hunger and sex are inherent in human nature (Analects). Later on, the argument about human nature was raised between two main Confucian philosophers. Mencius asserted that human nature is essentially good, because human beings have an innate sympathy, which drives people to be humane. Hsun Tzu declared that all human beings are born greedy, jealous, hateful, and lustful, so that life is full of competition, cheating, distrust, and debauchery (Tseng 1975).

Starting from different premises, Mencius held that people should cultivate and develop the good aspects in their nature, whereas Hsun Tzu advocated that they should repress their inborn evil by propriety and music. Most of the later advocates of Confucius followed Mencius' thinking; therefore, for centuries the most popular book of enlightenment starts with the sentence: "In the beginning of life, all men are by nature good. It is the practice that makes people who are naturally alike apart" (*Book of Three-Words*). Probably because of this book, many scholars have claimed that the Chinese believe human nature to be good (Weber 1951, Hu 1944, F.L.K. Hsu 1971.) However, one point should be clarified. Mencius did not deny the powerful evil part, nor did Hsun Tzu deny the subtle good part, of human nature. Classic studies show that their disagreement is based more on the emphasis of each on the good and the bad, than on the quality. Both admitted the good and evil features in human nature[7] and, most importantly, both stressed the significance of emotional control and self-cultivation to remove the evil from human nature and to maintain the "supreme harmony." Therefore, instead of further analyzing human nature, traditional Chinese scholars worked on how to practice the inner *kung-fu* of the mind by self-cultivation. "For the Confucian ideal man, the gentleman, 'grace and dignity' were expressed in fulfilling traditional obligations. The appropriate means of this goal were watchful and rational self-control and the repression of whatever irrational passions might cause poise to be shaken" (Weber 1951). Fulfillment of obligation to parents is still highly valued by the Chinese. Besides being morally filial to one's parents, the child should strive to achieve the parents' expectations and try one's best to honor them. De Vos's (1967) discussion on the relation between guilt and obligations toward parents among the Japanese can well be applied to the Chinese. Guilt feelings and shame feelings are more like the ends of a spectrum than a dichotomy. It is likely that the spectrum corresponds to the self-centered, concentric-circled social network. Only toward the most intimate family members can one feel guilt.[8]

Failure of Self-Control

What happens if one reveals affective problems to others? First, if the problem stems from an interpersonal relationship, it implies a moral weakness; i.e., the person has failed in self-cultivation, or, if the conflict is between family members, there is no harmony in the family. Second, if the problem arises from the relation between a man and his affairs, it implies that the person may be incapable of solving problems and that his ability to fulfill family obligations is questioned. All these implications bring shame to him or even increase his guilt toward his parents. Therefore he would rather hide his personal problems, in conformity with the Chinese saying, "Do not let out the ugly things of your family."

Many cases in Tseng's and in Kleinman's studies reveal that those with psychosomatic disturbances have talked about their problems only to their closest friends. (Tseng 1975:241, Kleinman 1980: cases 5 and 6). It is possible that the sense of shame and the behavioral rule of acting towards others according to one's intimacy to another prevents people from expressing their inner problems freely, even when they are in the presence of the Western-trained psychiatrist. This might account for the "heart-to-heart talks" reported to be the most significant method of psychiatry in China. "We were told that the most important form of treatment is the relationship between the psychiatrist and the patient" (Sidel and Sidel 1973).

Causes of Mental Illness Distinct from Physical Illness

With this understanding, we can turn to the Chinese concept of the individual's responsibility for getting sick. In traditional medicine, most physiological sickness is thought to be caused by a disequilibrium of *Yin* and *Yang*. For example, the disequilibrium of *Yin* and *Yang* in nature may result in wind, which causes headache, apoplexy, and dizziness; or cold, which causes cough, heartache, and stomachache; or hot, dry, wet, and so forth. Besides these causes, moral transgressions, attacks by spirits, and punishment by the gods or ancestors for wrongdoing are also cited (Morse 1934, Veith 1955, Gallin 1974). In modern times, there is a wide acceptance of Western scientific knowledge, and people easily find all sorts of reasons for their illnesses. However, relative to the broad range of explanations on physiological illness, the Chinese seem to put most of the responsibility for psychological trouble on the individual. Because the culture demands self-control, if a person fails in this, and thus develops psychological troubles, no one can really help except the person involved. That probably explains why traditional Chinese doctors do not treat the patient's psychologicl illness directly, but rather treat the physiological disorder which they realize might be related to the mental disorder. On the other hand, in cases of severe mental illness, blame might come to other family members. People may suspect that the illness is caused by harsh treatment by the patient's family members, or, at the folk level, by the gods or ancestors, as punishment for wrongdoing. All these ideas might contribute to the stigma attached to mental illness by the Chinese people.

Some studies have focused on traditional psychiatry in Chinese culture (Tseng 1974, J. Hsu 1974, Li 1972.) Tseng listed them as shamanism, drawing *chien* (signs engraved on bamboo strips) in the temples for divination, fortune-telling, and physiognomy (Tseng 1974). One interesting finding is that the biographical sketches of a Chinese traditional doctor show that geomancy, physiognomy, palmistry, and oracular consultations with the *I–Chin* (*Book of Change*) were all included in his professional training (Chuang 1972). *Book of Change* is one of the seven classic books arranged by Confucius. In traditional times, some elites were capable of learning from the book how to do the divination for themselves through a highly complicated manipulation of linear symbols. Confucius learned it in his late life, when he was very frustrated by his political encounters. It seems that the oracular consolation found in the book is the traditional way for Chinese elites to handle their own psychological problems. The philosophical basis of *I–Chin* is *Yin* and *Yang;* therefore it matches well with the rational Chinese elites' idea of an unknowable, nonanthropomorphic cosmology.

Although fewer educated people learn *Book of Change* in contemporary society, other methods of divination have not fallen into disrepute. On the contrary, people still go to fortune-tellers for instructions, and increasingly ornate temples are being built in Taiwan.

By analyzing traditional Chinese modes of psychiatry in terms of interpersonal relationships, we may gain insight into the question under discussion. In most cases, shamans, fortune-tellers, physiognomists, and *chien* interpreters are not acquainted with their clients. Rather, the relationship is usually one of strangers. Consulting these specialists on personal questions thus avoids shame and embarassment. Besides, all of them are mediators between humanity and supernatural beings; hence they should know and give instructions on people's problems without any intimate relationship.

Although the popular concept of mental problems implies that human beings are responsible for their sicknesses, most of the divination attributes causes to nonhuman sources, such as bad luck, attacks by spirits, ancestors' anger, etc. Nonetheless, these supernatural mediators always provide advice on how to act and how to change one's own temper. As a Chinese psychiatrist said, "It (*chien*-drawing) encourages a person to do as much as he can to improve his life; however, it puts the final responsibility on Heaven. So if the person fails and becomes depressed (the time when he would most likely go to the temple), divination puts the responsibility for failure on Heaven, and thus the person can better accept the frustration with less damage to his self-esteem" (Hsu 1974). Traditional psychiatry not only transfers the responsibility for mental problems to a more acceptable source, but actively tells people how to deal with their troubles.

To summarize, the Chinese postulate more sources for physiological illness, and the early oral indulgence might be unconsciously associated with a fondness for taking medicines. Taoism also reveals a strong tendency for people to seek immortality through magical potions. All kinds of advertisements for tonic medicines appear in the newspapers in present-day Taiwan. The traditional image of the student as the "white-faced scholar,"—elegant, gentle, and nonmuscular—remains undimmed in the popular minds.

In terms of sick role, physiological sickness is the legitimate occasion for people to show affection. One of the typical ways for Taiwanese elementary students to describe how their mothers love them is to say that, "When I am sick, my mother is very worried; she takes care of me day and night." It is always during one's sickness that one receives expressed concern and sympathy from others.

Therefore, when people discover that their social obligations are too hard to bear, some unconsciously escape to avoid their obligation (Tseng 1975,: cases 2, 3, and 8; Kleinman 1980: case 4, are all examples; see Appendix I). Physiological illness can also be a severe protest used by an indignant person, much like suicide. Since someone could be blamed for treating him badly and causing the illness, the sick man succeeds in silently making his charge by being sick (Tseng 1975: cases 4 and 7 illustrate this point very well). As Leites points out in his article on violence in China, "It is not far from hurting another to harming oneself" (Leites 1977). In addition, displacement is another function of psychosomatic symptoms. When some people are undergoing severe psychic conflicts, which are not acceptable to themselves, they displace them by somatization in order to disguise the real problems. (For example, Tseng 1975: cases 1, 5, 6; Kleinman 1980: case 6, also p. 158).

Summary

In the foregoing discussion, we have seen from three perspectives how Chinese culture gives meaning to experience and influences the handling of affective disorders. The characteristics of socialization, the Chinese social structure, and shared ideas all contribute to our understanding of the psychosomatic phenomena. Because of the impact of Western culture and the force of modernization, traditional Chinese methods of socialization and the indigenous social structure are undergoing drastic changes. However, the basic ideas about human nature have persisted, interacting with other dimensions of Chinese culture and functioning as a filter for foreign culture. Thus, the emphases on emotional control and self-cultivation, carried by all three dimensions, play significant roles in channeling the Chinese's affective experience.

APPENDIX

The following cases are from Tseng (1975) and Kleinman (1980).

A. Psychosomatic Illness as an Excuse To Get Away from an Excess or Undesirable
   Obligation

Case 1.   Mr. Chen, an 18-year-old high school student, visited the psychiatric
clinic complaining of dizziness, poor memory, and difficulty in concentration for
the previous 6 months. He requested a "brain wave examination" for his "worn-out
brain."

History revealed that the patient was the eldest son of a well-to-do family, who
was expected by his family to go to college after graduation from high school. The
entrance examination for college in Taiwan is so difficult and competitive that he
knew well that it would not be easy for him to pass the examination unless he
studied extraordinarily hard. Under such pressure he studied day and night, but
the more he studied the more he found it difficult to learn anything. Finally he
began to experience dizziness, poor memory, and difficulty in concentration, which
worried him a lot. Since, according to what he was told by a herb doctor, these
symptoms are signs of a "worn-out brain," the brain is in need of a rest and "brain
tonic" for recovery. His consultation at the psychiatric clinic ("brain hospital") was
therefore to find out his brain problem, rather than how to deal with his pressures.
With such an orientation he presented his "brain" symptoms and consequently was
only anxious to have a brain-wave examination (Tseng: case 2).

Case 2.   Mrs. Liu, a 28-year-old housewife and bank teller, visited the University
Psychiatric Clinic presenting her problems of "pain over shoulders, easy tiredness,
and insomnia" for about 2 months. In addition to medicine for her symptoms, she
asked for medical certification, as she felt that she needed to take a rest at home
for a short period of time. She explained that she and her husband were living
together with her husband's parents' extended family. Two months ago her father-
in-law had an attack of apoplexy and had been confined to bed since then. She, as
the eldest daugher-in-law, had to take care of him in the evening even though she
worked at the bank during the day. Being overburdened by such daily work, but
with no way to avoid the present situation, she felt unhappy and became irritable.
Frequently she quarreled with her husband and gave her children a difficult time.

The patient visited the psychiatric clinic to complain about her somatic discomfort, since it was a socially accepted way for her to obtain relief from her difficult
situation. She explained that she dared not complain to anybody that she could not
take such a great burden or cope with such responsibility. If she did she would no
doubt be criticized as a vulnerable person, and not filial to her parents-in-law, etc.
It would be much safer for her to complain of somatic illness, since somatic illness
is considered something beyond her own control and is really in need of special
consideration (Tseng: case 3).

Case 3. Mr. Sung, an 18-year-old man, was brought by his mother to the psychiatric clinic seeking a clinical evaluation and medical certificate excluding him from the draft. This thin and pale looking young man presented multiple somatic symptoms of dizziness, lumbago, abdominal discomfort, etc., even though all his physical checkups in the past had been negative.

The patient's mother insisted that her son was really physically weak and unable to tolerate life in the Army. According to her, her boy was born weak, and easily caught cold as an infant. In spite of her protective care he suffered frequently from illness. When he first began to go to school she asked the teacher to excuse him from classes in physical education, as she felt that he was too weak to attend such classes. The boy would use any slight discomfort as an excuse to avoid examinations and thus he was asked finally to leave the school before he finished the sixth grade.

When advised by his father to work in a factory he began to complain of many somatic symptoms such as back pain, dizziness, chest pain, etc., for which he would consult the herb doctor as well as the Western doctor for medication and treatment.

Now that he was 18 years old he was eligible for 3 years service in the Army. This worried both the patient himself and his mother very much since both of them believed that life in the Army would torture the patient. Accompanied by his mother, he visited several hospitals and clinics for physical checkups, hoping that some physical ailment would be detected that would prevent his being drafted. However, all the examinations revealed that he was physically sound. Therefore he and his mother finally followed the doctor's advice and requested a psychiatric evaluation (Tseng: case 8).

Case 4. Mr. Wang is a 26-year-old unmarried Taiwanese male, a government telegraph operator and night student in a junior college, who complains of dryness of throat of more than one year's duration. He has been to Western-style and Chinese-style doctors for his complaint without any relief. Recently he was referred by the Ear, Nose and Throat Clinic at National Taiwan University Hospital to that hospital's Psychiatry Clinic because his physical examination, x-rays, and blood tests have disclosed no abnormalities. Mr. Wang notes his chief symptom either begins or worsens when he is psychologically upset. But it is his physical symptom, not his psychological problems, that worries him. He is preoccupied by this complaint. He blames it for difficulty studying, poor school performance, lack of close friends, and family problems. It embarrasses him. He does not like to socialize with peers, date girls, or talk with others because of this problem. It makes him feel inferior to others and also leads him to fear losing face.

Besides this symptom, he reports insomnia with early morning wakening, weight loss, and periodic bouts of dizziness, rapid heart rate, sweating, and tremor of hands when he is under stress. In addition to these physical complaints, he reports some psychological complaints, which he feels are unrelated to the physical problems, including low self-esteem, feelings of shame and guilt, frustration with his job and schooling, chronic tension, and periodic feelings of sadness, hopelessness, and helplessness.

The third of six sibs, he is the only one who has not done well in school and who is neither in a profession nor studying to enter one. His academic performance has been so poor that he knows he cannot get his college degree, but he keeps attending classes because he fears his family will be ashamed of him and reject him if he cannot complete his studies successfully. He feels constantly frustrated, faced by an untenable situation that he declares "cannot change." He already believes that his parents and sibs look down on him, and he fears they don't really care about him. But he does not relate his personal and family problems to his physical complaints. Even though he recognizes that as the former worsen, the latter also become more severe, he rejects a psychophysiological explanation. When the dryness in his throat is most severe he thinks of nothing else but this "physical" problem. At such times, he worries continually about whether or not he can be cured.

On examination Mr. Wang is a thin Chinese male, appearing quite anxious. His speech reveals a partial impediment: he frequently uses the sound "ong," which he describes as a meaningless habit and which increases in frequency and loudness as he becomes anxious and feels under stress. Whenever he is asked to define or express his feelings or to talk about his school and family problems, he hesitates for long periods of time, looking off in space with tears in his eyes and repeating this same sound. The rest of his mental status exam is remarkable only for the feelings of sadness, hopelessness, and helplessness he reports. There are no delusions, hallucinations, evidence of thought disorder, phobias, or paranoid ideas. He has little insight into his problem and is able to characterize his feelings only with great difficulty and after receiving considerable help from the psychiatrist, who has to constantly prevent him from jumping directly from labeling his feelings "upset," in vague terms like *hsin-ching pu-hao,* to talking about his physical symptoms or social problems.

Psychiatric evaluation led to a diagnosis of mixed anxiety-depression syndrome with somatization and serious family and school problems. The patient rejected this diagnosis, refused to return to the Psychiatry Clinic, and discontinued his medication (a minor tranquilizer and an anti-depressant) after several days (an inadequate course of therapy) because of no symptomatic relief (Kleinman: case 4).

B. Psychosomatic Illness as a Way of Protest

Case 5.   Mrs. Wei, a 50-year-old housewife, was brought to the psychiatric clinic by her husband. She complained of fatigue, poor appetite, emaciation, and insomnia. According to her husband she developed these symptoms several weeks previously when their son, against their advice and their attempts to interrupt it, decided to go abroad for study and left immediately. The patient was very angry and upset, as she felt that her son had deserted them. She very soon became depressed, experiencing the symptoms just described.

When asked why she did not more directly present her problems of depression and anger over her son's leaving, and instead complained about her somatic symptoms of fatigue, poor appetite, etc., she explained that she wanted to let every one know how much she was hurt by her son through such suffering from (somatic) illness. According to her it was not serious to become depressed when someone in the family has "deserted." But if she were so depressed as to suffer from a physical illness, it signified the gravity of the hurt. By way of her somatic symptoms and complaints she was actually successful in obtaining others' sympathy toward her: her husband wrote a letter to their son abroad informing him that his mother was seriously (physically) ill, and the guilty son was finally urged to give up his study and return home (Tseng: case 4).

Case 6.   Mrs. Chen, a 50-year-old woman and mother of 3 children, was brought into the University Psychiatric Clinic via the Emergency Clinic, with the chief complaint of palpitation and "weak heart." Physical examination in the Emergency Room by an internist revealed no particular physical problems, but she was referred for psychiatric evaluation. When brought to the Psychiatric Outpatient Clinic she was escorted by her two daughters and one son-in-law. When the patient was interviewed it was not only she herself who complained of palpitation, but her daughters were also anxiously concerned about this. One of her daughters inquired anxiously whether there was any possibility that her mother might have "heart disease," since she looked so weak. The other daughter meanwhile asked about the danger of apoplexy. In addition the son-in-law assured the doctor that there was no need to worry about fees as he could afford to pay for whatever was necessary to provide the best medicine for his mother-in-law's heart problems.
    After taking some time to calm the whole family, the psychiatrist then began to inquire how the patient first started to suffer from palpitation. She said that it first started the night before her visit to the emergency room, when she accidentally discovered that her husband had secretly been spending a large amount of money fooling around with a mistress. Obviously the patient was manifesting such somatic symptoms as a way of showing her anger toward her husband, and at the same time obtaining attention from her family (Tseng: case 7).

C. Psychosomatic Illness as a Displacement of Deep, Unacceptable Psychic Conflicts*

Case 7.   Somatization may involve several family members or an entire family. For example, one lower-middle-class Taiwanese family I studied in Taipei complained of backache affecting all the family members when they visited a shaman. This was perceived by each individual as something attached to their backs and experienced by them as a heavy weight or "burden." One month before a daughter-in-law had died in a motorcycle accident which the family feared might have been a suicide. The family members held deeply ambivalent feelings about the dead woman. She had been discovered stealing money from the family business, which she sent to her father and brothers, and subsequently had quarrelled repeatedly with her in-laws, demanding that her husband leave and take with him his share of the business. On several occasions she had threatened suicide, saying that if she and

*Most of these cases are associated with strong guilt feelings.

her husband were thwarted her ghost would haunt the family in revenge. After her death the family became terrified that her ghost would "attack" them. They also feared the retribution of the dead woman's father, who was believed to possess knowledge of sorcery. During the period of mourning, the symptom of backache was experienced by each member of the family. They did not complain of the terror they experienced, their ambivalent feelings, or their acute grief. The backache substituted for these problems. It isolated the family's distress, strengthened family bonds, and sanctioned their desire for help. The shaman treated them in part with exorcistic rituals to drive away the ghost, but also reassured them about their fears (Kleinman: p. 158).

Case 8.   Mr. Yeh, a 48-year-old veteran soldier, visited the University Psychiatric Clinic with the chief complaint of a "cold sensation over the body, and frequent attacks of palpitation and anxiety" for almost 1 year. He had migrated to Taiwan from Mainland China when young. He is not married and has no close friends or relatives. As an old soldier, he depends entirely upon the army for financial as well as psychological support. He had visited an herb doctor once and was given an herb to "raise his body temperature," but in vain. Later, he consulted internists several times and was treated for "common cold" for his symptoms of chills. As there was no improvement he was referred for psychiatric evaluation.

During the first session of diagnostic interview, when asked how he developed the somatic symptoms of chills and palpitation, he brought from his pocket a piece of paper to show the doctor certain information. On the paper, entitled "Self-analysis of the cause of illness," he reported that he had been saving money for several years for his future security, particularly for life after his retirement. Every month when he got his payment and went to the bank to deposit money in savings he would become tense and anxious without knowing why. It was one year ago when he was on his way to the bank that he met one of his friends in the street. His friend teased him, saying that no matter how much money he had saved it would be no use if he became sick. As a response to such alarming comments he immediately developed the cold sensation over his whole body, with palpitation and anxiety. Since then he has suffered periodically from such symptoms. At the end of the paper he concluded by speculating that "My illness might be related to my constant worry over the possibility of losing my money."

Surprised by the patient's own insightful interpretation of his illness, the psychiatrist asked why he had not complained about the part concerning his emotional problem, i.e., worrying about losing his money as he described in his report, and why he instead complained only of somatic symptoms. He explained that according to his knowledge, every person has emotional problems; therefore, he had not thought that he should consider this as a "problem." He was concerned about his somatic symptoms of cold sensation primarily because, according to his knowledge of Chinese medicine, this is a serious sign of weakness—an indication of deficiency of *Yang,* the male element—and requires urgent care (Tseng: case 1).

Case 9.   Miss Lo, a 26-year-old college-graduate–secretary, visited a psychiatric clinic requesting psychotherapy for her problems. She complained that she had many problems and was in need of psychiatric help. However, she had difficulty in clearly presenting the problem bothering her. She tended to focus on the somatic symptoms she had, i.e., the feeling of trembling of her hands. This attractive and intelligent patient kept being concerned with her somatic problems for several sessions, until she was able to reveal that her shakiness would occur whenever she met any man with whom she was acquainted. She described her shaking symptoms as having first begun three years before, when she met one of her previous classmates on the street who, in greeting her, inquired about her recent life and particularly about her marriage.

It took a while for the patient to stop focusing on her mysterious somatic complaints and to begin revealing her actual personal life. The patient's father, a government underground agent, had left home for some place on a special assignment when the patient was twelve. He had not yet returned though he had left 14 years ago. The patient missed her father very much, as he was very fond of her. But there was nothing she could do about it, except to keep hoping that her father would reappear suddenly one day. When she was 18, she became acquainted with one of her father's previous friends, a married man her father's age, with whom she eventually became sexually involved. This involvement with a married man was considered by society as the most disgraceful event that could happen to a young girl. When it was discovered by her mother, she was scolded for her promiscuousness and forced to stop the relationship immediately.

Several years later, when she was 22, she happened to meet another friend of her father's with whom, as before, she could not resist a sexual involvement. Of course, the relationship was again interrupted when it was discovered. However, after the repeated episode, she began to wonder herself why she felt so disgraced by her promiscuous behavior, but, at the same time, still had the uncontrollable desire to do such things—acting as if she were a prostitute.

From her personal history it is easy to understand the nature of the feeling of tremulousness that occurred whenever she was close to any man with whom she got intimately acquainted, with the fear of becoming promiscuously involved again. She was constantly afraid of being discovered by others for her disgraceful personal history. Thus, she developed shaking symptoms when she was asked about her recent personal life by her previous classmate. This also explains why she took so long in being able to work on her emotional problems after focusing on her somatic symptoms during psychiatric treatment (Tseng: case 5).

Case 10.   Mr. Wang, a 34-year-old unmarried man, visited the psychiatric clinic for his obsessive fear of being scratched or bitten by cats. During the initial contact with the psychiatrist he kept worrying about the possibility of being scratched or bitten by a cat without knowing it and asked the psychiatrist to give him a physical check-up again and again. Whenever he found any unusual mark on his skin, or if he experienced any slight discomfort, he complained about it and wondered whether it was caused by the scratch of a cat or not.

After struggling for some time with such obsessive somatic fears and resistances to work on his personal life, he finally revealed the story of the development of his obsessive fears. It was several months prior to his first visit to the psychiatrist that he dropped in on one of his close friends at home. When he got to the house no one answered his knock, but since he found the door open he walked right in. As he looked about the rooms to see if anyone was home, he happened to walk into the bedroom in which his friend's wife was sleeping. He found her lying on the bed clad only in very light pajamas. Surprised and embarrassed by appearing to peep into such a seductive scene, he was about to withdraw from the room when he suddenly stepped over a cat and was bitten by it.

He had been born the only child in a well-to-do family. As a child he was very much protected by his mother and was never allowed to engage in any strenuous activity or to risk any danger. Although very intelligent, he was also very timid. He was not confident about his masculinity, and was not married yet, even though nearing middle age. After the episode of intrusion into the woman's bedroom, and of being bitten by her cat, he developed an excessive fear of being scratched or bitten by cats. For him it was easier to focus his problems in this manner rather than worry directly about the troubling event of intrusion into his friends's privacy (Tseng: case 6).

Case 11.   Mr. Hung is a 60-year-old retired Navy captain from the China mainland, a widower living alone in Taipei. He has suffered from the following constellation of symptoms over the past two years: weakness in all extremities; tremor of hands; unsteadiness of gait; heart palpitations; easy fatigue; profound weight loss; and insomnia. Full medical and neurological work-ups revealed no organic pathology on several occasions. Medical doctors told him he had neurasthenia. Since tranquilizers did not help and since Western-style medical doctors spent very little time talking to him about his problem and led him to believe there was nothing further they could do for his condition, Mr. Hung began visiting the clinic of a noted acupuncturist, a friend who had retired from the Navy. There, over the last six months, he has begun to feel much better with return of strength and appetite, increase in weight, improvement in gait, and greatly improved sleep pattern. He spends three full mornings each week in this Chinese-style doctor's clinic. He receives a half hour of acupuncture therapy and some herb teas each visit and spends the remainder of the morning sitting in the clinic talking with his friend and the patients who come there. He feels that his friend's acupuncture has benefited him, but admits also that his friend has inspired confidence in him, helped him relax, and encouraged him to socialize—things that have been problems for him since the onset of his disorder.

Mr. Hung was in good health upon retiring from the Navy three years ago. However, over the next year, he experienced severe financial reverses in his business ventures that left him without any income other than his small government pension.

These reverses destroyed both his savings and the plans for retirement he had made. He found himself deeply disturbed and ashamed. He felt that he had failed in life and had brought shame on himself and his family. He feared his friends would ridicule him if they knew his plight. He felt unable to express his sadness to anyone. And he began to avoid his friends and his grown children. He experienced his depressive affect as a "pressure" on his head and chest. Whenever he felt sad or wished to cry, he associated his despondent feelings with the somatic sensations. His depression came to mean not the psychological symptoms but the physical ones:

"First the bad financial problem caused my depression on the heart and brain. [He demonstrates this with his hands as a physical pressure, a pressing on heart and brain.] Then that depression pressed further on me causing my nerves to become weak and also my heart to become weak . . . Now I take tonic and get acupuncture to make my heart and brain stronger."

Mr. Hung would tell me he was depressed, but he described that in somatic terms. If I asked him about his personal feelings, he would not tell me anything other than that he was getting better. He mentioned repeatedly that his financial problems caused his sickness (which he believed to be a physical disorder), but if I asked him how this made him feel, tears would come to his eyes, which his facial muscles would strain to hold back, and he would look away for minutes at a time. He told me that these were things that were better not talked about, that he never talked about them with anyone, *even with himself,* that after all they were getting better; then he would politely but firmly introduce another topic. Even after four months, when his depression had largely subsided, Mr. Hung refused to talk about what his feelings had been like. In fact, on one occasion he told me that he himself did not know what they were like since when they came to mind he felt his somatic symptoms greatly worsen and became preoccupied with the latter. He also admitted that he spent most of the time watching television, reading, collecting stamps, or playing card games in order to keep his "mind blank." Keeping his mind blank seemed to him important because he felt his physical symptoms less at such times. Even at the time of my last visit, he could talk about his financial reverses in detail but could not say how they affected him beyond stating they depressed his heart and brain, thereby hurting his nerves and bringing on all of his physical complaints (Kleinman: case 6).

NOTES

1. The Chinese character for "temper" (p'ī-chi) combines the word for "spleen" and "*chi,*" which means "air," "spirits," "morale," or "anger."
2. Veith has argued that filial piety imposes a dual obligation upon the family which keeps Chinese mental patients from being set apart from their accustomed surroundings, and that the architecture of Chinese traditional country houses permits easy seclusion of a disturbed family member (Veith 1955).

Although architecture has changed to Western apartment style today, there are still many

Chinese mental patients hidden at home. However, filial piety is not breached by the admission of physiologically ill family members to the hospital.

3. Kleinman follows Klerman's definition to characterize depressive syndrome as depressive affect, insomnia, weight loss, dry mouth, and an apparently limited number of related psychological complaints (Kleinman 1977).

4. One criticism of Solomon's study is that most of his samples are from middle-class mainlanders' families in cities (Barnouw 1979). However, Wolf did her fieldwork in a small Taiwanese village. All the methods of child training mentioned here appeared in both studies.

5. I revise the concept of concentric circles to a more detailed diagram to explain the basic social structure of traditional Chinese society. See Fig. 16.1.

6. It is a well-known fact that there is some distance between the Chinese elites and the folk culture. But one feature of Chinese society has been social mobility through education. Thus, in the past, if a poor family managed to provide their smartest son with an education, once the man passed official examinations, he became an elite and raised the social class of his family. The line between elites and peasants in traditional Chinese society was based more on education than on economic or blood condition. Therefore, the ideas of the great tradition could find channels to interact with those of the popular tradition. This might explain the reason why Chinese families always put strong emphasis on children's education, and why school performance is seen as the most important way for children to fulfill their obligation and to honor parents. Besides, in contemporary Taiwan, because of compulsory education the distance between elites and peasants has been reduced. In the Chinese great tradition it was not forbidden to the common people to contribute ideas and thoughts.

7. As mentioned before, scholars like Solomon, Tseng, and Hsu—who study the Chinese personality and child-rearing practices from a psychological view—stress the frustration, dissatisfaction, and bitterness in the socialization process. Contrasted to this, a Chinese sociologist's humanistic approach on the Chinese personality focuses on those virtues consciously emphasized in generation after generation: For example, the morally articulated feelings *ching-tsao* (情 操), which were of such concern to Confucians as being able to reduce the anxiety, fear, and grief connected to death, and which could satisfy the desire felt by all civilized people to live a high-level social, cultural, and moral life. The sociologist thinks that the process of submitting to authority was not only painful and frustrating but also involved important feelings of gratification (Yang 1972).

Metzger thinks that the argument originates from different assumptions about behavior. In the psychological approach, the assumption is mainly about one's quest for "direct gratification," that is, survival, appetitive satisfaction, wealth, power, and prestige. In the humanistic approach, emphasis is put on an individual's "basic desires" for "Knowledge of a sense-making, cognitive and moral order, involvement in feelings and symbols intimating transcendence of death, a sense of moral worth and the associated pleasures of extending feelings of affection toward others, and feelings of solidarity, including the opportunity to devote oneself to one's group" (Metzger 1978:23).

I think that this argument might also come out of the underlying different assumptions of human nature. The ideas about "basic desires" in the psychological approach seem to be derived from Freud's concept of the id. Hence, this approach stresses that the Chinese way of socialization, frustrating as it is to children, is satisfying these innate, more biological impulses. On the other hand, the sociologist's concept of human nature seems to come out of the traditional Confucianism. Thus in his discussion, not only biological desires are contained in human nature, but also drives for sympathy, benevolence, knowledge, righteousness, and so on.

8. It is likely that, in Chinese society, the sense of *pao* (報: retribution, repayment, reward—Yang has written an excellent article on the topic [1957]) is associated with the sense of shame or guilt. As in many primitive societies, the Chinese are very concerned about reciprocity, from which I suspect that the concept of *pao* originated. It is an important virtue that one should repay another's kindness or show gratitude. One failing to do so should feel ashamed (Hu 1944). However, according to the Chinese idea, since no one can ever repay one's parents for giving life, rearing, and training one, one should practice filial piety to show gratitude toward parents. Thus, guilt feeling arises when one feels ambivalent towards one's parents, fails to carry one's family obligations, or cannot achieve parental expectations. On the other hand, the feeling of shame is always in proportion to the degree of unfamiliarity, except that before a stranger one feels neither guilty nor ashamed. That is to say, in a group of friends, one may feel more shame toward the friend with whom one is less well acquainted.

REFERENCES

Barnouw, Victor. 1979. *Culture and Personality*. Homewood, Ill.: Dorsey Press.

Cannon, Walter B. 1940. " 'Voodoo' Death." W.A. Lessa and E.Z. Vogt, eds., *Reader in Comparative Religion*. New York: Harper & Row.

Chuang, Yu-min. 1972. *Chinese Acupuncture*, trans. D.K. Shin. Hanover, N.H.: Oriental Society.

De Vos, George. 1967. "The Relation of Guilt toward Parents to Achievement and Arranged Marriage among the Japanese." R. Hunt, ed., *Personalities and Cultures*. Austin: Univ. of Texas Press.

Fei, Hsiao-tung. 1948. *Hsiang-tu Chung-kuo [Rural China]*. Shanghai: kuan-char-sheh.

Gallin, Bernard. 1978. "Comments on Contemporary Sociocultural Studies of Medicine in Chinese Societies." A. Kleinman, P. Kunstadter, E.R. Alexander, and J.L. Gale, eds., *Culture and Healing in Asian Societies*. Cambridge: Schenkman.

Hsu, Francis L.K. 1971. "Psychosocial Homeostasis and 'Jen': Conceptual Tools for Advancing Psychological Anthropology." *American Anthropologist*, 73:23–44.

Hsu, Jin. 1974. "Counseling in the Chinese Temple: Psychological Study of Divination by 'Chien' Drawing." W. Lebra, ed., *Culture and Mental Health Research in Asia and the Pacific*, vol. 4. Honolulu: Univ. of Hawaii Press.

Hu, Hsien Chin. 1944. "The Chinese Concepts of 'Face.'" *American Anthropologist*, 47:45–64.

Kleinman, Arthur. 1977. "Depression, Somatization, and the New Cross-Cultural Psychiatry." *Social Science & Medicine*, 11:3–10.

——— 1980 *Patients and Healers in the Context of Culture*. Berkeley: Univ. of California Press.

Klineberg, Otto. 1938. "Emotional Expression in Chinese Literature." *Journal of Abnormal and Social Psychology*, 33:517–20.

Leites, Nathan. 1977. *Psychopolitical Analysis*, ed. E.W. Marvick. New York: Halstred Press.

Li, Yih-yuan. 1972. "Shamanism in Taiwan: An Anthropological Inquiry." W. Lebra, ed., *Culture and Mental Health Research in Asia and the Pacific*, vol. 4. Honolulu: Univ. of Hawaii.

Lin, Tsung-Yi, Kenneth Tardiff, George Donetz, and Walter Goresky. 1978. "Ethnicity and Patterns of Help-Seeking." *Culture, Medicine and Psychiatry*, 2:3.

Mendelson, Myer. 1960. *Psychoanalytic Concepts of Depression*. Springfield, Ill.: Thomas.

Metzger, Thomas A. 1977. *Escape from Predicament: Neo-Confucianism and China's Evolving Political Culture.* New York: Columbia Univ. Press.

Morse, William R. 1934. *Chinese Medicine.* New York: Paul B. Hoeber.

Price, John. 1968. "The Genetics of Depressive Behaviour." A. Coppen and A. Walk, eds., *Recent Developments in Affective Disorders: A Symposium of the Royal Medico-Psychological Association.* Ashford, England: Headley Brothers.

Sidel, Victor W., and Ruth Sidel. 1973. *Serve the People: Observations on Medicine in the People's Republic of China.* New York: Josiah Macy, Jr., Foundation.

Singer, K. 1974. "Society and Rights of the Mentally Ill: A Historical Retrospective in the Chinese." *Mental Health and Society,* 1:49.

Solomon, Richard H. 1971. *Mao's Political Revolution and the Chinese Political Culture.* Berkeley: Univ. of California Press.

Tseng, Wen-shing. 1972. "On Chinese National Character from the View Point of Personality Development." Y.Y. Li and K.S. Yang, eds., *Symposium on the Character of the Chinese: An Interdisciplinary Approach.* Taipei: Institute of Ethnology, Academia Sinica.

    1973   "The Concept of Personality in Confucian Thought." *Psychiatry.* 36:191–202.

    1974   "Traditional and Modern Psychiatric Care in Taiwan." A. Kleinman, P. Kunstadter, E.R. Alexander, and J.L. Gale, eds., *Culture and Healing in Asian Societies.* Cambridge, Mass.: Schenkman.

    1975   "The Nature of Somatic Complaints among Psychiatric Patients: The Chinese Case." *Comprehensive Psychiatry.* 16:237–45.

Veith, Ilza. 1955. "Psychiatric Thought in Chinese Medicine." *Journal of the History of Medicine and Allied Science.* 10:261–68.

Weber, Max. 1951. *The Religion of China,* trans. and ed. Hans H. Gerth. New York: Free Press.

Wolf, Margery. 1970. "Child Training and the Chinese Family." M. Freedman, ed., *Family and Kinship in Chinese Society.* Stanford: Stanford Univ. Press.

Yang, Lien-sheng. 1957. "The Concept of 'Pao' as a Basis for Social Relations in China." J.K. Fairbank, ed., *Chinese Thought and Institutions.* Chicago: Univ. of Chicago Press.

Yang, Martin M.C. 1972. "Familism and Chinese National Character." Y.Y. Li and K.S. Yang, eds., *Symposium on the Character of the Chinese: An Interdisciplinary Approach.* Taipei: Institute of Ethnology, Academia Sinica.

17

Mental Health, Traditional Beliefs, and the Moral Order among Yemenite Jews in Israel

Phyllis Palgi

The purpose of this chapter is to demonstrate that in the field of health, particularly mental health, the Yemenite community in Israel draws from its traditional system as an accessory to the modern medical system, which in itself does not as yet satisfy the community on an emotional level.

According to the World Health Organization, health is a state of complete physical, mental, and social well-being, not merely the absence of disease and infirmity. This definition implies that one cannot understand the body without understanding the mind, and that body and mind have full meaning only in relation to society (Firth 1959). What does the word "health" mean both in concrete terms and symbolically to the Yemenites; what is its major connotation in their culture? The underlying philosophy and basic concepts of the Yemenite health system will be identified and presented as part of the configuration of their culture in general. An attempt will be made to narrow the area in which the relationships between health and other aspects of life are more closely bound together. The emphasis will be on the mutual relationship of basic health concepts and the Yemenite world view, which is dominated by an all-pervasive but rigid moral order. Furthermore, I will try to identify patterns of overt behavior during illness and the interpretation of the Yemenite view of causation, which will provide clues to both manifest and latent stress points in the culture.

Sources of the Traditional Yemenite Health System

All Middle Eastern Jewish communities have retained certain beliefs and practices stemming from early Babylonian, Egyptian, and Greek cultures—as well as from their own ancestral Hebrew culture. These beliefs and practices have become incorporated into evolving Middle East health systems, an integral part of which have been drawn from the more complex system found in the monotheistic religion of Judaism. The latter fact suggests that to learn about Yemenite traditional healing beliefs, a link between health and morality must be explored. From the classical anthropological point of view, the Yemenite health system may be characterized primarily as a folk system. Following the analysis of Saunders (1958), folk medicine differs from scientific medicine in that it is generally the common possession of the group, so that what one adult knows about illness and its treatment is usually known by all others.

> Although knowledge of the origins of folk medical practices and beliefs may have largely been lost, the practices and beliefs themselves are often so rooted in tradition that they seem a part of the natural order of things. . . . Folk medical law is transmitted from person to person and generation to generation by informal methods. . . . The expected attitude toward a given element of folk medicine is one of uncritical acceptance. Failure does not invalidate a practice or shake the belief on which it is based . . . If he [the patient] dies, the reason is not that the remedy was inappropriate, but that the patient was beyond help [p. 199].

The structure of the Yemenite health system includes preventive and curative aspects and is classified into diagnostic and therapeutic components. The Western dichotomy usually made between physical and mental illness, is much less applicable to the Yemenite system—although not totally inappropriate.

During the period in history when most of the Jewish communities were concentrated in the Muslim orbit, the body of knowledge of the famous medieval Arab physicians as well as the beliefs and practices of the local native folk societies became incorporated into the accepted Jewish system. In modern times, particularly during the second half of the present century, Western medicine has been introduced into the Middle East and was adopted on a selective basis and in varying degrees, according to the general technological level of the particular country or region. Thus, one may find that a partially developed modern medical system exists side by side with a well-developed time-honored folk system, or that the former has become an overlay upon the traditional system.

In Yemen, the Jews—who were entrenched for centuries in their isolated cultural niche and who had little or no contact with modernity—became very set in their ways and, on the whole, continued practices developed during medieval times. Modern medicine barely reached them except at a very minimal level in the capital town of San'a, where there were some hospital facilities. In fact, immediately upon arrival in Israel, in the first stage of resettlement, it was the confrontation with a modern medical system that became one of the most frightening aspects of the new life for the Yemenites. Israeli medical personnel were shocked by these immigrants' lack of knowledge regarding health matters. In particular, the high infant mortality rate among the Yemenites was an emotional issue even for doctors and nurses in a child-centered society like Israel.

Thus, in the first encounter between the Yemenite immigrants and the Israeli community, the health situation was a fertile ground for many mutual misunderstandings, tensions, and incriminations. Yet, significantly, the Yemenites, who during the past 25 years have clung to tradition in so many respects, have shown an unusual flexibility when faced with illness. It was the conservative, highly conforming Yemenites who eventually bridged the gulf between a folk system and a Western, scientifically based medical system. Today, Israeli Yemenites use both systems, either successively or simultaneously, the latter strategy being particularly common in cases of psychological problems or mental illness. This aspect will be stressed in this chapter.

As might be expected, after a quarter of a century of contact with modern medicine, the traditional system is not as intact and coherent as it was in the "old country." However, the successful traditional healers in Israel still have a large clientele. Apparently neither the healer nor the patient feels that there is a basic conflict in practice or in ideology between the old and the new system. True enough, visits to the traditional healers were not usually divulged by the patient during a visit to the "scientific" doctor, it being assumed that the latter would not understand the traditional system and might even ridicule it. Healers, on their part, prefer secrecy out of fear of being charged with the illegal practice of medicine, or are wary of some other official authority like the tax collector. More recently, as a result of the influence of anthropology in Israel, some psychiatrists have shown an interest in traditional therapeutic measures and have encouraged their patients to speak openly about their visits to folk healers. In fact, in certain circles, it has become almost chic to pay special attention to the opinions of the latter.

The body of medical knowledge comprising the traditional system, which had become crystallized into a coherent system by the medieval Islamic period, was drawn in the main from the following sources (Kepach 1961):

Jewish Sources

1. Rambam's writings in the twelfth century on medicine and Jewish philosophy had a major influence on Yemenite beliefs. His work, in turn, was heavily influenced by that of the Greeks. (The majority of his works were written in Arabic.) (*Encyclopedia Judaica* 1971:2: 778).

2. The other source, lesser known, but nevertheless important in medieval times, was the work of doctors such as Rabbi Yichia Al Tabib and the Yemenite doctor known as "Zacharia, the doctor." The latter was famous for the grasses and herbs he used for medicinal purposes. There were healers who linked their nature cures with astrology. For instance, Jacob Alkandi and Harara stressed the importance of the right day of the week or month or the right time of the day for healing treatment.

3. The Talmud spelled out very clearly specific health rules and regulations. It was also an important source of legitimation for recognition of the potentially dangerous nature of spirits as well as the power of the evil eye.

4. Kabbala and Zohar contributed, in the main, mystical aspects of diagnosis and treatment based on a combination of astrology and Jewish religious precepts.

The Yemenites seem to have had no problems in integrating Rambam's rationalistic approach with that of the mystics. They simply ignored the fact that Rambam, for instance, was against the use of amulets and cameos, which is basic to the Yemenite preventive medical practice. In other Jewish communities, a major controversy raged between the followers of these two opposing schools of thought, at one period even leading to violence. In the twentieth century, before emigration from Yemen, a small intellectual elite group among the Jews gave attention to the existence of a basic contradiction between the two main approaches. The controversy did not, however, touch the masses.

Arab Sources

1. Certain medical books reached Yemen, the most famous of which was *Zad Al Misasir* by Ibn al Hadad.

2. Prescriptions from the Kor'an and various Middle-Eastern folk beliefs became incorporated not only into the Jewish health system, but also into the Muslim legal system. Here, too, full support was given to the all-pervading influence of spirits, *jinns* as they were called in Arabic, which, it was believed, could enter into human beings or animals and take control of their behavior. The Muslim legal system accepted this belief as valid.

As Kroeber (1948) has pointed out, in all societies, cultural influences from different sources may become fused to form one coherent system. Linton (1936) has stressed the extent to which individuals are unaware of the origin of their customs and beliefs, most times assuming that they originated in their own tradition. When practices and beliefs are contradictory, dissonance may be resolved by regarding the disparate aspects as acceptable alternatives. In Yemen, as in Israel, Jews would turn to Arab healers, particularly when their own people failed to effect a cure, and vice versa.

In broad terms, one may say that Yemenite medicine was a subsystem within the total overall Middle-Eastern system of medicine. In Yemen itself the rigidity and religious fanaticism of Muslims and Jews alike, as well as the degree of isolation, enhanced the similarity of beliefs between the two ethnic groups. At the same time, the overall ethnic identities were kept scrupulously disparate. To understand this seemingly contradictory statement, one should know that the ethnic differences reasserted themselves whenever the medical beliefs merged into the religious system, which was the basic dividing line between the two communities. As has been pointed out earlier, whenever there was no obvious religious clash, Jews would easily consult Arab specialists and vice versa.

Fatalistic View of Illness

Yemenite Jews shared with both the Muslims and other Middle-Eastern Jewish communities the belief that, in the final analysis, illness and its cure was dependent on God's will. In a more direct way illness could be attributed to the work of some supernatural force like evil spirits or the evil eye; thus holy words and names of angels were involved in the curing process. The concept of natural disasters or some other external event causing illness did exist, but it was never quite clear whether affected individuals did, after all, bear some responsibility for bringing upon themselves the misfortune. This was the case even if the misfortune was regarded as the result of the evil design of other human beings, or through unfortunate combinations of events, which together combusted and produced a situation loaded with supernatural dangers.

The traditional system places no importance on the concept of awareness; on the contrary, at most times it strengthens the projective system and works towards cancelling out the evil effect of the alleged sorcery. However, the system is based upon the fact that there is almost invariably a recognition of the personal involvement between the victim and the persecutor.

On the basis of empiric experience, when the illness is brief or slight, a practical common-sense attitude is adopted: appropriate herbs, purgatives, or pastes are used, and little time is spent in discussing causation. Even a minimal ceremony might be performed to expunge the evil eye. All such techniques are comparable to minor surgery. Again, in view of the capricious nature of the evil eye, if the illness or mishap is temporary it is not considered necessary to search too deeply, or pinpoint the person who caused it. However, if the illness persists, and the patient suffers considerably and becomes unable to fulfill daily functions, then home remedies are no longer considered efficacious. At this point an expert in folk medicine will be consulted, and an explanation for the onset of illness will be sought as an essential part of the diagnostic and hence therapeutic process. It is suggested here that, in view of the all-pervasiveness of religion in Yemenite life, the explanation will invariably be found within the moral order. The nature of the Jewish religion— heavily dominated as it is by clearly expressed ethical principles referring to interpersonal human relations, as well as to religious precepts pertaining to behavior toward Almighty God—in itself helps support the moral approach.

Role of Spirits

In the Yemenite medical belief system, a very important role is attributed to spirits. Thus the nature and habits of spirits as viewed by the Yemenites warrant discussion in some detail. Yemenite beliefs about the spirit kingdom and spirit activity have persisted for centuries and are passed on from generation to generation. These beliefs, however, have been somewhat shaken since immigration to Israel, and some uncomfortable questions have been raised. However, the beliefs still linger on. The fact that the Talmud refers to the existence of spirits has strengthened the ideological connection between religion and health beliefs and contributed to the perseverance of the beliefs as well as their integration into life as a whole.

A visit to a learned Yemenite rabbi who holds an official position in the Israeli

Rabbinate confirmed this view. We sat in his study, which included an extensive library. When we turned to the subject of spirits, he rose from his chair, moved to the couch, sat upon it cross-legged, and pointed to the Talmud and some other ancient-looking books, saying "It is written there that there are *shedim* but how they came to Israel is something I cannot explain." He continued, "They should not be here. Israel is the Holy Land and they cannot live in the Holy Land. How did they cross the border?" He based his evidence that *shedim* did come to Israel on the fact that there are people in Israel who are mentally ill, which in itself is proof of possession by spirits. The rabbi was troubled and had no answer. "The doctors also have no answer," he said. "They lock people up in hospitals, and that solves nothing." The rabbi was trying to prove that it is not the "primitiveness" of the Yemenites that brings them to support the belief in spirits, but rather that the modern world is slowly beginning to understand the power of such supernatural creatures. However, he appeared puzzled and confused on the issue.

According to Yemenite Jews, the holiness of the Land should be strong enough to prevent spirits from crossing its frontiers. Furthermore, spirits do not like light, and since Israel is well lit, the spirits should be unable to function. Traditional Jewish Moroccan beliefs also support this contention. However, the fact remains that people display behavior considered to be a result of spirit intervention.

A psychotherapist reported a case to me regarding a husband and wife who were concerned that the disturbed mental state of the wife might be attributed to the work of a *shed*. This woman would fall into a trance-like state. While in the trance, she shouted, talked nonsense, appeared to be totally unaware of what was happening to her, and called for her dead sister. When she awoke she was perfectly logical and coherent. They consulted a *chacham* ("sage," in Mid-Eastern communities, "rabbi"), who diagnosed her situation as being one of spirit possession. According to the *chacham*, the woman bumped into a *shed,* and as revenge he came to take possession of her soul from time to time. The husband was a learned and religious man, and he too believed that *shedim* should not be found in the Holy Land. Both husband and wife felt helpless and in desperation they turned to psychiatric counseling for advice and treatment. The *chacham* apparently placed no blame on the possessed one, but located the encounter between the wife and the *shed* in her sister's home. According to further information, it appeared that the patient had guilt feelings about her anger and jealousy toward her late sister. The treatment of the *chacham* was a cleansing treatment to drive out the *shed*, which represented the badness in her. At the time of the report the patient continued to wear the cameo given to her by the *cacham,* and also continued to see the "official" therapist.

According to the Yemenites, the night is dangerous because of the spirits, and, therefore, one should never go out alone in the dark; three people should always be together. This suggests that humans have some capacity to ward off spirits. At night there may be more than ten thousand mischievious spirits lurking about, yet three human beings are enough to keep them away. A general concept of territorialism exists. Humans must be careful not to trespass in a blatant fashion or disturb the spirits unnecessarily. At the same time, a Yemenite must bear in mind that the spirits are expansionist in nature, and that there is a constant struggle on the part of the demons to extend the zone of their influence by means of marriage and inheritance (Kagan 1968). Thus, procedures must be established for humans to make contact and threaten the spirits or make compromises and conciliatory gestures toward them.

Basic Characteristics of Spirits

Spirits are more numerous than humans. Although they have the power to fly anywhere, they prefer to live in the house together with ordinary humans and are affected by the atmosphere of the home they inhabit.

All spirits like dark and damp places. The evil spirits prefer dirty and neglected places almost exclusively but may be found also near wells or springs or in forests and on mountain tops. In view of the nature and function of toilets, it is understandable that it was thought that toilets attracted spirits. Similarly, the Talmud cautions against exposure to dirty water and, for instance, advises against sitting under a drain pipe leading from the roof, because dirty water might drop down, inviting the evil spirits.

Spirits are good, bad, or neutral. Apparently they resemble human beings in this respect. Their degree of goodness is correlated positively with their degree of etherealness. Spirits combining fire and wind are the best, whereas spirits made of fire, wind, water, and dust are bad. The good are the most invisible; hence, if one feels or, in some form or other, sees a spirit, it is probably an evil one.

Yemenites have ways of evoking good spirits. If a powder is made from the placenta of a black kitten together with that of the kitten's mother, both of whom must be from the first litter, and the powder is rubbed on a person's eyes, good spirits may thereby be summoned. The tears of a donkey are also considered effective as a means of spirit revelation. Such techniques are not usually used by the ordinary person, but rather by the *mori,* who specializes in working out a person's fortune. The good spirits are important for the specialists who need information about the future. The specialists, however, are cautious; they claim that they can get information only about the near future.

Giridi (1945) claims that by studying the Talmud the Yemenites learned that spirits have three characteristics in common with angels and three with human beings. The spirits have wings like angels, their movement within the universe is unlimited, and there are no barriers to their hearing ability. Their human-like features are their mortality, their reproductive potential, and their need and desire for food and drink. They can reproduce, not only by sexual intercourse with their own kind, but also by cohabitation with humans. As a rule they are invisible, but they have various ways of making their presence felt or can appear in different forms, both human and animal. Rabbi Shmuel ben Yoseph Adani describes their basic constituents as various combinations of fire, wind, water and dust (Giridi 1945).

A Description of a Successful "Mori"

In Israel today there is a successful *mori* that the Yemenites suspect of being a charlatan. However, because of his ability to summon the spirits he has gained fame and power.

The *mori* lives not far from Tel Aviv in a neighborhood of immigrants from Middle-Eastern countries. The *mori*'s room is separated from the waiting room by a curtain. Children played, pushed, tusseled among themselves. The walls were dirty and the floor uncarpeted. I could see a lounge leading off the waiting room, which was shabby but better kept, and was obviously for family guests. The *mori*'s wife was in the kitchen cooking, and the pungent smell of food frying in oil filled our nostrils. The room the *mori* himself occupied was no sanctum. The children popped their heads in from time to time to ask the *mori* questions or to request small sums of money. The clientele included both sexes, most from Middle-Eastern countries but by no means exclusively Yemenite. Among them was a man of Rumanian origin accompanied by his teenage daughter. Talking with him, I concluded that the daughter had been diagnosed by a psychiatrist as suffering from schizophrenia.

This *mori* impressed me differently than the previously mentioned dignified rabbi. He, too, sat cross-legged on a bed and was surrounded by books, but the room was filled with bric-a-brac such as beads and dried beans. Next to him was a spittoon into which he coughed and spat loudly. From time to time he shouted to his wife and children. He was boastful of his powers over the spirits and his ability to diagnose and counteract sorcery. He smiled lasciviously when he spoke of sexual matters. In my presence he received a man who complained of a large number of vague physical and psychological symptoms. The *mori* said that he was not sure whether this client was possessed or not. He got up from his couch, walked to the door, lowered the blind, and, in the dark, behind the blind, on the verandah, he conducted his conversation with the spirits. He spoke in esoteric Aramaic terms. A second voice with a Yemenite accent was heard answering him. It was all done very quickly. The atmosphere in the room, where two other patients and I waited for the results, was tense. The *mori* returned tired but triumphant. He said that the spirits informed him that his client was not possessed by one of them; thus the *mori* concluded that the patient was ill because of the evil eye or some other sorcery. The *mori* dealt with the case accordingly.

Spirit Involvement with Human Beings

One of the outstanding features of the spirits is their deep involvement with human beings. The spirits could serve humans either for good or bad purposes, depending upon the character and motives of the humans with whom they were in contact, and also, of course, upon their own character. Usually, their evil intent dominates. A Yemenite explained to me how another Yemenite wished to harm him and was able to do so because the former cohabited with a female spirit, who served him as an "army of soldiers serves the general." The enemy had particularly strong evil powers and could perform sorcery with sperm that he obtained after intercourse with the female spirit. The family of the accused claimed that it was not true, because it was impossible to import his female spirit from Yemen to the Holy Land.

The spirits play a predominant role in the sexual aspects of human life. Various sexual dysfunctions, prohibited erotic behavior, and fantasies are closely associated with demon intervention. The evil spirits, sometimes called "angels of destruction," are more prone to reveal themselves, because of their malicious involvement with humans and their intent to harm them.

In Jewish demonology, Lilith is the most dangerous of all demons. She is not, however, the only female demon. Lilith is mentioned in the Talmud and also in the Kor'an under the name of Ziat Bint Silkes. Kagan (1968) traces the development of the idea of female demons, their behavior, and their characteristic traits. Like most Jewish traditional groups, the Yemenites attribute a number of disasters to Lilith's activities, such as possessing persons, terrifying them or making them mentally ill, and in various mysterious ways, Lilith is capable of causing a person's death.

From my own field experience, Lilith or other female demons became apparent in some kinds of forbidden sexual behavior or in fantasies. Kagan reports that in the early legends there were merely chance matings between human men and female demons and that only in the Middle Ages was the motif of marriage introduced. It is very common in Jewish communities of the Middle East to keep a 24-hour watch over the newborn child, particularly a male, for a period of at least one month. It is feared that the jealousy of a sterile female demon might drive her to strangle the child. One reason why men should not sleep alone, when in remote places far away from home, is that they are liable to be seduced by these female demons.

According to Kagan marriage to a female demon is punishment for a sin. However, Yemenites do not necessarily endorse this statement.

Case Studies on Spirit Possession

Case 1.   The following is the account of Mrs. Yonah, a Yemenite woman suffering from severe anxieties and phantom pregnancy, who was hospitalized in an open psychiatric hospital. She no longer fulfilled most of her tasks as a wife and mother and claimed that some members of her husband's family were trying to harm her through magical means. It took intensive interviewing to discover what was worrying the woman. My knowledge about Yemenite spirits made it possible for me to build the necessary rapport with Mrs. Yonah so that she was able to admit to her terrifying secrets.

Mrs. Yonah, aged 30, was born in Yemen and came to Israel at the age of 16. She is illiterate and lives in a conservative Yemenite neighborhood. She works as a maid in an upper-middle-class modern home. At 20 she married a young man from her own neighborhood, despite opposition from her family, who claimed that they did not know the groom's family, and "he is not like one of us." They objected to his general behavior and his life-style. He was far less religious and less traditional than her family. When the future Mrs. Yonah insisted that she was in love with this man and would not give him up, her family finally consented to the marriage. However, soon after the marriage she realised that she had become an outsider in the eyes of her own kin, who looked upon her as being willful. Her husband's mother accepted her in a cursory fashion, but the rest of his family, particularly his siblings, openly rejected her, and she suddenly felt very much alone in the world. Because she did not become pregnant during the first three years of marriage, vague hints began emanating from her husband's family that he should divorce her. Out of desperation she did three things. She prayed incessantly to God, visited a *mori,* and finally went to a gynecologist. She now has three small boys and is not sure which procedure was the effective one.

Mrs. Yonah spent a great deal of time telling about the injustices, insults, and possible evil eye to which her husband's kin had subjected her. It seemed clear to her that misfortunes that befell her were a direct result of the evil eye given to her by her husband's siblings, who were jealous that she had given birth to another son.

Finally, in whispered tones, she confessed to what she believed was the major cause of her inability to function. Since the birth of her third child, her husband usually insisted upon anal intercourse, and on the rare occasions that they did have sexual relations in the accepted fashion, he practiced coitus interruptus, an act forbidden by Jewish law. Furthermore, he would insist upon approaching her before she was ritually clean; in other words, he would not wait out the prescribed number of days after she had completed her menstrual period, so that she could perform the ritual ablutions. Mrs. Yonah described these details sitting far away from any other patient or staff member. She had not previously been able to discuss these unmentionable details, because she was terrified about the punishment, and because she was so ashamed.

She began to understand her situation only after she had confided in a member of her husband's family, a practicing *mori.* Although he was not a very knowledgeable or skillful practitioner, because he did not have any secret books, he was an expert in Yemenite pharmacopoeia. This *mori* had dropped in to visit her after hearing that she had not been well, and had offered his professional services. She told him about her husband's demands, and also told him that despite the fact that she could not be pregnant and was menstruating regularly, she felt life in her womb.

The *mori* thought that she might have become pregnant by a *shed,* for, as he had explained, they swarm round spilled sperm. This meant that she was carrying an embryonic *shed* in her womb and might be possessed from time to time by a female *shed,* particularly at the time of coitus. Her confused thoughts supported the *mori's* thesis. For a rather large sum of money, the *mori* claimed that he could rid her of this undesirable supernatural pregnancy. She paid him eagerly, and he brought an ointment for her to rub over her body in a ritualistic fashion, particularly over her stomach. The ointment burned her skin, and brought on heavy vaginal bleeding, which the *mori* tried to stop by administering additional medicines. She felt desperately ill and began to suspect that he was practicing sorcery, especially since he was a member of her husband's family. She became desperate and neglected her housekeeping and the care of her children. This finally led to a serious row, when her husband came home one Friday afternoon and found that she had made no Sabbath preparations. When he threatened to beat her, she ran to her eldest brother, leaving the children at home. She waited for her husband to fetch her, but he refused to do so until there had been a full family council.

She was taken to the family doctor, who prescribed pills for her "pains and her nerves" and referred her to a psychiatrist. The psychiatrist hospitalized her in an open psychiatric setting. Her husband visited her often in the hospital. She described with some pride how he brought her slippers, food, and clean clothes.

Mrs. Yonah felt relieved after telling this story. She believed that she had been forced into committing a sin by her husband, even though he viewed life differently than she. Though he has become attentive to her, she does not trust him and does not know how to interpret his solicitous behavior.

She has two explanations for her husband's changed attitude toward her. He is either genuinely sorry for what he and his family have done to her, or he is guilty about his sexual behavior and wants to be sure that she does not tell any of the hospital staff.

In summing up the situation, she said that she felt abandoned by her own kin, ridiculed by her spouse's family, and contaminated by her husband's sinful behavior. Furthermore, she still feels uncomfortable with her husband's family and friends, who consider themselves an integral part of modern Israeli society, to which she knows she can never belong.

Case 2. The following story was told by Mrs. Simcha. Her grandfather, since deceased, was traveling alone through a mountainous area in Yemen, thought to be inhabited by *shedim*. A female demon entered his body and possessed him for the remainder of his life. She became in fact his "real" wife and was so jealous of his human wife that she would not allow him to have sexual relations with the latter. The wife accepted the situation when she realized that the she-demon was powerful, dangerous and capable of killing her out of jealousy. Mrs. Simcha explained that although her grandfather should not have gone alone into the mountains, he could not be blamed for what had happened. It was simply a matter of very bad luck. It was generally accepted that if a she-demon was passionately in love with a man, no one could remove her. As far as his human wife was concerned, she regarded her husband's impotence as a sickness inflicted upon him by supernatural causes. A subsequent meeting with the grandfather's widow revealed an extremely strong, independent, and domineering woman.

Case 3.   Mr. Saadia, a dour, introverted man, owns a butcher shop in a Yemenite neighborhood. He is not well liked, but his wife is. Mrs. Saadia has a good relationship with her children, whereas their father is seen as a cold and distant figure. She is careful in the presence of her husband, but he is aware that she is the focus of the house.

One evening, Mr. Saadia returned home after a difficult day at the shop. He went to his room to rest. No other members of the family were at home. Suddenly, he felt a warm pressure on his back and had the feeling that he was being strangled. He went to see a *mori,* who said that a *shed* had come to plague him because he had not kept a promise. In addition, the *mori* suggested to him that he regularly chew *khat,** and then the *shedim* would no longer bother him.

There are three significant facts that led to the diagnosis and treatment prescribed by the *mori.* The first is that butcher shops, being spattered by blood and offal, are considered natural places for attracting *shedim.* The second is that *khat* is a mild toxicant widely used in Yemen, much like tranquilizers in Western society. Finally, that Mr. Saadia had made himself vulnerable to spirits.

Because of the taboo against masturbation, the admonition not to sleep alone was meant to protect men from temptation. It is expected that women are never alone. However, clinics report numerous cases of women who are fearful of the effect on their children of their own destructive or illicit sexual thoughts.

Almost invariably, bad thoughts are attributed to the interference of spirits or the evil eye. The person afflicted with bad thoughts considers himself ruled by the power of the spirits, the evil eye, or some other combination of supernatural forces. Here one sees the syncretism of both Muslim and Jewish folk beliefs to the basic Talmudic tenets.

Members of the family or friends of the afflicted one usually express their sympathy. However, these expressions may not be sincere. It is a cultural imperative that one must express sympathy for anyone who has met with misfortune. In any case, these expressions do not mean that the afflicted person may not in some way be responsible for his own misfortune. However, once a person is suffering, what brought the misfortune on is irrelevant.

Evil Eye

The ancient concept of the evil eye continues to have a strong grip on people throughout the Mid-East and North Africa. It is a phenomenon found in many different cultures, but the concept diffused throughout the present Muslim orbit and Christian Europe from ancient Mid-Eastern civilizations. During the Middle Ages it became an integral part of both Jewish and Christian life and became one of the daily fears throughout the *shtetl* of the Jewish Pale in Eastern Europe from

Khat is Arabic for the fresh or dried leaves of *Catha edalis, Celastraeae,* an excitant of the central nervous system widely used by the Yemenites.

the fourteenth until the early twentieth century. Lilienthal records over 80 anti-evil-eye practices among Eastern European Jewry (*Encyclopedia Judaica* 1971, 6: 1000).

In the Muslim world, when a person admires another and possibly adds a few words of praise, the danger of the evil eye is so great that he must utter *t'bark Allah* "May God be blessed" (Westermarck 1926:417). In contemporary Israel, when a compliment is given, particularly to a child, the expression in Hebrew, "B'li ayin harah" ("May there be no evil eye") is common in ordinary conversation, especially among the middle-aged foreign-born. The expression is also used when speaking to persons who have recovered from illness.

Much of the Yemenite view of the evil eye is shared by other Jewish communities that have lived for centuries in the Muslim orbit. According to Trachtenburg's (1939) historical data, the Jewish comprehension of the evil eye is a synthesis of two early versions of the phenomenon. The Babylonian view was that certain harmful properties were inherent in the evil eye, and that unfortunate men are born *jettarori* (endowed with these properties). They shed rays of destruction with every glance, frequently unaware themselves of their dread influence. Some *jettarori* may be recognized by the peculiar and striking cast of their eyes, but others pass unnoticed until an unfortunate experience unmasks them. They are to be found "in all stations of life" (p. 55). The ancient Palestinians viewed the evil eye as a temporary situation, which became effective only when the person feels envy or hatred. "We may see that this belief is a hypostatization of the evil which man discerns in invidiousness, a translation of a profound poetic truth into the language of superstition" (p. 56).

The literature refers to the magical power of the eye, which can work benevolent wonders for the entire community. The sage Shimon bar Yochai, venerated throughout the Middle East by all Jewish communities, was thought capable of transforming an evil person into a "heap of bones by the burning fire in his eyes" (*Encyclopedia Judaica* 1971:6: 998). Trachtenburg observes that several Talmudic rabbis were considered to possess such powers, but he stresses that this was a minor theme. If one accepts the idea that these pious and virtuous men were considered to be people born with destructive psychic power in their eyes but exercised it for good purposes only, then one may also accept Trachtenburg's view that the evil eye is a product of a synthesis of the two early versions of the phenomena.

The evil eye is considered by many to be a possible cause for a wide range of misfortunes that befall mankind. Westermarck (1926), referring to Muslim and Berber Moroccan society of which the Jews were an integral part, particularly in the sharing of magical beliefs, wrote: "It is said that the evil eye owns two thirds of the graveyard or that one half of mankind dies from the evil eye or that the evil eye empties the castles . . . and fills the graves" (p. 414).

The evil eye is usually, although not exclusively, attracted to a situation that manifests health, happiness, success or beauty. Children, in particular, are considered natural objects for the evil eye, and parents must never show either to the child or to anyone else that they are proud or pleased with them. Persons involved in an important happening are more susceptible than others. Brides and bride-grooms, pregnant women, or nursing mothers are all targets for the evil eye (Van Gennep, 1960).

When Israel first became a state one of the difficulties of getting mothers to come to infant clinics was that the mothers thought their babies could be exposed to evil eyes en route. Mothers would arrive at the height of summer with their babies fully wrapped up and covered from head to foot so that no one would see the child naked. However, mothers had no problem in breast-feeding their infants in public, for then only the mouth of the baby need be exposed. The breasts of the mother were not regarded as an erotic part of the body.

Bearers of the Evil Eye

From whom does the evil eye emanate? Potentially anybody and everybody can give the evil eye. This supports Trachtenburg's view that the Yemenites believe the evil eye is a natural human enmity that emerges under certain sets of circumstances.

On the basis of my empirical experience over a period of 20 years of contact with the Yemenites, I find that women more often than men have been suspected of being the bearer of the evil eye. This is apparently true for the Mid-Eastern and North African Muslims as well. Westermarck (1926) observed that in Morocco, "Women are allowed to eat first at feasts; otherwise they might injure the men with their evil eyes . . . it is believed that misfortune would befall any person or animal at whom a bride looked before she had seen her husband at her arrival at his house" (p. 420). Shiloh (1969) also maintains that women throughout the Middle East are more prone to possess the evil eye.

Since the presence and power of the evil eye is so commonplace, it is thought that most times the person does not intentionally cause harm. It is felt that it is simply in the nature of man, and apparently even more so in the nature of woman, to feel envious. Envy is aroused when one sees something he or she would like to possess, a material, nonmaterial, or human object. Thus, as moral principle, a person should fight envious feelings, although there are situations that trigger these feelings, and then, willy-nilly, the evil psychic power goes into action.

Case Studies on the Evil Eye

Case 1.   Mrs. Mazal, a middle-aged Yemenite woman, tells how she inadvertently became victim of an evil eye. In Yemen, on her wedding night, a friendly young Arab woman entered the house to pay her respects. She looked at Mrs. Mazal, beautifully dressed, with envy in her heart but at the same time expressed her genuine admiration by saying, "What beautiful eyes you have." After the ceremony, Mrs. Mazal became almost blind and remained so for many months. She was taken to an Arab healer. She carried out his instructions, but it took many months before her eyesight was fully restored. (Mrs. Mazal was married very young, even before she began menstruating. She was emotionally unprepared for married life; this leads one to suspect that she was suffering from hysterical blindness.)

Case 2. Mr. Zaccariyah, a 45-year-old Yemenite, had been given the evil eye by both a male and a female. He fell from a ladder, broke his leg, and had to be operated on, and now, after many months he is still suffering from the effects of the fall. When I asked him how it happened, he explained that the ladder had suddenly split into two. The ladder was in perfect condition and Mr. Zaccariyah was always steady on his feet. While talking to me he became thoughtful and suddenly the explanation for his misfortune became clear. Some time before the accident, he was working in a nearby Muslim town. An Arab woman looked at him and admired how he could climb the ladder like a young man. Clearly, he said, she had given him the evil eye, for he had never before fallen from a ladder.

On another occasion, he was given the evil eye by an Ashkenazi Jewish worker who was jealous of his prowess as an electrician. This worker said he could not understand how a Yemenite who had not studied the trade and could not even read a plan could work faster and better than he. That night when Mr. Zaccariyah came home from work, he saw that a rash had spread over both his hands. The rash went away only when he stopped working on that particular job.

The evil eye can penetrate one's dreams. This is considered very dangerous and must be dealt with immediately. If not, the child of the person who had the dream might die.

Theories about the Evil Eye

Westermarck (1926), in his interpretation of the significance of the evil eye, introduced the element of fear, not only fear of the envy of others but one's own fears about the future. He wrote, "In accordance with one of the laws of the association of ideas, which generally play such an important part in magical beliefs, namely, the law of association by contrast, the praise or admiration of something good readily recalls its opposite—the more so as the future is always uncertain and fortune is not to be relied upon" (p. 418).

Freud (1917–1919) arrived at essentially the same conclusion as Westermarck. Freud's psychoanalytic approach is based on the premise that every person knows that envy is part of human nature, and, therefore, if someone has something very valuable, he will arouse envy in others, since, if he were in the place of the other, he would certainly feel envious.

According to the Yemenite view, the influence of the evil eye is enough to cause illness and misfortune but not severe mental illness, which is the work of the spirits. For protection, infants and children are provided with amulets, which are tied on their arms or hung around their neck as preventive measures. It is generally accepted that fearful and anxious persons are very susceptible and open to the evil eye, since fear is in itself a cause of ill health or misfortune.

Responses to the Evil Eye

In most families there is a grandmother, an aunt, or some other female who is competent to control the effects of the evil eye. If the situation becomes serious and the misfortune persists, a specialist is consulted. The treatment was and still is more or less standard. The healer interviews the afflicted person, learning all he can about the situation. After referring to the "books" he can inevitably reveal the name of the malevolent agent. A piece of cloth from a garment of the evil carrier must be obtained. This is burned in a metal box, and the afflicted one breathes in the smoke. Mrs. Mazal, for instance, said that she was cured in this way. She added that urine obtained from a small boy was thrown over the burning fire before she inhaled the smoke. Others have their heads covered while breathing in the fumes. Embedded in the cloth covering their heads are small pieces of paper on which the specialist has written the names of appropriate angels. All the specialists have knowledge derived from the Kabbala, which enables them to find the combination of names of angels that must be written on ritually clean paper or parchment and that is appropriate to the individual situation. Astrology is also involved, and the stars of the client and the client's parents are consulted.

There is a great similarity between the techniques used in the different Middle-Eastern and North African countries in handling the pernicious effects of the evil eye. However, there are some regional innovations. Moroccan Jewish women in Israel explain that if a woman who has had some known family problem arrives at a wedding, the mother or other female relative of the bride would run her tongue around her mouth and whisper prayers. An Egyptian Jewish woman who had only one child and was unable to bear another child went to a circumcision ceremony of the newborn son of one of her close friends. To her embarrassment, she was first ignored, and then she heard the whisperings of prayers, obviously designed to neutralize the evil eye which she might inadvertently give.

For the Yemenites, the evil eye mechanism serves several purposes. It is a means of expressing feelings as well as an instrument of social control. Rambam, in his demand for moderation based on Judaic principles, stressed the dangers of extreme emotions, such as anger, jealousy, or pride. Jealousy, for instance, is injurious both to the person who is the object of jealousy and to the jealous person. The Yemenites emphasize the sanctity of both the home and the community through the sexual purity and modesty of its members, who use supernatural means to help them cope both with their misfortunes and with their emotions. The key to understanding the role of the belief in spirits, the evil eye, or the power of forbidden obsessive thoughts within the Yemenite health system, lies in the Yemenite concept of the nature of humans and of the ideal moral order.

REFERENCES

Bialik, N., and Y.C. Rabnitzki. 1956. *Books of Legends Based on the Talmud*. (In Hebrew.) Tel Aviv: Dvir, 6:620–55.

Burton, A. 1974. "The Nature of Personality Theory." A. Burton, ed., *Operational Theories of Personality*. New York: Brunner–Mazel, p. 7.

Encyclopedia Judaica 1971. Jerusalem.

Firth, R. 1959. "Acculturation in Relation to Concepts of Health and Disease." I. Galdston, ed., *Medicine and Anthropology*. New York: International Universities Press, p. 132.

Freud, S., 1917–1919. *The Complete Psychological Works of Sigmund Freud,* vol. 17. London: Hogarth Press.

Giridi, S. 1945. *From Yemen to Zion.* (In Hebrew.) Tel Aviv: Massada.

Kagan, Z. 1968. "Marriages of Humans and Female Demons in Fable and Folklore." (In Hebrew.) *4th World Congress of Jewish Studies,* vol. 2.

Kepach, J. 1961. *Yemenite Customs.* (In Hebrew.) Jerusalem: Ben Zvi Institute.

Kroeber, A. 1948. *Anthropology.* New York: Harcourt Brace.

Linton, R. 1936. *The Study of Man.* New York: Appleton–Century.

Saunders, L. 1958. "Healing Ways in the Spanish South West." E. Jaco, ed., *Patients, Physicians and Illness*. Glencoe, Ill.: Free Press, p. 199.

Shiloh, A. 1969. "The Inter-Action of Middle Eastern and Western Systems of Medicine. A. Shiloh, ed., *Peoples and Cultures of the Middle East*. New York: Random House.

Trachtenburg, J. 1939. *Magic and Superstition.* New York: Behrman's Jewish Book House.

Van Gennep, A. 1960. *The Rites of Passage.* Chicago: Univ. of Chicago Press.

Westermarck, E. 1926. *Ritual and Belief in Morocco,* vol. 1. London: Macmillan.

Zborowski, M. 1969. *People in Pain.* San Francisco: Jossey–Bass.

18

Psychotherapy:
Brave New World
or Requiem
for Misguided Idealism?

Igor Grant

Psychotherapy as we know it started becoming part of medicine at the end of the nineteenth century; the closing years of the twentieth century are witnessing a sustained attack on these techniques, to the extent that psychotherapy's survival as a medical treatment is in serious jeopardy. Ironically, the pressures on psychotherapy are largely culturally determined: they stem from two central concerns of mainstream American society in the last half of this century and from two specific concerns of the subculture of mental-health gatekeepers. The two general societal concerns are the economy and freedom (civil rights, reaction to intrusiveness of big government); the two subcultural concerns of mental health professionals are the mind–body problem and the scientific basis (or lack thereof) of psychotherapy. In this chapter I shall endeavor to show how, at a time when the indications, effectiveness, and limitations of psychotherapy are coming into sharper focus, political, economic, and philosophical considerations threaten its very survival.

What is psychotherapy, and why are they saying all those bad things about it? Meltzoff and Kornreich (1970:6) propose:

> Psychotherapy is taken to mean the informed and planful application of techniques derived from established psychological principles, by persons qualified through training and experience to understand these principles and to apply these techniques with the intention of assisting individuals to modify such personal characteristics as feelings, values, attitudes, and behaviors which are judged by the therapist to be maladaptive or maladjustive.

This is a good and comprehensive definition, though somewhat cumbersome. For most purposes I would propose as equally serviceable the following: "Psychotherapy is an interpersonal process whereby patients or clients work toward achieving desired changes in thinking, feeling, or behavior with a therapist, a professional trained in the behavioral sciences."

Psychotherapy has been classified in many ways: according to unit of intervention (individual, conjoint, family, group); by time (brief, long term); in terms of goals (support, insight, behavior modification); according to philosophical orientation of the therapist (learning theory, psychodynamic, client centered, cognitive); or by the degree of therapist involvement (directive, nondirective).

The Mind–Body Problem

Within the company of mental health and medical professionals the first criticism of psychotherapy boils down to a recycling of an age-old preoccupation with mind–body dualism. Szasz (1978) states, "There is, properly speaking, no such thing as psychotherapy. Like mental illness, psychotherapy is a metaphor and a myth" (preface, xvi). He continues, ". . . if the conditions psychotherapists seek to cure are not diseases, then the procedures they use are not genuine treatments" (introduction, xviii). Albee (1977) agrees, saying, "The really fundamental question, ultimately, is whether persons with the kinds of problems dealt with in outpatient, traditional psychotherapy are really *sick* . . ." and ". . . there is a great deal of evidence to support the position that people have emotional problems in living that are produced by the problems inherent in an industrial civilization and that these problems should not be regarded as illnesses . . ." (p. 721). This neo-Cartesianism has gained legitimacy through the evolution of a whole school of "biological psychiatry," some adherents of which would admit as psychiatric illness only those disorders that are genetically transmitted or that show manifest brain disturbance.

"Concepts with Blurred Edges"

The problem seems to be that some otherwise thoughtful physicians and behavioral scientists are attempting to create mutually exclusive classes in an event field which is better thought of in terms of Wittgenstein's "concepts with blurred edges" (1953). A heart attack is clearly a biological event, and a sickness; sociologists might also see it as a social role, and social workers as a problem in living. Does classifying a heart attack as a cardiac illness exclude it from the realm of social problems? Clearly not. Indeed, there is mounting evidence that "problems in living," be they occupational hazards, family or work stress, or unhealthful living habits, have an etiological and potentiating role in many medical conditions, and that psychotherapeutic interventions are sometimes helpful in rehabilitation. With regard to myocardial infarction, specifically, several studies suggest that cardiac patients undergoing brief psychotherapy experienced reduced mortality and better quality of life subsequently than untreated controls (Olbrisch 1977).

Behavior is both biological and social; it reflects the activity of the neurobiological apparatus; and information derived from the context (culture) in which the behavior occurs serves to modify this neurobiological function. The well-accepted ability of the environment to alter neuroendocrine activity appears to have been overlooked by Szasz (1978) when he dismissed psychotherapy from ranks of "literal treatment," partly on the basis that there is no organ or part of body being treated. If we need to specify an organ, then I suggest that the neuroendocrine system is the target of psychotherapy. And if we believe that antidepressant drugs ameliorate depression by altering neuroendocrine activity, then specific psychotherapy may do the same. Rush et al. (1977) noted, for example, that 20 sessions of cognitive therapy with outpatient depressives conducted over 12 weeks produced better improvement than imipramine in a dose range of 150–250 mg. administered daily for the same length of time.

Has Psychotherapy a Scientific Basis?

The second criticism of psychotherapy by mental health experts has been on scientific grounds. Actually, "pseudoscientific grounds" might be a more accurate term, as many of the critics appear either to have misinterpreted research findings or to have applied inappropriate experimental standards to human research. Eysenck (1952), reviewing outcome in 8053 cases from 24 studies, concluded 28 years ago that the spontaneous rate of improvement among untreated neurotics was about two-thirds in two years, and that treatment did not improve on this rate. Many authors have challenged Eysenck's findings, the most important criticism being that he greatly overestimated spontaneous remission, apparently by applying more liberal outcome critieria to untreated cases than to treated. The real spontaneous improvement rate may be closer to 43 percent (Bergin and Lambert 1978). At the same time, five major reviews of psychotherapy results published since 1970 have all concluded that treated persons do better on a variety of outcome measures than untreated, wait-listed, or placebo-treated persons (Meltzoff and Kornreich 1970; Luborsky et al. 1975; Smith and Glass 1977; Gomes–Schwartz et al. 1978; Bergin and Lambert 1978). Further, the various studies are beginning to identify characteristics of clients and therapists and technical considerations that relate to improvements (Bergin and Lambert 1978).

Ultrascientism

A second trend in the "scientific" criticism of psychotherapy is perhaps best characterized "ultrascientific." It is exemplified by authors who criticize experimental design, forgetting the limitations of human research involving a clinical method. On this basis Rachman (1973), in supporting Eysenck's original conclusions and attempting to refute Bergin's (1971) reanalysis of 14 of the studies Eysenck reviewed, was able to exclude all but two investigations as having no evidence worth considering! (Bergin and Lambert 1978). Such ultrascientific manipulation of data lends credence to Cummings's "Warning: research may be hazardous to your health" (1977:713). As he cogently points out, there has yet to be a definitive experiment to support the surgeon general's warning on cigarette packages. Indeed, portions of the clinical evidence on which the surgeon general based his conclusions are even now apparently being refuted by carefully designed experiments supported by the tobacco industry, which fail to demonstrate a causal link between smoking and lung cancer in humans (Cummings 1977). Cummings suggests that to understand many medical problems we will have to look at the weight of evidence from clinical experience and human studies, flawed though these might be in certain technical detail. If the preponderance of evidence favors a conclusion that psychotherapy has benefit, then why the debate? Not surprisingly, when information contains some ambiguities, and particularly when it concerns an emotionally charged issue such as the manipulation of thoughts, feelings, and behavior, then facts will tend to be interpreted less in accordance with scientific principles than with beliefs. This brings me to the question of the cultural context of psychotherapy, to some dominant concerns in current American society and their potential impact on the future of psychotherapy.

The Concept of Freedom

Freedom has been a concern of American society since its inception; but in the past two decades this concern has crystallized into two different forms in the politics of the left and the right. For liberals, the cutting edge has been desegregation and civil rights; for conservatives, the battle cry has been less government, less taxation, less regulation. Each of these viewpoints has had impacts on psychotherapy.

The radical left is concerned with visible oppression, "whether it be of women by men, blacks by whites, patients by psychiatrists, or everybody by capitalism" (Kovel 1976:249). The left rejects conventional psychotherapy as "bandaids for the bourgeoisie" and believes that therapy should be delegitimized as an institution. Kovel summarizes this position succinctly: "And since regarding human troubles as correctable by psychological means, or by individuals, saps the urge to unite as a class against the common oppressor, the delegitimization of therapy would deprive capitalism of one of its handiest props" (ibid.). A more polished articulation of these sentiments may be found in the writings of R. D. Laing and his followers, whose blend of Marxism, psychoanalysis, and existentialism has criticized Western societies, including traditional families, traditional conceptions of mental illness, and traditional approaches to psychotherapy.

The conservatives of the right, coming from a tradition of Thoreau-like individualism and Emersonian self-reliance, tend to criticize psychotherapy on different grounds: it is a frill, a crutch for the self-indulgent. In hearings before the Senate

Finance Committee in August 1978, Martin L. Gross asserted that psychotherapy was a hoax, worthless for nonpsychotic problems, which are simply normal anxiety. "He also asserted that a person's 'natural temperament' exists at birth and 'parents have very little to do with the emotional balance of children' " (Holden 1978:794).

For Szasz the problem is somewhat different. Psychotherapy is dangerous precisely because it might work; and since it is not "literal treatment" but rather "religion, or rhetoric or repression" (Szasz 1978:190), it threatens people's freedom. This threat comes from the fact that whereas there are strict constitutional safeguards concerning imposition of religion or repression on Americans, such safeguards do not extend to medical treatments. Thus, government, or the dominant culture, can surreptitiously impose thought or behavior control by defining certain acts as sick and requiring them to be treated. Some support for the potential of political misuse of psychiatry comes from the USSR experience. However, as Field (1977) notes, the position of physicians in contemporary Soviet society differs sharply from our own: there the physicians are state functionaries and lack both professional organization and autonomy. This facilitates being coopted as instruments of ideological control. In any case it seems unreasonable to delegitimize psychotherapy simply on the basis that there are potentials for its abuse in a sick society.

Economic Considerations

I have said that the second general concern of contemporary American society is the economy. Inflation, stagflation, and rising energy and health-care costs are constantly on our minds. From a culture that once believed that anyone could have everything, given hard work and a little luck, we are confronted with the painful realization that goods and services of all kinds are becoming more expensive and increasingly scarce. I consider that the battle for psychotherapy will be fought on the economic battlefield, as perhaps befits a capitalistic society. The issue will be whether, and to what extent, third-party payers—the U.S. government, in particular, under Medicare, Medicaid, or national health insurance—will pay for people to receive psychotherapy. The opposing viewpoints are already solidifying.

On the one side, Albee (1977) argues that there should be "no coverage for any outpatient (psycho) therapy except in cases of genuine organic illness" (p. 721). His basic reason is that such coverage would represent a subsidy to the rich from the poor. As evidence he notes that psychiatrists and psychologists are upper- or middle-class obsessives who do not understand the problems of people in lower classes; that blue-collar auto workers have not utilized psychiatric services even when these were provided free by union contract; and that psychiatrists are woefully maldistributed geographically—50 percent are in five states, the majority in the Northeast. Senator Edward Kennedy shares some of Albee's concerns: "We would be asking the 86 percent of American families whose earnings are under $20,000 per year to pay the lion's share of the cost of a health care service which is rendered to individuals in families whose incomes are over $20,000 per year" (Kennedy 1975:151–52). McSweeny (1977) shares these concerns, but stops short of recommending deletion of psychotherapy as a health benefit under national insurance. Instead, he proposes treatments more appropriate to the poor (e.g., structured learning therapy), utilization of indigenous workers who might have more in common, culturally, with their clients, and restricting the absolute amount of psychotherapy benefits.

Finally, the overall costs and benefits of psychotherapy are of concern. It is evident that unrestricted access to certain forms of psychotherapy would quickly bankrupt an insurance plan. One sobering example concerns Blue Cross/Blue Shield under the Federal Employee Health Benefits Program in Washington, D.C. According to Cummings (1977), in the years 1971–1973, 2.3 percent of those seeking psychotherapy exceeded outpatient costs of $10,000 per year and accounted for approximately 25 percent of the total psychotherapy dollar. In addition, this 2.3 percent accounted for 66 percent of the *national* figure spent by Blue Cross/Blue Shield for the "over $10,000" group.

The case for including psychotherapy as a benefit under national health insurance has been well stated by Cummings (1977). He counters Albee's "subsidy of the rich by the poor" contention by stating that such inequities are not inherent to psychotherapy as treatment, but to psychotherapy as sometimes practiced and delivered. After two decades of experience with the San Francisco Kaiser–Permanente plan, he observed no systematic difference in utilization of the psychotherapy benefit by people of different occupational or ethnic groups (except that Asian Americans utilized less). Further, he notes that 5 percent of all MediCal (California Medicaid) recipients utilized psychotherapy. This contrasts with the national average of 2.5 percent. These figures suggest that psychotherapy services, properly organized, will be utilized by people of all socioeconomic groups.

Of equal importance, Cummings provides evidence from the Kaiser–Permanente experience that when properly provided in a medical setting (that is, with emphasis on brief therapy), the costs of a psychotherapy benefit are more than offset by savings in medical utilization. For example, Follette and Cummings (1967) compared utilization of inpatient and outpatient services of all kinds in two groups of people who presented with medical complaints but were thought by physicians to have substantial emotional problems. One group received one of several forms of therapy: single session, brief therapy (mean of 8.5 sessions), or longer term therapy (mean, 33.9 sessions); the second group received no therapy. Inpatient utilization declined for all three therapy conditions, but not in the controls. Outpatient utilization dropped in the single-session and brief-therapy groups (the long-term therapy patients offset medical visits with psychotherapy visits). The biggest drop in utilization of services occurred in the treated patients during the second year of follow-up, the declines being in the order of 60–75 percent. Since a large proportion (perhaps as high as 60 percent) of visits to doctors (family doctors, in particular) are by patients who demonstrate emotional rather than physical etiology, it appears that a properly structured psychotherapy benefit would reduce substantially that cost accruing to a health insurance plan which is incurred by patients who somatize psychological difficulties.

Conclusion

In summary, I would say that from a scientific standpoint it can be asserted, more convincingly than ever before, that psychotherapy is a useful medical procedure whose curative properties are slowly becoming clarified in terms of client, therapist, and technical variables. Much remains to be done, especially in developing effective brief techniques that address varying client needs. Some preliminary ideas on matching patient and method have been proposed by Burke et al. (1979), and these should be subjected to test. In a culture of activist consumers, more attention also needs to be paid to informed consent: outlining benefits and risks, costs and procedures, expectations and responsibilities. As the personal and technical attributes of effective therapists become better understood, a method for evaluating their competence will have to be developed (Sakinofsky 1979). These and other advances are all possible. The question remains, will psychotherapy as treatment weather the political and economic storms that lie ahead?

REFERENCES

Albee, G.W. 1977. "Does Including Psychotherapy in Health Insurance Represent a Subsidy to the Rich from the Poor?" *American Psychologist*, 32:719–21.

Bergin, A.E. 1971. "The Evaluation of Therapeutic Outcomes." A.E. Bergin and S.L. Garfield, eds., *Handbook of Psychotherapy and Behavior Change*. New York: John Wiley & Sons, 217–70.

———, and M.J. Lambert. 1978. "Evaluation of Therapeutic Outcomes." S.L. Garfield and A.E. Bergin, eds., *Handbook of Psychotherapy and Behavior Change*, 2d ed. New York: John Wiley & Sons, 139–89.

Burke, J.D., H.S. White, and L.L. Havens. 1979. "Which Short-Term Therapy? Matching Patient and Method." *Archives of General Psychiatry*, 35:17–186.

Cummings, N.A. 1977. "The Anatomy of Psychotherapy under National Health Insurance." *American Psychologist*, 32:711–18.

Eysenck, H.J. 1952. "The Effects of Psychotherapy: An Evaluation." *Journal of Consulting Psychology*, 16:319–24.

Field, M.G. 1977. "Psychiatry and the Polity: The Soviet Case and Some General Implications." *Annals of the New York Academy of Sciences*, 285:687–97.

Follette, W.T., and N.A. Cummings. 1967. "Psychiatric Services and Medical Utilization in Prepaid Health Plan Setting." *Medical Care*, 5:25–35.

Gomes–Schwartz, B., S.W. Hadley, and H. Strupp. 1978. "Individual Psychotherapy and Behavior Therapy." *Annual Review of Psychology*, 29:435–71.

Holden, C. 1978. "Senators Hear Case for Psychotherapy." *Science*, 201:794–95.

Kennedy, E.M. 1975. "Commentary." J. Marmor, *Psychiatrists and Their Patients*. Washington, D.C.: Joint Information Service of the American Psychiatric Association and National Association for Mental Health, 151–52.

Kovel, J. 1976. *A Complete Guide to Therapy: From Psychoanalysis to Behavior Modification*. New York: Pantheon, 1976.

Luborsky, L., B. Singer, and L. Luborsky. 1975. "Comparative Study of Psychotherapies:

Is It True That 'Everybody Has Won and All Must Have Prizes?' " *Archives of General Psychiatry*, 32:995–1008.

McSweeny, A.J. 1977. "Including Psychotherapy in National Health Insurance." *American Psychologist*, 32:722–30.

Meltzoff, J., and M. Kornreich. 1970. *Research in Psychotherapy*. New York: Atherton.

Olbrisch, M.E. 1977. "Psychotherapy Interventions in Physical Health: Effectiveness and Economic Efficiency." *American Psychologist*, 32:761–77.

Rachman, S. 1973. "The Effects of Psychological Treatment." H. Eysenck, ed., *Handbook of Abnormal Psychology*. New York: Basic Books.

Rush, A.J., A.T. Beck, M. Kovacs, and S.D. Hollon. 1977. "Comparative Efficacy of Cognitive Therapy and Pharmacotherapy in the Treatment of Depressed Outpatients." *Cognitive Therapy and Research*, 1:17–37.

Sakinofsky, I. 1979. "Evaluating Competence of Psychiatrists." *Canadian Journal of Psychiatry*, 24:193–205.

Smith, M.L., and G.V. Glass. 1977. "Meta-Analysis of Psychotherapy Outcome Studies." *American Psychologist*, 32:752–60.

Szasz, T. 1978. *The Myth of Psychotherapy*. New York: Anchor Press/Doubleday.

Wittgenstein, L. 1953. *Philosophical Investigations*. New York: Macmillan.

PART FIVE

Modern Medicine: Social Structure and Ritual in Biomedicine

MEDICINE, WHETHER WE CONSTRUE IT AS A "SCIENCE," A "FIELD," A "DISCIPLINE," AN "art," or a "calling," is a part of culture. Like any other part of culture—be it !Kung subsistence, Aztec sacrifice, Crow kinship terminology, or academic anthropology— medicine has an element of unrecognized internal "logic," and is influenced by other nonmedical cultural phenomena in a multitude of ways. Since medicine is perhaps the most deliberate of applied sciences, it becomes a particularly compelling challenge to understand both the logic and the influence.

The language of discourse in any part of culture organizes what participants think, what they "see." What we "see" is the endpoint of what we think we see. As an example, the organization of education has as much of an effect on students as does its content. Medical students necessarily view themselves quite differently from the patients under study. They have learned to solve problems with corpses. They have learned their lessons of cause and effect on static objects, developing a cross-sectional rather than a longitudinal orientation to problem solving. The ethos and mystique of a profession grows out of the transformed shadows of its cultural survivals: corpses are passive and are not colleagues; there is the implicit expectation that the patient will assume the same attributes. Indeed, the most obvious *behavioral characteristic* of the cadaver is its patience. Whatever is learned from the corpse has to be learned anew from the living body, but the *affect* and the *context* of the original lessons are never erased (Romanucci–Ross 1982).

This cross-sectionalizing of the inherently longitudinal is as apparent in larger historical contexts as it is in biographical ones. How incredibly fortunate we are that Fleck's monumental (troubling, challenging, and provocative) *Genesis and Development of a Scientific Fact* (1979) is about a problem in *medicine* (the "fact" that the Wasserman reaction is related to syphilis) rather than one in physics or chemistry! Whatever else we may learn from Fleck, we need to keep constantly in mind his definition of a "fact" as a *"stylized signal of resistance in thinking"* (ibid:98), a roadblock in the flow, a cross-sectionalization of the longitudinal.

Ways of seeing, or knowing, or doing, or thinking, are *stylizers* of cultural processes in any culture. Activities and stylizers of activities are never free of the effects pre-determined by the social structure with its implicit mechanisms for self-perpetuation.

Clinical decision making should be dictated only by what is considered good for the patient by the physician, but actually many decisions converge at this very point. Much of the decision making can occur in a hospital where technical aspects of patient care, cost of care (from personnel salaries to "empty bed expenses"), and competition with other hospitals mean that these decisions are influenced by a conglomerate of business interests. The board of trustees are advocates and surrogates for community interests (Who is bringing money and business into the community? Do we want to go into the health sciences business? Will this attract other businesses?). This does not mean that the community does not want emergency services, and an assurance of medical quality, as well as decisions consistent with present medical knowledge. It may mean, however, that cost–benefit does not have the same meaning to the patient as it does to other individuals and groups. Policy decisions, then, are products not only of the sum of all individual decisions made by good doctors but also products of resources, personnel, and the science and art of he "possible."

The "field" of the art and science of medicine, then, is a culture, an island of cognition, affect, social structure and institutions, codified language; it has boundaries which include members and exclude others. As an information system, the field of medicine is a relatively closed system of knowledge; it has many vested interests in remaining that way. Physicians who stray too far from the properly defined and encoded "clinical perspective," or from what is generally deemed to constitute proper "basic research," are likely to be shunned, or at least ignored, by peers and superiors. This is a most serious control system, as, rhetoric to the contrary, the most lauded work is done not by individual practitioners but by teams: a recent article in the *New England Journal of Medicine* listed some 96 "authors." The rewards in this culture are for those who go deeper and deeper into the thesaurus of the medical lexicon, into the most technical aspects of diagnosis. The accomplishments that elicit the most praise are those displaying the finest motor, auditory, and visual skills, or the most ingenious measurement and quantification. That which cannot be measured is deemed, more or less, not to exist; at best it is ignored in any notions of causality. Agonies and ecstacies of scientific meetings (corroborees?) center around complex new technologies that require ever more years of training for organ-system specialists. A physician is much more likely to receive the plaudits of colleagues for inventing a new machine than for healing a sick patient. (At a recent international meeting on nuclear medicine in cardiology, one physician, having heard praises of the sensitivity and precision of certain radioactive isotopes, remarked—inviting near-certain censure— that he would like to see more sensitivity and precision in history taking!)

This culture of medicine is organized as much by these implicit structures as it is by its overt functions of easing suffering and curing the sick. And as such, it behooves us to try to understand how these structures influence the whole healing process.

In this section, Felker analyzes the process of surgery as if it were a secular ritual that reflects and shapes social relationships. Ritual in the operating room resolves tensions and transforms them into social acclaim. The core of ideology in surgery is an orientation to *action,* coupled with a massive reliance on science and technology. The omnipotence of the surgeon is coupled with an American passion—the body is a machine (with or without resident ghost, depending on philosophical persuasion). "Teamwork" is exalted, and the family image in the operating room disguises contractual relationships. Ritual obscures endemic structural conflict as it masks an absolute division of labor based on class and sex. Overt egalitarianism obscures a rigid class structure. These social forms, regardless of content, influence the entire medical process in many nonmedical ways; medicine is as much a social as a rational institution.

Radine specifically examines some of the social and political forces operating in the area of care for mentally and developmentally impaired patients. He analyzes a bureaucratic structure designed to protect the rights of these patients, examining the relationships between the central office, the field staff, and the hospital staff in terms of anthropological theories about pollution and anomaly, so that we might understand the strains within and between various belief systems and subsystems in the medical culture. The field staff of rights advisors, caught between the office and the hospital, are in an impossible position, neither this nor that; they are perceived as "polluted." As such, the central office marshalls a series of rituals of demarcation and control, limiting the effectiveness so deeply desired by the agency.

Embedded in a larger culture, the medical culture is influenced in ways no one intended, again influencing patients in unknown and, perhaps, undesirable ways. The "field" of medicine is meshed within a much larger and even more complex field.

To understand medicine, we must understand the culture within which it exists. To understand the effects of medicine on the sick, we must understand the ways in which such complex social and conceptual forces affect the human organism. This is the challenge accepted by those who study the anthropology of medicine.

REFERENCES

Fleck, Ludwik. 1979. *Genesis and Development of a Scientific Fact,* ed. Thaddeus J. Trenn and Robert K. Merton. Chicago: Univ. of Chicago Press (orig. pub. 1935).
Romanucci–Ross, Lola. 1982. "Medicalization and Metaphor: Their Meanings in Culture." Martin W. DeVries, Robert L. Berg, and Mack Lipkin, Jr., eds., *The Use and Abuse of Medicine.* New York: Praeger.

19

Ideology and Order
in the Operating Room

Marcia Elliott Felker

The Problem

Rising criticism of surgical practice in America has focused on the excessive number of surgeons (Bunker 1970:136), the estimated number of unnecessary surgical procedures (Brown 1979:214), the increasing numbers of surgical procedures, surgical mishaps and surgical malpractice claims per year (Lander 1978:51), the performance of surgery by noncompetent physicians (*Hospitals* 1975:78), and the amazing tolerance of incompetent and over-operating physicians by hospital boards and peer review groups (Freidson 1970:179; Millman 1977:118). America's surgeons are renowned as innovative and skilled, utilizing the finest in technological aids to surgery and postoperative support systems. However, approximately 11,900 Americans die every year from the surgery itself (Brown 1979:214). The death rate and other critiques are public knowledge, yet Americans still seek and accept surgery with alacrity. How can this paradox be interpreted?

This chapter will consider the ideology underlying surgical choices and examine the order that surgery as a ritual creates from the disorders existing in the individual, the medical system, and wider social frameworks. Clearly, we cannot separate out the symbolic, ideologic, political–economic, and contradictory factors of social life, analyzing them in isolation. They all create, modify, reflect and extend social situations, playing back and forth upon one another in a dialectic moving social relations through time. What follows will therefore explore the interaction between these social factors, which interaction ultimately contributes to the high rate of American surgery.

Ideology is here presented as the justificatory dimension of culture, which establishes and defends patterns of belief and value. Ideology functions to make social institutions possible by providing concepts that make institutions meaningful to people, and that motivate people to support these institutions. As "schematic images of social order" (Geertz 1973:218, 231), ideology appears as a set of "certain 'natural' ideas, an ordinary way of thinking, 'common sense', which govern the way people normally act, their feelings of themselves as individuals" (Coward and Ellis 1979:67).

Based on Moore and Myerhoff's premises (1977), we will examine surgery as a secular ritual, granting that the step-by-step procedure of surgery is instrumental in ensuring that efficient technological intervention occurs. However, the ritual itself both reflects and helps shape social relationships and ideas, as do all rituals, an important factor influencing the high incidence of surgical procedures.

A brief overview of accumulating discordances in the American health-care system will be presented as these impact upon the incidence of surgery, but this subject has been cogently analyzed by others in recent years (Ehrenreich and Ehrenreich 1971; Krause 1977; McKinlay 1977; Mechanic 1976; Navarro 1976) and will not be dwelt upon here. We will critique the process of surgery as a purely functional occurrence, clarifying the ideology that legitimates surgery as a highly valued occurrence, and challenging current perspectives on potential social change within the health-care system. Surgery as secular ritual is posited as an inappropriate but effective vehicle for the creation of order out of indeterminate and ever-fluctuating social circumstances.

Contradictions in the Background

Accelerating rationalization and fragmentation of the health-care system has led to an increase in the number of full-time specialists (more than 70 percent) compared to general practitioners (Knowles 1977:2), and an increase in the number of physicians who are salaried employees (58 percent in 1973) compared to solo practitioners (McKinlay 1977:168). General practitioners live on, slightly altered and often derided, as new specialists called "primary care physicians," undergoing several years of postgraduate training as do those physicians beginning training in internal medicine, obstetrics, and surgery. In the present system, physicians must specialize to survive and be successful.

Salaried physicians work in office-based group practices, as interns and residents, full-time hospital employees, industrial physicians, and in teaching, research, and administrative positions. Part of this trend has to do with the prohibitively high cost of establishing a solo practice. Medical sociologists believe that these changes in physicians' activities are manifestations of a long-term structural movement within the health-care system toward bureaucratization and ultimate loss of professional autonomy for physicians. Yet medical schools and the AMA continue to proffer an ideal of the solo practitioner.

The ideology of professionalism is inherent in the role of physician. Larson (1977) has observed that "the model of profession passes from a predominantly economic function—organizing the linkage between education and the marketplace—to a predominantly ideological one—justifying the inequality of status and closure of access in the occupational order" (p. xviii). It is under the aegis of "profession" that market exchange relations (sale of expertise) were extended into an area historically seen as human service. Ultimately, as we have seen, "professionalism" has become an ideology disguising the fact that more than half of contemporary physicians are wage earners rather than solo practitioners enjoying full autonomy at work.

Third-party payments (insurance companies, Medicare–Medicaid, Workmans' Compensation) and prepaid health programs (health maintenance organizations) have led patients to believe in their right to physicians' expertise, changing the patient–practitioner relationship from that of patient compliance to that of patient demand (McKinlay 1977:176). The ultimate in care demanded by patients is access to the latest, most scientific surgical techniques available.

Public dissatisfaction with an impersonal health-care system and lack of alternative choices has led to the filing of malpractice suits and other attempts by the public to enforce physician accountability, and to the practice of "defensive medicine" by physicians. Escalating costs from these and other factors are greeted with horror by the public and the government, and are mostly paid by the public through increased taxes, higher insurance premiums, and inflation.

The illnesses that typically afflict American society today are no longer infectious diseases, but chronic and degenerative diseases associated with aging—primarily heart disease, stroke, and cancer. Still oriented toward "cure," physicians endure many frustrations in treating chronic illnesses, finding themselves at best simply able to maintain patients on a trajectory that includes a decreasing quality of life.

More and more of the gross national product is being spent on patients who have illnesses that cannot be cured (McKinlay and McKinlay 1977:415), in the form of disability payments, cost of repeated hospital admissions, life-time maintenance drugs, and interim surgical procedures to repair, replace, remove, or insert parts. Many of these patients are no longer part of the tax base because of advanced age, illness, or poverty, which in itself contributes to chronic illness (Lerner 1975). The social costs of lingering illnesses are inestimable, sooner or later posing ethical questions concerning the high rate of illness caused by industrial toxins both in and out of the workplace.

As part of the "medical–industrial complex" that includes drug manufacturers, laboratories, insurance companies, research–teaching hospitals, medical schools, nursing homes, health-care technology and commodity manufacturers, blood producers, exporters to Third World nations, etc., the medical system is big business (Ehrenreich and Ehrenreich 1971).

As such, it must expand to survive, and does so admirably, earning, for example, $2.4 billion profit for private investors in 1976 (Rodberg and Stevenson 1977:109). Part of this expansion occurs in operating rooms, as more intricate and expensive technology is created and sold to help surgeons increase their skills and effectiveness. This in turn enables surgeons to offer the public a greater number of operative procedures than was previously possible, up to a thousand by a count taken in 1973 (Child 1973:91). As the number of operations per year increases, the number of surgical mishaps and complications also increases.

Many of the contradictions and tensions within the health-care system are generated by its goals and structure. These in turn are created out of social, economic, political, and ideological forces found in the wider society. Physicians cope with these problems from within the medical system, so that in the end, they are both participants in and victims of its disorder.

Ideology and Surgery

As set forth by Geertz (1973), ideologies play roles in "defining (or obscuring) social categories, stabilizing (or upsetting) social expectations, maintaining (or undermining) social norms, strengthening (or weakening) social consensus, relieving (or exacerbating) social tensions" (p. 203). Ideologies relating to the medical system are varied, operating along the fluctuating lines described above. Some of these are an orientation to action and task, reliance on science and technology, utilitarianism, expertise, individualism, success, progress and change, physical attractiveness, "man controls nature," cleanliness, comfort, daily life organized by the clock, male-oriented society, family, education, the "curability" of illness, and so forth. Some of their influences are discussed next.

Aspects of Health-Care Ideology

Most commonly, an indeterminate illness is initially treated by a general practitioner or an internist. Should there be indecision as to the need for surgery, an action ideology will bias the train of events toward operating. The surgeon consulted is trained to operate; the family and the patient are anxious; a decision to operate in uncertain situations will clear the air, making everyone feel that "something is being done" (Parsons 1951:466).

Another ideology supporting surgical intervention is the American passion for science, expressed in an inordinate belief in medicine's efficacy because of its use of technology, its "scientific" approach to diagnosis, and highly publicized surgical "miracles." A third ideology is a view of the human body as a machine composed of many parts, which can become diseased or wear out, and which can be repaired, replaced, or removed by surgeons so that life can go on.

A very powerful ideology is that the physician, especially the surgeon, is omnipotent; he has actual life and death control over anesthetized patients. We place surgeons on pedestals through our belief in their skills and abilities to heal by cutting. The mystique of "laying on of hands," once a priestly function, has been magnified by the symbolism of hands *inside* our bodies in a healing effort. Additionally, the public has ascribed an ideology of service to surgeons, and usually do not hold them responsible for failures in efforts of intervention, a blamelessness also ascribed to priests.

The similarities between a religious ritual of renewal (communion) and a medical ritual of renewal (surgery) are too marked to bypass. Consider the associations presented in Table 19.1.

Table 19.1.   Associations between Surgery and Religious Communion

	Communion	Surgery
Setting:	church	hospital
Sanctified area:	apse	operating room
Officiate, special clothing:	priest	surgeon
Ritually prepared for renewal:	penitent and priest	patient and surgeon
Ceremonial area:	altar	operating table
Assistants:	acolytes	surgical residents
Transforming substance:	bread and wine	anesthetics
Symbol of power to change:	cross	scalpel

It is no wonder that we tend to deify surgeons, or at least to grant them supernatural powers, for they often must play the role (Nolen 1970: 272).

Last, we should examine the twin ideologies of "kinship" and "teamwork," enabling a group of widely divergent people to work together harmoniously. In looking at the social variables associated with operating room personnel, and the social action necessary for efficient and functional performance, we come across an enigma.

We find surgeons at the top of the medical system's status hierarchy, with all the power embedded in that position. Surgeons are highly paid for their work by the patient or by a third-party agent. They utilize a work setting provided for them at no cost, and may request additional tools or technology. They are provided assistants whom they do not reimburse themselves. They have the authority to request or reject certain of these assistants according to personal needs or preference. They schedule their work at times suiting their own convenience (except for traumatic emergencies), and may exhibit personal behaviors of either serenity and good will or antagonism and irritability, according to what is "natural" to them and the occasion. They may, in their autonomous roles, choose to attempt new surgical techniques or to adhere to outmoded procedures, with little peer accountability. Statistically, they are white upper-middle-class or upper-class males.

On the other hand, their supporting personnel are nurses and technicians, mostly female, of working or lower-middle class, and often of ethnic minorities. They are salaried workers, earning a fraction of what the surgeon earns. As employees with little status in the medical hierarchy, their individualized behavior is restricted; there is little power to make changes in the work situation; and working hours are determined by others. The high turnover of hospital workers adds to the reality of their impersonality and interchangeability. Their jobs are at risk if they discuss technical errors or inadequacies observed in individual surgeons, question decision making, object to "unnecessary" surgery, or protest verbal abuse from those in authority. With such profound differences in socioeconomic status, education, and autonomy among participants in surgery, how is it that surgery flows smoothly?

An explanation can be found in the associated ideologies of kinship and teamwork. Schneider (1968) investigated the social relations embedded in American kinship: relations of nature (by blood) and relations of contract (by marriage). He then described the cultural definition of "natural" relations (between kin) as "enduring, diffuse solidarity," with specific relations between members differentiated by age and sex. "Older and male" dominate "younger and female," justified by the ideology of enduring, diffuse solidarity, and by relations of trust, loyalty, responsibility, and mutual support, or "doing what is good for or right for the other person, without regard for the doer" (p. 60).

Critiques of Health-Care Ideologies

Barnett and Silverman (1979) point out that these features are not neutral parts of a cognitive system, for they promote solidarity *and* allow personal domination. Moving from the home to the workplace, Barnett and Silverman posit that in the wider society, individuals who are personally dominated (Indians, women, Blacks, children, etc.) are not seen as individuals in the same sense as are other individuals. These less-than-individuals can be dominated behaviorally and economically via an ideology of "equivalent selves freely agreeing to contractual arrangements in a free marketplace" (p. 64). Personal domination and domination in other domains mutually shape each other, and can be substituted for each other. Promotion of enduring, diffuse solidarity appears, then, as a way of dealing with and perpetuating inequalities of domination (pp. 59–69).

It should come as no surprise, in examining the structure of social relations in the operating room, to find a father figure (chief of surgery), a mother figure (operating room supervisor), and children figures (nurses, technicians). Nor is it unexpected to find males taking active, decision-making roles as surgeons and anesthesiologists, and females taking supportive roles, handing surgeons their instruments, helping them to gown and glove (nurses gown and glove themselves), cleaning up after surgery, etc. Although the interns *could* pass instruments to surgeons, and nurses *could* hold retractors and tie knots in sutures, they do not, for these activities do not fit the "natural" gender role differences attributed by Schneider's (1968) American informants to males and females within the family.

Female physicians are covertly and overtly excluded from surgical specialization, which is still considered a male domain, and almost twice as many male graduates choose to enter surgical careers as do women (Weisman 1980: 816, 823). Women's "natural" biologic deficiencies are believed to make them unfit for this division of medicine (Quadagno 1978: 250).

Finally, those who work in operating rooms, or in any bureaucratic organization, are familiar with use of the kinship metaphor by management in urging employees to work together cooperatively, "like one big family." Where this ideology is used,

Barnett and Silverman have asserted that it operates to disguise contractual relations which have their origin in purchase and sale. A family image is linked precisely to domination of owned by owner, with the owner (management) retaining the right to fire or sell the members of its "family" (Barnett and Silverman 1979:75–76). In work situations infused with a kinship ideology, participants fall into "natural" relationships of domination and submission, supported by enduring, diffuse solidarity. Social relationships are enhanced and this, in turn, stimulates productivity: in our case, smoothly flowing surgical procedures. Hospital administrators and surgeons dominate operating-room nurses and technicians, one group abundantly rewarded for productivity, the other meagerly rewarded and stressed.

Added to this is the ideology of teamwork, which is deliberately promoted by bureaucratic organizations to stimulate congenial working relationships among hierarchically divided workers. Teamwork is described to participants as an egalitarian, collegial enterprise (Leininger 1976). In the operating room, teams ostensibly work in this manner in planning and executing surgery for the good of the patient. Yet teams are far from egalitarian or collegial on even the most superficial examination, especially within the medical system.

Most teamwork in medicine is a matter of the professional peers in a group (nurses, doctors, therapists, etc.) relating to one another, with very little constructive social action across lines of professional division of labor. A hierarchy of specializations, with physician at the top, soon develops in any group, flavoring and directing the outcomes. Teamwork in the operating room is no exception to this rule. Wilson (1954), in particular, has noted a plethora of sexist and hierarchical incidents in the operating room, all paradoxically labeled "teamwork." Personal informants confirm that the same actions and attitudes continue today.

Nolen, writing of his own surgical education, spoke of the shared joy when everyone worked well as a team and "things were going right," but noted that "a surgeon had to be able to get through a case with a clumsy assistant, an inattentive scrub nurse and an apathetic anesthesiologist." An experienced scrub nurse, Nolen stated, often knows more about the operation than the surgeon, but must be extremely diplomatic if she offers any advice during the procedure (Nolen 1970:240).

The power of kinship and teamwork ideologies legitimates and masks the impermanent and stratified structural situation of operating-room employees, allowing them to maintain a service orientation and feelings of self-worth within their jobs. Social inequalities are viewed simply as individual differences of skill and ability in a land of equal opportunity (Seidler 1980:127) where those who have *more* skills and abilities dominate the social action of work. Therefore, it is only "natural," because they are female, for operating-room employees to be in a low-paid, nonautonomous, tightly bounded work situation; and it is only right that professional surgeons, whose special expertise is derived from extensive education, are highly paid, powerful entrepreneurs in their common effort to "save lives" (still another ideology).

Yet it is the class structure of our society and its supporting ideologies that place women and minorities in positions such that only a few can acquire extended educations and special expertise. Similarly, it is the ideology of fee-for-service medicine that allows the surgeon to accrue a disproportionate share of the rewards for "teamwork." We can postulate that operating-room supervisors and chiefs of surgery, acting as agents of the hospital and the medical profession, will find it more efficient and more profitable to maintain a "traditional" division of labor for surgery, and will resist changes in operating-room work relationships analogous to those now taking place in the wider society (feminist movement, hospital employee unions, civil rights laws, affirmative action, etc.).

Order and Surgery

Moore and Myerhoff (1977) describe secular rituals as collective ceremonial forms that "dramatically attempt to bring a particular part of life firmly and definitely into orderly control" (p. 3). Ideas, values, and social relationships, which are inherently invisible most of the time, are objectified and reified, while "the form of the ritual itself is an essential carrier of its own unique message" (p. 19). The messages conveyed often concern matters about which we are in doubt, presented as if these matters are unquestionable. The action itself may be reassuring, expressing potency and optimism, especially in uncertain, anxious situations (p. 24).

The stereotyped, sequential process of surgery, described in detail by Wilson in 1954, undoubtedly originated well before that time; this stylized activity continues today with little variation and can be anticipated and relied upon by the participants. Among other things, the resultant predictability allows surgeons and nurses to participate with competence in operative procedures at *any* hospital, not simply where they currently work.

For the doctors, nurses, and technicians, the sheer repetition of routine step-by-step surgery—the social order embedded within the ritual, the conversations occurring in the locker rooms and during surgical procedures, and the stress and relief from stress—presents surgery as a "natural" healing methodology, the social relationships as ordinary ways of behaving, the ideologies as common-sense thinking, and the stress and its release as good things for individuals to experience.

We can analyze ritual in the operating room to discover how this activity reflects and helps shape social relationships and ideas for surgeons and patients; we can examine surgery as order in response to current pressures on the medical system; and we can determine what unique messages are carried within the ritual form of surgery. We will consider surgery in four contexts: as a personal enterprise for the individual physician, as it relates to the medical system, as it exists within the medical–industrial complex, and as it exists within society.

Surgery as Individual Enterprise

Disorder for medical students and interns derives from the need to decide on general practice versus a specialty, and, if a specialty, which one? They receive two messages: first, the value of solo practice, whether as general practitioner or specialist, and second, the reality of bureaucratization of the medical system and "proletarianization" of physicians. They have remained in the student role long after reaching adulthood, with limited incomes, while nonphysician friends their own age have been moving up in their chosen careers, buying homes and becoming active in social life.

There are several social factors that make surgery an attractive specialty for many neophysicians. It is predominantly male, quite remunerative, with accompanying prestige and privileges, and so highly regarded by the public that surgeons are regarded as a kind of culture hero (Parsons 1951: 467; Sidel and Sidel 1977:9). This status is in itself a powerful enticement for surgical specialization.

While the medical student assists in surgery he spends dozens of hours holding retractors, listening to discussions of technique and the "perks" associated with the role of surgeon, observes the autonomy and control exhibited by the surgeon, absorbs the drama inherent in the ritual, occasionally puts in a few skin stitches and picks up a few skills. All this makes a lasting and often favorable impression on many medical students.

We live in a society that idealizes individuality, personal enterprise, success, the small businessman made good, autonomy in one's work, etc. However, the present economic situation militates against the achievement of these ideals. They are more likely to be realized by a physician than by a white-collar worker, but for those persons who choose to become physicians, completion of a residency program initiates the hard economic reality of setting up an office for practice. Space itself, laboratory and other diagnostic equipment, examining tables, X-ray machine, instruments, etc., represent a large initial investment, usually requiring additional debt for the physician on top of that incurred during a prolonged education.

This situation is considerably eased for the surgeon, who enters a structural situation wherein the profit-making portion of his work takes place in a physical setting in which he has no personal investment. The hospital where he applies his knowledge and skill provides the diagnostic equipment, the operating suite, tools and other technology, supporting personnel, and special clothing. Additionally, as scientific research devises new and more expensive technology for surgical use, he need not worry personally about acquiring this equipment in order to attract patients or to perform the newest procedures, for the investment in these new items is made by the hospitals in which he operates.

This economic boon can easily influence choice of specialization, for, as French (1981) has observed, unmanageable debt on graduation, expected to average $50,000 in a decade, "may force young physicians to choose higher paying careers, prescribe more revenue-producing procedures, or vastly increase their patient loads" (p. 565). The physician whose initial and continuing investment in the tools of his trade is minimized is able to retain more of his long-term gross income for living expenses, debt payment, or capital investment.

The indeterminate situation that forces specialization decisions upon young physicians, originating in the wider political–economic milieu, is resulting in a rapidly increasing number (averaging over 4000 a year) of board-certified surgeons in the

United States (Haug and Kuntzman 1979:17). Ideologies, particularly powerful in America, that present the surgeon as a demigod, and the secular ritual of surgery itself, which demonstrates the social status and economic benefits to be derived from a career as surgeon, are resolving disorder for many new medical-school graduates as they "choose" surgery for their specialty. Of the filled residency positions in America, 31.4 percent were in surgical specialities in 1977 (ibid.: 9).

Thus we are ensured that the incidence of surgery will increase. Studies have indicated that where different areas of the country with similar population have varying numbers of surgeons, the area with more hospital beds and more surgeons has a statistically higher incidence of surgery (Lewis 1969).

Surgery within the Medical System

Disorder for surgeons within the medical system is found first in the often vehement criticism by lay persons and peers of the surgeons' alleged veniality, performance of "unnecessary" surgery, many surgical mishaps and fatalities, and attitudes of infallibility and superiority. Second, the surgeon is in the position of entrepreneur within the operating room, yet is himself dependent upon others in order to perform his work. Third, surgeons need technically competent surgical assistants, for few operative procedures can be performed by a single surgeon. Last, surgeons must keep in practice, for unused skills deteriorate (along with the patients underutilized skills are practiced upon), and new skills are learned imperfectly if not attempted frequently. The above disorders are all resolved through the power of surgery's structural form.

In discussing the performance of surgery as ritual, we draw on Turner's work on communitas (1977: 96,134), noting that actual participation is in itself an aspect of that which is being expressed. By performing, the surgeon accepts his professional activity as "the natural order of things" and indicates his acceptance to others. As a public act, surgery delivers messages of status, expertise, knowledge and skill, autonomy, domination, and the use of science to control nature. The action itself—controlled, ordered, temporally and spatially bounded—relieves doubts, establishes conventions, and affirms its own morality in the face of criticism. Ideologies that sustain the surgeon in his choice of specialization are made visible, offered to others, and accepted by them by their own participation. Thus the hierarchical dimension of ritual enables the surgeon to incorporate others into the performance as willing assistants.

As we saw when discussing kinship and teamwork, the powerful communal aspects of ritual melt away differences in socioeconomic status and autonomy while ideologies of altruism, utilitarianism, teamwork, use of individual skills, saving lives, and efficiency are emphasized. The repetitive, stylized form of surgical ritual and its communicative, participatory, and collective aspects augment one another, enabling surgeons to work as leaders of goal-oriented groups, rather than as bosses of individuals who have divergent goals and priorities. Surgical ritual therefore functions to disguise the actual social relations within the operating room and hospital.

Surgery must be seen as a business enterprise, for cash profit is being made by the surgeon, the hospital, the manufacturers of the technology and commodities being used, and the insurance companies, which pay for much of the work being performed. Moreover, in any hospital employing residents, the ritual of surgery disguises the fact that new surgeons are being trained at the same time that profits are being made for others. While the surgeon works, and often without an attending surgeon's assistance (Ritchie and Cohen 1980:321), the surgical resident learns his trade, develops his skills and techniques, and practices on the patient; many residents are being taught by and eventually replacing a few surgeons.

The public ultimately pays for the bulk of the resident's privately owned skills and knowledge, through taxes that support medical schools and teaching hospitals, through insurance premiums, and through the offerings of their bodies in time of need as the instruments of residents' learning. The metaphor of "offering" is used deliberately, since the death rates from surgery, anesthesia, and postoperative complications are so high (Couch et al. 1981).

Finally, surgery as a secular ritual is the manifestation of the cure-and-action ideology in biomedicine. For the disorder inherent in situations where internists are unable to do more than prolong the trajectory of the patient's chronic illness, where patients are in despair over medicine's apparent inability to fulfill expectations of cure, and where surgeons need to relieve their own anxiety regarding doubtful prognosis (responsibility to "do everything possible"), resort to surgery provides acceptable—even necessary—relief from uncertainty.

Where successful, surgical results may be attributed either to actual physiological alterations or to the well-known placebo effect, wherein patients have otherwise unexplainable relief from distressing symptoms and prolonged feeling of well-being after surgery (Moerman, Chapter 9; idem 1979:66; Beecher 1961:1103). Unsuccessful surgery has been studied by Couch and associates (1981), who examined recurrent factors contributing to errors in surgery. They list misplaced optimism concerning need, outcome, and the surgeon's skill; unwarranted urgency; and insufficient restraint and deliberation (p. 636). All of these factors can be seen to relate to uncertainty in patients' conditions or in physicians' anxieties.

Surgery within the Medical–Industrial Complex

Disorder for surgeons as part of the medical–industrial complex, which is in turn embedded in a capitalist economic system, is found in the need for survival through economic growth. With the number of American surgeons so high and rising—one in every seven MDs (Sidel and Sidel 1977:76)—there arises a need to devise new types of surgical procedures if everyone is to be kept busy. Fads in surgery come and go; frontal lobotomy, tonsillectomies, and hysterectomies are prime examples. Surgeons must also maintain their dexterity through regular performance, a type of career anxiety.

Moreover, since individuality and creativity are personal attributes emphasized in entrepreneurs, one suspects that few surgeons would be content to perform only routine operations such as appendectomies, tonsillectomies, and hysterectomies for very long. As entrepreneurs, surgeons who are full-time specialists are risk takers: they are willing to try new, unproven (Partsons 1951:468), or stylish procedures that have prestigious appeal (Couch et al. 1981:636). Hence the development of more challenging types of surgery, such as brain and eye surgery, kidney and heart transplants, joint replacements, and continuing research on lung and liver transplants.

However, because surgeons are dependent upon referrals from colleagues for much of their business, their risk taking must have a reasonable success rate. Few physicians will continue to refer patients to a surgeon whose results are poor (too many patients die or have serious complications).

From a hospital administrator's standpoint, surgery is a profitable sector within the hospital, frequently exhibiting a brand of drama that generates good public relations and stimulates philanthropic donations. Boards of directors are therefore easily persuaded to approve plans for expansion of surgical suites, their satellite postoperative intensive-care units, and acquisition of complex surgical technology.

Manufacturers of medical technology have extensive research and development facilities, for new surgical procedures often require new commodities as support systems. This includes equipment for precise preoperative diagnosis (CAT scanners), for use in the actual performance of surgery (heart–lung machines), and for postoperative monitoring of patients who have undergone extensive, life-threatening surgery (cardiac-output monitoring equipment). Surgeons often work closely with these manufacturing corporations, which, in turn, send their representatives into operating rooms to teach surgeons exactly how to use their new equipment. Once again, since hospital growth is often substantially financed through public sources, the public is involved in paying for the cost of the expansion of production.

Surgery within Society

As a secular ritual, surgery creates order for the state and for society. The two are linked through legislative, judicial, and regulatory mechanisms dominated by the corporate class (reified as the state) and imposed on the other classes (reified as society). The corporate class represents about 1.3 percent of the labor force, and makes most of the decisions governing the lives of the upper-middle, lower-middle, working, and unemployed classes (Domhoff 1971; Navarro 1976).

Serious illnesses today are predominantly chronic and degenerative. Onset is slow and insidious, and no particular events mark their beginnings. By the time a person realizes that a physician's care is needed, the process is often advanced enough to require hospitalization for precise diagnosis. Treatment is then instituted, which presumably will maintain the patient in a state of intermediate health. We see here a contradiction in expectations and goals, for many times neither the patient nor the physician is satisfied with "maintenance" of intermediate health in place of "cure."

The etiology of these illnesses is multiple, having to do with environmental pollution, workplace stress and hazards, personal habits encouraged by manufacturers of products detrimental to good health (sugar-saturated foods, drugs, cigarettes, whiskey) and supported by culturally created ideologies, socioeconomic and physical stress, and a medical system emphasizing cure rather than prevention. Furthermore, all too many illnesses are iatrogenic (acquired through medical intervention), both in and out of the hospital (Couch et al. 1981, Steel et al. 1981, Illich 1977).

Since the medical system follows an outmoded ideology of illness as individually acquired (defective immune system, susceptibility to particular microbes and toxins, failure to follow good health practices, etc.) and cellularly expressed, instead of finding illness inherent in the socioeconomic, industrial, and political forces operating in our society, it follows that illness must be individually cured rather than socially prevented.

Members of society, taking their cues from the medical system's focus on cure, find it difficult to accept illness as incurable, and often push physicians for more vigorous intervention than regular check-ups and life-time maintenance doses of medications. Surgery is often requested and received in an effort to find some meaning and resolution for the otherwise unexplainable illnesses that create havoc in individual lives.

The contradictions between reality and attribution of etiology, and between reality and treatment, are resolved through the ritual of surgery, which sanctions illness as an individual phenomenon for the benefit of the state, and legitimates the significance of illness for the benefit of society, reaffirming the value of individual life. In return, however, both the state and society exhibit marked ambivalence. The state financially supports surgical expansion, while encouraging measures intended to lower the incidence of surgical procedures. Society financially rewards and idolizes its surgeons, while expressing litigious resentment of the power surgeons hold over its members' lives.

Surgery benefits society in yet another fashion. Here we refer to illnesses that are especially abhorrent to Americans, such as cancer (Sontag 1979), and those that affect parts of the body more esteemed than others, such as the face, the brain, and the heart. (The importance of these parts can be attributed to ideologies valuing, respectively, physical attractiveness, active and lucid participation in life, and life itself.)

One of the criticisms of the medical system's recent phenomenal growth has been directed toward the "medicalization" of personal physiological states previously accepted as being within normal limits. Here we refer to the growth of plastic or reconstructive surgery. Examples are face-lifts, augmentation or diminution of breasts, "smiley" operations (a quarter-moon-shaped piece of tissue with underlying fat is removed from the lower abdomen), buttock reconstruction, nose straightening, etc. These operations are sought and gratefully endured by persons who accept the current ideology of attractiveness in physical appearance. Granting that much plastic surgery is both necessary and desirable for patients with birth defects, or who have undergone extensive and disfiguring tissue removal (cancer surgery), or who have experienced trauma, it is also apparent that a profitable new market is burgeoning in this field of surgery.

Surgeons have devised ingenious techniques for intervening in these particular problems, thereby enhancing society's respect and gratitude for surgeons, for the medical system with all its faults, and for a state often willing to finance such surgery.

Ideology and Order versus Social Change

We have discussed various disorders in society and in the medical system, which surgery resolves. But what exactly might result if surgery could not react to disorder? We must first ask whose disorder and from whose perspective? For whose benefit is order perpetuated?

Surgical order maintains a class and gender division of labor in the operating room, presenting this division as the natural order of things to operating-room personnel, medical students, interns, residents, and the wider society, which views this ordering via the media (television serials, dramas, movies, and books).

Surgical order maintains the high regard and financial status of physicians who become surgeons.

Surgical order defuses peer and public criticism of unnecessary surgery, surgical fads and failures, iatrogenesis, and increasing costs, in that surgery's successes are often spectacular, and it concentrates on individuals in an era of bureaucratic indifference and personal powerlessness.

Surgical order creates capital for individual surgeons, hospitals, manufacturers, and insurance companies.

Surgical order mystifies the reality of complex industrial society's illnesses for the benefit of big business and the state, thus quelling potential social protest concerning the exchange of individual health for economic expansion.

It is not difficult to see that the order created serves an elite class of surgeons and other profit takers while purporting to serve society. What other ways are there to deal with the disorder previously described?

We might subscribe to a national health service, providing preventive health care as well as primary care at the community level, thus lowering to some extent the necessity for extensive surgical interventions at late stages of illness.

We might limit the number of physicians allowed to specialize in surgery, and require that they distribute themselves evenly throughout the nation, as in Great Britain and Sweden.

We might use nurses and technicians in primary health-care delivery, and train them to perform minor surgery, which is, after all, a learned skill.

We might place limits on elective surgery and a moratorium on the development of technology that involves excessive costs aimed at a few select illnesses.

We might set and enforce occupational health and safety standards and antipollution laws.

We might stop subsidizing the tobacco industry; we might prohibit intense advertising, aimed at captive audiences, of unhealthy and nutritionally valueless food products (e.g., television commercials for child audiences).

It is instructive to listen carefully to the rejections and demurrers made in response to proposals such as these. Who protests, from whose perspectives are the protests made, and who benefits from the status quo? Who provides the research data "proving" that the above suggestions for change are impossible to implement, and who funds that research? More important, what are the implications for society if these changes are *not* made?

Conclusion

In conclusion, it is appropriate to return to Moore and Myerhoff on secular ritual:

> Ceremony can make it appear that there is no conflict, only harmony, no disorder, only order, and that if danger threatens, safe solutions are at hand, that . . . unity is immediate and real because it is celebrated . . . Ritual can assert that what is culturally created and man-made is as undoubtable as physical reality . . . The connection between ritual and the unquestionable is often at the core of its doctrinal efficacy as much in social and political settings as in religious ones [1977:24].

From this perspective, the reward in examining secular ritual is that we get a glimpse into the way people in society represent their situations to themselves. Our analysis gives us a glimpse of the ways in which surgical ritual reflects and shapes American social relationships and ideas. Out of understanding, perhaps we may find some direction for changing those social relationships and ideas. A decrease in the incidence of surgical procedures in America would be an indicator that such social change is occurring.

REFERENCES

Barnett, Steve, and Martin Silverman. 1979. *Ideology and Everyday Life: Anthropology, Neomarxist Thought, and the Problem of Ideology and the Social Whole.* Ann Arbor: Univ. of Michigan Press.

Beecher, H.K. 1961. "Surgery as Placebo." *Journal of the American Medical Association,* 171:1102–7.

Brown, E. Richard. 1979. *Rockefeller Medicine Men: Medicine and Capitalism in America.* Berkeley: Univ. of California Press.

Bunker, John. 1970. "Surgical Manpower: A Comparison of Operations and Surgeons in the United States and in England and Wales." *New England Journal of Medicine,* 282:135–44.

Child, Charles. 1973. "Surgical Intervention." *Scientific American,* 229 (3): 91–98.

Couch, Nathan P., Nicholas L. Tilney, Anthony A. Rayner, and Francis D. Moore. 1981. "The High Cost of Low-Frequency Events: The Anatomy and Economics of Surgical Mishaps." *New England Journal of Medicine,* 304:634–37.

Coward, Rosalind, and John Ellis. 1979. *Language and Materialism: Developments in Semiology and the Theory of the Subject.* London: Routledge & Kegan Paul.

Domhoff, William. 1971. *The Higher Circles: The Governing Class in America.* New York: Vintage Books.

Ehrenreich, Barbara, and John Ehrenreich. 1971. *The American Health Empire: Power, Profits and Politics.* New York: Random House.

Freidson, Eliot. 1970. *The Profession of Medicine.* New York: Dodd, Mead.

French, Frances D. 1981. "The Financial Indebtedness of Medical School Graduates." *New England Journal of Medicine,* 304:562–65.

Geertz, Clifford. 1973. *The Interpretation of Cultures.* New York: Basic Books.

Haug, James N., and Kathleen Kuntzman, eds. 1979. *Socio-Economic Factbook for Surgery 1979.* Chicago: Department of Surgical Practice, American College of Surgeons.

Hospitals. 1975. "Stricter Controls Needed To Regulate Surgical Procedures." 49 (1 Nov.):78.

Illich, Ivan. 1977. *Medical Nemesis: The Expropriation of Health.* New York: Bantam Books.

Knowles, John. 1977. *Doing Better and Feeling Worse: Health in the United States.* New York: W.W. Norton.

Krause, Elliott. 1977. *Power and Illness: The Political Sociology of Health and Medical Care.* New York: Elsevier.

Lander, Louise. 1978. *Defective Medicine.* New York: Farrar, Strauss & Giraux.

Larson, Magali Sarfatti. 1977. *The Rise of Professionalism: A Sociological Analysis.* Berkeley: Univ. of California Press.

Leininger, Madeleine. 1976. "Two Strange Health Tribes: The Gnisrun and the Enicidem in the United States." *Human Organization,* 35(3):9–14.

Lerner, Monroe. 1975. "Social Differences in Physical Health." John Kosa and Irving Zola, eds., *Poverty and Health: A Sociological Analysis.* Cambridge: Harvard Univ. Press.

Lewis, Charles. 1969. "Variations in the Incidence of Surgery." *New England Journal of Medicine,* 281:880–84.

McKinlay, John. 1977. "The Changing Political and Economic Context of the Patient–Physician Encounter." E. Gallagher, ed., *The Doctor–Patient Relationship in the Changing Health Scene.* Washington, D.C.: U.S. Department of Health, Education, and Welfare.

    1979   "A Case for Refocussing Upstream: The Political Economy of Illness." E. Gartley Jaco, ed., *Patients, Physicians and Illness,* 3d ed. New York: Free Press.

McKinlay, John, and Sonja McKinlay. 1977. "The Questionable Contribution of Medical Measures to the Decline of Mortality in the Twentieth Century." *Milbank Memorial Fund Quarterly,* 55:405–28.

Mechanic, David. 1976. *The Growth of Bureaucratic Medicine: An Inquiry into the Dynamics of Patient Behavior and the Organization of Medical Care.* New York: John Wiley & Sons.

Millman, Marcia. 1977. *The Unkindest Cut: Life in the Backrooms of Medicine.* New York: William Morrow.

Moerman, Daniel. 1979. "The Anthropology of Symbolic Healing." *Current Anthropology,* 20:59–66.

Moore, Sally, and Barbara Myerhoff. 1977. *Secular Ritual.* Amsterdam: Van Gorcum.

Navarro, Vicente. 1976. *Medicine under Capitalism.* New York: Prodist.

Nolen, William A. 1970. *The Making of a Surgeon.* New York: Dell.

Parsons, Talcott. 1951. *The Social System.* New York: Free Press.

Quadagno, Jill. 1978. "Occupational Sex-Typing and Internal Labor Market Distribution: An Assessment of Medical Specialities." Howard Schwartz and Cary Kart, eds., *Dominant Issues in Medical Sociology.* Reading, Mass.: Addison–Wesley.

Ritchie, Wallace P., and Lawrence H. Cohen. 1980. "Surgical Residencies Reviewed by Surgical Residents." *Surgery*, 88:315–25.

Rodberg, Leonard, and Gelvin Stevenson. 1977. "The Health Care Industry in Advanced Capitalism." *Review of Radical Political Economics*, 9:104–14.

Schneider, David M. 1968. *American Kinship: A Cultural Account.* Englewood Cliffs: Prentice–Hall.

Seidler, Victor J. 1980. "Trusting Ourselves: Marxism, Human Needs and Sexual Politics." S. Clarke, T. Lovell, K. McDonnell, K. Robins and V.J. Seidler, eds., *One-Dimensional Marxism: Althusser and the Politics of Culture.* London: Allison & Busby.

Sidel, Ruth, and Victor Sidel. 1977. *A Healthy State: An International Perspective on the Crisis in United States Medical Care.* New York: Pantheon Books.

Sontag, Susan. 1979. *Illness as Metaphor.* New York: Vintage Books.

Steel, Knight, Paul M. Gertman, Caroline Crescenzi, and Jennifer Anderson. 1981. "Iatrogenic Illness on a General Medical Service at a University Hospital." *New England Journal of Medicine,* 304:638–42.

Turner, Victor. 1977. *The Ritual Process: Structure and Anti-Structure.* Ithaca, N.Y.: Cornell Univ. Press.

Weisman, Carol, David Levine, Donald Steinwachs, and Gary Chase. 1980. "Male and Female Physician Career Patterns: Specialty Choices and Graduate Training." *Journal of Medical Education,* 55:813–25.

Wilson, Robert. 1954. "Teamwork in the Operating Room." *Human Organization,* 12(4):9–14.

20

Pangolins and Advocates: Vulnerability and Self-Protection in a Mental Patients' Rights Agency

Lawrence B. Radine

The last fifteen years were a period of dramatic growth in the legal system's recognition of the rights of institutionalized mental patients and retarded residents. By the mid-70s, landmark federal court decisions required state-run institutions to provide mental patients and developmentally disabled (mentally retarded) residents with humane, individualized, and professional treatment.[1] By the end of the decade most states had updated and consolidated their mental-health statutes.

In many states these comprehensive mental-health codes included some kind of monitoring, regulatory, or enforcement apparatus. These rights-protection systems varied a great deal: some were complaint-receiving; others were oriented toward litigation. But some of the rights agencies had an even larger mission: to bring about fundamental change in institutions. This chapter is an analysis of one of the more comprehensive agencies.

The Bureau of Recipient Rights

The bureau of recipient rights, a branch of the state department of mental hygiene (DMH), was a state-level rights-monitoring agency whose primary goal was to protect the rights of mental patients and retarded residents who entered the state's two dozen public facilities.[2] The bureau consisted of a central office in the state's largest city and "rights advisers" (RAs) stationed at each of the 12 mental hospitals and 12 facilities for the developmentally disabled. At the time of my research, the bureau employed about 70 people (including clerical staff), and about 15 of these people worked in the central office.

366

Any observer who visited the central office would have been struck by its intensity. The office was pervaded by a sense of urgency. This atmosphere was especially apparent in staff meetings, which were brisk, well organized, and informative. The director was impressive in her ability to keep track of a myriad of details, taking an interest in a large number of cases, often reviewing them herself. She had a rare talent for remembering the facts and issues of each of the cases. The director often discussed impending DMH policy developments along with the bureau's plans for responses. In discussing strategies for coping with new policies, the director imbued her staff with a sense of involvement and urgency. Sometimes the meetings would close with a brief discussion of the interest the agency had attracted from the federal government or a news team. The impression was one of a busy, fast-paced office doing work of real social significance.

The office's modern, modular furniture—with movable partitions and open office geography—facilitated communication within the bureau. (The director's office was the only one with floor-to-ceiling walls and a door.) As a result, staff members, already informed through meetings of developments outside the bureau, could learn more details through easy communication with other staff members.

The meetings and informal communication produced a well-informed staff and contributed to the formation of an office culture. This culture (a central topic in this chapter) included expectations of competency, commitment, and a shared sense of urgency.

The bureau contrasts with popular preconceptions of regulatory agencies: central office officials, representing no single profession, generally identified with their agency's goals. They really cared about unresolved patient complaints.

But in talking with some of the agency's field staff (RAs who were stationed at the 12 psychiatric hospitals), I found that they shared very little of this impression of the central office. Rather, for the most part, they were quite alienated from the central office. Many felt that the central office was cold, dictatorial, and naive about hospitals.

The central office was only dimly aware of this alienation of its field staff. It had its own problems of internal strain to deal with. Its relations with the department and other outside organizations created continuous difficulty for the central office. Urgency all too often became desperation. Added to its considerable internal pressure was the suspicion frequently expressed by outsiders that the rights agency was ineffective and should be done away with.

In this chapter, I will show that these demands and pressures created in the agency a sense of vulnerability and fueled a preexisting idealism that characterized the leadership of the agency. The sense of vulnerability and the agency's idealism led the central office to insulate itself from its own field staff and from the hospitals it was monitoring. This distancing interfered with the overall operation of the rights agency, reducing its capacity to supervise its field staff supportively. My purpose here is to develop a thesis about agency vulnerability and to show how a pervasive sense of vulnerability, combined with regulatory idealism, leads to dysfunctional behavior.

Pollution Theory

The central office's relationship with its field staff was seriously troubled by distrust and misunderstanding, and much of this seemed to have overtones of ideological purity or "contamination." "Contamination" may seem an odd word to use, but in fact the choice (by central office staff) of this word seems very revealing.

Contamination or pollution is a central concept in the theories of the anthropologist Mary Douglas (1966, 1975). Douglas uses the concept of pollution as a key to understanding the dynamics of strains within belief systems. She links the experience of threat or vulnerability to rituals of protection and demarcation. The usefulness of Douglas's perspective for this explanation of the problems of the bureau of recipient rights lies both in identifying pollution as a central, unifying concept and in associating pollution-protective behavior (such as shunning) with organizational and cultural strains. A brief review of this theoretical perspective follows.

Anthropologists view belief systems as systems of categories; objects or events in the world are placed in one category or another, depending on the rules of correspondence in the belief system (Needham 1979). Scientific paradigms, such as those developed in physics or physiology, rely as much on systems of classification as do the beliefs of the Lele tribe in Central Africa. Both sorts of systems contain rules of correspondence that place objects and events into the categories of the classification system.

When talking about cultural, rather than scientific, belief systems, the classification system can be linked with the form of social organization. The peculiar character of each society's classification system may depend in part on organizational features, such as the extent of consolidation of political power, division of labor between the sexes, relationships with other societies, and so forth. The classification categories and the rituals that define them perform many functions for the society and may be expressive as well as instrumental in their uses.

Dealing with the Pangolin

What makes Douglas's work so interesting—and where she goes beyond other social anthropologists—is her interest in what happens when reality does not fit the classification system. This failure of the belief system to account for events or things can occur in a number of ways. For example, if the belief system describes various categories of animals in nature, then an anomalous creature would challenge the adequacy of the system of classification. Such a creature, for the Lele tribe of Central Africa, is the pangolin. This mammal, also called a scaly anteater, defies all classification by the Lele. It is an animal, but instead of bearing litters, it bears its young only one at a time, like humans. It is a mammal, but is scaly rather than furry. Although it looks like a heavy lizard, it lives in trees like a squirrel or monkey. To add to its odd character, the pangolin does not even run away if someone goes up to it to attack it. The pangolin is an anomaly—a challenge to the Lele classification system.

Categories are delineated from one another by boundaries. An anomaly, like the pangolin, could be something that is located at the boundary between two categories or even suspended in an undefined space between two categories.

Events or situations that are anomalous pose challenges to belief systems. For example, a culture may define a successful hunt as a consequence of carrying out certain magical rituals. If one day tribesmen faithfully follow these rules of magic, but the hunt yields nothing, an anomalous situation is engendered and must be accounted for in some way.

Anomalies are fairly common occurences in society and some are not necessarily threatening. Other anomalies may pose a more disturbing threat. Because a symbol system in large measure constitutes one's view of reality, a serious ambiguity can cause one's sense of well-being to be threatened. The anomaly itself can be threatening and upsetting because it seems unpredictable, unacceptable, and perhaps incomprehensible. If the anomaly is in a key area of the culture, it suggests that the belief system is seriously amiss, and that something must be done about it.

Anomalies occasion various responses. Probably the most typical is shunning or avoidance. A second response would be physical control, including destruction. A third response would be to settle for one or another interpretation, to force the anomaly into an existing category: a "monstrous" human birth, Douglas notes, might be considered a hippo and put gently in the river to join its fellow animals. Another response would be to label the anomaly as dangerous; this is less than satisfactory because it does not resolve anxiety. The fifth response would be to make the anomaly in some sense sacred: to use it to call attention to a different level of existence. Here a specific anomaly can act as a symbolic lightning rod to draw other anomalous situations to it in a safe and controlled way. Replete with ritual, the anomalous object can be used to symbolize and explain various ambiguous situations.

The pangolin elicits several of these responses from the Lele. The predominant response is avoidance, because, as an anomaly, the pangolin is dangerous. But sometimes the creature is used in a metaphorical sense as well. A prestigious secret cult turns it into a ritual object, killing it and carrying it about in the village in an elaborate ritual. By controlling the pangolin, the Lele feel that they control the anomalies it represents. This dual role—anomaly and metaphor—allows the Lele to cope with other ambiguous or anomalous situations without upsetting their belief system. (There is no certainty that the pangolin is put to this metaphorical use by the Lele—it is simply one of several possibilities.)

The responses to anomalies in nature comprise one set of cultural mechanisms that can be referred to as pollution-protective behavior. Broadly conceived, pollution may be viewed as any experience in which matter is seen as out of place. A reaction to pollution may occur when something that belongs in one category or place comes in contact with something that should be kept separate, in its own place. When the cross-category contact occurs—either as an event, like contamination of food by dirt, or by its sheer anomalous existence, like sea creatures without fins and animals that chew their cuds but do not have unitary hooves for the ancient Israelites—the reaction is commonly disgust and avoidance.

To deal with possible pollution, cultures develop rituals of demarcation, transformation, protection, and purification. These rituals function both to identify the boundaries of the categories and to express the attachment the society has for its values. Such rituals may range from simple, private activities, such as hand washing, to elaborate patterns of social action, such as graduation ceremonies.

Whereas concerns about pollution probably can be found everywhere, one might be led to ask why some societies seem to have a great deal of anxiety over pollution and go to such great lengths to protect themselves from contamination. One might also ask why such concerns are more pronounced in some areas of a single culture than in others.

Douglas assiduously avoids propositional statements such as those that might direct one to look for an intensity of pollution concerns here or there, but she does offer hints about this issue within what one anthropologist described as a volcano of insights.* Pollution-protection behavior is probably related to a sense of vulnerability. The insecurity that is tied to vulnerability causes more intense fears over pollution and more protective behavior. But what is vulnerability?

Types of Vulnerability

Vulnerability occurs at various levels. One level of vulnerability involves a whole society experiencing a sense of threat from another. Vulnerability may occur in relationships between individuals or classes and may arise from internal political instability or corruption of accepted political (or other) roles. Vulnerability may be a feature of the belief system itself. Critical, central areas within the belief system may be built on contradictions that do not map reality well, and the exposure of these flaws would be a serious threat to the system. Vulnerability may arise from other sources, including individual personalities and even the technical or environmental bases of the society.

There is no reason to assume that one should look to only one level of threat. I suggest that the area of greatest concern is where the sense of threat at various levels (ideological, organizational, and so on) happens to coincide; this is where the most pronounced pollution-protective activities occur. The impetus to protect from threats is a social force, and when the social forces all point in the same direction, the effect is cumulative. Although such an unhappy coincidence may not happen often, it did occur with particular force within the bureau of recipient rights.

The vulnerability that Douglas directs us to look for was present in the bureau of recipient rights at three levels. One was organizational: the agency suffered from a lack of support within state government and elsewhere. The second was personal: it derived from a reasonable concern over the possibility of failure that might result from an unreasonably ambitious task structure. The third came from the idealism—or rather, lack of realism—that typified the patients' rights ideology itself. All three

*Personal communication from Prof. Daniel Moerman, 17 Nov. 1979.

levels of threat aggravated the regulatory idealism that characterized the leadership of the agency. I will consider each of the three levels in turn, and, in the course of the discussion, I will describe a pattern of regulatory idealism.

Organizational Vulnerability

The bureau's political environment was generally either hostile or indifferent. The DMH and the state legislature were continuous sources of concern for the agency. Other organizations, such as the major urban newspapers, various advocacy groups, and advisory committees, occasionally affected the agency. The bureau had little visibility outside of mental-health or governmental circles; hence very little public support could be depended on.

The political vulnerability of the agency was a consequence of its odd organizational position. When the bureau was created by legislative enactment in 1974 as part of the state's new, comprehensive mental-health code, the legislature chose to place the agency inside the DMH. The director of the bureau reported to the director of the DMH, as did the directors of the hospitals and facilities. This "internal" structure was viewed by some critics as senseless, because the agency would then be a branch of the very department it was charged with monitoring. Predictably, the most serious and continuous difficulty in the political environment came from the DMH itself.

A latent conflict of interest existed in the reporting of complaints of rights violations. These statistics of complaints at each facility were published by the agency and were a matter of public record. The bureau had an interest in seeing these numbers high, so that it could not be accused of "covering up" or some other form of ineffectiveness. The department, in contrast, faced unending public-relations problems, and these difficulties were certainly not ameliorated by reports of thousands of complaints at its facilities. Beyond remarks about the bureau wanting to use the complaint volume for "empire building," this conflict did not often come out in the open. Rather, it seemed more subtly to separate the bureau from the rest of the department, and thus created some tension.

Of more portent, however, were conflicts that arose in the process of writing departmental policies and procedures (which the facilities had to follow), and in the stands that the department took on certain issues. The bureau was not a true regulatory agency, in that it was not empowered to write rules, policies, and procedures, and in that it lacked any direct enforcement powers. Any position statement on rights could only come from the department, or the attorney general. However, the department did not support all of the patients' rights sections of the code as strongly as the bureau, considering several sections to be something of a bother, and many other sections impossible to comply with. Furthermore, many department functionaries wanted the bureau to be a purely monitoring type of agency and to involve itself less in what they felt were administrative matters. However, the bureau understood its mandate to require it to be actively involved in the writing of departmental policies[3] and it energetically—some department functionaries would have said abrasively—attempted to do just that. Despite the agency's high visibility in the department, the process of policy writing within the department eventually came to exclude the agency from participating in the important initial stages of drafting of the rights-related policies. Once the policies were in draft form, the department could then scarcely ignore the bureau, and it would be asked to comment on the policies, just like any other branch within the department. This subtle exclusion led the bureau to feel that its input was unwelcome, despite the fact that its comments had often been incorporated in final versions.

The exclusion experienced by the bureau was interpreted both as a lack of appreciation for the patients'-rights mandate of the mental health code and as a lack of departmental support for the agency. Central office staff sensed hostility from some department functionaries as they pushed for policy changes. Of course, they expected this lack of support, and consequently regarded a supportive DMH director as a sine qua non of an effective "internal" system. This they lacked, and a deep sense of vulnerability was the result.

The major urban newspapers were a source of pressure on the department, forcing it to attend to patients' rights. One newspaper published a 15-part, front-page series about an atrocity scandal involving abuse of the retarded at one of the department's facilities. This scandal resulted in the ouster of the facility director and the director of the DMH (ironically, the only DMH director who had actively supported the bureau), and, in the aftermath of various "blue ribbon committee" investigations and hearings, in a considerable expansion of the bureau staff.

The atrocity stories did not place much blame on the bureau. The RA at the facility was presented by the newspaper as "unable to clean things up," but was not shown to be a part of the administrative laxity that had allowed the abuse to occur.[4]

The scandal intensified the legislature's concern about the department. Even before the scandal, it had kept close watch, through its committee and staff structure, on conditions in the state's hospitals and facilities. The scandal and the investigations that followed intensified the legislature's belief that the department had withheld information and balked at implementing the legislature's statutory initiatives. The growth in the bureau from 70 to more than 120 officials was the result of various political pressures on the department, which would ordinarily have opposed the expansion of its bureau. In contrast, the legislature endorsed this growth, after its committee investigations revealed rights problems.

Nevertheless, the legislature could not be depended upon by the agency for reliable, long-term support. Increased size only brought increased demands on the agency. With remarkable ambivalence, the legislature continued to view the bureau as suspect because it was part of the department. It therefore did not trust bureau data about the volume and distribution of rights violations any more than it would trust department figures on other topics that might prove politically embarrassing.

Officially, the bureau could never raise an issue with the legislature directly: it could only respond to questions. The department had official channels for initiating communications with the legislature; to circumvent these channels by attempting to communicate directly with the legislature regarding a dispute over some rights-related policy could cost one one's job.

Since the legislature's suspicion of the department spilled over onto the bureau, the legislature contributed to the bureau's sense of vulnerability. Even when expanding the agency, the legislature had serious questions about the bureau's effectiveness and independence from the department.

Taken together, the legislature and the department exerted contradictory demands on the agency and created a difficult course for its leadership to chart. If it took too aggressive a stance, the department would be antagonized. Yet no proof of effectiveness would satisfy the legislature.

Task Structure and Regulatory Idealism

Perhaps the reactions of suspicion, coolness, and indifference expressed toward the bureau by various organizations—such as the legislature, the newspapers, and advocacy groups—are manifestations of the disappointment politically informed Americans have experienced in the past regarding regulatory agencies. The idea that regulatory agencies are "captured" by the industries they are supposed to regulate is a popular conception in American political life. Although the capture theory may be oversimplified or even misleading, there is a widespread expectation that regulatory agencies should be viewed with a jaundiced eye. This cynicism was reinforced in the case of the bureau of recipient rights because the agency was part of the departmental bureaucracy and thus not even formally independent.

This cynicism about regulation was accompanied by expectations (in the legislature and elsewhere) that the bureau should produce some rather dramatic changes in the facilities. Given the cynicism about the agency, only a dramatic impact could convince these observers that the bureau was not ineffective. This demand for strong, clear evidence of effectiveness led to the second source of vulnerability, the bureau's unbounded task structure.

Despite the central office's focus on departmental policy making, it defined its overall task very broadly, almost insuring that it would be mostly incapable of achieving its goals. Much of the excessively wide goal structure came from the bureau's legislative mandate. According to the mental-health code, the bureau was empowered to do anything (everything?) possible to see that patients' rights were protected.[5] This meant that the agency was to be far more than a mere complaint-handling mechanism. The bureau leadership felt that all levels of the agency had to be active in all aspects of the mandate: monitoring of complaint resolution within the facility, staff education, patient information, and administrative activities, such as review of local policies.

Added to this unbounded task structure was an unboundedness along a different dimension. The bureau was expected to see that the various patients' rights as guaranteed in chapter 7 of the code were protected in the two dozen state-run facilities; but these rights encompassed about 90 different issues, including abuse, neglect, physical restraint, telephone and mail rights, confidentiality, access to money, treatment suited to the patient's condition, and "least restrictive alternative" form of treatment. No guide for prioritizing these rights was available from the legislature or the department, and the bureau itself ordinarily made no attempt to set priorities. Why did the bureau accept such an impossibly broad responsibility?

One reason is that the central office of the agency identified with the cynics' argument about regulatory agencies. It was very concerned about independence. Whereas it could not maintain independence in fact—the director of the bureau could be fired at any time by the DMH director—it did attempt to maintain it in spirit. Another reason is that it, too, wanted to produce dramatic results. The agency tended to gauge its success in terms of policy changes rather than the facilities' day-to-day practices.

"Taking Things Seriously": Regulatory Idealism

But primarily the central office took on its vast mandate uncritically, as a consequence of its way of viewing its work. The central office people took life very seriously. They wanted to do more than "shuffle papers." The inflated mandate seemed congruent with their goals: they wanted to bring change to a system that they saw as in serious need of change, perhaps fundamentally flawed. Taking things seriously is a core characteristic of an organizational style I shall call regulatory idealism.[6]

Idealism, one dimension of taking things seriously, involves not only strong attachment to values, but also commitment per se. In other words, one should believe in believing, perhaps because it is so clear that so many other people do not. Idealism and a "belief in believing" would be predictable traits in recruits for the central office of recipient rights, just as idealism, enthusiasm, and attachment to principles are traits that are highly valued and encouraged both in academia— especially in liberal arts—and in voluntary advocacy groups, such as the American Civil Liberties Union, the Sierra Club, and the Association for Retarded Citizens. But these traits are less valued in large state bureaucracies. I sometimes encountered department bureaucrats who at one time had been idealists, but who had long since been "ground down." They found that ideals and enthusiasm did not work out in the department, due perhaps to barriers to goals and a general lack of support from other functionaries. These few individuals sensed their loss and quietly regretted it. But, given the way the department worked, this was probably the more appropriate style. Generally, the way to get along in the department, they said, was to be somewhat uninvolved with goals, never to express irritation, to be ready to compromise on anything, and to work on projects that made the department look good to the legislature or the public.

But, of course, this was not the bureau's style. It strongly advocated writing policies that would more fully implement patients' rights. It appeared determined and unwilling to compromise. Many of the rules it wanted implemented would not have helped the department look good, at least in the short run.

Taking oneself seriously is costly. It blinds one to the realities of other people's goals. Change is difficult to bring about in organizations generally because other groups have other goals. The bureau's central office accepted this fact, but also tended to dismiss it, as the other groups' goals were not seen as legitimate, but rather self-serving and lazy, or simply out of date, ignorant, and paternalistic, not to speak of being proscribed by the code. Playing down the legitimacy of others' goals produces an awareness in the others that their goals are held in contempt. This impression led many staff at various levels within the department to reject the bureau and partly explains its isolation.

Taking things seriously also has personal consequences. The stance makes it difficult to distance oneself from the job: one can come to feel singularly responsible for too much. There was a sense in the bureau's central office that without the bureau, patients would be in serious trouble. Taking things seriously can lead to a kind of narcissism, an elevation of one's own importance.

Perfectionism

Regulatory idealism involves a kind of perfectionism, which, along with some optimism, can lead idealists to believe that, given intelligent strategy, they will prevail. Bureaucratic life is like a series of games, as many observers have noted, and implicit in the notion of a game is the idea that one can win. So, from the vantage point of this notion, perfectionism brooks no failure. One should be knowledgeable in the rules of the game; one should be an effective game player (or, perhaps, a jungle-fighter). Such perfectionism demands not only skill at bureaucratic maneuvers, but clairvoyance as well. It assumes that the world is predictable and rational, even in its irrationality. One who understands the forces at play can foresee what will happen and hence can prepare for it.

There is little room in this way of thinking to allow that anyone might reasonably fail. Yet, in the matter of rights protection, the forces arrayed against the bureau were so great that it is difficult to believe that any amount of foresight and skill could have led consistently to success.

The bureau leadership was not so conscious of the possibility of globally failing as it was of being *accused* of failure in one area or another. The agency was always vulnerable to such accusations of failure, and its excessively broad mandate, coupled with very limited political power, led to a sense of near desperation. For example, the bureau felt that it could not prioritize rights unilaterally, because defining some rights as less important than others might make the agency vulnerable to criticism from some quarter. The agency could not possibly accomplish all of its tasks, yet would be readily labelled as corrupt and ineffective if it did not try. The bureau was afraid lest it miss anything. RAs' complaint handling was reviewed in part to see if additional rights issues implicit in a complaint on a subject might have been missed. There was always a concern that a patient might be seriously hurt or killed, while the bureau had previously detected nothing at the facility or on the patient's ward that would indicate anything amiss. An accusation of failure could come from neglecting to "cover all of the bases" or from appearing to be insufficiently aggressive in the pursuit of patients' rights, thereby proving the critics right—"regulatory agencies are no damned good." Given the perfectionism of regulatory idealism, there is no resolution possible for this vulnerability. The unbounded task structure was congruent with the agency leadership's desire to take on all challenges.

I have established thus far that the threat to the bureau existed on two levels: one was organizational, arising from a lack of support from the department, the legislature and others, and the other was internal. The internal threat arose from an interaction of, on the one hand, concern about accusations of failure deriving from an unrealistic and unbounded task structure with, on the other hand, the personal traits of regulatory idealism. The threat to the bureau came from yet another direction—the agency's ideology.

Ideological Vulnerability

The rights chapter of the mental-health code was more than a mandate: it formed the basis of the agency's ideology. The patients' rights chapter of the law, a statement of principles and values, provided the agency with a belief system that placed the bureau, patients, and hospitals into categories of good and evil; virtue and corruption. Its ideology was subject to disconfirmation, however, whenever it confronted the key subjects of its categories, the patients and the staff; this created an additional source of vulnerability for the agency.

"Recipients," Not "Patients"

The code demanded a fundamental alteration of the hospitals' prevailing view of patients and of what was appropriate in terms of the care, treatment, and control of patients. Rather than use the word "patient" or "retarded resident," the writers of the code, in the rights chapter, usually used the term "recipient." The connotation is that of a contractual relationship, rather than a paternalist–dependent connection. The term implies a freedom of choice and a legal equality between the provider of service and the recipient. The recipient, it would seem, may choose not to continue as a recipient, if the services proffered are not satisfactory. The conception of two contracting parties stands in stark contrast to the conventional "benevolent conspiracy" among the doctor and the hospital ward staff, where the doctor gives orders to the patient and the entire institution takes responsibility for controlling and protecting the insane—hence irrational, irresponsible, and dependent—patient.

The code views recipients as potentially able to understand their illnesses and their course, just as one might understand the course of an infectious disease. Mental illness here is no longer a fundamental alteration of identity. The image is of a citizen who happens, right now, to have this disability, which should not be taken to encompass the whole person. By partitioning mental illness, the code can render the patient "normal" in the sense of legal rights, but still admit the reality of mental disorder.

This partitioned conceptualization of mental illness is a major point of the ideology. The rights chapter of the code begins with an assertion that the mental illness is not legally incapacitating by separating the act of commitment from the judgment of competency. Whether involuntarily committed or not, all adult patients and retarded residents can vote and have access to a lawyer—and some can retain a driver's license, get divorced or married, or form any other contract, without the hospital's or the state's interference.

Hospitals as "Evil"

If the mental patient and retarded residents are uplifted and validated in the code, the hospitals and facilities are discredited. The code contains numerous sections that restrain the hospital staff from brutalizing, mortifying, or otherwise degrading its patients. These include protection from verbal, physical, and sexual abuse, restrictions on the use of physical restraint and seclusion, the provision of a "safe, sanitary and humane living environment," and the overall promotion of basic human dignity. The ideological significance of these clauses lies in the fact that they need to be stated at all. The code, in specifying these rights, acknowledges the conditions that critics of total institutions have ascribed to hospitals and facilities for the disabled.

In practice, this ideology as adopted by the bureau contains some difficult contradictions. At the risk of some oversimplification, one might say that the central office's ideology placed the hospitals in the category of evil, because the institution was seen as the source of the problem. Yet the agency felt that its task, at its core, was somehow to induce the facilities and hospitals to adopt the patients' rights ideology.

Despite the self-stigmatizing implications of hospitals' attachment to the code, some potential for this identification was possible. The hospital directors I interviewed seemed to identify to some extent with the code. One, perhaps an extreme case, exulted spontaneously in an interview, "I think the mental health code is a tremendous document." Some facility directors found the code was useful from an administrator's point of view, because it provided them with a tool to upgrade care and ward attendants' behavior.

As a result of its placement of hospitals in the evil category, the central office of the bureau did not, in my view, differentiate the facility directors' interests from those of other staff, such as ward attendants or psychiatrists. The fact that the facility director was responsible for the hospital but ordinarily did not treat patients directly produced potentials for many kinds of goal conflicts within the hospitals. Similarly, goal conflicts sometimes emerged among various professions as a consequence of differences in their professions' ethics or views of patients, and these differences could have been used as a vehicle to institute discussions about patients' rights reforms.

Even if the central office had fully recognized the potential for support among facility directors and others, it might not have been able to exploit that support effectively because of the inviolable values it was promoting. The fact that the belief system was so imbedded in fundamental American values and in state and constitutional law meant that, as a set of values, the ideology's legitimacy was beyond dispute. In consequence, this legitimacy put the central office in an unambiguously "correct" position, at least in the abstract. Knowing that one is right prevents one from questioning oneself and is a component of regulatory idealism. Being right means that one need not persuade and negotiate quite so much, because there is so little legitimacy in other points of view.

This description of central office orientation could be described as moral absolutism, but I think that that characterization oversimplifies. The bureau did not operate the hospitals, nor was it responsible for the cure of patients. Without such leavening of disparate responsibilities, its singular ideology became paramount. What appears to be moral absolutism resulted more from the task of regulation than from personal authoritarianism.

Despite the central office's firm attachment to its values and categories, it was partially aware that staff at the hospitals did not fit the categories so simply and neatly. The central office staff knew of some differences in orientation among staff members and among the facilities and hospitals. Contact with the hospitals and facilities, to the extent that it occurred, inevitably demonstrated this diversity and thereby threatened the adequacy of the categories.

Sources of Strain in the Rights Ideology

If the practical identification of evil was ambiguous and troublesome, the characterization of virtue (the partitioned concept of the mental patient) was even worse. The code's assumptions about patients and residents did not fit facility and hospital staffs' experiences with them, and staff had an endless supply of examples of patients' and residents' mental incompetency and irrationality. One staff member told me of an incident where a retarded resident wandering about the grounds of a facility drowned in a river because she literally did not know the difference between a river and a road. Involuntarily committed mental patients sometimes just walked off hospital grounds, to be later picked up by the hospital security staff hitchhiking on the interstate route. Adolescents, staff members would say, misuse the rights complaint system to harass staff members who will not give them something they want or to "get back" at a staff member they do not like. Abuse, it was said, is far more likely to come from other patients than from staff; and given privacy partitions or private rooms, patients assault each other, unobserved by ward staff.

Of course, there are answers to all the examples hospital staff brought up. There should be better monitoring, more staff, better understanding of the rules and their exceptions, and so forth. But whatever the rationale, the point is that concrete information about patients tended to threaten the bureau's ideology.

For their part, the patients provided little help for the bureau's ideology. Most were remarkably uninterested in the patients' rights system. Few identified with the system or supported it in any way. Not only were patients uninterested in the rights system, many of the concerns they did have trivialized the rights ideology. The fact that so many rights complaints seemed petty stood in stark contrast to the ideological intensity and commitment of the central office, and demonstrated a significant gap between the rather grand, ethically grounded, and therapeutically modern rights ideology and the patients themselves.

The more contact the central office had with the hospitals and facilities, the more its ideology would have been challenged. It would have been confronted with some of the untherapeutic consequences of some of the departmental rights regulations that it had helped to formulate. It would have learned in detail that hospital activities are too differentiated to fit well into categories of good and evil, and that staff noncompliance may arise as much from inability as from unwillingness to comply. A full appreciation of these complexities would have necessitated a reorganization of the bureau's ideology. The embattled bureau was under too much stress to take that on.

I now have identified threats to the bureau of recipient rights on three levels: organizational insecurity, task unboundedness leading to the possibility of failure, and the contradictions of an idealistic ideology as it faces reality. These combined to produce a pervasive sense of vulnerability as the sources of threat tended to intersect at the nexus between the central office and the hospitals and facilities.

Vulnerability and insecurity, I have argued, can be expected to generate concerns over pollution from anomalies. If the hospitals and facilities were the prime source of iniquity—and of the bureau's problems with ideology and effectiveness—the concerns over pollution should appear there. The central office's only continuous linkage with the hospitals and facilities was through its field staff of rights advisers.

Anomaly, Pangolins, and Rights Advisers

The rights adviser (RA) is the central office's pangolin. Situated at the boundary between the central office and the hospitals, the RA does not fit fully into either category. The RA exists in a kind of undefined space, an anomalous position. The RA, officially connected to the bureau, but physically part of the hospital, could be dangerous for the central office, according to Douglas's pollution theory.

The central office's view of the rights adviser was fraught with contradiction and concern. Even the term "adviser" symbolizes the ambiguity of the position. The bureau leadership preferred that term when the rights system was originally put in place in 1975 because it did not want to be seen as an antagonist in the department, but rather a working component within it.[7] This cooperation should extend from the main office of the department down to its hospitals and facilities. From an administrative point of view (the central office was, after all, part of the central administration), explicitly structured antagonists within a bureaucracy do not make sense; hence the bureau consistently avoided using the term "advocate."

Yet, on the other hand, the central office knew that its job, and the job of the RAs, often meant pressuring functionaries to do things they did not want to do. Of necessity, this work involved a great deal of conflict, and to keep up this pressure the rights bureau had to maintain its sense of mission and not cave in to the department at any level. So, although it was unwilling to describe itself as an advocacy organization, it nonetheless wanted to maintain independence. This meant that the central office wanted a special kind of person for its field staff positions—people with the ability to stay independent and push singlemindedly for the bureau's goals, and yet to serve as adviser, not advocate.

Central Office's Fear of RA Cooptation

The central office's concern was not so much that its field staff would fail to recognize this rather subtle distinction, but that such staff would abandon their sense of mission entirely. The central office saw its RAs in perpetual danger of being coopted by the hospital. Cooptation, the idea that one would sell out or allow one's principles to collapse through inclusion by the opposition, is a modern pollution belief. The central office felt that all RAs were contaminated to some extent by the sheer fact of their continuous contact with the hospitals. But some could be more contaminated than others, and the central office staff used the term "coopted" for the more thoroughly contaminated of its RAs—the ones who saw things from the hospitals' point of view, not the bureau's.

The definition of RAs as contaminated led to behavior that is quite predictable from Douglas's theories. At the very least, RAs were shunned by the central office. I do not recall seeing an RA in the central office on an informal basis during the entire year I was connected with the bureau. Central office staff did not invite any of its field staff to its parties or other social gatherings. The only times RAs came individually to the central office were for official purposes. Of greater portent, the bureau did not promote its experienced RAs into central office operations. Clearly, promoting RAs into its own midst would have polluted the central office.

Cooptation of RAs was perceived as a serious threat for reasons beyond the concern of individual pollution of central office staff. Effectiveness was one of the central office's chief concerns, and failure to be effective was an ever-present fear and source of vulnerability. The central office's definition of effectiveness rested in part on a stance of opposition to the administration, precisely because the critics and the public would expect the agency to be captured by the organization it was trying to regulate. A coopted RA might collude with the hospital in covering up bad conditions or in not reporting some violations. If that were exposed, it would undermine the bureau.

Cooptation also meant ineffectiveness in that the coopted RA might shrink from forcing the hospital to comply with rights rules. The central office's goals involved much more than just complaint handling, and in order for this mission to succeed, the RAs would have to share in that vision. Cooptation, then, would detract from attempting such broad reforms.

Why were RAs seen as so susceptible to cooptation? Surely the answer must extend beyond mere proximity. Part of the answer lies in central office hiring policies for these jobs. In some sense, the central office viewed many of its RAs as second rate. The Civil Service Commission restricted the bureau's choices to people already on its localized "registers" or lists. In many facilities, this meant hiring people who were already working for the facility, but who for some reason wanted a change. And some were "inherited" from the facility directors' choices for the positions. The central office would have much preferred to hire people with less contact with the hospital.

Another part of the central office's explanation for RA cooptation lies in the nature of the RAs' work relationships. The most important relationship at any facility was with the facility director, and the responsibility for correcting rights violations was the facility director's.

RA effectiveness was nearly impossible for the central office to determine. Complaint volume, a readily available measure, was notoriously unreliable as an index of RA effectiveness. Even if the central office had had meaningful effectiveness measures, the RAs would have had considerable control over that information. The central office, therefore, had to rely all the more on its RAs' dedication or attachment to regulatory idealism.

But this dedication was already suspect, and, in itself, very difficult to assess. Even if an RA were uncoopted at one point, one could never tell when, because of close association with the iniquitous hospital, the RA might be transformed. Not able to rely on confidence alone, the central office had to resort to other methods.

Supervisory Methods

The expectation of seducibility allows the use of social controls in a manner that otherwise might be difficult to justify: pangolins must be handled with caution. In general, these controls conveyed—accurately—a sense that the central office distrusted its RAs.

Central office supervision of RAs was based on two procedures: conferences held at the central office and continuous review of RA reports on recipient rights complaints. Although these types of supervision are social controls, they can also serve as rituals of protection from pollution.

Conferences

The distance between the central office and the field staff on informal matters, already referred to, was apparent in the structure of the conferences with RAs. RAs would come to the central office or a nearby conference center to be updated on new reporting procedures, changes in regulations, or similar topics. The conferences resembled large classroom lecture situations, where various members of the central office would lecture the audience of RAs. Sometimes the program included an RA talking to the assemblage on implementation of some specific issue in the code. In some contexts this lecture format is alienating, however informative it may be. It establishes distance and separation between the central office and the field staff. The RAs sit like students in the audience. Although a student can give a presentation to a class, there is little ambiguity as to who is the professor and who is the student.

The conferences not only set the RAs apart from the central office, they also set the central office as the authority, the expert. RAs either asked questions or displayed their attributes of cleverness, energy, or independence, by talking about their efforts at the hospital. Either behavior further consolidated the relationship as one in which RAs were distinctly subordinate.

These conferences did not permit the RAs to form any kind of group solidarity or to collaborate with one another.[8] Lunch was on central office terms, with central office people at each of the tables. Some RAs commented in interviews that the only time they could talk to one another privately at the conferences (held every few months) was in the restrooms.

Bureau conferences resembled the rituals of protection and demarcation that Douglas found in Central African tribes. They separate out the polluted from the pure, acting on two levels. One level is instrumental: influencing others, reinforcing social pressures, and consolidating power through the fear of danger from pollution. The rituals are an exhortation to righteousness. The other level expresses the general view of the social order.

Reviews of Complaint Processing

The central office's reviews of RA's complaint handling also displays these elements of ritual uncleanness combined with social control. The process, in brief, worked as follows. The RA, upon receiving a complaint, would investigate and determine whether a right had been violated. This determination might lead to a request to the facility director to remedy the situation. The investigation, determination, and recommendation for action would be presented in a written recipient right report. Ostensibly, the report was the RA's response and explanation to the complainant, typically the patient. But each report was also sent to the central office for review. The central office review assessed whether all the rights issues in the original complaint had been responded to and whether the remedial action was adequate. Often the central office staff could not understand the terminology used in the report and, in a written request, asked the RA for clarification. The RAs resented this intrusion, since they felt that everyone at the hospital understood what had been said. In other reviews that rankled RAs minor technical errors were pointed out, such as mislabelling a violation, or missing an additional rights issue in a complicated complaint.

The RAs resented these reviews (called intervention sheets) out of all proportion to the number they received: some RAs (along with their assistants) processed hundreds of recipient rights complaints each month, and the interventions numbered only a dozen or two every couple of months, and, for some RAs, only a few for the entire year. Some viewed the reviews as the central office's attempt to protect itself.

Further, they resented the reviews because they felt that the interventions were useless for improving their work. It shifted their reporting style away from the local audience and added to the "bureaucratic" burden of their jobs. For a time some reviewers were student interns and this fact caused tremendous resentment among the RAs because they felt that the students were completely unqualified to render judgment on the adequacy of RAs' work.

The RA as Metaphor

It may be apparent by this point that in suspecting its field staff of cooptation, the central office was accusing the RAs of precisely the same corruption of which the "public" accused the central office. The identification of the RA as the entity to be acted upon and controlled was no mere passing the buck. The response to the RA was based on a dual reaction, just as the Lele responded to the pangolin in two different ways. The pangolin was both an anomaly per se and a metaphor for all kinds of other anomalies and problems faced by the Lele. The powerless, identifiable, and contaminated RA was a convenient metaphor for the agency's larger problems. Through its control over the RA, the agency could believe that its larger, more difficult, problems would somehow also be controlled.

For example, the rights advisers could have been a primary source of ideological disconfirmation for the central office, because they faced the hospitals every day. If they spoke of conscientious hospital staff members whom they knew, that might pose a difficulty for the central office. Similarly, if the RAs expressed complaints about difficulties in dealing with patients, they risked having the central office identify them as agents of the enemy. In this manner the central office could either prevent its field staff from presenting difficult, threatening ideas, or respond with rationales that kept the ideology intact. Some RAs knew that talking of their militance toward their facility directors would put them in good stead with the central office.

Given the central office's perfectionism, it naturally assumed it was training and reviewing its RAs in the best possible way (given its crucial lack of a middle layer of management). Viewing RAs as beleaguered, it was apparently unaware that the RAs interpreted their overwork and other pressures as a consequence of excessive demands from the central office.

Central Office Misunderstandings

RAs could never be as pure as central office ideology would demand, because their work required so much cooperation. Nor could they see themselves as the sole barrier to ruin, another dimension of regulatory idealism, because they knew too much of the variety of hospital staff and the distribution of hospital staff good will, and may even have agreed with some of the staff's problems with the administrative rules.

RA cooptation, despite all of the central office controls, could still, therefore, occur, and that per se would be anomalous, given the central office's expectation of its own bureaucratic expertise. An explanation would be necessary. Here it could be said that outside forces intervened, just as sorcery beliefs explain tribal failures at control. The power of the facility directors to seduce the RAs was a convenient way to deal with this difficulty.

The concept of cooptation resulted in serious misunderstanding of the RAs' work at the hospital. Their effectiveness relied heavily on a good working relationship with the facility director, because the RA had no direct power to tell the hospital staff anything. So, in order to interview an M.D. or an attendant as part of an abuse investigation, the RA had to be certain that the director would compel cooperation by his staff. The RA also relied on the facility director for corrective action in response to the recipient rights complaints. Typically, the RA would ask the facility director to discipline the staff member if improper behavior (such as patient abuse) had occurred, or would write a policy memo to the staff to change some procedures that the RA had determined violated patients' rights.

In some instances, the RAs conflicted with facility directors, but much more often the relationship was more cooperative. Some rights advisers had managed to get themselves accepted as members of the hospital administrative staff and were included in a variety of administrative meetings. I sat in on several hospital administrative staff meetings where some decision was being considered and someone, usually the facility director, would turn to the RA and ask, "Well, what does recipient rights think of this?" The RAs seemed to think their involvement in meetings was a useful way to accomplish their goals. A few fought to get included in such meetings, but others attended with little fuss.

With the rest of the hospital staff, there was even more variety: at one moment the RA might be invited to train new staff or update the nursing staff on some new regulation; at another, the RA might be confronting a staff member with a serious allegation of misconduct. The point here is that the RA was cooperative at some times with some people and confrontational at other times.

The hospital RAs I interviewed were probably nearly as isolated from the hospital as they were from the central office. As much as they were a part of the border of the bureau, they were also part of the border of the hospital itself. Although they got along with the facility directors and other hospital staff for the most part, they were not part of the hospital's informal network. To describe the complexity of the RAs' negotiations and other activities, therefore, as either globally coopted or pure is fruitless in terms of understanding their work. RAs were fairly independent of the hospital and did what was possible.

Concerns about Pollution: Consequences

The RAs would have welcomed supportive, educative supervision. Because of their minimal informal involvement with their facilities and their difficult jobs, they needed support from the rights system, but the absence of experienced RAs in the central office meant that it literally could not effectively supervise and train its RAs.

Despite their difficulties with the central office, a few RAs were interested in a promotion to the central office. The central office's expansion and relatively high staff turnover created several openings during the period of my interviews, but no RAs were offered any of these jobs.[9] RAs generally understood that there was no chance for mobility within the bureau, but had various explanations for it. One felt somewhat charitably that any RA's attachment to some specific rights issue might jeopardize the central office's political work at a higher level. Another RA was more bitter, saying that any disagreement would put one in disfavor with the central office.

Whereas the RAs were aware that the central office was pushing them to be more militant with facility directors, their perception of their lack of promotion opportunities seemed to be tied to their view of the central office as intolerant of disagreement. Some RAs spoke of central office pressure to "order their facility directors around," whereas, they said, the central office then complained of poor relationships between RAs and facility directors. RAs never understood that the central office viewed them as contaminated by their hospitals. And, of course, the central office never understood the nature of the RAs' work.

Rights protection is a line of work that draws people with strong values, and these people also seem to have a strong need for approval and support. Although it is understood that such support will not come from one's enemies, it should come from somewhere. As for the RAs, most felt no sense of support or approval from the central office.

Options of the Central Office

It is difficult to see how the central office could have been very different, given the external forces acting on it. It was in a lose/lose situation. Its style could have been a little less abrasive, and it could have been more skilled at gaining assent, but that would not have mattered very much. It faced a highly ideological task in a nearly impossible situation of constraints and demands. It is inevitable that it would have been concerned with its own purity and with the corruptibility of its border functionaries, and that these concerns would seriously disrupt its operations.

The state, in serious financial difficulties in 1981, cut some of its services, and many of those cuts came from the DMH budget. The department, faced with a massive budget cut, decimated the bureau, cutting its staff from 122 to 34 (the only other area of large cuts was in training and development). At this writing, there are 8 staff members in the central office (6 professionals and 2 secretaries) and about 26 in the field (7 of these are stationed by court order in the facility that was the subject of the atrocity stories). The central office's sense of vulnerability and the RAs' insecurity have both proven to be well founded.

NOTES

1. For various points of view on the consequences of these "right to treatment" decisions, see Golann and Fremouw (1976). The landmark right to treatment case is *Wyatt v. Stickney,*

325 F. Supp. 781 (M.D. Ala. 1971). This case appears under several different references because the Alabama Mental Health Department Director, Stonewall B. Stickney, was succeeded by other officials while the case was still under review, and because two parallel class actions were pursued: one for the mentally ill and the other for the mentally retarded.

2. I had served as a consultant to this agency in 1978 as a consequence of an NIMH postdoctoral fellowship at the University of Michigan at Ann Arbor. After spending nearly a year with the agency on a part-time basis, I was asked to design and direct a study to be funded by the National Institute of Mental Health evaluating the effectiveness of the rights agency. The study was a survey of about 500 patients and 600 staff members at the 12 state-run psychiatric hospitals. As a subproject within the study, I conducted in-depth interviews with the rights advisers and facility directors at the 12 hospitals in 1979. I want to express my appreciation to NIMH for funding both the fellowship and the evaluation project. I also want to thank the staff and administrators of the 12 hospitals and the rights agency for their tremendous cooperation, interest, and candor. These people provided their support and gave of their time in ways far beyond the call of duty. The cooperation of the Department of Mental Hygiene is also to be acknowledged. The names of the state agencies have been modified to protect the confidentiality of the respondents. Daniel Moerman, J. Patrick Dobel, and Geoffrey Eley were very helpful in critiquing this essay and suggesting ideas, and I am very grateful to them.

3. The department's administrative rules require the bureau to "draft department policies, procedures, and standards required by statute or rule relating to the rights of recipients."

4. At that time, prior to 1978, the rights advisers were hired by and reported to the facility directors. Direct supervisory authority over the rights advisers was transferred to the bureau of recipient rights in May 1978, a little more than a year before my interviews. The bureau of recipient rights had replaced about half of the rights advisers by the time I interviewed them.

5. The code reads, "[The bureau] shall receive reports of and may investigate apparent violations of the rights guaranteed by this chapter, may act to resolve disputes relating to apparent violations, may act on behalf of recipients of mental health services to obtain remedy for any apparent violations, and shall otherwise endeavor to safeguard the rights guaranteed by this chapter."

6. Idealism and idealistic commitment are in no way restricted to liberal, leftist, or emancipatory points of view. A recent study of conflicts within antitrust activities in the Federal Trade Commission shows free-market economists so strongly attached to their principles as to seriously interfere with FTC lawyers' choice of cases (Katzmann 1980).

7. The person who was the department director in 1975 created the term "adviser" in consultation with the soon-to-be director of the bureau. The bureau director originally served as a consultant to the department in the writing of the administrative rules and the planning of the rights system. Once implemented, she became director of the bureau. The department directorship thereafter changed hands several times.

8. When the bureau was approaching a size of 120 staff members, it regionalized supervision. Some of these barriers were muted as a result. RAs met less formally, in regional meetings, and the bureau even hired two former RAs in regional positions. This development occurred as my field research was drawing to its conclusion.

9. Civil Service ratings of some of the new, regional positions within the bureau added an additional barrier to promoting RAs.

REFERENCES

Douglas, Mary. 1966. *Purity and Danger: An Analysis of Concepts of Pollution and Taboo.* London: Routledge & Kegan Paul.

  1975   *Implicit Meanings, Essays in Anthropology,* Part I. London: Routledge & Kegan Paul.

Golann, Stuart, and William J. Fremouw, eds. 1976. *The Right to Treatment for Mental Patients.* New York: Irvington.

Katzmann, Robert A. 1980. "The Federal Trade Commission." James Q. Wilson, ed., *The Politics of Regulation.* New York: Basic Books.

Needham, Rodney. 1979. *Symbolic Classification.* Santa Monica, Cal.: Goodyear.

List of Contributors

George J. Armelagos, Department of Anthropology, University of Massachusetts, Amherst

Marjorie Mandelstam Balzer, Russian Research Center, Harvard University, Cambridge, Mass.

Memory Elvin-Lewis, Department of Microbiology, School of Dentistry, Washington University, St. Louis, Mo.

Nina L. Etkin, Department of Anthropology, University of Minnesota, Minneapolis

Lorraine Evernham, Departments of Anthropology and Public Health, University of Hawaii, Honolulu

Marcia Elliott Felker, Whittaker International Services Co., Arlington, Va.

Kaja Finkler, Department of Anthropology, Eastern Michigan University, Ypsilanti

Igor Grant, Department of Psychiatry, School of Medicine, University of California, San Diego

James W. Herrick, Department of Anthropology, College of Technology, State University of New York, Utica

Margaret S. Keith, Department of Anthropology, University of Massachusetts, Amherst

Clara Sue Kidwell, Department of Native American Studies, University of California, Berkeley

Daniel E. Moerman, Department of Anthropology, University of Michigan, Dearborn

Phyllis Palgi, Sackler School of Medicine, Tel Aviv University, Tel Aviv, Israel

Gretel H. Pelto, University of Connecticut Health Center, School of Medicine, Farmington

Pertti J. Pelto, University of Connecticut Health Center, School of Medicine, Farmington

Lawrence B. Radine, Department of Behavioral Sciences, University of Michigan, Dearborn

Allen F. Roberts, Center for Afro-American and African Studies, University of Michigan, Dearborn

Spencer L. Rogers, Museum of Man, San Diego, Cal.

Lola Romanucci-Ross, School of Medicine and Department of Anthropology, University of California, San Diego

Paul J. Ross, Department of Anthropology, Washington University, St. Louis, Mo.

Laurence R. Tancredi, M.D., Department of Psychiatry, New York University Medical Center, New York, N.Y.

Jen-Yi Wang, Department of Anthropology, Harvard University, Cambridge, Mass.

Robert Welsch, Department of Anthropology, University of Washington, Seattle

Index

Typography and Binding design by Jeanne Ray Juster
Edited by Jenna Schulman
Set in VIP Garamond by Trade Composition Inc., Chicopee, Massachusetts
Printed and Bound by Edwards Brothers, Inc., Ann Arbor, Michigan